HUDSON BAY COMPANY
BRITISH POSSESSIONS
CANADA
Lake of the Woods
L. SUPERIOR
Sault Ste. Marie
L. MICHIGAN
L. HURON
L. ONTARIO
L. ERIE
VIRGINIA
Quebec
Montreal
Ottawa R.
St. Lawrence R.
Disputed Territory
Claimed also by N.H.
NEW HAMP.
Portsmouth
Boston
MASS.
CONN.
R.I.
NEW YORK
Oswego
Albany
Ft. Niagara
MASS. AND N.Y.
Detroit
MASSACHUSETTS AND VIRGINIA
CONNECTICUT AND VIRGINIA
Claimed also by New York
Claimed by New York
PENN.
N.J.
Pittsburg
Philadelphia
Trenton
MD.
DEL.
Baltimore
Ohio R.
Vincennes
VIRGINIA
St. Louis
Kaskaskia
Richmond
Norfolk
Cape Hatteras
Cumberland R.
Nashville
NORTH CAROLINA
Tennessee R.
SOUTH CAROLINA
Wilmington
Cape Fear
Charleston
Savannah
GEORGIA
Claimed by Spain until 1795
Mississippi R.
Natchez
SPANISH POSSESSIONS
Pensacola
New Orleans
St. Augustine

The Library of

Crosby Hall

Political and Social Growth
of the American People
1492-1865

Political and Social Growth
of the American People

$$\boxed{1492-1865}$$

BY HOMER CAREY HOCKETT

*Professor of History at the Ohio
State University*

$$\boxed{1865-1940}$$

BY ARTHUR MEIER SCHLESINGER

*Francis Lee Higginson Professor of History
at Harvard University*

Adams — James J — Revolutionary War Cavalry Genl. — oly Cgatil

A Caravan Encamped

Political and Social Growth
of the American People
1492 - 1865

BY HOMER CAREY HOCKETT
PROFESSOR OF HISTORY AT THE OHIO STATE UNIVERSITY

THIRD EDITION
New edition of *Political
and Social Growth of the
United States, 1492-1852*

The Macmillan Company

New York · 1940

PREFACE

SEVEN years have elapsed since the appearance of the second edition of this history. To gain the space required for the treatment of these momentous years it has been necessary to extend the terminal date of the first volume to 1865, the close of the Civil War. This extension, in turn, has required some compression in the discussion of the beginnings of the American people, and the omission of most of the story of the European background.

The preparation of the present edition presents the opportunity once more to incorporate in the references many significant works of recent publication, and to rewrite the text to an extent which justifies calling the edition a substantially new work. Most of the maps have also been redrawn, and for the first time illustrations are introduced. The adoption of a new format is in keeping with these new features.

H. C. H.

CONTENTS

LIST OF ILLUSTRATIONS

LIST OF MAPS

Political and Social Growth
of the American People
1492 - 1865

Chapter I

EUROPEAN BEGINNINGS IN NORTH AMERICA

SPANISH COLONIZATION

THE American nation is debtor to the whole earth. Aside from the native peoples, its inhabitants are descendants of immigrants from every country of Europe, and from Africa and Asia. England, indeed, was the source of its language and its political institutions, but each incoming stock has made its contribution to its culture. In the beginning Spain and France played a large part in the exploration and occupation of lands now within the limits of the United States, and each of these nations left a permanent impress upon the regions which it occupied. For this reason, in spite of the fact that these powers were dispossessed, it is desirable to notice the character of their activities.

The three chief colonizing powers, Spain, France, and England, differed markedly in their methods of settlement and of control of their American subjects; and in the New World the subjects of each of these nations not unnaturally followed, with necessary modifications, habits already developed in their European homes.

The early Spanish navigators hoped to find a route to Asia, and when they began to suspect that a continent lay between them and the land of silk and spice, they made prolonged efforts to find a waterway through it to the "South Sea." Although they failed, knowledge of the geography of much of the Atlantic coast was a by-product of this quest. Effecting a crossing of the continent in the narrow Central American-Mexican region, they attained the Pacific coast early in the sixteenth century, and explored it at least as far north as Oregon. On land, the Spanish accomplished, before 1550, a rough reconnaissance of the region lying south of a line drawn from Chesapeake Bay to San Francisco Bay. But Spain's American empire lay chiefly south of the Rio Grande; aside from St. Augustine in Florida (founded in 1565) and its dependent mission stations, and Santa Fé in New Mexico (dating from about 1608) with similar outlying stations, Spanish colonization made no progress north of the present Mexican boundary before the closing years of the seventeenth century.

Spain's colonization was a crown undertaking. As such her policy followed lines first worked out during the reconquest of the Spanish Peninsula from the Mohammedans. The Indian like the Moor was to be conquered; but in the case of the former there was added the hope that he might also be converted to the true faith. Moreover, his lands were to extend the empire while his labor filled the coffers of his royal and ecclesiastical masters.

Isabella and her successors allowed private adventurers to bear the burden of conquering a new Spain in America, but no one could migrate to the New World without the royal permission. By authority of the crown rules were framed governing conquest, land grants, relations with the natives, and commerce. The early *conquistadores* invested their own fortunes, usually assuming the entire expense of their adventures. Only in the case of particularly promising projects did the crown take a share in the hazards. Yet always close supervision was maintained over every detail of the colonizing process, and a portion of whatever profits were realized was due the government.

In practice the leader of an expedition, having "pacified" a district, enjoyed the right to govern it and dispose of the lands, in the monarch's name, to his followers, assigning with each tract a number of natives to perform the necessary labor upon it. The white conquerors were never numerous enough to supplant the natives, nor had they any relish for the task of producing wealth by means of their own labor. These holdings worked by Indians were called *encomiendas,* and the holders *encomenderos;* they were an adaptation of the feudal method of disposing of conquered territory in Spain. This method of colonization was most successful, from the Spanish viewpoint, among the sedentary Indians of the Ana-huac Plateau in central Mexico.[1] These natives, already in semibondage to their Aztec rulers, were industrious by habit and docile in disposition.

Somewhat in contrast with life on the *encomienda* was that of the natives who were not brought within that system. Long accustomed to living together in their own villages or *pueblos,* they received protection, after 1551, through the crown grant of so-called municipal status, under which they enjoyed important liberties, especially inalienable control over their village lands. The Spanish were forbidden to plant new settlements within a certain distance of such native towns. With such protection the aboriginal stock was enabled to survive and preserve a modicum of its own culture, under a thin veneer of Spanish civilization.

A potent agency in extending the frontier was the mission. Members of the Jesuit and Franciscan orders, in particular, were zealous in carrying the cross into the wilderness. The aim of the missionaries was both to Christianize and to civilize their converts. The mission was a school of industry as well as religion. Each had its range for cattle, sheep, and horses, its grain fields, vegetable gardens, orchards, and vineyards. The care of all these was taught, and the men were instructed also in carpentering and wine-making. Spinning, weaving, sewing, and cooking were taught to the women. The inten-

[1] Nothing is said here of the establishment of the Spanish power south of Mexico. The process differed in detail, but bears little relation to the history of the United States.

tion was, as soon as the converts were trained for self-support, to "secularize" the mission by transferring its lands to them and relinquishing the "cure of souls" to parish priests.

By the repetition of this process, more or less successfully, the missionaries eventually carried Catholic Christianity to the upper Rio Grande Valley, the plains of Texas, the shores of the bay which bears the name of the founder of the Franciscan order, and the coasts of what are now the states of Georgia and Florida. The *padres,* seeking sites for new mission stations, became the first makers of the trails leading from the Rio Grande to the Pacific. Their success was greatest where, as among the pueblos of the Rio Grande Valley, the Indians were already peaceful and productive, and was least in the arid regions where roamed the Comanche and other predatory tribes.

The missionaries, however zealous in advancing the faith, were no less imbued with the passion for empire. As they spread the Spanish influence northward and westward their progress became increasingly a process of conquest, in which the priest and the soldier advanced side by side, and the mission rested less often upon the consent of the natives. Military posts (*presidios*) were found necessary to protect the missions and to maintain the frontier. Even military force proved incapable of pushing the frontier into the Great Plains and holding it against the marauding Apache and Comanche. In short, all of the agencies of Spanish expansion were balked in succession by the forces which they encountered; the *encomienda,* the mission, the *presidio* found each in its turn a natural limit beyond which it could not go (in the eastern Gulf area it was sheer neglect!) and their combined momentum left the Spanish in the end with but a slight hold upon what is now our great Southwest and the coast of the Gulf of Mexico. Yet considering the meagerness of the man power which pushed the bounds of civilization outward, the area brought under control is astonishing.

Whatever its shortcomings, the Spanish treatment of the natives compares favorably with that of the English. The Englishman regarded the red man as an obstacle to be thrust from his path; English colonization was almost a mass migration to a sparsely inhabited region the occupants of which were certain to be dispossessed. The Spanish, on the contrary, aimed at complete assimilation of the aboriginal stock, in race, religion, and culture. The difference in policy was due in part to the small numbers of the Spanish colonizers in proportion to the Indian population. Spain was not crowded, thanks to the extensive areas taken from the Moors, and actual necessity did not drive her people to seek homes abroad. Rather, only adventurous unmarried men, for the most part, migrated, and these in many cases married native women. The result was the early appearance of a large population of mixed blood. The conquerors had no racial antipathies which stood in the way of intermarriage, and there are today relatively few Mexican families which preserve the European blood in its purity.

Among the earliest measures of the crown relating to the colonies were regulations designed to secure for Spain a monopoly of the commerce with them. Foreigners were not allowed to migrate to them, nor to visit them for purposes of trade. Even the intercourse of the Spaniards was strictly regulated. At stated intervals, government fleets sailed from Cadiz or Seville for designated colonial ports: of these Vera Cruz was for a long time the port of New Spain (Mexico). The trade of the merchants was limited to these fleets. All colonial exports had to be brought to the ports, where fairs were held for the exchange of goods.

Few commodities except the precious metals could bear

the cost of transportation for long distances, and remote settlements like those in New Mexico were condemned to stagna-
tion or illicit traffic. Smuggling was punishable with extreme
severity, but the rigidity of the commercial system encouraged
it, and, assisted by official corruption, it flourished.

Despotic in rule at home, it was not to be expected that the
Spanish monarchs would encourage political liberty in their
dependencies. Nor did the temper of their American subjects, whether native or immigrant, demand it, although they
chafed more or less under the restrictions on trade and the
exactions of the omnipresent tax-gatherers. When first
founded, the *pueblos* had their own officials, who were appointed by the leader or elected by the residents; but apathy
commonly permitted the local offices to become purchasable
or hereditary. The towns were allowed to send procurators
to the provincial government, but these agents were mere pe-
titioners who had no share in legislation.

The crown governed the dependencies through the Council
of the Indies. The colonies were divided into viceroyalties,
with subdivisions for purposes of local administration. The
chief representative of the king (the viceroy or captain-
general) presided over a body known as the *audiencia,* which
was a civil and criminal court of last resort except in extraordinary cases, as well as a supervisory administrative body,
charged with directing trade and finance and with the general
preservation of law and order. Colonial officials were appointed by the crown and were almost invariably sent out
from the homeland. Self-government in the English sense,
by officers acting under laws made by representative assemblies, was nowhere to be found in the Spanish dominions, except in the limited control over local matters which the inhabitants of some of the towns enjoyed.

Spanish colonization in the New World has received scant
justice from historians of English blood. The Spanish con-

querors were not mere blood-stained wielders of the sword, as they have been so often pictured: they put an end to the human sacrifices of the Aztecs; they bore the cross; they

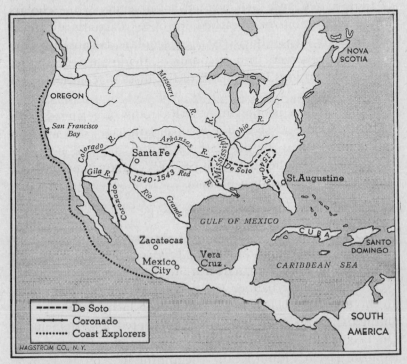

SPANISH EXPLORATION AND SETTLEMENT IN NORTH AMERICA

brought useful plants and animals; they began the cultivation of the citrus fruits, sugar, cotton, and olives; they introduced cattle, swine, sheep, horses, and mules, so that, as one of the early chroniclers phrased it, the natives "blessed the beasts which relieved them from burden-bearing"; in brief, they gave to America all that they themselves had of practical civilization and religious aspiration.

Before either France or England had occupied a foot of American soil, Mexico City had a population of fifteen thousand whites and ten times as many natives. Lima, the capital of Peru, contained two thousand Spanish families. There were schools, hospitals, and other public institutions in each of these cities, and each boasted a university with scholars whose reputations had reached Europe. Partially medieval still in their mental horizons, these scholars, because of their priority as observers in new countries, made particularly notable contributions in the fields of linguistics, geography, and natural history.

"Fifty million people in America today are tinged with Spanish blood, still speak the Spanish language, still worship at the altar set up by the Catholic kings, and still possess a culture largely inherited from Spain." Many thousands of these are within our own borders.

FRENCH ACTIVITIES

While the Lions of Castile were showing Europe the way to colonial empire, the kings of France were distracted by civil wars or busy with schemes of expansion nearer home. Nevertheless their banner was carried to the St. Lawrence. In three voyages between 1534 and 1541 Jacques Cartier examined the great northern river, attempted a settlement at Quebec, and reached the bold height which still bears the name he gave it, "Mont Real." Beginning in 1562 the French made several efforts to establish settlements on the coast of Carolina, Georgia, and Florida. It was these attempts which prompted the Spanish to found St. Augustine and to send missionaries northward and westward to extend their influence over the natives. The opposition of the Spanish, added to other difficulties, caused the failure of the French in this quarter.

Fishermen from Brittany probably visited the Banks of Newfoundland in the early years of the sixteenth century. But despite these activities the French failed to gain a permanent foothold in America until the seventeenth. In 1605, a commercial concern began a settlement at Port Royal, near the present Annapolis, Nova Scotia, and from this germ came the colony of rough fisher folk and trappers called "Acadia."

With the founding of Quebec on the St. Lawrence by Samuel de Champlain in 1608, a far more important chapter began in the history of French effort. This settlement commanded a natural highway leading to the Great Lakes and the heart of the continent. The transition from the St. Lawrence to the Mississippi is easy; at many points the low watershed between the two great drainage basins is crossed by portages. On the Fox-Wisconsin route only a mile and a half of boggy plain separated the two river systems; indeed, during spring floods the waters of the two often mingled at the portage, permitting the passage from the Great Lakes to the Mississippi entirely by boat.

The great river flowing by the cliff of Quebec from the mysterious woodland of the West lured the French into the vast interior. Champlain's commercial company had little interest in the development of the agricultural possibilities of Canada. Larger profits and quicker returns were to be had from the fur trade; and the pursuit of trade led the French to trace the intricate network of the streams, to find the portages, to reveal the geography of the Mississippi Basin.

Champlain himself was active in exploration. In 1609 he examined the lake which bears his name. Soon afterwards he accompanied a war party of Algonkins from the St. Lawrence against the Iroquois Confederacy. Hostile from this time, the Iroquois made the shores of Lake Ontario so dangerous for the French that their first excursions to the westward followed the Ottawa River and Lake Huron.

Champlain visited Lake Huron in 1615, and by 1634 his agent Nicolet was penetrating the forests of far-off Wisconsin. Three decades later Radisson and Groseilliers penetrated westward and northward of Lake Superior, possibly touching the upper waters of the Mississippi.

Frenchmen were not eager to exchange the contentment of the homeland for the fickle savage neighbors and the long cold winters of Canada, or New France, as it was called. At the end of fifty years, when the French islands in the Caribbean Sea contained fifteen thousand whites, the population of New France had not yet reached three thousand, and this scanty number was scattered from the shores of the Atlantic to the banks of the Wisconsin, a distance of more than fifteen hundred miles. Many times that number might have found sustenance within a few miles of Quebec.

This dispersion was due in part to restrictions on the fur trade which drove many to engage in it without license. The wide wilderness offered a secure retreat for these adventurous spirits. Fear of arrest and punishment prevented them from frequenting the vicinity of Montreal or Quebec, and led them to seek a market among the Dutch or their English successors in New York, through their Indian allies of the Iroquois League as middlemen. Many a "wood-ranger" (*Coureurs de bois,* the French called them) made his home in the wilds, taking a squaw for mate and rearing a dusky brood in a native village on the banks of the inland waters.

Close behind the explorer-trader went the missionary. The Jesuits in particular carried the cross to the remotest regions with a heroic devotion never surpassed in the annals of the Church. By 1670 their stations on the Upper Lakes dominated the tribes of the farther Northwest, and through them they sought to develop the native culture along Christian lines, rather than to cover it with a veneer of French civilization. The priest and trader sometimes became companions in exploration, as when Father Jacques Marquette and Louis Joliet crossed to the Mississippi by the Fox-Wisconsin route and descended as far as the mouth of the Arkansas (1673).

Greatest among the seventeenth-century explorers was the Sieur de la Salle. Coming to Canada in 1666, he spent several years in trading among the eastern tribes and in the Ohio country. Then he conceived the idea of developing the fur trade of the Mississippi Valley on a grand scale. Visiting France to promote his project, he obtained the grant of a monopoly of the fur trade of the Valley. After misfortunes which would have discouraged a less resolute man, he began the descent of the river early in 1682, and reached its mouth in April. Two years later, having visited France again in the meantime, he came by sea in command of an expedition seeking the mouth of the Mississippi with the purpose of planting a colony there. Missing the goal, the party landed on the Texas coast, where after suffering great privation, La Salle's mutinous companions murdered him (1687). A few survivors succeeded in reaching the Illinois country.

The net result of La Salle's dream was the awakening of interest in the lower Valley. It was a dozen years, however, before a new expedition under the Canadian-born Sieur d'Iberville began a settlement at Biloxi (1699) in the present state of Mississippi.

A few years later the Mississippi was reëxplored in the hope of finding mines of copper, lead, and other metals. In disregard of the protest of the Spanish, who claimed the coast of the Gulf both to the westward and eastward, the French gradually extended their settlements, founding settlements near Mobile in 1702, New Orleans in 1718, and planting outposts on the Red and Arkansas rivers. Their occupation of the territory came in the nick of time, for an English expedition in quest of a site for a colony on the lower Mississippi turned back in 1699 on meeting a French vessel which had barely preceded them on the river. Traders from the Carolinas and Virginia had reached the Mississippi by this time, and they relaxed their activity not a whit after the coming of the

French. With the opening of the eighteenth century the lower Mississippi Basin and Gulf Plains became the scene of a keen rivalry involving Spanish, French, and English.

The second quarter of the eighteenth century was a time of considerable French activity west of the Mississippi. Marquette and Joliet had abandoned their descent of the river when they became satisfied that it flowed into the Gulf of Mexico, and not into the Pacific, as they had imagined; but the hope remained that by ascending its branches a way might be found to the "Sea of the West." The trade of new regions served as a continual lure to exploration. The native tribes of the Great Plains were visited, the Osage, Arkansas, and Rio Grande rivers explored, and in 1739 two brothers, Pierre and Paul Mallet, are believed to have crossed the plains to the Spanish settlements in New Mexico.

About the same time Varenne de Vérendrye was planning the extension of the fur trade westward from Lake Superior. By a chain of forts he hoped not only to command the trade of the country around the Lake of the Woods and Lake Winnipeg, but also to extend French influence so far that "the discovery of the Western Sea may be accomplished." From one of these posts Vérendrye's son Pierre crossed the northern plains in 1742–1743, going at least as far as the Black Hills.

Monopolistic commercial companies played a large part in the early history of the French colonies, but the paternalistic government maintained such close supervision that private initiative was almost stifled. In the eighteenth century both New France and Louisiana were under the crown, and were governed much like provinces in France, the most highly centralized country of western Europe. A governor appointed by the king headed the military as well as the civil administration, checked by another official (*intendant,* or *commissaire-ordonnateur*) who controlled expenditures, was chief justice in civil cases, and as agent of the king (or colonial ministry) watched the governor's conduct. This double-headed admin-istration divided authority and led to continual friction and quarreling. In New France the bishop was also an official of no slight importance, sharing civil and judicial power with the governor and intendant. From the body of the inhabit-ants, on the nomination of the governor and bishop, the crown appointed annually a number of councilors, who with the officials mentioned possessed all executive, legislative, and judicial powers, subject only to appeal to the government at Paris. The council was dominated by the three great officials, as were the local officers, and the colonists in general were without any voice in government.[1] On the other hand, in the remote Illinois country at least, the inhabitants of each village controlled local affairs in large degree.

A form of feudalism known as the "seigniorial system" was introduced into Canada at an early date, and was the basis of the tenure of land so far as agriculture was pursued. It was also the basis of an order of nobility. Many of the names which one meets in the history of Canada bear the title "Sieur" (Seigneur), the sign of the feudal lord. The tenants (*habitants*) cultivated their lands in narrow strips, paid a portion of their produce to their lord, patronized his mill and oven, and labored for him a few days each year, like the peas-ants of France and Germany. Although the seigneurs liked to spend their winters in Quebec, they were usually poor, and worked with their hands, like their tenants. The latter were happy and contented as a class, and the social barrier between them and their lords was so slight that it was often crossed by means of marriage.

Clerical bodies held large areas of land, and usually main-tained a more efficient cultivation than the lay farmers. New France did not produce the hardy frontier-farmer type so

[1] There was a similar council in Louisiana. Ecclesiastically Louisiana was under the Bishop of Quebec.

prevalent in the English colonies, although in the remote settlements, such as those in the Illinois country, most of the feudal features of the land system disappeared, replaced by individual ownership.

Permanent settlements were begun in the Illinois country

FRENCH EXPLORATIONS AND SETTLEMENTS TO 1763

at about the same time that the beginnings were made near the mouth of the Mississippi. La Salle had established Fort St. Louis on the Illinois River in 1682. A mission was opened at Cahokia in 1699; a rival one was founded at Kaskaskia near by in 1700. Fort Chartres and Prairie du Rocher, in the same vicinity, date from 1720 and 1733. At Detroit the French appeared in 1701, for by that time they could navigate the lower lakes without danger from the Iroquois. Vincennes on the Wabash (1732) and other outlying posts marked the spread of the diffuse French population.

In origin the Illinois settlements were the result of expansion from the St. Lawrence Basin, but circumstances tended to associate them with Louisiana. The Fox Indians of Wisconsin were enemies of the French and interposed a barrier between Canada and the Mississippi. The river also afforded an easier outlet for the produce of the villages on its banks than did the route through the Lakes. Illinois was finally (1731) incorporated with the southern province, and governed by a deputy of the intendant. By the middle of the eighteenth century the little cluster of villages, while maintaining some activity in the fur trade, had become noted as the chief agricultural community in the French mainland possessions. Quantities of produce were taken eastward to Detroit, but especially southward to the settlements along the lower river and to the French West Indies.

Canada also exported a little wheat and flour, but the agricultural production of French North America as a whole scarcely sufficed for its own needs.

ENGLAND IN AMERICA: VIRGINIA

England's rulers, like their neighbors across the Channel, for a long time showed little interest in lands beyond seas. Although the first European who explored the coast above Chesapeake Bay sailed under the English flag, he was an Italian (John Cabot, 1497) whom the penurious Henry VII allowed to embark at his own expense. Upon his return the king gave him a trifling present for finding "the new isle," a discovery on which his successors based their claim to half a continent.

It was not until 1578 that Englishmen made their first serious attempt at colonization. Sharing the belief, by that time current, that great advantages were to be derived from overseas enterprise, Queen Elizabeth, as lord of vacant lands under the feudal law, gave a patent for an American fief to Sir Humphrey Gilbert. Gilbert lost his life in a storm at sea; but within the six years allowed him for establishing a settlement, his half-brother, Sir Walter Raleigh, secured a renewal of the patent in his own name. In 1584 Raleigh sent an expedition to select a site for a colony on Chesapeake Bay, but his agents chose Roanoke Island, in Albemarle Sound. Several times during the next few years recruits were sent to Roanoke, but in each case, on one pretext or another, they abandoned the settlement. The last attempt was made in 1587. After landing his passengers the master of the vessel returned to England for supplies, arriving just at the moment when the country was threatened by Spain's Armada. He was detained by the war crisis, and when the colony was visited again, in 1591, the whites had disappeared. The best conjecture is that they had found homes among some friendly native tribe.

Early in the next century some of Raleigh's friends decided to make another trial. Taught by experience that great losses must be expected before profit could be realized, they abandoned the feudal grant and organized a joint-stock company.

Before proceeding further it is important to note that the character of English colonization was shaped in large measure by the middle class. In Spain and France the rise of this class was checked by the growth of strong monarchies; but in England it was never more than temporarily halted; and eventually, through the growth of the system of representation in Parliament, it gained control of the government. While, therefore, in tracing the achievements of Spain and France in the New World, the student is much concerned with the institutions and policies developed by autocracies, in studying English colonization, on the contrary, the customs and institutions of the middle class are more significant, because of the prominent rôle of this class in the national life. The policies of the government, in fact, were shaped by the wishes of the dominant groups among the English population.

For this reason the history of English commerce is significant in connection with American history. The beginnings of trade, both domestic and foreign, were made at the initiative of the merchant class organized in the gilds of the medieval towns. Even in the extension of commerce to foreign countries, the king's part was generally little more than to approve by charter the plans of the merchants' organizations, and to promote these plans, on occasion, by the negotiation of treaties. At the beginning of the sixteenth century (1503) one of the most notable of these groups, known as the "Merchants Adventurers," received its first charter from the English crown. It was the forerunner of the great trading corporations which were to extend their operations to far-off India and America.

The charter of the Merchants Adventurers provided for a governor and twenty-four assistants to manage the company's business. This management included jurisdiction over the Englishmen who resided abroad as agents or employés of the company. Commercial organizations operating in foreign countries thus possessed political functions which in the case of the communities established in the New World became the germs of governments.

The group of promoters who revived Raleigh's project took as its model the charter of the British East India Company, in which the total capital was divided into shares, each of small amount, to be sold to many persons. The device brought together a larger sum than any one person could command, and if the undertaking brought no profits, no investor was liable beyond the sum paid for his shares. Without some system of limited liability it is difficult to see how the beginners of English colonization could have commanded the capital necessary to obtain a permanent foothold.

Upon application of the promoters King James granted them (1606) a charter for two such companies, known respectively as the "London Company" and the "Plymouth Company." To each was given a tract of land with exclusive rights of settlement and trade.

Under a new charter of 1612 the London Company became a self-governing corporation, with the privilege not only of managing its business affairs but of governing the people in the plantation. It was authorized to hold a meeting in London four times each year, known as the "general court," at which a majority of the stockholders present could elect officers and make "such Laws and Ordinances for the Good and Welfare of the said Plantation" as they thought "requisite and meet," so long as they were not contrary to the laws of England. For the transaction of routine business there was a smaller body including the officers chosen by the general court. From this time the London Company was commonly known as the "Virginia Company."[1]

The stockholders were of two classes: those who bought shares and remained in England were known as "adventurers," while those who emigrated were called "planters." Many of the planters were men of little or no means, for the

---

[1] A second charter of 1609 is passed by as a mere step in the transition from the first to the third. Its most notable feature was the new definition of the bounds of the company's grant—along the coast two hundred miles each way from Point Comfort, and "up into the land throughout from sea to sea, west and northwest." The terms "planter" and "adventurer" are used in the second charter.

company was glad to give a share of stock to an able-bodied man who would "adventure his person." The company undertook to maintain the planters at the common expense for a period of years, but during that term all products were to be sold for the benefit of the common treasury. At the end of the period the profits and the lands in the "plantation" were to be divided among the stockholders of both classes.

Success in the undertaking required that the colony should not only sustain itself but produce something which could not be grown or made in England and for which there was a considerable demand. Such a staple was found in the native tobacco plant. Its cultivation was begun about 1612 and within a few years it became the chief product, affording Virginia its economic basis.

But the company did not prosper. The plan did not supply the incentive needed to draw forth the best efforts of the planters, and harsh measures were required to keep them at work. The severe discipline and the unwholesome climate caused much discontent, and with the high death rate made it difficult to obtain immigrants. A great step forward was taken when the joint-stock period ended in 1616. Although the company had made no profits, a "land dividend" of one hundred acres was awarded to each planter. Soon after this a grant was promised for each immigrant—to be given to him if he paid the cost of his passage across the Atlantic, otherwise to the person who did so. This practice, with the size of the grant fixed at fifty acres and known as the "head right," became the basis of the Virginia land system.

About the same time the company began to offer large tracts to "societies" which would purchase shares of stock. These societies were expected to find their own immigrants to supply the labor needed on their "particular plantations," as they were called.

Under the stimulus of these new plans Virginia began to grow rapidly. Plantations appeared along the banks of the James, both above and below Jamestown. They were usually far apart, for tobacco growers desired plenty of room to expand operations. Another class of inhabitants also appeared. These were the "indented" servants, who were bound to work for a time (about four years on the average) for the person who defrayed the cost of their passage. The owners of particular plantations imported many such servants, some of whom were promised lands of their own upon the expiration of their terms.

These changes in the economic system were accompanied by changes of equal importance in the government. For six years after the granting of the charter of 1612 the planters were ruled and the business managed by governors and councilors chosen by the general court and sent out to Virginia. As stockholders the planters were probably entitled to vote in the general court if it had been possible for them to attend its sessions. Soon after the adoption of the new land policy, therefore, the company established a Virginia branch of the court, as the most feasible means of giving the planters an active share in the management. The governor and council were still to be chosen by the general court, but Governor George Yeardley's instructions of 1619 directed him to call upon the free inhabitants of each plantation to choose representatives to join with him and the council, at Jamestown, in passing ordinances for the welfare of the colony.

The settlements were grouped for this purpose into eleven "boroughs," and the representatives were called "burgesses." The ordinances passed by the assembly were subject to the approval of the general court, while those of the general court were equally subject to the approval of the assembly. The Virginia assembly of 1619 is memorable because it marks the extension to America of the British principle of representa-

STATUE OF POCAHONTAS

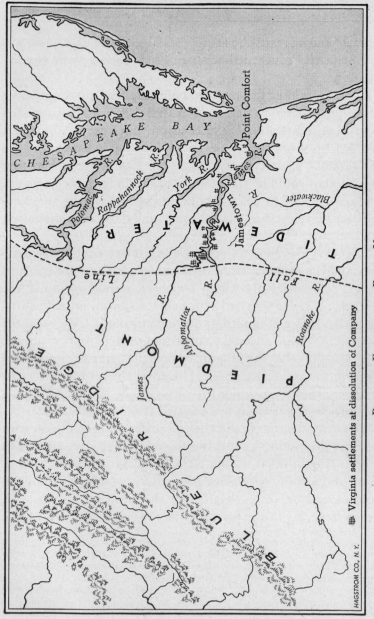

PHYSICAL FEATURES OF EARLY VIRGINIA

⌗ Virginia settlements at dissolution of Company

HAGSTROM CO., N.Y.

21

tion, although it must be remembered that the enterprise was
still primarily concerned with business rather than government.

A few years after this notable event the Virginia Company's
career was brought to a close. An Indian massacre in 1622 led
to a royal commission of investigation which revealed so great
a loss of life from this cause and from disease that an action
was brought against the company of a kind similar to that
which today would be called an application for a receivership.
The sequel was, in 1624, a court decree dissolving the company and placing the "plantation" under the administration
of the crown.[1]

With this judgment Virginia ceased to be a trading corporation, and the changed circumstances emphasized the political
aspects of colonial life which had been secondary under the
company. There was little immediate alteration of the government so far as the settlers were concerned. After a short
interval they were allowed to continue to elect representatives
to an assembly, but the king instead of the company appointed
the governor and councilors. The governor became the agent
of the crown, acting under the terms of the royal commission
and such instructions as were issued from time to time.

The earnest entreaties of the colonists had much to do with
the king's decision to continue the assembly. In America as
at home Englishmen were attached to representative government, and already they were particularly jealous of the principle of taxation by legislators of their own choosing, as is
shown by an act of the assembly of 1624 declaring "That the

[1] It was long believed that the policies of the liberal faction in the company were due to a deliberate design to establish a virtual republic in Virginia, and that the dissolution of the company was the result of the king's
apprehensions as to the effects of the discussions in the general court upon
his own control of Parliament. These views seem to have been overstressed;
probably the emphasis should be placed on the desire of the company to
make the colony prosperous and profitable, and cn the discredit brought
upon the management by its mistakes and misfortunes.

Governor shall lay no taxes . . . upon the Colony, its lands or goods, other way than by the authority of the General Assembly."

The assembly lost the right of assenting to measures decided upon in England relating to Virginia, and its acts became subject to veto by the governor. Gradually the government in the colony conformed to the pattern of that of the mother country. After many years (about 1676) the burgesses and councilors separated into two houses; the one suggests the British House of Commons, the other the Lords. It was but natural that in the new country Englishmen should follow in general the forms which long usage had made habitual.

SELECT BIBLIOGRAPHY

(A full list of the books and articles cited in the bibliographies at the close of the chapters in this volume, with places and dates of publication, will be found in the Appendix.)

The following comprehensive works are useful for broad periods of American history:

The American Nation: A History, is a series comprising twenty-eight volumes, prepared under the editorship of Albert Bushnell Hart. Each volume is the work of a recognized authority on the period which it covers, and while the merits of the studies vary, the series as a whole is one of the most useful of the works which cover all or a large part of our history. A valuable feature is the chapter on the authorities used, which appears at the close of each volume.

The Chronicles of America, consisting of fifty volumes edited by Allen Johnson, is likewise the product of a group of scholars. Each volume gives a fairly complete treatment of a single topic. While the style is intended to be popular, the series maintains a high level of accuracy and trustworthiness.

Newer than either of the preceding is *A History of American Life,* edited by Arthur M. Schlesinger and Dixon R. Fox. When completed, this work will contain twelve volumes, each by a specialist. As the title indicates, the scope is broad, with emphasis upon social and intellectual rather than political history.

For this reason the series stands almost alone among general histories. The final chapter in each volume is a careful survey of the authorities and sources. Individual volumes of all these series are cited in appropriate connections.

The Narrative and Critical History of America, in eight volumes, edited by Justin Winsor, was the first notable product of co-operative historical effort in this country. It is a work of great learning; its discussions of historical sources are especially authoritative. However, it was published a half-century ago, and needs to be supplemented at many points by newer works. It stresses the extension of geographical knowledge, political development, and diplomatic relations. The great bulk of the series is devoted to the colonial period.

John Fiske's *Historical Works* cover the period from the discovery of America to the adoption of the Constitution. They are noteworthy for literary excellence, but in scholarship leave somewhat to be desired.

George Bancroft's *History of the United States,* beginning with the first efforts at colonization and ending with the ratification of the Constitution, is written in a tone of extravagant patriotism, and, at times, with inattention to the sources.

Edward Channing's *History of the United States,* the six volumes of which narrate the history of the country from the age of discovery to the close of the Civil War, is a notable work of recent scholarship.

The History of the United States by Elroy M. Avery, in seven volumes, supplies a readable narrative ending with the year 1806. It is especially valuable for its maps and illustrations.

The Rise of American Civilization, in three volumes, by Charles A. and Mary R. Beard, is a recent thoughtful and stimulating interpretation.

An excellent collection of extracts from contemporary accounts is to be found in the ten volumes of *Original Narratives of Early American History,* edited by John F. Jameson. Another valuable collection of illustrative source material is *American History Told by Contemporaries,* in five volumes, edited by Albert B. Hart. It covers the whole period from 1492 to 1919. A series of official documents of great utility to students has been collected in three volumes by MacDonald: *Select Charters, Select Documents,* and *Select Statutes.* In *Documents of American History,*

Commager has collected illustrative materials of many kinds.

References, including citation of sources, for almost every phase of colonial history, are given in the bibliographies in Chitwood, *History of Colonial America,* and Sanders, *Early American History.* These textbooks are themselves valuable for collateral reading on the colonial period.

The maps of the *American Nation* series are available in one volume. The most elaborate map book is Paullin, Atlas of the Historical Geography of the United States. Various aspects of American development are treated pictorially in Gabriel, ed., *The Pageant of America.*

Spanish Colonization. The events in Europe which bear upon the discovery and early colonization of America are reviewed by Cheyney, *European Background of American History,* Channing, *United States,* I, and Abbott, *Expansion of Europe.* The extension of geographical knowledge is the theme of Beazley, *Dawn of Modern Geography.* It ends with the year 1420, but the story is carried forward by the same author in *Prince Henry the Navigator.* Baker, *A History of Geographical Discovery and Exploration,* is a recent publication covering ancient as well as modern times.

Most of the lives of Columbus are voluminous; that by Markham combines brevity, accuracy, clearness, and readability. Duff, *The Truth about Columbus and the Discovery of America,* is one of the latest efforts to summarize modern views. Fiske, in the *Discovery of America,* tells the story of the Spanish explorations, conquests, and settlements in his usual fascinating way. See also the more recent works by Chapman, *Colonial Hispanic America,* Cotterill, *A Short History of the Americas,* and Jones, *An Introduction to Hispanic-American History.* Bourne, *Spain in America,* is an excellent discussion of the whole subject indicated by the title. Kirkpatrick, *The Spanish Conquistadores,* Maynard, *De Soto and the Conquistadores,* and Richman, *The Spanish Conquerors,* deal with the initial explorations and settlements. Moses, *The Establishment of Spanish Rule in America,* gives a good account of the system of government. Priestley, *The Coming of the White Man,* discusses the social and economic life of New Spain. To these references may be added Lowery, *Spanish Settlements within the Present Limits of the United States (1513–1561)*; and, for contemporary accounts, Hodge, *Spanish*

Explorers in the Southern United States, and Bolton, *Spanish Explorations in the Southwest* (both in the *Original Narratives* series).

One of the means by which Spanish expansion was accomplished is described in Bolton, "The Mission as a Frontier Institution in the Spanish American Colonies" (in his *Wider Horizons of American History*). The Spanish occupation of California is the theme of Chapman, *The Founding of Spanish California,* and *A History of California.* The story of the journeys by land and sea to California is told in Cleland, *Pathfinders.* Caughey, *History of the Pacific Coast,* gives much space to the Spanish period in California.

French Activities: England in America. Bourne, Channing, Fiske, Priestley, and Winsor, in the works mentioned above, deal with the French and English efforts in the sixteenth century. The standard history of the work of the French for the period is Parkman, *Pioneers of New France.* Later are Winsor, *Cartier to Frontenac,* Munro, *Crusaders of New France,* and the volume on Canada in the *Cambridge History of the British Empire.* Mulvey, *French Catholic Missionaries in the Present United States,* is especially good for the Illinois country.

Wood, *Elizabethan Sea Dogs,* treats of romantic phases of the English-Spanish rivalry in the later decades of the sixteenth century. Beer, *The Origins of the British Colonial System, 1578–1660,* analyses the economic background of the English attempts at colonization, and marks out the lines within which most recent studies of British expansion and colonial administration have been carried out. Older studies of value are Seeley, *The Growth of British Policy,* Seeley, *Expansion of England,* and Egerton, *Short History of British Colonial Policy.* Robinson, *Development of the British Empire,* is a good general textbook which tells the story of expansion well. Biggar, *The Precursors of Jacques Cartier;* Brebner, *The Explorers of North America;* and Williamson, *The Voyages of the Cabots,* deal with the history of discovery. For source accounts, see Burrage, *Early English and French Voyages,* and Grant, *Voyages of Champlain* (both in *Original Narratives*).

In addition to Channing and Winsor, the following general accounts of the English colonies become important with the beginnings of Virginia: Andrews, *The Colonial Period of Ameri-*

can History, a work still in progress, is by the leading American scholar in the field. *Our Earliest Colonial Settlements,* by the same writer, is a brief but illuminating survey. Doyle, *The English Colonies in America,* is the standard English treatise. Volume I deals with Virginia, Maryland, and the Carolinas.

Osgood, *The American Colonies in the Seventeenth Century,* is a careful and critical account of institutional history. Fiske, *Old Virginia and Her Neighbors,* tells the story of the southern colonies. Johnston, *Pioneers of the Old South,* covers the same ground more briefly. A scholarly political history of Virginia is Wertenbaker, *Virginia under the Stuarts.* The same writer is author of *The First Americans, 1607–1690.* Three books of great merit, all by Bruce, are: *The Economic History of Virginia in the Seventeenth Century; The Institutional History of Virginia in the Seventeenth Century;* and *Social Life of Virginia in the Seventeenth Century.* See also the *History of Virginia* by the same author, and Stanard, *Story of Virginia's First Century.*

Chapter II

PURITAN COLONIZATION

THE PILGRIMS AND PLYMOUTH

THE love of adventure, the hope of gain, and the desire for political and religious liberty have been the mainsprings of emigration from the Old World to the New. While the Virginia Company was vainly seeking profits on the banks of the James River, other Englishmen, self-exiled for conscience' sake, were making homes on the shores of Cape Cod Bay.

Back of the beginnings of New England is the religious history of the motherland. The Anglican Church, which had separated from the Roman under Henry VIII, took definite form under Elizabeth (1558–1603). As then established it was a compromise and included both Catholic and Protestant elements.[1] Extremists on both sides were therefore dissatisfied; Catholics were offended by the departure from the old faith, while Protestants were displeased by the retention of what they termed the vestiges of Romanism.

The discontented Protestants, called "Puritans," did not agree among themselves. The Nonconformists believed in one national church, and were content to remain within the establishment, departing from its practices, so far as they dared, in the direction of "purer" forms of worship. They desired more preaching and simpler ceremonies. Some of them (the Presbyterians) wished to substitute Calvin's plan of church government for the episcopal system. There were

---

[1] The acts establishing the national Church made the ruler its head instead of the Pope and provided for its support by taxation. No other religious organization was recognized as legal.

28

other Puritans whose dissent was so decided that they withdrew from the Anglican communion. Desiring the separation of church and state and congregational control in religious matters, they were called "Independents," or "Separatists."

James I (1603–1625) disliked the Nonconformists extremely. He feared that their agitation for changes in the Church would end in the curtailment of his prerogative. He therefore formed a close alliance with the Anglican party, and put his view in the epigrammatic form, "no bishop, no king." The king had good reason to fear the Puritans, for in truth they were the heart of the political group which stood for the powers of Parliament as against his claim to rule by "divine right."

The Separatists were objects of the king's particular displeasure. One congregation of them, to escape his persecution, left their home at Scrooby in Nottinghamshire and fled to Holland. For several years they dwelt in Leyden, where they enjoyed religious liberty; but as their livelihood could be won only by labor as wage-earners, and their surroundings were non-English, they became discontented. They desired a new home where they might maintain an English community and become independent in worldly estate.

When they heard of the particular plantations in Virginia, they planned to settle in that colony, and their application for lands was promptly granted when the liberal faction gained control of the Virginia Company. On the voyage the vessel, the famous *Mayflower,* ran out of her course, and near the end of the year 1620 landed her passengers on the shores of Cape Cod Bay. Winter being at hand, the company decided to remain. After some days spent in seeking a proper site, a point on the west side of the bay, already known as Plymouth, was chosen. There was here a satisfactory harbor, a brook with good water, a good site for a fort on a near-by hill, and much cleared land. Moreover, the neighborhood was un-inhabited, the native population having been destroyed by a plague.

This region was beyond the bounds of the Virginia Com-pany, and by planting their settlement on lands for which they had no grant the Pilgrims became "squatters." They proceeded by an act of "squatter sovereignty," to set up a government. Before landing the men drew up the "May-flower Compact," forming a "civil body politic," each member of which pledged himself to submit to the will of the majority.

The Mayflower Compact was not an assertion of independ-ence, but arose from necessity, since for the time being there was no other means of preserving order. Nor can the com-pact properly be called a constitution, as it did not provide a plan of government. This was left to evolve as needed. At first public business was carried on by a "general meeting" of the men. This assembly determined what was for the good of the colony and dealt with offenders, exercising both legisla-tive and judicial functions. For executive duties it chose a governor and one or more "assistants." [1]

It was not long before the general meeting became imprac-ticable, as settlement scattered more and more widely. Then it was decided that each community should send delegates to the general court, which took the place of the original general meeting, and hold its own "town meeting" for local business.

[1] The Mayflower Compact was an application to civil affairs of the Sepa-ratist theory of church government by members of the congregation. The act of the Pilgrims in thus setting up a provisional government was the first of a long series which have distinguished our history. Whenever Anglo-Americans have found themselves in the wilderness, thrown upon their own devices, they have promptly resorted to the expedient of erecting "homespun" governments. Repeated experiences of this kind undoubtedly did much to develop the American creed that "governments derive their just powers from the consent of the governed." The roots of the doctrine, to be sure, are English. The creed was formulated in England notably by the philosopher John Locke, late in the seventeenth century, and in France by Jean J. Rousseau in the eighteenth. America offered many opportunities for the pioneers to put the theory into actual effect.

Each "town" also had its church, the members of each congregation choosing their own pastor and transacting all business relating to ecclesiastical ·affairs. Plymouth colony thus became a little republic. The democracy of Congregationalism tended distinctly towards democracy in government.

The Leyden congregation was so poor that the money for the removal to America had to be borrowed from capitalists in London. To meet this debt the men of the colony established fishing stations and posts for trading with the Indians on the coast of Massachusetts and Maine and in the valley of the Connecticut River. For sustenance they relied upon the produce of their fields and fisheries.

Conditions of life were hard in the Plymouth colony. In spite of the mild winter half of the original company died during the first three months in America. Yet the survivors did not lose heart. Their numbers were recruited before the autumn by newcomers, and the first harvest, supplemented by the migrating wild-fowl, sufficed to remove the fear of immediate want.

But Plymouth did not increase rapidly either in wealth or population. The first group of settlers numbered only about one hundred, and although others came from Leyden during the following years, that source of immigrants was soon drained. Thereafter Plymouth grew chiefly by an overflow from Massachusetts Bay. In effect Massachusetts gradually absorbed the smaller colony. Although a land patent was obtained from the New England Council (the successor of the Plymouth Company of 1606), all efforts to secure a royal charter failed, and Plymouth was finally (1691) incorporated with its neighbor.

MASSACHUSETTS BAY

The Massachusetts Bay colony, which became by far the most populous and powerful of the New England communities, was not founded until Plymouth was nearly a decade old. It owed its origin to the discord between the Puritan party and the king. James I was a man of scholarly tastes, who contrasted favorably in personal morals with his Tudor predecessors. But he lacked the Tudor tact. In his own opinion he was responsible to God alone for his conduct as ruler. Parliament, he thought, should provide funds for the government without meddling with the way in which it was carried on. He could not avoid applying to Parliament for funds, however, and the House of Commons, the stronghold of Puritanism, would not grant money unless he would enforce the laws against Catholics and treat Nonconformists leniently. Because of the friction which came with every effort to deal with Parliament, James summoned it as seldom as possible; in the twenty-two years of his reign there were but eight sessions.

Under Charles I, who came to the throne in 1625, the situation grew still worse. When Parliament refused taxes for an unwise war, Charles levied forced loans. Parliament then drew up the Petition of Right, which the reluctant king accepted in 1628 in order to obtain a money grant. In the growth of the British constitution the Petition of Right ranks in importance with the Great Charter wrested from King John in 1215. It made illegal the collection of money without authority of an act of Parliament.

Almost immediately another dispute arose. The House of Commons tried to punish some of the Anglican clergymen who leaned towards Catholicism. The king forbade the proceedings and decided to be rid of the troublesome Puritans. He therefore dissolved Parliament in 1629 and did not summon another session until 1640. In France and elsewhere rulers were setting up autocratic monarchies and Charles hoped to do the same. He and Archbishop Laud began to enforce conformity with a strong hand, while the disheartened Puritans turned their hopes towards New England as a land of promise.

The way was already prepared for a Puritan migration. The Plymouth Company of 1606 had done little more than license trading and fishing vessels to visit the New England coast. Among a number of stations which its licensees had established was one at Cape Ann. In 1628 some of the owners of this station purchased lands from the reorganized Plymouth Company, and in the next year they obtained a royal charter. This charter was much like the third one of the Virginia Company. It created a trading corporation, which was made proprietor of any colonies which it might set up within its grant, and given the right to govern them in accordance with English law. As in the case of the Virginia Company, the stockholders, called "freemen of the Company," met in general court to manage affairs and elect officers consisting of a governor, deputy governor, and eighteen "assistants."

Upon the abrogation of the Virginia Company's charter, the king had declared his intention of retaining the government of future colonies in his own hands. If Charles I had foreseen the results of creating "The Governor and Company of Massachusetts Bay," he would doubtless have adhered to this resolution of his father, for during the summer following the dissolution of Parliament in 1629 the Puritan leaders set on foot a plan to utilize the new trading corporation in founding in the New World "a bulwark against the Kingdom of Anti-Christ." To bring this about it was arranged, by an agreement signed at Cambridge, that all stockholders who did not wish to emigrate to America should transfer their rights under the charter to the members of the company who would go. John Winthrop, who had been prominent in the contest between Parliament and king, was chosen governor, and by March, 1630, he and others were ready to sail. During that year seventeen vessels carried some two thousand persons to Massachusetts Bay. Thus began the "Puritan Exodus," or "Great Migration," which peopled Massachusetts in the course of a decade with sixteen thousand souls.

The lands around Boston Bay filled up rapidly. Salem, Boston, Charlestown, Watertown, and Newtown (Cambridge) were founded within a year or two. The coast plain was narrow, and the higher levels back of the plain were strewn with glacial boulders which made cultivation of the soil difficult. The early towns were generally located on level terraces only slightly above the reach of high tide. In the cultivation of these lands and in the neighboring fisheries, along with the Indian trade, the early inhabitants found their occupations. Settlement spread inland less rapidly than along the coast, for want of navigable streams such as made tide-water Virginia a "sylvan Venice." The soil did not lend itself to the production of a single staple like tobacco, but was tilled for food. The dispersing influence of the plantation was lacking, and the congregational system in the church made for compact settlement.

In none of the early colonies did the English know how to deal with the wilderness. Occasionally a man showed exceptional capacity to adapt himself to the primitive environment. John Smith of Virginia, Edward Winslow and Captain Miles Standish of Plymouth, were quick to learn woodcraft and the art of dealing with the natives. In many ways, such for example as the cultivation of maize, the natives became the white men's teachers. It took time to evolve the bold and adventurous type of pioneer who loved the wilds and feared no danger or privation. Most of the early-comers were merely transplanted English villagers who were pitifully unprepared to face the hardships of an untamed land.

The Bay colony paid its full toll in human life and suffering before the day of security and comfort was attained. Al-

though free from the fevers which plagued the Virginia lowlands, New England endured far greater extremes of heat and
cold than either Virginia or the British Isles.   Deaths from
exposure in winter were not uncommon.   During the first few
years the influx of population overtaxed the capacity to produce food, and semifamine prevailed.   Upon women and children the severities of life fell like a blight.   In Plymouth the
first May found only four women alive of the eighteen who
landed in January, and many indeed of those who came to
Massachusetts Bay merely passed through "on the way to
Heaven."

The leaders were disappointed but not discouraged by the
unexpected privations.   Winthrop abandoned hope of improving his temporal fortune with the words "we may not
look for great things here."   Thomas Dudley, his associate,
found conditions "short of our expectations."   But the chief
purpose of these men was not material gain; according to
Winthrop they sought to build "a City of God on earth," and
New England they called the "New Canaan."

In contrast, the motives of many of the inhabitants were
purely worldly.   Economic conditions were especially bad in
the English counties where Puritanism was strong.   Besides,
within the tract granted to the company there were seven
little settlements in 1630, remnants of the fishing and trading
ventures licensed during the twenties.   The total population
of these was small, but the Puritan chiefs added to this element by bringing in many indented servants.   Winthrop
alone had twenty such servants in his household.   While
many persons of this class may have been honest and capable,
they came as a rule from the least promising portion of the
English nation.

The great body of the Puritan immigrants belonged to the
middle class of small farmers, tradesmen, and craftsmen who
felt the continual pressure of poverty and were accustomed to

follow the lead of the minister and squire. With these, religious and economic motives were doubtless mingled in
varying degrees.[1] Of the two thousand who came in 1630
only about twelve were "freemen of the Company" and
signers of the Cambridge agreement. This handful of aristocrats therefore composed at the time the entire body of
stockholders and the agreement placed all of the privileges
granted by the charter in their hands. They composed the
general court, and by its election all of them were also assistants.

This small group thus had the legal right to govern all of
the other emigrants to Massachusetts; but some of the others
soon demanded admission to the company. As the malcontents with their families represented a considerable fraction
of the population, the assistants feared that if they refused
their demand, there would be an exodus to Plymouth or some
attractive unsettled spot. On the other hand, to grant it and
admit the new members to the general court might cost the
old group its control.

To retain their power the assistants violated the charter.
They decided to admit the new freemen, but allowed them
only the privilege of voting for assistants "when these are to
be chosen," reserving to themselves the legislative power and
the choice of governor. By this unwarranted action they
transferred the legislative function from the general court
to the court of assistants. At about the same time they
"ordered that for time to come no man shall be admitted to
the freedom of this body politicke but such as are members
of some of the churches within the lymitts of the same."

All might now have gone smoothly had not the laws passed

[1] Some years after the founding of Massachusetts Bay, a minister, exhorting
the inhabitants of one of these villages to continue "a religious people . . .
the main end of planting this wilderness," drew forth the retort: "Sir . . .
our main end was to catch fish!"

by the assistants favored the upper classes by limiting the
wages of artisans and laying penalties upon the poor man
whose stock wandered from the woodland to the unfenced
fields of his betters. Perhaps some rumor of the true nature
of the charter raised doubts of the competence of the court of
assistants to pass any laws. In any case, in 1634 a group of
freemen from several of the towns asked Winthrop to show
them the charter. He produced it, but frankly told the delegation that the freemen did not have men among them who
were qualified to share in legislation; he intimated that the
assistants would lend an ear to the suggestions of a committee
chosen by the freemen. From this time on the towns sent
deputies to act with the assistants at each meeting of the general court, and the "suggestions" of the deputies speedily
became in practice a share in legislation.

By these steps the freemen regained their charter rights,
but the leaven of democracy worked slowly. The freemen
were for a long time only a small fraction of the population,
and because of the requirement of church membership were
in effect chosen by the ministers. Besides, they were too
thoroughly imbued with belief in the superiority of the gentry
to choose farmers or artisans as officials, and the influence of
the aristocracy, lay and clerical, continued to be enormous.
The aims of the magistrates (officers and members of the
court of assistants) and clergy were so identified and their
coöperation so close that the government is sometimes described as a "theocracy." The deputies really represented
the orthodox church members, and as the popular element in
the law-making body, only slightly offset the influence of the
assistants. The viewpoints of the two groups were different
enough, nevertheless, to cause some friction, and after an unusually warm dispute in 1644 they decided to sit as two
houses.

In the events narrated we can trace the evolution, step by step, of a constitution from the charter of a commercial corporation. A colony which, like Massachusetts, enjoyed self-government is called a "corporate" colony, to distinguish it from the proprietary and royal types, in both of which a large degree of control was exercised from without.

The Massachusetts Puritans professed allegiance to the English Church but put into practice the purified service which they had advocated in England. In effect they really separated from the English Church and gravitated towards the congregational system of Plymouth. Yet the union of church and state was preserved and a Puritan establishment resulted. As Winthrop put it, he and his associates had come "to seek out a place of cohabitation under a due form of government both civil and ecclesiastical." In addition to the denial of the franchise to all non-members of the church, no churches were allowed except of the approved type, and the clergy assembled in synods were habitually consulted on political questions.

The religious aims of the founders of the "New England Canaan" are further shown in the code of laws known as the Body of Liberties, which was adopted in 1641.[1] Although the code embodied many principles of English law, its penalties for criminal offenses were based in great part upon the Old Testament. From this source the "Bible Commonwealth" drew the decree of death not for murder alone, but for blasphemy, idolatry, and the practice of witchcraft. The Body of Liberties is also an evidence of the disposition of the colonists to legislate for themselves, according to the needs arising from their local situation, rather than to copy the laws of distant England. Finally they imposed a certain restraint upon the magistrates by providing a set of fixed prin-

---

[1] The Body of Liberties was superseded in 1648 by an enlarged code known as *The Laws and Liberties of Massachusetts.*

ciples to guide them in making judgments, in place of their mere discretion.

It must not be supposed that events in New England passed wholly unnoticed by the king. Malcontents from the colony complained that the Puritans were setting up an independent church and state, and as early as 1634 a royal commission ordered Massachusetts to submit its charter for scrutiny. The colonial authorities delayed their reply and sent an agent to persuade the English officials to forego their inquest. Meantime fortifications were erected and other preparations made for defense. The crown took steps to enforce the surrender of the charter, but decisive action was prevented by the disturbances in England which led to the Civil War of the forties.

The demands of the king were a part of his plan for enforcing conformity throughout the British dominions. New England escaped chiefly because of distance. In Scotland the Presbyterian "Covenanters'" resistance caused the failure of the king's experiment at rule without Parliament. By various devices, including the exaction of "ship-money," through the enforcement of an obsolete law, Charles succeeded for a decade in raising funds, but when his ecclesiastical policy provoked armed resistance in Scotland, an army became necessary, and the only way to obtain sufficient money for the payment of the soldiers was to call Parliament and ask for a grant. Parliament demanded reforms before it would vote taxes, and the quarrel which followed culminated in war between its supporters and those of the king. Broadly speaking, the king's camp contained the Anglicans, while the Puritans of all varieties upheld the cause of Parliament. Beginning in 1642, the Civil War ended seven years later in the triumph of the parliamentary party and the trial and execution of Charles I. The interregnum which followed was ended in 1660 by the restoration of the Stuart line.

These events directly influenced the progress of colonization. The Puritan emigration coincides with the period of
Charles' personal government. With the meeting of Parliament in 1640 the movement was checked. In fact, many
Puritans returned to England, and the triumph of their party
there gave the impulse for a considerable migration of
Royalists to Virginia, where the English Church was established by the laws.

Social distinctions, almost wanting in Plymouth, were
marked in Massachusetts Bay. Slaves were never numerous,
but Indians and Negroes of this status were at the bottom of
the scale. Indented servants came next. The third class
included those who did not own land or pursue a trade as independent workmen but labored for hire. The farmers and
skilled craftsmen composed yet another group, forming the
main body of the Puritan population, and inferior socially
only to the small class from which were drawn the magistrates
and ministers. The last were the gentry, who alone enjoyed
the then significant title of "Master," since transformed into
our universally used "Mister."

The gentry belonged to the social rank which in England
composed the House of Commons and as country squires or
magistrates held the county offices. Many of them, especially
the clergymen, were trained in the universities. They were
aristocrats by tradition and profession. They were brave
and honorable idealists, but the moral quickening of their
religion had not completely freed them from the narrowness
and bigotry which their times had inherited from the Middle
Ages. Social distinctions were to them real indexes of worth.
They could suffer from the pinch of rising prices without
perceiving why smiths and carpenters should raise their scale
of charges. Women's activities were restricted to the home,
and when they appeared in public, as at "meeting," they were
expected to maintain a modest silence.

EXPANSION AND UNION IN NEW ENGLAND

In Massachusetts the occupied area was extended, not as in Virginia, by granting land to individuals but by the incorporation of new towns by groups.[1] The first step was an application to the general court. If the court approved the petition, the group was recognized as incorporators of the town and a tract of land was assigned to the corporate body. The incorporators then laid out the lands and assigned plots to their own members and others at their will, the more important persons receiving the larger plots, in favored locations. Meadows, pastures, and woodlands were held in common, as they had been for ages in the village communities of the Old World.

The town soon became one of the most significant of the institutions of New England. It early gained the right of sending representatives to the general court. It also became the unit of local self-government. The town meeting was the body through which the inhabitants acted. It passed by-laws providing for local interests, it elected officers to administer these laws, it chose the deputies to the general court. In different towns the privileges of the inhabitants varied somewhat. Only freemen of the company could vote for deputies in any of them, but in other respects some of the towns gave non-freemen equal rights. Some of them, in short, were little democracies. Although, taking the population as a whole, only a small percentage of the adult men were fully enfranchised, so many were in constant contact with public business that Thomas Jefferson, many years later, called the town meeting "the best school of political liberty the world ever saw."

Massachusetts soon became the mother of other colonies.

---

[1] Note that the word "town" in the New England sense means "township" rather than "village." It is also used to denote the corporate body.

A fur trader named John Oldham found a trail leading to the Connecticut River and brought back such a glowing report of the lands in the river valley that a new migration was begun in that direction.   Lacking good land, and somewhat dissatisfied in other ways, some of the Newtown people and others from neighboring towns, under the lead of Thomas Hooker, the Newtown pastor, started the movement in 1635. Within two years Windsor, Hartford, and Wethersfield had been founded, and the total population was about eight hundred.   In 1639 a plan of government was adopted, known as the "Fundamental Orders of Connecticut."

Like Plymouth, Connecticut was a squatter colony, for the founders had no legal title to the lands taken, and the Fundamental Orders, like the Mayflower Compact, rested on the assent of the people.   But being more specific than the earlier compact as to the frame of the government, they mark another step in the evolution of the idea of a written constitution.

The Connecticut government and church were very much like those of Massachussetts, but the Fundamental Orders, instead of requiring the voter to be a church member, left his qualifications to be determined by the town.   In 1659, however, a property qualification was adopted by the general court which stood with slight change until the nineteenth century.   After nearly a generation Connecticut obtained a royal charter (1662) which gave a legal sanction for the institutions which had been set up without permission.

While the settlements on the Connecticut River were taking form, another appeared farther west at New Haven, on Long Island Sound.   The New Haven people differed but little from the Puritans of Massachusetts and Connecticut, but most of them came directly from England.   The story of New Haven repeats the tale of government-making which we have noted in the case of Connecticut, but this colony was united with Connecticut when it was given a charter.

About the time that Connecticut received its first white inhabitants other groups from Massachusetts began the settlement of Rhode Island. These emigrants did not leave voluntarily, like the pioneers of Connecticut, but were expelled on account of their religious views. Winthrop and his like were not advocates of toleration. Liberty of worship, said one of them, is liberty "to blaspheme, . . . to seduce others from the true God, . . . to tell lies in the name of the Lord." Having left England as a chosen people under the guidance of God, in quest of a land where they might establish the kind of society which seemed good to them, they were prompt to cast out all who differed in opinion. Dissenters were to enjoy "free liberty to keep away." Hence it was that Roger Williams and Anne Hutchinson and their disciples were banished for disseminating doctrines which the Puritan leaders held to be false.

Williams, escaping from a ship on which he was held for deportation to England, came with five others in 1636 to the head of Narragansett Bay and founded Providence. A little later a party of Mrs. Hutchinson's followers founded Portsmouth on the island in the bay. Still later a third town was begun at Newport. These and other settlements were at first unconnected. Each had its government resting upon the voluntary agreement of the inhabitants. In spite of rivalries there was a strong tendency to unite under a general government, and after several half-successful experiments a permanent union was formed under a charter granted by Charles II in 1663.

There was no favored church in Rhode Island. Owing partly to the influence of Williams who preached toleration —a rare doctrine in that age—and partly to the fact that the colony was the common refuge of several sects, it was from the first the home of religious freedom. There were many contentions among the sects, and Rhode Island was regarded by her neighbors as a hotbed of disorder; to them she seemed a "receptacle of all sorts of riff-raff . . . the sewer of New England." But she clung to freedom of speech and worship even while they drove out heretics and hanged Quakers. America offered a unique opportunity for experiments in new types of society for which Europe had no room. Rhode Island and Maryland took the lead in making the first experiments in "full liberties in religious concernments."

New Hampshire and Maine were the scenes of early efforts at colonization by proprietors, but both of them owe more to Massachusetts than to any proprietor. Some of her religious exiles went to these northern districts, and the expansion of her shipping and trade interests sent others. Her charter could be construed to include portions of both New Hampshire and Maine, and she gradually extended her control over them. In the case of Maine the union lasted until the nineteenth century, but New Hampshire was detached in 1679 and made a royal province.

All along the New England coast the native tribes had been almost destroyed by a plague shortly before the coming of the Pilgrims. In consequence there was little trouble between the settlers and the Indians for several years. From the Puritan viewpoint, God had sent the plague upon the natives to make the waste places safe for his elect. Nevertheless, as the English extended their settlements, they recognized the moral obligation to pay the Indians for their lands. The red men, however, regarded their sales only as admitting the whites to share in the use of them. The migration into the Connecticut Valley caused the first war, by crowding the Pequot tribe into a narrow space between the white settlements and the hostile tribes of the Narragansett Confederacy, which dwelt upon the west shore of the bay of the same name. In 1637 the hard-pressed natives murdered and plun-

dered John Oldham, the trader, and committed other acts
of violence. To punish them a joint force was raised by
Massachusetts, Plymouth, and Connecticut, which surprised

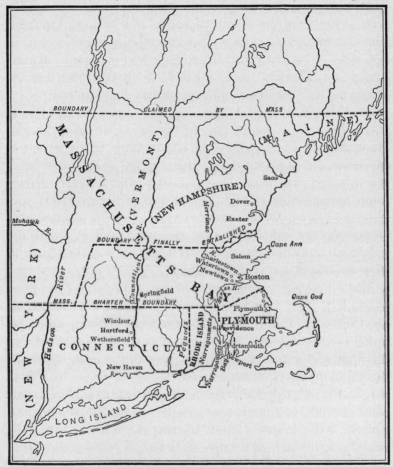

CHIEF NEW ENGLAND SETTLEMENTS BY 1640

the Pequots and almost exterminated them. Their lands
were thus opened for occupation by the conquering race.

The Pequot War revealed the advantages of coöperation in

meeting a common danger. Massachusetts, Plymouth, Connecticut, and New Haven were so similar in their institutional life that before 1640 synods representing the clergy of all four were held to promote a common policy in church affairs. Some disputes had arisen by this time over boundaries and other questions, and the need began to be felt of an organization able to deal with questions involving the interests of more than one colony.

Out of this situation came the New England Confederation of 1643. A Board of Commissioners was created, consisting of two men from each colony. At the annual meeting the vote of six was to determine action on any business within their powers, which included the making of war and peace, the promotion of justice between the confederates, and the rendition of fugitive servants and criminals. The Confederation worked none too well. Massachusetts exceeded in population the other three members combined, and on more than one occasion refused to be bound by the decision of their commissioners. The incorporation of New Haven with Connecticut against her will almost destroyed the Confederation. The experiment in coöperation is important historically because it shows the tendency of the colonies to unite as they became conscious of common interests. In this way, and also in the powers given to the commissioners, the Confederation foreshadowed the union under the Constitution. In 1643 New England and the Chesapeake Bay colonies were, of course, too far apart to dream of acting together. Even Rhode Island, because she was not orthodox, was repeatedly denied membership in the Confederation.

SELECT BIBLIOGRAPHY

Channing, Doyle, Osgood, and Tyler all have good chapters on the New England colonies. Of works dealing only with New England the standard is Palfrey, *History of New England*. Although rather old it is still useful. Fiske's volume on this group of colonies is *Beginnings of New England*. Newer studies are Andrews, *Fathers of New England*, and Adams, *Founding of New England*. A good non-political account is Weeden, *Economic and Social History of New England*.

In addition to these more general works, the following are of especial value for particular colonies:

Plymouth. Dexter, *The England and Holland of the Pilgrims;* Goodwin, *The Pilgrim Republic;* Plooij, *The Pilgrim Fathers from a Dutch Point of View.*

Massachusetts Bay. Morison, *Builders of the Bay Colony,* contains sketches of the leaders.

Rhode Island. Richman, *Rhode Island, Its Making and Its Meaning;* Carpenter, *Roger Williams.*

Connecticut and New Haven. Clark, *A History of Connecticut;* Calder, *The New Haven Colony.*

Expansion and Union in New England. The works cited provide adequate treatment of this topic for the general student. Osgood's discussion of the land system, the evolution of colonial governments, and the New England Confederation are especially good.

For contemporary illustrative material, see *Original Narratives of American History*, VI, VII, VIII, X. A fairly accurate historical picture of the life of women at Plymouth and Boston Bay is given in Bell, *Women of the Wilderness.*

Chapter III

FILLING IN THE COAST PLAIN

MARYLAND

A LITTLE while before Pastor Hooker led his flock to the fine bottom lands of Connecticut the beginnings of a new colony were made near the mouth of the Potomac (at St. Mary's, 1634). This was Maryland, which Charles I had granted to Cecil Calvert, second Lord Baltimore.

Maryland arrests attention chiefly because it was the first successful proprietary colony. Unlike the charters of Virginia and Massachusetts, the grant to Lord Baltimore was not in form a charter creating a trading company, but a patent for a feudal fief. The model for it was found in the terms on which the County of Durham, in England, was held from the king. The patent gave the proprietor the right to make laws "with the advice, assent, and approbation of the freemen." He construed this provision to mean that the colonists might approve or reject bills which he drew, but the representatives of the settlers insisted that it gave them the right to enact laws subject to his veto, and he somewhat reluctantly accepted their view. So far as the colonists were concerned, this concession placed them in a position quite like that of the people of Virginia after the dissolution of the company. In course of time the bicameral system evolved in Maryland, as in Massachusetts and Virginia, but the members of the upper house, or council, were selected by the proprietor instead of by the people or the king. The governor, also, was the appointee and agent of the proprietor. Maryland, in short, was governed much like Virginia, with the proprietor taking the

48

king's place. It will serve as the type of the proprietary colony.

Baltimore offered a thousand acres to any man who would import five others to settle upon the land, and over them the grantee was given the rights of an English "lord of a manor." Few manors were ever created; with land so plentiful and easily acquired, few men were willing voluntarily to accept the status of dependent tenants. As in Virginia many immigrants came as indented servants. For them the inducement was held out of a grant of fifty acres when their terms of service expired. Moreover, they could readily obtain additional acres, and needed only laborers to become planters themselves. For many years the poor servant's opportunity to rise in the social scale was better in Maryland than in Virginia, until the latter adopted the practice of making grants to ex-servants. The more shiftless of the Maryland servants were content, when their time was up, to "squat" on ungranted lands of the proprietor.

In other features the history of Maryland was not so different from that of Virginia as to call for particular study. To this statement there is one notable exception. Baltimore was a Catholic, and many of his coreligionists were among the early immigrants. Yet from the outset the proprietor welcomed Christians of all sects and granted them full political as well as religious equality. In this liberality Maryland antedated even Rhode Island, and anticipated by several decades the amelioration of the practice of the homeland. When after a few years the Protestant immigrants seemed inclined to adopt the harsh anti-Catholic code of England, the assembly passed a Toleration Act (1649) which insured religious liberty for all who professed belief in the Trinity.

Maryland's liberality made the province an asylum for Nonconformists from Virginia, as Rhode Island was a refuge for the dissenters of neighboring settlements in New England.

VIRGINIA, 1622–1676

By the time Maryland was founded Virginia had fully recovered from the set-back given by the Indian massacre of 1622, and was again growing rapidly. A census taken in 1635 showed a population of five thousand. Plantations had taken up the lower valley of the James and its tributaries and were spreading to the northward beyond the York. When the Civil War ended with the execution of the king, Virginia proved to be a congenial refuge for the discomfited supporters of the alliance between the crown and the episcopacy. Far from changing the trend of development in the colony, the coming of the "Cavaliers" gave added impetus to the growth of the plantation system, since many of them were men of wealth.

In the development of Virginia there was no such activity of groups of men as has been described in New England. Grants of land were made directly to individuals. The diffuse population required a large territorial unit for purposes of local government, and nothing like the New England town was possible. In 1634 the assembly divided the colony into eight counties, modeled after the shires of England. These replaced the earlier boroughs. New counties were created from time to time as settlement spread. In each the free adult white males annually voted for two burgesses to represent them in the assembly. With this act the average man's participation in government began and ended. There was no county meeting with functions like those of the town meeting in the North. The duties of local administration were performed by county officials appointed by the governor and council.[1] The chief of these were the sheriff, the lieutenant (commander of the militia), and the justices of

[1] Some local administration, especially in the relief of the poor, devolved upon the vestrymen of the parish, under the supervision of the county court. The counties were divided into parishes in 1641.

the court. Usually, if not always, the elected burgesses as well as the appointed officers were wealthy planters, but sometimes they were "graduates" from the yeoman class.

It has often been said that Virginia was aristocratic and that Massachusetts was democratic. But the statement requires qualification. The range of the voter's activity was narrower in the southern province, but for a long time the franchise was less restricted. Later in the century a few great planters formed a powerful clique which for awhile, in alliance with the governor, monopolized the seats in the council and dominated the government. Bacon's Rebellion (see pages 84–85), however, did something to check the tendency to control by a privileged few. On the whole the burgesses were fairly responsive to yeoman opinion. The Virginia system developed a keen sense of responsibility on the part of the governing class, and trained men for leadership as few other plans have ever done. It was no accident that so many statesmen of the first rank in the early days of independence hailed from the Old Dominion.

EXPANSION, 1650–1676

Tide-water Virginia, with an area more than one fifth as large as that of England, afforded ample room for the expansion of that province during the seventeenth century. By the middle of the century immigrants were crossing the Potomac from the Maryland side and taking lands in the "northern neck." Among them were the ancestors of George Washington, John Marshall, and other great men of later times. The newcomers from the north, reaching the banks of the Rappahannock, met other pioneers coming from the old settlements on the James and York.

The plantations continued to hug the river banks, and the quest for good lands pushed the frontier to the fall line along the streams while great spaces between them remained al-

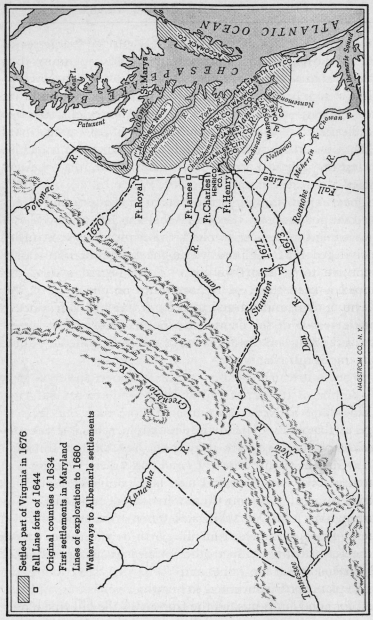

Legend:

- Settled part of Virginia in 1676
- □ Fall Line forts of 1644
- ▨ Original counties of 1634
- First settlements in Maryland
- Lines of exploration to 1680
- Waterways to Albemarle settlements

SETTLEMENTS IN THE CHESAPEAKE REGION BY 1676

HAGSTROM CO., N. Y.

Map labels: ATLANTIC OCEAN, CHESAPEAKE, Kent I., B., Patuxent, Potomac R., St. Marys, Northern Neck, Rappahannock R., York R., Chickahominy R., JAMES R., Nansemond, ACCOMACK CO., ELIZABETH CITY CO., YORK CO., WARWICK CO., CHARLES CITY CO., JAMES CITY CO., HENRICO CO., WARROSQUOIAKE CO., Blackwater R., Nottaway R., Meherrin R., Chowan R., Albemarle Sound, Ft. Royal, Ft. James, Ft. Charles, Ft. Henry, 1670, 1671, 1673, Fall Line, James R., Staunton R., Roanoke R., Dan R., Greenbrier R., Kanawha R., New R., Tennessee R.

most unbroken wilderness, traversed only by bridle paths. During Indian disturbances in the forties, military posts were erected at the falls of the chief streams, and by 1650 interest was awaking in the more remote interior. Within the next generation explorations to the west and southwest reached the Carolina Piedmont and the upper waters of the Tennessee and Great Kanawha rivers beyond the Appalachian watershed—the first visits of Englishmen to the "western waters."

These expeditions opened the fur trade with distant tribes, and tempted some of the planters at the fall line to divide their attention between tobacco growing and the Indian trade. To and from these westmost plantations the traders came and went, and their ways of life began to show the characteristics of the typical American frontier.

The agricultural advance halted at the fall line until a decade or two of the eighteenth century had passed. However, ascending some of the streams which fall into the James from the south, the whites found themselves in touch with other streams which led them to the Roanoke, and soon after the middle of the century they began settlements on Albemarle Sound in North Carolina.

New England's expanding population spread southwestward along the coast to the mouth of the Hudson. Inland it followed mainly the valley of the Connecticut River, which contained the only considerable body of good land. Its course led settlement northward instead of westward. The earliest river town in Massachusetts was Springfield, which was founded soon after Hartford and its neighbors of the Connecticut colony. By 1676 the valley was occupied as far as Deerfield, although the strip of settled land along the coast was as yet hardly thirty miles wide.

Just when the Indian war broke out in Virginia (see page 84), the expansion of New England was checked by King

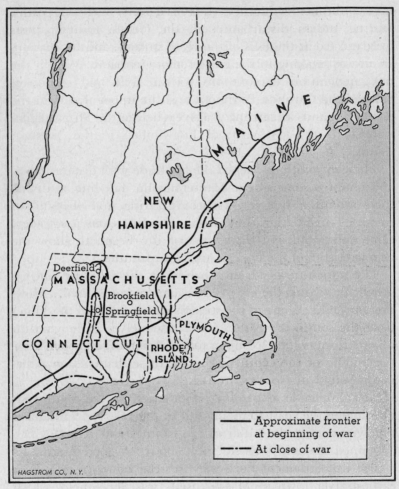

EFFECT OF KING PHILIP'S WAR

Philip's War, in which the tribes made a united effort to resist the white advance. Using their favorite tactics of surprise, the natives fell upon the exposed towns with savage
fury. Beginning in the summer of 1675 the conflict raged
desperately for two years. Of ninety towns forty were at-

tacked and twelve destroyed. The frontier was driven back and the whites lost a thousand men. In the crisis the New England Confederation was revived and the united strength of the colonies was brought to bear in the struggle. The Indians were finally crushed, and when next New Englanders suffered the horrors of Indian war, their enemies were remoter tribes in alliance with the French of the St. Lawrence Basin.

THE OUSTING OF THE DUTCH

The confusion in England during and following the Civil War was not conducive to the planting of new colonies. The execution of Charles I was followed by an Interregnum when Oliver Cromwell ruled with a strong hand supported by the army; but after his death came reaction and the "Restoration" in 1660 of the Stuart line in the person of Charles II. Then the country, weary of strife over religious and political dogmas, turned again to worldly matters. The new king had spent the years of the Interregnum in exile, and an easy-going, pleasure-loving disposition led him to avoid repeating the offenses of his father and grandfather, lest he be compelled "to go again upon his travels." Desiring to please, he lent himself readily to the schemes of men who began to push plans of commercial and territorial expansion with great vigor.

One of the aims of these "mercantilists" was to destroy the Dutch maritime power. The Dutch states had recently won their independence from Spain and had conquered the East Indian possessions of Portugal, which state had superseded the Italian cities in the trade with the remote parts of Asia. With an enthusiasm born of freedom and success they had then begun to look around for other opportunities, and during the early decades of the seventeenth century no Europeans were more active than the shrewd and energetic Nether-landers in the occupation of the world beyond seas. In emulation of Spain, France, and England, a little nation of only two million souls spread its activities over four continents, and did not learn the value of concentrated effort until it had lost nearly all of its holdings except the Spice Islands. An unkind fate permitted the Dutch to weaken the monopolistic systems of Spain and Portugal, only to lose the preëminence to the rising power of England.

About the time of the coming of the Pilgrims to Plymouth the Dutch West India Company was formed with an ambitious program embracing projects as widely separated as the slave traffic on the African coast, rivalry with the Portuguese in Brazil, and trade with the North American Indians. Until they were driven from the Connecticut Valley by the men of Plymouth, the activities of the Dutch in the Indian trade extended from the Connecticut to the Delaware, which they called "South River." On the site of New York City they built the village of New Amsterdam; but Fort Orange on the Hudson, near the modern Albany, was the key-point for the fur trade.

Excursions from this post first made known the geography of the New York lake region, and the course of the Delaware from source to mouth. Central New York was the home of the most powerful native confederacy of North America, the League of the Iroquois. The five (later six) tribes composing this alliance were the terror of the other natives, from New England to the Mississippi, and from Canada to Carolina. With the nearer natives on the lower Hudson the Dutch had serious conflict; but with the Iroquois, owing to the mutual benefits of trade, they had the happy fortune to establish friendly relations which were never greatly disturbed.

The primary interest of the Dutch Company in New Netherland was trade rather than the extension of political dominion. Some agricultural activity was found to be required, however, for the support of those who were engaged in trade. Like the Virginia Company, the Dutch organization tried to shift the burden of bringing in settlers to private shoulders. The device employed for this purpose, called the "patroonship," was similar to the particular plantation in Virginia. It was a grant of land to an individual or group of men on condition of importing immigrants. The Dutch went beyond the English, however, in giving to the patroon the political as well as the economic rights of a feudal lord over his tenants.

Several patroonships were attempted, but the only successful one was Rensselaerswyck, established by Kiliaen van Rensselaer. It embraced the present counties of Albany and Rensselaer, completely surrounding the company's post at Fort Orange, and maintained a degree of independence which well-nigh thwarted the company's purpose. The miscarriage of the patroonship led to other plans to induce immigration. Lands were offered on liberal terms to persons of small means, and sometimes free passage was provided, as well as house, barn, tools, and animals. Peasants from Holland, indented servants who had served their time in Virginia, and New Englanders in numbers were attracted to New Netherland. They settled on Long Island, on the mainland near the mouth of the Hudson, or at Fort Orange, for most of the Hudson Valley, as one contemporary put it, was "little fitted to be peopled," having only "here and there a little corn land, which the Indians had prepared by removing the stones."

Comparatively few of the permanent immigrants came from Holland. In that land of religious liberty there was no persecution to drive men forth as in contemporary England. Nor were the inducements to remove sufficient to cause an exodus to a wilderness ruled by a commercial monopoly, for New Netherland lacked the liberal features of government found in the English colonies. Although the governor was appointed by the political authorities at home, the company enjoyed almost sovereign power, and ruled its subjects as despotically as did the autocrats of New Spain. In fact, the governor and council in New Netherland may fairly be likened to the viceroy and *audiencia* of the Spanish provinces. There was no representative assembly, and the people had only a limited voice in local affairs. The lack of political privileges caused much discontent among the English element, and their constant agitation seemed to be about to win the right of representation when Dutch control came to an end.

The Dutch Reformed Church was the established form of worship in New Netherland, and public offices were held only by its members. Other Protestant groups were tolerated in varying degrees. Presbyterians and Congregationalists were allowed to worship publicly, but other dissenters were restricted to services in their homes. Quakers and Jews were decidedly unwelcome, and all residents were subjected to strict laws designed to promote morality.

The Dutch had slight success in the Delaware Valley. They tried to maintain a trading post in what is now New Jersey, almost opposite the site of Philadelphia, and patroons and others attempted to settle on Delaware Bay. Their failure was due in large part to the hostility of the Indians. The Swedes fared better. They built Fort Christina on the site of the future Wilmington, in the late thirties, and it was soon the center of a group of small hamlets. The Dutch regarded the Swedes as intruders, but being allies in the Thirty Years War then raging in Europe, they contented themselves for the time with a protest by the governor at New Amsterdam. With the end of the war, however, came the bloodless conquest of New Sweden (1655) by a force from New Netherland.

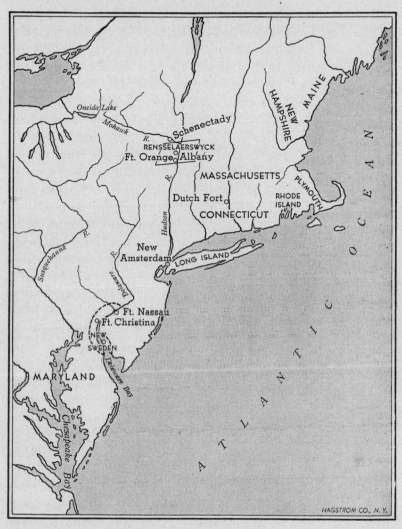

REGION OF DUTCH AND SWEDISH ACTIVITY, 1609–1664

The elimination of New Sweden was the prelude to the conquest of New Netherland by the English, who claimed the whole coast from Nova Scotia to Florida, and regarded the Dutch as interlopers. Indeed, the enterprises of the last-mentioned were not readily distinguishable from projects of permanent occupation. Although the drift of New Englanders into the Hudson Valley may have been inspired by the hope of crowding out the Dutch, and although Delaware Bay was within the grant to Lord Baltimore, the English had made no actual attempt, before the middle of the century, to oust their rivals from any locality except the Connecticut Valley. By the mid-century, however, the growing maritime interests of the Netherlands had aroused the English, who were resolved to win and maintain the supremacy on the seas. A large share of the commerce of the English colonies was carried in the ships of these enterprising competitors. To regain this trade and to encourage English shipping, Parliament began to pass restrictive laws known as "Navigation Acts." One of these, dating from 1651, forbade the importation into England, or any English possession, of goods from Asia, Africa, or America, except in vessels owned by Englishmen or English colonists, and manned chiefly by English sailors. Imports from European countries might be brought into the English possessions only by English ships or ships of the producing country.

This act was aimed directly at the Dutch, and with other causes led to war, during which an attack was planned (1655) against New Netherland. The forces of New England were to be employed; but Massachusetts held out against the other members of the New England Confederation, and the war ended without hostilities in America.

Similar causes brought on a second war in 1664. The English now thought the time ripe for ejecting the Dutch. An expedition against New Netherland was carefully planned and was actually on the way across the sea before war was declared. Reenforced by some Connecticut volunteers it appeared before New Amsterdam and received its surrender.

NEW NETHERLAND BECOMES NEW YORK

The region of which the Dutch were dispossessed, from the Connecticut to the Delaware, was given to the king's brother, the Duke of York.[1] The duke in turn transferred the portion between the lower Hudson and the Delaware to Lord John Berkeley and Sir George Carteret, retaining the Hudson Valley and Long Island for himself, under the name of New York.

Ten thousand Dutch inhabitants accepted the change of masters quite readily. Their property rights were respected, holders of petty offices were allowed to serve out their terms, and the Dutch local government was replaced so gradually as to cause no annoyance. Complete religious liberty was allowed, and those who wished to leave the province were permitted to do so. Few availed themselves of this privilege, and the descendants of the Dutch stock form to this day an important element in the New York population.

The English inhabitants were sorely disappointed because the conquest did not bring representative government. Perhaps because the people had no representation during the Dutch period, the duke's patent, unlike Baltimore's, did not require their assent in legislation. Instead it gave him "full and absolute power . . . to . . . govern and rule," so long as his laws were not contrary to the laws of England.

At the outset Governor Richard Nicolls told the English that they might "assure themselves of equal if not greater freedoms and immunities than any of his Majesty's colonies in New England." In fulfillment of this promise he pro-

[1] An agreement with Connecticut fixed the boundary between that colony and New York, but the Vermont region was in dispute between New York and New Hampshire until after the Revolution.

claimed the "Duke's Laws," based upon the New England codes and including some features of the system of town government. They permitted the freeholders (landowners) of each town to elect local officials, but the town meeting, with its right to pass local laws and to choose delegates to the legislature, was wanting. The law-making body consisted of the governor and his council aided by the "Court of Assizes," which was also a judicial tribunal.

The English inhabitants were dissatisfied with the Duke's Laws. To them Nicolls' promise meant the right of the freeholders to elect deputies to act with the governor and council in law-making. The history of New York for a generation after the conquest turns on the struggle for this right. In 1683 the duke seemed to be on the point of yielding; he allowed Governor Thomas Dongan to permit the election of an assembly, but upon his accession to the throne in 1685 as James II, he changed his mind. Three years later he was overthrown by the Revolution of 1688, and in the general reorganization which followed New York gained at last the coveted privilege.

THE CAROLINAS

The conquest of New Netherland filled in the gap between the English possessions in New England and on the Chesapeake. At the same time new colonizing efforts were made in the territory claimed by Spain. Lords Berkeley and Carteret were members of a group of courtiers who were eager to undertake colonial ventures. Lord Berkeley's brother William, governor of Virginia, was also of this group. To them and others, eight in all, the king gave a patent in 1663 for lands south of Virginia, under the name of Carolina. As later defined the tract extended from the southern limits of Virginia (36° 30′) to the thirty-first parallel, and to the Pacific on the west.

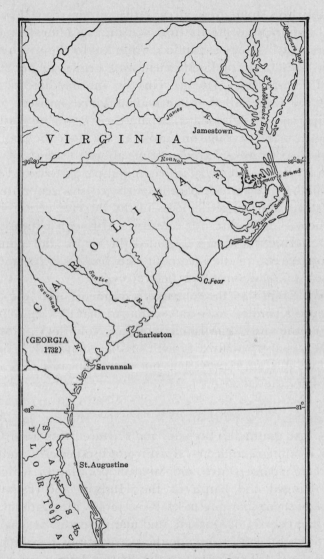

BEGINNINGS OF CAROLINA AND GEORGIA

63

Within this grant were already the settlers on Albemarle Sound, who had come in from Virginia. They formed a nucleus which slowly expanded, while far to the southward, on the coast, a second settlement was begun in 1670 and named Charleston. Attempts in the intermediate region, near Cape Fear, failed. The wide interval between these occupied centers necessitated separate governments and led at length to the division of Carolina. In each the ordinary type of proprietary government came about in time.

Owing partly to their later origin and partly to broad belts of "pine barrens" which paralleled the coast a few miles inland, there were no settlements in the interior of the Carolinas before the eighteenth century. Although almost from the beginning fur traders ascended the rivers and trafficked with the natives in the Piedmont, this back country did not receive its inhabitants much before 1750.

In economic life, the southern settlements near the coast developed a plantation system similar to that of Virginia, but owing to the tardy establishment of these colonies this characteristic was also chiefly a growth of the eighteenth century. Religious toleration prevailed, but the Anglican Church was favored by the laws.

THE JERSEYS AND PENNSYLVANIA

The land granted to Berkeley and Carteret was named New Jersey. Immigrants from New England, especially, came to add to the sparse Dutch and Swedish population which already fringed the banks of the Hudson and Delaware. Through successive purchases New Jersey gradually passed under the control of Quakers, and many persons of this faith came from England to escape the persecutions to which dissenters were still subjected in the British Isles. For a time the province was divided into two parts, known as "East Jersey" and "West Jersey," with separate governments.

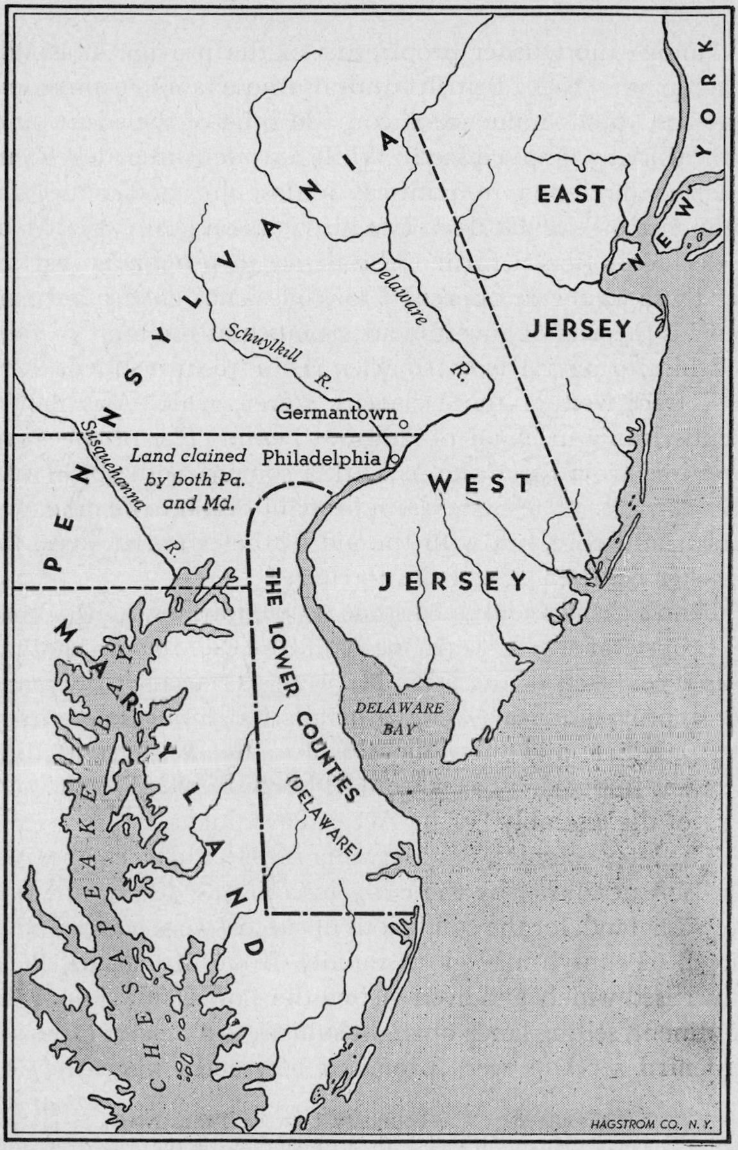
NEW YORK
EAST
JERSEY
WEST
JERSEY
PENNSYLVANIA
Delaware R.
Schuylkill R.
Germantown
Philadelphia
Susquehanna R.
Land clained by both Pa. and Md.
THE LOWER COUNTIES (DELAWARE)
DELAWARE BAY
MARYLAND
CHESAPEAKE BAY
HAGSTROM CO., N. Y.

BEGINNINGS OF NEW JERSEY, PENNSYLVANIA, AND DELAWARE

Among the Quaker proprietors of the province was William Penn, son of a British admiral, whose family connections gave him much influence at court in spite of the adoption of the faith of a despised sect. While a student in college Penn became interested in political philosophy, and under the influence of Friends' doctrines his views on government took a decidedly liberal turn. The desire to provide an asylum for those who were oppressed for conscience' sake, and to try out his theories of government, as much as the hope of gain, led him to obtain from Charles II, in 1681, a patent for a vast tract west of the Delaware River, which was named Pennsylvania in honor of Admiral Penn. The next year he acquired from the Duke of York a somewhat doubtful title to Delaware. The latter claim brought him into dispute with Lord Baltimore, but with the aid of the powerful duke the Quaker courtier gained the territory.[1]

Penn's charter contained some restrictions upon his powers as proprietor which were not found in the earlier grants of this type. Acts of the assembly were to be sent to England for approval; appeals were to be allowed from the courts of the province; and the obligation to enforce the navigation acts was imposed. Taxes were to be laid only with the consent of the assembly "or by Act of Parliament."

The later colonies, Pennsylvania in particular, escaped the hardships endured by the early inhabitants of Virginia and New England, for the conditions of success were better understood. Pennsylvania grew rapidly from the start. Penn advertised widely and even visited the Low Countries on the continent, selling lands outright subject to a modest quitrent. Indented servants were promised fifty acres when they at-

---

[1] A further dispute over the boundary between Pennsylvania and Maryland was not settled until 1760. In accordance with the agreement then reached between the heirs of Penn and Baltimore, the present boundary was surveyed by Mason and Dixon, in 1767. The arrangement gave Pennsylvania a strip many miles wide within the original Maryland grant.

tained freedom. Religious liberty was promised to all who believed in the existence of God, although only Christians were to be allowed to take part in government.

Penn's first immigrants settled along the Delaware. Philadelphia was laid out upon its banks in 1682. The next year Germantown was founded near by, by Dutch Quakers. Population then spread northward along the river and up the tributary Schuylkill.

The plan of government which Penn devised was artificial and clumsy but unusually liberal, for the voters were allowed to elect the council as well as the lower house. The proprietor depended upon the governor, whom he appointed, to protect his interests. A few years showed that his rights were not sufficiently guarded by this arrangement, and in order to regain the usual right of a proprietor to appoint the members of the council, he agreed that it should relinquish its share in legislation. As a result, Pennsylvania, unlike the other colonies, had a legislature of only one house.

The settlements on the lower Delaware, known as the "lower counties," were for awhile under the same government as those around Philadelphia, and sent their representatives to sit in the assembly; but Delaware was given a separate assembly in 1703.

GEORGIA

A half-century passed after the founding of Pennsylvania before the English filled in the last gap along the coast plain. James Oglethorpe, founder of Georgia, was, like Penn, a philanthropist; he sought to open a new door of opportunity for the prisoners for debt in English jails, while the government wished to forestall the Spanish in occupying the vacant territory, still claimed by both nations, lying between Florida and South Carolina. Parliament therefore, for the first time in the history of British colonization, granted financial aid. A secondary object with Oglethorpe was to provide an asylum for the persecuted Protestants of Catholic countries; hence, in 1733, Germans from the Salzburg came to the new colony. Scotch Highlanders came too, and located not far from the Spanish settlements.

The character of the settlers and the purpose of the undertaking seemed to forbid the usual type of government. The colonists were given no part in it, and control was vested in a board of trustees for a period of twenty-one years, after which Georgia was to become a royal province. Slavery was prohibited, as well as the importation of intoxicants, and the amount of land which might be held by one person was limited in order that settlement might be compact and easily defended. These restrictions so hampered the growth of the province that one by one they were given up. Progress was more rapid after the change to a royal province in 1752, and at that time a representative assembly was established.

SELECT BIBLIOGRAPHY

Maryland. Andrews, *Founding of Maryland,* and *History of Maryland;* Mereness, *Maryland as a Proprietary Province;* Hall, *Narratives of Early Maryland (Original Narratives)*.

Virginia, 1622–1676. See Bibliography for Chapter I. Andrews, *Virginia: The Old Dominion,* covers the seventeenth and eighteenth centuries in an interesting manner, The studies of Bruce become invaluable for this period of Virginia history.

Expansion, 1650–1676. The story of the explorations which opened the fur trade to the west and southwest from the fall line in Virginia is told, with accompanying documents, in Alvord and Bidgood, *First Explorations of the Trans-Alleghany.* The spread of the New England population is dealt with in Mathews, *Expansion of New England.* On King Philip's War see Britt, *Great Indian Chiefs.*

The Ousting of the Dutch. Dutch and Swedish colonization is covered by Fiske, *Dutch and Quaker Colonies,* and by Goodwin, *Dutch and English on the Hudson.* A standard work of the old type is Brodhead, *History of the State of New York.* Volume

I treats of the Dutch period. Priestley, *The Coming of the White Man*, describes Dutch life in New Netherland. The story of the conquest is told by Andrews, in *Colonial Self-Government*, by Channing, *United States*, II, and by Winsor, *America*, III. See also Jameson, *Narratives of New Netherland, 1609–1664* (*Original Narratives*).

New York under the English is dealt with in Brodhead's second volume, and Fiske, *Dutch and Quaker Colonies*. See also Roberts, *New York*.

The Carolinas. Ashe, *History of North Carolina*, is best for that province. McCrady, *South Carolina as a Proprietary Province*, is a good modern work. See also Salley, *Narratives of Early Carolina, 1650–1708* (*Original Narratives*).

The Jerseys and Pennsylvania compose the subject-matter of Fisher, *The Quaker Colonies*. Sharpless, *A Quaker Experiment in Government*, and Jones, *The Quakers in the American Colonies*, are standard books. Of the several lives of Penn those by Fisher, *The True William Penn*, and Hodges, *William Penn*, best deserve mention. See also Pound, *The Penns of Pennsylvania and England*; and Hull, *William Penn and the Dutch Migration to Pennsylvania*. For contemporary matter see Myers, *Narratives of Early Pennsylvania* (*Original Narratives*).

Georgia. For the founding of Georgia see Greene, *Provincial America*, Channing, *United States*, II, Coulter, *Short History of Georgia*, Ettinger, *Oglethorpe*, and Avery, *History*, III. Crane, *Southern Frontier, 1670–1732*, studies the expansion of the Carolina frontier and the beginnings of Georgia.

Chapter IV

SEVENTEENTH-CENTURY
COLONIAL LIFE

SINCE the days of Columbus America has been the land of the heart's desire, where men have believed that their dreams might come true. Coronado dreamed of the seven cities and Ponce de Leon of the fountain of youth; the first Virginians of gold mines and spices; Calvert, Penn, and Oglethorpe of freedom for the oppressed; Winthrop and Cotton of a holy land where God's chosen people should dwell in righteousness. None of these dreamers found his vision realized, least of all those who sought selfish ends. The social idealists failed too, but not without leaving a deep impress upon the culture of the communities they founded.

Besides the purposes of the founders, several factors shared in the shaping of colonial life. Back of the colonists with their particular ideas was the general English culture-complex, including a series of attitudes on such matters as education, care of the poor, regulation of individual conduct, and political and legal procedure. Repeatedly, in shaping the course of their incipient states, the New-World leaders drew upon this inherited fund of social experience and practice.

There was, secondly, the influence of the new environment —a rugged reality which awoke men from dreams to face the cold, harsh fact that for a considerable period the mere preservation of life demanded the most unremitting and extreme exertion. For many of the colonists the necessity of severe toil continued so long that it came to seem a part of the normal order. Labor came to be regarded as a virtue in itself—a view which in New England intensified a Puritan tendency to undervalue the uses of leisure.

The environment not only drove men to toil as the condition of survival, but dictated their occupations. The working out of these influences, which were in the ultimate sense beyond the control of the founders, often proved inimical to their original purposes.

NEW ENGLAND

The miscarriage of the plans of the Puritan leaders in Massachusetts began when they yielded to popular pressure and increased the number of freemen. Nevertheless, by restricting the privilege to the members of the orthodox churches, by exiling dissenters, and by close collaboration between magistrates and ministers, they were able, during their own generation, to maintain the "theocratic" polity. Their supremacy was short-lived, but it covered the formative period, and enabled the founders to give a semi-permanent cast to the fundamental institutions of the commonwealth.

The Massachusetts leaders would gladly have kept their New Canaan wholly free from contaminating contact with other communities. Most of the original colonists, being of the peasant class, were certain, both from experience and the character of their new home, to continue the pursuit of agriculture. That occupation offered the best prospect of the self-sufficing economy which the community must have if it maintained its isolation. But New England agriculture never much more than provided food for the local population. The need of other things compelled the people both to diversify their industry and to resort to commerce. The necessity of producing something to give in exchange for what they obtained through trade was an additional reason for developing other industries besides agriculture. In the conditions which

surrounded them, in short, were the seeds of an economic
development which was destined to play a large part in
thwarting the Puritan ideal.

New England possessed great advantages for the export of
furs, fish, and lumber. The fur trade and the fisheries, indeed, had their beginnings even before permanent settlement. It was inevitable that, in connection with the fisheries
and lumber-cutting, such crafts as ship-carpentry should soon
appear. In addition, local needs promptly called others into
existence, such as black-smithing, wood-working, cabinet-mak-
ing, tanning, shoemaking, spinning and weaving, and house-
carpentry.

In spite of the considerable division of labor, agriculture
was the basic industry, and employed most of the time of at
least nine tenths of the people. Many farmers resided in
hamlets about which lay the arable fields, granted to the
town when first incorported, their individual plots being
held through allotment by the town meeting. The system
of tillage was crude and wasteful. Few plows were in use
during the seventeenth century. Those employed were such
clumsy affairs that two or three ox-teams were required to
draw one; in the course of a day an outfit of this kind
scratched the surface of an acre of ground to a depth of three
inches. The cost of a plow, moreover, was so great that the
owner served his neighbors as well as himself, and few farmers
undertook to replow within several years. Most seasons, the
seed was poked, along with a herring, into the old hills; the
cultivating was done by hand with hand-made tools. There
was little understanding of the value of rotating crops, the
tiller relying chiefly upon the practice of letting the land lie
fallow for one or more seasons when threatened with exhaustion of fertility.

Stock-raising was as unscientific as crop-growing. The
cattle of a whole town grazed as one herd on the common

pasture. Under such methods both stock and tilled land deteriorated rapidly.

The limited amount of arable land on the narrow coast plain, the necessity of supplementing agriculture, and the proximity of good sea-fishing led to such a rapid growth of the fishing industry that as early as 1640 New England was exporting a part of the annual catch. Half a century later the occupation had become so important that, in homely phrase, all New England "smelled of fish."

The fisheries called shipbuilding into existence. The colonists had hardly constructed habitations before they were taking to the sea in vessels of their own making. The first of these, "The Blessing of the Bay," was launched at Boston in 1631, upon the to-be-historic date of July 4. Before the century closed thousands of men were engaged in the ship-yards of Boston, Salem, and other seaports, turning out the vessels demanded by the fisheries and the growing commerce.

The New England skippers traded with New Amsterdam, the Chesapeake Bay colonies, the West Indies, and England. From the last they brought manufactured goods in exchange for furs, tobacco, and lumber. The West Indies supplied the chief market for fish, and paid for them in sugar, molasses, indigo, and cotton. The Catholic countries of southern Europe also presented a promising market, offering wines and sugar in return. By 1660, many vessels made voyages twice yearly from the New England ports. After 1676, the trade in Guinea Negroes began to be a profitable branch of commerce.

The growth of commerce introduced a new class into the social grouping of New England. Before Boston was ten years old, merchants began to bid for a share of the influence enjoyed by the gentry. By the beginning of the last quarter of the century the one colony of Massachusetts contained no less than thirty merchants who possessed fortunes rated at

£10,000 or more. The commercial gentry were not merely an offshoot of the original Puritan stock. Rhode Island, in particular, was the home of several Jewish merchants who had migrated thither from the Low Countries. Whatever their origin, they introduced a new social ferment with results to be noted presently.

A chronic shortage in the supply of labor was characteristic of the whole colonial period. In a new country there was so much to be done, from the mere holding at bay of savage nature to the use of its resources in setting up civilized ways, that hands were never numerous enough. Every community needed workers of all kinds; towns offered lands and even homes to attract craftsmen. The labor of skilled artisans was well rewarded. They habitually trained their sons to follow their trades, and the class held a respectable rank even in the somewhat exclusive society of provincial New England.

The dearth of labor was so great that for a long time even indented servants were welcomed. Conditions in the North were not conducive to the use of Negro slaves. Neither the diversified crops of the small farm, nor the crafts, were suited to the capacity of the "raw" Negroes, fresh from Africa. Nor did they do better as seamen, or stand well the exposure of the fisheries.

But white servants were numerous. Young men of this class sometimes spent their period of service as apprentices to craftsmen. After that there was ample opportunity to get on. Conditions made for high wages, and through application and saving many a servant became a craftsman or farmer.

The occupation of the artisan shaded into that of the farmer on the one side and that of the manufacturer on the other. Spinning and weaving were carried on in homes from the beginning, and employed whole families on winter evenings. Similarly, in the earlier years, the grinding of grain was a household task, every home using a hollowed block of wood as a rude mortar. This occupation was soon taken from many homes, however, since milling was one of the first industries to become specialized. A wind-mill was erected near Boston in 1631, and the next year the first water-mill was set up (at Dedham). Soon on every stream and hill rose water- and wind-mills, lightening the home tasks of the families of the neighborhood. Fulling mills also appeared in many places. Both Massachusetts and Connecticut were producing linen and woolen cloth by 1640 or soon after, and within the first generation such goods became articles of export. By 1699 the trade had grown so great as to attract the attention of Parliament, and an act was passed forbidding any colony to export woolen cloth.

The very nature of the Massachusetts theocracy compelled it to strive to shape the lives of individuals into conformity with the pattern which it regarded as correct. Only by success in so doing could it hope to set up and perpetuate the ideal order at which it aimed. Necessarily, then, it sought to regulate and censor the conduct of every member of the community. These efforts were by no means confined to the preservation of order, the punishment of crime, and the promotion of education; they included the enforcement of Sabbath observance, the fixing of prices and wages, the regulation of the use of liquor and tobacco, and extended to matters which have come to be regarded as even more purely private concerns. The system may be illustrated by the function of the tithingman, who supplemented the sermon of the pastor by supervising the conduct of about ten families throughout the week. His task was not merely that of a modern pastor's friendly visitation; it was his duty to see that the children were properly catechized, and to check any dereliction on the part of parents. Evidence of indifference on their part, or signs of worldliness, such as extravagance in dress, was noted, and was likely to be followed by the stern admonition of the elders.

Looking back from our own times, the Puritan régime appears to best advantage in the field of education. Some forty or fifty of the early leaders, including most of the ministers, were graduates of the English universities, especially Cambridge, and were thoroughly imbued with the necessity of an educated ministry. Reliance upon the schools of the far-away motherland for the training of their successors seemed too precarious, and within the first decade of Massachusetts Bay the initial steps were taken to create in Harvard College a suitable agency for this important task. This purpose carried with it as a corollary the provision of secondary schools to give boys a preparatory education.

The Puritan ideal in education, however, included hearers as well as preachers of the Word of God. All church members should be able to listen intelligently and to read the Scriptures for themselves. There was a naïve confidence that universal education would promote rather than hinder unity in the true faith. In the matter of training children, much reliance was placed on parents. But for various reasons it was soon found necessary to supplement the home. Several of the Massachusetts towns established schools before there was any legislation of a general character. The first act applying to the whole colony was passed in 1642. It made it compulsory for all parents and guardians to see that children were taught the primary branches. Such instruction might be given in the home or in a school if one were available. Another act, passed in 1647, sought to provide universal school facilities while still leaving it optional whether children should be sent to them or taught at home. This law required every town of fifty or more families to maintain an elementary school, while towns of one hundred or more households were required in addition to maintain a college preparatory (grammar) school.

In the elementary schools boys and girls were taught reading, writing, arithmetic, and the catechism. Girls seldom went beyond this, except in practical subjects such as sewing, and in etiquette. The secondary schools were open to boys even if they did not contemplate entering Harvard. Like the English schools after which they were patterned, they placed the chief stress upon the Latin classics, adding advanced instruction in writing and mathematics. In the curriculum of these schools the Puritans, tied to British tradition, failed conspicuously to adapt the education of youth to the needs of a pioneer community. Owing in part to this fact and partly to the cost of maintenance, few grammar schools were established, and those were attended chiefly by youths preparing for the clerical profession. The Act of 1647 was not rigorously enforced.

From the standpoint of financial support, the schools were of several types. Some were private, maintained by tuition fees; some depended upon voluntary contributions supplemented by sums voted by the town. The latter were called "free schools" owing to the fact that they were open to all without specific charge. Families able to do so were expected to make contributions, but poor families sent their children without any payment, and the appropriation of funds raised by taxation was depended upon to prevent a deficit. Such schools became the prevalent type, and were found in all of the New England colonies except Rhode Island. They were not free public schools in the sense in which the words are now used, but they did foreshadow them.

In keeping with the spirit of the age, flogging and other severe disciplinary measures were customary. Such a science as child psychology was undreamed of, and rare were the teachers who possessed sympathetic insight into the mind of childhood. Mere stupidity was readily confused with will-fulness, and corporal punishment was the panacea for both. Worst of all, the purpose of instruction was not to teach the young to think for themselves, but to bring them up in the way they should go. The Puritan philosophy called for the suppression of self-expression, and made education an instrument for confining the mind with the fetters of orthodoxy.

Not until 1690 did New England begin to provide text-books of its own creation. The first was the *New England Primer,* which continued in favor until the Revolution of 1776. During most of the seventeenth century texts were imported from England. The favorite form was the quaint hornbook—a sheet of paper containing the alphabet and some Scripture verses, pasted on a paddle and covered with a transparent film of horn to protect the printed surface.

It would be an error to think of Puritan education as motivated solely by religious objectives. Two other purposes were quite important. One was the desire to increase the supply of skilled workers, the other the necessity of dealing with the problem of pauperism. Both of these grew out of conditions due to the practice of indented servitude. Times were hard in England during the last decades of the sixteenth century and early part of the seventeenth. The enclosing of agricultural land for sheep pasture, with the resultant displacement of labor, caused an oversupply in the wage market, and wages remained stationary while prices were rising. So great was the depression of the laboring class that about the year 1600 four days were required to earn as much as one sufficed to earn a century earlier. In parts of England a third or more of the people depended on charity for support during the very years when labor was scarce in all of the American settlements.

A good many unfortunates who learned of the larger opportunities overseas entered voluntarily into contracts to labor for four or five years to repay the cost of their transportation. Such persons were often intelligent and energetic enough to contribute a valuable element to the provincial population. This was not true of the whole class of indented servants, for many of them were sent to America by the judges of the criminal courts, who wished to rid England of troublesome characters. The indented servants to be found in the colonies consequently included many persons who had been convicted of wrong-doing of one kind or other. Conviction for felony did not necessarily mean that the convict possessed a vicious character, for in a country where at least one hundred and fifty offenses were punishable with death, the crimes for which a less penalty was inflicted were mostly of a trivial sort. Nevertheless many of these petty criminals, guilty perhaps of nothing worse than vagrancy due to lack of employment, were dissolute and shiftless; and while some of them responded to the stimulus of larger opportunity in America, many remained unchanged, a dead weight to be carried by society.

So great was the need of laborers that some of the colonies were well-disposed even towards these convicts. New York went so far, in 1693, as to ask to have all the inmates of Newgate prison sent to her. Elsewhere indented convicts had been the source of much trouble. In Massachusetts, families of indented whites (perhaps not wholly of the convict class) which had gained their freedom seem to have been particularly in the minds of the lawmakers when they passed the Education Act of 1642. The act refers to "the great neglect in many parents and masters in training up their children in learning and labor"; and apparently anticipating considerable disregard of the obligation which it imposed, it made it the duty of the selectmen of all towns to apprentice the children of negligent persons to those who would bring them up properly. A proper bringing-up was understood to include instruction in some useful trade or employment, in reading, and in the principles of religion. The law combined certain features of the English Statute of Apprentices of 1562 and the Poor Law of 1601, but went beyond both by adding the provisions for instruction in reading and religion.

Such a far-reaching scheme of education was well calculated to prevent children from contracting idle habits and becoming public charges, but it did not prove to be a complete preventive of pauperism. Additional legislation was found to be necessary to prevent vagrancy and willful idleness. Vagrancy was punished by whipping, and town officers were required to compel the able-bodied to work. Near the end of the century, in the larger towns, houses of correction began to be built, to which such persons might be committed. In smaller places they were confined in ordinary jails, where sometimes they proved only too content to stay at the public expense. The problem then became one of getting rid of them. The favorite plan was to "sell" them into service for a time.

Similar plans were followed throughout the New England colonies. In general each town was responsible for maintaining its own poor, and possessed the right to determine what persons might come in as residents, or even as visitors. Great precautions were taken not to admit persons who might become public charges. Resident paupers were often sent from house to house, each family taking its turn in providing support. Most of the relief to the worthy poor was provided thus in homes. Officials sometimes "farmed out" the impotent and aged to the lowest bidder. In cases of illness or misfortune temporary relief was given according to the need.

As early as 1642 Plymouth required all shipmasters bringing in strangers to secure the town against all responsibility for their maintenance. This device was destined to wide adoption. Boston suffered from being the chief town and seaport. In 1679 its officials complained that all sorts of persons came by land and sea. "The towne is fild with poore idle and profane persons which are greatlie prejuditiall to the inhabitants." This problem grew worse, and the town repeatedly called for assistance from the provincial government. Such conditions forced it to take the lead in establishing public almshouses, houses of correction, and workhouses.

THE SOUTH

Aside from New England, Virginia and Maryland were the only colonies which developed a very distinctive life during the seventeenth century. New York, Pennsylvania, and the Carolinas were begun so late as to be still in the incipient stage at the end of the period. A review of conditions in Virginia, with perhaps a glance at her neighbors, will therefore complete this survey.

Southern life may be the better understood if one keeps in mind certain original differences between the North and South. Virginia had no group of leaders with a consistent social ideal, such as controlled Massachusetts during the formative period; at least she did not after the dissolution of the company. From early years individual initiative had much freer scope for action. Natural influences resulted also in a different type of economic activity, which centered, as has been noted, around the tobacco plantation.

It was easy to obtain land for the large-scale production of tobacco. Head-right certificates were purchased and sold, and fifty acres could be obtained for each certificate on condition of "seating" within a certain time (by which was meant the clearing and cultivating of a small acreage and the erection of a cabin), and the payment of a small annual quitrent to the king. Even these slight requirements were laxly enforced.

The right to the labor of indented servants was purchasable, but the scarcity of white servants limited the size of plantations. It has been estimated that in the tobacco colonies of

Virginia, Maryland, and North Carolina not fewer than one hundred thousand servants completed their terms and became free during the seventeenth century. It seems probable that at no time was more than one eighth of the population under indenture. The labor of Negroes who were permanent bondsmen was obviously more desirable than the temporary servitude of persons of the white race. Negroes were brought to Virginia as early as 1619, but the Dutch, Spanish, and Portuguese controlled the trade through most of the century and found a more satisfactory market elsewhere. If all the Negro slaves of Virginia in 1670 had been distributed in lots of fifty, they would have supplied only forty estates. It was not until the eighteenth century that Negro slavery eclipsed indented white servitude on the plantations.

These facts make it evident that seventeenth-century Virginia is not to be thought of as made up of large plantations owned by rich men. The great majority of the inhabitants had come at their own expense, receiving fifty acres for each adult member of their families, including a servant or two. Many more had come as indented servants, either voluntarily or under sentence of the courts. As in New England, the more energetic of these became landowners when freed. From these two sources there arose a sturdy yeomanry. The typical landholding was small, and approximately two thirds of the owners held no slaves, but cultivated their plantations with their own hands. In at least a few cases ex-servants rose to the rank of wealthy planters and were sent to the assembly. The more shiftless, upon attaining their freedom, formed the class known as "poor whites."

The cultivators, both great and small, were called "planters." They sought the bottom lands along the navigable streams. The most productive soils were found there, and they wished to load their tobacco upon ocean-going vessels at their own wharves. From England they received in payment not cash but whatever goods they needed. There was little place for the retail merchant or the free handicraftsman. The lack of these classes and the dispersion of the population delayed the growth of towns until late in the eighteenth century.

The planter's task was that of a pioneer. Often his holding was heavily wooded, and it was necessary to clear a space before he could plant. Sometimes this was done by cutting down the trees, but more often they were merely girdled and left standing for the first season or two. The ground between the deadened trunks was broken up with spade and hoe, for, just as in New England, plows were almost unknown. While tobacco was the staple, small grains and root crops were raised for food; and by the middle of the century orchards of apple, pear, and peach trees were not uncommon in the older districts. Cattle and hogs ranged the woods and required little care, as they fed on the natural grasses or beechnuts and acorns. Game was abundant, and that yeoman was poor indeed who did not possess a gun, which he used as a means both of recreation and of supplementing the produce of his land.

Few great planters followed the migrations to the west and south. It was the poorer men, as a rule, who were pushed by social and economic forces towards the outer rim of settlement. Rich planters who had acquired large tracts of the best lands in the fertile river valleys had little reason to seek new homes, while indented servants who were out of their time, or yeomen immigrants, could hardly get land at all except in the newer parts of the colony. In the second half of the century the migration of the poorer whites was accelerated also by the increasing competition with servile labor in the tide-water section. The white servant might have been a trained craftsman, but as a free man he usually preferred to become a cultivator of land of his own rather than work for hire at a trade. The scarcity of free artisans compelled the planter to employ servants as craftsmen, and the more this was done, the less free men cared for such occupations. The eastern regions of the tobacco colonies were thus deprived of their most intelligent class of workers.

At the same time a sectional cleavage appeared. The large planters became fearful that the poorer element might gain control of the assembly, and to preserve their power Governor William Berkeley withheld writs for the election of burgesses during the whole period from 1661 to 1676.[1] In 1670 the assembly thus irregularly prolonged imposed a property qualification upon the voters.

While the common people were still angry over this reactionary law the Indians of the Piedmont began to give trouble. The governor was so slow in taking steps for the defense of the frontier that the people in the danger zone believed he was trying to avoid hostilities in order to save his profits in the fur trade. Exasperated at last beyond endurance by a man who "bought and sold their blood," the frontiersmen took matters in their own hands, and chose one of the fall-line planters, Nathaniel Bacon, Jr., to lead them against the savages. The governor, enraged in his turn, refused to give Bacon a commission, and his followers turned their arms against the administration. Gaining the upper hand for a time, the insurgents called an assembly which restored manhood suffrage; but Bacon died during the turmoil, his discouraged followers submitted, and their work was undone. "Bacon's Rebellion" (1676), so called, shows how decidedly the frontier tended to foster an independent and democratic spirit.

The southern colonies developed no such system of schools as distinguished New England. The dispersion of population made the maintenance of schools impracticable save in the few communities where settlement was fairly compact. But it must not be forgotten that schools, even in Massachusetts, were only one of several agencies for educating youth. Physi-

---

[1] Some authorities believe that there was an election in 1666.

cal conditions in the South, as well as the more individualistic spirit of the people, caused more stress to be placed on these other agencies, especially the home. In Anglican theory, education was a function of the parents or Church rather than of the government. Therefore no such legislation as the Massachusetts acts of 1642 and 1647 are to be found upon the statute books of Virginia. It was assumed that, normally, parents and masters of young persons would care for their education without compulsion. Many parents and masters did, in fact, give the young both practical training and instruction in reading. Well-to-do planters often employed tutors, and clergymen frequently supplemented the efforts of the heads of households in their parishes.

In cases where these agencies failed to protect society against the consequences of neglect on the part of the natural teachers of children, the authorities stepped in, as in New England, taking children from those in charge of them, and placing them as apprentices on terms which gave some assurance that they would be so trained as to become self-supporting. The aims were to reduce idleness and unemployment and to increase the number of skilled artisans. Practically, the government was thus forced to share in the work of education, but not until the eighteenth century were masters required to give apprentices some book education, in addition to vocational and religious training. Workhouses, where trades would be taught to young people, were contemplated, but apparently not provided.

Owing to the larger number of indented whites, the presence of Negroes, and the smaller opportunity for free artisans, the southern colonies found even more serious than the northern the problem of the idle, the shiftless, and the poor. From an early date Virginia suffered from the large number of "vagrant, idle, and dissolute persons." In 1670, following the exposure of a plot of servile insurrection, the assembly forbade the further introduction of convicts,[1] and made the alteration in the suffrage laws already referred to, with a view to withholding the ballot from the ex-servant class until they had proved their worth.

The responsibility for looking after the dependent and delinquent classes devolved upon the parish vestrymen. They apprenticed children of poor families, aided the unfortunate according to their necessities, and levied taxes to meet the cost of relief. Incapables were usually placed in private homes, under an agreement as to terms of compensation. Other relief was given either in money or by temporary assignment to the care of a competent person or family. Cases are recorded where patients were even sent to medicinal springs at the expense of the public. Efforts were made to find work for the able-bodied poor.

SELECT BIBLIOGRAPHY

The entire volume by Wertenbaker, *The First Americans,* is devoted to the subject-matter of this chapter, and covers many aspects of colonial culture for which there is not space in this book. Most matter of this kind is only to be found scattered through the general works already mentioned, or in monographs. The following works may be mentioned as being among the most important for the several subjects indicated. Some of them are better suited to the needs of specialists than of general students:

Industry. McFarland, *A History of the New England Fisheries;* Forman, *Rise of American Commerce and Industry;* Clark, *History of Manufactures in the United States, 1607–1860;* Tryon, *Household Manufactures in the United States, 1640–1860.*

Religion. Cobb, *The Rise of Religious Liberty in America;* Earle, *The Sabbath in Puritan New England;* Goodwin, *The Colonial Church in Virginia.*

---

[1] Parliament repealed this measure in 1717, opening eighteenth-century Virginia to a new flood of immigration of doubtful value.

Education. Cubberley, *Public Education in the United States;* Dexter, *A History of Education in the United States;* Finney, *Brief History of the American Public School;* Heatwole, *History of Education in Virginia;* Knight, *Public Education in the South;* Martin, *The Evolution of the Massachusetts Public School System.*

General. Wright, *Literary Culture in Early New England;* Dow, *Domestic Life in New England in the Seventeenth Century;* Earle, *Child Life in Colonial Days;* Parrington, *Main Currents of American Thought;* Dexter, *Colonial Women of Affairs;* Beard, *America through Women's Eyes* (the story of woman's rôle in our history) ; Jernegan, *Laboring and Dependent Classes in Colonial America, 1607–1783;* McKee, *Labor in Colonial New York.*

There are several economic histories which discuss some of the topics touched upon in this chapter. In this connection Weeden, *Economic and Social History of New England,* and Bruce, *Economic History of Virginia in the Seventeenth Century,* should be mentioned again. Bogart, *Economic History of the United States,* and Faulkner, *American Economic History* should be added.

Chapter V

LOW TIDE IN THE COLONIES

RELATIONS WITH ENGLAND

THE Restoration of the Stuarts to the English throne in 1660 marked the triumph of religious as well as political reactionaries. The Puritan party in Parliament was eclipsed and several new laws were enacted against dissenters. Another generation was to elapse and a revolution was to occur before the Protestant sects gained the legal right to worship in their own way (by the Toleration Act of 1689) ; recognition of the Catholics was to be still longer delayed. Yet with the accession of Charles II the period ended in which religious controversy was the chief concern, for, as we have seen, the main interests of the group to which the king now lent ear were economic. With men of the type now dominant the extension of trade had always been a chief consideration in colonization. It was men of this "mercantilist" class who had made most of the early attempts to settle America. At first they operated, as in the case of Virginia, through private companies to which the king granted concessions. From the Restoration on they gained more and more influence in the government, and in the eighteenth century practically became the government. Their rise is closely associated with the growth of the power of Parliament at the king's expense, and as their influence increased, British colonial policy more and more embodied their views.

British mercantilism, like that of the other states of western Europe in the same era, aimed at national self-sufficiency. Accordingly, colonial industry should be made to supplement English industry, in order that it might help to free the empire from dependence upon foreign countries. Economic strength had a political purpose, the safety of the nation in its rivalries with other powers, especially when those rivalries led to wars. The professed intent of the British mercantilists was not merely to advance the prosperity of the commercial class, or of England, but to promote the welfare of the empire as a whole.

Charles II was hardly seated securely before the mercantilists began to devise a policy for the suitable control of the American dependencies. In the very year of the Restoration, Parliament passed a navigation law which excluded all foreign vessels from colonial ports. It also required the colonists to send certain enumerated products only to England or another English colony. The main purpose of this provision was to bring the products of the West Indies to the mother-country, but as tobacco was included in the list of enumerated goods Virginia and her neighbors were also affected. In 1663 a second act added the requirement that all articles bound for the colonies from European countries must first be brought to England and there reshipped for the colonial ports.

Charles II, working in harmony with the mercantilists, after some tentative plans, appointed (1675) a Committee of the Privy Council for Trade and Plantations (commonly called the Lords of Trade) to administer these laws and give general supervision to colonial matters. The purpose of the laws was to build up English shipping. A prosperous merchant marine was regarded as the foundation for the powerful navy which was essential for the protection of the colonies as well as England.

By destroying Dutch competition these acts gave New England the lion's share of the carrying trade of the empire and greatly benefited her shipbuilding industry. The restrictions in the acts may have been meddlesome but they were not deliberately unjust, and valuable privileges were granted as off-sets. Thus while tobacco could be shipped only to England, it enjoyed a monopoly of that market, for its importation from any other source than the English provinces was forbidden.

None the less the crown had difficulty in enforcing the acts, for the colonists chafed under the restrictions. During the Interregnum the tobacco colonies had profited by the temporary freedom from control, and had greatly extended their market through the employment of Dutch carriers. They now found their trade not only confined, but burdened with a heavy duty upon tobacco consumed in England. The acts increased freight costs and the prices of imported goods, while decreasing the net returns on tobacco. Many a Virginian found his profit gone under the new system.

Evasions and violations of various kinds resulted. Enumerated articles were shipped first to another colony and thence to Europe. New England shipmasters imported goods directly from European countries and distributed them throughout the colonies. The cost of such commodities was reduced somewhat, perhaps twenty per cent, below the prices quoted by British merchants.

The colonial governors were required to enforce the acts of 1660 and 1663, but they performed this duty so laxly that special collectors of customs had to be appointed with salaries paid by the English government. Their performance of duty sometimes led to violent resistance—to an insurrection in North Carolina and to the murder of a collector in Maryland. In Massachusetts the stand was taken that acts of Parliament were not in force unless reënacted by the colonial assembly. The collector for New England, Edward Randolph, found that colonial juries would not convict persons charged with violations of these laws; nine cases prosecuted by him resulted in eight acquittals. In the ninth the shipmaster was fined, the money going into the colonial treasury while the costs were assessed against the collector. Taught by experience that Americans were likely to be guided by their interests rather than by their sense of loyalty, Randolph urged the government to set up admiralty courts to try such cases. These courts would be free from local influence, because they dispensed with juries and left the decision on points both of fact and law to judges appointed by the crown.

The self-willed conduct of Massachusetts in other matters irritated the king. She had long been a thorn in the side of the Stuart rulers. During the Civil War and ensuing disorders in England she had acted very much as if she were an independent state. Soon after the Restoration, therefore, the king demanded that her people take an oath of allegiance; that the courts render justice in his name; that freedom of worship be granted to members of the Church of England; that execution of Quakers cease; and that a freehold qualification for voting be substituted for the religious test. When royal commissioners visited New England to see how these commands were obeyed, they found that only one—the issue of writs in the king's name—had really been complied with,[1] and they departed in high dudgeon, declaring: "The king did not grant away his Sovereigntie over you when he made you a corporation. When [he] gave you power to make wholesome laws and to administer Justice by them, he parted not with his right of judging whether those laws were wholesome, or whether justice was administered accordingly or no."

The obstinacy of Massachusetts at last led the Lords of Trade to advise the king that its government was conducted without the slightest regard for the authority or revenue of the crown. The outcome was a court process and judgment annulling the charter, in 1684.

---

[1] Massachusetts dropped the death penalty for Quakers from her laws in 1661 and temporarily abandoned corporal punishment.

By this time it was apparent that the charters of the corporate and proprietary colonies interfered with the plans of the
government.   Down to 1679 Virginia was the only royal
colony, but the design was now formed of changing all of the
chartered colonies to the royal type and uniting them to sim-
plify administration of the trade acts and other laws.   Following the Massachusetts case the Lords of Trade determined
to proceed against the charters of Connecticut and Rhode Island and the patents for the Jerseys and Delaware, and to
unite all of them with New York and Massachusetts under
one governor.   Only the one charter was actually annulled,
but Sir Edmund Andros was sent in 1686 as governor-general
of the "Dominion of New England," with authority also over
New York and the Jerseys, where he was represented by
deputy governors.

James II probably carried the changes farther than the
Lords of Trade intended.   He ordered Andros to discontinue
the representative assemblies.   This done, Andros ruled New
England with the aid of a council appointed by the king, although its members came from the colonies composing the
Dominion.   Landowners were required to secure new deeds,
for which fees were exacted, and to pay an annual quitrent
in recognition of the king as grantor of land.   In spite of the
abolition of the assemblies the towns were required to collect
taxes, and when some of them refused, town meetings were
forbidden save for the purpose of electing officers.   The New
Englanders, like the New Yorkers of the same period, protested vigorously against taxation without representation,
again foreshadowing the stand taken eighty years later.

THE REVOLUTION OF 1688

James, less cautious than his brother, asserted the royal prerogative in accord with his grandfather's theory of divine
right, and revived the conflict which had made the seven-

teenth century a long struggle for supremacy between king and Parliament. He held the claims of English municipal corporations under their charters in as light esteem as he did those of the corporate colonies, and, being himself a Catholic, he suspended the laws which excluded Catholics and dissenters from office. By this conduct he offended both the Anglicans who had supported divine right and the anti-Anglicans who held that the king was subject to the law.

The "bloodless revolution" drove James to seek refuge at the friendly court of Louis XIV of France. Parliament signalized its victory by giving the vacated throne to Mary, the Protestant daughter of the deposed monarch, and her husband, William of Orange, head of the Dutch state, and prescribing the terms on which the throne should be held thereafter.[1]

To justify the turning of a hereditary ruler out-of-doors and choosing his successors, the parliamentary party appealed to the compact theory—that rulers derive their powers, not from divine right, but from the people, through an agreement to set up government for the protection of their lives, liberty, and property. The philosopher John Locke played the rôle of chief apologist. In language which found an echo in the Declaration of Independence in 1776, he wrote: "Whensoever the legislative shall . . . endeavor to grasp . . . an absolute power over the lives, liberties, and estates of the people, by this breach of trust they forfeit the power the people had put into their hands for [the preservation of their rights] and it devolves to the people, who have the right to resume their original liberty, and by the establishment of a new legislative (such as they shall think fit) , provide for their own safety and security, which is the end for which they are in society. What I have said here concerning the legislative

[1] By the Bill of Rights (1689) and the Act of Settlement (1701). The latter insured the Protestant succession by barring the Catholic descendants of James II.

in general holds true also concerning the supreme executor [king], who having a double trust [as part of the legislature as well as executive] acts against both [trusts] when he goes about to set up his own arbitrary will as the law of the society."

With the overthrow of James II came the downfall of Andros and the end of the Dominion of New England. The denial of the right of representation was contrary to the spirit of the English revolution, and Connecticut and Rhode Island were allowed to resume their governments. The people of Massachusetts had high hopes of recovering their lost charter and making it the basis of a more liberal government. A new charter was granted in 1691, but it did not restore all of the former privileges, for the governor was to be appointed by the crown. The council, however, was to be chosen by the assembly subject to confirmation by the governor, and Plymouth and Maine were incorporated with Massachusetts. It was at this time that New York won the privilege of a representative assembly, but in that province this liberty rested not on a charter but upon the less secure basis of royal instructions. The Jerseys were restored to their proprietors, but they voluntarily surrendered their patent in 1702, and the two colonies were united as one royal province.

Although liberal principles underlay the revolution, it did not alter the direction which colonial policy had taken. The influence of the mercantile class, now acting with the landed aristocracy, become greater than ever. A new motive for desiring effective control over American resources in men and money arose with the beginning of the wars with France, the first of which broke out soon after the ejection of James II. They therefore continued to aim at the thorough administration of the navigation system, at the reduction of the colonies to the royal type, and at intercolonial union.

A new navigation act was passed in 1696, to correct defects

in the earlier ones, and admiralty courts were established as Randolph had recommended. In the same year the Committee of the Privy Council for Trade and Plantations was superseded by the Board of Commissioners for Trade and Plantations (the "Board of Trade"). The membership of the new body was not confined to Privy Councilors, but included other men who were experts in the work to be done. Its functions included the general supervision of colonial affairs.

THE DECLINE OF CULTURE

The revocation of the first Massachusetts charter dealt the theocracy its death blow. Under the new charter, property replaced church membership as the basis of the suffrage franchise, and toleration was guaranteed to all Protestants. Although the Congregational Church remained the legally established one, the other political props which had bolstered up the power of the clergy were destroyed. In particular, the magistrates ceased to be their allies, and thenceforth their influence was reduced to that which they could command through their intellectual and moral force and capacity for leadership.

Long before the abrogation of the charter the influence of the clergy had begun to wane. One of the principal causes was the growth of commerce and the increase of wealth. Wealth and leisure undermined the devotion to religious ideals and activities. The infiltration of inhabitants who had never shared the Puritan purposes was another factor tending in the same direction; while the mere coming-on of the second and third generations within the families which formed the core of Puritanism brought more or less of a reaction from the stern asceticism of the founders.

The progress of the reaction is indicated by the adoption, in 1657, of the "Half Way Covenant." Admission to church

membership had up to that time been conditional upon a
public profession of spiritual rebirth, but the time had come
when many who had no consciousness of regeneration found
membership desirable for many reasons. The new arrangement recognized them as identified with the Church in what
we may term associate membership, upon their signifying
general accord with its work and aims.

These changes in the religious sphere were paralleled by a
general decline in culture. The New England colonies, Massachusetts Bay above all others, had enjoyed at the outset a
highly educated leadership. It is doubtful if any other group
of pioneers ever equaled this colony in the proportion of
members who had received the best training of their age.
Winthrop, Cotton, and the forty or fifty other Oxford and
Cambridge men who ruled early Massachusetts were, besides,
persons of virile mind who would have held their own intellectually in any surroundings.

But a new country is not conducive to the refinements of
life; the conquest of a wilderness is so engrossing a task that
they cannot even be preserved without serious impairment.
By means of Harvard College the founders of Massachusetts
made a noble effort to keep the torch of learning burning
brightly while they felled the forest, built themselves cabins,
and attacked the stubborn soil. But the light of Harvard
shone alone throughout the seventeenth century,[1] and little
by little the civilization imported by the first-comers dwindled, reaching its lowest point, perhaps, during the opening
decade of the eighteenth.

It must be remembered, too, that the main purpose in establishing Harvard was to provide instruction of the kind
thought proper for clergymen. Every minister, it was as-

[1] William and Mary, the second college established in English America,
dates from 1697.

sumed, should know the languages in which the Scriptures were written, as well as the Latin of the great works of the Church Fathers down to Calvin. Such studies, plus the Bible itself, were regarded as covering all necessary knowledge of law and government as well as theology. Even if it could be supposed that Harvard approximated the English universities in the presentation of these subjects, it is certain that neither it nor any other American instrumentality afforded facilities for keeping abreast of European knowledge of law as taught in the Inns of Court, or medicine as presented elsewhere.

Even England and the other European countries were still in almost medieval darkness so far as natural science is concerned. Since the days of Columbus some notable inventions, such as the telescope and microscope, had been added to man's equipment for observation, but the premises on which he based his thinking were not yet much changed. The seventeenth century was nevertheless a great age in intellectual history. Within its first quarter Sir Francis Bacon set forth the first clear statement of modern scientific method. He was ably seconded by the Frenchman Descartes (1596–1650), who rejected the assumptions derived from authority (the Bible and teachings of the Church) and insisted that reasoning must rest upon evidence. In the application of these principles, the great name of the period is that of Sir Isaac Newton (born 1642), with whom modern science is generally reckoned to have begun.

It was long before the influence of these men produced any perceptible effect upon the mental outlook of mankind at large. Even yet, its full force has perhaps reached only a portion of the intelligentsia. It was slight indeed upon the contemporaries of these thinkers. Few if any of the most learned compatriots of Bacon would have challenged the belief that

James I, by his touch, had cured hundreds of his subjects of the scrofula.[1] And hardly a breath of the new scientific thought reached America.

It is obvious that real medical science could hardly exist in such an atmosphere. The thinking of the wisest was still dominated by the concept, inherited from early ages, that disease is caused by diabolical influences. Logically, natural remedies for supernatural evils seemed futile. Divine assistance, obtained by prayer, was regarded as the most appropriate remedy for bodily ills.

The best medical practice still followed the precepts of ancient and medieval authorities. The opening of the western continents added at least one valuable drug to the pharmacopœia—cinchona (quinine), which in the second half of the seventeenth century greatly reduced the mortality from malaria. Some worth-while lessons were learned, also, from the Indian "medicine men," who in addition to worthless nostrums compounded some rather effective cathartics and emetics from herbs.

But the practice of medicine was not based on science. At best it was empirical; at worst it drew upon current superstition for remedies which were useless, if not actually harmful. An example of the professional lore of the time is found in a letter written by a London physician to the governor of Connecticut, in 1643, in which he prescribes the following cure for smallpox, plague, purples, and poison: Place live toads, caught during the month of March, in an earthen pot; cover, surround with charcoal, and burn; powder the remains; give dose according to the strength of the patient. The com-

[1] The superstition that this disease, called the "King's Evil," could be cured by the laying on of hands by the ruler, prevailed throughout Christendom. Such was the state of credulity that one of the ablest surgeons in England testified that he had frequently been eye-witness to such cures. Charles II "touched" nearly a hundred thousand victims of scrofula and epilepsy during his reign.

mon failure to perceive the relationship between cause and effect appears in a prescription for ague: Pare the patient's nails, place them in a linen bag, and tie about the neck of a live eel. Keep the eel in a tub; when it dies the patient will recover.

When such notions were prevalent on both sides of the Atlantic, it is hard to believe that colonial medicine was worse than English, or that it declined during the century. Yet in England there was a recognized course of preparation, and practice was restricted to persons who were "properly" trained. Few trained physicians found their way to America; at the end of the century Boston is said to have had four. Ministers sometimes treated persons who would otherwise have been wholly without care. Barbers were most generally relied on for the bleeding which was supposed to let "hostile humors" out of the system. In the South, the planters and their wives did most of the "doctoring." There was little or no effort to protect the public from quacks, who, to be sure, were hardly distinguishable from honest practitioners.

Both birth and death rates were high. Families of twelve to twenty children were common, usually the offspring of one father and successive wives. The mortality of infants under two years of age was approximately twenty per cent; that of the mothers was also excessive.

The supernaturalism which tainted medicine affected every phase of life. Every natural phenomenon for which the age had no simple explanation—every unusual occurrence—was regarded as supernatural. Destructive storms were the work of malignant spirits, and comets were portents of dreadful events. Cotton Mather, the most learned New Englander of the second half-century, attributed the death of his child to a demon, and his own escape from yellow fever to a guardian angel. Belief in witchcraft was ever in the background of men's thinking, and needed only some unusual stimulus to cause it to break forth in such a frenzy as that which smote the Puritan colonies in the years following 1688.[1]

The witchcraft delusion is a striking evidence of the low state of provincial civilization. It was closely associated with efforts of the clergy to counteract the forces which were depriving them of their former prestige. Greatly afflicted by the "sins of the times," which were corrupting "the very heart of New England," the ministers preached in vain against the worldliness which was breaking down the "walls of Zion." Increase Mather at last conceived the idea of collecting and publishing the evidence which to him proved God's special concern for New England. Published in 1684 under the title, *Essay for the Recording of Illustrious Providences,* Mather's book, widely read, set everyone talking about supernatural occurrences, including cases of witchcraft.

It was not long before the excitement produced the result which might have been predicted. The children of a Boston mason named Goodwin accused a "queer" old woman of bewitching them. This afforded Cotton Mather, the son of Increase, an opportunity to study the cases of the supposed victims. Like his father a believer in witchcraft, he gained by his observations the material for another book intended to convince readers that disbelief in witches, angels, and evil spirits was heresy. He succeeded not only in intensifying the belief in such beings, but in arousing the expectation of additional manifestations of their activity. Accusations of professed victims multiplied, especially in the Salem neighborhood, and at least nineteen persons were put to death as witches before the reaction set in. The credulity of even that age was overtaxed when it was asked to believe that so many agents of the devil were abroad as the number of accusations

---

[1] This outbreak was only the worst (so far as the colonies are concerned) of several which occurred during the century. Western Europe was swept during the first years; England suffered during the middle years; and New England experienced a mild attack at the same time.

indicated. The conviction followed that, in the excitement, the trials had been conducted without due regard to evidence of guilt, and that many innocent persons had been sacrificed. The confession by one of the "bewitched" girls that her whole performance was an imposture confirmed this conviction. Although the reaction did not lead many to perceive that the belief in witchcraft was itself an error, the whole unfortunate affair hastened the dawn of a more rational spirit.

The frenzy spent its force within New England. Although almost every colony had one or more witch trials at one time or other, only the intense religiosity of Puritanism supplied the proper medium for a panic. In the indifferent air of Virginia, persons inclined to become accusers hesitated to bring charges before an impartial court, lest they be punished for failure to substantiate them.

In Massachusetts it was the class least interested in religion which first denounced the persecution. The whole episode was unfortunate in its results upon the clergymen who clung to the old concepts. Their campaign in behalf of the faith of the fathers ended in their own discomfiture. The ministers to whom the people were to hearken in the new century were to bring a message which was altered in many respects.

While Anglicans of the southern colonies escaped the disgrace of the witchcraft persecution, they were no more successful than the New Englanders in preserving the Old-World heritage. The scattered population, which was an important factor in preventing the rise of a system of schools, had equally unfortunate effects upon the ministrations of religion. If a parish was large and populous enough to support a pastor, it was too large for him to do his work properly. Pastoral calls could at best reach only a few parishioners, and distance (families often lived ten or fifteen miles from the church), poor roads, and bad weather kept most of the people from the services on Sunday. Pastors often faced empty pews.

Chapels here and there throughout the larger parishes helped to bring pastor and people together once every month or two; lay readers filled the intervals between such visits.

The hard life of the minister, and the inadequate compensation, paid in tobacco at a price which usually overvalued it, kept down the supply of able men. There was a chronic dearth of ministers and many of the parishes were pastorless. Under such circumstances unworthy clergymen were sometimes employed, and retained in spite of complaints of swearing, drunkenness, or fighting.

The solicitude of the Bishop of London and his Virginia representatives, especially Commissary Blair, led to the founding of William and Mary College (1697) for the purpose of training young Virginians for the ministry. Before its work was well begun it was destroyed by fire (1706). Full observance of the Anglican ritual could not be secured in a country devoted to plantation industry; and despite the best efforts of the ecclesiastical authorities, the influence of the Church continued its downward course throughout the colonial era.

SELECT BIBLIOGRAPHY

Relations with England, 1660–1700. The interrelations of the European nations which form the background of the British colonial system are treated in Abbott, *Expansion of Europe,* II. Beer, *Old Colonial System, 1660–1754,* continues the study presented in *Origins.* A standard but older treatise is Seeley, *Expansion of England.* Osgood, *American Colonies in the Seventeenth Century,* III, is also excellent on the early phases of the imperial system. Andrews, *Colonial Self-Government,* and Channing, *United States,* II, are brief but good. For the years following 1691 see also Adams, *Revolutionary New England.*

The Revolution of 1688. The best single volume on this subject is Barnes, *The Dominion of New England.* See also Andrews, *Narratives of the Insurrection (Original Narratives).*

The Decline of Culture. Wertenbaker, *The First Americans;* Murdock, *Increase Mather;* Wendel, *Cotton Mather, the Puritan*

Priest; Kittredge, *Witchcraft in Old and New England;* Burr, *Narratives of the Witchcraft Cases (Original Narratives)* ; Bruce, *Institutional History of Virginia in the Seventeenth Century;* Eggleston, *The Transit of Civilization;* Haggard, *The Doctor in History.* See also Bibliography for Chapter IV.

Chapter VI

EIGHTEENTH-CENTURY DEVELOPMENT

AT THE close of the seventeenth century Britain's American provinces gave little promise of the progress which the eighteenth century was to witness. A scant two hundred thousand souls inhabited a mere fringe along the seacoast, broken by patches of swamp and forest, and nowhere extending far inland except along the courses of the navigable streams. Even in Virginia three generations had not pushed the frontier beyond the fall line, but two more generations were to find the population, increased ten-fold, penetrating the Alleghanies and pouring into the Ohio Valley in a constantly swelling stream.

The new century was to bring equally momentous changes in the outlook and spirit of the people. If the seventeenth century filched from them little by little the civilization which the first settlers had brought from England, the eighteenth atoned by fostering the rise of a native culture; and as American life expanded and grew in vigor it took new directions, diverging from its British stem in interests, ideals, and habits until a political separation became inevitable.

THE WESTWARD MOVEMENT

At the opening of the eighteenth century the New England population had reached the Massachusetts-Vermont line. In New York expansion had been slow in getting under way. Just when New Netherland was coming under its English masters a few Dutch families had settled at Schenectady, the Mohawk-River gateway to the land of the Iroquois. For more than half a century Schenectady remained a lonely outpost on the exposed frontier. In 1698 over fifteen thousand of the eighteen thousand inhabitants of New York were still on Long Island or near the mouth of the Hudson.

The lack of representative government long caused immigrants to avoid the province. The narrowness of the Hudson Valley and its stony soil were additional deterrents. The land system was uninviting. Oftentimes as the result of fraud on the part of the recipients of land grants, large holdings prevailed and formed the basis of a provincial aristocracy which controlled political and social life. On some of the great estates a system of tenantry existed which was quite out of keeping with the prevalent freehold tenure in America. Small landowners were crowded out, and young men sometimes left New York for other provinces where lands could be obtained more easily and held more securely.

The expansion of New York on a notable scale began in the eighteenth century when the frontier was thrust up the Mohawk by German immigrants. Driven from their homes in the valley of the Rhine by persecution and hard times, like the Dutch who had founded Germantown, they came to New York by thousands during the first quarter of the century, and their settlements on the Mohawk marked the farthest advance of the frontier in the province before the Revolution.

In Pennsylvania the opening of the century found population on the banks of the Delaware and its navigable tributaries, with a few outposts on the Susquehanna. Through the mountain wall which barred the advance of the farmer the Susquehanna and Delaware led northward to the Indian country of the "finger lakes," inviting the adventurous trader to compete with New Yorkers in the commerce with the redskins. Although by the royal patent of 1664 the western boundary of New York was a line drawn due north from the source of the Delaware, the prosperity of that province rested so largely upon the fur trade of the lake country that vigorous efforts were made to forestall the Pennsylvanians. The assertion of a protectorate over the Iroquois was the means of compelling the southern traders to turn their attention elsewhere.

Threading the passes of the mountains traced by the western branches of the Susquehanna, the Pennsylvanians now came upon the upper waters of the Allegheny and began to traffic with the tribes of the Ohio Valley. It is not unlikely that they crossed the mountains as early as 1725; before the middle of the century their posts were to be found at several points in the Ohio country, between the river and Lake Erie.

Prominent in this trade were the so-called "Scotch-Irish." They were Protestants of Ulster, in northern Ireland, who came to Pennsylvania in great numbers, and to the other colonies to a less extent, in the early eighteenth century, because of British laws which discriminated against the people of the smaller island in favor of English commerce and of the Anglican Church.[1]

Germans, who had shared in the making of Pennsylvania from the beginning, continued to come in great streams. Some of those who had gone to New York came later to Pennsylvania by way of the Susquehanna. Others came directly from the Fatherland. Many of them were from the Rhine Palatinate, and possessed so little of this world's goods that they were compelled to defray the expense of their transportation by pledging their labor for a term of years, like the indented servants of the previous century.

Greatly to the annoyance of the government officials, the free immigrants were disposed to help themselves to lands when they could not pay for them. The Scotch-Irish declared that "it was against the laws of God and nature that so much

[1] The "Scotch-Irish" were people from the Scottish lowlands who had been colonized in Ireland by James I as a means of holding the native Irish in check.

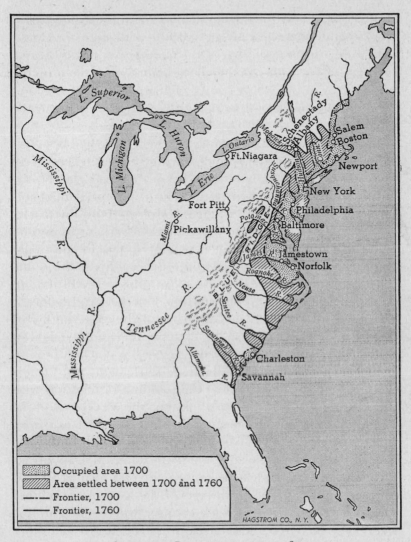

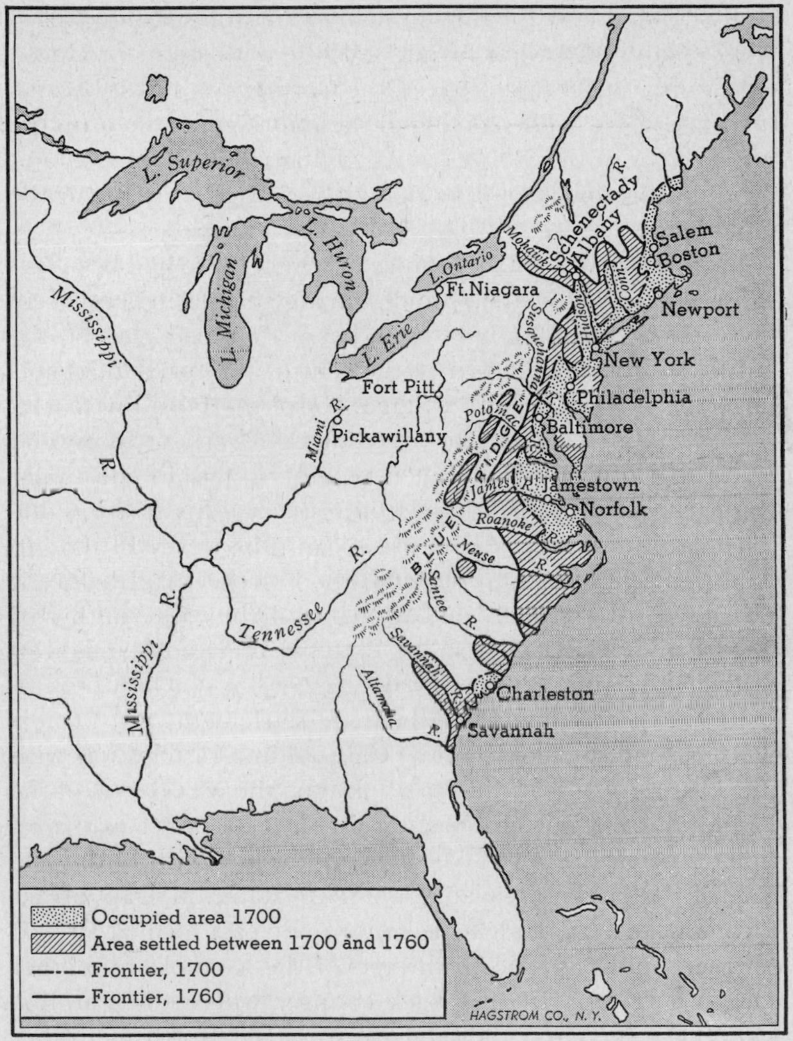
L. Superior
L. Michigan
L. Huron
L. Ontario
L. Erie
Ft.Niagara
Fort Pitt
Pickawillany
Miami R.
Mississippi R.
Tennessee R.
Mohawk R.
Schenectady
Albany
Hudson
Conn.
Salem
Boston
Newport
New York
Susquehanna R.
Philadelphia
Potomac
Baltimore
James R.
Jamestown
Norfolk
Roanoke R.
Neuse R.
Santee R.
Savannah R.
Altamaha R.
Charleston
Savannah
BLUE RIDGE
Occupied area 1700
Area settled between 1700 and 1760
Frontier, 1700
Frontier, 1760
HAGSTROM CO., N. Y.

SPREAD OF POPULATION, 1700–1760

land should lie idle while so many Christians wanted it to work on and raise their bread." While both stocks produced many a fur trader and pioneer, the Germans as a class became thrifty farmers. The coming of these foreigners filled up the lower valley of the Susquehanna, giving rise to Lancaster and neighboring towns, and bringing the settled area up to the mountains.

Virginia was the only province in which there had been any considerable westward advance during the seventeenth century. By 1675, as we have seen, her people had reached the fall line. Just at the turn of the century French Huguenots formed a settlement on the James above the falls, the first in the Piedmont. Fourteen years later Governor Spotswood brought a number of German redemptioners to the upper Rappahannock to work local iron ores. To his zeal was due the organization a little later of two counties in the Piedmont. The pioneers moved in only tardily, however, and before it was filled up Germans and Scotch-Irish moving southward from Pennsylvania crossed the Potomac and took lands west of the Blue Ridge (1730–1750).

In North Carolina the Albemarle settlements did not expand beyond the mouth of the Chowan until after a war with the Tuscarora Indians in 1712.[1] In fact the occupation of the Piedmont of both Carolinas was due largely to the continuation of the movement of Germans and Scotch-Irish, with some English, from Pennsylvania. Where Staunton Gap breaks through the Blue Ridge the convenient pass formed an exit for the pioneers to the headwaters of the Roanoke and other southern rivers. In that back country where the Carolina rivers take their rise the pioneers from the North met other newcomers, who were pushing in from the coast. Among these latter came, about the middle of the century, Scotch

---

[1] After their defeat this tribe was removed to New York and became the sixth nation of the Iroquois League.

Highlanders, exiled by the government of George II for supporting the efforts of the Stuart "Pretenders" to regain the English throne.

This interior country remained for two generations a region of small farms and few slaves. Many of the men of this new frontier were more interested in hunting, or in the Indian trade, than in agriculture. In religion the groups which first took possession of this upland region represented many sects.

THE FRONTIER

In one sense, the first English colonists in America were all frontiersmen. The primeval woods formed the somber background of their rude cabins, and the howl of the wolf was the nightly accompaniment of their slumbers. However, they suffered but a temporary deprivation of their accustomed ways of life, and speedily transformed their surroundings. It was in the "back settlements" of the mid-eighteenth century, stretching from the Mohawk to the Savannah, that the typical frontier society first took form.[1] From this frontier onward,

[1] A vivid picture of the mid-eighteenth-century frontier is given by Schnell, a missionary representing one of the German sects in Pennsylvania, who in 1743–1744, made a journey on foot along the entire frontier from Pennsylvania to Georgia. Unarmed, except with a hatchet with which to cut a path through the forest, he ascended the Shenandoah Valley, penetrated the Blue Ridge to the Virginia Piedmont, and passed southeastwardly through North Carolina to the sands of the beach which he followed to Charleston. Six years later, on another journey through the Shenandoah Valley, he found a sleeping place each night in a settler's hut, and swimming James River, came to an Irish settlement near the site of Fincastle. Here the people "lived like savages," having no clothing but deerskins, and no food except deer and bear meat and Johnny-cakes. For thirty miles after leaving this settlement he saw no house.

A few years later George Washington, while engaged in the survey of the estate of Lord Fairfax, visited this same back region of Virginia. Of conditions at that time he wrote: "I have not slept [sic] above three or four nights in a bed, but, after walking a good deal all the day, I lay down before the fire upon a little hay, straw, fodder, or bearskin, whichever is to be had, with man, wife and children, like a parcel of dogs and cats, and happy is he who gets the berth nearest the fire."

the real pioneer kept in the van of the movement westward and formed the "cutting edge" of civilization in its attack upon the wilderness. His type was permanent. His isolated cabin of rough logs, often without floor or windows, stood in the midst of a tiny clearing where a few trees had been felled or perhaps only deadened to make room for a little patch of corn. His few hogs ranged the neighboring woods, fattening on acorns and beechnuts until needed for the table. But he "loved the gun and scorned the plow." His long muzzle-loading flint-lock was his most intimate friend, and hunting was at once recreation and business, the source of food, raiment, and income. Venison supplied the larder and deerskin took the place of cloth in the making of garments. Peltries he bartered for the few commodities which he could not provide for his family through his own efforts. Of these the chief were salt, ammunition, and hardware, brought by the trader or obtained by occasional visits to a post or distant town.

Accident and disease were met with rough readiness; barring wounds, if alive, the frontiersman was usually well. Life was a prolonged adventure with danger ever near. Any night might bring the savages to burn, scalp, and torture. Wild almost as the Indian, certainly as bold and freedom-loving, the frontiersman endured hardship as his daily lot and despised the soft life of the old communities, while his Amazon-like companion dauntlessly reared a numerous brood and skillfully wielded ax and gun, sometimes even against the Indian. Europe could show nothing so primitively simple as the life of these pioneers.

The constant threat of danger imparted a semimilitary aspect to the life of each new region in turn. Every frontiersman expected to join his neighbors at times in expeditions against hostile natives. New settlements reflected the prevalent insecurity in the means employed for defense, strong palisades replacing the walls of the European towns. Jamestown and Plymouth were so enclosed, and the palisaded fort or village accompanied the westward movement until it halted on the shores of the Pacific.

URBAN LIFE

America was by no means all frontier as the colonial period drew to its close. While the towns on the coast still lacked many of the pleasing features of the maturer culture of the Old World, they had far more in common with eighteenth-century Europe than with the United States of our own day. At the wharves were rows of warehouses for storing articles of sea-borne commerce. Creaking windlasses, hand-turned, slowly swung heavy casks and bales to and from the wooden sailing vessels, a hundred of which would hardly have shipped the cargo of one modern ocean freighter. By the waterside massive two-wheeled carts, horse-drawn, rumbled to and fro. In the closely-built districts were the shops of retail merchants and craftsmen, whose families occupied the upper stories of the houses. Farther off were the homes of the wealthier people.

Nowhere were the ears greeted by the whir of machinery. No tall chimneys belched forth smoke to dull the brilliance of the sunlight. No shriek of whistle disturbed the perpetual calm. Locomotive and factory were deep in the womb of the future. Void were the avenues of street-cars and automobiles, of telephone poles and lamp posts. Water-driven grist-mills and saw-mills of primitive type marked the limit of man's success in harnessing nature's forces.

In the houses of the wealthy were fine imported furnishings, but conveniences were unknown. Heating arrangements were most primitive and there was an utter absence of sanitary plumbing. Open fireplaces provided the only opportunity for cooking and the only source of artificial warmth. In winter they consumed enormous quantities of wood at an alarming cost, yet did not redeem the houses from almost arctic cold. In such a domicile many of the habits now deemed essential to decency were quite impossible. Each morning a Negro servant kindled the fire and assisted the master to dress, but a scanty washing of hands and face was the nearest approach to a bath.

All work moved at the pace set by hands, horses, and sails. Did one wish to send a message, no telephone at his elbow emancipated him from bondage to the ubiquitous servant. Amanuenses with goose-quill pens laboriously wrote letters in triplicate, one for the office records, the others to guard against the mishaps attendant upon transmission to distant correspondents. These letters, if placed at once upon a vessel bound to England, would be delivered in from four to ten weeks at a cost of a shilling each; if the destination were a neighboring province, a week or less might suffice for carriage. But if a message were not ready for the sailing of the fleet for England, it might wait for six months, if not a whole year, for another opportunity.

Amusements were few. In Boston neither music nor drama afforded diversion. Plays were forbidden, and music either in the home or outside was seldom to be heard. A "consort of music" was given at the court room in 1732, but a dozen years passed before there was another. Rare animals were exhibited now and then. Within one six-year period Boston enjoyed opportunities to view a sea lion, a lion, and a polar bear. Sleight-of-hand performers, rope-walkers, and puppet shows came more often, but were probably the delight of the populace rather than of the gentry. Gentlemen preferred to stroll with their ladies on the Common, or to drive to a country inn for dinner. Some of the richer families had country seats where they gave great house parties. The men loved fishing and shooting, too, and paid many a visit to the woods and streams. For more extended outings there were cruises along the coast of Maine.

Dances were the chief social events, and the great annual ball given by the governor was the climax of the season. Both men and women appeared on 'these occasions in resplendent attire. Silk, satin, velvet, and broadcloth, of many hues, and ornamented with buckles, buttons, and lace of silver and gold, found a fitting setting in parlors walled with elaborately carved or painted panels. Even in the dim light of tallow or bayberry candles such a gathering was a brilliant spectacle.

Puritanical Massachusetts forbade the sale as well as the use of playing cards, but the law was disregarded by the fashionable set, and merchants of high standing sometimes impaired their fortunes by gambling. The use of strong drink was universal and as a class the aristocracy vied in bibulous habits with their poorer neighbors who indulged their convivial propensities in the public houses or taverns. Yet a drunken man in the streets was a rare sight, and excessive drinking was condemned, although usually on economic rather than moral grounds. No organized temperance movement arose until many years after the close of the colonial era, although John Adams must have uttered the thought of many when he remarked that "if the Ancients drank wine as our people drink rum and cider it is no wonder we hear of so many possessed with devils."

The slow processes of production meant long and toilsome hours for those who worked with their hands. Wage-earners in the modern sense were relatively few, and organizations of workers as distinguished from employers quite unknown. In the shipbuilding industry, for example, the yard owner might be himself a shipwright, and wield hammer and saw elbow to elbow with the little group of journeymen and apprentices who formed his working force. Of these the journey-men worked for wages, but the apprentices, who were young men learning the craft, worked for their "keep" as members of the master's household. The intimacy of master and man made the members of the group sympathetic, and prevented the antagonisms which in later times have divided "capital" and "labor." That the lot of the northern workmen was happy as compared with that of the same class in England is indicated by the immigration of ship carpenters.

Love of display, social gayety, and the desire to get on in the world suggest that eighteenth-century Boston had lost much of the piety of earlier days. If so, she made outward atonement by the strict observance of the Sabbath. This vestige of seventeenth-century Puritanism still survived in full vigor. At sundown on the seventh day of the week every counting-house, shop, and tavern closed and remained shut for the space of twenty-four hours. During that interval neither man nor beast left the town, or walked by the water-side or on the Common.[1]

As late as 1723 the Harvard library contained none of the writings of Addison, Bolingbroke, Swift, Steele, Dryden, Pope, or Locke. A generation later it is described as contain-ing "above five thousand volumes" on theology, the classical languages and literatures, history, biology, mathematics, and philosophy.

The Boston public library had been started in 1673 and until destroyed by fire in 1747 was kept in a room of the Town House. Its great folios certainly did not circulate, but were doubtless consulted more or less at least by the clergy. Books were in demand, as the number of printers and booksellers shows. The Exchange was surrounded by the shops of book dealers, who displayed the works of Latin and Greek writers

---

[1] Washington, when President, was once stopped by a Connecticut tithing-man for driving on Sunday, but was allowed to proceed upon explaining that he was on his way to divine service.

in profusion but found little need of carrying in stock "contemporary" literature (although Addison's *Spectator* seems to have been widely read) , or even the classics of Milton and Shakespeare.   Five printers supplied the retailers with reprints of English books and with the works of American writers.   The latter were chiefly sermons.   Even the efforts at poetry dealt mostly with theological themes.   A "best-seller" in its day was Wigglesworth's *Day of Doom,* which has been called the "epic of fire and damnation."   In this age of the beginnings of the English novel the colonies produced no fiction.

No newspaper appeared in the seventeenth century.   The *Boston News Letter,* first issued in 1704, was the pioneer Anglo-American journal.   For fifteen years it had no local rival, but by 1730 the Boston public was supplied with news of "the most remarkable occurrences, Foreign and Domestic," by three weekly papers.   They afford even more evidence than the printed books that literary impulses were astir. They offered encouragement to writers of prose and verse, and printed some essays in the vein of the *Spectator* which showed promise.

At the close of the colonial period Boston had a population of twenty-five or thirty thousand.   New York, older but less populous; Philadelphia, the junior of the New England metropolis by fifty years yet now outranking it in numbers; Charleston in South Carolina, almost contemporary with Philadelphia in origin—these were the "great towns" of the Atlantic seaboard.   Salem in Massachusetts, Newport in Rhode Island, Baltimore in Maryland, and Norfolk in Virginia, while much smaller, were also important places.

While in culture and in material civilization all of the towns were much alike, there were some noteworthy differences.   New York, like Boston, had many narrow, crooked streets, while Philadelphia and Charleston were laid out with streets crossing at right angles. Philadelphia streets were well lighted as well as paved, and had sidewalks of flat stones. Charleston was unpaved, except for brick footways about six feet wide, separated from the drive by a line of posts. Its streets were foul and ill-smelling, and neglect of sewage made it unsanitary. It was subject to annual epidemics of smallpox, yet as the favorite residence of the South Carolina planters it was noted for its gay and lively society. Yellow fever was a frequent summer plague in the coast cities as far north as Philadelphia.

Many New York houses were built in the style introduced by the Dutch colonists, with gables on the street. Philadelphia and Charleston were cities of brick. Three-story structures of uniform design gave the former a monotonous appearance that drew unflattering comment from visitors. In Charleston only the better houses had glass in the windows. The Anglican churches of these two cities were stately edifices, in pleasing contrast with the homely meeting-houses of Boston. All had bells, and Christ Church, Philadelphia, had a set of chimes.

The Puritan strictness, which so carefully guarded Sabbath observance and banned dramatic performances, was not in evidence south of New England. The Philadelphia Quakers were quite as strict as the Puritans, but the community did not take its tone from them. Plays were a constant diversion of the upper class in the middle and southern colonies for twenty years before the Revolution. The first theater was built in Williamsburg, Virginia, in 1716, and New York had a "play house" by 1733. Taverns, court rooms, and warehouses were utilized before the erection of special buildings. The earliest theater buildings made little advance over these makeshift accommodations, but despite all handicaps patronage was sufficient after 1750 to support a small number of professional actors.

Musical instruments, such as spinnet, pianoforte, and violin, were quite common in the South, and Charleston had a St. Cecilia Society. Cards, dancing, gay parties, and hunting were in vogue everywhere, while horse-racing (not unknown in New England) and cock-fighting were followed with special devotion in Virginia and the Carolinas.

In New York and Philadelphia the schooling of children instead of being provided for by the public was regarded as the duty of the religious bodies. Schools were of the parochial or private type, and probably reached a smaller percentage of the boys and girls than the schools of Boston. In New York the Anglican Church, through the Society for the Propagation of the Gospel in Foreign Parts, established a number of elementary schools. In Philadelphia the Friends were especially active. Each of these towns had its college. King's, the forerunner of Columbia University, was founded by the Anglicans in 1754, while, in contrast, the Academy out of which grew the University of Pennsylvania (1755) was promoted by citizens of Philadelphia without regard to sect. Several of the smaller towns had institutions of higher education, the chief of which were William and Mary College, at Williamsburg, Va., Yale at New Haven (1701), and the College of New Jersey at Princeton (1746). Charleston had neither college nor public schools. Wealthy families employed tutors, and others sent their children to small private schools taught by the rector—or in the pioneer regions, the Presbyterian pastor. During the years just preceding the Revolution numerous academies sprang up in the South. In these many prominent men received their final schooling, or prepared for entrance to Princeton. Many young people grew up untouched by any instruction other than that which parents could give.

None of the colleges provided instruction in professional branches except theology, until the University of Pennsylvania opened a school of medicine in 1765. The boy who determined to become a lawyer or physician served a kind of apprenticeship, "reading law" in the office of an established practitioner until he could pass a mild examination for admission to the bar, or attending a physician and observing his methods until he absorbed such knowledge as his mentor possessed. A few fortunate young men attended English schools and universities, or studied law at the Inns of Court. Most of these came from the middle and southern colonies, and the superiority of the training obtained in the British Isles was a factor in the intellectual leadership of the statesmen of these provinces during the Revolution.[1]

Free libraries supported by public funds were practically unknown. Only a few men of means accumulated private collections of as many as a thousand volumes. Philadelphia, Charleston, and some of the smaller places, among them Salem, organized library associations, the members of which raised funds by subscription for the purchase of books to be used on the circulating plan. Most famous of these was the Library Association of Philadelphia; founded (1731) as the result of Benjamin Franklin's efforts, it is still in existence.

By the end of the first quarter of the eighteenth century enterprising publishers in all of the important centers had followed the lead of Boston in establishing newspapers. For the most part they had only a local circulation, but they gained steadily in importance as disseminators of information and quickeners of thought.

In the intellectual and material equipment of provincial

---

[1] The legal profession did not assume an important position in America until the eve of the Revolution. Colonial magistrates and legislators drew their notions of law largely from the Bible or "common sense," and lawyers were looked upon with suspicion. At almost the last moment American students in England derived from legal studies a large part of the arguments which inspired the great pamphlets, resolutions, and other documents of the revolutionary era.

America nothing is more conspicuous to the modern student than the lack of knowledge of science and its applications. In this respect, however, the colonies were not far behind the rest of the world. Little advance had yet been made beyond the fifteenth and sixteenth centuries, and geology, botany, zoölogy, chemistry, anatomy, and physics as we conceive them today were still blank pages in the book of human knowledge. All that was known on these subjects was briefly summed up under the term "natural philosophy." At the close of the colonial era only a generation had passed since Newton had gone to his grave (1727). Franklin was in the midst of the experiments which brought him international fame and honorary degrees from Yale and Harvard for "improvements in the electric branch of natural philosophy." Not until the era of American Independence did the discovery of oxygen lay the foundation of chemistry, and another dozen years passed before Jenner announced the theory of vaccination. Anaesthesia awaited the 1840's.

Astrology, alchemy, and kindred superstitions still held sway over the minds of intelligent men, and medicine was on a par with these pseudo-sciences. The medical books in common use dated from the previous century, and at best perpetuated the lore of the Middle Ages. There was much brewing of concoctions of herbs and barks, to which were sometimes added worms, wood lice, or vipers, making a broth quite worthy of Macbeth's witches. Melancholia was thought to be due to worms in the brain, and fever was supposed to yield to the application of salt herrings on the soles of the feet. None the less medicine was honored as one of the learned professions, and physicians deserved respect for their practical skill in the simpler forms of surgery and in the use of laxatives and purgatives. Too often, however, their treatment was sadly overdone.

COUNTRY LIFE

The great majority of Americans cultivated the soil for a livelihood under conditions perhaps midway between those of the frontier and English rural life. In general, land was so abundant and cheap that the cultivator found it easy to obtain possession of all that he could till, without the necessity of sharing the fruits of his labor with a landlord. His toil was hard and incessant and his pleasures and comforts few; yet as compared with the peasant-tenant class of Europe from which he sprang he enjoyed independence and a rude plenty.

The stubborn soil of New England, even when with infinite toil it had been cleared of stones and timber, responded reluctantly to the efforts of the husbandman. The colonist who came to plant was driven to the sea. Many a farmer was also a sailor, at least in his youth, and on occasion made a hand on a fishing vessel. The farm belt hugged the coast, and in Massachusetts still extended hardly more than thirty or forty miles inland. The Connecticut Valley, the only exception, maintained its contact with the sea by way of the river rather than by overland connections with Boston Bay.

The typical cultivator was a freeholder. His small, one-story house of logs or rough-hewn boards was unpainted, and unheated except by the fireplace in the room which served as kitchen, dining- and living-room, and in cold weather as bedroom. Strings of dried apples, pumpkin, and peppers hung in festoons from the ceilings. A large slab fitted with long pegs for legs did service as a table. Wooden trenchers, which were often merely square blocks hollowed out by hand, held food and served as plates from which two or more persons ate, sometimes with forks or wooden spoons, often with fingers. Homespun garments were the rule, made from wool grown by the farmer, spun and woven and made up into suits and skirts by the women of the household.

Toilsome as was the farmer's life, food at least was abundant. Soil, forest, and stream amply supplied the larder and yielded some surplus for the market. Fruits and vegetables, butter, cheese, barreled beef and pork, and wooden articles such as bowls, staves, ox-bows and ax-helves, whittled out by firelight in the winter evenings, were carried to town by ox-cart or sled, and brought a little ready money in the form of paper currency.

Rural life was even more monotonous than that of the town. Few homes contained any books except the Bible, psalm-book, and almanac. The last was magazine, cyclopædia, and speller, all in one. It guided the farmer in sowing and reaping and in treating disease in man and beast; contained the record of expenses, crops, and the weather; and even vied with the Bible as the record of births and deaths.

The meeting-house was the center of intellectual and emotional stimulus and of solemn sociability. The village tavern and schoolhouse were also important places for group gatherings. At the tavern were posted notices of elections, sales, and other matters of public interest, and there men gathered to make trades, swap yarns, and discuss politics.

At meeting-house, schoolhouse, or tavern the men of each community assembled from time to time in town meeting, to pass by-laws and choose selectmen, constables, and other petty officers. Once a year each town meeting chose the deputies to the General Court. In town meeting as elsewhere social rank counted. The voice of the gentleman was heard rather than that of clerk, mechanic, or farmer, and deputies were much more likely to be selected from the "best families" of each locality than from the plain people.

Immigration was infusing foreign blood into the Puritan stock, although the country felt this influence less than the towns. Such names as Faneuil, Bowdoin, and Magee betray non-English origins. The total mass of foreigners in New

England was not great, but it showed quite diverse elements, including French, German, Dutch, Scotch, and Irish. So many of the newcomers intermarried with Puritan families and were assimilated that the population retained its homogeneity. It was becoming, however, a new "Yankee" race—a "new Nordic amalgam on an English Puritan base," differing from the English in character, dialect, and ideals.

The era of improved roads had not yet dawned even in Europe in 1760. In America roads existed, of a kind, along the coast, and it was possible to go from Boston to New York in four days, with three days added if the journey was continued to Philadelphia. For the most part, the streams were unbridged and crossing was possible only by ford, ferry, or canoe. No hill was leveled, no valley filled, in road construction, and the surfaces were innocent of any harder finish than the native soil. The best day's journey seldom exceeded forty miles, and twenty-five miles was a good average. Under favorable conditions travel by water was less arduous and as rapid, but with light winds two weeks might be consumed in such a voyage as that from New York to Albany.

The traveler journeying southward from New England found the character of country life gradually changing. In southeastern Pennsylvania he encountered the Germans on the most productive lands to be found anywhere in the colonies. Huge barns sheltered their stock and stored their grain, while smaller, simpler structures sufficed for the housing of the family. Negro servants were rare here, for the Germans despised the blacks and would not work beside them. Wife and daughters shared with husband and sons the labor of the fields, raising wheat for export and contenting themselves with Indian corn for their own sustenance. Dwelling in communities of their own kind and speaking a foreign tongue, the "Pennsylvania Dutch" formed an element which alarmed the English, as they seemed to be unassimilable.

Crossing the Potomac the traveler entered still another realm, where the roads became even more wretched, the inns more intolerable, and the population more diffuse. When Thomas Jefferson went to Williamsburg in 1760, at the age of seventeen, to enter William and Mary College, few Virginia towns contained more than a dozen houses. Williamsburg, the provincial capital, had about two hundred dwellings, and the new town of Richmond about as many. While Norfolk, the center of trade with the West Indies, was larger, Virginia—in fact, the South in general—was distinctly a region of country life. In most counties the courthouse and jail, although perhaps destined in later times to become the nucleus of a village, stood alone, unless flanked by a tavern or store.

In the absence of towns the country store, where almost everything could be bought, was becoming an important institution. Planters sometimes "kept store" in addition to their other activities, or set up their sons as storekeepers, as did Patrick Henry's father. But the plantation worked by Negro slaves was the central feature of southern life.

The house of the wealthy planter was of wood or brick, and, like the Washington home at Mt. Vernon, often stood upon elevated ground commanding a view of a river. The kitchen stood apart from the house, freeing it from odors and heat. Well-kept grounds, ornamented with flowers and trees, surrounded the mansion. In the rear was the vegetable garden, and still farther removed were tobacco-barns, granaries, stables, the dairy and poultry houses, and the quarters for the Negro slaves. These last consisted of cabins of logs or rough planks, each cabin containing a bed, chairs, and a few cooking utensils.

The typical plantation consisted of four or five thousand acres, part of which was cultivated while part was woodland. The nearest neighbors were usually two or three miles distant. Many planters had much more land, and the population of their estates, mostly black, might run into the hundreds. It was necessary to possess a much larger tract than could be cultivated at any one time. Tobacco, grown year after year in the same field, without crop rotation or use of fertilizers, exhausted the soil, and most plantations contained areas of abandoned land. The cultivated acreage at any one time was but a fraction of the whole. A large freehold, as compared with a northern farm, was required for the support of one family.

The low price of tobacco, due in part to the British commercial legislation, taught the more intelligent planters to diversify their industry, and, like medieval lords, to make their establishments as nearly independent as possible. Hence they trained their slaves as carpenters, coopers, blacksmiths, tanners, shoemakers, spinners, weavers, and distillers, as well as house servants and field hands. Lumber, fuel, meat, grain, fruit, vegetables, wool, cotton, flax, rough furniture, shoes, flour, brandy, cloth, casks, all these were often produced on the estate. Articles for the "great house" and the personal use of its white occupants were generally brought from England, and the extravagance of the average planter (or his family) kept him in a chronic state of debt.

The planter who took his business seriously and was his own manager could not indulge in indolence. Yet a love of leisure was characteristic. There was much exchanging of hospitality, and entertainment was often on the grand scale. Idle hours were turned to good advantage by the few men of intellectual tastes. Some of the best private libraries in America were gathered in the homes of Virginia gentlemen. William Byrd II, who had been educated in England, possessed at his estate of "Westover," near Richmond, nearly three thousand volumes. He was a writer as well as a reader, and his *History of the Dividing Line* (the story of the survey of the boundary between Virginia and North Carolina) makes an effort, with some success, at literary grace.

The planter's children were taught by tutors who were inmates of the house, or by the parish clergyman, or they attended a "neighborhood school" maintained by subscription. If the young men went to college, they attended William and Mary like Jefferson, or Princeton, like Madison; or sometimes went abroad, like Byrd. A substantial part of the education of many Virginians who attained prominence—Washington, Jefferson, Madison, and others—was gained through careful reading in their own homes.

The rural population was much given to games and sports. Fox-hunting and horse-racing were favorite exercises of the aristocrats, and public gatherings often gave occasion for boxing and wrestling matches and other contests of skill and strength. Elections and court sittings brought together at the courthouse men from all parts of the county to indulge in such sports, to listen to speeches by prominent men, and to drink the liquor which candidates for the assembly always provided in the greatest abundance at such times.

ECONOMIC DEVELOPMENT

The eighteenth century was a time of rapid industrial development. New England, where the fisheries were from the beginning one of the chief occupations, enjoyed a great expansion of this pursuit. Under the stimulus of an increasing market in Europe the whale fisheries also developed from an intermittent longshore business into a well-conducted enterprise which sent Yankee vessels into every corner of the Atlantic. Shipbuilding, which shared the benefits of the navigation acts, was on the increase. The advantage of abundant material offset the high wages paid to laborers, and Yankee shipwrights became so skillful that their product was readily salable in Europe and the other colonies. Shipbuilding was the chief New England manufacture in this epoch. Rum, distilled from West Indian molasses, was the next most important manufacturing enterprise of this section.

Boston, Salem, and Newport were the centers of New England's commerce. Hundreds of native-built ships cleared yearly from these ports laden with lumber, the products of the fisheries, or rum. The Catholic countries of southern Europe had become the chief buyers of fish, the poorer grades going to the West Indies to feed slaves. Lumber was sold in the same markets, while most of the rum was exchanged on the Guinea coast for gold, or Negroes to supply the slave market of the Spanish colonies. As the fur trade of New England declined, its important place was more than filled by the demand of New York traders for Yankee rum, to be used in their own traffic with the Indians. From the West Indies came in the round of trade goods of European manufacture, sugar and molasses, and cash in the form of Spanish silver coins. Few exports went to the mother-country. New England paid for English manufactures with the coin derived from the West Indian trade.

The middle colonies grew even faster than New England. By 1750 Pennsylvania, although founded so much later, took rank with Massachusetts and Virginia as one of the three most populous colonies. The merchants of Philadelphia supplied much of the capital for the fur-trading ventures of the Scotch-Irish and bought for export the surplus produce of the German farmers. From New York and Philadelphia the furs, grain, and flour of the middle colonies, like the fish and lumber of New England, went to the markets of southern Europe, the West Indies, and the Carolinas. Manufacturing here took the form of flour-milling, utilizing the grain of the extensive arable areas in southeastern Pennsylvania and the Cumberland Valley. Among the non-English inhabitants were many mechanics who set up small manufacturing plants to supply their neighborhoods with a variety of articles, such as stoves and other iron products, glass, paper, and cloth. Such small-scale manufactures were carried further in the middle colonies than anywhere else in North America.

In the South, North Carolina soon adopted the plantation of the Virginia type, with slave labor. Tobacco was the chief crop, while in South Carolina indigo and rice, grown in the swamp lands along the coast, were the important staples. Negro slavery was especially necessary on the plantations in the marsh region, which was unwholesome for whites. The planters tended to congregate in Charleston, leaving their estates to be managed by overseers, and the result was a harsher type of slavery than that in Virginia, because it lacked the sympathy which sprang from frequent contact between owner and slave. The growth of chattel slavery was stimulated by the slave traders. The British Royal African Company, organized in 1672, monopolized this traffic for several years. In the Treaty of Utrecht (see page 138) England exacted from Spain the privilege of supplying her colonies with slaves. Independent traders, some of them New Englanders, now claimed a share of the profits, and developed both the Spanish and English colonial market to the utmost. By the middle of the century Negroes composed nearly half of the inhabitants of Virginia, while in South Carolina they were far more numerous than the whites.

The scarcity of white craftsmen compelled southerners to make use of Negroes not only as field laborers but wherever workers were required. If the black race had not supplied numerous individuals of ability and intelligence, the diversified industry of the plantations, already referred to, would not have been possible. Many planters thus were enabled not only to produce tobacco, wheat, and meat for export, but to manufacture articles of various kinds for sale. Some even gathered small groups of trained slaves to work in specially equipped buildings, producing woolen, linen, or cotton cloth, shoes, or other articles for the market. The lumber industry in its various branches employed large numbers of Negroes, and there were many black ship- and house-carpenters, cabinet makers, wheelwrights, and coopers. In short, most of the labor of the Southland, whether skilled or unskilled, was performed by slaves.

The presence of the Negro created some grave problems. According to law, the status of children followed that of the mother, the child of an indented white woman being regarded as free. Vicious women of this class not infrequently became the mothers of mulatto children, who although classed as Negroes were recognized as free. Thus, in part, arose the class of free Negroes. Through the apprentice system, the authorities sought to supply such children with some degree of training and education for adult life, in order that they might be self-supporting.

No public provision was made for the education of slaves, and they received little training from their masters except along practical lines. Masters hesitated to impart "book learning," believing that it made the slaves restless and discontented. Even instruction in the Christian religion was restricted by fear of the consequences. Christian Europe had long since abandoned the idea that one Christian could own another. The enslavement of pagans was a different matter, and Indians and Negroes suffered accordingly. Kindly-disposed masters found themselves in a dilemma, however, when impelled to seek the conversion of their slaves: would they not become free upon being baptized? The property interests of the dominant race thus made war upon its humane impulses until it was decided that conversion did not alter the Negro's status. Even then many masters feared that Christianity would spoil their servants by developing notions of race equality. Of course most slaveowners were quite as indifferent to the slave's spiritual well-being as they were to their own.

In contrast with the commerce of the northern and middle colonies, the chief trade of the southern provinces was with England. British or Yankee ships carried the plantation products to London, where some merchant acted as agent for the planter, selling his crop and purchasing the goods desired in return.

The people of the back settlements at first lived as self-sufficing family units, existing by hunting and the most primitive agriculture. Gradually the inland counties became farming communities, producing grain and stock, even in the Piedmont portions of the Carolinas and Virginia. A few men of wealth penetrated to the back settlements and took large tracts of land which they tried to cultivate with slave labor, but most of the settlers were poor men who disliked slavery and cultivated their small farms with their own hands. It was not until after the colonial period that the plantation reached the Piedmont and displaced the small-farm economy. By the end of the colonial era the back settlements were producing an agricultural surplus which found a market in the tidewater for consumption or export. This productivity relieved Charleston and tide-water South Carolina, for example, of dependence upon Pennsylvania for foodstuffs, and created a demand for roads and other improved means of transportation to bring the output of the interior farms to the coast.

RELATIONS OF FRONTIER AND COAST

The wealth and culture of provincial America were to be found in the coastal regions and were little in evidence among the fur traders and farmers who were pushing westward. By the time the frontier had reached the mountains there was a sharp contrast between the society of the coast lands and that of the back country.

The settlement of the new regions was welcomed by the people of the coast as a protection against the Indians, but in every colony those in possession of political control took care to prevent it from passing out of their hands. Even when the population of the new districts exceeded that of the old, the system of government was such as to keep the interior communities in subordination to the minority on the seaboard.

In New England, where there was the nearest approach to equality, few of the dwellers inland were eligible for seats in the upper houses because of the high property qualifications. In the southern colonies the planters dared not share power with the non-slaveholders of the Piedmont. Everywhere the property-owning class feared that popular government would lead to taxation of those who possessed property for the benefit of the poorer class. In Pennsylvania the immigration of foreigners aroused the apprehensions even of Franklin. The ease with which they acquired land made the ordinary property qualifications for voting and officeholding an ineffectual barrier.[1] New communities were therefore tardily organized as counties, and then only allowed from one to four representatives each, while the old counties where dwelt the "Quaker aristocracy" enjoyed eight each—more than either their relative wealth or numbers warranted.

Virginia allowed each of the new counties, like the old ones, two representatives in the lower house, but made them so large that their delegates represented many more inhabitants than did those from the tide-water counties. In South Carolina the Piedmont had no separate representation before 1773.

The men of the back country did not meekly accept their position of inferiority. Many of them, including the Scotch-

---

[1] At the close of the colonial era seven colonies imposed a freehold qualification upon the franchise; the other six accepted personal property as an alternative qualification. For officeholding the requirements were higher than for voting.

Irish Presbyterians and some of the German sects, held the Calvinistic theology with its democratic implications. Under the primitive conditions of the frontier these doctrines and the actual equality of men inevitably begot the ideal of political equality. The backwoodsmen forgot those artificial distinctions which had no meaning in the realities of their lives, and used arguments which anticipated those of the Revolution, in their demand for equal rights.

Although allowed so slight a share in the government of their provinces, the frontiersmen actually regulated the affairs of their everyday lives, and their actual liberty and self-reliance made them all the more impatient with the restraints put upon them by the governing class. Before the Revolution a sharp contest had begun between the people of the coast and those of the interior in most colonies. The unenfranchised workmen of the towns were potential allies of the men of the back districts in this contest for more liberality in government; in this division is to be found moreover one of the bases of the political parties of later times.

GROWTH OF LIBERALISM

The democratizing influence of the frontier was one of several liberalizing forces in American life. In Britain, social rank and political privilege were associated with the possession of large landed estates. Because of the scarcity of land a small portion of the population was able to maintain itself as a dominant aristocracy. Similar ideas but not similar conditions prevailed in early America. The most influential colonial leaders were naturally imbued with the aristocratic notions of the English society from which they came. Hardly less than the Stuart kings the Puritan leaders believed themselves to be chosen of God to govern. John Cotton, the minister at Boston, and for a long time the most influential of the Massachusetts clergymen, declared that he did not conceive that God "did ever ordain democracy as a fit government for either church or commonwealth. If the people be governors," he asked, "who shall be governed?" In similar vein Winthrop held that "the best part is always the least, and of that best part the wiser part is always the lesser." Democracy has "no warrant in Scripture." "Among nations it has always been accounted the meanest and worst of all forms of government."

The New World, with its limitless expanse, was not hospitable to a landed aristocracy, even when favored by legislation. Laws of primogeniture (inheritance of the entire landed estate by the eldest son) and entail (prohibition of the sale of a landed estate by the heir) disappeared from American statute books by the time the colonial population cast off England's leading-strings, and the vestiges of feudal land tenure were doomed to follow later. The possession of land, as a qualification for voting and officeholding, in a country where its acquisition was easy, did not constitute an insuperable barrier; and the democratic ideas of the frontier tended to permeate the whole of society.

The scarcity of men in proportion to the vast natural resources inviting enterprise tended to enhance the value attached to the human factor in production. This not only meant relatively high wages, but it is a striking fact that throughout America the penal code was ameliorated long before the mother-country modified her ancient laws. At the outbreak of the Revolution no colony designated more than twenty offenses as punishable by death, while England exacted the extreme penalty for no less than one hundred and fifty.

The progress of humanitarianism and democratic ideals is shown also in religious history. It has already been hinted that toleration of dissenters was promoted by American conditions, and while vestiges of discrimination outlasted the colonial period, political disabilities based on religious grounds disappeared rapidly during the eighteenth century. Reference has been made to the persistence of Calvinistic theology in the orthodox Congregational churches.   The greatest preachers of the period, such as Jonathan Edwards, professed the same creed as their predecessors of the previous century; but the temper of the times had changed, and both pastors and people were responsive to new sentiments.   The doctrine of predestination no longer suited the mood of men who had shaped their earthly careers successfully by dint of individual force, and something akin to the rationalism becoming prevalent in European intellectual circles was capturing the minds of provincial Americans.   Edwards wrote a profound essay on the freedom of the will without proving anything except that his intellect, commonly acknowledged to be one of the greatest America had produced, was devoted to a by-gone issue.

Nevertheless in another way Edwards led his times forward, for he embraced wholeheartedly the movement to make religion a matter of fervid personal conviction and conduct rather than a cold and formal profession.   This movement, known as the Great Awakening, after sweeping western Europe, had its colonial beginning in Edwards' church at Northampton, Massachusetts, in 1734.   Continued by George Whitefield, an English Methodist, during a visit to America, it won converts by hundreds, with important results.   By stressing the value of the soul, it enhanced the importance of the common man in the body politic as well as in the religious organizations.   It thus reënforced the philosophy of human rights on which the Revolution was to rest, and at the same time released a humanitarianism which found expression in the founding of orphanages, and in missionary undertakings among the Indians and Negroes.

Conservatives looked askance upon the movement; hence the radicals sometimes formed new sects.   Thus arose the

New Lights, as an offshoot of the Congregationalists. Similarly, several new colleges were founded, representing the new thought-currents. Among these were Princeton, Brown, Rutgers, and Dartmouth, the last growing out of an Indian mission-school.

A famous illustration of the American tendency to develop new types of liberalism is found in the Zenger libel case. Peter Zenger, publisher of a New York newspaper, was prosecuted in 1734 for writing articles criticizing the government. His counsel, Andrew Hamilton, offered to prove the truth of the statements—a plea which meant, in effect, that a true statement is not libelous. Such was not the law, however, and the presiding judge ruled that the jury could pass only upon the fact of publication. In spite of the ruling, Hamilton persuaded the jury that Zenger's strictures on the government were true and obtained a verdict of "not guilty." Although the decision did not establish Hamilton's contention beyond controversy, it indicated a tendency of colonial law to diverge from that of England in the direction of greater individual liberty.

SELECT BIBLIOGRAPHY

Nearly all of the topics treated in this chapter are discussed in Adams, *Provincial Society.* See also Greene, *Provincial America,* Osgood, *American Colonies in the Eighteenth Century,* and Kirkland, *History of American Economic Life.* Chitwood, *A History of Colonial America,* covers economic and social life in Chaps. XX–XXVIII; Sanders, *Early American History,* devotes Chaps. XVIII–XXV to Colonial Civilization.

The Westward Movement; The Frontier. Ford, *Scotch-Irish in America,* Hanna, *The Scotch-Irish,* and Faust, *German Element in the United States,* are important books dealing with the race elements which contributed most largely to the early pioneer stock. For the general significance of immigration see Schlesinger, "The Influence of Immigration on American History," in *New Viewpoints in American History.* Turner, *The Frontier in Amer-*

ican History, develops in a series of essays the significance of the westward movement. Turner is the pioneer scholar of the modern school to exploit this theme.

Urban Life; Country Life. Andrews, *Colonial Folkways.* Alice M. Earle has written several books on the manners and customs of the colonial period. Among them are: *Child Life in Colonial Days; Colonial Dames and Goodwives; Colonial Days in Old New York; Customs and Fashions in Old New England; Home Life in Colonial Days; Stage Coach and Tavern Days.* See also Benson, *Women in Eighteenth Century America.*

Economic Development. Weeden, *Economic and Social History of New England;* Andrews, "Colonial Commerce," Bell, "West India Trade." See Bibliography for Chapter IV.

Relations of Frontier and Coast. Turner, "The Old West," in *The Frontier in American History;* Hockett, *Western Influences on Political Parties to 1825,* 9–22. Nettels, *Roots of American Civilization,* interprets the period as a struggle between the people and the large property owners.

Growth of Liberalism. Parrington, *The Colonial Mind,* Book II; Porter, *A History of Suffrage in the United States.*

Chapter VII

THE STRUGGLE FOR THE
MISSISSIPPI VALLEY

RIVALRY OF THE FRENCH AND ENGLISH

FROM the outset the progress of French settlement was watched with jealous eyes by the English. Not long after the founding of Acadia a band of half-piratical men from Virginia raided Port Royal (1613). A few years later (1622) the king granted the region (called by the English Nova Scotia) to a proprietor who tried to colonize it in spite of the presence of the French. Every occasion of conflict between the two powers in Europe was the signal for hostilities in America, and even in the intervals of peace the indefinite boundary between New England and Acadia was the cause of constant friction.

During the second half of the seventeenth century the two countries became rivals for the fur trade of the interior. Radisson and Groseilliers, the discoverers of the Hudson Bay country, offended by their treatment at the hands of the French authorities, turned to the English, and the Hudson's Bay Company was chartered (1670) as the result of their efforts.[1] Its posts on the shore of the bay were readily reached by ocean-going vessels during the ice-free months, and ease of transportation gave its traders a great advantage over the French of the lake country.

Englishmen also reached the Upper Lakes and undersold the French; or the friendly Fox Indians and French wood-rangers came down to the eastern shores of Lake Erie to meet

---

[1] The promoters belonged to that group which was so active in all sorts of schemes of colonial expansion under the second Charles.

the Iroquois or New Yorkers. This competition in the lake region was a source of great distress to the Canadians, and in 1673 and 1678 the governor of Canada built forts at the site of Kingston (Fort Frontenac) and at Niagara, to cut off the English from the northwest trade.

The Iroquois country was another field of rivalry. These tribes, dependent on the English at Albany for goods, were jealous of their position as middlemen between New York and the western Indians. In 1680, encouraged by the English, they began a war on the Illinois tribes to break up their traffic with the French. On the other hand, Jesuit missionaries won considerable influence over the Iroquois. The English considered the Jesuits as political agents of the French government, and tried to supplant them with English priests. In 1684 Governor Dongan obtained the acknowledgment by chiefs of the League of the dependence of the Iroquois upon the government of New York, and took them under its protection. Thereafter hostile encounters between the Canadians and Iroquois tended to embroil the English and French governments.

While Anglo-French relations from Hudson Bay to the Mississippi mouth were thus tending towards armed conflict, the spark which brought war was lighted in Europe. William of Orange, whom the Revolution of 1688 brought to the English throne, was already the chief enemy of the French king, Louis XIV, having led in the formation of an alliance to check his projects of expansion towards the Rhine. The pleadings of the exiled Stuarts added to the old enmity embroiled Louis with England in the first of a series of wars which ended only with the overthrow of Napoleon in 1815.

In 1689, when "King William's War," as it was called in America, began, wide stretches of wilderness separated the settlements in Canada from the English even in New York and New England where the frontiers were nearest. In

America, therefore, the war was not fought by armies drawn up in battle array after the European manner, but on the French side consisted chiefly of a series of forays against the English settlements by parties of Indians led by a few whites. These raids fell first upon outlying towns in New Hampshire and Maine. Early in 1690 came an attack on Schenectady, in the Mohawk Valley. It was fortified, as was usual on the frontier, with a palisade of logs set upright, the lower ends planted in the ground. Taken by surprise, it was burned and many of the inhabitants slaughtered or captured.

On the other side, Connecticut and New York troops attacked Montreal, and a naval expedition from Massachusetts captured Port Royal. The war was ended, without permanent results for either participant, by the Peace of Ryswick, in 1697.

Only five years elapsed before hostilities began afresh. "Queen Anne's War," as the War of the Spanish Succession was called in America, like its predecessor, found its chief causes in Europe. It was waged to preserve the balance of power, England, Austria, and Holland joining to prevent the virtual union, as they feared, of France and Spain through the accession of a French prince to the Spanish throne.

In America the fighting was of the same character as in King William's War. In the end the Bourbon prince retained the throne of Spain, but at the price of great concessions in the Peace of Utrecht (1713–1714). Besides other changes in the political map of Europe, Gibraltar went to England. France yielded Newfoundland, Nova Scotia (conquered by New England militia in 1710), and the Hudson Bay Territory; and recognized the British protectorate over the Iroquois.

Unfortunately the treaty did not define the boundary of Nova Scotia, and although peace prevailed between the two countries for more than thirty years after Utrecht, quarrels and hostile encounters continued along the disputed border.

After Queen Anne's War the rivalry of France and England became world-wide, and a renewal of conflict was inevitable. Each had its chartered company seeking to control the commerce of the Far East. On the Guinea coast the rival traders competed for the commerce in gold and Negroes; while the dim forest glades of America witnessed many a dark encounter the story of which has never been told.

The next armed conflict between France and England took place during the general War of the Austrian Succession, 1744–1748 ("King George's War" in America), which owed its inception to causes quite apart from their own enmities. During the long peace after 1714 France built the strong fortress of Louisburg on Cape Breton Island, commanding the approaches to the St. Lawrence, guarding her interests in the fisheries, and encouraging the Acadians, now British subjects, to remember their former allegiance. When war broke out in 1744 this stronghold became a shelter for privateers and a base for possible expeditions against the British colonies. Its reduction therefore became a prime object in New England. Governor William Shirley of Massachusetts took the lead in organizing an expedition which with some aid from the British navy succeeded in taking Louisburg in 1745. Shirley would have followed up this success by an attempt at the conquest of Canada, but the British government gave him no encouragement, and the remainder of the war, so far as it concerned America, was a repetition of the old dismal story of Indian raids against the northern frontier.

To offset the success of the British, the French gained a position in the Low Countries so menacing to England that at the Peace of Aix-la-Chapelle (1748) she purchased the evacuation of the Netherlands by restoring Louisburg, to the great dissatisfaction of the Americans, who felt that their interests were sacrificed.

THE FRENCH AND INDIAN WAR

The peace of Aix-la-Chapelle left unsettled the old dispute over the Acadian boundary and did nothing to remove the causes of rivalry in the Mississippi Valley. Even while the peace commissioners were still disputing, the shadow of a new war fell across the upper waters of the Ohio. English land speculators as well as fur traders were now becoming active west of the mountains, seeking control of choice locations in anticipation of the coming of settlers. In 1749 a group of Virginia gentlemen, in association with several prominent Englishmen, organized the Ohio Land Company, and sought for it a grant of a half million acres on the Ohio River, below the "forks." The next year they sent Christopher Gist to "spy out the land." These plans were the cause of special alarm to the French. Even before Gist's journey the governor of Canada dispatched a party under Céleron de Blainville (1749) from Lake Erie to the Allegheny River and thence down the Ohio, to assert the French claim. At the Miami River the expedition turned north, crossing to the Maumee and returning to Canada by way of Detroit. They found the Indians friendly to the British, with whom their trade was large, and saw that vigorous action was needed to hold the country against the English advance. Céleron's expedition was therefore followed by an attack (1752) by Indians under French control upon an Indian town on the Miami River (Pickawilliny) which was a center of British influence, and by the building of forts at Presqu'île and on French Creek, as the first of a chain intended to bar the English from the Ohio country.

The year 1753 found the people of two nations engaged in a race for possession of the same territory, each determined to repel the other's encroachments upon its "undoubted limits." It was under these circumstances that Lieutenant-Governor

Robert Dinwiddie of Virginia decided to send George Washington with a formal message to the French commandant on French Creek demanding the withdrawal of the French as

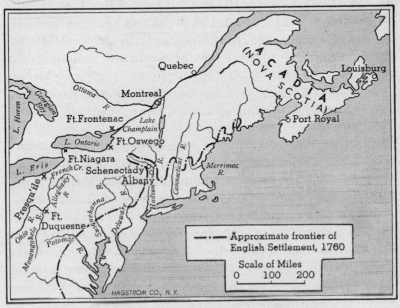

THE FRENCH AND INDIAN WARS, 1689–1763

trespassers. Washington, then a young man of twenty-two, was already familiar with life in the wilderness through experience as a surveyor on the Virginia frontier.

The reply to the British demand was a polite refusal. It was followed by the building of Fort Duquesne at the forks of the Ohio, the key to the entire Ohio Valley. Meeting this challenge, the Virginia government sent Washington a second time with a force to drive out the intruders if they would not go peaceably. While still some distance from Fort Duquesne, Washington learned through scouts of the approach of an armed party with hostile intent, as he supposed. He surprised and defeated it, thus shedding the first blood in the new war; but a few days later, pressed by a superior force, he was compelled to surrender. The enemy was left in possession of the disputed country.

These events in the American backwoods involved Europe in another general conflict, the French and Indian War (in Europe called the Seven Years' War). England would gladly have confined the struggle to the western hemisphere; she withheld a declaration of war until 1756.

In the campaign of 1755 the chief objective of the English was the recovery of the forks of the Ohio. General Edward Braddock was sent from England to command the combined force of regulars and colonial troops collected for this purpose. The two elements of the army did not harmonize. Colonial officers of the highest grade were ranked with British captains and jealousy destroyed the morale of the forces. American tactics, learned in the school of experience, in combat with savage foes in the woods, differed radically from those of the open battlefields of Europe. The discord, combined with Braddock's tactless disregard of advice and inadaptability to his new surroundings, led to disaster. After a toilsome march across the mountains, as the army neared its destination, it fell into an ambush. From the shelter of the forest the unseen foe fired upon the regulars, who were unable to make effective reply. The provincials, of whom Washington was one of the officers, fought frontier-fashion, from behind trees, covering the retreat of the shattered army.

Against the western border, left exposed by this failure, the French now directed the savages, for most of the tribes quickly turned to the side which seemed to be winning. "It is incredible," wrote a French captain, "what a quantity of scalps they bring us. . . . These miserable English are in the extremity of distress, and repent too late of the unjust war they began against us." To Washington, in command of a few hundred militia, fell the hard task of defending as best he could the harassed frontier.

The years 1756 and 1757 brought fresh disasters for the English. The Canadian forces led by the able Marquis de Montcalm gained control of western New York and the Lake Champlain district. In the crisis there came to the front one of the really great Englishmen of the century, William Pitt, who, as the dominating personality in a new ministry, became the organizer of victory.

When England declared war in 1756, a diplomatic revolution took place in Europe. France, the ally of Prussia in the previous struggle, growing apprehensive of her rising power, joined her foes, Austria and Russia, while England acted with Prussia. Ambitious for the place of predominance among the states of Europe, France aspired also to rank as the greatest colonial and maritime power. Grasping at both objects she dissipated her resources in the effort to put huge armies into the field while increasing her navy at the same time.

Pitt discerned the error of France and concentrated his effort upon the building up of British sea power, letting Prussia fight the battles of the alliance on the continent. British sea power eventually won the war. Moreover, Pitt put aside the incompetent army officers who owed their rank to seniority or favoritism and promoted young men to the positions of responsibility. He appealed also to the loyalty of Americans by giving fairer recognition to colonial officers and undertaking to pay for the operations of colonial troops outside of their own jurisdictions.

The population of the English colonies outnumbered that of the French about thirteen to one, but it was impossible to muster it in full force. The assemblies had to be appealed to separately in carrying forward war plans. The English provinces were in little danger of actual conquest, but the success of the French would have stopped British expansion. The task of the English, therefore, was to break down the French defense of the Ohio Valley and Canada.

The superiority of the British navy began to tell in 1758, cutting off supplies and reënforcements for the Canadian armies, and coöperating with the land force under Jeffrey Amherst in a successful attack on Louisburg. Despite minor reverses in the Lake Champlain Valley, the year was one of victory. Fort Frontenac on Lake Ontario was taken, and an expedition under General John Forbes occupied Fort Duquesne. The new Fort Pitt at the forks of the Ohio was a monument to the British statesman.

Again, in the summer of 1759, a fleet in the St. Lawrence cut off succor for the French and enabled James Wolfe to lay siege to Quebec, the chief stronghold of Canada. Nature was the ally of the defenders. Almost inaccessible cliffs guarded the approaches from the river side, and Montcalm hoped to avoid a combat until the early northern winter compelled his enemy to raise the siege. Wolfe, however, in mid-September, found a path which enabled him to scale the heights and force Montcalm to battle. The prize of victory was the possession of Quebec. The next year saw the fall of Montreal and the completion of the conquest of Canada.

Pitt aimed at victory so complete that England could dictate the terms of peace; but the final triumph was delayed by Spain's entry into the war in 1761. The Bourbon allies hoped that their united fleets might more than match the sea power of the English. The naval war of the final years only added, however, to the series of British successes, and involved Spain as well as France in the disasters of defeat. By the treaties of Paris in 1763 France yielded to Great Britain Canada and all claims to territory east of the Mississippi, while Spain, in order to recover Cuba which Britain had taken, ceded

Florida.[1] New Orleans went with Louisiana to Spain, but with this exception England now held the whole of North America east of the Mississippi. France retained only two little islands in the St. Lawrence, of importance to fishermen. In the Far East, also, the fruits of British generalship were garnered by the diplomats at Paris in the expulsion of France from India.

THE PROBLEM OF THE WEST

"Heirs apparent of the Romans!"   In these words an exulting Englishman described his race as successive victories in the Seven Years' War foretold a triumphant end. On sea and land, in every clime—on the battlefields of Europe, in the tropical jungles of India, in the dark forests of North America —the banner of St. George had contended against the *Fleur-de-lis* until France, defeated, exhausted, humiliated, accepted the victor's terms. With their defeat the French Bourbons made their exit from the North American mainland and the curtain fell upon the dramatic and colorful history of New France; the turbid waters of the Mississippi marked the eastward limits of the dominions of decadent Spain, and half a continent spread its invitation before the restless feet of the sturdy race whose multiplying paths ran westward from the margin of the Atlantic.

The Peace of Paris marked, indeed, a signal triumph for England over her rivals in the race for world-wide empire. The treaties swept away all European opposition to English expansion to the Mississippi; but, dramatically, victory marked the beginning of a controversy with the American colonies which ended in the sundering of the great empire built up in long rivalry with France and Spain. Perplexing

[1] This is equivalent to saying that Spain, like France, relinquished her claim to all territory east of the Mississippi. The boundary between the Spanish, English, and French claims in the Gulf region had been ill-defined.

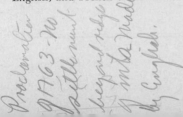

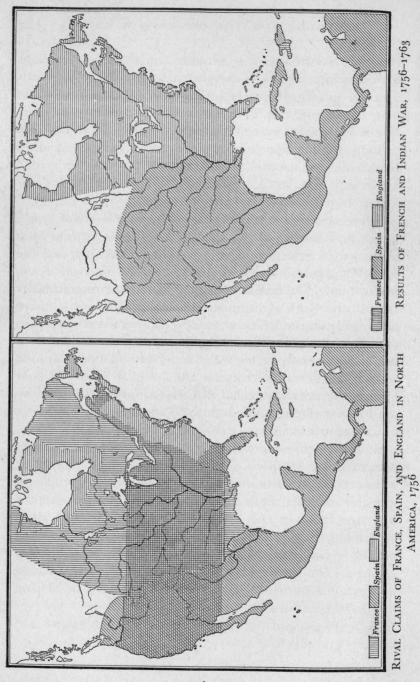

RIVAL CLAIMS OF FRANCE, SPAIN, AND ENGLAND IN NORTH AMERICA, 1756

RESULTS OF FRENCH AND INDIAN WAR, 1756-1763

questions confronted the ministry when peace was made. Should white settlers be permitted to go beyond the Alleghanies, and if so, on what conditions? What policy should be followed with respect to the Indian occupants? What additional provision was needed for the defense of the augmented empire? Finally, how should the great debt incurred in the war be met, and how should the vast sums be raised which were needed for this purpose and for administration?

The Indian problem required immediate attention. The time had come when Indian relations could no longer be left to the governments of the separate colonies. Sad confusion had resulted from the diversity of provincial laws, and the natives had suffered many wrongs at the hands of unscrupulous whites. The ministry resolved to take the responsibility for Indian affairs as an imperial matter. The Six Nations, while sympathetic with the British, had on the whole maintained a neutral attitude during the war, but the more remote tribes in the Ohio Valley and Northwest had sided with the French, chiefly through fear that the success of England would mean the loss of their lands. The advance of the British farming frontier alarmed them, while a French victory would not disturb their occupation or trade relations.

As the war drew to a close the restlessness of the Indians warned the English of danger. Unprincipled Frenchmen were playing upon the fears of the natives to keep them at war even after the white contestants had ceased to fight. In 1763 the tribes of the Northwest made a concerted effort against the English. The great chief Pontiac brought the natives far and wide into his plan for striking a blow which would drive them back across the Alleghanies. At the same moment attacks were made on the posts at Mackinac, Detroit, Presqu'île, and Fort Pitt.

Such attempts of the natives to defend their homes and hunting grounds have always ended in the same way. How-

ever severe the punishment suffered by the whites, the check
has been but temporary, and the flood has afterwards advanced more irresistibly than before.   In 1764 two well-led
expeditions to the Ohio country reduced the tribes to submission.   By autumn of 1765 the British had the situation
well in hand.

The ministry, anticipating hostilities, had tried in vain to
avert them by a royal proclamation relating to the regions acquired by the war.   The Spanish and French settlements along
the Gulf of Mexico were designated as the Provinces of East
and West Florida, while for the French inhabitants of the St.
Lawrence basin the Province of Quebec was erected.   Between these two lay the broad domain west of the mountains
where dwelt the natives.   This the proclamation provided
should remain in the hands of the Indians, and all grants of
land therein were forbidden "for the present."   The purpose
of this prohibition was perhaps primarily to assure the natives
that their rights would be respected and encroachments prevented until, by negotiations from time to time with the
proper officers, they might agree to relinquish portions of
their territory.   The ministry was also desirous by this means
to preserve the fur trade from the injury which it would sustain from an inrush of settlers.

Indian affairs were placed in the hands of two superintendents, Sir William Johnson for the "Northern District," and
Captain John Stuart for the "Southern."   The districts were
subdivided, with subordinate officials in each division to enforce a uniform code for the protection of the Indians against
traders and speculators.   Purchases of lands were to be made
only by the superintendents.

Within a few years most features of this plan were abandoned because of the cost, but the rule of land purchases by
the superintendents was retained.   Two great tracts were acquired in 1768 and 1770.   The first, bought from the Six Na-

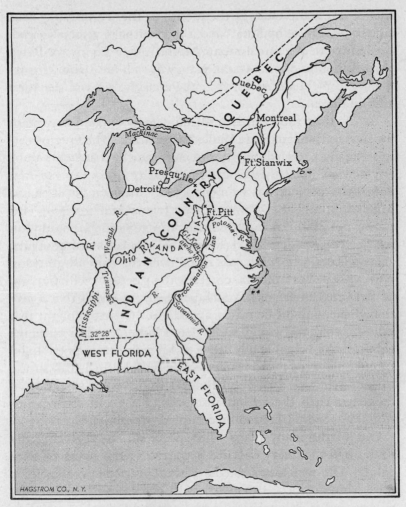

DISPOSITION MADE OF CONQUESTS IN FRENCH AND INDIAN WAR
(Northern boundary of West Florida was fixed in 1764)

tions by Johnson in the Treaty of Fort Stanwix, extinguished
their claim to all lands east and south of a line running irregularly from the upper Mohawk to the Allegheny River and

thence down the Ohio to the mouth of the Tennessee. The second purchase, by Stuart from the southern tribes, secured the lands east of a line drawn from the upper Tennessee River to the mouth of the Great Kanawha. These two treaties opened central and southwestern Pennsylvania and the West Virginia area.

By the time the French and Indian War ended many plans for new settlements were under discussion. The entire coast was already parceled out in provinces, and if there were to be any new colonies, they would of necessity lie in the interior. A favorite project was to erect a new province between the Mississippi and the Wabash. That triangle of territory contained the old French settlements, which would be seed-plots for future growth. The scheme was favored by some of the army officers, who were concerned over the expense of transporting supplies from the coast for the garrisons which might be stationed in the old French posts, and thought that a portion of them might be raised by settlers. Others thought that interior colonies would yield new kinds of products which would make valuable additions to English commerce. Land speculators were more interested than any other class in the various schemes, but the distant Illinois country attracted them less than the region just beyond the old settlements, which was more likely to be occupied promptly.

Out of the many plans which were discussed during the sixties one took very definite form, under the name of Vandalia. The promoters sought a grant from the crown for a tract which coincided roughly with the cession obtained by Stuart, that is, West Virginia and eastern Kentucky. Franklin, in England, labored to secure favorable action, and Samuel Wharton, a Philadelphia Quaker, crossed the ocean for the purpose of lobbying with members of Parliament.

The question of new settlements brings out very well the

weakness of the ministries of that period as makers of policies. Frequent shifting of the political kaleidoscope made for vacillation and indecision, and prevented the pursuit of a consistent program. There were differences of opinion concerning the desirability of new colonies. While some of the ministers were favorably disposed, others believed that remote settlements would be of little value and hard to control. Lord Hillsborough, president of the Board of Trade, took this view, and held that the Proclamation of 1763 was intended to bar the whites permanently from the transalleghany lands. Lord Shelburne best represents the other position. He was a friend of Franklin, and of America, and liberal in his views.

Notwithstanding the fact, as Hillsborough urged, that the tract desired by the Vandalia Company lay within the charter bounds of Virginia, the ministry decided to make the grant, thus apparently setting Virginia's claim at nought, much as Charles I had done when he carved Maryland out of her unsettled domain and gave it to Lord Baltimore. The outbreak of the Revolution prevented the consummation of the project.

While speculators were proposing and ministers debating schemes of settlement, the frontiersmen were paying scant heed to government plans or proclamations. Before 1763 only the merest beginnings of settlement had been made west of the mountains, in Pennsylvania and Virginia. The breaking down of the French barrier was the signal for overleaping the one interposed by nature. The densely wooded ridges of the Alleghanies lying in the path of the pioneers had hitherto diverted them southwestward along the valleys between the ranges, to the Shenandoah Valley of Virginia and the upland country of the Carolinas. Only the adventurous hunters and traders had followed the stream courses through the ranges, except here and there a squatter who had built a lonely cabin along the trails of the fur-seekers.

With peace came a rush through the passes. Southwestern Pennsylvania, western Maryland, the mountains of (West) Virginia and northeastern Tennessee began to receive their inhabitants. By 1768 a cluster of "stations" dotted the branching waters of the upper Tennessee on both sides of the boundary between Virginia and North Carolina. Hither in the early seventies came the Scotch-Irishman James Robertson from the North Carolina frontier, and John Sevier, the Virginia Huguenot.

Opening out from the settled valleys of upper Tennessee into Kentucky was the mountain gateway known as Cumberland Gap. Kentucky, included within Virginia's charter grant, was a no-man's land, unoccupied by native tribes but used by many as a hunting ground. Practically unknown to the English before the French and Indian War, it now became for them also a hunting ground. Its well-watered blue-grass lands of wonderful richness formed a natural pasturage which with the numerous salt licks had ages ago attracted the mastodon and other extinct mammals as they now drew the deer and bison. Most famous of all the white hunters who visited this paradise in the sixties was Daniel Boone, whose Quaker parents had followed the stream of migration from Pennsylvania to the North Carolina Piedmont while Daniel was a youth. Trained from boyhood to handle gun and knife, and inured to the life of the wilderness, his name became the symbol of all that is characteristic of the hardy pioneer-stock which was about to sweep into the Ohio Valley.

SELECT BIBLIOGRAPHY

The French in North America; Rivalry of the French and English; The French and Indian War. The works of Francis Parkman, under the general title of *France and England in North America,* give the classic account of French expansion in the New World, the rivalry with the English, and the final overthrow of

French dominion. For literary excellence as well as sound scholarship these volumes have not been surpassed in historical writing in America. In *Montcalm and Wolfe,* which tells the story of the last French and Indian War, Parkman reaches his highest level.

Abbott, *Expansion of Europe,* II, gives the Old-World background of the Anglo-French rivalry in America. Mahan, *Influence of Sea Power on History, 1660–1783,* discusses international relations with especial reference to the decisive part played by Britain's navy.

Thwaites, *France in America,* is a convenient one-volume summary, of the whole topic stated in the title. Wrong, *The Rise and Fall of New France,* is fuller and more scholarly. Fiske covers the subject in *New France and New England.* Recent and brief is Wrong, *The Conquest of New France.*

Several volumes of the *Chronicles of Canada* are of interest on this topic. Such are Leacock, *Dawn of Canadian History,* and *Mariner of St. Malo-Cartier;* Colby, *Founders of New France,* and *Fighting Governor;* and Munro, *Seigneurs of Old Canada.* Wrong, *Fall of Canada,* is a readable yet critical account of the last years of the French power.

Sources: Kellogg, *Early Narratives of the Northwest* (*Original Narratives*).

For Louisiana under the French, see Thwaites as above, Parkman, *La Salle and the Discovery of the Great West,* and Gayarré, *History of Louisiana.*

The Problem of the West. Parkman, *The Conspiracy of Pontiac,* tells the story of the Indian war of 1763. Carter, *Great Britain and the Illinois Country,* contains an excellent account of the projects of new colonies in the West after 1763. Alvord, *The Mississippi Valley in British Politics,* discusses the whole problem of the West from the point of view of the English government; he deals with the same theme more briefly in *The Illinois Country.* Roosevelt, *Winning of the West,* takes up the story of the actual movement of population after the Peace of Paris. Winsor, *The Westward Movement,* covers the same ground with less attention to the life and experiences of the pioneers and more to the formal political and diplomatic history. With these two writers may be compared Henderson, *The Conquest of the Old Southwest,* a more recent publication of popular character.

Boone's story is well told in Thwaites, *Daniel Boone,* and Bruce, *Daniel Boone and the Wilderness Road.* For the beginnings in eastern Tennessee see Driver, *John Sevier.* An important phase of Washington's career is the subject of Ambler, *George Washington and the West.*

Chapter VIII

ENGLAND AND THE COLONIES

RISE OF PARLIAMENTARY GOVERNMENT

LOGICALLY, the Revolution of 1688 meant the supremacy of Parliament over king, but the subordination of the king actually came about so slowly as almost to escape observation at the time. The Frenchman Montesquieu, who wrote a great book (*L'Esprit des Lois*, 1748) praising the British government because it separated the legislative, executive, and judicial branches, misinterpreted the facts, for as the royal influence declined executive powers passed to ministers who were members of Parliament and responsible to it.

One of the high points in the history of the passing of the royal power was the abandonment of the veto of acts of Parliament. It was used for the last time in 1707. In 1714 the accession of George I of the German state of Hanover consigned the kingship almost to insignificance. George was already advanced in years, only slightly acquainted with the English language, and not inclined to vex himself with British problems. He preferred to leave them to the ministers, and when the second George came to the throne in 1727 the position of the ministry was already too firm to be shaken.

The ministry framed policies, but if these were not supported by the necessary legislation, its functions were at an end. A new ministry possessing the confidence of the majority in the legislature, especially in the House of Commons, must then be formed, or an election held to determine whether the voters would uphold the ministry by returning a majority of members in sympathy with their program.

This development made the legislature the supreme power in the government. Blackstone, in his *Commentaries on the Laws of England* (1765), expounded the doctrine of parliamentary supremacy. "I know of no power," he wrote, "which can control the Parliament."

In the nineteeth century parliamentary government became responsible to the masses of the people, but in the eighteenth it rested on a basis which was far from popular. The members of the upper house—the Lords Temporal and Spiritual—held their places as they still do by right of birth or position in the Church. In the House of Commons members, although elected, were chosen under a very restricted franchise. In the incorporated towns only those residents voted who belonged to the small group which held the corporate privileges.[1] In the rural districts the usual test was the possession of land with a rental value of forty shillings or more per annum.

The apportionment of seats in Parliament had not been revised for something like two centuries, and some of the towns or "boroughs" represented had declined until they were almost or entirely without inhabitants. Other towns had grown up, and some of them had become populous, yet members still sat in the House for the ancient boroughs while the new towns were without representation except as parts of the shire in which they were situated.

The owners of great estates were very influential in controlling the votes of the small landowners. Perhaps, as a rule, the latter voted as a matter of course for the candidate preferred by the local aristocrat. In case of the "rotten boroughs," as they were called, the choice of members became practically a power of appointment by the owner of the land where the borough had stood. Corruption was rife, and the

---

[1] *Cf.* the freemen of the Massachusetts Bay Company.

buying and selling of votes and of seats in the House was a common practice.

Instead of being representative of the nation Parliament was the representative of the merchants and landlords. The merchants were especially influential in the towns, and as wealth increased with the growth of commerce they came more and more closely into alliance with the landed aristocracy, partly through intermarriage, and partly through the purchase of estates for their own families.

When George III came to the throne in 1760, he determined to regain the ground lost by his predecessors. Born and bred in England, he "gloried in the name of Briton." He indulged in no dreams of absolutism such as that of the monarchs of France and Prussia, but relied upon his control of patronage. By skillful distribution of offices he was able to gain control over the choice of a good many members of Parliament and thus built up a faction of his own known as the "King's Friends." These were able at times to defeat the ministry, and even, by coalition with other factions, to form a majority. Control of the Commons meant control of the ministry, in effect the personal rule of the king.

In all this George III carefully observed the forms of parliamentary government and ministerial responsibility; he simply played the game of the politicians and beat them at it. Through his mastery of Parliament and the ministry he became chiefly responsible for some of the measures which brought on the American Revolution. He was a well-meaning man of good character and high sense of honor, but he lacked statesmanship and was unusually headstrong. His influence reached its height in the ministry of Lord North (1770–1782). The failure to crush the American revolt discredited his leadership, and the current set again in the direction of parliamentary rule, but with a tendency towards liberalism which brought democracy at length through great reform acts in 1832, 1867, and 1884.

BRITISH MERCANTILISM IN THE EIGHTEENTH CENTURY

The aims which the British mercantilists originially had in promoting the colonization of the New World were never realized. They had hoped that the American colonies would supply the products which the English needed to free them from dependence upon other countries. With the partial exception of ship-building materials, this hope had proved vain, but as time passed, the aims of the mercantilists were gradually brought into conformity with the possibilities, and the colonies were made to contribute to the prosperity of the mother-country through the stimulus they gave to the carrying trade, the market they afforded for English manufactures, and the staples which some of them yielded, such as tobacco and rice.

The dominance of the mercantile and landed classes in the English government is a fundamental fact in explaining the relations between Britain and the colonies in the eighteenth century. Many persons in these classes owned plantations in the West Indies, and there were occasions, then as now, when men yielded to the temptation to seek private gain at the general expense. The island colonies, moreover, were more highly regarded by the mercantilists than those of the mainland. The records of the Board of Trade indicate that in the year 1700 the island of Barbadoes was thirteen times as valuable, and Jamaica nine times as valuable, to England as was New York.

Inevitably, control over colonial industry was gradually extended. Some of the new regulations were in line with the provisions of the navigation acts. Such was the law of 1733 called the "Molasses Act." To force the continental colonies to buy their sugar and molasses from the British

West Indies, and thus to build up the plantations there, the act laid prohibitory duties upon these articles when brought from the foreign sugar islands. This legislation is a good illustration of the union of policy and private interest; while in harmony with the idea of fostering colonial industries which supplemented those of Britain, it was enacted at the behest of a lobby of Englishmen who owned plantations in Barbadoes and Jamaica—and it is said that the agitation for the law originated with a resident of Boston who had a similar interest in the islands.

In keeping with the earlier policy also was the addition of naval stores, furs, and rice to the list of enumerated articles. Finding that the rice growers suffered from this restriction, a concession was made permitting that commodity to be sent directly to the countries of southern Europe, although it was still to go to the north of Europe by way of England.

A new departure was the regulation of manufactures. The prosperity of the rising factories of England must not be endangered by colonial competition. So thought the rulers. By successive enactments Americans were forbidden to make woolen cloth and hats for sale outside of the colony where made, and manufactures of iron were restricted to the making of bar- and pig-iron. Such laws were hardly needed, since there was as yet little incentive in the colonies to manufacture. Recognizing this, the English economist, Adam Smith, whose book on *The Wealth of Nations* (1776) started a reaction against the whole theory of mercantilism and is regarded as the beginning of modern economics, called the restrictions "impertinent badges of slavery." [1]

[1] "Land is still so cheap, and, consequently, labour so dear among them, that they can import from the mother country, almost all the more refined or more advanced manufactures cheaper than they could make them for themselves. . . . In their present state . . . those prohibitions . . . are only impertinent badges of slavery imposed upon them, without sufficient reason, by the groundless jealousy of the merchants and manufacturers of the mother country."—*Wealth of Nations*, Book IV, Chap. VII, Part II.

Other laws sprang from the need of some general supervisory authority which could make uniform rules in matters affecting the interests of the colonies collectively, where separate action tended to confusion. Such were the acts creating a general postal service and regulating the currency. All of the colonies suffered from the lack of specie, and from time to time tried to make good the deficiency by issuing circulating paper. The whole matter of the currency was taken up by Parliament, as closely related to imperial commerce, and several acts were passed to regulate the value at which foreign coins should circulate throughout the provinces, or to prohibit paper money issues.

It is difficult to find any example of parliamentary legislation for the colonies previous to 1763 which is not connected with the regulation of their external relations. Other kinds of legislation were proposed, including laws for raising a revenue by an excise, or a stamp tax. Especially during the wars with France there was strong temptation to levy troops and raise money by direct parliamentary action. But Parliament in the end always refrained from legislation which would have touched the "internal police" of the colonies. In matters affecting only its own inhabitants each colony was allowed to enjoy "home rule."

THE CROWN AND THE COLONIES

While except in their external relations the colonies were hardly touched by parliamentary acts, the crown was a very real factor in their government. Colonial administration, in other words, was a function of the crown rather than of Parliament. The governor in the royal colonies was the agent of the crown in holding his province in line with the policies of the home government. He had a veto upon the acts of the legislature, and was under instructions to work for certain kinds of legislation and to withhold approval of other kinds.

An example of the former class would be laws for raising troops or revenue for the French wars.   His veto was to be given to all acts which tended to injure British commerce, such as those restricting the slave trade, or favoring American debtors at the expense of English creditors.

Strictly speaking, colonial laws were not in force even after receiving the governor's signature until approved by another crown agency, the privy council in England.   Many were actually disallowed because they were in conflict with the laws, interests, or policies of Britain.   Moreover, the privy council, which in earlier centuries had possessed judicial powers and lost them so far as England was concerned, developed in the eighteenth century the function of a court of appeals for cases tried in the colonial courts.

The immunity of the chartered colonies, especially the corporate ones, from the control exercised in the royal provinces was a source of increasing dissatisfaction to the British politicians, and several proposals were made to set aside all of the charters by parliamentary act.   The Whigs, however, always sensitive to property rights, looked upon charters as vested interests of the holders and defeated all such proposals. They sought the same end quite successfully by other means, such as purchase and forfeiture.

A number of chartered colonies had been converted into royal provinces during the last two decades of the seventeenth century.   Thus New Hampshire had been detached from Massachusetts in 1679 and New York had become royal through the accession of the proprietor to the throne (1685). Misgovernment furnished the pretext for voiding the charter of Carolina and erecting two royal provinces (1728).[1]   The Georgia charter provided for the reversion of government to the crown after twenty-one years.   Negotiations were carried

[1] The king took over the government of South Carolina about 1719, owing to disturbances, and a few years later acquired the proprietary rights by purchase.

on for many years with the Penn family for the purchase of their rights in Pennsylvania and Delaware, but without success, and these two provinces with Maryland remained proprietary until after independence was won, when the proprietors' rights were purchased by the states. At the close of the colonial period eight of the thirteen colonies were royal, and the influence of the crown had increased correspondingly. Connecticut and Rhode Island remained corporate.

Even in the colonies which retained their charters the royal influence was considerably extended. The crown had established the right (first set down in the charter to Penn) to confirm the appointment of governors for the proprietary colonies and to require them to give bond to execute the British laws relating to America. The right of appeal from the provincial courts to the privy council was also extended to the proprietary provinces. Even in the corporate colonies the right of appeal was asserted with increasing success. The collectors of customs and the admiralty courts are examples of imperial agencies which were everywhere independent of provincial control.

All of this administrative machinery was supervised in England by the Board of Trade. Besides drafting instructions for the governors and other crown officials, the Board gave colonial laws their first examination, and under the advice of the law officers, recommended their acceptance or rejection by the privy council. The latter held the real authority, as it included the great ministers who acted nominally for the king but really for the aristocracy which dominated Parliament.

In part because the ministry desired to have at hand a source of information relative to American affairs, some of the larger colonies supported representatives in England known as the colonial agents. These men were often skillful lobbyists and sometimes succeeded in preventing the passage of acts which would have been detrimental to the interests of their constituents. The most famous of them was Benjamin Franklin, of Pennsylvania. His success led other colonies to appoint him as their agent, and on the eve of the Revolution he was virtually an informal ambassador of the American people.

It must be remembered that the British control, whether by acts of Parliament or through the crown administrative agencies, was devoted mainly to securing the interests of the empire as a whole. In spite of the elaborate machinery and of the royal governor's share in every act of legislation and administration, the Americans had large freedom of action. In most matters with which each government dealt no one was concerned except the inhabitants, and the governor allowed them to have their own way as a matter of course.

Britishers when appointed to colonial offices were likely to remain at home, enjoying their income while their duties were performed by a deputy who was often a provincial bound to those whom he governed by intimate ties. This practice helps to explain the lax enforcement even of the laws of which the British were most tenacious. The Molasses Act, for example, was almost a dead letter. By false papers, by covering the cargo from foreign ports with a layer of molasses-casks from the British West Indies, by slipping into some obscure inlet to make a landing—all these practices with the connivance of dilatory officials—colonial skippers set the statute at nought. The duties collected were negligible. To be sure, the act was not intended as a revenue measure, but the foreign molasses brought into Rhode Island alone, it is estimated, would have yielded something like £28,000 if the duties had been paid.

Even where the colonial will was in direct conflict with the governor's instructions the Americans frequently had their way. In such contests the weapon of the provincials was the control of the purse. Without acts for raising and appropriating money the governor's administration was paralyzed. For his salary also he was dependent upon the legislature in almost every colony. He was the servant of two masters, the crown and the assembly, and not seldom compromised his instructions to save his income. It was therefore sometimes possible to avoid the veto and give legislation an effective life of weeks or months before news of the royal disallowance could be received. Or, as emergency measures, acts might be passed for limited periods, and reënacted from time to time, so that submission for approval might be avoided.

Especially during the French and Indian wars, when prompt action was needed in raising troops and funds, the necessity of dealing with so many provinces separately led bold minds in England to urge the short-cut of parliamentary action. The centralized power of the French government seemed much more efficient than the English system at times of crisis, and was regarded by many Englishmen as the model on which the British administration of the colonies should be reconstructed. Sober judgment indicated that at least some plan should be devised by which they would be brought into permanent coöperation, with a general legislative and executive body to deal with such a vital common interest as a war with the French. Several plans of union were suggested, some of them by Americans and some by British leaders.

The most notable of the proposals of union was the Albany Plan, which distinctly foreshadowed the Constitution of the United States. It was the work of a congress of delegates from seven colonies which met at Albany in 1754, at the instance of the British ministry, in the hope of bringing the colonies into joint action in the impending French and Indian War. The plan was drafted by Franklin. It provided for a council composed of delegates selected by the assembly of each colony, and a president-general appointed by the crown. This body was to have power to carry on wars in which the colonies were involved, and to raise troops and collect taxes for this purpose. In addition it was to control all relations with the Indians, including trade and purchases of lands, to superintend the laying out of new colonies, and to govern them until the crown erected them into distinct provinces.

These proposals were the fruit of actual experience and show a consciousness that the Americans could act to better advantage in union than separately. It was only advanced thinkers on either side of the Atlantic, however, who were able to appraise the plan at its true worth, and it was not put into operation. The British government thought that it savored too much of American autonomy, while the colonies, jealous of one another, needed another generation filled with sharp lessons to teach them the importance of union.

THE CONFLICT OF BRITISH AND AMERICAN OPINION

Several generations of life in the New World, under conditions so different from those in England, had given the Americans views which were widely different from those held by the British mercantilists. They regarded the provinces, not as establishments existing for the promotion of English commerce, but as commonwealths or states, comparable with England herself, inhabited by Englishmen associated together in all the manifold ways characteristic of political communities, and united with England only by having the same king. The train of events which had shifted authority from king to Parliament and made the merchants and landlords the masters of imperial policy meant comparatively little to them. They felt quite capable of managing their own affairs, and, indeed, were accustomed to doing so. Down to 1763 they were content with their lot under the colonial system as actually administered, although on many occasions they had shown irritation and a disposition to act according to their own judgment when the system pinched. Long enjoyment of immunity from parliamentary interference in matters of internal police had bred in them the belief that home rule was their right. The superiority of their charters to the enactments of their assemblies accustomed them to the concept of a superior law, and earlier English and European publicists supported the idea that the unwritten British constitution fixed limits to the powers even of Parliament.

Scholars are still disputing over the legality of the authority which Parliament sought to exercise in America after 1763, but apart from the question of law it was folly for Britain to attempt to rule Americans contrary to their wishes. At bottom this attempt was the effective cause of the Revolution. Political union was possible only under some plan which would recognize colonial autonomy—an idea practically inconceivable by eighteenth-century Englishmen.[1]

SELECT BIBLIOGRAPHY

Rise of Parliamentary Government. The changes in the British government after the Revolution of 1688 may be studied in Maitland, *Constitutional History of England,* or Pollard, *Evolution of Parliament.* Especially good on the ministerial system is Blauvelt, *The Development of Cabinet Government in England.*

British Mercantilism. Beer, *Old Colonial System, 1660–1754; British Colonial Policy, 1754–1765;* and *Commercial Policy of England towards the Colonies,* provide the most satisfactory survey of the subject. See also Egerton, *Short History of British Colonial Policy,* and Horrocks, *Short History of Mercantilism.*

The Crown and the Colonies. Dickerson, *American Colonial Government,* is a good study of British administration of the

[1] "The separateness of Britain and her colonies was based upon conditions beyond the power of man to change,—upon the broad expanse of the Atlantic, upon soil, climate, and geography."—Wertenbaker, *The First Americans,* 4.

colonies through the Board of Trade. Greene, *The Provincial Governor,* approaches the administrative system from another angle. See also Labaree, *Royal Government in America.* Kellogg, *The Colonial Charter,* is essentially a study of the efforts to reduce the colonies to the royal type.

The Conflict of British and American Opinion. Tyler, *Literary History of the American Revolution,* I, contains many quotations which illustrate opinions of Americans on questions of relations with England. Merriam, *History of American Political Theories,* contains a fairly good summary of American views. McIlwain, *The American Revolution,* is a recent brilliant defense of the legal soundness of the American denial of the authority of Parliament. Van Tyne, *Causes of the War of Independence,* is a dispassionate product of present-day scholarship. It stresses the divergent development of the two parts of the English world as the fundamental reason for the separation. Egerton, *The Causes and Character of the American Revolution,* is a discussion by a prominent English authority. Recent contributions to the literature of the subject are Coupland, *The American Revolution and the British Empire,* and Schuyler, *Parliament and the British Empire.* The discussion in the latter should be compared with that of McIlwain.

Chapter IX

THE CONTEST OVER TAXATION BY PARLIAMENT

THE POLICY OF GRENVILLE

BRITAIN'S success in the French and Indian War multiplied her problems. In the face of a stupendous war debt the safety of the enlarged empire demanded increased expenditures for defense. The tardiness of the response of colonial assemblies to calls for troops, and the poor discipline of the militia and volunteers which America had contributed had called out bitter complaints by British officers during the late wars. Reliance upon such resources was perilous in a sudden crisis like Pontiac's War. A force of two thousand regulars under imperial control, judiciously distributed among the border posts, would provide adequate protection in case of Indian uprising or trouble from the French in the new Canadian possessions.

Indispensable as this program seemed, it involved a serious expense. British taxpayers were already groaning under a burden which had been doubled by the war. Considerable economies might have been effected by purging the civil service of unnecessary offices created to reward the holders for political services, but the ministers lacked the courage to undertake drastic reforms. Besides, America was able to contribute something towards the cost of her protection, and it seemed only fair that she should be required to do so.

Two months after the signing of the Treaty of Paris there came to the head of the government as prime minister the man upon whom fell the chief burden of formulating the new defensive and financial program. This man was George Grenville. He was honest and conscientious and prized efficiency, but had little insight into the mind of Americans, and set about his task with slight anticipation of the reception in store for his plans.

It was clear to Grenville that the navigation system must be made a source of revenue in the colonies. He was amazed when his investigations revealed the extent of the evasion of the trade acts, and promptly tightened up the administration by appointing trustworthy collectors, sending vessels to patrol the American coast on the lookout for smugglers, and increasing the number of admiralty courts. In April, 1764, the Sugar Act was passed. It replaced the Molasses Act of 1733, and reduced the duty on foreign molasses from the prohibitory rate of sixpence per gallon to threepence, with the expectation that smuggling would cease and that the trade would yield a revenue. The new law laid duties upon a number of other imports, such as wines, silks, and coffee.

Grenville estimated that these imposts would yield about £45,000 per annum, while the cost of maintaining garrisons would amount to £360,000. Of this he planned that one third should be raised in America, but he was at a loss for the best means of doing it. Parliament passed a Billeting Act in 1765, which required the colonies wherein troops were stationed to provide them with quarters and certain supplies, and for the rest Grenville finally decided to recommend a tax requiring the use of stamps on a great variety of papers employed in everyday business transactions. He announced the plan nearly a year in advance of asking Parliament to pass the bill, to give the colonial agents opportunity to suggest an alternative means of raising the sum desired from the colonies. As they merely protested against any kind of direct tax, Parliament passed the Stamp Act in February, 1765, without debate. It was to go into effect on the first of November.

The Sugar Act and the enforcement of the trade regulations

aroused the merchants. A duty of even threepence per gallon
on molasses would kill the trade, they said, and injure British
as well as colonial merchants, since it was the source of the
specie for paying balances due England. Imports from the
mother-country must cease if the Sugar Act were enforced.
To aggravate the situation a Currency Act of 1764 forbade
the colonies to supply the deficiency of specie by issues of
paper money.

The remonstrances of the merchants aroused little public
attention. In an attempt to awaken the fears of the people
the Boston town-meeting declared that if Parliament could
tax trade, it could tax lands and houses. But in form the
Sugar Act was nothing new, and even the merchant class was
more concerned with its practical effects than with the significance of the shift from a duty to regulate trade to one designed to raise a revenue. But indifference quickly disappeared with the passage of the Stamp Act. As almost everyone
would have to use the stamps, the law brought home to every
American the claim of a distant legislature to the right of taxing communities which sent no representatives to sit in it.

Even before the passage of the Stamp Act, James Otis, of
Massachusetts, published a memorable pamphlet, entitled
Rights of the British Colonies Asserted and Proved (1764).
In this he drew a distinction between the *actual* powers of
Parliament and those which it *rightfully* possessed. Any act
contrary to natural or divine law would be void. On this
ground he denied that Parliament could rightfully tax the
colonies, because they were not represented in it.

In Virginia, Patrick Henry played a rôle somewhat like that
of Otis in Massachusetts. He came forward in the House of
Burgesses with resolutions declaring "That the General Assembly of this colony have the only and sole exclusive right
and power to lay taxes and impositions upon the inhabitants
of this colony." Supporting these resolutions, in a burst of

that eloquence which made him famous as one of America's greatest orators, he compared George III to Cæsar, Tarquin, and Charles I.[1]

Otis and Henry had pointed out the constitutional argument with which parliamentary taxation could be combated. The stamps were not to go on sale until November 1, and there was ample time to organize resistance. Otis proposed a meeting of delegates from all of the colonial assemblies, and in October, 1765, twenty-seven, from nine of the colonies, met in New York.

This "Stamp Act Congress" is memorable as the first effort of Americans to act together in opposing the policy of England. The resolutions adopted are the most authoritative expression of colonial opinion up to that time. Owning their allegiance to the crown, the colonists claimed also all of the rights and privileges of subjects within the realm. One of these rights was that no taxes should be imposed upon them without their consent. As their circumstances precluded representation in the House of Commons, it followed, they held, that no taxes could be consistently levied on them except by their respective colonial assemblies. It was the Stamp Act against which they directed this argument. As to the Sugar Act, professing "all due subordination" to Parliament, they protested against it as an unwise and oppressive restriction on trade. Apparently they regarded the duty as a trade regulation rather than a tax, and the failure to denounce taxation in this form seemed to give assent to its legality.

Meantime opposition had shown itself in other ways. The

[1] The speaker of the house reprimanded Henry for this utterance, which he said was treasonable, whereupon Henry apologized, declaring that he was ready to prove his loyalty to the king with the last drop of his blood. Heroic tradition transformed the speech into the following defiant utterance: "Cæsar had his Brutus and Charles the First his Cromwell; and George III—." Then as those about him exclaimed "Treason! Treason!" he concluded— "may profit by their example. If that be treason make the most of it!"

merchants, to give weight to their contention that enforcement of the acts of trade would destroy their power to purchase British goods, organized a boycott on imports from England. There were several outbreaks of mob violence, in one of which the mansion of Thomas Hutchinson, chief justice of Massachusetts, was pillaged. Under the pressure of public opinion all of the stamp agents had resigned before November 1 arrived. Business was temporarily embarrassed for want of stamps, but soon went on as usual in entire disregard of the law.

As for the Billeting Act, the Americans in their excited state of mind could see in the presence of the troops only evidence of a determination to intimidate them into submission.

When Parliament met and took up the American situation, a change of ministry had taken place, and Grenville was no longer in position to defend his policies from the vantage ground of the premiership. His friends insisted that the repeal of the Stamp Act would be a surrender to rebellion. With the support of Chief Justice Mansfield, reputed to be the greatest lawyer of his time, they maintained the doctrine of parliamentary supremacy and ridiculed the idea that Parliament might lay an import duty, as in the Sugar Act, but not an "internal" tax, such as the Stamp Act provided. They held that the colonies, like the new cities of Manchester and Sheffield, were virtually represented in the House of Commons.

The new ministry was in a quandary. It must restore order in America. English merchants were feeling the effects of the boycott and were asking for the repeal of the Stamp Act. But how could it be done without admitting defeat? The House called Franklin before its bar and interrogated him. He gave his opinion that the colonists would resist all internal taxes. Duties on commerce he thought they would accept unless mayhap the arguments in Parliament convinced them that they were wrong in making any distinction between internal taxation and taxation at the ports. If troops were used to enforce the law, "they would not find a revolution, but they might make one."

Parliament was not indisposed to make concessions. Some of the most influential members upheld the colonial view that parliamentary taxation was unjust and illegal. Pitt was one of these, and Lord Camden was another. Colonel Isaac Barré declared that he "rejoiced that the Americans had resisted," and referred to them as "Sons of Liberty." It was finally determined to repeal the act, but to assert the theory of parliamentary supremacy in unmistakable terms. In March, 1766, therefore, the repeal was voted, and at the same time a Declaratory Act was passed asserting that Parliament possessed authority to "bind the colonies and people of America, subjects of the crown of Great Britain, in all cases whatsoever." Pitt would have added, "with the exception of taking money out of their pockets without their consent." The rejection of his qualifying clause was ominous.

The repeal of the Stamp Act closed the first act of the dramatic contest which began in 1763. Many Americans celebrated the event with demonstrations of joy and loyalty. If they noticed the Declaratory Act at all, they thought of it as mere words used to cover the retreat of the discomfited party, and not as a threat of further attempts at taxation. That the other parts of Grenville's program remained in force also attracted little notice.[1]

Nevertheless discontent and apprehension continued to be

[1] At the same time that the Stamp Act was repealed the provisions of the Sugar Act were modified. The duty on molasses was reduced from threepence to one penny per gallon and the impost on certain articles exported from England was to be collected on *exportation* instead of at the colonial port, lest the colonists object to "taxation at the ports." The changes made the act more clearly than ever a revenue measure, yet Americans overlooked it as completely as they did the Declaratory Act.

widespread, for the issue remained unsettled, and the government still needed revenue. The times called for a constructive statesman who could devise a means of harmonizing imperial necessities with colonial ideals of self-government. Few men on either side of the ocean saw the nature of the problem or gave it any thought. Franklin was one of the few. Otis was another. In England, liberals like Pitt, Camden, and Shelburne were at least disposed to avoid arousing colonial resistance anew, and for a time it seemed that they might win support for a conciliatory policy. Pitt, now made Earl of Chatham, was called upon to form a new cabinet, and both Camden and Shelburne became his associates. A ministry so constituted was not likely to revive the odious program of taxation. In Parliament, Shelburne advocated generous treatment of America, and urged that the provincial governors be charged to avoid giving offense.

However, many members of Parliament were incensed against New York because its assembly had failed to comply with the requirements of the Billeting Act. Even Pitt and Shelburne shared the disposition to discipline the province, and it was agreed to suspend its assembly until it came to terms. Moreover, illness incapacitated Pitt at the critical moment and removed his wholesome influence from the cabinet. Charles Townshend, Chancellor of the Exchequer, a man more clever than judicious, was thus enabled to obtain the adoption (1767) of a plan which thwarted the good intentions of the liberals and precipitated a second contest with the colonies over the question of taxation.

THE TOWNSHEND SYSTEM

Townshend's policy on the whole was a continuation of Grenville's. The elaborate machinery for managing Indian affairs was given up on account of the expense, but as to the keeping of troops in America, the enforcement of the trade acts, and the raising of a revenue, Townshend soon showed that he was in harmony with his predecessor. The act of Parliament suspending the legislative functions of the New York assembly coerced it into making an appropriation to give effect to the Billeting Act. Since the right of that province to a legislature rested upon the grant of the king, its suspension by Parliament was a pronounced assertion of supremacy. If the rights of legislation and appropriation were not immune from invasion, it was difficult for Americans to see that they had any inviolable rights whatever.

The Chancellor promptly took steps to enforce the navigation acts. He procured the passage of a law creating a Board of Customs Commissioners to sit at Boston, and specifically authorizing the use of writs of assistance in the search for smuggled goods.[1] As to taxation, he boasted that he knew a way to raise a revenue in America without arousing resistance. What he had in mind was new duties on imports which would take advantage of the implied admission, in the resolutions of the Stamp Act Congress, of the legality of taxation at the ports. The act passed at his suggestion laid duties on paint, paper, glass, and tea.

That this was a revenue measure could not be overlooked. The Sugar Act had declared that it was expedient to raise a revenue in America and had been little noticed; but three years of discussion had intervened since its passage, and the repetition of this phrase was not lightly passed by as before. Besides, the new act declared that the proceeds were to be used for the support of British officials in America, thus menacing the control over crown officers which the legislatures held through the power of the purse. Townshend was ex-

[1] Writs of assistance were general search warrants. Otis had first come into prominence in 1761 as a defender of colonial rights by an argument against the use of such warrants.

perimenting with colonial opinion, planning to add to the list of dutiable articles if the first attempt succeeded, until a considerable revenue was obtained.

As Franklin had hinted might be the case, the Americans now began to deny the right of Parliament to tax them in any way whatever. The lead in bringing them to the new point of view was taken by the Quaker, John Dickinson, in his "Letters of a Pennsylvania Farmer." "I have looked over every statute relating to these colonies from their first settlement to this time," he wrote. "Though many of them imposed duties on trade, yet those duties were always imposed with design to restrain the commerce of one part, that was injurious to another, and thus to promote the general welfare. The raising of a revenue thereby was never intended." "If Great Britain can order us to come to her for necessaries we want, and can order us to pay what taxes she pleases before we take them away, or when we land them here, we are as abject slaves as France and Poland can shew in wooden shoes, and with uncombed hair."

The merchants had been alarmed by the riotous outbreaks against the Stamp Act, fearing that lawlessness would divert the attention of the English government from the sound reasoning of the Americans. They were careful to exert their influence to preserve order during this new dispute. But they had less faith in petitions and remonstrances than in measures which would "touch the pocket nerve." Since the English seemed more sensitive to loss of profits than to arguments, non-importation agreements were again resorted to. The merchants of Boston, followed by those of New York and Philadelphia, entered into covenants to discontinue importation until the Townshend Act was repealed. In the southern colonies the planters took the lead in organizing the boycott.

A new device was resorted to in 1768, as a kind of substitute for another intercolonial congress. This was the Massachusetts Circular Letter. It set forth the views of the assembly, and copies were transmitted to the assemblies of the other provinces inviting their replies and concurrence.

"The House have humbly represented to the ministry," so ran the letter, "their own sentiments, that his Majesty's high court of Parliament is the supreme legislative power over the whole empire; that in all free states the constitution is fixed, and as the supreme legislative derives its power and authority from the constitution, it cannot overleap the bounds of it, without destroying its own foundation; . . . that it is an essential, unalterable right, in nature, engrafted into the British constitution, as a fundamental law, . . . that what a man has honestly acquired is absolutely his own, which he may freely give, but [which] cannot be taken from him without his consent; . . . that the acts made there [in Parliament], imposing duties on the people of this province, with the sole and express purpose of raising a revenue, are infringements of their natural and constitutional rights. . . ." The obvious conclusion is, as the resolutions against the stamp tax had declared, that the people of each province could rightfully be taxed only by the provincial legislature in which they were represented.

Although couched in respectful terms, in England this letter was regarded as seditious, and Lord Hillsborough, now holding the newly-created office of Secretary of State for the Colonies, attempted to suppress discussion of it. Peremptory orders were sent to the royal governors to dissolve the assemblies of their provinces if they began to discuss the letter, while through the governor of Massachusetts a demand was made upon the assembly for its recall. When the assembly refused to rescind its action, the houses of Parliament joined in an address to the king proposing the arrest of colonial agitators for trial in England, under an ancient and almost forgotten law for punishing treasonable plots made outside of the realm.

Notwithstanding the desire of the merchants to avoid violence, outbreaks occurred. In Boston the cargo of John Hancock's sloop *Liberty* was landed in defiance of the revenue officers, who later seized the vessel (June, 1768). Such deeds, and the defiant attitude of the legislature, brought down upon Boston two British regiments which were quartered in the town to overawe the inhabitants (October, 1768). The presence of the troops led to irritating incidents involving the soldiers and the less self-controlled elements of the population.

The climax came in the affair known as the "Boston Massacre," in 1770. Beset by a mob of boys and young fellows who threw snowballs and clubs a squad of soldiers fired into the crowd and killed four persons. In the trial which followed John Adams defended the soldiers, and the commanding officer was acquitted because it could not be shown that he had given orders to fire. Two of the privates were convicted of manslaughter and given slight punishment. The affair had little real significance, except that it gave the radicals an opportunity to excite popular resentment against England. For several years, each anniversary of the "massacre" was made the occasion for a new appeal against "British tyranny."

Again the British government reconsidered its course. Townshend died. The new administration headed by Lord North was subservient to the king. The elements composing it were united in their belief as to England's rights over America, but the Townshend revenue law was costing too much in proportion to the sums it was bringing into the treasury. It was therefore determined to repeal the duties with the exception of a tax of threepence per pound upon tea. This was to be retained because, as the king said later, there must always be one tax to keep up the right. Thus, much as in the repeal of the Stamp Act, the government beat a "strategic retreat" but made no concession in principle.

As in the former case also colonial opposition relaxed. The non-importation agreement was abandoned except as to tea; but the merchants were growing weary of sacrificing profits and kept up the boycott on this article only half-heartedly. Although most of the tea used was smuggled in from Holland, little heed was given to the importation of small quantities which paid the tax. Even John Adams notes in his diary that he "dined at Mr. Hancock's . . . and drank green tea, *from Holland, I hope, but don't know!*"

DIVISION OF OPINION IN AMERICA

Another reason for the lax observance of the tea boycott was that the merchant class, which led the opposition to Parliament at the beginning, was becoming fearful of the radical agitators whose conduct they could not control. They found that leadership was slipping from their hands. The arguments based on constitutional principles had kindled a fire among the masses. With the British government on the one hand and the American radicals on the other, the upper classes were in a serious predicament. To press their complaints against England was to encourage the popular clamor, which might lead to worse things than British misrule. There was, indeed, an important group of Americans who were becoming convinced that the parliamentary party was right. An excellent example is found in Thomas Hutchinson. Although he disapproved of the Stamp Act, he was the chief sufferer from the violence which it stirred up—an experience which confirmed his dislike of radicalism. About the time of the repeal of the Townshend Act he was made governor of his province, and in this position he became an open champion of the British viewpoint.

The continuance of agitation after 1770, then, was due to radicals who aimed at reforms both in British and domestic relations. They determined not to allow the people to lose sight of the purpose of Britain in retaining the tax on tea. In Massachusetts their chief was Samuel Adams, upon whom had fallen the mantle of Otis.[1] It was he who drafted the Massachusetts Circular Letter of 1768, and who used the Boston Massacre to arouse the prejudices of the people. He was careful to let no occasion pass which might serve to keep alive the anti-British feeling. In 1772 it became known that the king planned to pay the Massachusetts judges, whose salaries had been appropriated by the general court, from the customs receipts. Adams thereupon urged the appointment by the Boston town meeting of a committee of correspondence to keep in touch with other towns. The plan spread, and it proved to be an effective means of bringing the radicals together.

In Virginia, to mention only one other province, the social cleavage separated the great planters from the plainer people. The former chafed under the burden of their debts to British merchants, who were favored, as they believed, by the currency laws of Parliament. They resented also the interference with their land speculations in the West, by such British regulations as that imposed by the Proclamation of 1763. Moreover, the planters then as later were extremely individualistic and opposed to centralized government. Yet in Virginia as in the northern colonies, the zeal of the original leaders began to flag somewhat after the repeal of the

---

[1] In 1769 Otis printed an article which drew upon him an assault by a British official. Insanity followed and he disappeared from public life. Both Samuel and John Adams were much influenced by Otis. The "brace of Adamses" were cousins. In contrast with the conduct of Samuel, John, as legal counsel for the officer who commanded the soldiers in the massacre, secured his acquittal of the murder charge. The state of public sentiment may be inferred from the fact that he did not forfeit prestige as a radical leader.

Townshend Act, and this allowed the leadership to pass to a group of young men, most of whom were from the western counties.

Prominent among the young leaders were Thomas Jefferson, James Madison, and Patrick Henry. They thought that the older members of the Virginia assembly were not "up to the point of forwardness and zeal which the times required." Moreover, they were imbued with the democratic reforming spirit of the "West," and disliked the domination of the planting aristocracy only less than they did that of England. The three men named led a movement which eventually undermined the Church Establishment and the aristocratic system of land tenure, with its laws of primogeniture and entail.

Following the adoption of the committees of correspondence by Massachusetts, Henry, Jefferson, and Richard Henry Lee secured the appointment of a committee of the House of Burgesses to correspond with similar bodies in the other provinces. The radicals elsewhere secured similar action, thus creating an intercolonial organization.

While the radicals were thus busy the great majority of the people were unmindful of any probability of renewed contention. Indeed, all these preparations might have been to no purpose had not the British government blundered again. The ill feeling engendered by the controversies between 1763 and 1770 might gradually have declined if there had been no new occasion for friction. With the exception of more rigid trade regulations and the presence of troops, relations with England were on substantially the same basis as before 1763, and most provincials were content. In 1773, however, Parliament passed a new tea act which revived controversy without affording even the prospect of benefit to the treasury.

The tea trade was a monopoly of the East India Company.

The company had a great quantity of tea stored in England, the market was glutted, and the company was in financial straits. If the American market could be reopened, the company would be relieved, especially if excused from paying duty in England on tea reshipped to the colonies. This duty was twelve pence per pound, which so much exceeded the cost of transportation across the Atlantic that, if remitted, tea would cost the consumer less in America than in England. The new act not only granted this "drawback," but allowed the company to appoint agents at the principal colonial ports to receive the shipments and sell the tea. The relaxation of the boycott, nominally maintained since 1770 because of the tax of threepence, misled the ministry into supposing that larger quantities could be marketed if the price were lowered. Relief to the company was only one object of the act. Although the duty in England was remitted, that payable at the colonial port remained unchanged, for, as Lord North admitted, "the king meant to try the case in America."

For the time being the new act brought the merchants and radicals once more into alliance. The business of both legitimate tea importers and smugglers was threatened by the new methods of the East India Company, while the king's purpose was a direct test of colonial devotion to the principle of no taxation by Parliament. Once landed and the duty paid by the agents, there was no doubt that the tea would find its way into the channels of trade and the whole American position against a duty for revenue would be undermined. The interest of the merchants no less than the principles at stake required that the tea must not be landed.

At Philadelphia, New York, and Charleston the company's agents were persuaded to resign. When the tea ships arrived at the first two ports, since there was no one to receive the cargoes and pay the duty, the shipmasters sailed back to England with their freight. At Charleston the tea was placed in storage by the revenue officers for want of payment of the duty.[1] At Boston, however, two sons of Governor Hutchinson held commissions as agents. They would not resign, and the governor would not permit the issuance of clearance papers for the return of the ships. With the issue thus drawn the radicals boarded the ships disguised as Indians (December 16, 1773) , and "next morning tea lay strewn like sea weed along Dorchester beach!"

THE COERCIVE ACTS

With the "Boston Tea Party" the British plan of raising a revenue in America came to an abrupt termination. Begun in good faith by Grenville, it had degenerated in the course of a decade into a policy of "shifts and devices," as Edmund Burke declared. Provocative as had been the conduct of the king's government, moderate men like Franklin thought the Tea Party a blunder, for it was certain to force larger questions to the fore. Disregard of property rights put America in the wrong in the opinion of liberal Englishmen whose friendship was needed, and seemed to call for measures of coercion. The early months of 1774 brought the enactment of five laws, two of which were the direct consequence of events in Massachusetts.

The first of these acts, the Boston Port Bill, forbade commerce with the guilty city until the inhabitants should compensate the East India Company for the destroyed tea. The bill punished the innocent with the guilty, but the next law, the Massachusetts Government Act, by an extraordinary assertion of parliamentary authority, set at utter disregard the most precious rights of Americans. It remodeled the government of that colony, converting it into a royal province of the standard type. No longer were councilors to be elected,

[1] The Charleston consignment was sold at auction by the revolutionary government after hostilities began.

as provided by King William's charter of 1691. Instead they were to be appointed by the crown as in other royal provinces. Judges and some other officers were also to be no longer chosen by the people. Town meetings, hotbeds of sedition in the British view, were to be allowed only by permission of the governor, except for the performance of their routine functions.

Provincials regarded their charters as contracts which could be set aside only for cause duly proved before a court of competent jurisdiction. Since they emanated not from Parliament but from the king, provincial opinion regarded them as quite outside the sphere of Parliament's authority. The idea of converting the chartered colonies into royal provinces by act of Parliament had never before won favor even among the supporters of parliamentary supremacy.

A few liberals in Parliament vainly opposed the act. Said one: "The Americans have the same veneration for their Charters that we have for the magna charta." Another referred to the proposed changes as a "violation of the law of nature." Whatever might be the correct theory of Parliament's relations to the colonies, statesmanship called for efforts at mutual understanding; but the majority was too much stirred to heed good counsel.

The next two statutes renewed the Quartering (Billeting) Act of 1765 and permitted the trial of royal officials in England on charges brought against them in the colonies. In view of the fair trial given to the perpetrators of the Boston Massacre this Administration of Justice Act seemed insolent, and was in harsh contrast with the proposal to carry Americans to a less friendly locality for trial.

The fifth measure, the Quebec Act, was a consequence of the French and Indian War rather than of the friction with the colonies, but coming simultaneously with the other acts and giving additional cause for discontent, the Americans classed it with them. The Treaty of Paris had promised that England would respect the religious liberty and legal customs of the French in Canada, and one purpose of the law was to carry out these pledges.

It also extended the boundaries of the Province of Quebec to include the Northwest. The Proclamation of 1763 had reserved this triangular area between the Ohio and Mississippi rivers as part of the Indian country. The few whites—French *habitants* and English traders—resident in the region had been left without government except such as might be exercised by the commander of the military forces. The union with Quebec now brought the region under the civil government of that province. The natural associations of the French residents, by race, religion, and trade, were with their kinsmen of the lower St. Lawrence.

However, the government of this Anglo-French province of Quebec was not representative, and its extension to the Mississippi and Ohio rivers tended to keep Englishmen from settling in the Northwest. The discouragement of English settlement in order to preserve the region for the fur trade was, in fact, an important purpose of the act. Scotch merchants of Montreal were rapidly gaining command over the trade and employed many of the French in the business.

The act disregarded the charter claims of Virginia, Massachusetts, and Connecticut to portions of the Northwest, and thwarted the plans of land speculators and promoters of projects of new colonies. These, it appeared, would have to be content with lands south of the Ohio, where the cordiality of the ministry towards the Vandalia project indicated that other grants might be made.

The religious prejudices of the Protestant inhabitants of the Atlantic colonies were aroused, moreover, by what could be interpreted as a plan to build up a strong Catholic province on their flank and in their rear.

If the Tea Party angered the British, the Coercive Acts—
"Intolerable Acts," the colonists called them—inflamed the
provincials even more.   In Massachusetts Hutchinson was
replaced by General Thomas Gage, who as both civil and
military governor was to execute the new laws affecting that
colony.   The radicals in their turn resolved to ignore the new
government and called for the election of a "provincial congress" to act as a provisional government in planning resistance.

Whether this bold course would be supported by the other
colonies was the crucial question.   Many of the moderates
thought that the quarrel should be ended by paying the East
India Company for the damage done to it, but the radicals
would not consent to this course, and they gained ground
daily.   The popular movement brought the voteless workingmen of the towns into union with the back-country people
who clamored for proportional representation in the assemblies, and led to the meeting in several colonies of irregular
bodies in which the common people were represented and
began to influence the course of events.

The radicals urged that the cause of Massachusetts was the
cause of all.   The Boston Port Act was to go into effect June
1, 1774.   The Virginia House of Burgesses set aside this day
for fasting and prayer.   For this the governor dissolved the
assembly.   Some of the members then reassembled at the
Raleigh Tavern and issued calls for a continental congress
to consider the "united interests of America," and for a convention in Virginia to elect delegates.   The choice of delegates to the First Continental Congress by every province but
Georgia was the answer to the question whether America
would support Massachusetts.

The Congress assembled in Philadelphia in September,
1774.   From only two or three colonies came delegates chosen
by the assemblies; in others the choice was made by "con-

ventions" or irregular bodies composed with little attention to the legal right of the members to vote. The Congress was fairly representative of colonial opinion, however, for it included conservative as well as radical elements. Divergent views had therefore to be reconciled if the body was to speak with the "united voice of America."

The conservatives were led by Joseph Galloway, of Pennsylvania. They hoped to formulate some plan of reconciliation which would safeguard rights in future; and their program was set out in the "Galloway Plan." It proposed a union of the colonies quite like that contemplated by the Albany Plan of twenty years before, with control over the common interests of the colonies; but a new feature was the provision that no measure relating to such interests should become law without the concurrence of Parliament and the general council of the colonies. In essence this council was to be a third house of Parliament.

The Galloway Plan was a worthy effort in the direction of an imperial constitution. Although cumbersome it might have worked well enough to lead to something better; but it was unacceptable to the radicals, who insisted that the British must be forced to recognize the colonists' view of their rights. Consequently it was decided to draw up a Declaration of Rights and Grievances as a kind of ultimatum.

The discussion of the contents of this Declaration showed the divergence of view as to what American rights were. Some held that Parliament was without legislative power over the colonies, while others clung to the opinion that it had authority in matters of general concern. Some ambiguity resulted from the attempt to frame a statement which all could accept. In the end the Declaration claimed all of the rights derived from "the immutable laws of nature, the principles of the English constitution, and the several charters or compacts." Some Americans had long maintained that even the navigation acts were not binding in the colonies unless re-enacted by their legislatures. This idea seems to have been behind the provision of the Declaration which denied the legislative supremacy of Parliament but promised acquies-cence in measures for the *bona-fide* regulation of trade. Ex-ternal taxes were thus excluded, while the necessity was rec-ognized of some central body for controlling commerce.

In connection with the Declaration a demand was made for the repeal of a number of laws which were held to contravene colonial rights. A petition to the king was prepared looking to the same end, and an appeal to British public opinion was attempted through an Address to the People of England. No petition was sent to Parliament, whose authority was now so nearly repudiated. Canada was invited to make common cause in an address to the inhabitants of Quebec. Finally, in adjourning in October, the Congress resolved to reassemble in the following May in case the appeal for redress of griev-ances proved fruitless.

Another measure was intended to "put teeth" into the de-mand for justice. This was the agreement known as the "As-sociation." It revived and extended the non-importation agreements which had proved efficacious on former occasions, and threatened non-exportation to England and the West Indies after a year in case American demands were not heeded. Members had great faith that commercial coercion would again win concessions. A Maryland delegate believed that it would mean nothing less than bankruptcy for the English, while Richard Henry Lee declared that the same ship which carried the news of the Association to England would bring back redress. To enforce the agreement a system of commit-tees was to be organized throughout the colonies.

The efforts of the Congress seemed for a time likely to bring results. Pitt, now Lord Chatham, commended the Declara-tion of Rights for "solidity of reason, force of sagacity, and wisdom of conclusion." He hoped for some agreement, such as Galloway had outlined, which should define the powers of Parliament and the colonies respectively and prevent further controversy. Burke pleaded for a return to the old régime of the days before 1763. Many merchants, alarmed at the prospect of a new interruption of trade, petitioned for such a modification of program as would avert that disaster.

The king, however, was determined not to yield, and an election showed that he had the support of the voters. He refused to receive the petition of the Continental Congress. A motion by Chatham for the withdrawal of the troops from Boston received only eighteen votes in the House of Lords. Both houses by large majorities pledged their support to the king in putting down "rebellion," and in the course of the winter military and naval preparations were hurried forward. Lord North, indeed, proposed to exempt from parliamentary taxation any province whose assembly would pledge itself to raise a stipulated sum for imperial purposes, but the offer, coming at the same time with the warlike preparations, was regarded by the provincials as an attempt to divide them.

Meantime, in America, party divisions crystallized, with the radicals, now called "Whigs," in the ascendant, especially in Massachusetts and Virginia. Conservatives began to fear that Whig plans must end in separation from England, and many who opposed the course of the British thought that such a cure would be worse than the disease. One part of these continued to act with the Whigs, still hoping for reconciliation. Another part believed that the Whig party was hopelessly under the influence of extremists, and sharing Hutchinson's opinions, became the party of the "Loyalists," or Tories." It had a numerous following among the wealthy families in every colony who had social and political position and feared the rising power of the people. Many of the merchants in Massachusetts, New York, and Pennsylvania chose this side. The Quakers had strong loyalist leanings, in part because peace was their creed. Even John Dickinson hesitated long enough to bring himself under suspicion of toryism. The planters, on the contrary, were as a class moderate Whigs, and in Virginia worked well with the radical leaders

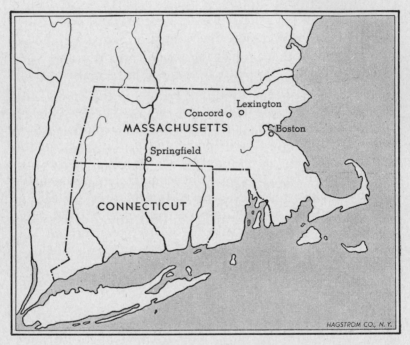

LEXINGTON AND CONCORD

from the western counties. Farther south loyalism was strong in the back settlements. The old conflict between coast and interior caused the frontiersmen to lean to the side opposite to that taken by their antagonists.

Taking the colonies as a whole the Loyalists were numerous and of the most prominent class, but they agreed only in fearing that resistance to England might be carried too far. Lack of a positive program reduced their weight to the minimum.

On the other hand the Whigs were active and well knit. Their local committees suppressed the utterance of Loyalist opinions and rigidly enforced the Association by social ostracism, and if need be by physical violence.

The Whigs understood that the unyielding attitude of the king might lead to armed resistance as their own next step. The winter of 1774–1775 was therefore spent in collecting military supplies and drilling the patriot militia. They had no intention of starting hostilities, but by the spring of 1775 the situation was such that conflict was inevitable. Lord Dunmore, governor of Virginia, almost came to blows with the colonial militia, while Gage in Massachusetts found the authority of his government confined substantially to Boston.

In the gray light of early morn on April 19 a detachment of red-coated soldiers was in motion along one of the rude lanes serving as roads which led northwest from Boston. Word had come to Gage that the Whigs, led by Samuel Adams, were collecting arms and ammunition at Concord village. To prevent mischief, the governor had resolved to seize these stores, and, if possible, to arrest Adams. Hoping to accomplish his purpose by surprise, the troops had marched all night; but from rustics seized along the way they learned that the countryside was apprised of their approach. Now, as they entered Lexington through which their road led, they found upon the green about the meeting-house a company of provincial militia drawn up as if to dispute their passage.

Ordering his men not to fire unless the word was given, Major Pitcairn rode towards the Americans and commanded them to disperse. In view of the great disparity of numbers, Captain John Parker, commander of the militia, likewise gave the order to withdraw. The provincials were in the act of obeying when suddenly a single shot rang out. An American may have fired it, or in the confusion a red-coat may have mistaken Pitcairn's command. None the less, this shot, American or British, was the opening gun of the Revolution. Britain and her subjects had drifted into a war from which thirteen colonies were to emerge independent states.

After a brief engagement the troops proceeded to Concord where they overcame further resistance, but their return to Boston was converted into a rout by the Americans who lined the road and fired from the cover of the stone walls and trees. "Though we beat them in the fight they beat us in the race," said the Americans. Gage made light of these encounters in his report to the British War Department. Not so the Americans. The news of Lexington and Concord spread with amazing rapidity, and soon all of New England was represented in the force gathered at Cambridge for the siege of Boston. Throughout the colonies the spirit of revolt was unleashed. Patriots seized the reins of government and royal officials found that their power had vanished almost over night. Instead of the redress of grievances hoped for, the Second Continental Congress found the country at war.

SELECT BIBLIOGRAPHY

Channing, *United States*, III, covers the years 1761–1789. Howard, *Preliminaries of the Revolution*, and Becker, *The Eve of the Revolution*, deal with the years preceding the resort to arms. See also Adams, *Revolutionary New England*. Van Tyne, McIlwain, Egerton, Coupland, and Schuyler (see Bibliography for Chapter VIII) are indispensable for this chapter. Schlesinger, *The Colonial Merchants and the American Revolution*, is an excellent critical interpretation from the economic point of view. A brief sketch by the same writer is *New Viewpoints*, Chap. 7. Andrews, *Colonial Background of the American Revolution*, interprets the movement from a broad, international point of view.

The most satisfactory history of the whole revolutionary era is Fisher, *The Struggle for American Independence*. Fiske, *The American Revolution*, is rather popular and uncritical. Excellent histories by Englishmen are those of Trevelyan, *The American Revolution*, and Lecky, *England in the Eighteenth Century*. The chapters from the latter relating to the quarrel between England

and the colonies have been published as *The American Revolution* (edited by J. A. Woodburn).

The *American Statesmen* series contains Tyler, *Patrick Henry,* Hosmer, *Samuel Adams,* and Morse, *John Adams.* A standard life of Dickinson is Stillé, *Life and Times of John Dickinson.* An adequate life of Otis is badly needed. Harlow, *Samuel Adams,* is a new and authoritative life. Still more recent is Miller, *Sam Adams, Pioneer in Propaganda.* Several excellent studies of Franklin have appeared of late, among them Crane, *Benjamin Franklin, Englishman and American;* Faÿ, *Franklin, the Apostle of Modern Times;* and Van Doren, *Benjamin Franklin.*

Lincoln, *The Revolutionary Movement in Pennsylvania,* gives some insight into the division of opinion in the colonies. An interesting point of view is presented in Clark, *British Opinion and the American Revolution.* The constitutional arguments, especially those of the colonists, are given in Hockett, *Constitutional History of the United States, 1776–1826,* pp. 72–95.

Chapter X

THE WAR FOR INDEPENDENCE

EARLY CAMPAIGNS

THE Congress assembled May 10, 1775. Few if any members desired independence as the goal of the struggle in which the country had become involved. Two months before, Franklin declared that he had never heard a word from any one in favor of independence. John Jay said later that the first talk of separation was heard in the autumn of 1775.

In explanation of resistance to a king to whom they professed loyalty the Congress issued a Declaration of the Causes and Necessity of Taking up Arms. This document placed all the blame upon the ministers. "We are reduced to the alternative of chusing an unconditional submission to the tyranny of irritated ministers, or resistance by force. . . . The latter is our choice. . . . We have counted the cost of this contest, and find nothing so dreadful as voluntary slavery. . . ." In the hope of retaining the moral support of English Whigs, who in Parliament had "nobly and strenuously asserted the justice of our cause," the Declaration assured them that "we mean not to dissolve that union which has so long and so happily subsisted between us," and concluded with a prayer that the Ruler of the Universe may "dispose our adversaries to reconciliation on reasonable terms." Had the British government at this time shown the conciliatory disposition which it did after Burgoyne's defeat, it can hardly be doubted that separation would have been avoided.

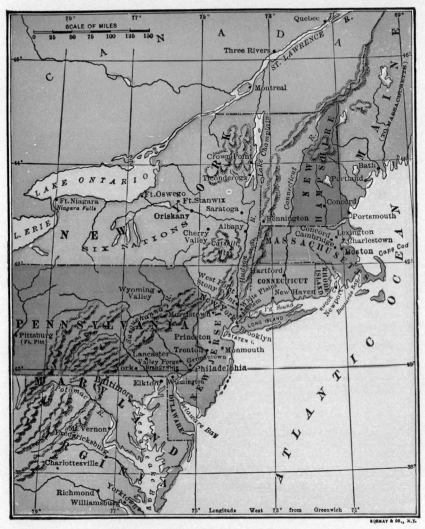

THE NORTH DURING THE REVOLUTIONARY WAR

1775	IN THE NORTH	IN THE SOUTH	IN MIDDLE STATES	IN WEST
Apr. 19	Battles of Lexington and Concord			
May 10	Capture of Ticonderoga			
May 12	Capture of Crown Point			
June 17	Battle of Bunker Hill			
Nov. 12	Capture of Montreal			
Dec. 31	Assault on Quebec			
1776		Battle of Moore's Creek Bridge		
Feb. 27				
Mar. 17	British evacuate Boston			
June 28		British repulsed at Charleston		
Aug. 27	Battle of Long Island			
Sept. 15	British occupy New York			
Nov.-Dec.			Washington retreats to Pennsylvania	
Dec. 26			Battle of Trenton	
1777				
Jan. 3			Battle of Princeton	
Aug. 6	Battle of Oriskany			
Aug. 16	Battle of Bennington			
Sept. 27			British occupy Philadelphia	
Oct. 17	Burgoyne's surrender			

CAMPAIGNS OF THE REVOLUTION

1778	IN THE NORTH	IN THE SOUTH	IN MIDDLE STATES	IN WEST
June 18			British evacuate Philadelphia	
June 28			Battle of Monmouth	
July, 4/5				Capture of Kaskaskia
Dec. 29		British capture Savannah		
1779				
Feb. 25				Capture of Vincennes
1780				
May 12		Surrender of Charleston		
Aug. 16		Battle of Camden		
Oct. 7		Battle of King's Mt.		
1781				
Jan. 17		Battle of Cowpens		
Mar. 15		Battle of Guilford C.H.		
Oct. 19		Surrender of Cornwallis		

Pending its response Congress did not shrink from military measures. It took control over the army at Cambridge, appointed officers, and called upon the provincial governments to raise arms and men. The conditions of American life had not developed military men, and Congress was compelled to rely upon civilians as officers. Henry Knox, who served with the artillery throughout the war, was a young Boston bookseller. Nathanael Greene, who won a reputation second only to that of Washington, was a Rhode Island blacksmith who was expelled from the Society of Friends because of his eagerness to fight his country's battles. Washington, notwithstanding the fact that he had served with distinction in the French and Indian War, and that his military ex-

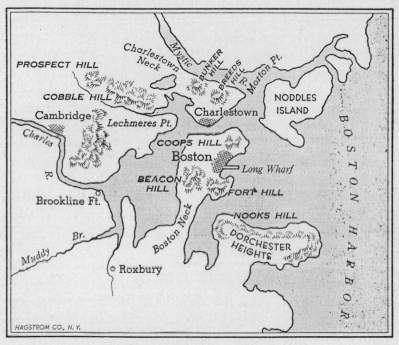

BUNKER HILL AND BOSTON

perience was quite as extensive as that of any of the Whig leaders, was essentially a civilian. In choosing him as commander-in-chief Congress could not foresee that he was destined to win fame as one of the great commanders of modern times. Indeed, his appointment was due in part to the fear that jealousy would prevent southern Whigs from serving wholeheartedly under a northern leader. Considerations of expediency, and faith in Washington's integrity and judgment, moved Congress quite as much as confidence in his military capacity. At it proved, his moral qualites quite as much as his generalship made his name an anchor for the hopes of his countrymen in the dark days of the war.

Events now moved rapidly. Before Washington could reach Cambridge the Battle of Bunker Hill had been fought. In the middle of June the Americans tried to force Gage from Boston by planting batteries on high ground in Charleston. The position was on a peninsula, separated from Boston by Charles River, and the Americans might have been forced to retire by the simple and safe expedient of threatening their single narrow path of retreat along the isthmus. Gage preferred to show his belief in the superiority of the British regulars by sending Sir William Howe to take the position by assault. This was accomplished, but only after two repulses, and then only because of the exhaustion of the ammunition of the Americans. They lost less than half as many men as the British, and "all the advantages of victory were on their side."

Blundering generalship marked the British conduct of the war in its early stages. Gage, and William Howe who soon succeeded him, rested inactive while Washington organized the patriot army, drilled the men, taught them the necessity of discipline, and made ready to occupy Dorchester Heights, south of Boston. When he took this position, early in March, 1776, Howe was at the mercy of his guns and agreed to evacuate the city.

Thus early in the war New England was rid of hostile troops. During the winter the Americans had directed a movement against Canada. The way for this expedition had been opened in May, 1775, by the pioneers of Vermont, who, under the lead of Ethan Allen and Benedict Arnold, attacked and captured the forts at Ticonderoga and Crown Point. These posts commanded the valley in which lay Lakes George and Champlain, the natural pathway to the St. Lawrence. If Montreal and Quebec could be taken, the Patriots hoped that the Canadians would join in the war, and that Great Britain would soon be forced to concede satisfactory terms of peace.

Late in the year a force under Richard Montgomery followed the Lake Champlain route and succeeded in capturing Montreal (November, 1775). Another force under Arnold marched against Quebec by way of Maine, suffering great hardships in the wintry woods. Uniting before Quebec, the two commands made an unsuccessful assault, in which Montgomery fell (December 31). In spite of reënforcements Quebec could not be taken, and Montreal, useless without it, was abandoned.

The Americans kept the foe on the defensive in the North during the first year. In the South the British made an attempt against the Carolinas, expecting help from the Loyalists of the interior. A body of North Carolina Tories set out for Wilmington, expecting to meet the British fleet there, but they were intercepted and defeated at Moore's Creek Bridge by a Whig force. In June came a futile attack on Charleston. Disdaining the tedious process of siege, the fleet tried to batter down the log fort on an island in the channel; but the solid shot buried themselves harmlessly in the soft palmetto logs, while the fire from the fort inflicted severe damage on the vessels.

THE MOVEMENT FOR INDEPENDENCE

The first year's fighting was inconclusive. Apart from the capture of Boston neither side had won a notable success. Yet the situation had altered greatly. The appeal of Congress for reconciliation had made far less impression upon the king than the news of the Battle of Bunker Hill. His answer to both was to proclaim that the Americans were rebels and to forbid commercial intercourse with them. Parliament followed with an act blockading the provincial ports. Many English Whigs opposed a warlike program. Even some of the army officers had no heart for the task of coercion which was assigned to them. For the time being, however, the king had his way, and ere long was hiring German soldiers to reduce his American subjects to obedience.

As the winter of 1775–1776 passed the hope of reconciliation grew faint; more and more the logic of events forced steps which could hardly be reconciled with the theory of civil war. The last vestiges of British authority disappeared even in the royal colonies, leaving control in the hands of the revolutionary organizations. These served as temporary or provisional governments, but their status was too indefinite to be satisfactory. Under the advice of Congress province after province adopted governments of a more formal kind, based on the authority of the people, and disarmed those who refused to join in the effort against England. In March, 1776, Congress decided to appeal to France for aid. The cessation of commercial intercourse with England necessitated new trade relations, and in April, in disregard of the navigation acts, colonial ports were opened to vessels of all nations.

In spite of the widening breach the tide of opinion set but doubtfully towards independence. In this crisis of indecision Thomas Paine, a recent immigrant from England, wrote *Common Sense*. "Reconciliation is . . . a fallacious dream. . . ." Everything that is right or natural pleads for separation. The blood of the slain, the weeping voice of nature cries, ' 'Tis time to part.' Even the distance at which the Almighty hath placed England and America is a strong and natural proof that the authority of the one over the other was never the design of Heaven. . . . Freedom hath been hunted round the globe. Asia and Africa have long expelled her. Europe regards her like a stranger, and England hath given her warning to depart. O! receive the fugitive and prepare in time an asylum for mankind." Published in pamphlet form and scattered broadcast—a copy for every three families within three months—this bold and incisive argument for independence was the seed of "a new method of thinking" in the minds of hesitating men.

In the early months of 1776 there was evidence that the southern colonies were ripe for the change. By May Congress had gone so far as to recommend that each colony form a government based on the assumption that all authority under the crown was at an end. The provincial convention of Virginia had already in this same month drawn up a state constitution, at the same time instructing the Virginia delegates in Congress to propose a resolution of independence. Such a resolution was offered on June 7 by Richard Henry Lee. Still the moderates hung back and the vote on the resolution was postponed, but the radicals were able to secure the appointment of a committee to draft a declaration.[1] While the committee worked the friends of independence strove to secure a favorable vote on Lee's resolution, and on July 1 it received the support of nine state delegations. On a later vote assent was unanimous.

The formal declaration reported by the committee was adopted on July 4. This justly famous document, prepared by Jefferson, falls logically into three parts: The first sets forth principles which are regarded as self-evident—that men are by nature endowed with certain inalienable rights; that governments are instituted to preserve these rights; that governments derive their just powers from the consent of the governed; that the governed may alter or abolish their government if it proves destructive of the ends for which it was established.

[1] The committee consisted of Jefferson, Franklin, John Adams, Roger Sherman, all radicals, and Robert R. Livingston, a moderate.

These ideas did not originate with Jefferson. They had been developed by John Locke nearly a century before. No doctrines were more familiar to Americans in the revolutionary era, and Jefferson merely gave them a new application. They were not the principles to which appeal had been made during the controversy with Parliament. For a dozen years the British constitution had been invoked in vain in defense of American rights. Now resort was had to natural rights, which were conceived of as above all constitutions.

The second part of the declaration enumerated the acts of the king which were destructive of the purposes for which governmental relations existed between the crown and the colonies. The declaration differed from earlier statements of grievances in laying the blame for infractions of American rights upon the king; he, it asserted, has done the wrongful acts, although in some of them he "has conspired with others," *i.e.*, Parliament.

The third part, or conclusion, is that "these united colonies are, and of right ought to be, free and independent states." Reduced to a single statement, the declaration meant that the king, having repeatedly violated his "compact" with his American subjects, had forfeited his claim to their allegiance.

The declaration was received with wild rejoicings, "as though," said Samuel Adams, "it was a decree promulgated from heaven." America had turned a sharp corner. Hesitation was no longer possible. From this moment every man was either a Patriot or a Loyalist. And from this moment the Loyalists suffered much at the hands of the Patriots. Many were driven into exile in Canada, the West Indies, or England, losing their immovable property through acts of confiscation. Others joined the hostile armies or took refuge within the British lines upon the occupation of New York and other coast towns. In modern warfare peaceable resident subjects of an enemy country are usually protected in their personal and property rights. In a revolution which divides a people against itself, such treatment is not likely to be accorded to the members of the losing party, even when non-combatants.

But it cannot be said that the conduct of the Loyalists was inoffensive. Even in Boston, which was the very hotbed of the Revolution, they boldly promised some "fine hangings" when the king's men came back. Their aristocratic instincts provoked many a sneering comment on the humble origin of continental officers. Throughout the country many of them gave all the aid they dared to give to the king's cause. In the later years of the war bands of Indians and Tories from Canada returned to burn, plunder, and scalp on the frontiers of New York and Pennsylvania. Other Loyalists took part with British sailors in raids upon the coast. The fairest-minded Americans, such as Franklin and Washington, were inflamed against the Tories, and it is hardly surprising that they were generally regarded as traitors. "A Loyalist," said the Patriots, "is a thing whose head is in England, whose body is in America, and its neck ought to be stretched."

Besides forcing a sharp cleavage between Patriots and Loyalists, the declaration made it much easier to obtain foreign aid. France, especially, was now glad to help since success promised the break-up of the empire of her great rival. Although not yet ready to lend aid openly lest it involve her in war, she did not hesitate to do so secretly, while protesting to Great Britain that she was both neutral and friendly. Large quantities of munitions were "sold" to a company formed for the express purpose of turning them over on credit to the agents of Congress. Under this disguise the French government supplied the "rebels." [1]

The declaration also altered the military problem. Now

---

[1] International law permits the sale of munitions to belligerents by the *citizens* of neutral countries, but not by neutral *governments*.

that America aimed at independence England was certain to put forth much more vigorous effort. Could the United States withstand the might of a power three times as populous, and ranking first among European states in wealth and naval strength? To their advantage was the fact that the foe must be the aggressor; if they could hold out until she tired of the struggle, they would win. Their people would fight on their own soil, protected by a broad ocean across which all hostile forces must be transported.

A modern well-knit nation with a population equal to that of the states in 1776 (approximately two and a half million whites) could command an army of nearly two hundred and fifty thousand men. The Whig population alone must have included about one hundred and seventy-five thousand men of military age. But the states were only in the first stages of union, and there existed neither the strong central authority nor the public sentiment necessary to make the best use of the very considerable potential resources. The only centers of real authority were the new state governments. Congress had neither the power to draft men nor to lay taxes. For filling the ranks it relied upon the uncertain process of volunteering and upon quotas of state militia, assigned to service for short periods; for funds, upon contributions by the states, loans, and issues of paper money. Even the state governments, being in the experimental stage, dared not risk the odium which heavy taxation might bring upon them. Under such conditions we need not wonder that Washington's effective army never reached its potential strength and was often less than one twentieth of it.[1]

The personnel of the armies shifted so rapidly that, with the inexperience of the officers, it was difficult to create a fighting machine which could meet European regulars and profes-

---

[1] At its maximum, in 1776, including both continental troops and militia, the nominal army numbered about 90,000.

sional soldiers on equal terms. A great debt of gratitude is due the Europeans—Lafayette, Steuben, Kalb, Kosciusko, and others—who gave their skill to the work of organizing the army, and to the governments which made loans. Without aid from abroad, especially that which France gave, and the diversion of British strength which came when war was renewed in Europe, it is quite possible that the resistance of the Americans would gradually have been crushed.

CAMPAIGNS AFTER INDEPENDENCE

One of the darkest periods of the war came in the campaign which followed the Declaration of Independence. At the moment of its passage General Howe was preparing to drive Washington from the vicinity of New York, whither he had transferred his troops after the evacuation of Boston. Howe easily succeeded, for his men outnumbered the Americans four to one. But he let slip several opportunities to crush his opponents. For example, after defeating them on Long Island in August, he neglected to cut off their retreat to the mainland. One by one the American positions on the lower Hudson were taken, however, as the British carried out their plan of securing control of the Hudson Valley in the hope of cutting off New England from the other colonies.

Autumn found Washington slowly retreating across New Jersey towards Philadelphia with the foe in pursuit. The patriot army was dwindling, because the men were discouraged, and it was impossible to get recruits to replace the soldiers whose terms of enlistment were expiring. Howe did not press Washington to battle, for he did not wish to shed blood to hasten the end of what appeared to be a dying cause. He was, in fact, a critic of his country's conduct towards America, and his object now was to save the colonies for England without the loss of their loyalty and affection. He preferred the olive branch to the sword for the work in hand,

and proclaimed the royal pardon for all who would take an oath of allegiance. By December thousands of the inhabitants of the middle states had made their peace, and Washington wrote on the twentieth that "Ten days more will put an end to the existence of our army."

When winter came Howe placed most of his army in quarters at New York, scattering a few thousand men, mostly German mercenaries, in garrisons across New Jersey. He planned to place a garrison in Philadelphia. Meantime the end of his line rested on the Delaware at Trenton in an exposed position, but safe enough, in his judgment, from the insignificant force with which Washington had crossed to the Pennsylvania side of the river.

Something was desperately needed to reanimate the hope and courage of the Americans and refill the thinning ranks. That something was a military success. Washington "in very truth snatched victory out of the jaws of defeat" when he recrossed the Delaware on Christmas night, while he still had a force of four or five thousand, and surprised the Hessians at Trenton. By this movement he took a thousand prisoners. When Lord Cornwallis, Howe's lieutenant, took the field, Washington avoided battle and then bewildered him by striking another unexpected blow against the enemy at Princeton (January 3, 1777). Something like panic came upon the foe at this, and Howe drew in his lines to New York City, leaving Washington in possession of the State of New Jersey.

The Trenton-Princeton campaign "forever established Washington's reputation as a soldier." Yet even after this success the Americans might have been crushed at almost any time during the winter. Washington wrote in March: "If the enemy do not move, it will be a miracle. Nothing but ignorance of our numbers and situation can protect us." But Howe kept his soldiers in their comfortable winter quarters and by his negligence allowed the Patriots to weather the crisis.

Paine again brought his trenchant pen into action in the evil days before Trenton. His new pamphlet, *The Crisis,* beginning with the words "These are the times that try men's souls," along with Washington's victories, revived the spirits of the Patriots and swelled the number of recruits. When the army left its quarters in the spring of 1777, it counted about eleven thousand men.

Howe's great ambition now was to occupy Philadelphia. The capture of the city where Congress held its sessions he hoped would demoralize the government and discourage the insurgents. In September he defeated Washington at the approaches to the city and entered in triumph. By dividing his forces, however, he so weakened the army at New York that it was unable to aid in what the British War Office regarded as the main campaign of 1777. This was an invasion from Canada by way of Lake Champlain, to gain control of the Lake Champlain-Hudson River line, isolate New England, and crush the divided enemy piecemeal.

An attempt had been made along this line in 1776 when Howe was on the lower Hudson; but the forces employed were inadequate for the purpose and had been beaten back to Canada by Arnold's men. For 1777 the War Office planned that General John Burgoyne should enter New York by the Lake Champlain route, while Colonel Barry St. Leger led a secondary movement of Loyalist refugees and Indians down the Mohawk to unite with Burgoyne near Albany. Additional troops were to be detached from Howe's New York army to support Burgoyne.

Fort Stanwix on the upper Mohawk barred St. Leger's passage, and the German Whigs of the Mohawk Valley checked him in the Battle of Oriskany. Deserted by his Indians and baffled before Fort Stanwix, he returned to Canada. When Burgoyne reached the rendezvous, St. Leger, of course, failed to appear. A detachment sent into Vermont for supplies was roughly handled by Scotch-Irish militiamen under Colonel John Stark at Bennington, and Howe, preoccupied with his Philadelphia campaign, sent no supporting forces. Pushing slowly into hostile territory, farther and farther from his Canadian base, while the enemy gathered in increasing numbers, Burgoyne at length found himself almost surrounded. He tried to fight his way out, but several engagements failed to relieve his situation, and on October 17 the British cause sustained its severest blow thus far in the surrender of his entire army to General Horatio Gates, at Saratoga.

Burgoyne's surrender is rightly regarded as the turning point in the war. Creasy includes it in his list of fifteen decisive battles of the world's history. The frustration of the carefully laid plan of campaign gave the Americans for the first time grounds for enthusiastic confidence in the outcome of the struggle. Most important of all, it led directly to the French alliance.

THE FRENCH ALLIANCE

The secret aid which France had been giving the Americans has already been described. Many of the French people felt deep sympathy for the English colonists in their struggle with the British monarchy. Already French thought was permeated with the political philosophy of Rousseau, who carried the doctrines of natural rights even further than Locke. These ideas were undermining the French monarchy and preparing the way for the great revolutionary outburst of 1789. The kinship between the ideals of the Americans and those of the French liberals was too close to be overlooked.

The French government also "tingled with joy at American victories," but not from sympathy with American ideals. The

Count de Vergennes, minister of foreign affairs in the government of Louis XVI, was a statesman of the old school of crafty diplomacy. He saw in the American revolt an opportunity to weaken the imperial power which had recently vanquished France in the contest for domination in India and North America. Britain would be a less formidable rival in the future if shorn of her American possessions. Especially would this be true if, to reward those who aided them in winning independence, the new states diverted their valuable commerce from British to French channels and looked to France for guidance in international politics.

After the passage of the Declaration of Independence Congress appealed to both France and Spain for alliances. In France Franklin joined Silas Deane, the original envoy. The new American agent instantly won the heart of all classes; social Paris lost its head over him, finding something almost hypnotic in the character of the simple, unaffected man who kept his serenity and balance amid the artificialities of the world's gayest capital. Official Paris was less easily moved. Before committing his government openly Vergennes wished the revolutionists to show by some important success in the field that they possessed sufficient military strength to promise victory in case of an alliance; and to give additional assurance he besought Spain to join in the war. But Spain feared the effect of the example of revolt in the English colonies upon the loyalty of her own. Hatred of England induced her to give Congress some secret aid, like France, in the way of loans, but she would not make a treaty of alliance.

Vergennes' desire for Spain's aid delayed the success of Franklin's effort until news came of Burgoyne's surrender. Predicting that England would offer liberal concessions which America must accept unless France came to her help, that clever diplomat now urged Vergennes to espouse the cause of independence at once. Vergennes, regarding the reconciliation of England and the colonies as one of the worst evils that could befall France, decided to wait on Spain no longer, and early in February, 1778, he concluded two treaties with the United States.

One of these treaties dealt with commerce, and provided that each country should open its ports freely to the vessels of the other. The second was a treaty of alliance. By it France agreed to make common cause against England until the independence of the United States was recognized, and renounced all pretensions to territory on the mainland of North America. In return the United States promised to defend the French possessions in the West Indies "forever." Neither country was to conclude peace or truce with the enemy without the consent of the other.

Something more than a year after this Spain joined France in the war on England, but not as the ally of the United States. Conflicts in the interests of the two countries kept them apart. Spain had feared an Anglo-American reconciliation followed by an attack upon her possessions adjoining the English colonies in the Mississippi Valley. The Franco-American alliance removed this apprehension. She hoped to regain the Floridas, and Congress was ready to guarantee her possession of them as the price of an alliance, provided that the right of the people of the United States to navigate the Mississippi into and from the Gulf of Mexico were recognized. Navigation of the river was a vital matter for the settlements which were just beginning west of the Alleghanies, since they had no other outlet for their marketable produce. But Spain in possession of West Florida would hold both banks along the lower course of the stream, and a policy of excluding foreigners from the river below her northern boundary would well-nigh strangle the infant western communities. Moreover, although the United States desired the Mississippi as a western boundary, Spain interpreted the Proclamation of

1763 and the Quebec Act as having definitely extinguished the claims of the English colonies to lands beyond the mountains. In her opinion these regions were crown lands subject to conquest by any enemy of England.

In the darkest hours of the war Congress was willing even to waive the navigation of the river in order to obtain the desperately-needed aid of Spain. But Spain would not make an alliance; she refused even to recognize the independence of the American states.

Vergennes' pledges to Spain were confined to matters relating to Europe. His most important engagement was to aid her in recovering Gibraltar, which England had held since 1714. Despite this precaution Vergennes soon found himself in a delicate situation because of the rivalry of his two allies. He could not support the ambitions of either beyond the letter of his treaty obligations without incurring the charge of partiality. The embarrassment due to this three-cornered arrangement reached its climax during the peace negotiations.

CAMPAIGNS OF 1778

While the treaties with France were being arranged Washington's soldiers were enduring a terrible winter at Valley Forge near Philadelphia. "As the soldiers marched . . . to their winter quarters," says John Fiske, "their route could be traced on the snow by the blood that oozed from bare, frostbitten feet." In the midst of plenty the men starved and froze because Congress could not command supplies with its depreciated paper money, nor wagons and teams to bring in clothing, shoes, and stockings. Howe, in Philadelphia, paid gold and silver for the farmers' crops, and even "Patriots" sometimes yielded to the temptation to sell in the better market. Although the common soldier has been deservedly praised for bearing his misfortunes with fortitude, and laboring "barefoot . . . through mud and cold with a song in his mouth," the strain on the morale of the men was terrific, and nearly a fifth of them deserted. An efficient government would have prevented most of the suffering at Valley Forge, but Americans had yet to learn that lesson. The spirit of disaffection penetrated even to Congress and led to an intrigue which threatened to displace Washington as commander-in-chief.

The news of the French treaties came as an offset to the depression of this winter of horrors. As Franklin had predicted, the English government was ready at last to pardon the rebellion, forego taxation, restore the Massachusetts charter, consider colonial representation in Parliament—to concede any and all of the demands which the colonists had made previous to declaring independence. Even George III exclaimed that he who held the taxing of America to be justifiable was "more fit for Bedlam than a seat" in Parliament. Rockingham, Burke, and many other Whigs were ready to grant independence rather than continue the war, but recognition of independence at this juncture savored too much of a retreat in the face of the Gallic peril to be generally acceptable. On the other hand, the time had passed for holding the Americans within the empire by promises of reform. The prospect of independence was too alluring. Besides, the treaty with France amounted to an engagement that the United States would never restore the king's sovereignty as the price of peace. When therefore the royal commissioners came to Philadelphia to offer peace on terms which would have been welcomed two years earlier, Congress refused to enter into negotiations.

The entry of France into the war drew the attention of England for the time being from her lesser antagonist. Troops were withdrawn from the mainland for the defense of the British West Indies, and the approach of a French fleet under Count d'Estaing threatened to cut off supplies by sea for the army in Philadelphia, necessitating the evacuation of that place and the concentration of forces at New York and Newport.

The withdrawal of the enemy from Philadelphia gave Washington one of his rare opportunities to seize the offensive. Following Sir Henry Clinton, who had succeeded Howe, as he led his army across New Jersey, he chose a favorable moment for attack at Monmouth (June 28). The cowardly insubordination of General Charles Lee—the "damned poltroon" Washington is said to have called him—who retreated when ordered to attack, cost the American leader what should have been an easy and telling victory.

Still Washington hoped with the coöperation of the French fleet to drive the British from the port cities during the summer. D'Estaing, however, was a soldier, not a sailor, and notwithstanding the superiority of his fleet, respect for the seamanship of Admiral Richard Howe, his adversary, made him timid. Failure of coördination between the land and naval forces brought Washington's great expectations to nought. Eventually the Newport garrison was withdrawn, but the British hold on New York remained unshaken to the end of the war.

These operations of 1778 were the last major movements in the northern states. Thereafter the British contented themselves with raids which harried the countryside and plundered the towns within reach of New York. Such actions had little if any effect upon the outcome of the war, but aroused great bitterness. Connecticut especially was the scene of such raids, and those who suffered were afterwards given lands in the "Western Reserve," south of Lake Erie.

This same season of 1778 witnessed a notable campaign in the Northwest. The settlement of Kentucky had begun in 1774. Checked by Indian hostilities efforts were renewed in 1775, when Daniel Boone, as agent for a group of speculators under the name of the Transylvania Company, cut a wagon path from Cumberland Gap to Boonesboro. The same year saw the planting of several neighboring "stations." The Transylvania Company collapsed because it could not win the approval of the government, but the scanty population of Kentucky succeeded in weathering the storm of Indian attacks which came with the Revolution, and became the first detached nucleus of population west of the mountains.

The Kentucky settlements were organized as a county of Virginia, for when independence was declared, that state reasserted her claim to western lands under the charter of 1609. Left nevertheless to their own devices, the pioneers clung to their homes with dogged tenacity and struck blow for blow against their red foes. The pioneer period in Kentucky was a heroic age, and the story of the struggle of its people with the savages is a true epic. At last one of the leaders, George Rogers Clark, perceived that there could be no end to this kind of warfare so long as the British held the forts of the Northwest. From Detroit in particular the Indians were supplied with arms and incited to go against the border, not only in Kentucky, but in Pennsylvania and the West Virginia region. Clark therefore formed the bold project of carrying the war into the enemy's country.

As Virginia claimed the Northwest, Clark applied to the government of that state instead of to Congress. Receiving a commission to raise volunteers in the western counties, he gathered about 175 men, descended the Ohio, and marched overland from a point near its mouth to the group of old French towns near Kaskaskia on the Illinois side of the Mississippi. Here, as at most of the posts, only "the flicker of a red flag" showed that the land was British. No garrison held the fort, for as a measure of economy the French villagers had been formed into a local militia. It appears that they were secretly prepared to give the Virginians a friendly reception;

at any rate they were easily won to the American side by the news that France and the United States were allies. Through their connivance with their kinsmen at Vincennes on the Wabash, that post was also surrendered to Clark's men.

When the news of these midsummer happenings reached Colonel Henry Hamilton, lieutenant-governor of Canada in command at Detroit, he led in person a counter expedition for the recovery of the posts. He retook Vincennes without difficulty, and there waited for the end of winter before moving on Kaskaskia. But Clark, like a good soldier, struck first. Crossing the flooded prairies in February, 1779, he caught Hamilton off his guard and compelled him to surrender, sending him and his men to Virginia as prisoners of war. Hamilton was particularly hated by the frontiersmen, who called him the "Haar buyer," because they believed that he paid the savages for bringing in scalps. It is probable that he and other British officers enjoined their red allies to kill only in actual fighting, to spare non-combatants, and to scalp none but dead men. But the use of Indians by either combatant was certain to entail barbarities. The futility of humane exhortations to such warriors was exposed by Burke in the House of Commons with fine satire: "My gentle lions, my humane bears, my tenderhearted hyenas, go forth! But I exhort you, as you are Christians and members of civilized society, to take care not to hurt any man, woman, or child!"

Clark was never able to muster sufficient strength to attack Detroit. On the other hand, the British failed to recover their lost posts. Congress caused some demonstrations to be made against Detroit from Fort Pitt, and while never able to send out an effective expedition, checked the equally feeble British operations. Possession of the Illinois country by the Americans was not mentioned in the peace negotiations, but may have been a silent factor in the decision of England to concede the demand for the Mississippi boundary. Of greater influence, probably, was the desire of the ministry to regain America's friendship.

THE WAR IN THE SOUTH

By the close of 1778 the British were preparing a new offensive, this time in the South. With the aid of the Loyalists they hoped to overrun the southern states and recover at least a part of the revolted territory. Savannah was taken before the year ended. Little headway was made in 1779, but with the coming of fresh troops under Clinton in 1780 the march of events became swift and dramatic. Clinton laid siege to Charleston, while Banastre Tarleton, colonel of dragoons, by dashing cavalry attacks kept all American forces at a distance. Charleston surrendered in May. The British were elated, and Clinton called confidently on "every good man" to join the king's forces in the effort to "reëstablish peace and good government." In August the chief American force in South Carolina, under Gates, to whom Burgoyne had surrendered, was badly defeated at Camden by inferior numbers. Gates, whose incapacity was by this time patent, with the remnant of his army dared not stay his flight until he had put the safe distance of two hundred miles between himself and the foe. Then regaining a degree of courage he reported that he had "proceeded with all possible dispatch" to a point where he could reorganize his forces.

Events in the North added to the gloom. Clinton moved by sea from Charleston to New York, and Washington dared not detach troops to aid the southern states lest he seize the Hudson Valley. Then came Arnold's treason. Arnold, the victim of factional malignancy, had suffered rebuke for certain trivial offenses. He nevertheless retained Washington's confidence; but in the bitterness of his sense of injustice he abused this confidence by asking and receiving the command at West Point with the purpose of betraying this key to the

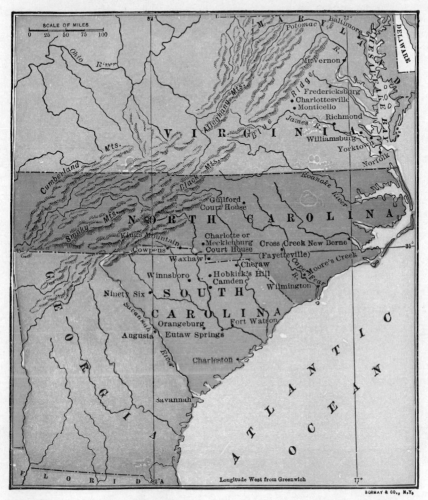

The Revolutionary War in the South

valley to Clinton. When the plot was discovered, he fled to the enemy, returning in 1781 with British troops to share in the fighting in Virginia.

Southern Patriots were almost in despair after Camden; they fled to the mountains and swamps; but they kept up an irregular warfare under leaders like Thomas Sumter, Francis Marion, and Andrew Pickens. The British, moving with artillery and trains of baggage wagons, were hampered by unbridged streams, trackless forests, and bewildering mountains, while a few hundred farmers, accustomed to fighting from behind trees and rocks, could assemble hastily, without uniforms, baggage, or cannon, strike a blow, and as quickly disperse.

Such was the stroke delivered at King's Mountain, in October. Cornwallis, the victor of Camden, now preparing to conquer North Carolina, sent Major Patrick Ferguson to recruit Loyalists in the back counties. Not far away were the Whig pioneers of the upper Tennessee country. These, joining with their friends east of the mountains, suddenly beset Ferguson's force and almost destroyed it.

The struggle between Patriots and Loyalists in the South in 1779 and 1780 was the most ruthless phase of the war. Loyalists taken with arms in their hands were treated, not as prisoners of war, but as traitors. The Loyalists retaliated whenever possible. The passionate hatred of former neighbors knew no bounds. Regular officers on both sides sought in vain to restrain their followers. After King's Mountain the victors executed several prisoners and spared not even the dead body of the opposing leader.

The check at King's Mountain delayed Cornwallis and gave the Whigs time to collect men for more vigorous resistance when he resumed his advance towards North Carolina in 1781. Nathanael Greene, by Washington's choice the successor of the incompetent Gates, was placed in command in the South, with Daniel Morgan as his chief subordinate. In January Morgan, attacked at Cowpens, showed himself more than a match for Tarleton. Then he joined Greene, and their combined forces fell back across North Carolina as Cornwallis advanced farther and farther from his base. When Greene thought Cornwallis sufficiently weakened, he turned upon him at Guilford Courthouse (March 15), and although beaten, inflicted such losses that Cornwallis retired to Wilmington on the coast.

This campaign showed the fundamental weakness of the British plans. Operating from the coast towns, each step forward necessitated the detachment of men to hold the country and cover communications. The forces available were never adequate for war on the scale attempted, and each advance sooner or later reached a point where the Americans were able to check it if not to inflict defeat. By the end of the summer of 1781 the enemy held only Charleston and Wilmington in the South.

The feebleness of England's efforts may not be understood unless one bears in mind her growing absorption in the European situation. In 1780 Russia, Denmark, and Sweden joined in an "Armed Neutrality League," menacing her with a general war unless she modified her practices towards neutral commerce. International law was still in a nebulous state, and the rights of neutrals were in dispute. England with her great navy made her own rules, much to the injury of other nations. The Dutch suffered from seizures of French goods on their carrying vessels, and contended that "free ships make free goods." On their part they harbored American war vessels and allowed their West Indian colonies to become the base for supplying the United States with munitions. These mutual injuries led to war between England and the Dutch Republic in 1781.

By this year the formidable array of maritime states either

actually at war or threatening war with Great Britain almost counterbalanced the sea power which was her chief reliance, and sea power was about to decide the war in America. "Nothing without naval supremacy," declared the Count de Rochambeau, as he embarked for the United States with new land forces. Washington recognized the same fact independently at about the same time. While he planned to attack Clinton in New York with the aid of Rochambeau's fresh army, his watchful eye, following the campaign in the South, perceived the opportunity for the master stroke.

Greene was in South Carolina, and Cornwallis, now in Virginia, had been chasing the "boy," as he contemptuously called the Marquis de Lafayette, commanding the Americans there. It was the old game of futile pursuit, and ended with Cornwallis' retirement to Yorktown on the narrow strip of land between the James and York rivers. If Count de Grasse, the French Admiral in the West Indies, would bring his fleet to the Chesapeake, while Washington and Rochambeau came down from New York, Cornwallis would be caught in a trap.

De Grasse reached the Bay on August 30, in time to drive off the British fleet which sought to keep open egress for Cornwallis by water. The land forces closed in during September, and on October 19, six years and six months after the Battle of Lexington, Cornwallis surrendered his entire army. British dominion ended almost on the spot where it had begun in 1607.

THE PEACE NEGOTIATIONS

So far as the United States was concerned the failure of Cornwallis ended the war. English opinion would not support further efforts to subdue America, although its loss was greeted with lamentations as marking the extinction of the glory and greatness of the empire and the establishment of the "uncontrolled superiority" of France in Europe. George

III declared that he would forsake England rather than acknowledge the independence of the colonies, but Lord North was forced to resign and the shaping of the American settlement passed from the hands of the stubborn monarch. A new ministry composed of men who had consistently advocated liberality towards America—the Marquis of Rockingham, who proposed the repeal of the Stamp Act in 1766; Burke, the advocate of conciliation; Charles James Fox, an outspoken sympathizer with the Americans; Shelburne, Franklin's friend of prerevolutionary days—faced the inevitability of a separation.

Since the French alliance of 1778 England had made several informal peace overtures, all based on the hope of restoring the status of America as a part of the empire. However favorable the terms offered, the United States could not entertain them, under the provisions of the alliance. Even after Yorktown peace could not be made, for France was still fighting. But as early as 1779 Congress appointed John Adams as peace commissioner and defined the terms of an acceptable treaty. These, in addition to independence, were: full rights in the fisheries off the Canadian coast, and the Mississippi River for the western boundary.

These demands were more than France was pledged to uphold, and to Vergennes seemed by their excess to threaten a prolongation of the war. Through his influence a modification was made in 1781. Franklin, John Jay, Jefferson, and Henry Laurens were joined with Adams in the peace commission, and the terms of peace were redefined so that independence was made the only indispensable condition. In regard to all other matters the commissioners were instructed to consult with the French minister, and ultimately to guide themselves by his advice.

Jefferson, then governor of Virginia, declined the appointment as commissioner, and Laurens, a South Carolinian, who had been the presiding officer of Congress and was at the time of his appointment a prisoner in England, was not released in time to take much part in the negotiations. Jay had been since 1779 the envoy of Congress in Spain, where he had not only failed to make progress towards an alliance, but had even been denied official recognition. Of the three men who acted Franklin alone, by temperament and experience, had a sympathetic understanding of France's position.

Vergennes' problem was to satisfy, so far as possible, the conflicting pretensions of his two allies, especially with regard to the Mississippi Valley, and at the same time to avoid making such heavy demands upon England as the price of peace that she would prefer to continue the costly and uncertain war. To give reasonable satisfaction to each belligerent and bring the war to a close would require some concessions by each nation. A compromise was necessarily Vergennes' aim.

Negotiations between the American and British commissioners were begun in September, 1782. Because Jay insisted that Great Britain must recognize the independence of the United States before discussing terms of peace, the commission given Richard Oswald, who began the negotiations for the British, authorized him to treat with the "Thirteen United States of North America."

The first step was to define the territory of the United States. It was the desire of the British to win the friendship of the former colonies by a liberal treaty. So act, Oswald was instructed, as to "regain the affections of America." Such a course might defeat the hope of France that the new nation, brought into being through her aid, would become her commercial and political satellite. If England could retain the good will of America and the lion's share of her trade, the ill results of independence would be substantially lessened.

Vergennes (or Rayneval, his secretary, who spoke for him), having to consider the interests of Spain as well as those of the United States, had already suggested to Jay that the territory south of the Ohio River, from the Alleghanies to the Mississippi, be reserved as Indian country, with the Tennessee River as the dividing line between the Spanish and American "spheres of influence," and that the Northwest remain under British control. Jay, remembering his humiliating experience in Spain and noting the Spanish slant of this suggestion (it had, in fact, been worked out by Rayneval in collaboration with the Spanish ambassador in France), construed it as evidence of an unfriendly disposition on the part of Vergennes.[1] In this opinion he was confirmed when Rayneval was sent in haste to London, presumably to present the French view to the British cabinet.

It is now known that Rayneval's errand had to do with another matter. But Jay, convinced of Vergennes' duplicity, formed the opinion that the commissioners could obtain a better treaty if they dealt with the British without French assistance. "Let us," he wrote to Congress, "be honest and grateful to France, but let us think for ourselves." Adams shared Jay's view, and Franklin finally consented to go on with the negotiations without consulting the French court.

The good faith of this course is open to question. England's policy of conciliation detached the United States, in effect, from her alliance. Many Americans then and since have believed with James Madison that "instead of coöperating with Great Britain" to take advantage of "the embarrassment in which France was placed by the interfering claims of Spain and the United States," the envoys "ought to have made every allowance and given every facility to it consistent with a regard to the rights" of America.

Nevertheless it is quite likely that the terms obtained were

---

[1] Vergennes was not actually hostile to the desire of the United States for the Mississippi boundary. He never insisted that it be abandoned, although he did suggest that it was extravagant.

better than they would otherwise have been. The British not only conceded the Mississippi boundary, but recognized the rights in the fisheries as unimpaired by the war and the new status of independence.

The treaty definition of the boundary was made in partial ignorance of the geography of the country through which the line ran. Beginning on the northeast at the mouth of the St. Croix River, the line followed that stream to its source. Thence it ran north to the "highlands," separating the streams flowing into the Atlantic from those falling into the St. Lawrence. Following the "highlands" to the upper waters of Connecticut River, and that stream to the forty-fifth parallel of latitude, it ran due west to the St. Lawrence, thence up that river and through the Great Lakes and the chain of small lakes beyond Superior, to the northwest corner of the Lake of the Woods. From this point it ran "due west to the Mississippi," thence south with the course of the river to the thirty-first parallel, thence east along that parallel to the Chattahoochee, down this stream to its junction with the Flint, thence straight to the source of the St. Mary's, and along its course to the sea.

At several points this line had subsequently to be adjusted. A dispute arose as to which stream was the St. Croix of the treaty; there proved to be no highlands forming a watershed as described; the line through the small lakes in the Northwest had to be run by actual survey; and it developed that the Mississippi would not be reached by a line running west from the Lake of the Woods. Sixty years elapsed before these boundary questions were finally disposed of.

Besides these disputes with England over the interpretation and application of the treaty, another serious one arose with Spain over the southern boundary. The generalship of Bernardo de Galvez, governor of Louisiana, had placed the Spanish in the British posts at Mobile and Pensacola, and in control of the east bank of the Mississippi as far north as the present Natchez. On the basis of these conquests and her relations with the neighboring Indians, Spain built a claim to extensive areas south of the Ohio River. As peace terms had not been agreed on between England and Spain when the negotiations with the United States were under way, the fate of the Floridas was undetermined. While fixing the southern boundary of the United States at the thirty-first parallel, therefore, a secret clause of the preliminary treaty provided that in case the British retained West Florida when they made peace with Spain, it should have its old northern boundary, fixed in 1764 at 32° 28'.[1] When peace was made with Spain, England found it necessary to yield the Floridas, which she did without definition of boundaries. Spain then not unnaturally claimed that the provinces ceded to her were the Floridas as bounded by the British while in their possession; and, moreover, that England could not cede to the United States territory that was not in her possession at the time. Beyond this strip in dispute under the terms of the treaty lay the larger region claimed by Spain on the ground of conquest. The United States claimed to the thirty-first parallel, Spain clung to her own view, and the quarrel dragged on until 1795.

Provisions of the treaty as to two other matters were also the cause of later disagreements. These were the stipulations that creditors in either country should encounter no legal impediments in attempting to collect debts due them in the other; and that Congress would recommend to the states restoration of the confiscated estates of Loyalists, or compensation of the losers. The purpose of the first clause was to enable English merchants to sue their American customers for

---

[1] The line 32° 28' is approximate. The boundary of West Florida as fixed in 1764 was the parallel of the mouth of the Yazoo River, and the stream changed its course from time to time.

prewar debts; but the states had passed laws of various kinds to prevent collection, so that the treaty right was nullified. The states moreover ignored the recommendations of Congress concerning the Loyalists. The British complained of the non-performance of the treaty, and made it the ground for

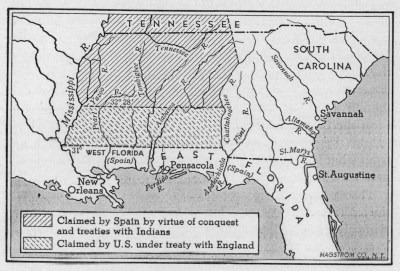

BOUNDARY DISPUTE WITH SPAIN UNDER TREATIES OF 1783

retaining a number of posts along the Canadian border which the treaty provided should be relinquished.

The preliminary treaty made in the autumn of 1782 became a definitive treaty when France and England made peace the next year (September, 1783). Americans had every reason to rejoice over the terms secured. Not so the French and British. "The English," wrote Vergennes to Rayneval, "buy peace rather than make it." Although the treaty was ratified, the ministry went down under the storm of criticism, and the new government was distinctly less friendly towards America.

One result of the change of ministry was the refusal to make a commercial treaty. The American commissioners hoped to conclude such an agreement in connection with the peace, but negotiations were postponed to a more convenient season. This proved unfortunate for the United States, for on account of the changed attitude of the king's government years passed before it was possible to obtain a treaty of commerce.

When Vergennes learned of the signing of the preliminary agreement, he complained to Franklin of the violation of the instructions of Congress. "I pray you to consider," he wrote, "how you are to fulfill those [obligations] which are due to the king." Franklin could only reply that nothing had been done contrary to the interests of France, and Vergennes, although he might well have disputed the statement, did not press the matter further. To the French minister in Philadelphia he wrote, however, "If we may judge of the future from what has passed here under our eyes, we shall be poorly paid for all that we have done for the United States."

Thus was the United States ushered into the company of the nations of the earth. Many Europeans regarded its future cynically. Few believed that the feeble bonds of union would long hold the states together, much less stretch to the lands beyond the mountains without breaking. Nature herself, they said, had decreed that the Alleghanies should be the western limit of the new republic. Count de Aranda, the Spanish ambassador in France, wrote in quite another strain: "This federal republic is born a pigmy: A day will come when it will be a giant; even a Colossus. . . . In a few years we shall watch with grief the tyrannical existence of this same colossus." For a decade or more the predictions of the cynics seemed likely of fulfillment; but time has vindicated the foresight of the Spaniard.

SELECT BIBLIOGRAPHY

The military side of the war can be followed in the histories of the Revolution cited in Chapter IX, in Van Tyne, *The Ameri-*

can Revolution, and in Wrong, *Washington and His Comrades in Arms*. There is a substantial and trustworthy account by a British military man—Whitton, *The American War of Independence*. Roosevelt, *Winning of the West;* Henderson, *Conquest of the Old Southwest;* Bodley, *George Rogers Clark*, and *Our First Great West;* and James, *George Rogers Clark*, deal with the western phases. For naval warfare see Allen, *Naval History of the American Revolution;* Paullin, *The Navy of the American Revolution;* and Spears, *The History of Our Navy;* see also Mahan, *The Influence of Sea Power upon History, 1660–1783*—an epoch-making book.

Studies of special aspects of the war are: Anderson, *The Command of the Howe Brothers;* French, *The First Year of the American Revolution;* Nickerson, *The Turning Point of the Revolution, or Burgoyne in America;* and Wrong, *Canada and the American Revolution*. The situation in crucial states is dealt with by Eckenrode, *The Revolution in Virginia;* McCrady, *The History of South Carolina in the Revolution;* and *The American Revolution in New York*, prepared by the University of the State of New York.

For the Declaration of Independence see Friedenwald, *The Declaration of Independence;* Hazelton, *The Declaration of Independence,* and the book by Becker bearing the same title. The last is the most recent of the three.

On relations with France see Corwin, *French Policy and the American Alliance,* and Tower, *Lafayette in the American Revolution*. Phillips, *The West in the Diplomacy of the American Revolution,* is a valuable monograph on French and Spanish relations.

The diplomacy of the Revolution and the peace negotiations may be followed in Bemis, *The Diplomacy of the American Revolution;* and *Diplomatic History of the United States;* Latané, *History of American Foreign Policy;* and Sears, *History of American Foreign Relations*.

Useful biographies are: Guedalla, *Fathers of the Revolution;* Adams, *The Adams Family;* Chinard, *Honest John Adams* and *Thomas Jefferson;* Fisher, *The True Benjamin Franklin;* Morse, *Benjamin Franklin* (see lives of Franklin in Bibliography for Chapter IX) ; Monaghan, *John Jay;* Pellew, *John Jay;* Simms, *Life of Nathanael Greene* (old but still useful) ; Hendrick, *The*

Lees of Virginia; and, among many lives of Washington, the following: Corbin, *The Unknown Washington;* Fitzpatrick, *George Washington Himself;* Young, *George Washington* (a work by an Englishman who stresses Washington's military service). Studies of two of the notable foreigners who aided in the war are Gottschalk, *Lafayette Joins the American Army,* and Palmer, *General Von Steuben.*

An important collateral topic forms the subject of Manning, *British Colonial Government after the American Revolution, 1782–1820.*

Chapter XI

AMERICA IN TRANSITION

THE STATE GOVERNMENTS

THE story of the setting up of new governments in the states runs parallel in time to the story of the war. In response to the recommendation of Congress in the spring of 1776 Virginia was the first state to frame a constitution. This was in May, several weeks before Congress passed the Declaration of Independence. One by one the other states followed the example of Virginia, and by 1783 nearly all had adopted constitutions in place of the temporary devices of the early period of the war.

The Virginia instrument, drafted by George Mason as a member of the provincial convention, was put in force by that body without a vote of the people. This process was not quite satisfactory in a country where so much was being said about the popular origin of government, and as the other states took action a more consistent procedure was evolved. Delaware's course in August, 1776, marked a step in advance of that of Virginia, in that a convention of delegates chosen for the purpose drew up the new frame of government; but the Massachusetts convention of 1780 went still further and submitted its work to the voters for their approval or rejection.

Each of the new constitutions had a double purpose. The one aim was to provide a frame of government, the other to set forth the philosophy on which the constitution rested and to list the rights of man which the government was forbidden to violate.

It is a remarkable fact that as to its frame of government every state followed closely the model of its government before the Revolution. Connecticut and Rhode Island deemed it unnecessary to make any change at all; their charters being essentially constitutions of self-governing republics, they now merely proclaimed in a formal way that the charters were to be the constitutions of free and independent states. Americans were not dissatisfied with the forms of government under which they had been living. They were deeply imbued with the spirit of English institutions, and desired to follow beaten paths rather than to attempt experiments and innovations. The Revolution was directed against external control of internal affairs; it was a fight for home rule. The states therefore made only such changes as were required by the new status of independence. Governors, councilors, and judges could no longer receive their appointments from the English crown; the authority which the crown had exercised passed to the people, and the new constitutions vested the choice of all officials directly or indirectly in the voters.

The most considerable changes were in the governor's status. In some of the states that officer became elective by the voters; in others the choice was made by the assembly. In general the office was shorn of part of its powers. Choice by the assembly tended to subordinate the executive to the legislature. In some states the governor was surrounded by an executive council, which shared and restricted his responsibility. Quite generally he was deprived of the veto, which had been a vexatious power when used by the royal governors.

The whole series of limitations placed upon the governor reveals a suspicion of that office born of the continual friction between the colonial assemblies representing popular interests and the governor representing crown interests. This suspicion was illogical when the governor's authority was no longer derived from the crown. During the early days of independence the people reposed confidence chiefly in the elected members of the law-making body, because in the old days they had been the champions of colonial rights. It took them a generation to learn that this bias was without valid foundation.

Another notable characteristic of constitutions is that they were given written form. The charters and other instruments under which all of the colonies had been ruled had served virtually as constitutions, and had accustomed them to written schemes of government. Besides, many Americans had come to hold the view set forth in the Massachusetts Circular Letter, that "in every free state the constitution is fixed," and to apply it even to the unwritten British constitution. The idea of fixity was much more readily associated with a written instrument. Finally, the belief that the body politic results from a social compact led naturally to the view that the articles of compact, like business contracts, should be put in writing to avoid misunderstandings and disputes.

The constitutions attempted to define the powers and duties of each branch and officer of government and to prevent each from encroaching on the others. Abuses of power by executive and judicial officers could be checked by impeachment and removal by the legislature. The executive veto, where it existed, was a check upon the legislative power, and the two houses checked each other. The system of checks and balances did not effectively restrain the legislatures, for there was no explicit provision empowering courts to declare legislative acts void if in conflict with the fundamental law. However, they presently began to do so.

In carrying over the features of the colonial governments the constitutions generally retained the former restrictions on the right to vote and hold office. This fact is surprising at first thought, since the Revolution was truly a leveling movement. During the war the emigration of the Loyalists deprived the states of approximately one hundred thousand of their most intelligent and public-spirited inhabitants. Leadership fell to men of less training and experience, few of whom, outside of Virginia, belonged to the old aristocracy. The strength of the revolutionary party lay with the plain people, small farmers and tradesmen. Their philosophy, avowed in the state constitutions, was thoroughly democratic. The Massachusetts instrument, for example, declared that "the body politic is formed by a voluntary Association of individuals; it is a social compact, by which the whole covenants with each citizen, and each with the whole people, that all shall be governed by certain laws for the common good." "The people alone have an incontestible, unalienable, and indefeasible right to institute government, and to reform, alter, or totally change the same, when their protection, safety, prosperity, and happiness require it."

The other constitutions contained equivalent, if less explicit, expressions, embodying the philosophy which underlay the revolt against England; it so permeated thought that it was certain to find expression in the instruments of government. If one looked no further, one might easily conclude that the cause of extreme democracy had triumphed. But the clause of the Massachusetts constitution which dealt with suffrage restricted the right to vote to owners of a freehold of the annual value of three pounds, or other estate worth sixty pounds, and in this respect the Massachusetts constitution is again typical. In other words, the theoretical implications of the state constitutions were not given full effect. Four states retained a freehold qualification for the franchise; the rest required possession of a substantial amount of personal property. The Carolinas and New Jersey required legislators to be Protestants; Delaware demanded that they be Trinitarians, and Pennsylvania that they profess belief in the inspiration of the Bible. Massachusetts and Maryland excluded non-Christians from all offices.

The new governments were thus mildly aristocratic. Nevertheless, within a half-century the leaven of democratic doctrine was to bring about equality of political privileges for all white men. The immediate effects were not altogether happy. The violent overthrow of the old system and the philosophy of popular government weakened the bonds of society and lessened the respect felt for all governmental authority. The disorders of the years following independence may be in considerable degree ascribed to this cause.

THE CONTINENTAL CONGRESS

We have had occasion to note from time to time various plans of union from the New England Confederation of 1643 to Galloway's plan of 1774. The Stamp Act Congress is significant because it marked the first attempt to unite against the mother country, but it aimed only at a union of opinion in a temporary crisis. The rejection of Galloway's plan gave a similar character to the First Continental Congress.

Early in the sessions of the Second Continental Congress (summer of 1775) Franklin submitted a new plan of union, much like the Albany Plan, but more detailed. No action was taken upon it at the time. The following June, when Richard Henry Lee moved the resolution in favor of a declaration of independence, he offered a second looking toward a permanent confederation. Various delays prevented the adoption of anything of the sort until the war was almost over. Meantime the task of conducting the common business fell upon the Continental Congress, which met in session after session from May, 1775, to March, 1781.

The legal status of this body has been a matter of much discussion. Down to the Civil War the tendency in the North was to overrate its powers, in order to combat the arguments of southerners who held that the states were sovereign even under the Constitution. The present tendency is to regard

the Second Continental Congress as the successor of the
Stamp Act and First Continental congresses in the work of
uniting public sentiment. War made its task both more important and more difficult than that of the earlier bodies,
since from necessity it became the organ of common action
or coöperation.

Since Congress raised and directed armies, procured the
means of maintaining them, sent and received diplomatic
agents, and entered into treaties with foreign countries, it
performed the functions of a provisional or *de facto* government. Whether it was legally a government with authority
to do what it did is a very difficult question, and one of theoretical rather than practical interest. The delegates to the
first session were chosen by revolutionary conventions. After
the organization of state governments the delegates were appointed by the state assemblies and acted under their instructions. No state government felt itself bound by the deter-
minations of Congress if they ran counter to its judgment.
The effectiveness of congressional measures depended upon
the voluntary, not obligatory, support of the states.

The Congress has been likened to an assemblage of diplomats who as a body agree upon action to be taken by their
respective governments. The indispensable necessity of
union to meet the common danger gave its measures such
force as they possessed. As has been said, the lack of a real
government goes far to account for the small size of the continental armies, the sufferings of the soldiers, and the infre-
quency of aggressive movements. Full command over the
country's resources would have meant a different story.

THE ARTICLES OF CONFEDERATION

The need of defining the powers of Congress was one of
the reasons for proposing the Articles of Confederation.
More potent was the growing sense of permanent interests

in common which required some sort of general government. Not only the issues of war but many of the problems of peace could be handled for the common good and safety only by a common government. Lee's motion of June, 1776, led to the appointment of a committee to draft articles at the same time that the committee on the Declaration of Independence was chosen.

The chairman of the committee on articles of union was John Dickinson, who had removed from Pennsylvania and was now a delegate from Delaware. Dickinson's committee had before it the draft which Franklin had offered the preceding summer, and used it as the basis of its own work. The series of documents which ended with the Articles of Confederation runs back, therefore, with unbroken continuity to the Albany Plan.

The object of Franklin, and of Dickinson in his turn, was to decide what matters were of common interest, and therefore suitable to be intrusted to the care of the general government. Franklin's draft had added some items to the list in the Albany Plan, and Dickinson's committee added a few more. As to the frame of government, nothing more was practicable than to give responsibility for these common concerns to such a body as the existing Congress. As a result of the circumstances under which the Continental Congress had first assembled, the states enjoyed equal status, each delegation casting one vote. Franklin had proposed to change this so that the votes of the states would be in proportion to their populations, but Dickinson, representing one of the small states, struck out this provision and inserted one continuing equality of suffrage.

A week after the adoption of the Declaration of Independence Dickinson's committee made its report. Important as the business was, the debate proceeded slowly, for matters relating to the conduct of the war had right of way. It was not until the autumn of 1777 (November 7), some sixteen months after the presentation of the report, that a final vote was reached, under the impulse of the enthusiasm awakened by Burgoyne's surrender.

In the debate some disputes had arisen and some changes had been made in the plan. The equal representation of states had been confirmed, in spite of the protest of Franklin, who declared that the small states should not have as large a vote in Congress as the others unless they were willing to pay as much into the treasury. As to money contributions, the draft had proposed that they be made by the states in proportion to population, but a dispute had arisen over the question of counting slaves, and it had been decided that each state should contribute in proportion to the value of improved lands within its borders. Upon the insistence of the states which claimed western lands under their charter grants, control over these lands was denied to Congress.

After Congress had voted its approval of the Articles, they were sent to the states with the understanding that each legislature, when it approved, should instruct its delegates in Congress to sign on its behalf, and ratification by every one of the states was required before they were to be binding. Now arose a difficulty over the provision concerning western lands. Maryland, objecting to Virginia's claim, declared that the lands must be treated as a common possession of the states, and refused to ratify the Articles until the lands were ceded to the Confederation.

This domestic quarrel over the future of the West began long before it was certain that the lands could be held when peace was made. The "landless" states joined Maryland in demanding cessions by the "claimant" states, and the ratification of the Articles was long delayed. One by one, however, all of the states except Maryland gave their assent. She stubbornly refused to ratify without the cessions, and as her assent was indispensable the claimant states finally yielded. The Articles went into effect March 1, 1781.

When we compare the frame of government contained in this instrument with those which the states had adopted, we find striking differences. Not only was there no second branch of the legislature, but the familiar separation of executive and judicial functions from that of legislation was lacking. The powers which the Articles granted were vested in Congress, to be exercised by it or its agents. It was authorized to appoint such committees and "civil officers" as its executive business might require, and these were to perform their duties under its direction. There was the germ, but only the germ, of a judicial system in the power to provide courts "for the trial of piracies and felonies committed on the high seas," for "determining finally appeals in all cases of captures," and for the settlement of disputes between states.

This concentration of functions in one unicameral body places the Articles in a different category from the constitutions of the states. Moreover, the latter rested on the authority of the people in each state, and created governments acting upon and responsible to them. The Articles declared that the Union was a confederacy, or league of friendship, in which each state retained its "sovereignty, freedom and independence, and every power . . . not . . . expressly delegated to the United States in Congress assembled." The Articles rested upon the authority of the state governments (legislatures). Congress was responsible to them and not to the people, and did not act upon the people. It was the organ of common action of a league.

In this body each member state was entitled to the same number of delegates, two to seven. Each state legislature chose and paid its own delegates, or neglected to do so as it preferred. On all measures the delegation of each state cast one vote, provided at least two delegates were present. If the delegation was equally divided, its vote was lost. No important measure could be adopted without the concurrence of two thirds of the delegations, that is, the vote of nine states. Amendments to the Articles, after passing Congress, required the approval of every state, by vote of the legislature.

The member states were pledged by the Articles to observe certain rules of comity in their relations with one another, and to refrain from certain actions which were inconsistent with the purposes of the league. Thus citizens of each state were to enjoy freedom to come and go and carry on business in all of the other states, while fugitives from justice were to be given up on demand of the governor of the state from which they fled. The public records of each state were to be given full faith and credit by the others.

As has been said, both Franklin and Dickinson had tried to make a list of the matters of common interest to the members of the league, and by the time Congress sent the Articles to the states in 1777 the list had grown to a very respectable length. First and foremost, naturally, among the powers of Congress, was that of "determining on peace and war." Next was the responsibility for foreign relations in general —sending and receiving ambassadors and making treaties. Then, to promote uniformity for the benefit of trade, Congress was given exclusive power to fix the standards of coinage and of weights and measures. Relations with Indians "not members of any of the states" were committed to its care, likewise the postal service. The responsibility for paying the debt incurred in the War of Independence was laid upon it. Other powers were incidental to these main ones.

Some of these powers had been included in the Albany Plan, and every one of them had been wielded in colonial days by the imperial government rather than by individual colonies. Now that independence had come, Americans were turning to the task of creating for themselves some substitute for the British government in the performance of these functions. In general, the British system was the model which they followed.

Unfortunately, the former relations with the British had made Americans tenacious of certain views which they should now have given up. The long struggle against parliamentary taxation had grounded them in the belief that they should be taxed only by their own assemblies. It was still quite beyond the thought of most of them to give a power to Congress which had been denied to Parliament. Instead, the Articles allowed that body to estimate its monetary needs and then to make a "requisition" upon each state for its share. The laying of the taxes to raise this and all other revenues was reserved to the states.

There was a similar defect of power in relation to the regulation of commerce. The regulation of commerce was one of the functions of Parliament which most colonists admitted as a necessity although they greatly disliked the workings of the navigation acts. The Articles consequently gave Congress only a partial and inadequate control over commerce. It was allowed to make commercial treaties, but the right to retaliate against any foreign country which discriminated against American trade was reserved to the states, and no control was given over interstate commerce.

In many ways the American league went beyond all precedents. Even such a union might have worked successfully for many years if the states had gone a little further in giving power to Congress. The lack of power to regulate commerce, the lack of power to tax, and the lack of power to act directly upon the people were fatal defects. Without these powers all of the others were mere shadows, and the Union itself a "rope of sand."

SOCIAL CHANGES

In so far as colonial society retained aristocratic features, they were much less associated with the ownership of land than was the case in England. In America pretensions to social distinction more commonly rested upon officeholding or wealth. Yet land ownership did not wholly lack social significance. The Virginia planter's social and political prestige as well as his economic status rested upon his landed estate. New York's three score estates of vast extent formed the chief basis of the aristocracy of that province; the estate of the Van Rensselaers spread over an area two thirds as large as the State of Rhode Island. In Maine, North Carolina, and elsewhere there were individual holdings of extraordinary size. The Fairfax lands in Virginia contained at one time six million acres. Those of the Penn family comprised a considerable percentage of the area of the province which William Penn had founded.

To this system of great holdings the Revolution brought the virtual end. The lands belonging to the crown, the Penns, and the Loyalists in general were confiscated and broken up in the course of a few years into many small farms. The Revolution thus gave a great impetus to the system of cultivation of small tracts by freeholders which became typical of America. The last vestige of the European system of feudal tenantry disappeared during the Anti-rent War in New York about 1840. Indeed, a landed aristocracy could not be permanently maintained in a country where land was so abundant and cheap. Large holdings were still sought, for resale at a profit rather than as the basis of social pretensions.

Outside of New England, the colonies had adopted the British laws of primogeniture and entail, devices designed to perpetuate the connection between aristocracy and land ownership. The abolition of laws of this kind had begun even before the Revolution, and within fifteen years after the Declaration of Independence they disappeared throughout America. Thereafter the more democratic system of equal inheritance prevailed.

Along parallel lines moved the attack on the established churches. On the eve of the Revolution nine provinces still recognized no church but the established one, and for its support they collected taxes. Congregationalism was thus favored in New Hampshire, Massachusetts, and Connecticut, and Anglicanism in most of the other colonies. The stronghold of Anglicanism was Virginia; but the Toryism of many of the clergy produced a reaction which reënforced the growing current of opinion against special privileges of all kinds. Hence liberal-minded members of that communion who were also revolutionary leaders led in the movement for disestablishment. When George Mason drafted the bill of rights for the first state constitution, James Madison persuaded him to include a declaration of the right of all men to the free exercise of religion. Then, with the aid of the dissenters, Madison and others promoted legislation putting an end to taxation for the support of the Church, abolishing the payment of ministers' salaries from public funds, and legalizing the marriage ceremony when performed by ministers of the dissenting sects. Maryland, the Carolinas, and New York followed Virginia's action while the Revolution was still in progress; but Congregationalism maintained its hold in New England for another generation.

All of these changes were more or less the results of the equalitarian thought of the revolutionary era. It was an important cause also of the first antislavery movement. A society seeking freedom for the black man was formed at Philadelphia during the opening days of the Revolution, "at a time," as the founders said, "when justice [and] liberty . . .

are the general topics." Other societies, to the number of thirteen, appeared within a short time, mostly in the slave-holding states. In 1780 Pennsylvania passed a gradual emancipation law—a manifestation of the desire to prove "sincerity of professions . . . by extending [freedom] to others." Some other northern states enacted similar legislation, and Virginia legalized manumission. Within a few years Virginia masters gave liberty to ten thousand bondsmen.

Partly from the same impulses and partly under the stimulus of reform movements abroad, the revolutionary period saw the beginnings of prison reform, the amelioration of laws concerning imprisonment for debt, and the general softening of the penal code. Even theology was affected by the prevalent philosophy, to the disadvantage of the churches which still clung to Calvinism. A theology which held that only a part of mankind was of the elect lost favor in an era of democratic professions, while those newer sects which held creeds based on the idea of the natural equality of men grew proportionately.

In other ways the break with England affected the churches. Independence necessitated the recasting of the constitution of the Anglican Church in the United States. With the passage of the declaration the king ceased to be its head. Some of the efforts to face the new situation seem ludicrous today; such was that of the vestry at Williamsburg, which crossed out the prayer for the king in the Prayer Book and substituted a petition to the Almighty on behalf of Congress! An American episcopate was established at the close of the war.

Methodism likewise severed its connection with the English Church and became an independent sect. Thomas Coke and Francis Asbury, who were at first called "Superintendents," became presently the first bishops of the denomination. In 1784 the Catholic Church in the United States was for-

mally constituted under a Prefect Apostolic. Changes were
in the air; states were adopting constitutions and attempting
to form a satisfactory union. The churches caught the spirit
and many revised their ecclesiastical constitutions.

These changes bore witness to the new consciousness of
independent nationality. New interest in past occurrences
was awakened, and several histories of states were added to
those already written for Virginia, Massachusetts, and Pennsylvania. One of the best of the new accounts was Belknap's
New Hampshire. The stirring within the churches bore fruit
in the founding of a number of new colleges.

The war also brought stimulating new contacts, especially
because of the presence of large numbers of soldiers from
France and other foreign countries, including the Hessian
mercenaries, many of whom remained when peace returned.
Through these contacts Americans gained new ideas, some
of which were of a very practical sort, resulting in the formation of agricultural improvement societies and the betterment of farm methods. George Washington became one of
the first American breeders of mules!

ECONOMIC READJUSTMENT

To set up an independent political household in the United
States was no slight undertaking. But the problems of the
new nation were by no means confined to the political sphere,
as the foregoing account of social changes indicates. The
years of war had seriously dislocated the social and economic
order as well as the political organization, and the confusion
and uncertainty of the half-dozen years following the peace
have fastened upon them the name of the "critical period of
American history."

The interruption of intercourse with Europe had forced
Americans to attempt to supply their own needs. As early
as the agitation against the Stamp Act efforts had been made

to foster the manufacture of cloth and other necessities in connection with the boycott on imports from England. Franklin had boasted a little later of the economic self-sufficiency of the colonies. During the armed conflict Congress did its utmost to encourage production along various lines by bounties and patents. Paper mills multiplied, and iron, leather, glass, and cloth manufactures increased. Considerable progress was made in the manufacture of guns, cannon, and ammunition, but the output was restricted by lack of some materials such as copper, and most of the needs of the army were met by importation.

Despite all efforts, American manufactures, still in the handicrafts stage, were at the close of the war far too weak to compete with the rising factories of England. For many years the United States was to depend upon England for most manufactured goods, and agriculture and commerce were to be her chief industries. Both of them had been badly damaged by the war.

While the war lasted, American seamen and shipmasters found a partial substitute for peace-time commerce in privateering. Possibly as many as ninety thousand men, manning five hundred vessels commissioned mostly by the New England states, pursued English merchant vessels on the high seas. From the profits Robert Morris is said to have enhanced his fortune by some £300,000, and others fared almost as well. But the most notable fruits of the practice were the improvement in the design of sailing craft, and the training of a courageous and enterprising class of sailors who, with the return of peace, were ready for adventures at the world's ends.

The irksome restrictions imposed upon colonial trade by the British navigation system had been contributory causes of the Revolution. Independence freed the Americans from these restrictions upon their trade with non-English countries, and notwithstanding the loss of their status as British subjects, they hoped that England could be persuaded to make a treaty allowing their intercourse with all parts of her empire to continue with the same freedom as in the former days. If there ever was a moment when such an agreement could have been obtained, it was when the Shelburne ministry, intent upon regaining the affections of America, signed the preliminary peace treaty in 1782. The change in ministry which came in consequence of the liberality of that treaty indicated that the hope of commercial favors was vain.

In April, 1783, Parliament by act renewed intercourse with the United States, but as a foreign country, subject to all applicable provisions of the navigation system. The Americans were excluded from the British West Indies, although the planters in the islands desired to trade with the United States. Canadian products brought in English ships cost them much more than the French and Dutch planters of the neighboring isles paid for goods from the United States carried in American vessels. Adam Smith advised that freedom of trade be permitted, and Pitt introduced liberal bills in Parliament. But the shipowners and Canadians protested, and the measures were voted down. Eventually, with the exception of products like fish, which competed with the industry of British North America, exportation from the United States to the British West Indies was allowed, but the goods had to be carried in English ships. As for exports to England, most products might be carried thither, even in American vessels, but in that case some articles were subject to higher duties than when brought in English bottoms.

Calculations of national interest swayed the British government, and its ancient policy was not much modified at the plea of the infant republic of the West. England had nothing to gain by concessions and nothing to lose by refusing to make them. The war was hardly over before it be-

came apparent that the French hope of supplanting England
in the American market was illusory. The habits of generations were too firmly fixed. While they sought some articles
of luxury from France, Americans preferred the staple manufactures of the English to the French goods of the same class.
British merchants hesitated for awhile to extend new credits
to their former customers whose prewar debts were still unpaid. But if Americans reëstablished their credit in England with some difficulty, they found it almost impossible to
obtain any elsewhere. English firms were soon accepting
orders from the states. In spite of restrictions, commerce
soon flowed back into its old channels. During the early
post-bellum years from seventy-five to ninety per cent of all
the trade of the United States was with England. In 1788
the new republic took approximately one twelfth of the
manufactured goods exported by Great Britain, and a half-
dozen years later the proportion had risen to about one fifth.

Freedom brought other losses besides that of the right to
enter British colonial ports. The bounties which England
had paid on the production of certain articles ceased, and
were sadly missed. American tobacco lost its special privileges in the English market, and depression followed in that
industry.

The recovery of the privilege of trading with the West
Indies became a prime object of diplomacy. John Adams,
sent to England as minister in 1785, was courteously received
by the king, but could not make headway with the ministry.
Despite the recommendations of Congress, the states had not
restored the property of the Loyalists, and had passed laws
sequestering debts due Englishmen. The British government therefore refused to make an agreement on commerce,
and charged the Americans with breaches of the treaty of
peace. The ministers intimated that they doubted whether

the Articles gave Congress power to make a treaty which the states would be bound to observe.

The inadequacy of the powers of Congress was, indeed, a chief root of the difficulty in negotiating treaties. If Congress could have imposed the same restrictions on British ships as American vessels were subjected to in England, it might have brought England to terms. That, at least, was Adams' conclusion from his humiliating experience. An amendment to the Articles had been proposed in 1784 to give Congress this very power, but only two states consented to part with their control.

Meantime Jefferson in France was faring hardly better than Adams. "We are the lowest and most obscure of the whole diplomatic tribe," he wrote. France, like England, was little disposed to treat the new republic with distinguished consideration. During the war she had given American vessels considerable liberty in her ports, both in the West Indies and in Europe, but concessions were made rather as a means of embarrassing the British than because of friendship for the United States, and with peace she like England resumed her navigation system. Spain pursued a similar course for like reasons.

Nevertheless within a year or two conditions began to improve slowly. In 1784 and 1785 France and Spain made concessions for their own convenience by which the vessels of the states were allowed restricted trade privileges in the West Indian ports. Treaties were concluded with some of the countries of central Europe, notably Prussia, embodying the most advanced contemporary views of international law. Unfortunately the amount of trade with these countries was small, so that the treaties were for many years hardly more than formal statements of ideals.

But the demand for American agricultural products grew,

and the open ports of the Danish and Dutch West Indies proved to be back doors to the neighboring British islands. A beginning was made, besides, in the Pacific. The first American vessel returned from China in 1785, and within a few years Yankee skippers were second only to the English in the trade with Canton. In conjunction with the Asiatic commerce came the development of the fur trade on the northwest coast. Ships from Boston and other New England ports rounded Cape Horn, carrying goods for the coast Indians, thence proceeding with furs to the Sandwich Islands (Hawaii), where conditions were favorable for wintering and curing the peltries. China was the great fur market, and silks, tea, and spices composed the return cargoes. Although Spain claimed the Pacific shores of North America, the "Bostons," as the natives called the American traders, outnumbered both Spaniards and English during the last years of the eighteenth century. The acquisition of Oregon and Hawaii by the United States long afterwards was in part the outgrowth of these early activities.

By the end of the Confederation period (1789) foreign commerce had regained its prewar prosperity, with added promise due to the new ventures. Boston, Salem, Newport, New York, Philadelphia, Baltimore, Norfolk, and Charleston shared in the profits. Through New York passed the trade not only of the Hudson Valley but of considerable portions of Connecticut and New Jersey. Its volume was sufficient to enable the great landowners who controlled state politics to shift the burdens of taxation largely from their own shoulders by means of customs duties. Evidence of the increasing prosperity due to commerce is found in the rise of real estate values. According to Franklin they had trebled in Philadelphia within a few years after the treaty of peace.

For this prosperity little credit is due the government of

the Confederation. Greater powers would undoubtedly have enabled Congress to promote the growth of commerce, but as it was, it grew from natural causes quite independently of the action of the government. Trade was so completely under the control of the states that their rivalries led to tariff wars which caused confusion and loss where prosperity should have been general.

THE CURRENCY QUESTION

The French and English armies and foreign loans had brought unusual quantities of coin into the country. It was largely used in buying supplies for the forces of both belligerents. The abnormal demand had sent prices to a high level and producers had prospered. Much of the money found its way eventually into the pockets of war profiteers and speculators, who spent their gains so freely that for a time after the war the value of imports far exceeded that of exports. This took coin out of the country again to pay for luxuries, and as it became scarce many a poor man found increased difficulty in paying taxes or other obligations which required hard money.

Men who were in debt therefore began to clamor for relief legislation—for stay laws deferring payment of interest or principal of debts, and especially for legal-tender paper.

The paper-money issue has been so perennial in the history of the United States that it is well to notice certain fundamental principles. Paper put out in large quantities to circulate as money, without an adequate specie reserve for its redemption (known as "irredeemable" or "inconvertible" paper), is likely to depreciate and cause changes in the general level of prices. Changes in the price scale are constantly occurring, through the operation of complex forces affecting the production and marketing of goods, and are usually slow and little felt. Even when slow, they may cause hardship, as in the case of obligations running through many years before maturing.

Ideally, the principal of a debt should be repaid in dollars of the same purchasing power as those borrowed. If their purchasing power increases (that is, if prices fall), the creditor receives a greater value than he loaned; if the change is in the other direction, he gets back a smaller value than he parted with. The debtor loses or gains inversely.

Legislation which affects the monetary system in either direction is very questionable, because it promotes the interest of one class or the other. Issues of irredeemable paper are dangerous for this reason. Depreciation, moreover, leads to a double scale of prices, one measured in specie, the other in paper, and the double scale aggravates the evils incident to changes in the price level.

The Second Continental Congress did its full part in demoralizing the currency, corrupting sound thinking, and teaching the people to demand paper money. When hard pressed for funds, it resorted to the issue of paper which it used in paying for whatever it needed. The receivers in turn passed on these "continental notes" to others in the course of their own business. These notes were mere promises that Congress would pay the bearer the amount printed on the face, not on demand, but at some unstated time in the future. To promote their circulation the states were asked to give them legal-tender character, and as Congress had no power of taxation, each state was requested to provide a tax for raising a fund which in time would pay off and retire its share.

This policy was adopted cautiously, and the quantity of notes authorized in the first years of the war was quite small. But the temptation to make new issues proved too great, and in proportion as the volume increased public confidence in the ability of Congress to carry out its promises of payment declined and depreciation proceeded. By 1779 one dollar of silver would buy twenty in continental notes. The next year the notes had dropped to half of this value.

Congress then adopted a policy of partial repudiation; the old notes were called in at forty dollars to one, in payment of taxes due the states. There were thus paid in and destroyed $120,000,000 of the $200,000,000 which had been issued. Then Congress put out notes of a "new tenor," one dollar of which was rated as equivalent to forty of the former issues.

This attempt to float new notes at par with specie did not stay the downward course of either series, and the currency of Congress finally became so nearly worthless as to give rise to the saying still in use—"not worth a continental." After the adoption of the Constitution, Alexander Hamilton, as Secretary of the Treasury, recommended the redemption of a limited amount at the ratio of a hundred to one, which was much more than the market value.[1]

Little could be done to improve the currency situation during the Confederation. Robert Morris, the able Superintendent of Finance appointed by Congress in 1781, understood the importance of a specie circulation, and had the advice of Gouverneur Morris, and of both Hamilton and Jefferson, in his efforts. It was Jefferson and the two Morrises who worked out our decimal system of coinage based on the Spanish dollar as the unit. But it could not be put into effect at once. The United States produced no appreciable quantity of the money metals, and foreign trade was the sole source of supply. In view of the adverse balance of trade and the scarcity of specie, recoining of foreign gold and silver

---

[1] A small percentage of the amount of a subscription for stock in the United States Bank might be paid in notes at this rate. The continental currency should be carefully distinguished from the certificates of indebtedness issued by the same authority. These were redeemed at par.

was put off, and the coins of France, Spain, and England formed a large portion of the hard-money circulation of the United States for many years.

With so scanty a supply of specie, the best use which could be made of it was to form a reserve for the redemption of a paper currency.[1] The Superintendent of Finance, in consultation with Hamilton, recommended in 1781 that Congress charter a Bank of North America. This institution, patterned after the Bank of England, began business in Philadelphia with a capital of $400,000 in specie.[2] Its notes, circulating at par, enabled business men to carry on their buying and selling without fear of losses due to fluctuations in the value of the currency. By 1789 two states had chartered banks, one operating in Boston, the other in New York.

These constructive measures did not meet the needs of the debtor class. With the fall of prices and the collapse of the continental currency, men who had incurred debts while their corn and wheat were bringing high prices found it harder to meet their payments than they had expected. The products of their labors brought fewer dollars, but their debts were not scaled down. The burden of their debts, if paid in specie or the notes of the new banks, was actually increased.

This was a real hardship. Not unnaturally they wished to avoid payment in the scarce specie, and demanded new issues of paper by the states under laws making it legal tender for debts. They did not desire the redemption of the issues, but wished the paper to depreciate gradually, operating as a tax, shifting the burden of debt from the poor and diffusing the loss throughout the community. In all of the

[1] Such a currency is very different from the irredeemable issues of the war period, being exchangeable for coin on demand. Such use of specie supports a sound circulation of two or three times as many dollars as are held in reserve.

[2] Doubts of the power of Congress to grant the charter led the Bank to reincorporate under a Pennsylvania charter. During the Civil War it became a National Bank, and has continued in business to this day.

states the advocates of paper money tried to gain control of the legislatures in order to enact their program.

The paper-money advocates of the Confederation period were almost identical with the rural classes which had before and during the Revolution sought democratic reforms. They had some moral support from the wage-earners of the towns who could not vote. The retention of conservative features in the state constitutions disappointed and angered the masses, who felt that the new governments did not rest upon their consent.

The philosophy by which rejection of the king had been justified was susceptible of dangerous interpretations. If governments derived their just powers from the consent of the governed, what obedience did individuals owe to a government which failed to secure economic justice? The limits of the revolutionary philosophy had not been defined.

Some extremists demanded the abolition of private property, contending that the property of all the people had been protected from confiscation by the joint exertions and common victory in the war, and should therefore become the common possession. In their eyes the state governments, with their machinery of courts for the collection of debts, took on more or less of the appearance of a mechanism for the exploitation of the masses by the few. The wealthy merchants and money lenders who made up the creditor class were the men who also controlled the legislatures, and the lawyers and judges seemed to be their allies in enforcing laws passed to protect property interests. Such thoughts tended to violence where no other means existed of redressing grievances, whether real or fancied.

In most of the states, on account of the restrictions on voting and the rules of apportionment in the legislatures, the conservatives were able to defeat the paper-money party at the polls and retain the upper hand in the assemblies. In some they won by narrow majorities only, and in Rhode Island the radicals gained control of the legislature and passed a legal-tender law. When creditors avoided debtors, unwilling to accept cheap money as required by the act, another bill was passed, permitting debtors to post notices declaring that they had vainly sought their creditors. Thereupon they were absolved from further obligation. As these notices began with the words "Know ye," the acts on which they rested were nicknamed the "Know ye laws." They gave rise to a famous case (Trevett *vs.* Weeden) —one of several during the Confederation which raised the question of the right of the courts to pass upon the validity of acts of the legislature.

In Massachusetts the paper-money party, defeated at the polls and rendered desperate by their debts, rose in insurrection. Farmers in the barren hill country of the western counties found a leader in Daniel Shays, a veteran of Bunker Hill, and broke up the sittings of the courts at Northampton and Worcester engaged in the trial of debt cases in which many of them were defendants. From the United States arsenal at Springfield they tried to get arms, and for a while laid the town under siege. This was in 1786. So general was the sympathy with the "rebels" that conservatives feared the state authorities would not succeed in restoring order. Governor James Bowdoin, however, sent out an army of militia which drove Shays in flight from Springfield and finally dispersed his followers. Popular sympathy saved all of the insurgents from punishment, and was supposed to account for the defeat of Bowdoin by John Hancock at the next election.

The conservatives found in these commotions additional reason for distrusting popular majorities. They were much concerned about the sanctity of contracts, and began to feel that some check should be placed on the power of the states to pass legal-tender laws. It seemed to them that new safe-guards of law and order were needed rather than more de-mocracy. They thought that Congress should be enabled to protect the states against domestic violence. They were humiliated by its inability even to defend its own property when Shays attacked the arsenal at Springfield, and demanded a stronger general government.

FINANCIAL FAILURE

While almost every phase of the history of the Confedera-tion shows the inadequacy of the Articles, the financial his-tory of these years is particularly dismal. The Articles laid upon Congress the duty of paying the war debt. Apart from the continental notes, the debt amounted to about $43,000,-000. Of this about $8,000,000 had been loaned by France, Holland, and Spain, the first named having supplied more than three fourths of the total obtained abroad.

Much of the domestic debt was represented by certificates issued in payment of soldiers' wages or for army supplies. Many of them had been given when necessity required the seizure of grain, wagons, horses, and cattle. The original receivers were fortunate if they were able to hold these evi-dences of debt. In most cases their own needs had compelled them to transfer the certificates to others who had ready cash and could afford to speculate on the chance of payment.

Under the circumstances the domestic debt was the last matter of finance to which Congress could turn its attention. First of all it must obtain funds to meet its own current ex-penses or cease to function. Next was the interest on the debt, especially the portion owned abroad. After that, if funds had been available, would have come the principal of the foreign debt, and finally the principal of the debt owed to Americans.

To provide for these needs the only resources made available by the Articles were requisitions on the states and new loans. No special provision was made for a revenue to be used in paying the debt. The land cessions, indeed, opened an additional source of income which, by implication, would be applied to this purpose; but so far as the Articles indicated, requisitions were to cover the needs of Congress for all purposes.

The insufficiency of this provision was realized by Congress almost before the Articles went into effect. To remedy it an amendment was submitted to the states, allowing Congress to collect a duty of five per cent on the value of all imports, to be devoted solely to the payment of the principal and interest of the debt. Rhode Island alone refused assent, thus defeating a proposal of the utmost consequence.

Experience soon showed the impossibility of providing for the debt through the use of requisitions. Congress asked for $10,000,000 during the first two years of the Confederation, and the states responded with less than $1,500,000. Requisitions yielded altogether, during the entire period of the Confederation, barely enough to meet current expenses, without paying even interest on the debt.

Congress tried again, in 1783, to secure additional financial powers by a "general revenue amendment," but with even less success than before. The necessity of making some payments on interest led to the borrowing of an additional $2,000,000 from Holland. But most of the interest went unpaid, the arrearage amounting in 1790 to many millions. Thus the public debt of a rich people increased continuously in time of peace because of the impotence of the government.

SELECT BIBLIOGRAPHY

State Governments. Nevins, *American States during and after the Revolution,* is the first comprehensive history of this topic. Brief accounts are given in Channing, *United States,* III, Chap.

XIV, Van Tyne, *The American Revolution,* Chap. IX, Morey, "The First State Constitutions," and Hockett, *Constitutional History,* I, 113–129. See also McMaster, *Acquisition of Rights of Man in America,* and Hockett, *Western Influences,* 22–27. There are a few good monographs which deal with particular states. One of the best of these is on Massachusetts: Cushing, *Transition from Provincial to Commonwealth Government.* The evolution of state constitutions from colonial charters is discussed by Morey, "The Genesis of a Written Constitution," in *Annals.*

The Continental Congress. Small, *Beginnings of American Nationality;* Van Tyne, *The American Revolution,* Chap. XI; and Van Tyne, "Sovereignty in the American Revolution."

The Articles of Confederation. McLaughlin, *The Confederation and the Constitution;* Hockett, *Con. Hist.,* I, Chap. VIII.

Fiske, *The Critical Period,* tells the story of the years of the Confederation and of the formation and adoption of the Constitution. It is one of the best of Fiske's books. McLaughlin, *Confederation and Constitution,* covers the same period; it was the first book to present the view now held of the nature of the problem of political organization which the United States faced after the Revolution. McMaster, *History of the People of the United States,* begins with the Confederation. It stresses the life of the people rather than political history, and while oddly organized is a mine of information. Its eight volumes come down to the Civil War. Schouler, *History of the United States under the Constitution,* also begins with 1783 and comes through the era of reconstruction after the Civil War. It is primarily a political history.

Social Changes. Jameson, *The American Revolution Considered as a Social Movement,* is a suggestive sketch. A forthcoming volume by Evarts B. Greene, in the *History of American Life* series, will cover the years 1763–1790. See also Nevins, *American States.* Humphrey, *Nationalism and Religion in America, 1774–1789,* is good on that phase of social history. Material illustrative of contemporary culture is to be found in Miner, *Our Rude Forefathers; American Political Verse, 1783–1788.*

Economic Readjustment. Channing, *United States,* III, Chap. XIII, is a good summary. Weeden, *Economic and Social History of New England,* is valuable. See also Carman, *Social and Economic History of the United States,* and East, *Business Enterprise* *in the American Revolutionary Era.* On manufactures see Clark, *History of Manufactures in the United States.* On privateering see Maclay, *History of American Privateers.* For the efforts to negotiate commercial treaties see Foster, *A Century of American Diplomacy,* Fish, *American Diplomacy,* and works on diplomatic history cited in Bibliography for Chapter X.

The Currency Question. Warren, "The Confederation and Shays's Rebellion," and Dyer, "Embattled Farmers," deal with the Massachusetts disorders. See also Hockett, *Con. Hist.,* I, 168–171.

Financial Failure. Dewey, *Financial History of the United States,* is a useful volume for the student of general American history. Chapter II deals with Confederation finance. Bullock, *Finances of the United States, 1775–1789,* is a study of especial value. See also Schlutz, *Financial Development of the United States.* Financial topics are dealt with in Oberholtzer, *Robert Morris, Patriot and Financier.*

Chapter XII

GROWTH OF THE WEST

THE WESTWARD MOVEMENT

NOTWITHSTANDING all discontent and tumult, America was stirring with vigorous life, as is shown by the increase of population and its expansion into new areas. The inhabitants were estimated at about three millions at the close of the war. By 1790 they numbered four millions—probably twice as many as the colonies contained in the days of the Stamp Act. Activity of speculation in western lands and the broadening current of migration westward showed confidence in the future.

At the close of the Revolution, settlements in western Pennsylvania, Kentucky and Tennessee were the only ones in the Ohio Valley. North of the river the native tribes enjoyed almost undisturbed possession. From the missions established, on the eve of the Revolution, by the Moravians at Gnadenhütten and Schoenbrunn in eastern Ohio to the French villages on the Wabash and the Kaskaskia, only an occasional trading post foreshadowed the coming of the white man. A sprinkling of Americans was to be found among the French at the old posts, followers of Clark who had remained and friends who had joined them. On the north bank of the Ohio as far as the mouth of the Muskingum, and along the east bank of that stream, squatters were making "tomahawk claims" in defiance both of the natives and the government of the United States.

South of the Ohio the first stages of pioneer life were already past. Cultivated farms and well-built houses were replacing the cabins in the clearings, and a steady tide of immigration was pouring in. Many of the newcomers hailed from Virginia and the Carolinas, coming by way of the headwaters of the Tennessee, Cumberland Gap, and Boone's "Wilderness Road." An easier route, save for the danger of Indian attacks, was the river. Virginians sometimes followed the Kanawha through the mountains to its mouth, but many of them preferred the longer but easier way down the Monongahela to the "forks of the Ohio." This was the favorite path also for the Marylanders who ascended the Potomac and then crossed to "Redstone" where Brownsville now stands, most of the way following the old trail of Washington and Braddock.

Across Pennsylvania the trails of the fur traders and the route followed by the expedition under General Forbes during the French and Indian War became the paths of the pioneers. The one chiefly used ran through Lancaster and Bedford to the village of Pittsburgh at the "forks." Upon this point all routes converged as all roads led to Rome in ancient days. Here or at Redstone the pioneer embarked on a flatboat and floated with the current to Limestone (Maysville) or the Falls of the Ohio (Louisville).

Settlers bound for the Nashville district in Tennessee crossed overland from the North Carolina settlements, or by boat followed the circuitous course of the Tennessee River to its mouth and thence ascended the Cumberland.

The Kentucky settlements contained fifty thousand or more people by the close of the eighties. Kentucky and Tennessee, being parts of Virginia and North Carolina respectively, were already open to settlement under the laws of those states when the Revolution ended. Very different was the situation in the Northwest. Interest in this region was growing, but authorized settlement had to await the completion of the cessions to Congress and the action of that body.

PITTSBURGH IN 1796

THE LAND CESSIONS

Maryland's refusal to ratify the Articles of Confederation started the movement for cession of the western lands to Congress. Seven of the thirteen states were numbered among the claimants of these lands. Connecticut, Massachusetts, Virginia, North Carolina, South Carolina, and Georgia based their claims on charter grants made by the Crown. New York, the seventh, rested its pretensions on its suzerainty over the Iroquois, who had maintained a shadowy superiority over the western tribes as far as the Mississippi and Ohio.

The validity of all these claims was open to question. The British government had repudiated them, in effect, by considering the Vandalia grant and by the Quebec Act. During the Revolution France as well as Spain had considered them extinguished by these acts of the British, and even Congress would have been less tenacious of the Mississippi boundary if it had meant only the territorial satisfaction of the claimant states. Clark's campaign under the authority of Virginia strengthened the contention of that state, but Maryland insisted that Clark's conquest was made possible only by the common military efforts in the East, and that therefore the winning of the region resulted from the common sacrifice.

In solicitude for the adoption of the Articles, Congress finally appealed to the claimant states to yield. New York, whose title was least defensible, responded first, and the others slowly followed. Maryland accepted the Articles in 1781, as soon as it became evident that she had won her fight, but the cessions were not completed until 1802. Georgia was the last to act. The Carolinas also made their transfers tardily, South Carolina in 1787 and North Carolina in 1790.

The cessions of the land north of the Ohio River were completed by 1786, through the action of New York, Virginia, Massachusetts, and Connecticut. Kentucky remained a part of Virginia, but that state yielded all claims to the Northwest with the exception of certain tracts to be distributed as bounty lands to her veterans of the Revolution. The largest of these lay between the Scioto and Little Miami rivers in the present State of Ohio. Connecticut also reserved an extensive tract lying south of Lake Erie, retaining for a time not only the title to the lands but jurisdiction. In this way she hoped to provide an outlet for her surplus population, and to compensate her citizens who had suffered from British raids during the war.

LEGISLATION FOR THE WEST

In appealing to the states for cessions Congress made promises which formed the basis of important legislation a few years later. One of these was that the lands ceded should be disposed of for the common benefit. At the time this pledge was understood to mean that the lands should be sold and the proceeds applied to the payment of the war debt. The other promise was that the West when settled should be formed into distinct republican states, which should become members of the Federal Union, with the same rights as the original states. In these pledges are found the germs both of the federal land system and of the principle on which the union of thirteen states has expanded into a sisterhood of forty-eight members.

After Virginia had made her cession and the movement seemed to be fairly under way, Congress took up the problem of providing a suitable government for the West. Thomas Jefferson was chairman of the committee appointed to draft an ordinance for this purpose. His report was adopted, after some changes, as the "Ordinance of 1784."

It divided the whole region between the mountains and the Mississippi into tracts each of which was to enter the Union when its population equaled that of the smallest of the original states. There were eighteen of these divisions. Previous to statehood the inhabitants were to have restricted rights of self-government under the supervision of Congress. Jefferson's draft provided for the exclusion of slavery from the entire West after the year 1800, but this clause failed to pass Congress.

The Ordinance of 1784 was prospective in its operation and never went into effect. At the time of its enactment the cessions had not yet been completed, and only two or three of the proposed states had any inhabitants. Before the conditions contemplated by the Ordinance came about, it was superseded.

In the meantime, however, Congress enacted the Land Ordinance of 1785, which dealt with the other phase of the task undertaken by its pledge to the states. It set out the plan by which the lands were to be disposed of, providing first of all for a system of surveys which has become known as the "rectangular," or "rectilinear" system.

By this method a "base line" is first laid out running due east and west. North and south across the base line, at intervals of six miles, meridians are marked off. Then lines parallel to the base line, six miles apart, mark off the surveyed area into blocks containing thirty-six square miles. Each of these blocks is called a "township," and each tier of townships between meridians is called a "range." The subdivisions of the township, each containing one square mile, are called "sections." Each section can be subdivided into halves and quarters, each quarter into quarters, and so on indefinitely.

The plan provided an admirably accurate system, in contrast with the "indiscriminate locations" which had been permitted by Virginia and some other colonies, and which had resulted in endless litigation. In part it was based on New England precedents, although the origin of some of its features is obscure. The system worked so well that it was

W ———— BASE LINE ———— E

6 mi. | 6 mi.

RANGE 6 mi. Meridian | RANGE 6 mi. Meridian

Township | Town-ship

6	5	4	3	2	1
7	8	9	10	11	12
18	17	16	15	14	13
19	20	21	22	23	24
30	29	28	27	26 / 25	
31	32	33	34	35 / 36	

26 b | 25 c c
b | c c
35 a | 36 b
d e e
d e e

SYSTEM OF LAND SURVEY

Township on enlarged scale showing sections and subdivisions

a = Section, 640 Acres; b = Half-Section, 320 Acres;
c = Quarter-Section, 160 Acres; d = Half Quarter-Section, 80 Acres;
e = Quarter Quarter-Section, 40 Acres.

applied to new areas from time to time as the settlement of
the West advanced, until it covered the whole of the public
lands. The Ordinance provided for a first survey to contain
seven ranges, along a base line running due west from the
point where the Ohio River crosses the boundary of Pennsylvania.

Besides the survey system, the Ordinance laid down the
terms and conditions on which lands were to be sold. Following an old practice of the New England colonies when laying
out new towns, section sixteen in each township was reserved
for the support of schools. The remaining lands of the seven
ranges were to be sold at auction to the highest bidder, for
cash, in plots of not less than one section. The minimum
price was fixed at one dollar per acre, but with competitive
bidding the actual selling price was expected to average considerably more. It was provided at first that an auction
should be held in each state, and to each was assigned for
this purpose a proportionate share of the tract to be sold.

This plan of sales was a departure from the land systems of
colonial days. In many of the provinces it became customary
to grant lands on such easy terms as to make them practically
free. This was due especially to the desire to promote settlement on the frontiers as a means of defense against the Indians. Such service was worth more than the money which
might be obtained by selling lands. Lands were also sold,
and speculators had become active in nearly every colony,
buying great tracts on special terms for resale. Often, however, they received the grants on condition that they colonize
them within a specified time with a certain number of settlers.

After the Revolution the straitened circumstances of the
public treasury and the burden of the war debt compelled
Congress to deal with the public lands as a source of revenue,
and for a time easy methods of acquisition found no regular
place in its system. The terms prescribed by the Ordinance

of 1785 shut out the poor men who would naturally become the actual settlers, for in those days the minimum sum required to purchase a section, $640, was a considerable for-

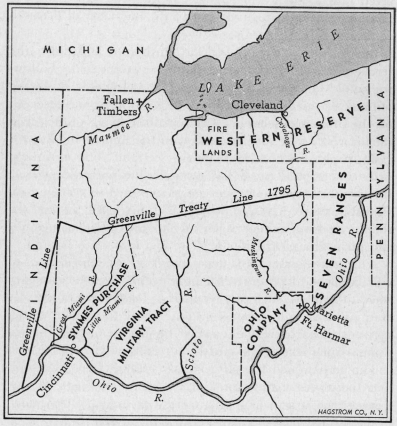

LAND PURCHASES, RESERVATIONS, AND SURVEYS IN OHIO

tune. It was expected that groups of settlers would buy whole townships, like the New England groups which formed new towns. This did not occur, and speculators were the chief buyers at the land auctions.

Land sold slowly under the Ordinance, and Congress

showed a willingness to make better terms than the Ordinance offered in special contracts with companies which wished to buy large tracts. As early as 1783 some officers of the continental army, whose arrears of pay Congress was unable to meet, had formed a plan to accept lands in the Ohio Valley in lieu of money, and to make a settlement there. The project led to the formation of the Ohio Company of Associates, consisting of New England veterans. In 1787 this Company sent an agent, Manasseh Cutler, to make a contract with Congress. He was able to purchase a tract of a million and a half acres on the Muskingum for a million dollars, to be paid in the certificates of indebtedness held by the members, then worth about twelve cents on the dollar.

In 1788 another organization, known from its promoter as the Symmes Company, and composed of New Jersey and Pennsylvania soldiers and speculators, obtained a contract for the purchase on similar terms of the lands between the Big and Little Miami rivers.

A part of the plan of Congress in dealing with the Northwest was not to permit settlement before surveys were finished, and not to make surveys until the Indian title had been extinguished. To prepare the way for settlement, Congress sent out agents immediately after the peace with England to make treaties with the tribes.

The Indians showed the greatest reluctance to negotiate. The British fur-trading interest, much discontented over the terms of the peace which assigned the fur-bearing Northwest to the United States, had persuaded the government to find excuses for delaying the surrender of the border posts situated on the American side of the boundary. Holding these posts, officials advised the Indians to refuse to cede lands north of the Ohio, and to make that river the permanent boundary of the American settlements. In short, notwithstanding the treaty, Britain sought to perpetuate her old plan of closing the

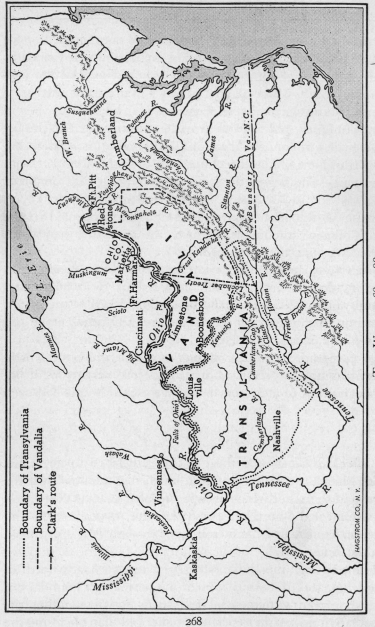

THE WEST, 1768–1788

Boundary of Transylvania
Boundary of Vandalia
Clark's route

HAGSTROM CO., N. Y.

Northwest to settlement, in the interest of the Indian trade.

With great difficulty the agents of Congress obtained several treaties, the last of which, signed in 1789 at Fort Harmar, at the mouth of the Muskingum, opened a large part of southern and eastern Ohio for white settlement. The Indians, however, refused to abide by the treaties, claiming that the chiefs had signed without authority, and Congress found the situation little changed for all its efforts. When the survey of the seven ranges was begun, the Indians prepared to take the war path, and the survey had to be abandoned for awhile.

This was the situation when the first contingent of the Ohio Company came from the East. Crossing the mountains of Pennsylvania, the party built a boat on the Youghiogheny, appropriately named the *Mayflower* in which these later Pilgrims floated down to the mouth of the Muskingum. There, opposite Fort Harmar and under its protection, they began the first authorized settlement of Americans north of the Ohio, naming it "Marietta" (1788). Almost simultaneously the Symmes Company began a settlement, while a third class of immigrants, crossing from Kentucky, contributed to the beginnings of a cluster of hamlets on the site of Cincinnati.

THE ORDINANCE OF 1787

Before this Congress had passed the Ordinance of 1787. By 1786, when the cessions by the states had placed the Northwest under its authority, it had become evident that the provisions of the Ordinance of 1784 were unsatisfactory. It was now believed that this ordinance provided for too many small states.

The new law applied only to the Northwest, leaving the region south of the Ohio to be organized whenever the cessions should be completed. The Northwest was to be divided eventually into not more than five nor less than three states.

While the process of occupation was in its early stages, government was to be in the hands of officials chosen by Congress, but as soon as five thousand adult males had removed to the territory, the qualified voters were to elect a house of representatives, while Congress appointed the governor. Congress was also to appoint the members of an upper house, or council, from a list of persons nominated by the representatives. This plan of government was much like that of Massachusetts before 1774. A delegate to sit in Congress without a vote reminds one of the colonial agent.[1]

Experience as subjects of Britain influenced the members of Congress in shaping their territorial—or as it might appropriately be called, "colonial"—system. Under the general plan first laid down in 1787, the whole wide space of the continent was to be occupied, as additional areas were brought under the flag by purchase or conquest and the westward movement called for provision for government in the new regions.

The American colonial system differed from that of England in one vital respect. She held her colonies in permanent subordination. It was this inferiority of status, at bottom, that caused the severance of the bonds between her and the thirteen colonies. The Ordinance of 1787 promised that whenever any one of the divisions of the Northwest attained a population of sixty thousand, it should be admitted to the Union forthwith, on terms of full equality with the original states. Thus the American system held before the colonists of the western frontiers the prospect of early admission to all of the privileges of partnership. This equality of new and old states is one of the unique features of American federalism, and goes far to explain the strength of the bonds of union.

[1] The Ordinance shows the temper of the times by property qualifications for voting and officeholding during the territorial régime.

The pledge of statehood was one of a number of articles of compact in the Ordinance which were declared to be unalterable except by common consent of Congress and the people of the territory. Other articles contained provisions similar to the bills of rights in the state constitutions, intended to safeguard freedom of worship, trial by jury, and property rights. One memorable paragraph read: "There shall be neither slavery nor involuntary servitude in the said territory, otherwise than in the punishment of crimes, whereof the party shall have been duly convicted."

This antislavery clause was the progenitor of a series of provisions which Congress applied to new territories in later years. During the controversy over slavery which preceded the Civil War, the program of the northern radicals was to extend this provision to all new territory. Hence this article of the Ordinance of 1787 was of epoch-making importance. Yet it is easy to overrate its effect. At an early date it was construed not to apply to the few slaves already in the territory, and later court decisions limited the prohibition to the territorial period. If new states entered the Union with all the rights and powers of the original members, the one class could no more be denied the right of choice in the matter of slavery than the other. The restriction undoubtedly operated in favor of settlement of the Northwest by opponents of slavery, so that when statehood came, free constitutions were preferred by the majority of the inhabitants. There was, nevertheless, a vigorous proslavery minority, especially in Illinois, which did not give up the hope of a proslave constitution until some time after the state had been admitted.

Oddly enough, these ordinances for the West, the constructive work of the Confederation period, were not warranted by any clause of the Articles. Congress had no better authority for what it did than the consent of the states implied in the acts ceding their claims to the western lands, and their subsequent acquiescence in the ordinances. To make them strictly legal an amendment should have been added to the Articles. The first Congress under the Constitution, with its fuller power, reënacted the Ordinance of 1787, and the appointment of the governor and other officials became, like other appointments, a power of the President acting with the advice and consent of the Senate.

In 1788 General Arthur St. Clair, a veteran of the Revolution, was appointed as first governor of the Northwest Territory, and the government was instituted at Marietta. A little later it was removed to Cincinnati and then to Chillicothe.

THE SOUTHWEST

South of the Ohio River the years of the Confederation brought discontent as well as growth. Under the jurisdiction of Virginia and North Carolina the people west of the mountains were too distant from the seat of government. The seaboard legislatures lacked the knowledge of conditions which they needed for the passage of suitable laws. Speculators held great tracts of land and kept out would-be settlers, and there was no local authority which could regulate their conduct. Not even adequate provision for defense was made. The organization of county governments failed to satisfy the pioneers. They desired to manage their own affairs and repeatedly demanded statehood.

Even in the days of the Transylvania Company the people of Kentucky had asked Congress to recognize them as a separate state. The desire grew with time and the increase of population, and the Confederation period brought almost continuous agitation for statehood. In western Virginia a parallel movement took place, and the settlements in the upper Tennessee Valley were equally eager for separation from North Carolina.

The passage of the Ordinance of 1784 encouraged these aspirations. The settlements on the upper Tennessee coincided almost exactly with one of the states projected in the Ordinance. Moreover, in 1784, North Carolina ceded this territory to Congress on condition that certain terms be accepted within a stated time. Congress did not accept the terms, but meantime the inhabitants, assuming that statehood was at hand, set up a government, took the name of the State of Franklin, elected John Sevier as governor, and appealed to Congress for recognition.

A similar situation existed on the northern frontier. On the eve of the Revolution pioneers from Connecticut, Massachusetts, and New Hampshire had entered the Green Mountains, which both New Hampshire and New York claimed. When independence was declared, the question of jurisdiction was still in dispute, and the "Green Mountain boys" proclaimed their independence both of England and of the claimant states, naming their state "Vermont."

All of the regions which desired statehood looked to Congress for support of their pretensions, but Congress dared not encourage them lest it offend the states interested. At most it could indicate a willingness to act when these states assented. Such a negative position did nothing to allay discontent. Nor was Congress able to care for other interests which to the western people were of vital importance. Because of the mountain barrier the only feasible outlet for the increasing produce of these new communities was the Mississippi. Spain now held both banks of that river in its lower course, and would not concede the right of navigation by Americans.[1]

[1] The Americans contended for the navigation as a *right*, while the Spanish maintained that it might be granted as a *privilege*, subject to regulation or withdrawal. Navigation was permitted during the Revolution, but after 1783 the river was closed. Then late in 1788 all western Americans were given the privilege of bringing their produce down to New Orleans subject to a fifteen per cent duty.

Her policy tended to make the Gulf of Mexico, almost surrounded as it was by her possessions, a "Spanish lake."

The settlers of Tennessee had an additional reason for dis-
satisfaction in the Indian situation. Between them and the
Spanish on the Gulf dwelt several powerful tribes—Chero-
kees, Creeks, Choctaws, and Chickasaws—occupying lands
lying largely within the bounds of the United States by the
treaty of 1783 with England, but claimed also by Spain.[1]
Fearing the Americans as neighbors and desiring, like the
English in the Northwest, to prevent settlement within the
Indian lands in order to protect her trade with the natives,
Spain encouraged the tribes to resist all encroachments of the
Americans and even to exclude traders from the states.

Unfortunately Congress was less competent to deal with the
Indians in the Southwest than on the north side of the Ohio,
for the claims of the states had not been relinquished and its
full powers over Indian relations were confined to those
tribes "not members of any state." Negotiations were undertaken with the natives of the Gulf region, but they encountered the opposition of Georgia, which claimed jurisdiction
over most of the territory in question. Treaties were nevertheless made, which served to assert, on paper, the sovereignty
of the United States as against Spain. The Indian problem
raised a clear-cut issue with the latter, whose own negotiations
met, or anticipated, each move of the United States.

RELATIONS WITH SPAIN

In 1786 Congress made an attempt to come to an understanding with Spain. John Jay, Secretary of Foreign Affairs,
opened negotiations when Don Diego de Gardoqui arrived
as minister. Jay asked him to agree to three concessions:

---

[1] It must be remembered that Spain claimed not only the strip between
31° and 32° 28′ but substantially all the territory lying between the Mississippi and Cumberland rivers. See pages 222, 224, and map, page 225.

The recognition of the thirty-first parallel as the boundary; the recognition of the right of Americans to navigate the river; and a treaty of commerce.

In return he had little to offer. Nevertheless Gardoqui was not unwilling to make a treaty. Fear of the ever-growing population of the transalleghany region was perhaps the chief reason for this disposition. A treaty of alliance containing a mutual guarantee of the western possessions of the contracting powers would lessen Spain's apprehension of American encroachments. Moreover, during the Revolution Spain had admitted American ships to her European ports upon the most-favored-nation basis. The United States had reciprocated, and after the war this arrangement had been continued informally. Both countries were conscious of the advantages of placing their commerce upon the firmer basis of a treaty.

Gardoqui was apparently unyielding on the boundary question, and really so on the right of navigation. Believing that a compromise might be reached, Jay appealed to Congress to modify his instructions. He desired permission to make a treaty *forbearing* for a term of twenty-five or thirty years insistence upon the claim of a right to navigate the Mississippi, provided that a satisfactory commercial agreement could be obtained. By the close of the term mentioned, he believed that the population of the West would have become so great that the logic of actual conditions would compel recognition of the right. As to the boundary, he thought it would be better "to yield a few acres than to part in ill-humour."

The vote of the state delegations in Congress on Jay's proposals stood seven to six, the southern states opposing unanimously. In this alignment Gardoqui read the failure of any treaty which might be agreed upon with Jay, since the approval of nine states would be needed to give it effect.

Spain now turned to an alternative plan of protecting her

interests in the Mississippi Valley against the disquieting advance of the American frontiersmen. Her force for the defense of her frontier numbered only five hundred men scattered among several poorly-built forts—a force utterly inadequate in case of a hostile demonstration on the part of these turbulent neighbors. Obviously the Spanish possessions would be much safer if these potential enemies could be converted into friends, either as subjects or dependent allies. If an alliance including a guarantee of territory could not be made with the United States, perhaps an arrangement of a similar kind might be effected with Kentucky. By this plan, wrote one of the Spanish officials, Kentucky "would forever constitute . . . a rampart for the protection of Spain."

This idea originated, not with the Spanish, but in the fertile brain of James Wilkinson, one of the pioneer settlers of Kentucky. Although he had been an officer in the American army during the Revolution, Wilkinson was a shrewd and unprincipled adventurer who finally won for himself immortality in that trinity of infamy to which Benedict Arnold and Aaron Burr have been assigned by American opinion. Wilkinson visited New Orleans in 1787, and managed to impress the officials there with the danger of an attack by westerners, aided by Great Britain, which might deprive Spain of Louisiana. He advised that Spain avert this danger by promoting a movement for the independence of Kentucky, to be led by himself. If Spain refused to concede the right of navigation to the United States, or to any westerners except Wilkinson and his friends, Kentucky would undoubtedly withdraw from the Confederation and treat with Spain. Wilkinson himself presently took the oath of allegiance to Spain and was granted a pension by the king. He professed to represent the opinions of the leaders in the western settlements.

It was the failure of the Confederation in the negotiations

with Spain which made possible this intrigue, and the affair is a capital illustration of the inadequacy of the powers of Congress. At every point touching the welfare of the Kentuckians and Tennesseeans that body seemed helpless. Aggrieved as they felt themselves to be, the westerners did not hesitate to weigh the advantages and disadvantages of union with the eastern states. The matter did not present itself to their minds as a question of treason or disloyalty. Such was one of the fruits of the revolutionary philosophy. The rumor that Jay's proposal had passed Congress caused great excitement. It showed an apparent willingness to sacrifice the West for the advantage of the old states, and brought the discontent in Kentucky to a climax. It was this disaffection which formed the basis for Wilkinson's conspiracy. The loss of the country south of the Ohio seemed imminent. Washington, referring to the uncertain sentiment of union there, declared that the West was "on a pivot," and that the touch of a feather would turn it either way.[1] Time proved that Wilkinson's influence was slight and that the majority in Kentucky preferred the prospect of early statehood to a precarious independence; but the questions at issue with Spain remained unsettled as an inheritance for the government of Washington.

SELECT BIBLIOGRAPHY

The Westward Movement. The general history of the West during the years covered by this chapter is to be found in Roosevelt, *Winning of the West,* and Winsor, *Westward Movement.* Clark, *The West in American History,* and Paxson, *History of the American Frontier,* are useful at every stage. Henderson, *Conquest of the Old Southwest,* and Hinsdale, *Old Northwest,* are useful for the respective areas dealt with. Briefer are Skinner, *Pioneers of the Old Southwest,* and Ogg, *Old Northwest.* The

[1] Washington advocated a canal joining the Ohio and Potomac rivers, to afford an artificial outlet for the West, believing it would counteract the influence of the masters of the Mississippi.

fullest and best treatment of the Northwest is that by Bond, *Civilization of the Old Northwest*. For Vermont see Jones, *Vermont in the Making*.

The Land Cessions; Legislation for the West. The best account of the land question is the work of Abernethy, *Western Lands and the American Revolution*. See also Treat, *National Land System*, and Hibbard, *History of the Public Land Policies*. On treaties with the Indians for cessions of land, see Mohr, *Federal Indian Relations, 1774–1788*.

The Ordinance of 1787. Barrett, *Evolution of the Ordinance of 1787*. A rare book, difficult to obtain.

The Southwest. See works by Roosevelt, Henderson, and Skinner cited above. Whitaker, *Spanish-American Frontier*, studies the American advance at the expense of the Spanish occupation. A pioneer work on this phase of history is Green, *Spanish Conspiracy*. The several movements for statehood are recounted in Turner, "Western State-making in the Revolutionary Era," in *The Significance of Sections in American History*. A reliable life of Wilkinson is needed. Wilkinson's *Wilkinson* is an attempt at vindication, by a descendant. Ambler, *George Washington and the West*, begins with his work as a young surveyor.

Relations with Spain. The best accounts are those of Bemis, *Pinckney's Treaty*, and Whitaker, *op. cit.*

Chapter XIII

THE FORMATION OF THE CONSTITUTION

STEPS LEADING TO THE CONVENTION

THERE was no lack of critics of the Articles of Confederation. To mention only well-known names, Washington, Hamilton, and Madison strove unceasingly to create sentiment in behalf of a more perfect government. Experience was also a faithful teacher. Each failure of Congress, each outbreak of disorder, added its quota of converts to the cause of a stronger general government.

The failure of all attempts at amendment of the Articles, however, was discouraging. It seemed impossible to secure the unanimous consent of the states to any change. Several proposals were made, now by state legislatures, now by members of Congress, again by public writers, for a convention of delegates from all of the states to consider the revision of the Articles, but Congress did not take kindly to the plan, and without its sanction a convention would be extra-legal. Besides, there was little hope that the recommendations of a convention would be accepted by the states.

In the midst of these perplexities Virginia and Maryland were seeking an agreement concerning commerce on Chesapeake Bay and the Potomac River. In general, interstate trade relations were in confusion, but these two neighbors had partially learned that coöperation is better than competition. In spite of conflicts over boundaries and other disputes they had from time to time in the past entered into agreements of various sorts, now for limiting the tobacco crop, again for joint campaigns against the Indians. Washington and Madison were eager to see the two states adopt a uniform commercial code, and at Washington's invitation, commissioners representing the two met at Mt. Vernon in 1785. This conference revealed the need of a wider agreement, and accordingly Virginia invited all of the states to send delegates to a convention at Annapolis the next year.

The announced purpose of the Annapolis meeting was to bring about nation-wide uniformity in legislation relating to internal and foreign trade. It was an attempt to take care of one of the great common interests by general agreement of the states to pursue a uniform course. Delegates came, however, only from five near-by states. These were too few for effective action. Moreover, the leaders desired to broaden the aims of the movement. They had been advocating a general convention, and the moment seemed propitious for bringing about such a meeting. Before the Annapolis convention adjourned, they carried through resolutions proposing to the states a convention to meet at Philadelphia in May, 1787, to recommend such changes in the Articles as would "render the constitution of the federal government adequate to the exigencies of the Union."

This resolution ignored Congress, which for some time took no action in support of the project. But the states responded so heartily to the Annapolis invitation that Congress, outflanked as it were, was forced to issue a call for the meeting. According to the terms of the congressional call, its recommendations were to be binding when approved by Congress and by the legislatures of every one of the states, in accordance with the amending clause of the Articles.

THE CONSTITUTIONAL CONVENTION

By the time appointed for the meeting eleven states had chosen delegates. New Hampshire delayed action until June; Rhode Island alone failed to send delegates. Most of the fifty-five members were already well known. About three fourths of them had served in Congress, and several were, or had been, governors and judges. The rest were business men, lawyers, and planters. Even the younger members were men of large experience in public or private affairs. There was a notable absence of radicals like Samuel Adams, John Hancock, and Patrick Henry, although the last named might have attended had he not refused a place in the Virginia delegation. Jefferson and John Adams, regarded as "moderate radicals," were still abroad.

Governor Edmund Randolph, tall, handsome, and dignified, headed the Virginia delegation, in which sat also Washington, Madison, and Mason. Washington, universally acclaimed as the foremost American, guaranteed the respectability of the Convention in public estimation by his mere presence. Madison, thirty-six years old, a diligent student of government, and a ready debater, was prepared for a leading part in the discussions. Mason had drafted the Virginia constitution.

Pennsylvania sent Franklin, the premier diplomat, now too old for strenuous labor, but endowed with a calm and philosophic wisdom which more than once poured oil on troubled waters when passions ran high. His colleagues noted for previous service or activity in the Convention were: Robert Morris, former Superintendent of Finance and himself active in the "big business" of the day; Gouverneur Morris, his former associate, a keen thinker and debater with aristocratic views; and James Wilson, a Scotch lawyer, who showed an unsurpassed grasp of the problems of the Convention.

From New York came Alexander Hamilton, who as aide on Washington's staff during the war had won his admiration and confidence by his brilliant and precocious genius. Delaware sent John Dickinson to improve if he could upon his former effort at constitution-making. In the Massachusetts delegation sat Elbridge Gerry and Rufus King, both destined to become prominent figures in politics, and Nathaniel Gorham, like Robert Morris a business man and land speculator.

Roger Sherman and Oliver Ellsworth, of Connecticut, were among the most active and able members of the Convention. William Paterson, of New Jersey, is best remembered as introducer of the small-state plan. Luther Martin, of Maryland, was one of the most consistent opponents of the program of the majority. John Rutledge, of South Carolina, was an ex-governor.[1] Charles Cotesworth Pinckney, a revolutionary general, became prominent later in politics and diplomacy. Charles Pinckney, cousin of the last named, a youth not yet out of his twenties, was the only member who came with a draft constitution in his pocket.

Although the Convention was not an "assembly of demigods," as Jefferson called it, the verdict of history agrees with the comment of Mason: "America has certainly upon this occasion drawn forth her first characters." But it cannot be said that these men represented a popular demand for a new government. Years ago one of the first historians of the Constitution (George Bancroft) wrote: "From the ocean to the American outposts on the Mississippi one desire prevailed for a closer connection." But there was no such unanimity; the rank and file of the people did not demand a strong central government. Talk about the "general interests" and "common welfare" meant little to men of the kind who had followed Shays. The problems of the Federal Government were far removed from the realities of the daily life of the masses.

The movement for the Constitution found its supporters, in short, among the conservatives who attributed the commo-

---

[1] Wilson, Ellsworth, Paterson, and Rutledge later became judges of the United States Supreme Court. Rutledge and Ellsworth were in turn Chief Justice.

tions of the time to an "excess of democracy," as Gerry phrased it, and desired to check these evils and promote business interests. The Philadelphia Convention was composed of men of the class that made the majorities in the state legislatures which chose them; it contained no representatives of the wage-earning and small-farming elements, for the one had no vote and the other was in the minority in the state assemblies. More than forty of the members were, or had been, holders of depreciated securities and were likely to be personally benefited in fortune by the adoption of a new plan of government and the establishment of the public credit. They doubtless believed, in addition, that the masses of plain people would benefit by the general improvement of conditions which a stronger government promised. Undoubtedly, however, the framers of the Constitution had the bias of the old governing class—indeed, they and the constituencies which sent them to Philadelphia were identical with that class—hence they came to do on the scale of the nation what they had already succeeded in doing in most of the states. Their ideal was not government by the people, although many of them would have professed faith in government for the people. The day of democracy had not yet come.[1]

The Convention began its sessions on May 25 with Washington as the presiding officer. Madison assumed the task

[1] This view follows in the main the thesis developed by Dr. Charles A. Beard, in *An Economic Interpretation of the Constitution*. This book is a brilliant analysis of the economic groups which pushed the movement for the new Constitution. These, concludes Dr. Beard, were: The holders of public securities; the professional money lenders; the great merchants; and the great landowners and speculators. Undoubtedly the primary motivation of the movement came from these groups. At the same time the present writer believes that much emphasis should be placed, as in the text, upon the view that the main features of the Constitution were determined by a process of evolution, which restricted rather narrowly the limits within which the Convention exercised a power of choice. The political philosophy of the "fathers" was derived from that of the English middle class which had triumphed over royalty in the Revolution of 1688. *Cf.* Farrand, *Fathers of the Constitution*, 162–163.

of reporting the debates for the information of posterity, and his notes, published a half-century later, are our chief source of knowledge of the proceedings. Contemporaries knew little of what went on, for the sessions were held behind closed doors. As in the Confederation Congress, the delegation of each state voted as a unit.

As soon as the work of organization was done, Governor Randolph presented a series of resolutions as a basis of discussion. These resolutions, probably drafted by Madison, were the result of conferences held by the Virginia delegates during the preceding days. Soon after the debate began some of the delegates showed dissatisfaction with the "Virginia Plan," and through Paterson offered a substitute (the "New Jersey Plan," or "small-state plan"). Neither was in the form of a draft constitution; each merely set forth in resolutions the chief objects sought.

The acrimony of the debate on the issue raised by the rival plans has led many students of the Convention to give undue importance to the difference between them, and to overlook the more significant fact that the members were so thoroughly agreed on their main task that it required little discussion. This main task was to see that all matters of general, not local, importance were brought within real control of the federal authority.[1] Even in drafting the Arti-

[1] The adoption of the Albany Plan would have provided representative machinery by which the several colonies could have acted together in general concerns, in cooperation with the British government. Franklin believed "that if the Albany plan of union had been adopted and made effective, the subsequent separation of the colonies from the Mother Country might not so soon have happened." For want of such machinery as the plan provided, the general powers had in fact been wielded by the British government, and the local by the colonies, prior to 1763. The controversy between England and the colonies arose because it seemed to the colonies that the British government by its measures, especially those relating to taxation, and by its doctrine of parliamentary supremacy, was disregarding the limits of its general powers and invading the local, or "internal police," power of the colonies. During the years following 1763 thinking Americans and a few Englishmen were groping towards a clearer conception of the principle

cles of Confederation the aim had been to intrust Congress with the care of the common interests, but extreme jealousy for the control of each state over its own "internal police" had marred the work. The years under the Articles had clarified men's vision and shown pretty definitely where the line ran between general and local concerns. The heart of the Virginia Plan was the declaration "that the National Legislature ought to be empowered . . . to legislate in all cases to which the separate states are incompetent, or in which the harmony of the United States may be interrupted by the exercise of individual [state] legislation." These words merely stated the aim, leaving until later the enumeration of the "cases to which the separate states are incompetent." The New Jersey Plan accepted this same principle and began the enumeration by demanding for Congress the powers of taxation and commercial regulation.

It is surprising how few other powers of a general character the Convention was able to think of, which were not already covered by the Articles. Naturalization, bankruptcy, patents, copyrights, the punishment of counterfeiting, and the power of coercion (really contemplated by both the Virginia and New Jersey plans) , exhaust the list. New restrictions on the states, however, aided in separating the functions of the general and state governments. For example, states were deprived of the power of coining money (held concurrently with Congress under the Articles) , of laying import duties, of emitting bills of credit, of making anything but gold and silver legal tender in payment of debts, and of passing laws impairing the obligation of contracts.

of "distribution of powers." If it had been grasped perfectly and applied courageously, it would have satisfied the colonists' demand for home rule on the one hand and the British demand for imperial control on the other; in essence it required nothing more than agreement as to what matters were "imperial," that is, of general concern, and what concerned the "internal police."

Clauses relating to taxation and commerce stood at the very head of the list of the powers of Congress in the first draft Constitution evolved out of the debates. In most comprehensive terms they authorized Congress "To lay and collect taxes, duties, imposts, and excises . . . to regulate commerce with foreign nations, and among the several states, and with the Indian tribes." But other clauses laid certain restrictions upon the use of these powers. Thus all duties, imposts, and excises were to be uniform throughout the United States; and direct taxes could be laid only in proportion to the population of the respective states. No tax could be laid upon exports from any state, nor could any regulation of trade or revenue give preference to the ports of one state over those of any other.

Some of these restrictions were made in deference to the desires of southern delegates who foresaw that in time Congress would probably be controlled by a northern majority, and feared that its new powers might be used to the detriment of southern industry.[1] The prohibition of export taxes, especially, arose from the fact that the southern states, as producers of staples such as tobacco and rice, sent abroad the great bulk of the fruits of their industry, and an export tax would fall with peculiar weight upon them. Another fear of the South was that Congress would use the power over commerce to prohibit the importation of slaves. Without some guarantee against this, Georgia and South Carolina would probably have rejected the Constitution. Hence Congress was forbidden to prohibit slave importations by the states prior to 1808.

None of the new powers was so vital as that of coercion. In fact, without it even with all the others the government must have failed as inevitably as the Confederation. Hamilton had seen the necessity of this power even before the adoption

[1] *Cf.* the controversy over the protective tariff, 1828–1832.

of the Articles, and had declared that Congress must have "complete sovereignty in all that relates to war, peace, trade, finance, and management of foreign affairs." By the words "complete sovereignty" he can only have meant coercive or compulsive power. In 1781 a committee of Congress, of which Madison was chairman, made a report arguing that from the necessity of such power it must exist under the Articles by implication. No result followed this report, for Congress dared not act upon this theory.

Washington again put the case in a nut-shell in 1786, when the fortunes of the Confederation were at the lowest ebb, by saying: "I do not conceive that we can exist long as a nation without having lodged somewhere a power which will pervade the whole Union in as energetic a manner as the authority of the State governments extends over the several States."

In such utterances we can trace the growth of the concept of a dual government, in which the states should retain authority over their internal affairs, while the general government, acting for the whole country, should wield full power over all matters that concerned the whole. Soon after the debates began in the Convention Gouverneur Morris explained that the existing government was "a mere compact, resting on the good faith of the parties [states]," while a supreme national government would have "a complete and compulsive operation." The Virginia Plan proposed to authorize the use of force against any state which was remiss in performance of its duties as a member of the Union. But Mason pointed out that "punishment could not in the nature of things be executed on the states collectively, and therefore such a government was necessary as could directly operate on individuals." Sherman proposed that the laws of the general legislature should be binding on the people of the United States.

The New Jersey Plan empowered the federal executive to use armed force to compel obedience to federal law by individuals as well as states; it also provided that the laws of the United States should be the supreme law, and that the state courts should be bound to uphold this supremacy even as against acts of the state legislatures.

Out of these elements the final provisions concerning coercion were constructed. The use of armed force against states was rejected as equivalent to civil war and as implying a union based on states. Even against individuals such force was feasible or desirable only in cases of insurrection involving formidable numbers. The outcome was provision for a complete judicial system for the enforcement of United States law, with recourse to military force, not only to "repel invasion," but to "execute the laws," in case of resistance.

In happy contrast with the Articles the scope of federal judicial power was made co-extensive with the legislative power, extending to "all cases, in law and equity, arising under this Constitution, the laws of the United States, and treaties made . . . under their authority."

The distribution of powers between the governments of the United States and of the states, with compulsive operation of the laws of both (where not in conflict) upon the same persons—in a word, the creation of a dual government—was the great achievement of the Convention, and in accomplishing it the friends of the Virginia and New Jersey plans united without great difficulty. The most serious controversy in the Convention came, as already indicated, over a matter of secondary importance. Having decided that the country needed a real government on a national scale, the delegates who sponsored the Randolph resolutions desired a Congress of two houses, with separate legislative, executive, and judicial branches, following the traditional model. Moreover, coming from populous states, they recurred to Franklin's contention of an earlier date, that the states should not have equal representation in Congress, as under the Articles, and proposed that in both houses the rights of suffrage should be in proportion to population or contributions to the common treasury. The members of the lower house were to be elected by the voters in the states, those of the upper by the lower house on nomination by the legislatures of the states.

The delegates of the small states urged that the enlargement of the powers of the existing Confederation would meet every exigency of the Union. The New Jersey Plan nevertheless accepted separate executive and judicial departments as well as new powers, but retained the one-house Congress and the equal representation of states.

There was in the two plans, as it turned out, nothing to prevent agreement except the difference concerning equality of representation in the legislature. The small states held that their equal vote was the essence of "federalism," and were fearful of a "national system" dominated by the great states through proportional representation.[1] In vain Madison and Hamilton pleaded that issues were not likely to arise which would array the large states against the small. Differences were much more likely to be sectional, they maintained, arraying the states of one part of the country against those of another part.

The small-state men were willing to accept even the two-house legislature, when they saw that it offered an opportunity to compromise. From proportional representation in one house and equal representation in the other a system "partly national, partly federal" would result. When the Convention voted for the first plan in the lower house, therefore, Ellsworth moved that equality be adopted for the upper.

[1] The phrase "proportional representation" has come in recent years to mean the representation of political parties in proportion to the vote polled. The student should avoid being confused by the change in the meaning of terms from period to period.

This motion failed and the chief crisis of the Convention resulted. The large-state leaders declared that they would not confederate on the basis of equal representation, and with equal emphasis the small-state men asserted that they would confederate on no other. A deadlock seemed to be reached and members began to talk of going home. Fortunately a majority were not willing to abandon the hope of compromise. A committee was appointed consisting of one member from each state for the purpose of formulating one. Franklin was the Pennsylvania member of the committee, and to him was due the suggestion which was made the basis of the report. Since the small states were ready to concede proportional representation in the one house, the situation demanded some makeweight to induce the large states to accept equality in the other. The report therefore repeated the recommendation of proportional representation in the lower house and equality in the upper, but added the condition that all bills for raising or appropriating money should originate in the lower house, and that those for the first purpose should not be amended by the upper. Thus the large states would control the public purse. After another bitter debate the report carried.[1]

Without a settlement of this issue of representation the Convention could not have proceeded. The agreement is therefore rightly regarded as the "Great Compromise." From this moment the cleavage between the large and small states ceased to be dangerous. Other disputes divided the Convention along different lines, but while some of them aroused much feeling, none threatened a break-up. Experience has

[1] The large-state delegations voted against the compromise, and some of their members were at first inclined to abandon the Convention and go home. By subsequent action of the Convention, the Senate was allowed to amend "money bills," thus destroying in part the advantage which the compromise had given to the large states. Two senators were allotted to each state, and allowed to vote as individuals instead of by delegations, thus further vitiating the original compromise.

proved that equality in the Senate has little value for the small states. Senators, as representatives of state governments in the "federal" branch of Congress, have been neither more nor less tenacious of state rights than representatives of the people in the "national branch." In other ways the equality in the Senate has had a very important influence upon the course of history. The Senate became a bulwark of sectional interests during the slavery contest, enabling the South with its minority population to prevent or delay the adoption of antislavery laws.

The agreement upon representation in the lower house according to population raised the question whether slaves should be counted for this purpose. The same question came up in considering the apportionment of direct taxes. The rule of apportionment provided in the Articles had been difficult to apply, and in general population was held to be a sufficiently accurate index of the relative wealth of the states. Southern delegates held, however, that slaves were not the equals of white men as wealth producers, and objected to a full count as an index of tax-paying ability. Since they desired the full count as a basis of representation, while northern men took the reverse position on each of these questions, another compromise was necessary, by which it was agreed that three fifths should be counted in apportioning both representation and direct taxes.

This three-fifths ratio had been proposed several times during the dozen years preceding, as a basis for the requisitions of Congress upon the states, but never before had it been discussed in conection with representation. In later years the North chafed under it because direct taxes were rarely levied and it gave the southern whites an influence in Congress out of proportion to their numbers.

A problem of real difficulty, although it aroused no heat, concerned the choice of the executive. After some debate a single chief executive was agreed to, but the best method of choosing him was a puzzle which long resisted solution. Choice by Congress threatened the independence of the magistrate, especially if his tenure of office was not limited to a single term. Reëligibility, which was likely to be highly desirable in some cases, called for some other method of election. A choice by popular vote seemed utterly impracticable, both because the people were regarded as incapable of making a wise selection, and because of the lack of a means of preventing a scattered vote. When the device of an electoral college was hit upon, it was acclaimed as one of the triumphs of the Convention.[1]

One of the primary motives impelling the states to union was the desire that the strength of all might be available for the defense of each in case of foreign attack or internal disorders. Shays' Rebellion had shown the inability of Congress to aid a state in case of insurrection. One of the Randolph resolutions looked toward a remedy for this defect, and a section was placed in the Constitution obliging the United States to protect each state against invasion, and, upon request, against domestic violence.

A great many provisions of the Constitution deal with mere matters of detail. The Convention soon discovered that its time would be fully occupied in debating and deciding major issues, and that details would have to be left to a committee. Near the end of July the results of the discussions up to that time were referred to a Committee of Detail. These results were still in the form of resolutions stating prin-

[1] Madison, Wilson, G. Morris, and others favored popular election of the President, the first two from democratic principles. Morris thought the people would never fail to prefer some man of distinguished character and national reputation, while if Congress made the choice, he feared it would be the work of intrigue, cabal, and faction. An executive chosen by Congress and impeachable by it he held would be a mere creature of the legislative branch.

ciples, and the task of the committee was to embody them into a preliminary draft of the Constitution.

Much of the committee's work was almost mechanical. That is to say, the Convention having decided upon a government for the United States, it was left to the committee to clothe that government with familiar attributes. From the state constitutions were borrowed the provisions relating to legislative procedure, privileges of members, and powers and functions of the executive. Substantially all of these can be traced back to the practice of the colonial governments, and most of them to earlier English usage. They were the time-hallowed accessories of governments of peoples of English blood.

The committee also transcribed from the Articles the powers of the old Congress, and added those new powers, notably of taxation, coercion, and commercial control, which discussion had so clearly indicated as necessary. Finally it arranged all this matter logically in the form of a Constitution, divided into articles and sections. Its report was made on August 6 and became the basis of the Convention's debates during the last weeks of its sitting.

It was during this final period that the commerce compromise was made, the method of choosing the President determined, and control of patents, copyrights, and bankruptcies added to the enumerated powers.

Despite all care the completed Constitution had some unfortunate omissions. Territorial expansion should have been provided for. Proposals to give Congress power to build roads and canals and to grant charters to corporations were voted down. An express power to regulate all industry of more than local scope would have been of the utmost importance a century later, but the framers could not foresee the vast industrial expansion of the future, and the small-scale enterprises of 1787 seemed to fall within the police power of the states. To meet unforeseen conditions the Constitution contained provisions for amendments. The chief method required the affirmative vote of two thirds of the members of both houses of Congress and the approval of the legislatures of three fourths of the states.

The duality of the new system of government implied a duality of citizenship. In the Convention men began to speak of Americans as citizens of their states and also of the United States. A definition of citizenship in the Constitution would have prevented much confusion in after years, but it was not until after the Civil War that one found its way into the organic law through the Fourteenth Amendment.

The Convention, in assigning powers to the new government, proceeded upon the theory that all powers not delegated to that government were reserved to the states. Nevertheless it seems to have been tacitly understood that there were powers which inhered in all governments, even if not specifically enumerated. An example of such a power, later assumed to belong to the Federal Government (as well as to the state governments) although not mentioned in the Constitution, is that of eminent domain. The impossibility of dealing specifically and without ambiguity with every such question made it certain that the interpretation of the Constitution would become more and more a matter of dispute as the years passed.

As would be expected from the personnel of the Convention, the system of government which was worked out for the United States was not more democratic than the contemporary state systems. The rejection of the idea of popular election of the President is but one illustration. Many utterances show that the Senate was designed to be, not only the federal element in the government, representing the states as such, but the conservative element representing the wealthy class.

Choice of senators by state legislatures was fixed upon for both of these reasons. A large majority of the Convention favored property qualifications for federal office, and attempts were made to decide what they should be. They are not found in the Constitution only because it was deemed best to leave them to be determined by Congress.

Even the so-called "popular" branch of Congress was not a democratic body, for it rested on the voting class and not on the masses. The suffrage clause of the Constitution reads: "The House of Representatives shall be composed of members chosen every second year by the People of the several states, and electors [voters for members of this house] in each state shall have the qualifications requisite for electors of the most numerous Branch of the State Legislature." This provision reached no lower into the social strata than the laws of the states, but it automatically democratized the House of Representatives as the states extended the suffrage.

The debates of the Convention show the aristocratic leanings of its members in yet another way. In each colony and state the class from which they came had had difficulty with the democratic populations of the frontier regions. The prejudices engendered by protracted struggles to preserve their dominance were carried by some members into the work of the Convention when it began to consider the future of the western settlements. These men disregarded the pledge of equality which Congress had made in 1780, and which it was in the very act of confirming in the Ordinance of 1787. "Property was the main object of Society," said Gouverneur Morris. "He thought the rule of representation ought to be so fixed as to secure to the Atlantic States a prevalence in the National Councils." He referred to the method by which the eastern part of his state had retained political control and urged its adoption on a national scale. Gerry moved that the representation of the new states should never exceed that of the old, and the group holding this view was strong enough to poll the votes of four delegations against five.

The report of the Committee of Detail provided for the admission of new states on terms of equality, but the conservatives were able to secure the adoption as a substitute of the colorless phrase "New States may be admitted by the Congress into this Union." The meaning of the provision was left undetermined, to become the occasion of a dangerous sectional controversy a generation later when Missouri applied for admission.

Madison, Mason, and Wilson advocated equal rights for new states. Wilson's penetrating mind shows to peculiar advantage in this discussion of the rights of the West. "The majority of the people wherever found," he urged, "ought, in all questions, to govern the minority. If the interior country should acquire this majority, it will not only have the right, but will avail itself of it, whether we will or no. This jealousy misled the policy of Great Britain with regard to America. . . . Like consequences will result on the part of the interior settlements, if like jealousy and policy be ours. . . . He could not agree that property was the sole or primary object of government and society. The cultivation and improvement of the human mind was the most noble object." Wilson was a prophet at once of nationalism and democracy.

In so far as the Convention was influenced by the writings of theorists Montesquieu was their guide. American practice had always conformed closely, however, to his theory that legislative, executive, and judicial functions should be vested in independent and coördinate branches of government, each balancing the others and possessing a check upon their powers for its defense against encroachments. The Constitution gave Congress power to impeach the executive officers and judges, and gave the President a veto upon the acts of Congress. The Senate checked the executive in making treaties and appointments, and the two houses acted as mutual checks. No power was expressly given to the judiciary to check the legislative branch, but remarks in the course of debate show that many members thought of the power to judge of the constitutionality of acts of legislation as inherent in courts under a written constitution, and as in accordance with the theory of checks and balances.

The theory that all powers not delegated to the Federal Government remained in the states or in the people was not set forth in any express clause in the Constitution, as the majority of delegates deemed it superfluous; but among the first amendments was one (the tenth) supplying the omission.

On September 17, 1787, an engrossed copy of the completed Constitution was read in the Convention and signed by nearly all of the delegates who were present. A few who had become dissatisfied did not remain for this event. According to the call of Congress, the Constitution, if approved by that body, would go to the state legislatures as an "amendment" to the Articles. The Convention, however, resolved upon a course that was really revolutionary. It proposed that ratification be by conventions of delegates in each state, chosen for the purpose by the voters, and that when the conventions of nine states had acted favorably, the Constitution should be binding upon those states. After some hesitation Congress submitted it to the states to be thus dealt with.

THE RATIFICATION OF THE CONSTITUTION

The opponents of the Constitution were at a disadvantage in the state contests. The secrecy with which the Philadelphia Convention had done its work kept them in ignorance of the new proposals until the moment of adjournment. In several states the conventions were called so promptly that the opposition had little time to study the Constitution and organize its forces. Moreover, the strength of the opposition was in the rural and interior parts, where the inhabitants were scattered and the diffusion of information slower than in the older, more compact communities. From Philadelphia southward, too, the rules of apportionment gave these back regions inadequate representation in the conventions, which followed the rules of the legislatures in this respect.

The friends of the Constitution were led by men who had attended the Philadelphia Convention and had come home knowing just what they wanted. Desiring to avoid the prejudice against nationalism by emphasizing the "federal" features of the new plan, they appropriated the name of "Federalists," which the opposition had first used, forcing it to accept the designation of "Antifederalists."

The Constitution being the program of the old dominant class, the question of ratification produced for the first time a nationwide division along lines of cleavage which had hitherto been only local. On the Federalist side were to be found the merchants, planters, lawyers, and speculators of the seaboard, while the Antifederalists included roughly the settlers of the isolated parts of New England, the people of interior Massachusetts who had sympathized with Shays, the Scotch-Irish and German pioneers of Pennsylvania, and the inhabitants of the Piedmont of Virginia, of the Carolina back country, and of Tennessee and Kentucky.[1]

Delaware was the first state to ratify (December 7). The second state to act—the first of the large states—was Pennsylvania. The Federalist leaders of this state deliberately hastened action in order to forestall opposition. The motion

[1] It must be remembered, in order to understand this sectional cleavage between East and West, that the wage-earning classes of the seaboard neighborhoods were for the most part unenfranchised politically. If their views had been considered, most of them would probably have acted with the Antifederalists.

for calling a convention was made in the assembly before official notification of the action of Congress was received. Only a month was allowed for the election of delegates, and six weeks before the date of meeting.

In the convention the Federalists, led by James Wilson, outnumbered the Antifederalists two to one, but came almost wholly from Philadelphia and the eastern counties. The delegates of the back-country farmers feared that the strengthening of the central government would cripple the states. They objected especially to the taxing power, and to the Senate as the stronghold of the moneyed interest. Perhaps because the outcome was not in doubt, Wilson met their arguments by advocating nationalism with a frankness which Federalists in more uncertain states hardly dared to emulate. The final vote was 46 to 23 for adoption.

By the middle of January, 1788, three other small states (New Jersey, Connecticut, and Georgia) had followed the example of Delaware, bringing the total to five. In none of these had the Antifederalists shown much strength, but now came a hard-fought contest in Massachusetts. In that state probably a majority of the delegates at first opposed ratification. As in Pennsylvania the rural classes disliked the reduction of the powers of the state which would lessen their freedom in what they considered their own affairs, such as the issue of legal-tender paper. The Federalists, led by the ex-members of the Philadelphia Convention (with the exception of Gerry, who took his stand with the Antifederalists), won their battle by clever tactics rather than argument. It was apparent that the delegates of the plain people would be greatly influenced by the course of the two popular men, John Hancock and Samuel Adams, who were undecided. The Federalists set out to win these men. In Hancock's case they succeeded by making him president of the convention and hinting at support for federal office later. Adams, not so eas-

ily flattered, was much impressed by the declaration of the
Boston craftsmen in favor of ratification. He and some others were inclined to advocate ratification only on condition
that amendments be made to the Constitution, but they were
finally persuaded to vote for unconditional ratification with
recommended amendments, which the Federalists promised
to support. The Massachusetts vote stood 187 to 168.

Massachusetts ratified early in February. Next came Maryland and South Carolina. Maryland was one state in which
an ex-member of the Philadelphia gathering led the opposition. Luther Martin left the Convention before it adjourned, exclaiming "I'll be hanged if ever the people of
Maryland agree to it!" On reaching home he published an
essay entitled *Genuine Information,* in which he gave his
reasons for disliking the Constitution. In spite of him the
Federalists in the state convention cast 63 votes to 11. In
South Carolina the seaboard, favored by the plan of apportionment and satisfied by the compromise on the slave trade,
outvoted the delegates from the Piedmont districts two to
one.

The ratification of New Hampshire in June was the ninth,
and gave that state the honor of putting the new instrument
of government into effect. Neither New York nor Virginia
had as yet acted. In these the lapse of time had permitted
the Antifederalists to perfect their organization and it was
doubtful what stand they would take.

In New York the opposition did not as in other states
center in a rural democracy, but in the great landowners of
the Hudson Valley, who did not wish the state to lose the
revenue from import duties which the Constitution would
take away. The rivalry of the landlords and mercantile
classes was of long standing, and the former controlled the
convention. Any advantage which the Antifederalists had
gained by the tardy meeting was offset, however, by the fact

that before the vote was reached the neighboring states had adopted the Constitution. The geographical position of New York, in the keystone of the arch formed by the Atlantic coast, made it impracticable for her to hold out against the decision of her neighbors. Hamilton and Jay helped to bring about a favorable decision by promising to join in requesting amendments after ratification. After all, the final vote was exceedingly close, the Federalists winning by a margin of three.

John Marshall, later to become chief justice, and Madison led the friends of the new plan in Virginia, ably opposed by Mason and Henry.[1] In the main the contest followed the now familiar lines. Madison and Marshall answered the zealous defenders of state autonomy by explaining that the states would retain all powers required for local functions (the "internal police" powers), while the Union would receive only those needed to protect the interests common to all the states. The promise of the Federalists, and of Madison in particular, to work for amendments, won some votes, and the final majority for the Constitution numbered ten.

It will be noted that the question of amendments played an important part in several of the states. The Antifederalists were generally disposed to withhold assent to the Constitution unless stipulated changes were made. But there was no interstate agreement among them as to what changes should be demanded. Even so they wrung from the Federalists the promises to support amendments in return for unconditional ratification. It may here be added that the first Congress redeemed these promises, although not to the entire satisfaction of the Antifederalists, by recommending to the states a number of amendments of which ten were accepted. Many of the objections of the Antifederalists seem trivial and even

[1] Washington was not a member of the Virginia convention, but used his influence, especially through correspondence, to promote ratification.

foolish in the perspective of history, and betray a lack of comprehension of the nature of the proposed dual government. Others, however, were well taken. The conservative ruling class had embodied its desires in the Constitution as turned out by the Convention. In the demand for amendments the Antifederalists voiced more nearly the will of the people at large, and the acceptance of their demands was in a sense the price paid by the Federalists to obtain the favor of the populace. The Constitution plus the ten amendments reconciled the contending factions, and both soon joined in enthusiastic loyalty to the new "charter of government," although differences of interpretation promptly appeared.

The first ten amendments constituted in effect a bill of rights, guaranteeing religious liberty, trial by jury, freedom of speech and of the press, etc., against the interference of the Federal Government. They abundantly proved their value in subsequent history. The tenth is an explicit statement of the principle of delegated powers: it became the corner stone of the doctrine of strict construction.

While the Constitution was before the states Jefferson, writing from Paris, wished "that the nine first conventions may accept the new Constitution . . . but . . . that the four latest . . . may refuse to accede to it till a declaration of rights be annexed." One state convention, that of North Carolina, actually did adjourn, hoping to force the adoption of amendments. When the first Congress took up the subject, the convention met again and ratified. Rhode Island, the one state which sent no delegates to Philadelphia, was also the only one which refused to act on the Constitution. Congress really forced her to yield at last (1790) by threatening a suspension of commercial intercourse.

Beginning in October, 1787, Madison, Hamilton, and Jay joined in preparing for newspaper publication a series of explanatory essays on the Constitution since known as *The Federalist*. They are still a valuable commentary, but it must be remembered that they were intended to allay the apprehensions of those who feared nationalism. One must expect exaggeration also in the arguments on the other side, such as Martin's *Genuine Information,* but we actually find in their recognition of the Constitution as the instrument of a national government the nearer approach to the view of our own day.

Looking back after more than a century and a quarter, the student is likely to conclude that the adoption of the instrument framed by the Philadelphia Convention put an end to the sovereignty of the individual states. Some of the framers talked, indeed, of "divided sovereignty," of the relinquishment by the states of a part of their sovereignty to the general government. What was done is more accurately described by the phrase already used: governmental *powers* had been "distributed."

Under the Constitution with its scheme of distributed powers there was no real basis for the conception of the Union as a league, formed by a contract of member states, and resting merely upon the obligations of good faith. Allegiance and obedience to the government of the United States as the supreme authority became due from every person subject to its jurisdiction, enforceable by the courts, and in case of necessity by armies and navies. The withdrawal of a state from the Union became likewise impossible (if the United States enforced its authority over its citizens within the seceding state), save as the result of successful revolution.

If the Constitution meant these things, however, hosts of people in all sections failed to grasp its true character. It became the instrument of a national government in days when the people at large were not yet conscious of national unity. Two generations were required for the national concept to master the minds even of the leading men in the majority section, while the South clung to the state sovereignty tradition until civil war and a policy of "blood and iron" destroyed it. But we must again recall that the Constitution was the work of representatives not of the masses, but of a comparatively small upper class. Nationalism was as far beyond the ken of the people in 1787 as democracy was foreign to the purpose of the dominant group.

SELECT BIBLIOGRAPHY

Steps Leading to the Convention; The Constitutional Convention. Recently published are two general histories of the Constitution: McLaughlin, *Constitutional History of the United States,* and a work by Hockett bearing the same title. Bancroft, *History of the Constitution* (included in his *History of the United States,* last revision, and also published separately), was for a long time the standard history of the Convention. It contains much matter which is still valuable, but its point of view is antiquated. Fiske, *Critical Period,* is also somewhat out of date in its treatment of the work of the Convention. McLaughlin, *Confederation and Constitution,* is excellent. Farrand, *The Framing of the Constitution,* is a recent summary by a scholarly specialist on this topic. *The Fathers of the Constitution* is by the same authority. Schuyler, *The Constitution of the United States,* is a still more recent summary. Warren, *Making of the Constitution,* tells its story largely by extracts from contemporary writings; a day-by-day account of the Convention. Beard, *An Economic Interpretation of the Constitution,* presents in brilliant array an abundance of evidence from a single point of view. For an excellent summary from a similar point of view, see Schlesinger, *New Viewpoints,* Chap. VIII.

Ratification of the Constitution. Fiske, McLaughlin, and Hockett give good brief accounts. See also Schuyler, and the general histories of McMaster and Schouler. The detailed history of ratification is still scattered in monographs dealing with particular states, and in many biographies, of which, as an example,

may be mentioned Spaulding, *His Excellency, George Clinton.*
A readable, popular book is Hendrick, *Bulwark of the Constitu-*
tion, which tells its story biographically.   The best life of Madison
is Hunt, *Life of James Madison.*   Smith, *James Madison,* is distinguished for compressed statement and for understanding.

Chapter XIV

THE ESTABLISHMENT OF THE NATIONAL GOVERNMENT

ORGANIZATION OF THE GOVERNMENT

WHEN formal notice reached Congress that the ninth state had ratified the Constitution, it took steps to prepare for the new régime. The first Wednesday in January, 1789, was fixed as the time for choosing presidential electors, and the first Wednesday in February as the day for casting their ballots. The first Wednesday in March was set for the meeting of Congress, with New York as the place.

The Antifederalists made efforts in some states to elect members of Congress. In Virginia they controlled the legislature and chose both senators. The great majority of the members of the first Congress, however, were Federalists, so that the new government was in the hands of its friends.

It was April before a quorum of members arrived in New York and the houses organized. The Constitution empowered the House of Representatives to choose its own presiding officer, or "Speaker," but assigned the duty of presiding over the Senate to the Vice-President. To act until the result of the electoral vote should be known the Senate chose a president *pro tempore*. The rules of procedure in both houses were adapted in the first place from the practices of the state legislatures and the Confederation Congress.

As soon as the work of internal organization had been done the houses turned to the business of counting the electoral vote. The constitutional provision for the choice of the President gave each state a number of electors equal to the sum of its representatives and senators, to be chosen as its legislature might prescribe. Several methods were used in the first election: three states used the general ticket; in five the legislatures made the choice; the rest divided the state into districts and allowed the voters in each to choose one elector. The first of these methods eventually became universal, but for many years the second was generally used.[1]

The electors met in their own states on the day appointed and each voted for two persons, one at least a non-resident of the state. The Constitution did not provide for any indication of preference for the presidency. From each state a certified list of the votes was to be sent to the president of the Senate, who was to open them in the presence of both houses. If a majority of the electors had voted for the same man he was to be the President. In case of a tie, or of no person having a majority, the House of Representatives was to make the choice, each delegation voting as a unit to preserve the equal influence of the small states as under the Confederation. If no person had a majority, the names of the five leading candidates were to come before the House. After the President was chosen the candidate having the next largest electoral vote was to become Vice-President. In case of a tie vote for the second place, the choice devolved upon the Senate.

This cumbrous machinery, which gave the Convention so much satisfaction, was expected to serve as a kind of nominating device. It was not expected that electors would often coincide in their judgment sufficiently to cast a majority for one man, hence the choice was expected to come to the House rather regularly. The framers of the Constitution failed to foresee the effect which the rise of political parties would have upon this system. The provision worked so badly that

[1] New York lost its vote in 1789 through a disagreement in the legislature as to the best method of choosing electors.

it was modified by one of the early amendments (the twelfth).

In the first election, however, no difficulty was encountered, for Washington's name was found upon the ballot of every elector. Their second votes were scattered among several men, but John Adams had more than any other candidate, although less than half of the total number.

Messengers were dispatched to notify Washington and Adams of their election, and to invite them to New York to take office. Washington, enjoying the life of a country gentleman at Mt. Vernon, and weary of public duties, was extremely reluctant to abandon his plantation. Nevertheless he set out for New York, greeted everywhere by the plaudits of the people, who made of his journey a veritable triumphal procession; and upon arrival took up his abode in a house so small—sad contrast with the spacious mansion on the Potomac—that three of his secretaries had to share one room. On April 30 he was inaugurated with great ceremony. Adams took his seat as president of the Senate, and the government was ready for work.

New York, now a bustling town of some thirty thousand people, ambitious to retain the government in its midst, presented to Congress a hall designed by the Frenchman, Charles l'Enfant, which was said to excel in architectural beauty any public building so far erected in the United States. In this "Federal Hall" Congress held its sessions until the government was removed to Philadelphia, in 1791.

The work of the first Congress was second in importance only to that of the Constitutional Convention. The Constitution, after all, was but a framework or skeleton which awaited the action of Congress to give it life. Its provisions were not self-executing, but needed legislation to put them into effect. The decisions involved were momentous, for they set precedents of almost constitutional force.

The Constitution referred only incidentally to "Executive

Departments" and "Heads of Departments." It rested with Congress to decide what offices were needed, to create them by law, and to define the duties of the officials. During the summer and early fall Congress passed bills creating three departments. First came the Department of Foreign Affairs (unfortunately renamed the Department of State). Then came the Department of War, followed by the Department of the Treasury. The head of each Department was to be a "secretary." In addition the offices of Attorney-General and Postmaster-General were established.

Under the Articles all civil officers had been appointed by Congress and were responsible to it. By the Constitution the power of appointment was vested in the President "by and with the advice and consent of the Senate." Washington offered the post of Secretary of State to John Jay, the associate of Franklin and Adams in the diplomacy of the Revolution, and Secretary of Foreign Affairs during the Confederation. The choice was a fitting one, since Franklin had passed the age for active service and Adams was Vice-President. When Jay declined, Washington turned to Jefferson, our representative in France. For the War Department he chose Henry Knox, of Massachusetts. This was a virtual continuation in office, since Knox held the corresponding post under the Confederation. Hamilton became Secretary of the Treasury and Edmund Randolph, Attorney-General.

Although the Constitution authorized the President to require the written opinions of heads of departments upon subjects relating to their respective offices, it said nothing about a cabinet. In making appointments and treaties the Senate was designed to be an advisory council. Washington's attempt to consult the Senate on an Indian treaty proved embarrassing, however, both to himself and to the members of that body. "A shamefacedness, or I know not what, flowing from the presence of the President, kept everybody silent," wrote Senator William Maclay, of Pennsylvania, in his diary. After the one effort the President adopted the practice of submitting business requiring the Senate's advice and consent in a written message, leaving it to deliberate at its convenience.

The failure of the upper house to function as an advisory body led Washington to create his own by calling upon the three secretaries and the Attorney-General for their opinions when matters of importance were to be decided. In this and other ways the first President, like the first Congress, created precedents which have become to all intents and purposes parts of our constitutional system.

While the Constitution expressly vested the appointing power in the chief executive and Senate, it was not clear on the matter of removals. Some congressmen thought that the power of removal was incidental to that of appointment, and belonged to the President with the Senate's consent. The view prevailed that administrative officers, from heads of departments down, were subordinates of the chief executive, and that the power of removal inhered in his office. Another precedent was set by this decision, but it did not escape challenge in later times when President and Congress were at odds.

The fundamental law vested the judicial power of the United States in "one supreme court" and such inferior courts as Congress might deem necessary. It also specified the cases in which the jurisdiction of the Supreme Court should be original. Here again much discretion was left to Congress, and the framing of the Judiciary Act of 1789 was an important part of its work of organizing the government. One group of congressmen disliked the idea of creating inferior federal courts, preferring to utilize the courts of the states in federal cases, with provision for appeals to the Supreme Court. They were outvoted by those who desired a complete federal system.

The Act provided for thirteen district courts, roughly one for each state, grouped in three circuits. For each district there was to be a judge. Appeals from a district court went to the circuit court. A session of this intermediate tribunal was to be held in turn in each district of the circuit, by the judge of the district and two Supreme Court justices. The Act fixed upon six justices for the Supreme Court, one to be chief and the others associates. As few cases were expected to reach the highest tribunal, it was not thought to be unfair to require the justices to make the round of the circuits periodically, a pair going to each annually.

An important paragraph stipulated that whenever a case before a state court involved federal law an appeal should lie to the federal courts unless the decision upheld the federal law. This clause gave great offense to the friends of states' rights.

Washington found at the very beginning of his term that he must protect his work from interruption by visitors. "I had no leisure to read or answer the dispatches that were pouring in upon me from all quarters," he declared. Desiring "to demean himself . . . in such a manner as to maintain the dignity of his office, without subjecting himself to the imputation of superciliousness or unnecessary reserve," he sought the advice of several men, among them Madison, Hamilton, and Adams, as to the official etiquette which would be suitable. Adams, whose head was somewhat turned by the popular acclaim over the new government, advised "splendor and majesty" to support "dignity and authority." Hamilton thought there was danger of "too much ceremony for the character of our government," and favored a simple manner to avoid exciting "dissatisfaction and cabal" in a country where "notions of equality are . . . general and strong."

Although Adams and a group of senators failed in the effort to decorate the executive with some such pompous title as "His Majesty," or "His Highness, the President of the United States of America, and Protector of their Liberties" (the Constitution itself gave the chief executive the simple title of "President of the United States"), the President did adopt enough of the grand style to draw the fire of criticism. When he rode with Mrs. Washington, he was attended by outriders in livery and the carriage was drawn by four or six horses with gay trappings and hoofs blackened and polished. Every Tuesday while Congress was in session he held a formal reception known as a levee, from three to four o'clock. At these he always appeared in black velvet knee breeches, yellow gloves, and cocked hat, wearing a dress sword in a scabbard of white polished leather. On Friday evenings Mrs. Washington held her "drawing-rooms," at which Washington desired to be regarded not as the President but as a private gentleman. From time to time the President invited diplomats, government officers, and members of Congress to formal dinners, but he and "Lady Washington" did not accept hospitalities.

FINANCIAL LEGISLATION

Even before it created the departments Congress passed a revenue law. Indeed, next to its own organization and the counting of the electoral vote, its earliest act was an exercise of the new power of taxation. Madison, kept out of the Senate by the Antifederalists in the legislature of his state, had turned to his neighbors as a candidate for the lower house, and it was he who moved the enactment of a five per cent duty on the value of all imports.

A Pennsylvania member asked that the duties be laid, not uniformly on all imported goods, but upon such as competed with domestic industry. At the same time that the necessary revenue was obtained, American production would then enjoy an advantage over foreign. The protective principle was thus introduced into tariff legislation at the very outset, although it was incidental to the purpose of raising a revenue. It was not until domestic manufactures developed on a considerable scale that protection became the dominant motive in framing tariffs.

The first tariff debate was typical of all that have followed in bringing out the conflict of interest of different sections of the country. Georgia, for example, which needed slaves, objected to any tax upon imported Negroes; Virginia, with slaves to sell, desired a duty. New England opposed an impost on molasses, the raw material of the rum distilleries of Rhode Island and Massachusetts, while other sections desired the revenue which it would yield.

The act as passed laid duties averaging about eight per cent. This first financial measure was framed hastily under pressure of urgent need, with little calculation of the relation of the probable returns to government expenditures. The more careful consideration of needs and policies was allowed to wait until the Treasury Department was instituted and Hamilton appointed Secretary. Meantime the public creditors became clamorous for appropriations to pay interest, at least, on the debt, and soon after Hamilton took office the House resolved that the Secretary of the Treasury should prepare a plan for the support of the public credit, to be reported to the next session. Accordingly Hamilton presented in January, 1790, the first of a series of reports in which was set forth his financial system.

This First Report on Public Credit dealt with the debt both of Congress and the states. The foreign debt amounted to nearly $12,000,000, the domestic debt was about $42,500,000 more, and the state obligations aggregated about $21,500,000. Hamilton proposed that the Federal Government should assume the state debts, and that the whole should be funded.   The essence of his plan of funding was that Congress should authorize the Treasury to accept the old securities at par in payment for new bonds.   The power of taxing made possible provision for punctual payment of interest on the new bonds and for their redemption at maturity.

Most of the securities issued by the Second Continental Congress had by this time passed into the hands of speculators who had paid much less than face value for them.   A vigorous fight was made in Congress against funding because payment of the securities at par would enrich these speculators. Madison proposed that they be paid the market value only, and that the difference be given to the original owners.   The plan was impracticable.

This disagreement marks the beginning of a breach between Hamilton and Madison which foreshadowed the rise of parties.   Hamilton's contention that the government was pledged to pay the debt to the legal holders, and that it could not establish its credit by beginning its career with an act of bad faith, was really unanswerable, and his recommendation prevailed.   The funding act established the credit of the government at one stroke.   In the rhetoric of Daniel Webster, Hamilton "smote the rock of national resources and copious streams of wealth burst forth."

Madison was also a leader of the group which tried to defeat the assumption of the state debts.   Hamilton urged that these debts had been incurred in the common struggle, and were a just charge on the common treasury.   He offered no adjustment in the case of states which had paid a portion of their debts, and he aimed by the scheme to win support for the central government.   There could be no better guarantee of its permanence, he thought, than to have a large number of men of wealth and intelligence looking to it as the source of income on their investments.   Such a device had steadied the throne of William and Mary after the Revolution of 1688.

A policy which tended to build up a moneyed interest was certain to encounter strenuous resistance. Comparatively few southern men had capital for speculative investments in government securities, and their representatives in Congress blocked the assumption project for a time. The contest followed sectional lines; but another issue between North and South which was pending at the same time made a bargain possible, an early instance of "log-rolling." Congress was discussing the permanent location of the national capital, northern men preferring a site on the Susquehanna or Delaware, southerners insisting on the Potomac. The arrival of the North Carolina delegation threw a new weight into the scales, and Hamilton made clever use of it. At his suggestion Jefferson, who had just returned from France to take his post in the State Department, invited a few influential politicians to a dinner party where southern votes for assumption were pledged in return for Hamilton's promise of northern votes to fix the capital on the Potomac. Jefferson later repented bitterly of his share in this transaction, claiming that he was duped by Hamilton before he got his bearings after his return from abroad.

In December, 1790, the Secretary of the Treasury submitted two more reports. One of these proposed a Bank of the United States, to be privately owned and managed subject to conditions prescribed by a charter of incorporation to be enacted by Congress. The capital stock was not to exceed $10,000,000; and the notes of the bank, backed by specie and government bonds, were to be receivable for all payments to the United States. The charter was to run for twenty years, and during that term no competing institution was to be sanctioned by Congress. The immediate interest of the government was limited to the privilege of subscribing one fifth of the capital stock, but for the protection of the public the Secretary of the Treasury was entitled on demand to statements showing the bank's condition.

Hamilton's purpose in making this recommendation was, in the first place, to provide a sound currency. The paper issues of previous years were disappearing, and the Constitution forbade further issues by the states. Owing to the scarcity of specie, however, the state governments were under strong temptation to charter banks without requiring that their paper be properly backed by reserves of gold and silver. The multiplication of unregulated banks might lead once more to floods of depreciated notes unless steps were taken to prevent. The establishment of a great central bank, pledged to the redemption of its notes on demand, would be such a step, for by supplying the channels of business with a sound circulating medium it would dominate the situation and make it useless for unsound institutions to put out their paper.

Hamilton held that such a bank "would be of the greatest utility in the operations connected with the support of the public credit," and mentioned particularly the aid which it could give the government in obtaining loans and facilitating the collection of taxes.

There were many friends of state banks who disliked the idea of a central bank with a monopoly of valuable privileges. Such an institution would give another opportunity of investment to the moneyed class and tend to create what would today be called a "money trust." Again Madison was the leader of the congressional forces of opposition, and in his speech against the bill he stressed most of all the argument that the Constitution gave Congress no power to grant a charter of incorporation.

When the bill was passed the fight was carried to the President. Washington called for the written opinions of his cabinet. Jefferson and Randolph submitted arguments against the act and Hamilton and Knox upheld it. Much to Jefferson's chagrin, Hamilton's opinion was a reply to his own, which had been submitted to the Secretary of the Treasury because the measure was financial. Thus Hamilton had the opportunity to make the final argument by way, so to speak, of rebuttal. Convinced by his reasoning Washington signed the bill.

In a final report made a year later (December, 1791), Hamilton dealt with the subject of manufactures. This document gives a view of the status of American manufactures at that time, and advocates the policy of a protective tariff for the purpose of promoting those especially which would "tend to render the United States independent [sic] on foreign nations, for military and other essential supplies." In his views on this matter Hamilton anticipated the arguments of Clay and Calhoun nearly a generation later. But the prevailing sentiment accorded with the laissez faire philosophy of the English economist Adam Smith, and the protectionist plea bore little fruit for many years.

In January, 1790, Hamilton had suggested an excise on distilled liquors as a source of additional revenue. When the assumption of the state debts required further taxation Hamilton recurred to the excise in a report which accompanied the one on the bank. He recommended also an increase in the duty on imported spirits, but thought the time inopportune for a general upward revision of duties. All of Hamilton's financial plans were tinged with political motives. In this proposal of an excise he seems to have had in mind the importance of making the power of the new government felt by the farmers of the western frontier. Along the border from Pennsylvania southward the making of whisky had become the rival of the New England rum industry. Separated from the coast markets by the mountains, the transportation of grain was out of the question, and the farmers would have found grain raising profitless if they could not have converted their crop into the portable and comparatively valuable form of whisky.

The same conditions that kept the crops of the western farmers out of the coast towns kept imported goods from reaching them, so that they were hardly touched by the tariff. The excise reached them only and seemed to single them out as subjects for special taxation. Their sturdy individualism was affronted; the excise was a form of tax which they had not expected. It reminded them of the internal taxes with which England had goaded the colonists to revolution, and Congress passed the bill in the face of predictions of trouble which were soon borne out by events.

The resentment which the western border felt against the excise took the form of active resistance in southwestern Pennsylvania. Meetings were held in which defiance was urged, and the collectors began to be threatened with personal violence. At length, in 1794, when warrants were issued for the arrest of some of the agitators who were destroying the property of persons who complied with the law, actual bloodshed occurred, and the malcontents began to gather under arms.

The federal authority was directly challenged by these proceedings. Jefferson, writing to Madison, denounced the law as "an infernal one," which would become "the instrument of dismembering the Union"; while Washington, spurred on by Hamilton, decided that the time had come to call out the militia to suppress the insurrection and enforce the laws of the Union. From Pennsylvania, Virginia, and Maryland he summoned fifteen thousand men who marched towards the scene of the disturbances. Meantime commissioners sent ahead were attempting to persuade the insurgents to disband. When the troops arrived no armed opponents were to be found. Some of the leaders were arrested and two were convicted of treason, but having vindicated the national authority Washington showed clemency and pardoned them.

The incident had both good and bad results. The demonstration of the government's ability to meet rebellion with overwhelming force was complete, and a new tone of respect was noted at once in men's references to the federal power. But the resort to military force did not win friends for the administration among the people, and, as with Hamilton's other policies, the political advantages of the incident accrued to the opposition.

FEDERALISTS AND REPUBLICANS

One important consequence of the discussion of Hamilton's financial plans was the rise of political parties. Those who followed him, being the administration party, retained the Federalist name. Madison was for a short time administration leader in the House of Representatives, but finding himself not in agreement with Hamilton, he swung into the leadership of the opposing group, which presently took the name of "Republicans," although sometimes called "Democrats" by the Federalists. Jefferson, Madison's senior and the patron and mentor of his young manhood, presently superseded him as the chief of the party.

Hamilton was of West Indian birth, his father being a Scotch merchant and his mother a French woman. He had come to New York on the eve of the Revolution as a student in King's College, but the stirring events of the hour had drawn him into public life. His brilliant ability quickly attracted attention, and his marriage to Elizabeth Schuyler introduced him into influential social and political circles. His rise was meteoric, and when called to the Treasury Department at the age of thirty-two, he was already a noted figure. In spite of small stature and slight build, his erect and digni-

fied carriage and mental force compelled respect in all with
whom he came in contact. For sheer intellectuality it is
doubtful if he has been excelled by any American statesman,
but in practical politics he lacked tact and persuasiveness
and was somewhat domineering in manner. He had set forth
his political philosophy in a speech in the Constitutional
Convention, in which he said: "All communities divide themselves into the few and the many. The first are the rich and
well born, the other the mass of the people. . . . The people
are turbulent and changing; they seldom judge or determine
right. . . . The British Government was the best in the
world."

As Secretary of the Treasury Hamilton was the constructive
genius of the administration. He built his hope of successful government upon the active interest of financiers, merchants, and speculators. They were the rich and well born
who would check the unsteadiness of the masses. Under such
a guide the Federalist party naturally attracted these elements, which were nearly identical with the old ruling class,
especially in the North.

Hamilton and his followers derived their creed from the
dominant English aristocracy. Jefferson represented the
spirit of the New World, begotten of frontier conditions.
He himself was born near the Virginia foot-hills, his father
being one of the early settlers in the Piedmont, and his philosophy of government was permanently influenced by his
boyhood environment. It harmonized with the philosophy
of Locke, which he himself had incorporated into the Declaration of Independence. While in France, moreover, he
had come into contact with the teachings of Rousseau, which
emphasized the happiness of the supposed state of nature
and stressed the natural equality of mankind.

Jefferson believed that a simple agricultural life was the
best basis for a free state, because it bred equality and indi-

viduality. Such was the natural life of America, with its "immensity of land courting the industry of the husbandman." Factories and wage labor he thought tended to destroy self-reliance and produce inequalities and class conflicts. He favored commerce with other nations as the means of exchanging the agricultural surplus for the manufactures of the Old World. Such exchange would "let our workshops remain in Europe." He preferred to let the foreign nations supply the ships, since the growth of an American merchant marine would entail a navy for its defense.

Jefferson did not believe in the possibility of democracy under all conditions. He could not trust the working classes in cities. His hope for the success of democracy in the United States was bound up with the continued preponderance of agriculture, and the wide, if not universal, distribution of land ownership. He would have required a small freehold qualification for the exercise of the franchise, and would then have made it the equivalent of manhood suffrage by granting estates from the public lands to all males.

He did not become a propagandist for these views while a member of Washington's administration, but he condemned policies which seemed to be conceived in the interest of the capitalists. In this he was the champion of the small farmers and the plain people in general, so that the alignment of parties followed in the main the old divisions based on economic and geographical differences. Most of the great southern planters drifted into the Republican party, however, not because they held Jefferson's liberal views, but because Federalist policies were unsatisfactory. As a class they had formed one of the groups which had promoted the movement for the Constitution; but the assumption scheme laid a burden upon them where, as in Virginia, the state debt had been partially paid; and Jay's treaty made them fear that their prerevolutionary debts would have to be paid. All of Hamilton's proposals tending to advance the interests of the owners of capital seeking investment favored the North, for such capital was scarce in the southern states; even the wealthy there were "land poor."

As associates in Washington's cabinet Hamilton and Jefferson were antagonists on practically every important question that came up. Their disagreement over the question of chartering the United States Bank is particularly memorable because it led to rival ways of interpreting the Constitution, and these became one of the chief differences distinguishing Republicans from Federalists.

In the opinion on the bank which Jefferson submitted he began by quoting the Tenth Amendment, which reserves to states or people all powers not delegated to the United States. Then examining the list of enumerated powers he found no mention of the right to incorporate a bank. Coming next to the general welfare clause, he held that Congress is not empowered by it to do just "anything they please" "but only to lay taxes" to provide for the general welfare.[1] The former construction "would render all the preceding and subsequent enumerations of power completely useless. It would reduce the whole instrument to a single phrase." Hence the general welfare clause does not authorize the charter of the bank.

Finally he considered the clause allowing Congress "to make all laws necessary and proper for carrying into execution the enumerated powers." "But," he reasoned, "they can all be carried into execution without a bank. A bank therefore is not necessary, and consequently is not authorized. . . . The Constitution allows only means which are 'necessary,' not those which are merely convenient for effecting the enumerated powers. If such a latitude of construc-

---

[1] "The Congress shall have power to lay and collect Taxes, Duties, Imposts, and Excises, to pay the Debts and provide for the common Defence and general Welfare of the United States."—Art. I, Sec. 8, Par. 1.

tion be allowed to this phrase as to give any non-enumerated
power, it will go to every one. . . . Therefore it was that
the Constitution restrained [Congress] . . . to those means
without which the grant of [an enumerated] power would be
nugatory."

The heart of Hamilton's answer lies in his interpretation
of the "necessary and proper" clause. "It is not denied [by
Jefferson] that there are implied, as well as expressed powers,
and that the former are as effectually delegated as the latter."
Implied powers are those which serve as "an instrument or
mean[s] of carrying into execution any of the specified powers. . . . The only question must be . . . whether the
mean[s] . . . has a natural relation to any of the acknowledged objects or lawful ends of the government. . . . If the
end be clearly comprehended within any of the specified
powers, and if the measure have an obvious relation to that
end, and is not forbidden by any particular provision of the
Constitution, it may safely be deemed to come within the
compass of the national authority." "The powers contained
in a constitution of government . . . ought to be construed
liberally in advancement of the public good. . . . It will
not be contended . . . that the clause in question gives any
new or independent power. But it gives an explicit sanction
to the doctrine of implied powers."

Some scholars regard this doctrine of implied powers as
Hamilton's chief contribution to the permanence of the
Constitution. In practice the difficulty of amendment proved
to be very great, but Hamilton's principles of construction
supplied an element of elasticity which made it possible for
the Constitution, without many formal changes of wording,
to be adapted to the changing needs of a rapidly developing
nation. A rigid framework, incapable of such adaptation,
must soon have been destroyed by the vital forces of the growing organism. The doctrine of implied powers has been,

not the means of destroying the Constitution, as Jefferson feared, but of preserving it. In theory, at least, the process of construction has not changed it, but only brought out what was inherent. The Republicans themselves, when they came to administer the government, had to abandon in large part their principles of strict construction.

Jefferson, knowing Hamilton's admiration for the British government, fell a prey to the fear that he and his "corrupt cohorts" were subtly seeking to undermine the foundations of the Republic to prepare the way for monarchy. To combat the influence of the "monocrats" he gave a clerkship in his department to Philip Freneau, really to enable him to publish an opposition newspaper. The bitterness of this sheet, which did not spare even the President, enraged Washington, who gave Jefferson a strong hint that he disapproved of the dual rôle which Freneau was enabled to play through his patronage. To his diary Jefferson confided his determination to retain Freneau, because he had checked the tendencies of the government which had been "fast galloping into monarchy."

Over his opposite-minded secretaries Washington presided with an even hand, giving added proof of his greatness. Inferior to Hamilton in intellectual power and to Jefferson in understanding of the people, he was the superior of both in judgment and solidity of character. When at the close of the Revolution the unpaid troops were on the point of mutiny, it was he who persuaded them to disband at the command of Congress, trusting to the future for justice. Hamilton was suspected at the time of being one of a group who would have welcomed an armed uprising as a means of teaching the country the necessity of establishing a government worthy of the name. There was danger of turmoil and bloodshed and of a military despotism in such a course, and Washington's essential confidence in the people appears in his insistence that they should have the opportunity to work out the country's political salvation in peace.

Next to nobility of character judgment was the outstanding quality in his statesmanship. For this reason he held a place second to none as early as the First Continental Congress. A rather silent man, he heard others patiently, but his decisions were his own, and they were seldom wrong. Few could have yoked together men so antagonistic in temper and opinion as the two great secretaries and evoked from each his best service. In matters relating to finance his convictions supported Hamilton. In foreign policy he held a middle course, differing from both advisers. In the strict sense he was also above party.

As the end of his first term drew near he desired to retire to private life. Hamilton demurred. The experimental stage of the government was not past, and the strife of parties and sections would endanger its permanence under any less commanding chief. On this point Jefferson and Madison joined their pleas with Hamilton's. The first wrote: "The confidence of the whole Union is centered in you. . . , North and south will hang together, if they have you to hang on." Washington yielded to this advice, and Republicans and Federalists united in giving him a second term (1792). Again the electoral vote was unanimous. But the Republicans refused to support Adams for the Vice-Presidency. For this post they named George Clinton, of New York, and gave him 50 electoral votes, while Adams, with the support only of the Federalists, received 77.

Adams ranks next to Hamilton as a leader of the Federalist party. Of rather humble origin, he was during the Revolution one of the popular leaders in Massachusetts. The equality of mankind, the social compact, and the consent of the governed were dogmas which he held in common with other "fathers of the Revolution." Except in his attitude towards

English policy in America, however, he was not a radical; and while he insisted upon the right of the people to choose their own plan of state government, he hoped they would be "wise enough to follow the English constitution" so far as circumstances permitted. He believed in the restriction of the suffrage to freeholders but wished to promote general ownership of land. In these particulars his views were much like Jefferson's.

As time passed he became distinctly less liberal. In his admiration of British institutions he resembled Hamilton. Like Hamilton also he believed that the rich and well born compose a natural aristocracy, the stable element in society. Holding the poor to be inclined to turbulence, he thought that the control of the propertied class would diffuse the benefits of security throughout the body politic. He would check this control enough to prevent oppression, for he feared the unrestrained influence of the rich more than Hamilton did.

Adams' views were quite in harmony with those of the classes which made up the Federalist party. He was not a skillful politician. He was able, honest, and patriotic, but lacked tact, was rather stubborn and pompous, and took himself too seriously. He had considered himself a presidential candidate in 1789, and was greatly offended when Hamilton became party to an agreement to divert a few votes from him to other persons, so as to insure Washington's election. A coolness between the two men dating from this time was the beginning of a factional division which at length split the Federalist party and contributed to its downfall.

SELECT BIBLIOGRAPHY

Organization of the Government. The twelve years of Federalist rule are most conveniently summarized by Bassett, *The Federalist System*. Volume IV of Channing, *United States,* begins with the constitutional era. Bruce, *Revolution to Reconstruction,* contains character sketches of the Presidents, skilfully portraying both faults and virtues. Hatch, *History of the Vice-Presidency,* shows that the holders of that office have rendered invaluable services.

Financial Legislation. Dewey, *Financial History,* is excellent from the economic standpoint; Lodge, *Alexander Hamilton,* supplies in addition the political data. Hutcheson, *Tench Coxe,* is a study of one of the leading economists of the formative years of the nation. See also general histories of Schouler and McMaster. An excellent account of the disturbances in western Pennsylvania is given in Baldwin, *Whiskey Rebels.*

Federalists and Republicans. Gordy, *Political History of the United States,* is inclusive in subject-matter, but gives special attention to the rise of parties. Ford, *Washington and His Colleagues,* is the work of a specialist in party history. Beard, *Economic Origins of Jeffersonian Democracy,* treats party divisions as the result of divergent economic-group interests. See also Hockett, *Western Influences,* 33–40, and *Constitutional History,* I, 260–267; Lynch, *Fifty Years of Party Warfare;* Munro, *The Makers of the Unwritten Constitution;* and Wiltse, *The Jeffersonian Tradition in American Democracy.*

Lodge, *George Washington,* Morse, *Thomas Jefferson,* Morse, *John Adams,* and Gay, *James Madison,* are helpful biographies. Lodge is somewhat of a hero worshiper. *Cf.* Ford, *The True George Washington,* and Thayer, *George Washington.* See Bibliography for Chapter X.

Chapter XV

THE FEDERALISTS AND
FOREIGN AFFAIRS

WESTERN QUESTIONS

THE dispute between New York and New Hampshire over the Green Mountain district was brought to an end in 1791 and Vermont was admitted to the Union as the fourteenth state. The next year Kentucky and Virginia reached an agreement on terms of separation and the fifteenth state took its place in the sisterhood. By this time both Carolinas had ceded their claims to jurisdiction over the lands west of the Alleghanies, and Congress organized their cessions as the Territory Southwest of the Ohio River, on the model of the Ordinance already adopted for the Northwest Territory, with the exception of the antislavery provision. The growth of population was so rapid that the Southwest Territory became the sixteenth state, under the name of Tennessee, in 1796. By 1800 its inhabitants exceeded one hundred thousand, while Kentucky was approaching a third of a million.

The early nineties were a time of great stress in the Northwest Territory. The beginnings of settlement around Marietta and Cincinnati aroused the natives, who had repudiated the treaties made during the Confederation. Depredations and murders became so frequent that General Josiah Harmar, in command of the garrison at the fort of the same name, was compelled to take the field. The Indians avoided battle, but cut off some detachments of Harmar's men and had rather the better of the contest. Governor St. Clair then took command in person of an expedition directed against

First Grist and Saw Mill in Ohio

the heart of the Indian country. Marching into the northwestern part of Ohio, remote from his base, he allowed his
army to fall into an ambush and be cut to pieces.

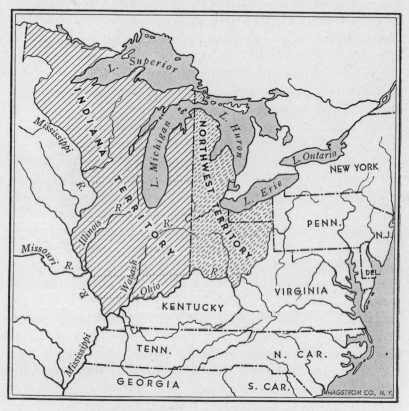

FIRST PARTITION OF THE NORTHWEST TERRITORY, 1800

This was in 1791. Warned at last that most careful preparations were essential to success, the government put General
Anthony Wayne—"the chief who never sleeps," the Indians
called him—in command, and nearly three years were spent
in plans for a decisive campaign. During these preparations
repeated efforts were made to agree with the Indians upon

terms of peace, but encouraged by the victory over St. Clair and the attitude of the British, the tribes refused to renew the repudiated treaties. In 1794, consequently, Wayne's army invaded the Indian country, laid waste the native villages and fields of the fertile Maumee Valley, and won a signal victory at the Battle of Fallen Timbers, a few miles from the present city of Toledo.

Forced by this event to come to terms, the tribes in 1795, by the Treaty of Greenville, agreed that the boundary of the Indian country should be pushed northward from the Ohio to the watershed separating its tributaries from the streams flowing into Lake Erie. All but the northwest quarter of Ohio was opened, and there was peace in the Northwest for sixteen years.

Its growth now rivaled that of Kentucky. Virginians came in great numbers to the Scioto Valley, and a mixed migration from New Jersey, Maryland, Virginia, Kentucky, and even New England entered the Miami country to swell the population of Cincinnati and begin new towns like Dayton and Hamilton, as well as occupy the farm lands in the Symmes Purchase. A stream from New England, especially Connecticut, flowed into the Western Reserve. By 1800 the number of inhabitants justified the partition of the Northwest Territory. The Ohio portion retained the old name, while the remainder was christened "Indiana Territory," with William Henry Harrison as governor.

Harrison was in Congress as delegate from the Northwest Territory. Before taking his new post, he, as spokesman of the pioneers, led Congress to pass a new land law (1800) which modified the Ordinance of 1785 in behalf of actual settlers. The main features of the new law were the introduction of the credit system and the reduction in the size of the tract which could be purchased to three hundred and twenty acres. Already (1796) the price had been advanced to a minimum of $2 per acre, but under the credit system it might be paid in four equal annual installments. Any man who had $160 in cash, plus small fees for surveying and registering, could command a farm of a half-section. Such was the scarcity of wage labor in the rising towns of Pittsburgh, Cincinnati, and Louisville that any able-bodied single man could soon earn enough above the cost of living to put himself in possession of a farm.

The credit system promoted speculation, and much land was purchased for resale. Many of the settlers bought from the speculators rather than at the government auctions. Nevertheless the new law was a quickening force in the movement of population into the Northwest. The Southwest was without this stimulus, for the unoccupied lands of Kentucky and Tennessee were under state control, and Georgia did not complete her cession until 1802. Even after that the Indians were in possession of much of the ceded area.

Only three years elapsed after the division of the Northwest before the first state carved from it came into the Union. Ohio was the "first fruit of the Ordinance of 1787."

RELATIONS WITH FRANCE, ENGLAND, AND SPAIN

Many problems arising from our relations with the countries of western Europe crowded upon the attention of the first administration, adding to the cares of a government already heavily burdened with the task of getting under way. Some of the most difficult of these problems grew out of the French Revolution. That memorable upheaval began simultaneously with the constitutional era in the United States. In 1789 the French monarchy, top-heavy "like a pyramid on its apex," confessed the failure of absolutism by summoning the first meeting of the Estates-General, or representatives of the nation, which had been called in one hundred and seventy-five years. Like the Long Parliament which marked the failure of Charles I's attempt at personal rule in England, the Estates-General demanded reforms as the price of its aid, and thus the Revolution began.

The Revolution ran through several stages. At the beginning it was in the hands of moderate men, like Count Mirabeau, who aimed at a constitutional monarchy and the abolition of the privileges of the nobility. But as many of the nobles fled to other countries and stirred them up to attack France, the course of events enabled the Republicans to overthrow the monarchists. They were in control by 1792, and when the king was found to be plotting with the *émigrés* he was deposed, and at the end of January, 1793, brought to the guillotine. Up to this time England was not a member of the coalition against France, but disputes now came to a head which brought her into the war.

American sympathies soon divided along party lines. The Republicans saw in the events in France the efforts of a great people to free themselves from oppression. The Federalists, on the contrary, were shocked by the violence which attended the revolution and saw in it proof of the turbulence of the masses when freed from restraint. In their admiration for England they became pro-British in their foreign policy, while the Republicans were equally pro-French. The rivalries of the powers involved the territories contiguous to the United States and touched our interests closely.

Soon after the outbreak of war between England and France word came that the Republic was sending a minister to the United States to replace the representative of the overturned monarchy. The news made it necessary for Washington to decide upon his course. Calling together his cabinet he submitted a number of questions. By the treaties of 1778 and a later consular convention the United States and France were allies; France was entitled to certain privileges in American ports, and the United States was bound to defend France's possessions in the West Indies. The cabinet disagreed as to whether the overthrow of the monarchy had abrogated the alliance. Jefferson held that the agreement bound the two peoples and that a change of government did not destroy it. All thought that the new minister should be received, and consented that Washington should issue a proclamation of neutrality. The proclamation announced the state of war in Europe, declared that the United States was at peace with all of the belligerent powers, and warned Americans against acts of hostility towards any of them.

Jefferson, believing that the alliance was still in force, called the proclamation pusillanimous notwithstanding his consent to it. His feelings were shared by the Republicans generally. Hamilton undertook to defend the President's course through arguments in the public press. Madison, prompted by Jefferson to take up his pen "and cut him to pieces in the face of the public," replied, and a lively debate followed. It was evidently Washington's belief that the United States was under no obligations to protect the French islands except in a defensive war. In the present case his view apparently was that France was the aggressor. Thus considered, the United States was not guilty of a breach of faith, although Washington was undoubtedly moved by a strong sense of the necessity of peace for his infant country.

The conduct of the new minister Genêt (addressed as "Citizen" after the revolutionary fashion) is a curious chapter in diplomatic history. Under the rules of international etiquette his first duty upon landing was to proceed to the seat of government and present his credentials before attempting any official act, but he was only twenty-eight years of age and his enthusiasm for the cause of the French Republic led him to act rashly.

Disembarking at Charleston, perhaps because his ship was

driven from its course by storms, he began at once to act as if the United States were the active ally of France. He issued a number of commissions as privateers to Charleston ship-owners, and their vessels began to prey upon English commerce. He also set on foot plans for a land attack on Spanish Florida by Americans of the southern states.

Then he set out for Philadelphia, passing through a Republican region in which he was everywhere hailed with enthusiasm. The contrast between Washington's cool dignity and the popular demonstration chilled Genêt like an arctic blast and led him to conclude that the President was not representative of the public sentiment. He did not demand fulfillment of the treaty of alliance, but insisted that the President call an extra session of Congress, apparently in the belief that the legislature would overrule his decision upon neutrality. Washington refused, but Genêt was nothing daunted.

Entering into correspondence with George Rogers Clark, he tried to organize a force of westerners to attack Louisiana. Clark, disappointed at the neglect of his claims for services during the War of Independence, and angry like others in the new settlements because Spain still denied them the use of the river, was ready for the part of leader. To pay the expenses Genêt sought advances on the debt due France, pretending that he would use the money in the purchase of supplies for the West Indies. One of the privateers commissioned at Charleston had brought in an English vessel, *The Little Sarah,* as prize. This, rechristened *The Little Democrat,* and fitted out as a privateer, Genêt planned to send by sea to the mouth of the Mississippi to support Clark's attack on New Orleans.

The designs against Louisiana and the Floridas were covered by Genêt's instructions, but finding the administration unresponsive he decided to carry them out secretly and in spite of neutrality. This led to a quarrel with the government over French rights in American ports. Washington held that while the treaties permitted France's prizes to be brought into our ports and denied that privilege to her enemies, they did not permit the refitting of the prizes for hostile use. Genêt would not accept so strict a construction of the treaties, but finally promised that *The Little Democrat* should not go to sea without notice.

Genêt's conduct at several points might have strained our relations with France if his government had supported him. He actually sent *The Little Democrat* to sea in violation of his promise. Washington then requested the French government to recall him. The request was granted readily, for another turn of events had supplanted Genêt's friends and the extreme democrats were in control in France. They sent Jean Fauchet as Genêt's successor, with instructions to arrest him and send him home. Washington refused the request for extradition and Genêt remained in America, marrying a daughter of Governor Clinton, of New York. Learning after Fauchet's arrival of the plans for the Clark expedition Washington took precautions to prevent it, although without funds there was little danger of its being attempted.

Relations with Great Britain were far from satisfactory during most of Washington's presidency. The king's government was slow in sending a minister and when finally George Hammond arrived the situation was little improved. England still refused to make a treaty of commerce. Although she desired to obtain a settlement of claims on behalf of creditors and Loyalists, these were inextricably entangled with the question of the border posts, which she wished to hold. Moreover, she was satisfied with the commercial situation, so long as the United States did not actually discriminate against her. She preferred, therefore, to procrastinate—to hold the posts and delay the making of a commercial

treaty. Negotiations led to little more than mutual recrimi-
nations on the subject of violations of the treaty of 1783, except that, through unofficial interviews with Hamilton, the
British minister gained inside views of American policy which
practically nullified Jefferson's efforts as Secretary of State.

The hostilities between the United States and the Indians
in the Northwest created a dangerous situation. The government officials in Canada supplied the Indians with guns
and ammunition, and encouraged them to withstand the demands of the Americans. In fact, they aided the natives by
every means short of joining in the hostilities—and Canadian
militiamen even engaged in the fighting, disguised as Indians.
The British government cherished the hope, for a time, that
the United States might accept its mediation in making peace
with the natives, and that a neutral Indian state might be
erected as a buffer between the United States and Canada.
Such an arrangement would protect the British fur trade and
safeguard the interests of the native allies, who had been
rather shabbily neglected in the treaty of 1783.

Under the circumstances there was danger that the American campaigns against the tribes would be regarded as a
hostile movement towards the border posts which were still
in the hands of the British. Wayne's advance was so construed by Lord Dorchester, in command at Detroit, who im-
prudently told the Indians that England and the United
States would soon be at war. An abandoned fort near the
site of the Battle of Fallen Timbers, fifty miles within American territory, was reoccupied, in order to halt any move of
Wayne's army in the direction of Detroit, and Wayne narrowly missed an encounter with it.

Meantime the war between England and France had
brought a new crop of troubles, due to the maritime code
which England saw fit to adopt. The war was a boon to
American ships, since as neutrals they enjoyed many immuni-

ties denied to vessels of the belligerents. As it was no longer safe for her own vessels to visit her colonies, France relaxed her navigation system (in February, 1793) and allowed neutrals unusual privileges in carrying colonial products to European ports. In fact a great part of the carrying for all of the countries of western Europe fell into American hands.

England regarded the relaxation of trade restrictions by her enemy as a mere war measure, and applied the "Rule of 1756" to counteract it. This held that a trade which France did not permit in time of peace could not be allowed in time of war. She also asserted that provisions were contraband and subject to seizure if bound for France. Under an Order in Council of November 6, 1793, she began to seize American vessels laden with the products of the French West Indies when bound for France. The United States denied the legality of both of these rules, and in addition rejected England's interpretation of the law of blockade. When England declared an enemy's port blockaded she seized vessels anywhere on the high seas if bound for that port (the "paper" blockade), while the United States maintained that the port must be guarded by a naval force stationed at that point, and that seizures might be made only when ships were caught in the act of attempting to enter a guarded port.[1]

The practice of impressment now also became extremely vexatious. Service on the British warships was hard, almost unendurable. Food was miserably bad, precautions against disease almost unthought of, and discipline brutal. Men-of-war avoided port more than the plague, for sailors deserted

[1] These advanced principles of maritime law had been agreed upon by the members of the Armed Neutrality League of 1780. "I could never find," John Quincy Adams wrote in 1796, of the British admiralty courts, that they "were governed by any other code" than " 'Rule, Britannia!' " The principles of the Neutrality League had been adopted by the United States in several treaties made during the Confederation period. Besides the rules governing blockades and provisions, they provided that enemy's goods on neutral vessels should be exempt from capture.

by hundreds on every opportunity. Only force kept the crews full. The character of life on board the vessels is indicated by Dr. Johnson's remark: "Why would a man be a seaman when he could get into a jail!" As a matter of fact, press gangs continually, in war time, ransacked prisons as well as merchant ships. For a long time it had been customary for the naval officers to board foreign merchant vessels on the high seas in search of deserters. The seizure of sailors on American ships began during the Confederation, and after 1793 became very frequent, for the rapid expansion of our merchant marine attracted many deserters. American sailors encouraged desertion by procuring "protections"—certificates that the holders were Americans—from local magistrates, which they were quite willing to transfer for a few dollars.

When every sailor whose native tongue was English was a British subject impressment seldom involved mistakes. After America became independent the case was different, and many a *bona-fide* citizen of the United States was seized along with deserters. England made no objection to the correction of errors, but long delays were unavoidable, and the victims and their families suffered great hardships. The United States government contended that seamen on board American vessels were to be treated as Americans. While admitting the right of British cruisers to search neutrals for munitions of war, it denied the right to search for deserters. It offered to seek them for arrest and return; but the British would not accept this as a satisfactory substitute for impressment. Nor would she recognize the right of expatriation.

France also began to make seizures. Her view of the Rule of 1756 and of the law of blockade was the same as that of the United States. She had no occasion to practice impressments, and her treaties with the United States exempted provisions from seizure. But if Great Britain did not respect the rights of the United States, France would be at a dangerous disadvantage if she did so herself.   Hence she disregarded her agreement, although, like her foe, she undertook to pay for provisions if seized.

The United States had cause for complaint against both countries, but Britain's offenses were far more numerous and grievous.   Even Hamilton called the order of November 6 "atrocious."   Especially harsh was the administration of it by the courts of vice-admiralty in the West Indies.   Within four months, about 250 American vessels were seized, more than three fifths of which were condemned.   Their crews were left stranded.

The news of these seizures and of Lord Dorchester's speech to the Indians arrived at almost the same moment.   Congress was already considering commercial retaliation, the Republicans believing that England might be brought to terms by such measures.   The Federalists, on the contrary, feared that restrictions would injure American trade even more than British, and perhaps lead to war.   With the report of the events just referred to, however, the tone of the discussions took a decidedly warlike turn, and preparations for hostilities were begun.

The Federalists still hoped that war might be averted, and decided upon an extraordinary effort of diplomacy.   In the crisis it seemed possible that a special envoy might gain a favorable hearing, since it seemed likely that Britain really preferred peace.

For this special mission the President chose John Jay, the Chief Justice, who accepted the appointment knowing, as he himself said, that "no man could frame a treaty with Great Britain without making himself unpopular and odious."   If any American were *persona grata* to the British ministry at this juncture, however, that man was Jay, for while Secretary of Foreign Relations during the Confederation he had believed that the British were justified in retaining the border posts. Although this opinion had been expressed to Congress in secret session, it had come to the knowledge of the British, who had reason to believe that Jay sympathized also with their views on other issues. Jay was in relations of close confidence with Hamilton, and the fact is that he, along with the Federalists in general, was willing to acquiesce, for the period of the war, in the British maritime code, provided the surrender of the posts could be obtained, together with favorable commercial arrangements.

Jay arrived in London at an opportune moment. Word of Dorchester's speech, Wayne's victory, and the American indignation over the Order of November 6 preceded him by a few days. At the same time the European situation was changing to the disadvantage of England. The coalition against France was weakening, and some of the Baltic powers were discussing the revival of the Armed Neutrality League. Hitherto Lord Grenville had temporized in his negotiations with the resident minister of the United States, Thomas Pinckney, satisfied that the United States would not go to war, and hoping that Indian successes would open the way for British mediation and the setting up of the buffer state. Now it appeared that concessions were necessary if war were to be avoided, a war which would mean the loss of England's best customer and the diversion of energy from the prosecution of the European contest. Moreover, the United States might join the League of Neutrals, and the League might abandon neutrality to fight for the freedom of the seas.

Jay was received cordially, Lord Dorchester was reprimanded for his indiscreet utterances, steps were taken to ameliorate the administration of the Order of November 6, and negotiations were begun promptly for a settlement of the issues between the two countries. Jay presented the American views on maritime law, but on these points Grenville would yield nothing. Through Hammond, Grenville soon learned that Hamilton had assured him that it was the settled policy of the United States to avoid entanglements with Europe. Thus Grenville, relieved of the apprehension that the United States might join the Neutral League, was enabled to continue the negotiations with an advantage over Jay of which the latter was quite ignorant.

The treaty, signed late in 1794, reached the United States early the next year. It provided that the border posts should be surrendered in 1796, allowed trade with the British East Indies, placed the commerce of the United States with the British Isles on a basis of "reciprocal and perfect liberty," and admitted American boats of not more than seventy tons burden to the West Indies. The last concession contained its own guarantee that the boats would not carry their cargoes to Europe, but as a further precaution to keep the carrying trade of the islands out of foreign hands, the treaty forbade the exportation from the states of the products of the West Indies (molasses, sugar, coffee, and cotton). Although intended to prevent re-exportation of goods brought from the islands, its terms applied equally to these articles if produced in the United States. The commercial clauses were to run for twelve years.

Joint commissions were agreed upon for settling the old question of the debts and for determining the northeast boundary. The claims on behalf of the Loyalists were dropped, as were those of the United States on account of slaves carried away when the British armies sailed for home. Claims on both sides arising from alleged illegal seizures of ships were referred to commissions. The disputed questions of international law were left as they had stood.

Washington decided to submit the treaty to the Senate rather than to attempt further negotiations or renew the risk of war. The Senate ratified after striking out the paragraph concerning West Indian trade, England consented to the change, and Washington proclaimed the treaty as part of the law of the land. But the agreement pleased no one. Although they accepted the treaty, the Federalists were disappointed because the commercial concessions were not greater; while the Republicans in Congress attempted at the next session, although in vain, to defeat its execution by withholding the necessary appropriations.

Republicans had denounced the negotiations from the first, as well as the choice of envoy. Had not Jay once tried to barter away our right to navigate the Mississippi? An agreement with haughty England was "a degrading insult to the American people: . . . and an insidious injury to France."

Notwithstanding the general dissatisfaction, the treaty did benefit the country in many ways. England relaxed in practice the maritime code which she refused to modify in principle. This was perhaps in part because trade was outstripping her tonnage. The commercial privileges given to Americans by the rejected article of the treaty were, at any rate, granted by executive order, and products of the French, Spanish, and Dutch islands when brought to the United States were allowed to be reëxported. In 1796 American vessels carried to Europe 35,000,000 pounds of sugar and 62,000,000 pounds of coffee.

In the case of *The Polly,* decided by the British admiralty courts in 1800, it was held that the vessel had not violated the Rule of 1756 by reëxporting a cargo from the French islands which had been landed in the United States and on which duty had been paid. While the direct carrying trade between the West Indian possessions of England's foes and Europe still incurred the penalties of the rule, this decision seemed to legalize the "broken voyage," and neutral shipping prospered. The burden of the duties paid in American ports and of the increased freight charges fell upon the ultimate consumer.

One of the beneficial consequences of Jay's treaty was that it aided the United States in obtaining a treaty with Spain. When the prospect of statehood counteracted her intrigues with the pioneers of the Southwest, fearful as formerly of the growing American communities, she became more tenacious than ever of her influence over the Indians. Much like England in the Northwest in the same years, she sought to maintain what was in effect an Indian buffer state between her settlements and those of the Americans. To maintain her supremacy among the Creeks, she employed a half-breed chief named Alexander McGillivray, who hated the Americans because as a Tory in the Revolution his property had been confiscated.

In an attempt to offset Spain's influence, Washington invited McGillivray to the seat of government in 1790 and paid him a liberal sum said to be in compensation for these losses. Thus mollified, he and the chiefs who accompanied him made a treaty; he accepted a military commission under the United States and promised both to promote the American trade among his people and to keep them at peace. The treaty was of slight effect and did nothing to pacify other tribes. Indeed, Indian relations in the Gulf region were in a state of confusion for many years. However futile, the dealings with the tribes endangered the peace between the United States and Spain. Dangerous also was a project affecting the east bank of the Mississippi near the mouth of the Yazoo River. This region was claimed by Georgia, under her charter, as well as by Spain and the United States. Instead of relinquishing her claim to Congress as all of the other states had done, Georgia granted lands to a company which proposed to make settlements. Such a defiance of Spain might provoke her to war, unless the settlers recognized her jurisdiction, which in turn would jeopardize the interests of the United States. Washington met the dilemma and avoided international complications by issuing a proclamation against the occupation of the tract.

Early in his presidency Washington renewed the effort to reach an agreement with Spain over the navigation of the Mississippi and the question of the boundary. Jefferson as Secretary of State believed that sooner or later some turn of affairs in Europe would aid the United States in obtaining the desired concessions. Spain's attitude did indeed vary with each change in the international alignment, and eventually Jefferson's faith was justified.

In 1790 Spain and England seemed about to engage in war over their rival claims on the Pacific coast. In this event, the former feared that an Anglo-American combination might strike at Louisiana and the Floridas; hence she invited the United States to send a diplomatic agent to Madrid to negotiate. When after a considerable delay William Short arrived for this purpose, the French Revolution had brought about the first coalition of powers against France, and of this coalition both Spain and England were members. While thus making common cause with England, Spain, of course, suffered less from the fear of an Anglo-American alliance. Hence it became her policy to procrastinate. For many months Short found it impossible to make any progress.

It was during this period that the Indian situation in the Southwest became acute. But in time Spain wearied of her connection with England, which proved to be of far greater advantage to the latter than to herself. She began secretly to plan to withdraw from the coalition and make her peace with France; but fearing the vengeance of England, she again changed her policy towards the United States. Again she

was ready to welcome an American alliance with a reciprocal guarantee of territory, to protect Louisiana and the
Floridas in case of attack by England.

Through the dilatoriness of Spain's representative in the
United States, the communication of the proposal of an alliance was long delayed. Meantime Jay completed his negotiations in England, and Pinckney was sent from London
to Madrid to bring matters there to a head.

In spite of the fact that the United States would not consider a treaty of alliance, Godoy, the minister with whom he
dealt, eager to prevent a *rapprochement* between England
and the United States, was ready to purchase the latter's
friendship by conceding the boundary which she desired.
On the question of the navigation of the Mississippi, however, he insisted that Spain would grant it as a privilege but
would not concede that it was a right. Even so, Pinckney
labored in vain for a time to obtain in addition the "right
of deposit," that is, the privilege of unloading goods at New
Orleans for storage until they could be transshipped to ocean-
going vessels. Without this privilege the navigation of the
river would have been of little use. At length, believing that
Godoy would not agree to this concession, which he regarded
as a *sine qua non,* Pinckney asked for his passports. At this
point, rather than allow the treaty to fail, Godoy yielded.

Pinckney's treaty was completed in 1795. It fixed the
southern boundary of the United States at the thirty-first
parallel, and conceded the privilege of navigating the Mississippi to its mouth, together with the right of deposit at
New Orleans for three years, with a stipulation that it would
then be renewed either at New Orleans or some other convenient point. The treaty contained no commercial clauses.
Trade between the two countries continued to rest upon the
basis of municipal law.

PARTY POLITICS

The year 1795 was a great one in the history of diplomacy. Within the twelvemonth treaties were signed or ratified with Spain, England, and the Northwest Indians. The vexed questions inherited from Confederation days were disposed of. These successes showed the efficiency of the new government and tended to create a spirit of confidence. The Federalists deserved the credit for these results. They had also established the financial system and proved that the government could cope with domestic disorders.

Yet party divisions were widening. The Republicans dropped out of the cabinet during Washington's second term, Jefferson resigning in 1793 and Randolph in 1795. Timothy Pickering, a staunch Federalist, became Secretary of State in that year. Hamilton also retired from office in 1795, Oliver Wolcott taking his place; but Hamilton continued to wield the power almost of a dictator over the Federalists. Jefferson called him a "colossus to his party." Adams, a man of independent views, was one Federalist who refused to follow him.

Outside of the administration the Republicans were growing in strength, and as Washington's second term neared its close they prepared for a vigorous contest in the next presidential election. Party organization was still so imperfect that no very satisfactory method had been devised for nominating candidates. For want of a better mode the members of the two houses met in caucuses of their parties and made recommendations. They were entirely without authority to do so, and had no power over the choice of presidential electors, but they were fairly representative of opinion in their parties and their advice carried weight.

In this way John Adams and Thomas Pinckney (negotiator of the Spanish treaty) became the Federalist candidates in 1796, while Thomas Jefferson and Aaron Burr were named by the Republicans. Adams was the logical candidate of his party, being far more prominent than any other leader except Hamilton, who, like many a later statesman, had made too many enemies to be an "available" standard-bearer.[1]

To prevent a tie and consequent failure of choice by the electors, it was necessary for them to scatter votes intended for the vice-presidential candidate. According to Hamilton it was agreed that equal support should be given to Adams and Pinckney by the Federalist electors. Within the circle of his confidential friends, however, he let it be known that in his opinion "if the chance should decide in favor of Mr. Pinckney, it probably would not be a misfortune." Some hint of this reached the ears of Adams' friends among the electors, in the form of a rumor that there was an intrigue on foot to bring in Pinckney over him, and to defeat it a number of them withheld their votes from Pinckney. Adams received 71 votes, and his rival Jefferson had 68, nine more than Pinckney.

Adams was rather glad than sorry that Jefferson, his friend of olden days, had defeated Pinckney. But the electoral system was not working satisfactorily, when one party could win the presidency and the other the second office. Burr moreover complained because the Republican electors did not support him equally with Jefferson, and before the next election public opinion came to require that an elector should not vote at his own discretion but according to the will of his party. The change illustrates the growth of party discipline. Equal support of party candidates, with a resulting tie and the necessity of choice by the House of Representatives, had its drawbacks, however, as the election of 1800 was to show. The root of the difficulty was the lack of provision for separate ballots for the two officials.

[1] A contemporary Federalist opinion characterized Hamilton as "an unfit head of the party, being radically deficient in the quality of discretion."

Washington was grieved by the rise of party spirit. He had hoped to unite men of all shades of opinion in the effort to govern the country for the good of all. Where he had failed Adams could not succeed. By consulting Jefferson with the thought of appointing a Republican as minister to France, he affronted the Federalists without winning the good will of the Republicans. He retained Washington's cabinet, but Pickering and Wolcott regarded Hamilton as the real head of the party and did not work in harmony with the President. In the end the factional breach was widened by the retention of Hamilton's friends, and a drastic reconstruction of the cabinet became necessary.

Washington, meantime, made the approach of the end of his service the occasion of a Farewell Address.[1] In it he appealed to all parts of the country to uphold the Union as the source of benefits for every section and interest, citing the Spanish treaty as an illustration of service which the Union had rendered the West.

A memorable passage dealt with foreign relations. The interests and policies of Europe, he said, differed from those of America. "Therefore, it must be unwise in us to implicate ourselves, by artificial ties, in the ordinary vicissitudes of her politics, or the ordinary combinations and collisions of her friendships or enmities. Our detached and distant situation invites and enables us to pursue a different course. . . . Why, by interweaving our destiny with that of any part of Europe, entangle our peace and prosperity in the toils of European ambition? . . . 'Tis our true policy to steer clear of permanent alliances with any portion of the foreign world. . . . Let [existing] engagements be observed in their

[1] The first paragraph announced his resolution to decline reëlection. Although he gives no hint of a belief that acceptance of a third term would form an objectionable precedent, his action did much to establish the doctrine that no President should serve for more than two.

genuine sense. But, in my opinion, it is unnecessary and would be unwise to extend them."

The Republicans took exception to the Address. Where "Union" was mentioned they read "Federalist party," for the deeds praised were the achievements of that party. They therefore appraised the utterance as a covert plea for their opponents.[1] Later generations, venerating Washington as the "Father of his country," have taken the Address as his political will and testament and have treasured his advice. They have, in fact, probably read into the passage concerning alliances with European powers a meaning which the author did not intend. Washington himself had leaned towards an understanding with France in 1792 as an offset to the weight of England and Spain upon our flanks. Though Europe was far away the powers of its western shores were our neighbors, as holders of colonies touching our borders on three sides. With Spain in Louisiana, on the Gulf coast, and at the mouth of the Mississippi, and with Britain in Canada, the transalleghany areas were fruitful soil for intrigues which threatened the allegiance of citizens and the territorial integrity of the United States.

The temptation was indeed great for the government to seek support through alliances, like the nations of Europe, but Washington had finally decided upon a neutral policy as a surer means of guarding national interests at the time, since

[1] The Address was put into its final form by Hamilton, at Washington's request, and some of its clauses seem to have been suggested by Hamilton. In this fact some recent historians have believed that they found evidence that Hamilton cleverly capitalized Washington's great prestige for the benefit of the Federalist party. On the other hand it is to be noted that the correspondence between Washington and Hamilton shows that the former scrutinized every word of the document attentively, so that it is difficult to believe that it contained any sentiment which was not entirely in accord with his own views. A careful study indicates that Hamilton's chief influence was in eliminating as undignified certain statements which betrayed Washington's sensitiveness to criticism.

an alliance would have linked the destiny of the young Republic with the fortunes of the ally. The advice in the Farewell Address was the outgrowth of the neutrality proclamation of 1793. In after years the warning against "permanent alliances" was transmuted into a doctrine of "isolation"— that *all* participation in the wars and politics of Europe should be avoided.

ADAMS AND THE BREACH WITH FRANCE

Although Jay's treaty relieved the tension in British relations it involved the United States in a misunderstanding with France. Our representative in that country at the time of Genêt's mission was Gouverneur Morris. His services were of great value, but his temper was aristocratic, and be became *persona non grata* after the fall of the monarchy. The Republic requested his recall at the same time that it acceded to the demand for Genêt's removal. Washington complied as a matter of international courtesy, appointing James Monroe in his stead.

Monroe was a Republican of the Virginia school, somewhat younger than Jefferson, and his devoted disciple. He had already won important rank in political life in state offices and as a member of Congress. Washington selected him partly because of his desire to preserve the bipartisan character of the government, partly because it was not likely that any Federalist would be acceptable to the French. The choice proved to be a bad one, for Monroe had not yet attained that judicial balance which characterized his later years, and conducted himself more as the representative of the Republican party than of the administration.

At the time of his arrival in Paris the only government France had was a Convention, elected by the radical democrats to draft a constitution. Delayed in this work by the prolonged crisis of war, the Convention was still acting as a provisional government, and to it Monroe presented his credentials. His reception was so cordial that he was carried away by his emotions and made an address pledging the cooperation of the two republics in the cause of liberty. The speech voiced sentiments appropriate to nations in alliance, and misrepresented the neutral views of the administration. The British government protested, and Washington admonished him to be more circumspect.

Jay's negotiations were in progress in England, but Monroe, insufficiently informed if not somewhat misled by his dispatches, repeatedly assured the French that the English treaty would contain nothing prejudicial to them. When the terms became known this was found not to be true. It was the desire and purpose of the American administration to adjust French relations on an entirely equitable basis, but France took the Jay treaty as evidence that the United States preferred the friendship of her chief enemy to her own.

Monroe like the French saw in the treaty evidence of a pro-British policy, and feeling that he had been duped, had no heart to defend it as he was instructed to do. On the contrary, his conduct became more than ever that of a partisan. When France proposed to send an envoy to the United States to seek a new treaty, he advised delay. The election of 1796 was at hand, with the possibility of a Republican victory, in which event he intimated the chances of success would be greatly enhanced. Monroe was doubtless moved by fear that failure of negotiations would mean war, but his conduct was indiscreet. When it was found that he was supplying friends at home with information to be used against the Federalists during the campaign, he was recalled.

The minister of France in the United States also violated the rules governing diplomats by working quietly in behalf of Jefferson's election. The defeat of the Republicans was followed by his recall, and for some time France was without

a resident minister. During Adams' term the situation between the two countries developed from bad to worse until
actual hostilities occurred.

Resentment against the pro-British policy of the Federalists
seems to be the clew to the strange conduct of France during
these years. Upon Monroe's recall in 1796 Washington sent
Charles C. Pinckney to Paris. The Convention had at last
framed a constitution which vested executive functions in a
Directory of five members. Charles Maurice de Talleyrand
was in charge of foreign affairs as a member of this Directory.
Pinckney arrived before Monroe left, but was informed that
France would not receive another minister from the United
States until her grievances were redressed. Wishing the full
responsibility for what followed to rest upon the French government, Pinckney lingered until officially notified that he
was liable to arrest as a spy. At about the same time Monroe's
departure was speeded with many marks of esteem.

The news of Pinckney's rebuff split the Federalists into two
camps. The extremists, including Pickering the Secretary of
State, were ready for war. For once, however, Hamilton's influence was on the side of Adams, who thought that another
effort should be made to reach a peaceful understanding. For
this purpose John Marshall and Elbridge Gerry, the latter a
Massachusetts Republican and ex-member of the Constitutional Convention of 1787, were joined with Pinckney as special commissioners. But they fared little better than Pinckney. They were not received officially, but indirect intima-
tions were given that they might be if a sum of money were
provided for the pockets of the members of the Directory and
a loan made to the government. Pressing the demand for a
douceur, Talleyrand's agents drew from the commissioners an
emphatic refusal. Their actual words were "no, no, not a
sixpence." Transmuted by the patriotism of the orators at
home, they have come down through the years in the ringing

sentiment "Millions for defense, but not one cent for tribute!"

While these proposals, especially the suggestion of a bribe, reveal the corruption of the French ministers, it is doubtful whether they expected the commissioners to accept them. It is likely that they were testing the spirit of the United States, and that they preferred not to reach an agreement. While dallying with the commissioners the Directory was trying, as we now know, to persuade Spain to retrocede Louisiana, partly because possession of that province would provide a source of supplies for the French West Indies, and partly because it would enable France, as was believed, to control American foreign policy through the power to throttle our western settlements.

When the commissioners found negotiations blocked by these demands, they prepared to leave France. Talleyrand thereupon invited Gerry, the Republican, to remain, and he, attributing the remonstrances of his colleagues to wounded vanity, consented in the hope of preventing a breach between the two countries.

As soon as these occurrences were reported to President Adams he ordered Gerry home and sent to Congress a message accompanied by copies of the dispatches from the commissioners. In these, letters were substituted for the names of the Frenchmen who had acted as Talleyrand's agents, and from this fact the whole episode is known as the "X Y Z affair." In the message Adams declared: "I will never send another minister to France without assurances that he will be received, respected, and honored as the representative of a free, powerful, and independent nation."

The war fever now ran high. The Federalists were reunited, and in spite of Jefferson's remonstrance that the French ought not to be held responsible for "the turpitude of swindlers," many Republicans acted with them. Some time before, work had been begun on six new frigates. The building of these was hastened and supervision of the navy taken from the War Department by the creation of a new Department of the Navy. The French treaty of alliance of 1778 was formally abrogated, and an act was passed authorizing the raising of an army. Up to this time merchant vessels had been forbidden to arm for defense against French cruisers, lest encounters inflame the war spirit of both peoples. Now the vessels of the navy were instructed to capture French ships interfering with our merchantmen, and engagements began to take place. For two years and a half the "Naval War of 1798" went on without a declaration of war on either side, with eighty-five captures of armed vessels to the credit of the new navy.[1]

No fighting occurred on land, but extensive preparations were made. Adams named Washington commander of the army. Since he was not expected to take the field in person, he, as titular chief, was in position to name the actual commander. Although Adams preferred Knox, whose claim was superior by right of seniority, he yielded at last, with very ill grace, to Washington's insistence, and appointed Hamilton to be major-general in command.

Hamilton now recurred to the idea of an English alliance and planned to conduct a land campaign for the liberation of the possessions of Spain, now the ally of France, while England coöperated by sea. To these far-reaching schemes Adams gave no countenance. He adhered to Washington's safer policy of avoiding foreign alliances, and resolved to restore peace if possible. That France wished for peace seemed to be shown by the fact that she had not replied to the attacks of the American navy by declaring war. Moreover, towards the end of 1798 the assurance reached our minister at The Hague, William Vans Murray, that a minister would be received by France with the respect demanded by the President's message.

[1] The Supreme Court ruled that a state of "limited war" existed.

The cabinet, in bad humor over the "affair of the major-generals," was committed to Hamilton's war policy, and Adams, also in bad humor, without even consulting it nominated Murray as minister to France. At the suggestion of senators he consented to add Oliver Ellsworth and W. R. Davie as special commissioners.

In the negotiations the United States sought the consent of France to the abrogation of the treaty of alliance and asked damages for the seizure of ships contrary to the terms of that treaty. France was willing to concede one demand but not both, and an agreement was finally made on that basis. The United States was released from the guarantee of the West Indies, and in return renounced all claims on account of injuries inflicted upon her commerce. The new treaty was signed September 30, 1800.

THE ALIEN AND SEDITION ACTS

Among the measures of the Federalists in 1798 were four which were directed against trouble-makers at home. At a time when Jefferson could seriously believe that Hamilton was plotting the overthrow of the Republic and the establishment of monarchy, it is little wonder that small men carried their attacks on officials to extraordinary lengths. Freneau's *National Gazette* made Washington regret that he had ever accepted office.[1] On the other hand, even federal judges denounced political agitators from the bench. Chief Justice Ellsworth, in a charge to a Massachusetts grand jury, thundered against "the French system-mongers, from the quintumvirate at Paris to the Vice-President and minority in Congress, as apostles of Atheism and anarchy, bloodshed and plunder."

[1] At one meeting of the cabinet Knox thoughtlessly displayed a cartoon called the "Funeral of George W-n," in which the President was placed on a guillotine. On seeing it Washington exclaimed in a rage that "that *rascal Freneau* sent him three of his papers every day, as if he thought he would become the distributor."

The English war with France which began in 1793 had encountered a good deal of opposition at first from liberal Englishmen who sympathized with the aspirations of the French people, but their criticisms had been hushed by repressive legislation. In consequence many of these liberals came to the United States. French citizens, too, were numerous in the states, and at a time when domestic and international politics were closely interwoven these immigrants took an active part in political discussions. Most of them having sought our shores in quest of ampler liberty leaned strongly towards the Republican party, supporting it with their pens, voices, and votes.

The existing naturalization law permitted foreigners to become citizens after five years' residence. This seemed to the Federalists too short a period for thorough Americanization. They felt, as Harrison Gray Otis expressed it, that something must be done "to prevent the indiscriminate admission of wild Irishmen and others to the right of suffrage." Although the granting of the ballot was a power reserved to the states, Congress had control over naturalization, and doubtless with the design of robbing the Republican party of an important source of votes in future, the Federalists passed a new naturalization act extending the required term of residence to fourteen years.

The second law, known as the "Alien Act," empowered the President to deal with undesirable resident subjects of a foreign government. "It was commonly supposed that the United States contained over thirty thousand Frenchmen, constantly engaged in intrigues against the government, and ready in case of invasion to rise as one man and murder their hosts." Under the act any alien whom the President deemed dangerous to the peace and safety of the country might be ordered to depart. If he did not obey, he was liable to imprisonment. The act was limited to two years.

The third law, or "Alien Enemies Act," was not limited in duration except that from its nature it could be in effect only during war. It gave the President extraordinary power to deport subjects of any country with which the United States might be at war, and to prescribe the restraints to which they should be subjected if allowed to remain in America.

The Alien Enemies Act may be justified as a measure of national self-defense, but the Sedition Act, fourth of the series, was an un-American law, much like the British measures just referred to. It treated political opposition as crime, and was aimed less at foreigners than factious citizens. It not only provided for the punishment of persons who conspired together to impede the operation of United States laws, but forbade any person to write, print, or utter any "false, scandalous, and malicious" statement "against the government of the United States, or either house of the Congress of the United States, or the President of the United States, with intent to defame . . . or to bring them . . . into contempt or disrepute." The Republicans and moderate Federalists secured with difficulty the inclusion of a clause permitting any person charged with such an offense to present evidence that his statements were true.[1] Hamilton, who was not in Congress, wrote urging the change. "Let us not," he advised, "establish a tyranny." This act was to expire with the term of the administration.

The alien acts were never enforced, the second one because war was not officially declared, the first because it appeared unnecessary. President Adams found it sufficient to give warning to a few agitators, and a number of Frenchmen left the country of their own accord while the Alien Enemies Act was pending. But indictments under the Sedition Act were numerous, and there were ten convictions. A Jerseyman, who had expressed a wish that the wad of a cannon fired as a salute to the President had hit him on the rear bulge of his

[1] *Cf.* the Zenger case, page 134.

breeches, was fined $100. Matthew Lyon of Vermont, while canvassing for reëlection to Congress, charged the President with "unbounded thirst for ridiculous pomp, foolish adulation, and a selfish avarice." He was punished with a jail sentence of four months and a fine of a thousand dollars.

The most famous of the sedition cases was that of Dr. Thomas Cooper, an English liberal and a good type of the class of men who left that country about 1793. He was a man of education and ability. He later became president of the College of South Carolina and a leader of that state during the days of the nullification controversy. He was tried in 1800 for calling President Adams incompetent, and saying that he had interfered with the course of justice. He offered to prove the truth of his statements by the testimony of Adams himself and certain members of Congress. They refused to appear as witnesses, however, and Cooper was fined $400 and imprisoned for six months.

THE REPUBLICAN TRIUMPH

In the judgment of Republicans, the course of the Federalists savored of centralization and militarism. They denounced the Alien and Sedition laws with particular wrath as iniquitous and unconstitutional. Congress by the First Amendment was expressly forbidden to pass any law abridging the freedom of speech or of the press. That, with control over personal rights in general, was reserved to the states. But they could not bring these laws before the federal courts in test cases with any hope that their views would be upheld. Nor would they have favored such a procedure in any event. The sedition trials were in effect test cases, which showed that the judicial branch of the government would support the legislative department.

Some Republicans despaired of checking the career of the dominant party, and suggested secession by the states of the

South and West, and the organization of a new republic. Jefferson, without denying the right of secession, pointed out the needlessness of such an extreme remedy. His penetrating political instinct taught him that the errors of the Federalists would bring their own punishment. To treat political utterances as crime is a fatal policy for any party which depends upon the votes of the people.

Jefferson's plan was to press the mistakes of the Federalists upon the attention of the voters. As the best means of doing this, it was decided to have resolutions passed by some of the state legislatures where the Republicans were in the majority, to be sent then to all of the states in the hope of arousing opinion against the obnoxious laws. Under Jefferson's inspiration Madison drew up one set of resolutions, which the Virginia assembly passed. Concealing his authorship on account of his position as Vice-President, Jefferson drafted another set, which was introduced in the Kentucky legislature by a member named John Breckinridge, and passed with slight changes by a large vote.

The Virginia and Kentucky Resolutions were the best criticisms made of the Alien and Sedition Acts, and ably presented the Republican view. They called on the other states to concur in denouncing the acts, and to unite in maintaining their rights. It was probably the expectation of the authors that these appeals would draw out similar resolutions in many states and create such pressure upon Congress that it would promptly repeal the laws. Beyond that they doubtless believed that the aroused voters would visit their disapprobation upon the party which had passed the laws, at the next election. The resolutions, in short, served the purpose of a party platform for the campaign of 1800.

The legislatures of the other Republican states failed to reply to the resolutions. Replies came, however, from Federalist states, and the whole discussion became plainly a party controversy. As might be expected, the replies expressed approval of the laws and maintained that the state legislatures had no right to pass judgment upon acts of Congress. That, they held, was the function of the federal courts.

The most important part of the Virginia and Kentucky Resolutions in the long run was the part which attracted least attention at the time. The opening paragraphs of each document advanced the compact theory of the Constitution. Of the two the Kentucky Resolutions were the more explicit. According to them the states as separate entities formed the Union by entering into a compact, the Constitution, delegating certain powers to a general government as a sort of agent of the states. Whenever, therefore, this agent exceeds its powers its acts are void. Nor is the agent the final judge of its powers—not even the federal courts, which are parts of the agency—but the states have the right to judge for themselves of infractions of the Constitution and of the mode and measure of redress.

The Virginia Resolutions held "that, in case of a deliberate, palpable, and dangerous exercise of . . . powers not granted by the said compact, the States, who are parties thereto, have the right and are in duty bound to interpose for arresting the progress of the evil, and for maintaining within their respective limits the authorities, rights, and liberties appertaining to them."

These premises warranted the legislatures in passing upon the Alien and Sedition Acts and declaring them unconstitutional and void. Just what more the authors had in mind has been a puzzle ever since. No contemporary explanation was given, and only one state noticed the compact theory in its reply. Many years later Jefferson and Madison attempted explanations which arouse the suspicion that even they hardly realized the import of their words when first used. It is difficult to avoid the conclusion that the resolutions mean that a single state may nullify the force of a federal act within its own borders, if it deems such act to be contrary to the Constitution.[1]

The formulation of the compact theory of the Union gave the belief in state sovereignty new life; in fact, from this time on it showed great vitality. Federalist New England adopted the Virginia and Kentucky doctrines during the War of 1812, and South Carolina justified nullification in 1832 upon the same grounds. Even the resort to secession in 1861 was a logical consequence of the views promulgated in 1798.

The feeling against France in 1798 aided the Federalists in the congressional election of that year. But the reaction against the Alien and Sedition Acts more than offset this gain, and the party approached the presidential election with discouraging prospects. The factional division came to an open rupture when Adams decided to send the peace commission to France. Pickering was disgusted at the President's failure to consult his cabinet, and was not in sympathy with his pacific policy. Supported by McHenry and Wolcott, Secretaries of the War and Treasury Departments, he neglected to draft instructions for the commissioners until the President called for his resignation. Then he refused to resign, compelling Adams to dismiss him. Intending to purge the cabinet of Hamilton's supporters, Adams also forced out McHenry, but Wolcott, whose equal culpability was unknown, escaped. John Marshall was called to the State Department, in recognition of the steady support Adams had received from a group of Federalists in the South.

The caucus nominated Adams and C. C. Pinckney, and

[1] The word "nullification" is used in a second set of resolutions passed by the Kentucky legislature in 1799, in reply to the resolutions of some of the other states: "A nullification by those sovereignties [the states] of all unauthorized acts done under color of that instrument is the rightful remedy." This phraseology leaves it uncertain, however, whether Jefferson thought the "sovereignties" could act separately and individually.

claimed for them the united support of the party. Hamilton's faction refused to be bound by the caucus. They had hoped to induce Washington to stand for election once more, but his death in 1799 put an end to their plans. Hamilton could not bring himself to uphold Adams, nor even to maintain a discreet silence. Offended by an uncomplimentary reference to his faction, he circulated among his friends a pamphlet criticizing the President's course in severe terms. When through Burr's agency the pamphlet came to light, it appeared to the public that Adams was without honor in his own political household.

By contrast the Republicans were harmonious and disciplined. Washington had observed with bitter humor that they had but to set up a broomstick and call it a Democrat to to command every vote in the party. Jefferson and Burr were named again by the caucus, with assurances to Burr that this time he should have equal support with Jefferson.

Burr's nomination in 1796 and 1800 showed the wish of the party to create an intersectional organization. Indeed, both parties adopted these tactics. A presidential candidate representing one section and a second candidate from the other promised the maximum support for the ticket. By accepting the subordinate rôle Burr advanced his fortunes at the expense of his New York rival, George Clinton, who was less ready to acquiesce in the leadership of Virginia. The Virginia-New York alliance thus begun lasted, with occasional interruptions, as long as the original Republican party.

The Republicans found many points at which to attack the Federalist administration. In spite of rising taxes the public debt had increased, giving color to the charge of extravagance. The *Aurora,* a notorious paper, constantly insisted that the Federalists had "picked a quarrel" with France in order to raise a standing army, form a British alliance, and establish a monarchy. All their measures, from Hamilton's financial schemes to the Alien and Sedition Acts, showed them, the Republicans declared, to be the party of the moneyed class and aristocrats.

The Republicans carried the electoral college by a vote of 73 to 65. As Burr, according to promise, received the same number of votes as Jefferson, an embarrassing situation resulted, since the tie threw the decision into the House of Representatives. The House assembled for the purpose of balloting in February, 1801. The intention of the Republicans to make Jefferson President was well understood, yet as the Constitution read the House was unrestricted in making its choice. If the Republicans had commanded a majority of members in a majority of the state delegations, the election of Jefferson would have resulted from the first ballot as a matter of course; but they controlled only eight states out of sixteen. The Federalists had six, and in two the parties were equally divided.

This situation made it possible for the Federalists to prevent an election until they were ready for it to take place, but hardly to decide it in Burr's favor as many of them would gladly have done, believing that Burr as a northerner would be more amenable to Federalist influence than Jefferson. In a party caucus it was decided to give him the preference. There is no proof that Burr made any promises to win their favor; on the contrary, he protested openly against a plan which was contrary to the will of his party.

After many ballots the vote still stood eight states for Jefferson and six for Burr, with two divided, and it was Hamilton's advice which finally broke the deadlock. In reply to the inquiries of friends he gave his frank opinion of both candidates. He denounced Burr, whose character he knew well, as "the Cataline of America." Jefferson, he thought, was not overscrupulous about telling the truth, and a "contemptible hypocrit," but he believed that he would pursue a "temporizing rather than a violent policy." In other words, he judged that Jefferson as President would be too astute to disturb in any serious way the structure which the Federalists had reared.

Following Hamilton's advice, on the thirty-sixth ballot some of the Federalists refrained from voting or cast blank ballots, allowing their Republican colleagues to throw the votes of the divided delegations to Jefferson and thus elect him.

Several important consequences followed the House election of 1801. Taken together with the experience of 1796 it proved the necessity of changing the method of casting the electoral votes and led to the passage of the Twelfth Amendment. This amendment required separate ballots for President and Vice-President, and has been called the constitutional recognition of the party system. It also reduced the number of names to go before the House, in case there was not a majority of the electoral ballots for any candidate, from five to three. The amendment was ratified in 1804, in time for the election of that year.

Hamilton's part in defeating Burr was the beginning of an enmity between the two men which, nourished by later events, led in 1804 to a duel which cost Hamilton's life.

With their defeat in 1800 the Federalists made their exit from the administration of national affairs. They had supplied the constructive ability needed to prove the experiment in constitutional government a success. They had organized the government, put its credit on a firm basis, vindicated the national authority, and greatly improved international relations through treaties with Spain, England, and France. Their work had been done so well that, as Hamilton predicted, the Republicans did not venture to make fundamental changes.

It may seem surprising that a party which had rendered such

services never succeeded in recovering from its first defeat. But for this there were several reasons. In the first place, as just stated, the Republicans built upon the foundations laid by the Federalists. In the second place the Federalists had continually offended by their aristocratic temper and acts. In so far as the masses enjoyed the right to vote they were effectually alienated and driven into the Republican ranks.

A very important part of the increasing strength of Republicanism was due to the rise of the West. The Kentucky and Tennessee frontiersmen came chiefly from that discontented stock of the Virginia and Carolina Piedmont which had in vain demanded political equality with the aristocrats of the tidewater. Even Federalists, when they migrated to the West, changed parties. It seemed that their principles could not withstand the strong solvents of the frontier. It was the younger and less prosperous men who felt most strongly the lure of the new regions, and whatever profession of Federalism they made was soon abandoned in their new homes. Their outlook on life was not that of the prosperous stay-at-homes. Pioneer conditions bred the ideas of equality and popular government for which Jefferson stood.

Southern Federalists also, for the most part, soon found Jefferson's party acceptable, and after 1800 Federalism had little vitality outside of New England.

SELECT BIBLIOGRAPHY

Western Questions. See books cited for Chapter XII. Ogg, *The Opening of the Mississippi,* is useful for the earlier West as well as for the topics included in the present chapter. For the Indian wars see Boyd, *Mad Anthony Wayne.* On the Ohio country before statehood see Downes, *Frontier Ohio.* A popular volume on Ohio before 1812 is Crouse, *The Ohio Gateway;* the best history of the state is Roseboom and Weisenburger, *History of Ohio.*

Relations with France, England, and Spain. Bassett, *Federalist System,* and Channing, *United States,* have useful chapters on foreign relations. Trescot, *Diplomatic History of the Administrations of Washington and Adams,* is fuller but somewhat antiquated. In addition to the diplomatic histories cited in bibliographies for preceding chapters, see Adams, *History of the Foreign Policy of the United States,* and Johnson, *America's Foreign Relations.* By far the best studies of the diplomatic relations with England and Spain are the two books by Bemis, *Jay's Treaty,* and *Pinckney's Treaty.* Illuminating studies of French policy towards the United States are: "The Origin of Genêt's Projected Attack on Louisiana and the Floridas," and "The Policy of France toward the Mississippi Valley in the Period of Washington and Adams," both in Turner, *The Significance of Sections in American History.* Excellent and more recent is Whitaker, *The Mississippi Question, 1795–1803.* On McGillivray see Caughey, *McGillivray of the Creeks.*

Party Politics. Bassett, Channing, McMaster, and Schouler are useful. Gordy, *Political History,* is more particularly devoted to party politics than any of these. See also Ford, *Washington and His Colleagues.* Stanwood, *History of the Presidency,* gives compact and accurate summaries of the presidential campaigns. Bowers, *Jefferson and Hamilton,* is as interesting as fiction.

Adams and the Breach with France. See works cited under preceding heads.

The Alien and Sedition Acts. The best studies of the Resolutions of 1798 are: Warfield, *The Kentucky Resolutions of 1798,* and Anderson, "Contemporary Opinion of the Virginia and Kentucky Resolutions."

The Republican Triumph. Use works already cited.

Chapter XVI

JEFFERSONIAN DEMOCRACY

THE REPUBLICAN SYSTEM

THE advent of Jefferson marked the first change in party administration, and the political atmosphere was charged with portents of impending events. There were New Englanders who believed that the Republican party was the American counterpart of French democracy, and that its triumph would be followed by excesses like those of the Reign of Terror in Paris. Jefferson's religious beliefs were misunderstood in the strongholds of orthodox Puritanism. His faith was close to that of the Deists, but many thought him to to be an atheist of the French type, and dire calamities were predicted in consequence of his elevation to office.[1]

Jefferson himself spoke of his election as a "revolution." In putting the ship of state "on her Republican tack," however, he took pains to reassure his countrymen. His first public utterance, the inaugural address, was an appeal to men of all political faiths. "We have called by different names brethren of the same principle," he said. "We are all republicans, we are all federalists."

Then, in the hope of winning general approbation, he set forth what he deemed to be the essential principles of government: "Equal and exact justice to all men . . . peace, commerce, and honest friendship with all nations, entangling alliances with none . . . a well-disciplined militia, our best reliance in peace, and for the first moments of war, till regulars may relieve them:—the supremacy of the civil over the

---

[1] Deism may be concisely defined as belief in God but not in revelation except through God's works. The Deists rejected all miracles.

military authority—economy in the public expense that labor
may be lightly burdened:—the honest payment of our debts
and sacred preservation of the public faith:—encouragement
of agriculture, and of commerce as its handmaid:—the diffusion of information, and arraignment of all abuses at the
bar of the public reason:—freedom of religion; freedom of
the press; and freedom of person, under the protection of the
Habeas Corpus:—and trial by juries impartially selected."

The effort to find the common ground on which all Americans could stand reduced some of these remarks to platitudes.
Others indicated views of the Republicans which genuine
Federalists did not share.   Such were the references to the
militia, economy, the public debt, and the mutual relations of
agriculture and commerce.   The main purpose of the address
came out in a private letter in which Jefferson indicated his
belief that many persons who were Republicans at heart were
in the Federalist ranks because of the late troubles with
France.   These he hoped to lead into the Republican fold
by cautious and conciliatory words and deeds.

Elsewhere in the address Jefferson stated his ideal: "A
wise and frugal government, which shall restrain men from
injuring one another, shall leave them otherwise free to regulate their own pursuits of industry and improvement, and
shall not take from the mouth of labor the bread it has earned.
This is the sum of good government."   Such an ideal is in
marked contrast with Hamilton's conception.   It reduced the
functions of government to the minimum, hardly more than
the preservation of order and defense against foreign attacks,
and reserved the largest possible sphere for individual action.
It was entirely in harmony with Jefferson's faith in a simple
agricultural state as the best basis for democracy.   A government with so few functions would not need by taxation to
"take from the mouth of labour the bread it has earned."

Hamilton's ideal of government was much less simple.

For him government was an agency for the promotion of the general welfare in manifold ways. Through its fostering care resources might be developed and industry stimulated. Economic strength would result, permitting the levy of heavy taxes for meeting the cost of performing many functions. The prosperity of commerce would justify the expense of a protecting navy, and national power would give the country a respectable position among the nations. Hamilton's theory was akin to that of the mercantilists and much closer than Jefferson's to the tenets of European statesmen.

In choosing his cabinet Jefferson again showed his desire to conciliate New England. He appointed General Henry Dearborn, of Massachusetts, Secretary of War, and Levi Lincoln, of the same state, Attorney-General. For Postmaster-General he selected Gideon Granger, of Connecticut. The last office, though not a cabinet position, was important because the holder controlled the appointment of numerous local postmasters and clerks.

The chief cabinet posts went to Madison, as Secretary of State, and Albert Gallatin, as Secretary of the Treasury. Madison, like Hamilton, was a small man, only five feet six in stature. Beside him Jefferson towered like a giant with his six feet two and one-half inches. The two men held each other in warm affection, and although the difference in their ages was but eight years, the contrast in physical appearance made their relations resemble those of father and son. Gallatin was by birth a Swiss, but he had come to America in 1780 while still a mere lad. For a time his home was in western Pennsylvania, the part affected by the Whisky Insurrection. He attended the meetings which preceded that outbreak, counseling moderation and opposing violence, but found his influence outweighed by that of the hotheads. He entered Congress during Washington's presidency, and at once showed a mastery of finance that made him a godsend to his party.

He alone among its members was able to cope with Hamilton's genius in that sphere on terms of approximate equality. In spite of his ability and loyalty his enemies in both parties would not forget his foreign birth and embittered his life by petty persecutions.

The first departure from Federalist ways appeared in the simplicity of the conduct of the new President. The inauguration took place in the new capital city on the Potomac. Its wild surroundings, in a district still only sparsely peopled, and its uncompleted buildings and streets, were more suggestive of the frontier than of the gayety and ceremonial of European capitals, and would have made elaborate display seem out of place. Jefferson, moreover, made a virtue of "republican simplicity." He walked up Capitol Hill to take the oath of office. He gave up the state carriage with six horses which his predecessors had used, and rode horseback unattended when he went out. Being a widower whose daughters were married and in homes of their own, his household lacked feminine management. The formalities at the executive mansion which had kept plain citizens at a distance gave way to the open house, and at times informality was allowed to slip over into slouchiness, as when on one occasion the President received a foreign diplomat in dressing-gown and slippers. Even worse, because of mild international complications which resulted, was the rule of "pêle mêle" in official etiquette —gravely adopted "to maintain the principles of equality"— "of gentlemen in mass giving precedence to the ladies in mass in passing from one apartment . . . into another." After one or two experiences with the working of the rule, the British minister declined the President's invitation to dinner "awaiting instructions from his Government."

In dealing with Congress Jefferson replaced the annual address, an imitation of the English king's speech from the throne, by the written message. In making the change he

explained that he "had principal regard to the convenience
of the Legislature," concealing his own preference for a
method of communication which would not display his lack
of readiness as a speaker. Indirection was one of Jefferson's
traits. He never, like Hamilton, announced aims boldly and
fought his way to them against all opposition. He preferred
the arts of management. Suggestion, advice, intimation, were
better means of attaining objectives than dictation. Within
the glove, however, was an iron hand, and few presidents have
dominated their parties so completely.

The Republicans had denounced the extravagance of the
Federalists and promised an economical administration.
They suspected Hamilton of desiring to perpetuate the public debt for political reasons, and resolved to get rid of it as
speedily as possible. The excise tax they had always disliked
because of its inquisitorial character, and they promptly repealed it. Notwithstanding the loss of this revenue, Gallatin's
careful calculations showed that by curtailing expenditures
the debt could be paid in sixteen years. The economies for
this purpose were made at the expense of the army and navy.
Although a military academy at West Point was authorized
in 1802, adequate support was withheld and the army was
sharply reduced. Naval construction ceased and the few
ships already built were tied up at the docks.

Jefferson's devotion to peace and his confidence in the
reasonableness of mankind led him to believe that the nation
was safe without armaments. Trusting the militia—the
citizen soldiery—as a sufficient first line of defense in case of
invasion, he planned a "naval militia" for protecting the
coast. Small gunboats were built and distributed among the
bays and inlets along the Atlantic, to be manned by the
farmers of the vicinity in case of attack. The boats proved
to be unmanageable in rough water, and, indeed, almost
useless.

Unexpected events—the Tripolitan War and the Louisiana Purchase—swelled expenditures far beyond Gallatin's calculations.   Nevertheless his policy of debt reduction went forward, for the receipts from customs rose rapidly, largely in consequence of importations due to the practice of the "broken voyage."   The European war era was the golden age of the American carrying trade, and the treasury reaped a harvest from duties on goods brought in and reëxported.

The President found the appointive offices occupied by Federalists.   Few men of his party had been appointed by Washington and Adams.   Monroe and Gerry, selected for diplomatic missions, were notable exceptions.   Republicans were eager for the spoils of victory and pressed Jefferson to remove the adherents of the defeated party to make room for his friends.   Jefferson would not do so; he wished to prove the sincerity of the appeal which he had made to the Federalists in the inaugural address.   The tests of a man's fitness, he said, should be, Is he honest?   Is he capable?   Is he faithful to the Constitution?   But some room had to be made for Republicans, and as the President remarked in rather grim jest, none of the Federalist officeholders resigned and few died.   So he removed the men whom Adams had appointed since the election, and in filling offices decided to choose Republicans until a parity of parties existed in the civil service. Once started on this course the time never arrived when he found it possible to make appointments without regard to party, and few indeed were the Federalists who received office at his hands.

His treatment of one group of appointments led to a notable court decision.   In February, 1801, in the last moments of Federalist majority in Congress, a law was passed authorizing the appointment of a number of justices of the peace for the District of Columbia.   Adams made the nominations so late in his term that—so the story went out—he was busy until midnight on March 3 signing commissions. Commissions were, in fact, found by the new administration upon the desk of the Secretary of State, signed and ready for delivery.

Jefferson thought it indecent for Adams to make such haste to put men into office who would serve under his successor, and instructed Madison not to deliver the commissions. Marbury, one of the "midnight appointees," applied to the Supreme Court for an order (writ of mandamus) directing Madison to deliver his commission. John Marshall, now Chief Justice, gave the opinion of the Court. Marbury, he held, was entitled to the commission, but the Supreme Court could not issue the writ because, according to the Constitution, Marbury's case was one which could come before the Court only on appeal. Although the Judiciary Act of 1789 seemed to provide for an original hearing in such cases by the Supreme Court, such a provision was void because it conflicted with the Constitution, which clearly specified the classes of cases in which the Supreme Court was the court of first resort. This case of Marbury *vs.* Madison (1803) is memorable because it was the first in which the Court passed upon the constitutionality of an act of Congress.

The Marbury decision greatly annoyed the Republicans. It seemed to them that the Court was placing itself above both the legislative and executive branches of government. If it could give orders to executive officials and set aside acts of legislation, was not the doctrine of equal, coördinate branches of government destroyed? They contended that while the Court was not bound by the opinion of the law-making body as expressed in statutes, neither could it bind either of the coördinate branches of the government by its opinions.

The Republicans, in fact, disliked the judicial system and thought that the legislature was much the safer guardian of the interests of the people. This was especially true now that they had the majority in Congress. They regarded the judges with all the more suspicion because they were Federalists. It seemed as if their antagonists, defeated at the polls, had fortified themselves in the judiciary, since judges were appointed instead of elected, and held office during good behavior instead of for fixed terms, like members of Congress and executive officials.

It was in their treatment of the judiciary that the new rulers showed the greatest tendency to interfere with the work of the Federalists. Even before the Marbury decision they had begun their attack. Besides the act under which that case arose, the Federalists had passed at about the same time a judiciary act making certain modifications in the court system as organized in 1789. The chief change was a provision for a distinct set of judges for the circuit courts, with a due complement of attorneys and marshals. From the outset the Supreme Court justices had demurred to the circuit-court duty required of them, not only because travel from district to district was an arduous labor, but also because they thought it bad practice for a judge to sit as supreme justice, in case of appeal, on the same causes which he had heard in the lower court. The Federalists welcomed the opportunity, moreover, when passing the new law, to place men of their own faith in the new positions. Adams had promptly nominated the judges and they had been confirmed by the Senate and were in office when the change of administration took place.

Jefferson referred to the new judges as "excrescences on the judiciary," and recommended that Congress repeal the act. The Republicans, exaggerating the cost, held that the law entailed needless expense, that the judges were not overburdened under the old plan, and that the purpose of the act was partisan. Repealing the law, they restored the original status of the circuit courts but added one judge to the Supreme Bench.

In one other way the Republicans showed that their control of Congress gave them the advantage over the Federalists intrenched in the judiciary. The power in impeachment cases is lodged by the Constitution in the two houses, the right to present charges belonging to the lower house, while the Senate hears the arguments and renders judgment. The grounds of impeachment are "treason, bribery, or other high crimes and misdemeanors."

At Jefferson's suggestion Congress turned the machinery of impeachment against John Pickering, judge of the New Hampshire federal district court. Pickering had appeared upon the bench in an intoxicated condition, and was clearly unfit for his position. In the course of the proceedings, however, it appeared that he was of unsound mind, and the question arose whether an insane man could be guilty of a misdemeanor in the ordinary legal sense. The Senate finally voted that he was "guilty as charged," thus evading the difficulty.

Encouraged by this success the Republicans next impeached Samuel Chase, an associate justice of the Supreme Court. Chase's real offense was partisan conduct. He had presided at some of the trials under the Sedition Act, and had shown prejudice against the accused. On another occasion, in a harangue to a jury, he had attacked the Republicans as a "mobocracy." In this case the Senate was unwilling to take ground which might lead to impeachments for mere differences of political opinion, and Chase was acquitted. The words of the Constitution imposed no check upon the discretion of the Senate when sitting as a court of impeachment, but public opinion and common sense tended to limit impeachments to cases of unethical conduct. The outcome of the

Chase trial possibly prevented the Republicans from proceeding against Chief Justice Marshall for his decision in the Marbury case.

THE LOUISIANA PURCHASE

The pacific course of Jefferson's first administration was interrupted by trouble with Tripoli. The Barbary States of the African coast of the Mediterranean had enriched themselves for many years at the expense of European commerce. Strangely the powers, instead of chastising the pirates, had as the result of their own rivalries, fallen into the habit of purchasing immunity by the payment of annual tribute. As part of the British Empire the American colonies had shared in the immunity from attack which this policy secured for British vessels. An unpleasant reminder of the price of independence was the seizure of some American vessels soon after the Revolution ended.

Against Jefferson's protest Washington's government adopted the European plan in dealing with the pirate states. Unhampered by the jealousies which tied the hands of the European governments, the United States, Jefferson believed, was strong enough to teach the corsairs a lesson. Therefore, when the ruler of Tripoli declared war in 1801, because of dissatisfaction with the present which the United States had sent him, he accepted the challenge. The Pasha meant by his declaration that seizures of American vessels would be resumed, and was little prepared for the action of the President in sending ships to blockade his coast.

Although marked by deeds of heroism, the war ran on for four years without decisive action, and in the end peace was obtained only by paying a ransom for captured American sailors. But the treaty provided that there should be no further tribute. The war developed a fine morale in the little navy, and trained a group of young officers who were to encounter British fighting ships a few years later.[1]

The most important event by far of Jefferson's first term was the purchase in 1803 of the Province of Louisiana, which spread its broad plains westward from the Mississippi River to the Rocky Mountains. First explored by Frenchmen before the middle of the eighteenth century, it received its name in honor of the king of France. At the close of the French and Indian War it had become the property of Spain. At that time a few traders of French blood had reached the site of the modern St. Louis, but thence southward to Red River wilderness prevailed, except for a lonely post or two on the Arkansas. Most of the inhabitants dwelt in New Orleans or near by. Apart from a few Spanish officials the St. Louis settlements remained French during the Spanish period, with numbers augmented about 1763 by newcomers from the eastern banks of the Mississippi, who found English rule distasteful.

Among the inhabitants of Spanish Louisiana the occasional American was conspicuous because of his rarity. The interest which the people of the United States felt in the transmississippi region was hardly that of possible settlers. Rather it was the interest of rivals who were jealous of the power which through possession of the mouth of the Mississippi held the economic life, and perhaps the political destiny, of the entire interior valley in its hand. The Spanish closure of the river and intrigues with the early settlers of the West had jeopardized the hold of the United States upon the transmontane country and taught statesmen the danger that would be involved in having a strong power in Spain's place. No one was more aware of this danger than Jefferson.

---

[1] During the War of 1812 the pirate states took advantage of the embarrassment of the United States and renewed their captures. In 1815 a strong squadron was again sent to the Mediterranean and the corsairs were forced to sign treaties which ended their depredations.

While Secretary of State, in 1790, the threat of war between England and Spain drew attention to the probable effects on the United States. If war came, England would, in all probability, attack and seize Louisiana and the Floridas. Then, as Jefferson said, she would embrace us on one side by her possessions and on the other by her fleet. Such a situation would be perilous in the extreme, for it would destroy the American balance of power, as Jefferson called it. It was to the interest of the United States to have Spain remain in possession of Louisiana and the Floridas rather than to have them pass into the hands of a more powerful nation.

But the war cloud of 1790 blew over, and the real danger came not from England but from France. Although by the alliance of 1778 that country renounced all pretensions to territory in North America, the Revolution had hardly closed before she began efforts to regain Louisiana. Genêt's plans for expeditions organized on American soil bore witness to this ambition. After 1795 when Spain and France made peace, French influence grew apace. Appeals were made to Spain's fears of American encroachments, and she was urged to retrocede a province which only the strong arm of France could defend. French representatives in the United States significantly pointed out to their home government that the Mississippi Valley was a natural unit, that a river did not form a good international barrier, and that one nation was destined to rule the whole interior of the continent from the Appalachians to the Cordilleras.

Spain resisted the pressure of her neighbor until Bonaparte became First Consul. He eagerly embraced the plan of a revived colonial empire, and in characteristic manner obtained the coveted cession by means which left the weaker party little choice. Almost at the same instant that the treaty of 1800 with the United States was signed, Spain retroceded Louisiana by the Treaty of San Ildefonso. Bonaparte promised never to dispose of the territory to any other power than Spain, and also to create a kingdom in Italy for the Spanish king's son-in-law. He afterwards violated both pledges without compunction.

This Treaty of San Ildefonso was made secretly. France and England were still at war, and Bonaparte dared not allow the mistress of the seas to learn of his acquisition until he had an army on the ground to defend it. He prepared an expedition, therefore, for the double purpose of reconquering Santo Domingo and occupying New Orleans.

The eastern portion of the island of Santo Domingo was the most valued possession of France in the West Indies, and after 1763, in the western hemisphere. It was a rich source of sugar and other tropical products, and formed the nucleus of the plan of a revived colonial empire. It was valued for the same reason that the English mercantilists prized colonies the resources of which supplemented those of the British Isles. But it was not self-supporting; it did not produce its own food supplies, nor could France provision it, especially in war time. In this fact lay the value for France of peace with the United States, for from America came the means of subsistence for the island population. The possession of Louisiana would free France from this dependence upon the United States and complete the economic structure of her colonial empire.[1]

During the gloomy days of the Revolution in France, when she was hard beset by her foes, the slaves of the island had risen in revolt and drenched the soil with the blood of their masters. Under the lead of the remarkable Negro Toussaint Louverture a black republic had been set up and independence proclaimed. The career of the "gilded African," as Bonaparte called him, on a small scale paralleled his own

[1] Recall also the political influence which France would have over the United States through the possession of Louisiana.

and won for the Negro the name of the "Black Napoleon."

The preliminaries of the Peace of Amiens, made with England in October, 1801, gave Bonaparte a breathing space for putting his designs into execution. His army reached Santo Domingo early in 1802, and before summer had treacherously captured Toussaint and sent him to perish in a French dungeon. The blacks submitted, only to be roused again to frenzied resistance when the restoration of slavery was attempted. The war was thus prolonged until the heats of summer brought yellow fever to fight the battles of the islanders. The white army melted away and the reconquest of the island was given up. Without it Louisiana was less desirable, and the army of occupation had left its bones in San Domingan graves.

With the Treaty of San Ildefonso "the shadow of the Corsican fell across the seas." Rumors of the treaty revived Jefferson's fear of a strong power at the mouth of the Mississippi, and his pro-French sympathies did not for a moment blur his vision of the danger to America if France supplanted Spain. The French minister in the United States had warned his government, just after the election of 1796, that "Jefferson is an American and by that title cannot be sincerely our friend."

The President took pains to acquaint Napoleon with his views on the transfer of Louisiana in no uncertain terms. He wrote a letter to Robert R. Livingston, the American minister in Paris, declaring: "There is on the globe one single spot the possessor of which is our natural and habitual enemy. It is New Orleans, through which the produce of three eighths of our territory must pass to market. . . . [Spain's] pacific dispositions, her feeble state, would induce her to increase our facilities there, so that her possession of the place would be hardly felt by us. . . . Not so can it ever be in the hands of France. . . . The day that France takes possession of New

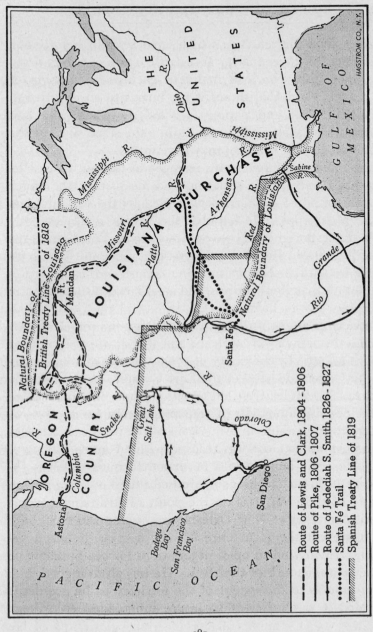

Route of Lewis and Clark, 1804 - 1806
Route of Pike, 1806 - 1807
Route of Jedediah S. Smith, 1826 - 1827
Santa Fé Trail
Spanish Treaty Line of 1819

THE LOUISIANA PURCHASE AND EXPLORATIONS OF THE WEST

Orleans, fixes the sentence which is to restrain her forever within her low-water mark. It seals the union of two nations, who, in conjunction, can maintain exclusive possession of the ocean. From that moment, we must marry ourselves to the British fleet and nation . . . and . . . make the first cannon which shall be fired in Europe the signal for tearing up any settlement [France] may have made. . . ."

The intensity of Jefferson's feeling was due to his conviction that France would seek and find means to unite under her control all of the territory watered by the ramifications of the Mississippi. He felt that the destiny of the country was at stake, and that, if he would not see the Alleghanies become its western limit, the designs of France must be frustrated even at the cost of a foreign alliance, such as he deprecated in his inaugural address, and an alliance at that with the England which he hated!

Some time after this letter was written news came that the Spanish officials at New Orleans had withdrawn the right of deposit granted by the treaty of 1795. In this action was erroneously seen the hand of the First Consul. Only in recent years has it been learned that the closure was due to an order of the Spanish monarch, in response to complaints of local officers alleging abuse by Americans of the privileges allowed them. An adjustment was reached without much difficulty. But before the tangle could be smoothed out the West, expecting the French legions and aroused almost to frenzy by the closure of the river, was on the point of striking the weak Spanish garrison at New Orleans and seizing the city.

To prevent the recurrence of such a crisis Jefferson instructed Livingston to open negotiations for the purchase of a tract at the mouth of the river. He was given a good deal of latitude as to the extent of the territory to be acquired, provided it was sufficient to insure unmolested enjoyment of navigation and transshipment of cargoes. To reassure the West by visible efforts Monroe, who was popular there, was dispatched as special envoy to aid Livingston in the negotiations.

These steps did not indicate that the threat in Jefferson's letter would be carried into effect. They seemed to mean that the government would not forcibly oppose the occupation of New Orleans, provided the tract asked for could be purchased. It is not likely, in any event, that Jefferson's threatening language had much to do with Napoleon's decision to part with the whole of Louisiana. The failure in Santo Domingo, and even more, conditions in Europe, were turning his thoughts from colonial empire. In March, 1803, it became certain that the Peace of Amiens would soon be ruptured, and he probably decided that the good will of the United States would be cheaply bought if obtained at the price of what, for want of an army of occupation, he could not hold against either the sea power of the British or the rifles of the frontiersmen. Regardless of his promises to Spain and of the French constitution, which did not permit the executive to alienate territory, he resolved to sell Louisiana to the United States.

On April 11, 1803, Talleyrand, discussing with Livingston the sale of the Isle of Orleans, suddenly asked, "What would you give for the whole of Louisiana?" Livingston, surprised beyond measure and somewhat deaf, could hardly trust his ears. Once convinced that the First Consul was in earnest the only question to be decided was the price. Although Livingston conducted the negotiations, he would not conclude them until Monroe arrived, and both signed the treaty dated April 30 which for 80,000,000 francs more than doubled the area of the United States. Livingston may be pardoned for exclaiming "This is the noblest work of our lives!"

When Jefferson learned what Livingston had done he was

perplexed. It was not from any doubt of the immense benefits of the cession that he hesitated. All of his fears for the future of the West were dispelled by the treaty. Relieved of the menace involved in the devious policies of European states, the great valley gave ample room for the peaceful expansion and development of the Republic. Possession of the lands beyond the Mississippi also suggested the possibility of removing the Indian tribes from the eastern states. But provision for the acquisition of territory was, as he said, a "*casus omissus*" of the Constitution. The treaty provided, moreover, that Louisiana should be "incorporated into the Union," and that the inhabitants should be admitted to all of the privileges of citizens.

Consistency required the President either to abandon the treaty or to seek the powers needed to authorize it. He decided upon the latter course, and drafted an amendment to give constitutional sanction for what had been done, without authority, on behalf of the nation. "Let us not," he urged, "make blank paper of the constitution by construction." But he found the Republicans whose advice he sought were not willing to risk the uncertain outcome of an effort at amendment. They adopted Hamilton's doctrine of implied powers, and in the power of making war and treaties held that there was ample warrant for acquiring territory.

Jefferson at length yielded his scruples, for delay was dangerous, as Livingston and Monroe were warning him that Napoleon might change his mind. In the face of vigorous protests by the Federalists, the Senate ratified the treaty and the houses joined in authorizing the President to receive the territory and to provide for its government. On the last day of November, 1803, the Spanish governor at New Orleans transferred Louisiana to the representative of France, and twenty days later the tricolor on the *Place d'Armes* was hauled down and replaced by the Stars and Stripes.

PLOTS AND CONSPIRACIES

These events filled the hearts of the Federalists with fore-bodings. In the promise of incorporation and citizenship they saw a pledge of future statehood for Louisiana, and it was against this provision that they directed their main attack while the treaty was before the Senate. They did not object to holding the territory as a permanent dependency, but denied the right of the President and Senate, as the treaty-making organ of government, to promise statehood. They maintained that new states could be admitted into the Union only by Congress, and that such states must be formed within the original territory of the Union.

The attitude of the Federalists was due to their belief that the increase of western states would mean the relative decline of the influence of New England. Gouverneur Morris wrote to Livingston: "Our party though with numerous exceptions opposed" the treaty; "for one reason, that it cost money the greater part of which we to the northward must pay, and it gains territory which will, in their apprehension, by giving strength to the Southern representation, diminish the Eastern influence in our councils." Senator Uriah Tracy, of Connecticut, complained that the relative strength which "admission gives to a Southern and Western interest is contradictory to the principal of our original union." Rufus King and John Quincy Adams were among the Federalists who saw in the acquisition the prospect of a politico-economic alliance between the South and the West, and of the perpetuation of the rule of Jefferson's party.

Some of the ultra Federalists even began to feel that the Union had failed to secure their dearest interests, and to consider secession and the formation of a northern confederation. "The people of the East," wrote Pickering to George Cabot, "cannot reconcile their habits, views, and interests with those of the South and West. The latter are beginning to rule with a rod of iron. . . . I do not believe in the practicability of a long-continued union. A northern confederacy would unite congenial characters."

The plans of the secessionists embraced New England and New York. In order to carry the latter with them they approached Burr. Jefferson distrusted the Vice-President, and deliberately cultivated the Clinton faction in New York, favoring it in federal appointments. Burr, indeed, in whose veins flowed America's best blood, whose ability was beyond question, and who was one of the most skillful political manipulators of his day, lacked the confidence even of his intimate political associates because of his predilection for unscrupulous intrigue. Angered by Jefferson's treatment, he now seemed ready to act with the New England plotters. If New York Federalists united with Burr's faction of the Republicans to make him governor of the state, he would be in position to promote the program of secession there.

It is quite unlikely that this scheme would have found much support among the people either of New England or New York. Jefferson's policy of conciliation had won wide approval in the northeastern states, as the election of 1804 was to show. When Hamilton's advice was sought by the malcontents he wrote: "Dismemberment of our empire will be a clear sacrifice of great positive advantages, without any counterbalancing good." He advised the New York Federalists to have nothing to do with Burr, thus for the second time contributing to his defeat for office. Burr in anger challenged him to a duel.

The encounter cost Hamilton his life and Burr the remnants of his reputation. Realizing that his career was blasted so far as the East was concerned, he turned to the West where the wilderness excited his adventurous genius. With the United States hesitating whether to seize West Florida in

defiance of Spain's claim—or mayhap Texas, to which the
Louisiana Purchase treaty gave even a better claim—the
Spanish borderlands were in a continual state of restless apprehension. Many were the Americans who trespassed on
Spain's rights in Texas during the opening decades of the
nineteenth century, with purposes ranging from the capture
of wild horses to the founding of independent states. Burr's
prominence made it certain that if he joined this crowd of
adventurers, his name would go down to posterity as the most
notorious of them all. His plans are obscure, but they aimed
at the formation of an independent state from the territory
either of the United States or Spain. His own words cannot
be reconciled, for he spoke sometimes of Louisiana and sometimes of Mexico as his objective. That his real design was
against the Spanish is the more plausible conjecture, as it fits
in with conditions and the temper of the people of the West
in these years.

In 1805 he began to collect supplies and men at Blennerhassett Island, in the Ohio River, near Parkersburg, West
Virginia. Before any action indicating his true purpose was
taken, suspicions arose which led his chief supporters to
abandon him. When finally arrested, he was charged with
treason against the United States. Treason is defined by the
Constitution as levying war against the United States, or
giving aid and comfort to the enemy in time of war, and it
could not be shown that the preparations at Blennerhassett
came within this definition. He was therefore acquitted and
disappeared from view, punished with such a load of obloquy
as the American people have never visited upon any other
man, not excepting Benedict Arnold.

General Wilkinson, who was Burr's accomplice, treacherously contributed to his downfall. It was he who had led the
secession movement in Kentucky. Now, while commander
of the United States' forces in the West he was a pensioner of

Spain and faithless to both masters. Although false to every trust he successfully covered his villainy during his lifetime, and bore a supposedly honorable (although incompetent) part in the War of 1812.

EXPLORATIONS IN THE WEST

Jefferson was a man of wide intellectual interests. A philosopher and lover of books, he had an insatiable curiosity about the physical universe and found the cultivation of his garden one of the most delightful of occupations. "Nature intended me," he wrote, "for the tranquil pursuits of science . . . but the enormities of the times . . . have forced me . . . to commit myself on the boisterous ocean of political passions." His correspondence ranged all the way from letters discussing botany with the Italian Philip Mazzei, to inquiries addressed to Kentucky pioneers about the "big bones" found at the salt licks. His curiosity was aroused concerning the unknown West long before Louisiana was acquired. In 1783 he wrote to George Rogers Clark suggesting an exploration into the transmississippi country. He recurred to the project while Secretary of State, but the presidency gave him for the first time means to carry out the scheme. At his instance Congress provided funds for an expedition led by Meriwether Lewis, his secretary, and William Clark, younger brother of the hero of Kaskaskia. Both held commissions in the army. These steps preceded the Louisiana treaty, the President deeming the scientific character of the undertaking inoffensive even though conducted on alien soil. Before the party set out, however, the transfer of Louisiana was completed, so that the explorers were within their own country until they crossed the Rockies.

Leaving St. Louis in 1804, the party went up the Missouri to the Mandan Indian villages near the present Bismarck,

The Landing of Captain Gray in the Columbia River, 1792

North Dakota, where it went into winter quarters. The next season the stream was ascended to its headwaters, where passes were found leading to the upper streams of Snake River. Down this the explorers proceeded to the Columbia, and thence to the Pacific, where the second winter was passed. The mouth of the Columbia had first been entered in 1793, by Captain Robert Gray, of Boston. Alexander Mackenzie, of the Hudson's Bay Company, had soon afterward crossed Canada to Vancouver Sound, but Lewis and Clark were the first white men to traverse any considerable portion of the Columbia River Basin. Their exploration gave the United States a claim to the "Oregon country" of which good use was made later.

Several other explorations of the newly-acquired territory were made at about the same time as the Lewis and Clark expedition. Some of these ascended the Red River but failed to reach its source owing to hostile Indians and even more to the jealousy with which the Spanish watched their border after the exposure of Burr.

Two notable journeys were performed by Lieutenant Zebulon M. Pike. In the winter of 1805 he made a search for the sources of the Mississippi but was unable to make trustworthy observations because of the snow-covered surfaces. In the summer of 1806 he went up the Arkansas River, penetrating the Royal Gorge, and gaining much geographical knowledge. Beyond the ridge Spanish soldiers were encountered, who took his party to Santa Fé and later to Mexico, under the fear that its errand was unfriendly. When released at last Pike returned home by way of Texas and Louisiana. The information which he gained about the northern provinces of Mexico through this enforced visit aroused interest in the United States and was afterwards a factor in opening the Santa Fé trail for trade with them.

DISPUTE OVER WEST FLORIDA

The Louisiana treaty involved the United States in a new dispute with Spain over boundaries. The treaty said that the United States was to receive the province "with the same extent that it now has in the hands of Spain, and that it had when France possessed it" before 1763. The French had claimed the Perdido River as the eastern boundary of Louisiana, but Spain had received nothing east of the Isle of Orleans in 1763, the part of French Louisiana lying between the Iberville and the Perdido going to England. When in 1783 England transferred this tract to Spain, Spain did not change the boundary between the provinces of Louisiana and West Florida. Spanish Louisiana, therefore, included nothing east of New Orleans. Did her retrocession to France include the tract east of the Iberville which had come to her through England as intermediate owner?

Livingston in perplexity asked Talleyrand what France intended to take under the Treaty of San Ildefonso. Talleyrand had in his possession at that moment a copy of the instructions prepared for the first French governor of Louisiana, in which the Rio Grande and Iberville were mentioned as the boundaries; but for some reason best known to himself —perhaps a wish to embroil the United States with Spain— he preferred to dissimulate. "I do not know," he replied. "You have made a noble bargain for yourselves, and I suppose you will make the most of it."

Livingston, although he knew that Spain had refused to include land east of the Iberville in the retrocession to France, and in spite of the fact that Napoleon informed them, soon after the signing of the treaty, that they had no claim to West Florida, taking the cue from Talleyrand, worked out a theory that Spain had retroceded West Florida inadvertently. Although the Spanish minister in the United States wrote to

Madison, several weeks before the treaty was ratified, protesting that in buying Louisiana the United States had really purchased stolen goods,[1] Jefferson not only ignored the protest, but, accepting Livingston's interpretation of boundaries, claimed the territory between the Iberville and the Perdido. Without awaiting the outcome of efforts to persuade Spain to accept this interpretation of the treaty, he asked Congress to extend the revenue laws to the district, although he located

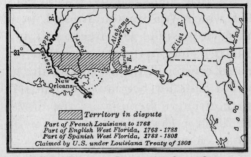

WEST FLORIDA DISPUTE, 1803–1819

the customs house on undisputed ground (1804). Then he turned to diplomacy.

Spain stood firm as to West Florida, but Talleyrand suggested that through French mediation the United States might be able to obtain the relinquishment of Spain's claim. Having failed to gain a means of influencing American policy through the possession of Louisiana, France now found it in Jefferson's hunger for territory. The President was kept dancing for several years to the Emperor's piping. In 1806 he persuaded Congress, not without considerable difficulty, to grant an appropriation for the settlement of the dispute through the mediation of France, but by this time Napoleon had lost interest because a favorable turn of fortune had made him careless of America's good will and money. The

[1] "In taking Louisiana," says Professor Channing, "we were the accomplices of the greatest highwayman of modern history."

settlement of this dispute over West Florida was not obtained until the whole of Florida was purchased by the treaty of 1819.

The acquisition of Louisiana influenced America profoundly. The acceptance by the party of strict construction of interpretation in place of amendment as a means of adapting the Constitution to new needs confirmed that process. The removal of European influence from the Mississippi Valley made real that "detached and distant" position of the United States which Washington stressed in his Farewell Address, and made possible that freedom from "entangling alliances" which Jefferson recommended in his inaugural. The undisputed control of the West gave the United States the geographical basis for becoming a great power, able to maintain in the western hemisphere the distinctive policy known as the Monroe Doctrine.

Two essential elements of that doctrine were already in evidence at the opening of the nineteenth century. Washington contributed one of them when he advised his countrymen to avoid permanent European alliances. Jefferson supplied the other when he resolved that Louisiana must not pass from the hands of Spain to any other European state, because of its vital relation to the welfare of the United States. These two elements—the principle of isolation and that of paramount interest—when joined with the principle of non-intervention in the message of President Monroe in 1823, constituted the famous doctrine which bears his name.

SELECT BIBLIOGRAPHY

The Republican System. Adams, *History of the United States of America during the Administrations of Jefferson and Madison,* is one of the best pieces of historical writing yet achieved in the United States. Channing, in *United States,* IV, and *Jeffersonian System,* is juster to the Republicans. Johnson, *Jefferson and his Colleagues,* is brief and readable. Bowers, *Jefferson in Power,* is readable and gossipy. Adams (James Truslow) expounds Jefferson's principles in *The Living Jefferson*. *Cf.* Chinard, *Thomas Jefferson*, and Wiltse, *The Jeffersonian Tradition*. Fish, *The Civil Service and the Patronage*, contains a section on Jefferson's policy.

The Louisiana Purchase. Adams's account of the acquisition of Louisiana takes insufficient note of the influence of European factors upon Napoleon's policy. *Cf.* Ogg, *Opening of the Mississippi*, Channing, *United States*, and *Jeffersonian System*, and diplomatic histories previously cited. See also Lyon, *Louisiana in French Diplomacy, 1759–1804*, and Brown, *Constitutional History of the Louisiana Purchase*.

Plots and Conspiracies. McCaleb, *The Aaron Burr Conspiracy*; Wandell and Minnegerode, *Aaron Burr*; more recent is Schachner, *Aaron Burr*. This last work presents new evidence which confirms old conclusions. Alexander, *Aaron Burr*, contains nothing new.

Explorations in the West. Roosevelt, *Winning of the West*; Dellenbaugh, *Breaking the Wilderness*; Ghent, *The Early Far West*; Gilbert, *The Exploration of Western America*; and Wilson, *Meriwether Lewis* (a mediocre biography).

Dispute over West Florida. Adams, *History of the United States*; Chambers, "West Florida"; Fuller, *Purchase of Florida*; and Cox, *West Florida Controversy, 1798–1813*.

Chapter XVII

THE STRUGGLE FOR NEUTRAL RIGHTS

RELATIONS WITH ENGLAND

THE general acceptability of Jeffersonian principles was shown by the reëlection of the President in 1804 by an overwhelming vote. Against C. C. Pinckney and Rufus King, the Federalist candidates, he carried even the New England states with the exception of Connecticut. Clinton, old-time rival of Burr, had profited by his fall, and reconciled temporarily to Virginia's leadership, received the Vice-Presidency in token that the intersectional alliance was intact.

The rupture of the Peace of Amiens in 1803 was followed by war on a scale never before equaled. Within a few years all of Europe was drawn into the struggle, and even the United States, despite its boasted isolation, was in the sequel unable to hold aloof.

The renewed conflict meant both prosperity and trouble for the United States. As in the previous decade the American carrying trade increased by leaps and bounds. In 1790 the total exports of the country were valued at about $19,000,-000. Five years later $26,000,000 worth of goods were brought from the French, Spanish, and Dutch possessions and reëxported. By 1806 the value of reëxports had risen to nearly $60,000,000; tonnage was increasing at the rate of 70,000 a year, requiring 4000 additional seamen every twelve-month; and the relatively high wages were attracting sailors from all of the maritime countries of Europe. Shipbuilding and subsidiary industries were proportionately active and absorbed most of the capital available for investment.

The rapid growth of this neutral commerce at length alarmed the British mercantile and shipping interests. They began to fear that the position of preëminence which they had enjoyed before the wars might be lost permanently. The decision in the case of *The Polly* encouraged a rival who was becoming a menace, and the courts were made to feel the pressure of public opinion. In 1805 came the decision in the *Essex* case. The *Essex* had brought a cargo from Spain to Salem. After it had been landed and the duty paid, it was reshipped to Havana and a drawback allowed for the duty. The highest authority in England held that the cargo was never intended for the United States market, and that, under these circumstances, the broken voyage violated the Rule of 1756 as truly as if direct and continuous.

The decision was regarded in America as a reversal of that in the case of *The Polly,* and the difference seemed to lie in the allowance of the drawback in the *Essex* case. The profitable reëxport trade thus faced the alternative of incurring the penalties of the Rule of 1756 or of carrying the burden of full duties. The British were charged with attempting to prescribe the duties which American commerce should bear in its home ports, as in colonial days. Under instructions from Madison, Monroe, who had gone to England as minister after the purchase of Louisiana, remonstrated with Charles James Fox, the Secretary of Foreign Affairs. Fox, during the Revolution and since, had been friendly, and obtained an executive order, or "Order in Council," which was in effect a substitute for the Rule of 1756 as interpreted in the recent decision. "Fox's Order," as it is called, dated May 16, 1806, announced a blockade of the coast of Europe from Brest to the Elbe River. Except between Ostend and the mouth of the Seine, however, naval officers had instructions to allow passage of inbound neutrals not laden in an enemy's port and outbound neutrals not sailing for one.

Thus trade *via* American ports was tacitly permitted without inquiry as to the payment of duties.

Meantime the question of impressments had again become acute. Within three years, according to a report of Madison, there were nearly twenty-three hundred cases. Impressments and complaints of seizures under the *Essex* decision led Jefferson to decide upon an extraordinary mission, and William Pinkney, of Maryland, was sent to England as Monroe's colleague for the negotiation of a new treaty. The commissioners were instructed to make no treaty which did not provide for the abandonment of impressments. That obtained, they were to seek the repudiation of the *Essex* decision and reparation for the seizures which had followed. These instructions were framed before Fox's Order was issued.

The discussion of impressments soon led to an *impasse*. To abandon the practice, Fox said, might result in the overthrow of British naval power on which the safety of the nation depended. Monroe and Pinkney on their part could not recede from the position that the flag of the United States must protect the crews of American vessels. This question was therefore dropped from the negotiations, with the assurance of the ministry that the greatest caution would be observed, in impressing British seamen found on American ships, not to violate the rights of American citizens.

At the request of the ministry the Americans, notwithstanding their instructions, took up the matter of commerce (Fox died before the negotiations were completed) and on the last day of the year signed a treaty which virtually accepted the *Essex* decision. Its chief provision was that reëxports should be regarded by the British as neutral goods in case they had paid certain duties in American ports. Jefferson did not even submit the treaty to the Senate, but under the urging of Madison instructed that negotiations be resumed. Early in 1807 a new ministry took office with George Canning as Foreign Secretary. To the proposal that negotiations be renewed he replied bluntly that such a course was wholly inadmissible.

Just at this moment occurred the *Leopard-Chesapeake* affair. The *Chesapeake,* Captain James Barron, was an American war-ship. In June, 1807, she left Chesapeake Bay for the Mediterranean, with new armament aboard which was to be mounted during the voyage. Reports had reached the Halifax station, in command of Admiral G. C. Berkeley, that the *Chesapeake* had shipped British deserters in her crew. He therefore ordered the *Leopard* to intercept her and seize any British seamen found on board. Coming up with the *Chesapeake* the *Leopard's* commander sent an officer to demand the surrender of deserters. Captain Barron replied that he knew of none among his crew, and refused to muster the men for inspection. As a matter of fact there were three Americans aboard who had formerly been impressed and had escaped, and one British deserter who had enlisted under an assumed name and had thus escaped Barron's notice.

The commander of the *Leopard,* upon receiving Barron's reply, opened fire. For fifteen minutes the defenseless *Chesapeake* sustained the attack, which killed three men and wounded eighteen. Just as the colors were struck a single gun was fired "for the honor of the flag." Then the British came aboard again and took away the four deserters.

The crippled *Chesapeake* made her way back to Norfolk to tell the tale of outrage. Never before had a government vessel been the victim of a press gang. The national honor was directly affronted. For the first time, in a surge of national emotion, Federalists and Republicans forgot their differences. "The affair of the Chesapeake put war into my hand," wrote Jefferson years afterwards. But the President did not choose war; he contented himself with ordering all British armed ships to leave American waters, while Madison prepared a demand for the punishment of Berkeley, reparation for the damages done, and the abandonment of impressments.

England was so clearly in the wrong in this affair that Jefferson and his Secretary thought she must now yield on all points at issue. When Canning heard of the insult to the flag, he voluntarily sent Monroe a letter of regret and promised reparation if British officers were shown to be culpable. But Jefferson refused reparation unless coupled with the abandonment of impressments, and this attitude made settlement impossible. As Canning said, "it showed a disposition to make a particular incident, in which Great Britain was in the wrong, instrumental to an accommodation in a case in which his Government held a different doctrine."

The climax of the impressment controversy had now been reached. The utmost endeavors to persuade England to give up the practice had been answered with refusal. With Canning's reply the alternatives left to the United States were to acquiesce or to attempt the maintenance of its rights by force, and since no warlike move was made, the decision of the administration, judged by its conduct, was acquiescence.

Monroe wrote urging that the country be put in a better state of defense. He believed the British navy was so occupied in Europe that the ministry would engage in hostilities with the United States only with great reluctance. The administration's course probably tended to confirm the opinion which he reported was prevalent in England, "that the United States are, by the nature of their Government, incapable of any great, vigorous, or persevering action." Randolph believed that the President should have convened Congress at once, following the *Chesapeake* affair, demanded redress, and recalled our minister; and that, if no redress were obtained within a reasonable time, he should have seized Canada to hold until justice was done. Jefferson's inaction relieved Canning of the fear of hostilities.

THE WAR OF ORDERS AND DECREES

By this time (mid-year, 1807) the European war had reached a state of deadlock. England, protected by the Channel like a huge moat, and by her "wooden walls," was beyond Napoleon's reach. He had, to be sure, gathered a host with the evident intent of invading the British Isles, but that possibility vanished with Nelson's victory at Trafalgar (1805) over the combined Spanish and French fleets. Thereupon, turning quickly from the coast, Napoleon struck his continental foes, winning in succession the battles of Austerlitz and Jena, and putting Austria and Prussia under his feet. By the end of 1806 he was the master of central Europe. The next year, by the Battle of Friedland, Russia too was forced to accept a peace (Tilsit) dictated by the Emperor.

With England in control of the seas and France invincible on land the war became an economic contest. Unable to reach his chief antagonist with armed forces, Napoleon devised his "Continental System." Under military pressure a combination of European states was formed, pledged to exclude British commerce from the markets of the continent. England's trade was the source of her economic strength, and to undermine it would be to destroy her power in war.

Fox's blockade, ordered with the intention of doing the United States a favor, gave Napoleon the pretext he needed for the inception of his system. In accordance with British practice the blockade was a "paper" one. France had hitherto agreed with the United States that the paper blockade was illegal, but Napoleon now decided that two could play at the game. He saw in the device a means of enforcing the Continental System, and of isolating England without a navy. Justifying his action by the plea of retaliation against Fox's blockade, he issued a decree from Berlin, in November, 1806, proclaiming a (paper) blockade of the British Isles. This, of course, subjected to capture any neutral vessel bound to or from a British port, but for want of ships it could be enforced only when such vessels visited the continent.

In 1807, by the Peace of Tilsit, the Czar engaged to close Russia's ports against Great Britain. Denmark and Portugal, neutral hitherto, were also compelled to choose between France and England, and saw the lesser danger in supporting the Continental System. The Italian states were likewise forced, and it became a part of Napoleon's aim to bring the conduct of the United States into conformity with his policy. If she did so England might be destroyed.

Realizing her danger, England resorted to retaliatory measures of similar nature; she chose war with the United States under the forms of peace rather than acquiescence in her enemy's designs. Early in 1807 the so-called "First Order in Council" forbade the coasting trade of neutrals between ports under French control. In November a Second Order blockaded the coast from Copenhagen to Trieste against neutrals unless they first entered and cleared from a British port and paid duties there. In other words, the United States was to be allowed to trade with Europe only subject to regulations intended to protect British commerce and to replenish the British treasury! Even more than the *Essex* decision the orders, if obeyed, would have degraded the United States to the level of colonies.

In December Napoleon countered with the Milan Decree under which ships were declared to lose their neutral character if they obeyed the Second Order, or even submitted to search on the high seas by British naval officers.

American commerce was thus caught as it were between upper and nether millstones. Trade with the continent could be carried on only by evading British cruisers. Our direct trade with England, France lacked the means of stopping, but the disastrous effects of the war of Decrees and Orders were shown by a fall of more than two thirds in the value of goods exported from the United States.

The President's remedy for all these wrongs was what he called "peaceable coercion." Jefferson is often called a pacifist. This is an error, for he was not a non-resistant on principle. He used force against Tripoli, threatened war with Spain over West Florida, and talked of a military and naval alliance with England during the Louisiana crisis. Yet he believed that in most cases the appeal to reason and interest was more likely to be availing than resort to the sword. When the belligerent powers seemed to attach so much importance to commercial restrictions as substitutes for military measures, it is hardly surprising that the chief neutral overestimated the effect which self-imposed restrictions were likely to have upon both belligerents. Our commerce is so valuable to them that they will be glad to purchase it when the only price we ask is to do us justice, thought Jefferson. American tradition, moreover, favored commercial coercion, and among the Republicans widespread sentiment demanded an attempt to secure justice by such means. They had withal but half-hearted sympathy with the carrying trade, holding that the legitimate function of commerce was to provide an outlet for our own surplus. During the years of expanding shipping Jefferson had declared that "this exuberant commerce brings us into collision with other Powers in every sea, and will force us into every war with European Powers." He was, perhaps, not loth to sacrifice it in the effort to preserve peace.

Monroe's unsuccessful negotiations, the promulgation of

the Orders in Council and the French Decrees, led to the experiment with the game of commercial war.[1] Indeed, even before the full scope of the Orders and Decrees was known, with the hearty support of his party but in the face of determined opposition by the Federalists, Jefferson's plan of an embargo was enacted into law in December, 1807. This act forbade the departure of all ships for foreign ports except foreign vessels in port at the time of the passage of the bill, which were allowed to depart in ballast or with cargoes already on board. Coasting vessels were required to give bond to land their freight at domestic ports.

Although impartial in terms the embargo did not affect France and England equally. It deprived the former of but little trade not already cut off by the Orders in Council. Federalists declared that the bill had "France" written on its face. "The Emperor," said the French minister at Washington, "applauds the embargo." It deprived Great Britain of her intercourse with America just when he was shutting her out of Europe, and cut off supplies from the West Indies which were supposed to be indispensable. It gave him also the pretext for a characteristic act of trickery. To avoid being shut up in port, many American ships had hastily put to sea while the embargo was on its passage, while others evaded the law in every possible way. Some of these under British license visited French ports, and in April, 1808, by the Bayonne Decree, were seized on the ground that they were outlawed by leaving home in violation of law.

Nor did the act produce the expected effect upon England. There was some distress among her poor who lost employment through the cutting down of the imports of raw cotton for the mills, but shipowners were benefited rather than injured. "Except with those directly interested," wrote one

[1] A non-importation act had been passed to aid Monroe's negotiation. It was to have become operative if his efforts failed, but was abandoned when Jefferson "pocketed" the treaty of 1806.

from London, "the dispute with the United States seems almost forgotten, or remembered only to draw forth ironical gratitude, that the kind embargo leaves the golden harvest to be reaped by British enterprise alone." The sarcastic Canning replied to Pinkney's suggestion that the embargo might be repealed in return for the revocation of the Orders in Council, by expressing concern over the law as an "inconvenient restriction upon the American people." Revolts in the Spanish colonies at just this time also opened new markets and sources of supplies for the British.

The embargo fell upon American shipping with a weight which almost crushed all that had survived the European Decrees and Orders. The masts of ships thrown out of use spread out before the port towns like "huge forests of dry trees." Seamen lost their employment and reëntered foreign service. The customs fell from $16,000,000 to $8,000,000, and Gallatin reported that in its effects upon national wealth and the public revenue the embargo was not materially different from war. The paralysis of shipping affected all subsidiary industries, and the loss of the foreign market brought down the price of the produce of the farms and plantations.

Despite their losses, the planters as a class stood manfully behind the program of their party, but public opinion in the commercial regions, especially New England, was so adverse that evasion of the law was general, and the administration found it necessary to recommend several supplementary acts for enforcing it. Congress, which had refused ships to protect trade, provided armed vessels to stop it. While these watched the harbors on the Atlantic, illicit traffic throve on Lakes Champlain and Ontario and at unguarded points on the northern and southern borders. Quebec and Halifax became depots for American commodities, and from them British goods were smuggled into the United States.

The enforcement acts inflamed the opposition and were

resorted to with great reluctance by the Republicans. They savored too much of the Federalists' methods of dealing with the resistance to the excise law in 1794. The administration party was not ready to uphold the embargo at the point of the bayonet. Moreover, the election of 1808 showed a distinct reaction in favor of Federalism, all of the New England states except Vermont swinging back into its ranks. In the last moments of his term Jefferson signed a repeal bill.[1]

THE ELECTION OF 1808

In the campaign of 1808 the Republican party was somewhat divided. In Virginia Monroe, embittered by Jefferson's rejection of his treaty with England and probably desirous of a less pacific foreign policy, contested the succession with Madison. Vice-President Clinton and his New York followers felt that the time had come for a northern President. A caucus of the Virginia legislature favored Madison over Monroe, and the congressional caucus named him for President with Clinton for a second time in the second position. Clinton publicly repudiated the vice-presidential nomination, and his friends in the electoral college gave him their votes for the chief magistracy. At that he had but 6, while Madison had 122. In the end Clinton accepted the vice-presidency. The Federalists cast 47 electoral ballots for C. C. Pinckney and Rufus King.

Although outwardly neutral, it was an open secret that Jefferson's choice was Madison. He was, indeed, in closer accord with the outgoing administration than Monroe, and

---

[1] The President bitterly resented the conduct of those Republicans who insisted upon the repeal. He held Joseph Story, one of the Massachusetts members, responsible. When a few years later President Madison proposed to appoint Story to the Supreme Bench, Jefferson advised against it, calling Story a "pseudo-Republican." But years afterwards Jefferson said that he signed the bill repealing the embargo to prevent open rebellion in New England. This was exactly the reason given by Story at the time, for advocating repeal.

the best person for the presidency if there were to be no change in policy. The Secretary of State was a master of argument, and his state papers dealing with the questions of neutral rights display the utmost keenness in penetrating the weak places in his adversaries' armor. This quality of mind made him an admirable member of the Federal Convention of 1787, where he probably rendered his greatest service to his country. In charge of foreign relations he became an inveterate note-writer, and unfortunately for his later reputation, he came to the presidency at a time when a man of vigorous action was needed.

MADISON AND COMMERCIAL COERCION

Some Republican members of Congress were inclined to think that war was the alternative of the embargo. Others still had faith in commercial restrictions. The outcome of considerable debate was a non-intercourse law, which went into effect a few weeks after Madison entered the presidential office (May 20). This law conciliated the domestic shipping interest by permitting commerce with all countries except France and England, and paved the way for negotiations by authorizing the President to suspend its operation against either of these upon the withdrawal of its restrictions upon American trade. From Canning's point of view the new act was preferable to the embargo, for it held out the hope that England might draw the United States into coöperation against France. He was willing to withdraw the Orders in Council in so far as they affected America, if the United States would allow British ships to capture vessels violating the American law by trading with France. D. M. Erskine, the British representative at Washington, whose wife was an American, misled by his desire for cordiality between the two nations, did not inform the Secretary of State of Canning's condition; instead he announced the coming of a special envoy to make a treaty, and the immediate suspension of the Orders.

Upon this Madison issued a proclamation in June (1809) restoring intercourse with England, only to be chagrined by Canning's disavowal and recall of Erskine. Non-intercourse was thereupon renewed, and when the special envoy, Francis J. Jackson, arrived, the chance of reaching an agreement was far from good. Slight as it was it was thrown away. Jackson explained the repudiation of Erskine in language which was understood to insinuate that the American government had known that he was violating instructions. Madison, who had taken the negotiations out of the hands of the stupid Secretary of State,[1] replied, "Such insinuations are inadmissible in the intercourse of a foreign minister with a government that understands what it owes itself"; and when he received Jackson's angry answer, refused to hold any further intercourse with him. For two critical years England was unrepresented at the American capital.

Erskine's conduct had placed England in a false light, for both France and the United States construed the supposed revocation of the Orders as evidence that she was yielding to pressure. But while not unembarrassed she was receiving large quantities of commodities, as under the embargo, by way of Halifax or other foreign ports near our border, whence they were conveyed in British ships. Thus in a degree the American law had the same effect as the British navigation acts, one aim of which was to give British vessels the carriage of American products.

The non-intercourse law was repealed after a little more than a year, but it gave Napoleon another opportunity to seize American ships. Under the Rambouillet Decree of March, 1810, several hundred vessels were confiscated on the

---

[1] Robert Smith, Secretary of State, was an unfortunate appointment, foisted upon Madison by factions opposed to Gallatin, whom he wished to appoint. Gallatin remained Secretary of the Treasury as under Jefferson.

ground that American law forbade their entry into French ports.

As a means of coercion non-intercourse was weaker than the embargo, and while it had led to negotiations they had miscarried. May 1, 1810, another act passed Congress known as "Macon's Bill No. 2." It repealed all restrictions on trade with the warring powers. If either would remove its own restrictions on American trade, however, the President was directed to renew non-intercourse with the other. Thus our treatment of each belligerent was made conditional upon the conduct of the other. It was hoped that both would yield if either did.

Macon's Bill No. 2 had at least the merit of benefiting commerce, as is shown by the increase in tonnage, the rise in the value of exports, and the greater revenue from customs. And it seemed at first that it might accomplish its purpose, for the French foreign minister announced to John Armstrong, American representative in Paris, that the Napoleonic decrees were revoked and would cease to have effect after November 1—it being understood that the English would revoke the Orders in Council, or that the United States "shall cause their rights to be respected by the English."

Madison accepted this conditional statement as a *bona-fide* revocation of the Berlin and Milan decrees, and demanded that England revoke her Orders. The notice to Armstrong was not followed by any public notice on the part of France, however, and the British refused to accept the French action as genuine. On November 2 Madison therefore proclaimed the renewal of non-intercourse with England, effective after ninety days, unless meantime the Orders in Council were withdrawn. But the French seizures of ships did not cease, and the British complained of the unfairness of non-intercourse with them alone when France was equally guilty of offenses.

Napoleon was playing a shrewd game. He probably did not wish England to revoke the Orders in Council; and by continuing to seize American vessels he made revocation impossible. But he did not condemn the ships seized, in order that the United States might cling to the belief that the decrees were not to be enforced, and thus be led to persist in non-intercourse with England. He doubtless aimed not only to encourage the United States to maintain non-intercourse, but to embarrass his enemy still further by inveigling the United States into war with her.

SELECT BIBLIOGRAPHY

Relations with England. An extraordinarily clear and readable account is that by Mahan, *Sea Power in its Relation to the War of 1812*.

The War of Orders and Decrees. Channing, *United States,* IV, gives an excellent summary of the French Decrees and British Orders in Council. See also Sears, *Jefferson and the Embargo,* and diplomatic histories previously cited.

Election of 1808. For this campaign as for others the best concise account is by Stanwood, *The Presidency*.

Madison and Commercial Coercion. See works cited under preceding heads.

Chapter XVIII

THE WAR OF 1812

THE RISE OF THE WAR PARTY

WHILE difficulties in the international situation were multiplying, the peaceful temper which the Madison administration had inherited from the Jeffersonian régime had gradually vanished. The generation which had fought the Revolution was passing from the stage, giving place to a younger one, less prudent and more inclined to action. The congressional election of 1810 brought defeat to half of the old members including many of the men of pacific views; their seats were taken by new men who owed their election to a growing impatience with the policy of peace at almost any price.

Among the men who entered the arena of national politics at about this time were those who were to be the foremost leaders in Congress until the eve of the Civil War. Henry Clay of Kentucky, John C. Calhoun of western South Carolina, and Daniel Webster of Massachusetts, who took his seat in 1813, attained such preëminence as to win the title of the "great triumvirate." Less well-known and yet important names are those of Richard M. Johnson of Kentucky, Felix Grundy of Tennessee, and Peter B. Porter of western New York. It will be noted that all of these except Webster were from new states or the frontier regions of old ones. With the same exception all were Republicans. To the same group of young Republicans belonged William Lowndes and Langdon Cheves, Calhoun's colleagues from South Carolina.

The events of the year following this memorable election of 1810 added fuel to a spreading fire. Madison read the signs

of the times as shown by the election and his administration
stiffened its tone towards England.   The election almost
coincided with the date set for the revocation of the Berlin
and Milan decrees.   With the renewal of non-intercourse
with England in the early months of 1811, Pinkney, minister
since the failure of the negotiations of 1806, was ordered
home.   No minister had been sent to Washington in place
of the dismissed Jackson, and this was made the pretext for
Pinkney's withdrawal.   Taken at this time, the action was
part of a studied effort to impress the British government
with the gravity of the displeasure of the United States.

Although a new minister to the United States was appointed before Pinkney left London, and although the
Marquis of Wellesley, Canning's successor, requested Pinkney
to remain, he would not do so because the British still refused
to recall the Orders in Council.   The new British minister,
A. J. Foster, nevertheless proceeded to Washington, and with
due formalities restored to the deck of the *Chesapeake* two
survivors of the quartette of sailors who had been impressed
four years before.

Notwithstanding reparation for the *Chesapeake* outrage
England was still firm in her insistence upon the Orders when
the new Congress assembled in November, 1811.   The new
men sealed their triumph by seizing control of the House and
electing Henry Clay as Speaker.   These Young Republicans,
Randolph referred to as "the boys," and dubbed "War
Hawks" because of their eagerness to take arms against England.   The War Hawks thought more in terms of the nation
and less in terms of local interests than had the Republican
"fathers" who formulated the doctrine of strict construction
and the Virginia and Kentucky Resolutions; the insults to
New England commerce they felt as a national affront even
more than did the skippers upon whom the losses fell.   But
it was events in the West which especially aroused their hatred

of the power which, with Grundy, they believed set on "the ruthless savages to tomahawk our women and children."

As in the days before Jay's treaty, the people of the Ohio Valley believed that England was behind the Indian resistance to their efforts to obtain land cessions. The Greenville treaty line had not long satisfied the land-hungry white man. That line left almost the whole of Indiana within the Indian country, and William Henry Harrison, as governor of Indiana Territory, was exceedingly zealous in opening new tracts for settlement. Treaty after treaty for this purpose at length stirred the tribesmen to make a concerted stand against further cessions.

The leader of this concert was Tecumseh, a worthy successor of Pontiac. His brother the "Prophet" introduced a supernatural element into the movement by preaching in the name of the Great Spirit a return to the aboriginal simplicity of life. Casting off the vices of the white men would be rewarded, he taught, by the aid of the Great Spirit in resisting them. Tecumseh aimed to organize the tribes of a vast territory to act as a unit in making land cessions, or, if necessary, war. Visiting Harrison, he made an eloquent plea for peace on the basis of the integrity of the territory of the Indians. Soon afterwards he visited the southern tribes (his mother was probably a Creek) hoping to win their support of his plan.

Taking advantage of his absence and believing that his activity threatened hostilities, Harrison led troops into a tract ceded in 1809 by a treaty which the natives had afterwards repudiated. His menacing approach to the Prophet's Town at Tippecanoe drew upon him an attack which was repelled only with difficulty and loss. This was in November, 1811. Because the Indians abandoned the village after the battle, Harrison became a hero in the eyes of the frontiersmen as the victor of Tippecanoe.

Notwithstanding the impending war with the United States, the British, throughout the whole period of Tecumseh's activity, endeavored to dissuade the Indians from beginning hostilities against the Americans. Possibly the British had in view the greater aid which might be rendered by a perfected confederation in case of an Anglo-American conflict. From their point of view, the clash at Tippecanoe was premature, for while it drove the major portion of the tribes into alliance with them, it injured the native morale and prevented the confederation from reaching its maximum numbers.

However pacific the advice given to the Indians, it was well known throughout the West that they were supplied with guns and powder by the Canadian government agents at Malden. This fact convinced the westerners that their hostile temper was due to incitement by the Canadian officials, and that the Indians could not be permanently pacified without displacing the British power in Canada. Land speculators probably encouraged a belief which promoted their plans to dispossess the natives, and the influence of the British was doubtless exaggerated. At all events, the clash between the races inflamed the West with a desire for war with England and for the conquest of Canada.

The election of Clay as Speaker is said to have been prompted by the belief that he was the only man among the Young Republicans who could curb John Randolph, the free lance.[1] Its deeper significance lies in the fact that the West

[1] Randolph is the most remarkable eccentric in our history. His membership in Congress was almost continuous for a generation. Beginning his career as a regular Republican, he soon gave free rein to his extraordinary personality and became a thorn in the side of Jefferson. His speeches were long and often incoherent, yet no public man has coined more telling phrases. He consistently opposed the war, and, like the Federalists, denounced the plan of conquering Canada, although for a different reason, viz., that it was contrary to southern interests and tended to arouse sectional antagonisms which were dangerous to the Union.

Clay's mastery of him is illustrated by an episode which occurred in May,

was beginning to be felt as a power in national politics, taking its place as a third section, holding the balance between the old North and South of the seaboard.

Clay was born in Virginia in 1777. His youth was spent in poverty, but his ambition and native ability attracted the attention of prominent men and won him the patronage of George Wythe, the state chancellor. Upon attaining his majority he, like many another youth, sought the new settlements in Kentucky and "grew up with the country." His gift of oratory won him speedy recognition. Before he reached the constitutional age of a United States Senator he was appointed to fill out an uncompleted term in the upper house of Congress. Then came his election to the lower house and the beginning of a brilliant career as Speaker. He was the first to recognize the possibilities of the office, and in his hands it was carried far in the direction of the commanding importance which it has possessed in recent times. He made it a position of party leadership, and through the power to control proceedings and to appoint committees aided in carrying out the program of the War Hawks.

Against the advice of the former leaders of the party, Madison, now in harmony with the War Hawks, sent in a message recommending "putting the United States into an armor and an attitude demanded by the crisis." Cheves and Lowndes reported for a special committee in favor of building twenty

1812. Randolph began to address the House in opposition to a declaration of war. No motion being before the body, a member raised a point of order and the Speaker, in spite of Randolph's protest that his remarks were introductory to a motion, ruled that the motion must come first. When Randolph moved a resolution "that it is not expedient at this time to resort to war against Great Britain," Clay again denied him the right to proceed until the motion was seconded. Randolph appealed to the House which sustained the Speaker's ruling. Finally, when Randolph had found a seconder and had again begun his speech, he was halted by a ruling that the House must vote on the question of considering the motion. By this time Randolph's ardor for his resolution had well-nigh spent itself in rage at the youthful Speaker. Randolph was a forerunner of Calhoun as a champion of sectional interests.

frigates to be followed by a dozen battle-ships. Such a fleet, they argued, could protect our ports against any force which the enemy could spare for an attack upon them. But the Jeffersonian antipathy to a navy could not be overcome. The majority of congressmen preferred to trust to privateering in case of war. After four long months of discussion Congress refused to appropriate money for naval construction, or to levy new taxes, but authorized an increase in the regular army and the enlistment of fifty thousand volunteers.

By the spring of 1812 the British government was ready to revoke the Orders in Council as soon as it could be done safely and with dignity. England was maintaining an army of 300,-000 men in Spain, to free the peninsula from the French, and to occupy Napoleon while Russia broke away from the Continental System. This army was well-nigh dependent upon America for supplies. Non-intercourse threatened the success of the peninsular campaign and meant scarcity of bread in England and actual distress in the manufacturing towns.

Napoleon was finally forced to show his hand by a new Order in Council, which declared that whenever the Berlin and Milan decrees should be absolutely and unconditionally revoked the British orders should automatically cease to be in force. The United States thereupon insisted that France produce indisputable proof that the decrees were no longer operative, and the foreign minister presented a decree dated a year earlier, which declared that the Berlin and Milan decrees were to be considered as non-existent, so far as concerned America, after November 1, 1810. There is no doubt that this document was drawn up in 1812 and antedated; but the British ministry chose to accept it, and on June 23 announced the revocation of the Orders.

It can hardly be maintained that fear of war with the United States led England to repeal the Orders in Council. Jonathan Russell, *chargé d'affaires* in London, wrote a short

time before this action was taken, "We have indeed a reputation in Europe for saying so much and doing so little that we
shall not be believed in earnest until we act in a manner not
to be mistaken." He could not see that the British apprehended a rupture with the United States. It would therefore
appear that the repeal, so far as American policy was a factor
in it, was a triumph for commercial coercion. Yet five days
before this event, which was clearly foreshadowed in the utterances of the British ministry during the spring, the United
States declared war.

With apparent blindness to the trend of events in Europe,
the preparations for war had gone on in the United States
during the early months of 1812. Hints were given Congress
before the first of April that the President believed that war
should be declared before adjournment. In April a ninety-
day embargo was passed, to insure that American ships would
be safe in port when war began. Although Madison told the
British minister that the embargo was not to be considered a
war measure, he sent to Congress on June 1 a message which
could only be construed as a recommendation of war.

In this message the President once more reviewed the familiar story of British aggressions upon neutral rights. The
indictment covered (1) impressments; (2) the "hovering" of
British cruisers near our coast to seize outbound vessels in enforcement of the Orders in Council; (3) the paper blockade;
(4) the Orders in Council. In addition the message alluded
to the Indian war, and adopting the view of the West, intimated that British influence was at the bottom of it. "It is
difficult," said Madison, "to account for the activity and combinations which have been for some time developing themselves among tribes in constant intercourse with British traders and garrisons, without connecting their hostility with that
influence."

These aggressions, the President held, amounted to war

against the United States. "We behold . . . on the side of
Great Britain, a state of war against the United States, and on
the side of the United States, a state of peace towards Great
Britain." "Whether the United States shall continue passive"
or shall oppose "force to force in defence of their national
rights," was a question which he recommended to the consideration of Congress.

WAR PLANS AND RESOURCES

The debate on the President's recommendation ended in a
declaration of war on June 18. At the moment when the
policy of peaceable coercion was nearing success, Madison's
message amounted to a public avowal that it had proved an
idle dream. Then came news of the revocation of the Orders
in Council. Indeed, most of the causes of war were removed
before hostilities began. The paper blockade and the "hovering," of which Madison complained, were incidental to the
orders and disappeared with their recall. Yet it is an error to
suppose that a cable, by bringing prompt news of the repeal
of the orders, would have averted war, for the Indian question and the old grievance of impressment were not affected.
Neither of these grievances justified war.

Americans should have looked to their own encroachments
upon the Indian lands rather than to British influence for an
explanation of the race friction in the Northwest. As for impressments, while they varied in frequency with the fluctuating needs of the British navy and the ups and downs of
American commerce, they had never been so frequent since
1807 as before, and it was extraordinary to make them a cause
of war in 1812 when they had been deemed insufficient in
1807. Since Grundy, a member of the Committee on Foreign
Relations, had said in the debate on the Committee's report
during the preceding winter, "I feel anxious not only to add
the Floridas to the South, but the Canadas to the North of

this empire"; since Clay had declared "The conquest of Canada is in your power. . . . Is it nothing to extinguish the torch that lights up savage warfare? Is it nothing to acquire the entire fur-trade connected with that country?"— the opponents of the war not without some justification charged that the real motive of the War Hawks was territorial conquest.[1]

Yet technically the impressment grievance must stand as the *casus belli* in 1812. The war message professed "a constant readiness to concur in an honorable reëstablishment of peace and friendship." Immediately after the declaration, the London *chargé* was instructed to propose peace on the basis of the revocation of the orders and the abandonment of impressments. At the same time the British government dispatched Admiral Warren to the United States to propose a suspension of hostilities in view of the recall of the orders. The ministry would not recede on the question of impressments, however, and the war was thus professedly fought—although vainly, as it turned out—to vindicate the rights of our sailors.

On any other ground it is difficult to justify the choice of antagonist. French seizures of vessels almost equaled those of Britain, and Napoleon's treatment of America had been marked, in addition, by the most offensive hypocrisy and deceit. Indeed, Madison consulted Jefferson as to the advisability of declaring war on both belligerents. But he could not strike France. She presented no vulnerable point for attack, while Canada lay almost undefended, as was thought, at our door. In effect the war with England was for France as good as an alliance, in spite of Madison's care to disavow all connections which might entangle the United States "in the con-

[1] Other members of Congress from the frontier states voiced views similar to those of Grundy and Clay. Harper of New Hampshire believed that the "Author of Nature" had marked the northern limits of the United States "by the regions of eternal frost."

tests or views of other Powers." Intent upon its own concerns
and oblivious of the great issues involved in the European
war, the New World Republic, in its provincialism, gave aid
and comfort to the would-be-master of the Old World.[1]

The country was fairly prosperous and potentially rich. At
the end of 1811 Gallatin reported that the public debt had
been reduced in ten years from $80,000,000 to $34,000,000.
With a population of nearly seven and a half millions the
nominal military strength was approximately a million men.
The prospect of success seemed excellent. England's preoccupation with the European conflict removed the danger of
an immediate attempt at invasion. Since the United States
sought to compel her to yield to certain demands, it must succeed in an aggressive campaign in order to dictate the terms
of peace.

A naval war, however, was out of the question. Thanks to
the practice afforded by the Tripolitan War, the naval officers
were experienced and skillful, but the Republic possessed less
than twenty vessels of war, only four of which were frigates
mounting more than forty guns. No ship in the entire fleet
was a match for a British seventy-four.[2] Canada was therefore the inevitable objective of the American attack, and the
War Hawks held the defensive capacity of the enemy's provinces in slight esteem. Clay boasted that Kentucky riflemen
unaided could capture Quebec and Montreal, and even Jefferson agreed that a campaign against these places was merely
a "matter of marching." "My plan," said Clay, "would be to
call out the ample resources of the country, give them a judicious direction, prosecute the war with the utmost vigor,

[1] It is only fair to say that the Republicans in general believed that the welfare of the peoples of Europe would be promoted by Napoleon's success. They
were suspicious of England as a monarchy in which old abuses were still
unreformed.
[2] A ship of the line was called a "seventy-four" from the number of cannon
carried. It was the most powerful type of fighting craft of that era.

strike wherever we can reach the enemy at sea or on land, and negotiate the terms of peace at Quebec or Halifax." [1]

Whether Canada should be held permanently was another matter. Jefferson was confident that the United States would strip Great Britain "of all her possessions on this continent," and agreed with the westerners that the cession of Canada "must be a *sine qua non* of the peace treaty." No official utterance of the administration, however, revealed any intention of utilizing the occupation of Canada except to obtain concessions in return for its surrender.

The test proved that the government was not able to command the country's actual resources in men and money. The Federalists had never become reconciled to Republican rule. Their rancor had smoldered but not died after the collapse of the secession plot of 1804. The policy of commercial restriction had revived the waning fortunes of the party, which showed large gains in the election of 1808. The war policy now showed the influence of the West, and Federalist dislike of the West had grown steadily since the purchase of Louisiana. In 1811, when the southern portion of the territory obtained from France asked admission to the Union as the State of Louisiana, Josiah Quincy, of Massachusetts, said in the House: "I am compelled to declare it as my deliberate opinion that, if this bill passes, the bonds of this union are, virtually, dissolved; that the states which compose it are free from their moral obligations, and that as it will be the right of all, so it will be the duty of some to prepare, definitely, for a separation; amicably, if they can, violently, if they must."

To the conflict into which the West had plunged the country the Federalists were bitterly antagonistic. Upon the passage of the declaration the Federalists in Congress met in cau-

---

[1] The overconfidence of the Americans was noted by a British observer, who reported as early as 1808: "It is amazing to hear them talk . . . of the extreme facility with which they can possess themselves of the British Provinces."

cus and issued an address denouncing the war as "a party and not a national war," entered into by a divided people. It was suicidal, they protested, to subject the bonds of union to the strain of war under such circumstances, and they disclaimed all responsibility for the disasters which they predicted. Taking the address as their keynote, the New England wing of the party continued their factious conduct throughout the period of hostilities. They hung flags at half-mast and tolled church bells upon hearing of the declaration. They made niggardly subscriptions to the government loans, contributing less than one dollar of every thirteen that went into the treasury. They obstructed the efforts of the administration to utilize the militia as a national army, attempted to nullify federal legislation, and finally called a convention supposedly to consider secession.

The sectional character of the war, and especially the responsibility of the West for it, are well shown by the presidential election of 1812. Madison's espousal of the belligerent program won him the support of the War Hawks in the congressional caucus in June. Elbridge Gerry received the indorsement for the vice-presidency. George Clinton was now dead, but the jealousy of New York towards the Virginia "dynasty" found expression in the candidacy of his nephew, De-Witt Clinton. Nominated by the Republicans of the state legislature, he was later indorsed by a convention of Federalists, as a peace candidate. The returns showed that the original states were almost equally divided; they cast 90 electoral votes for Madison and war and 89 for Clinton and peace, while the five new states cast their 38 votes for Madison, tipping the scales and showing that they held the balance of political power.

Madison, "master of ideas but not of men," visited all of the offices of the War and Navy Departments in person on the day after war was declared. The effect is indicated by the words of the observer who described him as "stimulating everything in a manner worthy of a little commander-in-chief, with his little round hat and huge cockade." Incitement of clerks to perform routine tasks was not the duty of the hour for the head of the nation. The competence of department heads, however, was a matter of infinite importance. William Eustis and Paul Hamilton, the Secretaries of the War and Navy Departments, were notoriously unfit for their great responsibilities, but in spite of warnings the President lacked the courage to place strong men in their places at the outset. In 1811, after performing the duties of Secretary of State himself for some time, he had dismissed Smith and appointed Monroe, his late rival, to the post. By this action Monroe became "heir apparent" to the presidency. He made a fair cabinet officer.

Quincy derided the administration as a "despotism," "composed to all efficient purposes of two Virginians and a foreigner." Gallatin, by far the ablest member of the official family, was so harassed by the continual hounding of small-minded politicians that after a year of war he welcomed the opportunity to exchange his cabinet post for a place on the peace commission. The failures of Eustis and Hamilton at length necessitated the appointment of other officials, but this was not done until great harm had been sustained.

The weakness of the executive departments was equaled by the incapacity of Congress to rise to the situation. The developed resources of the country were chiefly agricultural. The general prosperity depended in large measure upon the exportation of cotton, tobacco, corn, wheat, and flour, in exchange for imported manufactures. In spite of non-intercourse with England, foreign commerce in 1811 amounted to more than $100,000,000. Upon duties on imports the government also depended almost wholly for its revenues. Gallatin reported that the duties had fallen from $12,000,000 before commercial restriction began, to $6,000,000 in 1811, and a deficit was in sight for 1812, even with peace. War was certain to reduce commerce still further, curtailing revenues at the same time that expenditures rose.

Under such circumstances Congress performed little better than the Continental Congress of the Revolution. Although now possessed of the power of taxation, it was afraid to use it vigorously upon a people unaccustomed to heavy tax burdens. Gallatin, who for a decade had administered the treasury with scrupulous economy, seeking to wipe out the national debt and spare the people all needless taxation, saw all his work menaced by war; but when, facing the inevitable, he advocated internal taxes, the House rebuked the proposal of "unrepublican measures." [1] The tariff was indeed doubled, but the true alternative of direct taxes was loans which would saddle posterity with a burden not of its own choosing. Here too Congress was niggardly; and with most of the loanable capital of the nation in the hands of New England Federalists, Gallatin was unable to secure subscriptions even for the meager sums which Congress authorized him to borrow. The securities sold at much less than par, and bore rates of interest as high as seven and one half per cent.

Gallatin also recommended the renewal of the charter of the United States Bank, which expired in 1811. A strong institution of this type could have been used to excellent advantage by the treasury. But the Republican Congress had not yet escaped from the Jeffersonian tradition of 1791 and refused the recharter. [2]

[1] Necessity nevertheless compelled resort to a direct tax and an excise a year later.

[2] Lack of harmony between the administration and Congress was shown in other ways. For example, the administration recommended an increase in the regular army from 10,000 to 20,000 men. Congress voted to increase the number to 35,000, with enlistment for five years. The apparent zeal for a strong army was offset and recruiting retarded by the long term, and friends of the administration believed that the measure was adopted for the purpose of embarrassing the President.

The declaration of war was made with the army preparations still far from complete. There were at the time less than seven thousand regulars, distributed in widely scattered posts along the coast, near the Canadian border, and in the remote interior. Eustis *guessed* the number of new enlistments up to June 8 at about five thousand. The Republicans relied upon the state militia for the early campaigns, while regulars and volunteers were being recruited in adequate numbers.

The governors of the New England states refused, however, to honor the call for quotas of militia, and the United States found but a fraction of the desired number at its command.[1] Even these refused to fight on foreign soil, and proved useless

CAMPAIGNS OF THE WAR OF 1812

1812	IN THE NORTH	IN THE SOUTH
Aug. 16	Surrender of Detroit	
1813		
Aug. 30		Massacre of Fort Mims
Sept. 10	Perry's Victory on Lake Erie	
Oct. 5	Battle of the Thames	
1814		
Mar. 27		Battle of Horse Shoe Bend (Jackson's victory over the Creeks)
July 15	Battle of Lundy's Lane	
Aug. 24		Battle of Bladensburg
Sept. 11	Battle of Plattsburg	
Sept. 13		Attack on Baltimore
1815		
Jan. 8		Battle of New Orleans

[1] A decision of the Supreme Court in 1827 (Martin *vs.* Mott) upheld the President's right to judge of the necessity of calling out the militia. But the use of the militia as a national force, especially for warfare on foreign soil, has been beset with difficulties down to the present.

for the purpose of invading Canada. The response to the call for volunteers was meager also, and for all the government's efforts, the effective forces did not at any time exceed thirty-five thousand men.

Most of the fighting had to be done along the northern frontier in a wilderness still untouched by the art of the road-maker. The movement of large bodies of troops proved to be extremely difficult, and the proper coördination of attacks at widely separated points was almost impossible. The commissariat also was in continual confusion.[1]

Worse than any of the physical handicaps was the inefficiency of the officers from the Secretary of War down. At the beginning of the war two major-generals and seven brigadier-generals were selected. Their ages ranged from fifty-five to sixty-seven. Only three of the brigadier-generals had served in the regular army; Thomas Pinckney, junior major-general, and William Hull, one of the brigadiers, had records as officers in the Revolution. "The Creator," said Jefferson, "has not thought proper to mark those on the forehead who are of the stuff to make good generals." A period of actual warfare was required to bring to the front men of real military capacity. Meantime the campaigns suffered from the incompetence of the officers chosen, as it were, by a blindfolded administration.

THE CAMPAIGNS

Hostilities began with a triple movement for the invasion of Canada. Dearborn, the senior major-general, was to move from Lake Champlain and threaten Montreal; Stephen Van Rensselaer, a New York militia officer, and Alexander Smyth, of the regular army, were to strike the Canadian center in the neighborhood of Niagara; while Hull, from Fort Detroit, was

[1] A Kentucky officer who served under Harrison declared that no wagon could carry even the feed for its own team over the trail from the Miami to the Maumee.

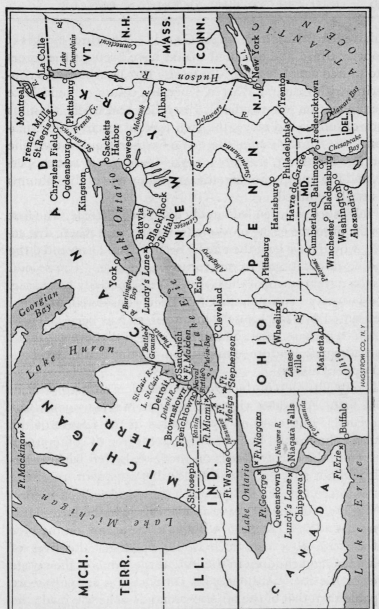

THE WAR OF 1812

HAGSTROM CO., N.Y.

425

to drive the British from upper Canada. The three strokes if properly timed and executed would have brought the forces into united action against Montreal. But Dearborn was conferring with Admiral Warren when his column should have been in motion towards the St. Lawrence, and when at last his army of militia did move, the men refused to cross the Canadian line. In the center there was further trouble with the militia. Moreover, the two generals there would not coöperate, and the unsupported attack essayed by one of the columns was easily repulsed.

Hull's success depended largely upon two factors. The first was the outcome of the movements farther east, where due activity would have kept the enemy occupied and prevented the sending of additional troops to upper Canada. The second was the naval control of the Great Lakes, especially Lake Erie. The necessity of this control had been considered, and had been urged by Hull himself, but no steps had been taken to obtain it, perhaps because Hull had judged that even without it an adequate land force might compel the British to abandon upper Canada.

The sluggishness of the other commanders allowed Hull to move first. A sudden vigorous blow at Malden might have succeeded. But, alarmed by the news of the failure of the eastern columns and by the danger to his line of communications from the enemy vessels on the lake, he fell back to Detroit without striking. Isaac Brock, his opponent, receiving as reënforcements the troops which should have been needed at Niagara, took the offensive and laid siege to the fort. Hull then surrendered (August) without firing a shot, on the plea that capture after resistance would endanger the lives of the women and children in the fort, at the hands of the savage allies of the foe. Although his conduct was scarcely more culpable than that of the other commanders, he was made the scapegoat. Tried and convicted of cowardice by a court martial, he was pardoned by the President out of consideration for his honorable record in the Revolution.

The whole season's campaign utterly miscarried, and ended with the British in occupation of Detroit. From this vantage point they threatened the entire Northwest, and actually carried the war into northern Ohio. The Wabash-Maumee line became the military frontier. Harrison, who succeeded Hull, was unable to hold ground on the River Raisin, in southern Michigan, but repelled attacks directed against forts on the Maumee (Fort Meigs) and Sandusky (Fort Stephenson, the modern Fremont) in 1813.

The misfortunes of 1812 had at least revealed the incompetence of the commanding officers. "We are literally borne down," commented Calhoun, "under the effects of errors and mismanagement." Among the changes made at the close of this year of disaster was the appointment of John Armstrong, of New York, as Secretary of War, partly to appease northern jealousy of Virginia. Of him Dallas (later Secretary of the Treasury) said, "He was the devil from the beginning, is now, and ever will be!" Under Armstrong the plan of campaign for the second year was substantially identical with that of 1812. Harrison aimed at the recovery of Detroit and the invasion of Ontario from that point, while new efforts were made against Montreal and Niagara. It had become clear that the control of Lake Erie was necessary for the success of the western phase of the campaign, and Captain Oliver H. Perry was given command of six vessels built on the lake. With these he met and defeated a slightly inferior fleet of the enemy, in September. Harrison was then able to force the British from Detroit and vicinity, to pursue them to the Thames River, and to win a considerable engagement on Canadian soil. Tecumseh's death in this battle disorganized his followers and prepared the way for the pacification of the northwest Indians some time before the peace with Britain.

In the Southwest the Creeks fell upon Fort Mims, on the Alabama River, in August, 1813, and massacred several hundred persons. Their pacification came, like that of the northern tribes, before the end of the war with England, in consequence of a severe defeat administered in March, 1814, by frontier militiamen in a battle which brought Andrew Jackson into prominence.

On the St. Lawrence James Wilkinson, who had replaced Dearborn, had ample opportunity to prove his incapacity. The operations near Niagara were again indecisive, preventing Harrison from following up his successes. However, events were slowly making it possible to discriminate between incapable officers and those who gave promise, and the names of Harrison, Jackson, Jacob Brown, and Winfield Scott began to inspire confidence.

The westerners' hope of conquering Canada ebbed with the reverses of 1812, but rose again with Harrison's successes, only to vanish in consequence of events on the southern frontier and in Europe. Grundy's coupling of Canada with the Floridas evinced a desire to frame a program of expansion which would enlist the support of both the northern and southern sections of the Union. The well-known opposition of the Federalists to the creation of new Republican states in the West and Southwest would, it was hoped, be dissipated by the prospect of new states to be carved out of the Canadian conquest. On the other hand the South could not be expected to support such a northward expansion without a *quid pro quo*. Coöperation of the sections, it appeared, might be insured by a plan of expansion in both directions.

If security and prosperity along the Canadian border seemed to require the expulsion of the British from their northern dominion, similar reasons operated in favor of dispossessing the Spanish along the Gulf coast. The situation in that region had been very grievous to the neighboring Ameri-

cans ever since the purchase of Louisiana. The possession by
Spain of a strip through which flowed the streams giving outlet to the inhabitants of the Georgia and Alabama settlements
was extremely inconvenient. Spain, moreover, embroiled as
she was in the European wars, seemed incapable of providing
a government for her Gulf provinces vigorous enough to preserve order.

In 1810 President Madison took advantage of an insurrection in West Florida to annex that province. The region involved was that which the United States claimed by virtue of
the Louisiana Purchase treaty. The revolutionists had declared independence and appealed to the United States for
annexation. Although the leaders were Americans and the
whole proceeding savored of conspiracy, Madison by proclamation took possession of most of the province, professing
that "in the hands of the United States it will not cease to be a
subject of fair and friendly negotiation and adjustment" with
Spain.

As the ally of England in the contest with Napoleon, it
seemed certain that, in case of war between England and the
United States, Spain's possessions on the Gulf would become
a base for England's attacks. Under such conditions Spain
was likely to become involved in the war, so that her provinces
would be legitimate objects of conquest. Even if war with
her were avoided, it appeared almost certain that the United
States would be compelled to occupy East Florida as a means
of preventing a similar move by the British.

As in the case of New Orleans before 1803, the interests of
the United States not only forbade the military occupation of
this adjacent region by an enemy in time of war, but precluded a transfer of permanent ownership to any other European power. Both Jefferson and Madison, during their terms
in the presidency, were constantly on the alert for any move
which seemed to tend in that direction. When England pro-

tested, on behalf of her ally, against the occupation of West Florida, the protest was unheeded, for Anglo-American relations were nearing the breaking-point. Indeed, Madison went further; fearing British occupation of East Florida, he asked and received from Congress, in January, 1811, authority to take temporary possession of that province also, on the ground that "the United States could not see without serious inquietude any part of a neighboring territory in which they have . . . so just a concern, pass from the hands of Spain into those of any other foreign Power."

Efforts of a government agent named Mathews to foment a revolution in East Florida preparatory to its annexation by the United States, following the precedent set in the case of West Florida, violated Spain's rights so patently that they were disavowed. The United States had no claim to East Florida such as formed a pretext for the former action. Only an attempt at occupation by a foreign power (so the administration tardily informed the repudiated agent) warranted the course permitted by the act of Congress. Nevertheless, like the crown refused by Cæsar, the territory was a prize which the government fain would have taken if a plausible pretext could have been found. Troops had been sent to support Mathews, and they were not withdrawn when he was dismissed. The government demanded as a prerequisite a promise of pardon for the Spanish subjects who had attempted revolution at Mathews' instigation. Delay in obtaining the amnesty enabled the government to leave the troops in the province until 1813.

Meantime, although England made no effort to acquire the Floridas, she used them as a base of operations against the United States. Mobile, in West Florida, and Pensacola, in the eastern province, remained in the hands of Spanish garrisons, and Spain was both careless of her duties as a neutral and unable to enforce them. British agents used these posts as centers from which to incite the Creeks and other southern tribes against the Americans. Creeks took refuge among the Seminoles of East Florida after their defeat in 1814, and continued hostilities. Jackson occupied Pensacola after the Creek campaign to prevent its use by the British, and in the course of his movements drove hostile forces from the nominally neutral ground.

With the withdrawal of the troops from East Florida in 1813, however, all thought of conquest in that quarter was dismissed by the administration. With the hope of such conquest departed also the grounds for southern interest in the conquest of Canada. Besides, the turn of affairs in Europe in 1814 destroyed the possibility of a military occupation of Canada even for the sake of its value in the negotiation of the peace treaty. For with the end of the European war in that year England was able to assume the offensive in America.

Napoleon, intending to chastise Russia for forsaking the Continental System which she had promised to support when she made the Peace of Tilsit, had led his armies deep into that country and occupied Moscow late in the autumn of 1812. There he found to his sorrow that possession of the Russian capital did not mean the conquest of the nation. The government and armies of the Czar forsook the vicinity, and the French found not even the means of subsistence in Moscow and the region roundabout. Napoleon was forced to forego his plan of wintering there and to attempt a midwinter retreat to central Europe.

The season proved to be exceptionally severe, and the sufferings of the ill-fated army as it plodded westward across the vast snow-covered plains are almost without parallel. Napoleon scented the coming uprising of the peoples of middle Europe at the news of his misfortune, and hastening on to France gathered a new army with which to face the united attack of Austria, Prussia, and Russia at the Battle of the Nations (October, 1813). Suffering here his first great defeat, he fell back to France, then to Paris, vainly striving to check the columns of his adversaries as they converged upon his doomed capital. Perceiving at last the futility of the effort, he chose to abdicate the imperial dignity rather than await deposition at the hands of his triumphant foes.

These events seemed to herald the return of peace in Europe. It only remained for the victorious powers assembled in the Congress of Vienna to redraw the map of Europe and decide the fate of the fallen autocrat. But he, banished to the Isle of Elba in the Mediterranean, escaped in the spring of 1815, and for a brief and splendid moment threatened to regain his lost glory. Then at the end of a hundred days came Waterloo, and amid its smoke and din the sun of fortune set forever upon the Corsican adventurer.

The last stage of Napoleon's career did not affect the American war, which closed six months before his final overthrow. In July, 1814, the Americans renewed the effort to invade Canada by crossing the Niagara River, no longer with the original hope of conquering a peace, but in order to make as formidable a showing as possible. Scott won a victory in a minor engagement at Chippewa, and soon after the united forces of Scott and Brown had the advantage in a hard-fought battle at Lundy's Lane. These engagements showed that capable officers were being developed and that American soldiers could fight well under good leadership. But the only use to which soldiership could now be put was to guard the territory of the United States; for, freed from the Napoleonic menace, England turned upon the little state which had been snapping at her heels while she grappled with the giant.

She planned to invade the United States at several points. A few weeks after Lundy's Lane, Sir George Prevost advanced from Canada along the well-worn route taken by Montcalm and Burgoyne in previous wars, seeking like them to isolate

New England. The American land forces defending Lake Champlain were greatly outnumbered, and the fighting strength of the British boats on the lake was double that of the American vessels. But in the face of these odds, Captain Thomas Macdonough succeeded by clever strategy in turning back the invaders in the naval battle of Plattsburg.

This was in September, like Perry's victory of the previous year. The month before, a British fleet entered Chesapeake Bay to create a diversion on behalf of Prevost. An army under General Robert Ross landed on the Patuxent and marched on Washington, encountering no resistance until it reached Bladensburg, five miles from the capital. There a force which outnumbered the British but consisted mainly of raw militia, under General W. H. Winder, awaited their coming. The commander was a politician, not a soldier, and the militia abandoned their excellent position and fled almost at the first attack, leaving the city at the mercy of the foe. Directions as to the route to be taken in the retreat were given before the battle, which has come to be known derisively as "the Bladensburg races."

A year before, York (Toronto) had fallen into the hands of Americans, who had pillaged and burned the Houses of Parliament and other public buildings. In retaliation the White House, the Treasury, and the War Office in Washington were now burned, at the command of Ross. The most important of the government records were hastily collected and carried to a place of safety. The President fled from the capital as ignominiously as the common herd, some of whom did not hesitate to revile him as the author of their misery. Armstrong was now sacrificed to appease the clamor of the people for a victim, and the war office was added to Monroe's responsibilities.

An attack upon Baltimore with the support of the fleet followed the capture of Washington. Improvised harbor de-

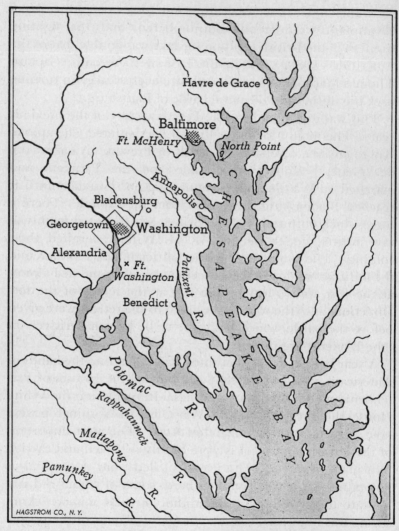

WASHINGTON AND VICINITY

fenses—chains stretched across the channel—kept the fleet beyond effective cannon range, however, and forces which were landed hesitated to press the attack.   After a brief siege the expedition reëmbarked to share in attacks on the coast of Maine and on New Orleans. The latter was the third point at which the British planned to invade the United States. Sir Edward Pakenham replaced Ross as commander of the expedition against New Orleans, which consisted of ten thousand veterans of the European wars.

Some months after General Wilkinson was transferred to the St. Lawrence, the command over the United States troops in the Southwest was given to Andrew Jackson. Jackson, a native of South Carolina, had "grown up" with Tennessee as Clay had with Kentucky. A smattering of legal knowledge acquired during his indigent and indolent youth, plus a great deal of native force, had made him a marked man from the early days of Tennessee statehood. He had served without distinction in the United States Senate during the presidency of John Adams. A natural leader of men, his resourcefulness and energy had shown to much greater advantage in campaigns against the southern Indians while a major-general of the Tennessee militia, and had won him the appointment to succeed Wilkinson.

When Jackson learned of the British plan to attack New Orleans, he collected all possible forces—piratical gangs from the coast islands and marshes as well as militia of the southwestern states—and with great energy prepared to defend the city. Pakenham made his own preparations cautiously, losing the opportunity to attack before Jackson's works were ready. These consisted of a barrier across the narrow strip of land between the Mississippi and the marshes bordering Lake Borgne. Along the strip ran the only practicable approach to the city on the east side of the river. On the west bank the American position was less strong, and by carrying it Jackson's main works might have been destroyed by an attack in the rear and from the river.

From caution Pakenham passed to rashness, misled possibly

by contempt for American militia. Occasional occurrences like that at Bladensburg were probably the basis of the belief of British officers, since the days of the French and Indian War, that militia could not withstand the charge of regulars.

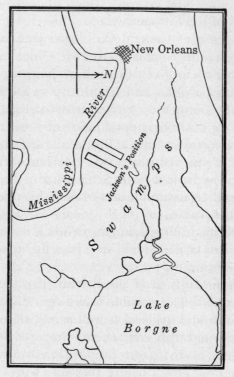

BATTLE OF NEW ORLEANS

On January 8, 1815, without awaiting the success of operations on the west bank, Pakenham attempted to carry Jackson's position by assault. Many of the militia were frontiersmen whose daily companion was the rifle. Every such man was a sharpshooter, and behind their breastworks their position was almost impregnable. The British general's decision was a fatal error. Two advances were repulsed by the deadly fire, with a loss of more than two thousand killed and wounded. Pakenham fell among his men, the attack was abandoned, and the expedition reëmbarked and sailed away. According to Jackson's report his own loss was sixty-three men.

The Battle of New Orleans was the chief victory of the war and made Jackson a national hero. Two weeks earlier peace terms had been agreed upon at Ghent. Under other circumstances a British victory at the mouth of the Mississippi might have meant the loss of Louisiana and revived the dangers associated with the occupation of that province by a European power. Such a result was anticipated and even desired by some of the Federalists who had opposed the acquisition of the territory in the first place. The success of the West in defending the approaches to the Mississippi Valley gave it greater self-confidence and soon led it to demand more recognition from the nation.

The British plan of invasion succeeded only at one minor point. Repulsed at Plattsburg, Baltimore, and New Orleans, they succeeded in taking a few places on the coast of Maine which they held until the peace. From the military standpoint the war must be pronounced a draw. Each belligerent successfully defended its own territory but failed in the attempt to carry the war to the enemy.

NAVAL WARFARE

The War Hawks had desired to increase the navy but had been defeated by votes of old-line Republicans with the aid of some of the Federalists. The vessels available for service at the beginning of the war were sent out to afford what protection they could to homeward-bound merchantmen and to attack British commerce. During the first season several duels occurred between them and British ships in which the Americans were victorious, to the great elation of the people. The

Constitution was the victor in two of these combats. In August she disabled the thirty-eight gun *Guerrière* in half an hour, and in December defeated the *Java* of about her own size. In other fights the *Wasp* beat the *Frolic,* the *United States* took the *Macedonian,* and the *Hornet* sank the *Peacock.* On the other hand the unfortunate *Chesapeake* was beaten by the *Shannon.*

It had been the plan of the United States to build its frigates slightly stronger than the standard British vessels of the same class, and in nearly every battle the American boat was of greater tonnage or threw a heavier broadside than its antagonist. Yet the English were so astonished at the series of victories that they imagined the frigates to be disguised ships of the line. They had felt the same contempt for American ships as for militia. Said Lord Brougham in Parliament, "The assembled navies of America could not lay siege to an English sloop of war!"

The truth is the American ships were more skillfully built than the enemy's; they were well handled, and the gunnery was good. The moral effect of their success was all the greater because of the immense prestige of the British navy. Apart from their effect on the morale of the people the sea fights were without influence upon the course of the war. On the contrary the battles on the lakes were well-nigh decisive.

The early victories induced Congress to make some additions to the navy. Nevertheless one by one the ships were captured or bottled up in port. It was the privateers after all that made the great showing in the war on commerce. Such enterprises attracted many shipowners and interested large numbers of citizens through popular subscriptions for the ventures. About five hundred vessels went out during the war with commissions to prey on the enemy's commerce. These boats gave additional evidence of the superiority of American shipwrights and seamen. By their swiftness they were able to

A Seaman of 1812

avoid danger, and risked combat only where success was certain. If they fought, they were sure to win; if they fled, they were sure to escape. Although the total captures of all kinds about equaled those made by the foe, English commerce suffered far less than American. Before the end of the war the blockade of the Atlantic coast practically stopped the entry and exit of boats.

THE PEACE NEGOTIATIONS

In the hope of freeing his ally from the embarrassment of war with the United States at the moment when Napoleon was beginning his invasion of Russia, the Czar tendered his good offices as mediator in September, 1812. Madison accepted, and appointed Gallatin and James A. Bayard, Federalist Senator from Delaware, to act with John Quincy Adams, then minister in Russia, as peace commissioners. England rejected mediation but indicated a willingness to treat directly with the representatives of the states. Clay and Russell, formerly *chargé* in England, were thereupon added to the commission, and negotiations were begun at Ghent in the summer of 1814. Britain's chief statesmen were absorbed in the discussions of the Congress at Vienna, and the conferences at Ghent were intrusted to men of little prominence, who, despite constant directions from their superiors, succeeded in making several blunders of which the American negotiators reaped the full advantage.

By conquering Canada the administration had hoped, through its relinquishment, to persuade England to abandon the practice of impressment. However, the first instructions to the American commissioners, formulated at the close of the disastrous campaign of 1812, when the probability of success in the invasion of Canada seemed slight, could demand nothing more than the restoration of the territorial *status quo ante bellum*. Without Canada in possession, serious modification of the terms of peace desired by the United States were found unavoidable. The demand that impressments be abandoned by express stipulation in the treaty was given up, and a similar recession was made in regard to the British principles of blockade. On these points the British could not be shaken, and in the end the United States had to be content with a treaty which was silent on the matters which had been the main causes of friction before the war.

The Americans on their part resisted with equal success the demands of the British. These, framed soon after Napoleon's abdication, were in their turn excessive. The English commissioners asked: (1) for a mutual guarantee of the integrity of the territory of their Indian allies as a *sine qua non* of peace;[1] (2) for military control of the Great Lakes, with a cession of territory in northern Maine to afford a direct route between Quebec and Halifax; and (3) for a concession in return for the renewal of the fishing rights of the United States within Canadian waters. The severity of these terms was such as to cause our commissioners to reply in effect that they could not be entertained unless America were completely conquered.

Back of the British demands was the expectation of success in the operations of Prevost and Ross. The news of the reverses at Plattsburg and Baltimore, and the threat of renewed hostilities in Europe because of disagreements at Vienna, made the British falter. Abandoning the *sine qua non* as to the Indian territory, they proffered a settlement on the basis of *status uti possidetis*—that the treaty should leave each belligerent in possession of the territory held when peace was made. The insistence of the Americans upon the *status quo ante bellum*—which would require the mutual restoration of conquered territory—was regarded by the statesmen of

---

[1] This demand represented the final effort of the British to realize their long-cherished ideal of an Indian buffer state in the Northwest.

Downing Street as the reply of stiff-necked Yankees who could not understand the logic of the war. But the American position was sound, according to the greatest military mind in the British Empire, the Duke of Wellington. In response to the appeal of the ministry that he take command of the Canadian army, the Duke declared that he could not conquer America without first regaining control of the lakes. Could he do this? He could not promise himself success. Evidently, in his judgment, the victories of Perry and Macdonough were decisive and the prolongation of the war unjustifiable. Nor did he regard the terms proposed by the ministry as warranted. "I confess," he said, "that I think you have no right from the state of the war to demand any concession from America. . . . You have not been able to carry it into the enemy's territory . . . and have not even cleared your own. . . . Why stipulate for the *uti possidetis?* You can get no territory."

While these consultations, unknown to the American commissioners, were disposing the ministry to acceptance of the *status quo ante,* Gallatin and his colleagues were drafting a treaty on this basis for submission to the British commissioners. Dissensions now appeared—not for the first time—within their own commission. Clay, champion of the new West which had arisen since 1783, was unwilling to purchase the renewed recognition of fishing rights by continuing the British liberty to navigate the Mississippi; Adams, true heir of his father as guardian of the fishermen, was ready to contest the point to the uttermost. With the patience which made him in a double sense a great peacemaker, Gallatin persuaded the disputants to agree to offer a renewal of both rights; but the British counter-proposal that these questions be left to be dealt with at a later time was finally accepted.[1]

[1] The fisheries question was covered by a convention or agreement made in 1818, by which the rights and privileges of the United States were curtailed somewhat as compared with the provisions of the treaty of 1783. Disputes

Already the Americans had consented to make peace with such Indians as were still at war, on the basis of restoring all their prewar rights, while rejecting everything in the nature of an international guarantee under which Great Britain might claim a right to intervene in their behalf in future. Other portions of the treaty related to matters not connected with the war. They provided for joint commissions to determine the boundary at several disputed points.

On December 24, 1814, Clay who had pictured the victorious hosts of his countrymen dictating terms of peace at Quebec, signed a treaty which added not a foot of territory to the United States; Adams, who had called impressment "man stealing," accepted a peace which was silent on the subject which had caused the war. Nevertheless benignant peace smiled again upon foes of kindred blood. In token of restored harmony the British delegates entertained the Americans at dinner on Christmas Day. "The roast beef and plum pudding was from England, and everybody drank everybody else's health." So wrote young James Gallatin, who had been his father's clerk during the long negotiations. "The band played *God Save the King,* to the toast of the King, and *Yankee Doodle.* Congratulations on all sides and a general atmosphere of serenity; it was a scene to be remembered. God grant there may be always peace between the two nations."

THE HARTFORD CONVENTION

While the peace negotiations were nearing their close New England discontent came to its climax. Again as in the revolutionary days the town meetings became centers for the discussion of grievances, and the state legislatures, like those of

---

grew out of the new agreement and the fisheries continued until the twentieth century to be a vexatious problem in Anglo-American relations. The British right to navigate the Mississippi was not renewed, since its sources were found not to be within British territory.

Virginia and Kentucky in 1798, passed resolutions denouncing the acts of the Federal Government. The Federalists now talked of the Constitution as a compact and spoke of the states as sovereign. In 1814 the Massachusetts general court used the very words in which the President had once maintained the right of a state to interpose its authority in cases of violation of the "federal compact"; and a few months later Connecticut passed an act intended to thwart the execution of a law of Congress for the enlistment of minors.

In consequence of the refusal by the New England states of the call for militia, the Federal Government had stationed no troops in that quarter, and when the British invaded the coast of Maine in 1814, New England was left to defend herself. Massachusetts thereupon asked the neighboring states to join with her in sending delegates to a convention to be held at Hartford, in December.

The Massachusetts, Connecticut, and Rhode Island legislatures, and counties in New Hampshire and Vermont, appointed delegates to the convention. Although the purpose stated in the call was to devise means of security and defense "not repugnant to their obligations as members of the Union," and to "procure such amendments to . . . the national constitution as may secure them equal advantages," it was generally believed that the leaders contemplated secession unless their demands were met.

Color was given to this conjecture by the utterances of some of the more radical Federalists. For example, one of them, writing in the Boston *Advertiser,* urged the convention to recommend that the states declare the Constitution "suspended," and the *Centinel,* another Boston newspaper, announced Connecticut's decision to send delegates to Hartford as the rearing of the "second pillar of a new federal edifice." "Refederator," who was quoted with approval by many papers, wanted, not the secession of New England, but the expulsion of the western states from the Union. *"Let the Western States go off,"* he argued; "then let us, who belonged to the old family [of original states], try, by the agency of such men as are to meet at *Hartford . . .* [to] revise our family compact." Gouverneur Morris, writing of the doings of Congress while the convention was sitting, declared that they were "indifferent to one whose eyes are fixed on a Star in the East, which he believes to be the day spring of freedom and glory. The traitors and madmen assembled at Hartford will, I believe, if not too tame and mild, be hailed hereafter as the patriots and sages of their day and generation."

Additional suspicion was aroused by the secrecy of the sessions, and to this day little·is known of what was said.[1] When after nearly three weeks the convention adjourned to meet again at the call of the presiding officer, the parallel with the course of the First Continental Congress was too striking to be overlooked, for the Hartford Convention had formulated certain demands to be presented at Washington, and the presumption was strong that some revolutionary action would follow rejection.

The demands took the form of amendments to the Constitution: apportionment of taxes and representatives in the House on the basis of free population; a two-thirds vote of both houses for the admission of new states, the interdiction of foreign commerce, or the declaring of war; the limitation of embargoes to sixty days; the disqualification of naturalized citizens for federal office; and the limitation of the President's tenure to a single term, no two Presidents to come in succes-

---

[1] The Journal of the Convention was published in 1823 to show the mild temper of the meeting. Members declared that it recorded every motion and vote, and that no proposal was made to divide the Union, organize a separate government, or form any foreign alliance. The man chosen as president of the gathering was George Cabot, one of the original founders of the Federalist party, but a moderate man, now sixty-two years of age. In 1813 he had said to Pickering, "Why can't you and I let the world ruin itself in its own way?"

sion from the same state. The first of these proposals sprang from the old dissatisfaction with the three-fifths compromise; the rest from sectional jealousy of the Virginia dynasty and the growth of the West. Sober afterthought questions whether any of the changes would have been wise.

Massachusetts and Connecticut appointed commissioners to present the proposals to the government at Washington. Yet in spite of appearances, most of the Federalists probably wished for nothing more than a redress of their supposed grievances. It is more than doubtful whether the majority of the people of any New England state would have supported secession. As an indication of their loyalty it is worthy of note that as many volunteers entered the army from Massachusetts as from Virginia.

In the columns of the *National Advocate,* a New York paper, appeared in January, 1815, the following mock advertisement: "Missing: three well-looking, responsible men, who appeared to be travelling towards Washington, disappeared suddenly from Gadsby's Hotel, in Baltimore, on Monday morning last, and have not since been heard of." The jibe was aimed at the New England commissioners. On their way to Washington they had learned of Jackson's victory at New Orleans, and news of the peace had arrived before them. Realizing that amid the universal rejoicing their errand would appear ridiculous, they had quietly turned their faces homeward.

SELECT BIBLIOGRAPHY

Mahan, *Sea Power,* is excellent on the whole war period and the peace negotiations. This writer, himself a naval officer, was the first historian to develop adequately the importance of sea power in the history of international relations. Henry Adams' treatment is able and full on all the topics of the chapter. Babcock, *Rise of American Nationality,* gives a good brief account of the war but pays slight attention to diplomacy. Paine, *The*

Fight for a Free Sea, is another brief account.   The Canadian point of view is presented in Wood, *War with the United States.*

Rise of the War Party.   A good life of one of the leaders of the "War Hawks" is Schurz, *Henry Clay.*   The newer biography by Van Deusen, *Life of Henry Clay,* is perhaps the best one-volume study.   Mayo, *Henry Clay,* is the first of a projected three-volume work.   A thorough study of Webster is that by Fuess, *Daniel Webster.*   For one of the important military leaders see Elliott, *Winfield Scott.*   Oskison, *Tecumseh and His Times,* is by an author who himself has Indian blood.

War Plans and Resources.   Bogart, *Economic History of the United States;* Dewey, *Financial History.* For the plans of the war party see Pratt, *Expansionists of 1812.*

The Campaigns.   McMaster and Schouler are briefer than Adams and more easily read.   Dutton, *Oliver Hazard Perry,* is a good biography.

Naval Warfare.   Roosevelt, *Naval War of 1812,* is an older work than Mahan's, but has fuller details on naval operations.

The Peace Negotiations.   See general histories and histories of diplomacy previously cited.   Of special importance is Updyke, *Diplomacy of the War of 1812.*

The Hartford Convention.   Lodge, *Life and Letters of George Cabot,* is best on the convention.   The work of Powell, *Nullification and Secession in the United States,* contains a brief account (Chap. V).

Chapter XIX

THE NEW NATIONALISM

THE War of 1812 was one of the most futile of conflicts, judged by the contrast between its objects and the terms of peace. The easy confidence with which the leaders had predicted a peace dictated at the Canadian capital contrasted sadly with the meager successes along the border. Neither force nor diplomacy wrested from England the recognition of neutral rights. Yet the war profoundly affected the American people. In spite of the inconclusive duel they had a sense of vindicated honor. The victories at the Thames and Lundy's Lane, the repulse of the enemy at Plattsburg and New Orleans, and most of all, the gallant performance of the seamen, appealed powerfully to the national pride; while the darker experiences—the lack of preparedness, the failure of the militia, the recalcitrancy of New England, the financial mistakes—were warnings to plan more wisely for the future.

The Republicans had been undergoing a process of nationalization since 1801. Jefferson had come to the presidency as the apostle of localism and the foe of centralized authority, but from the moment of his inauguration the logic of circumstances had proved stronger than his theories. After the purchase of Louisiana Gouverneur Morris wrote: "By downright demonstration it is shown that the republican party were not dissatisfied because the power of the Government was too great, but because it was not in their hands." In proportion, moreover, as the Republicans had gravitated towards the standard of strong government set up by the Federalists, the latter, as the party of the "Outs," had swung around to states' rights and localism.

Thus there had been an actual exchange of positions. But the opposition of New England to the war, culminating in the Hartford Convention, brought home to the whole country the dangers in the weakening of political authority towards which states' rights sentiments tended, and peace was accompanied by an access of patriotism and nationalistic feeling. Gallatin wrote in 1816: "Under our former system we were becoming too selfish . . . too much confined in our feelings to local and state objects. The war has renewed the national feelings and character which the Revolution had given."

AFTER-WAR READJUSTMENT

The spirit of nationalism had never before attained the vigor shown at the close of the second war with England. It pervaded all of the measures of reconstruction which followed the peace. One of its first manifestations is found in the plans for placing the army and navy on a peace basis. Madison's message of 1815 recommended adequate provision for the national defense. Clay, now returned from Ghent and reëlected Speaker, pointed to the unsatisfactory state of the relations with several European powers, and urged the retention of the direct tax as a measure of financial preparedness. New wars were not unlikely to come, and the former trust in pacific methods of preserving national rights was gone. There was no more talk of reducing the navy to the vanishing point, as in Jefferson's early plans. On the contrary, it was maintained at its full, though meager, war strength, with provision for some additions. The peace footing of the army was put at ten thousand men. Although this was but half the number recommended by Monroe, as Secretary of War, the action of Congress indicated that faith had been lost in the militia as a trustworthy first arm of defense.

Having provided for the military and naval establishments,

JOHN C. CALHOUN

HENRY CLAY   DANIEL WEBSTER

"The Great Triumvirate"

the Republicans, still following Madison's lead, set about restoring the currency. The evils of unregulated issues of paper, which Hamilton avoided by the creation of the United States Bank, had fallen upon the country when the Republicans refused to grant a renewal of the charter in 1811. Banks chartered by the states had multiplied, and while nominally specie paying, their issues were so little regulated that a total of possibly $170,000,000 was put into circulation upon the basis of specie reserves not exceeding $15,000,000. This was about four times as much as sound methods permitted.

Any unusual demand for specie, under such conditions, was certain to result in the suspension of specie payments. The shock came with the capture of Washington. All of the banks in the South and West suspended payments in the autumn of 1814, throwing the country upon a paper basis again, as at the close of the Revolution. Almost indescribable confusion followed. The paper of each bank had its own scale of depreciation, which varied with the strength of the bank and its distance from the point where the paper was in use. Tables, frequently revised to show the current value of the different notes in circulation in each community, were necessary to enable merchants to transact business at all, and even then the constant fluctuations discouraged activity in business through fear of loss by further depreciation. The government was involved also, since most of the money received for bonds was in the form of bank notes. Only in New England where specie payments were maintained did bank notes remain at par.

An attachment to state banks has been one of the striking manifestations of localism in the United States. In early days, when the issue of circulating notes was regarded as the chief function of banks, the business was one of the most profitable forms of investment. The idea of a great central institution endowed with special privileges by favor of government has always been repugnant to a large portion of the people, as tending to give a monopoly of such profits, and an undue control over credit, to a privileged few.

The necessity of a uniform currency, however, was felt even in colonial days, as shown by the parliamentary enactments fixing the value at which money of various kinds should circulate in the provinces. The Constitution recognized this need by giving Congress power to regulate the value of money; and Hamilton resorted to the United States Bank as the most expedient mode of exercising this power, in so far as it applied to paper.

With some hesitation Madison turned to Hamilton's ideas and suggested in the message of 1815 that if the operation of the state banks could not restore a uniform circulation, a national bank would "merit consideration." For the Republicans, such a course was a humiliating confession of error. But the confusion of the currency imperatively demanded remedial action, and they had no substitute to offer.

Calhoun was chairman of the committee which, working in touch with A. J. Dallas, the new Secretary of the Treasury, as the guiding spirit in financial reconstruction, reported a bill for the creation of a second United States Bank. The capital now authorized was $35,000,000. The government was to subscribe one fifth and to appoint a like proportion of the directors. The new bank was to issue notes redeemable on demand in specie. The charter was to run for twenty years; branches might be established in the states as needed; the bank was to be the depository of public funds unless they were removed by the Secretary of the Treasury for reasons satisfactory to Congress. It was to be exempt from federal taxation, but was required to pay a bonus of $1,500,000 for its charter.

In presenting the bill Calhoun insisted that it was the duty of Congress to regulate the currency and restore specie payments. So far was he from the position of Jefferson in 1791 that he waived discussion of the constitutional aspects of the question as "a useless consumption of time." Clay supported him heartily, attributing his change of mind since 1811 (when he had been among those who voted against rechartering the first bank) to "the force of circumstances and the light of experience." In April Madison placed his signature on the bill, thus virtually adopting the doctrine of implied powers which he had combated twenty-five years before.

The opening of the bank enabled the government to bring about a general resumption of specie payments. With the notes of the new institution in circulation, the Secretary of the Treasury was able to announce that, in accordance with a joint resolution of Congress, on and after February 20, 1817, government dues would be received only in the notes of the United States Bank and other specie-paying institutions. This and other measures of pressure compelled the state banks to get ready for resumption, and those which were not essentially unsound were able to do so by the date set.

Along with liberal provision for national defense and a new United States Bank, Madison's message recommended a protective tariff. The war had taught him the importance of building up such domestic manufactures "as will relieve the United States from a dependence on foreign supplies . . . for articles necessary for the public defence or connected with the primary wants of individuals." Here again the Republicans were adopting Hamilton's policies. Aid to manufactures for this very purpose had been advocated by him with little avail.

England, where the factory system was first established, thanks to the genius of the inventors of the steam engine and of power-driven machinery, carefully guarded the secret of the construction of the machines which gave her preëminence; but it was the greater profitableness of agriculture and commerce which long prevented serious efforts at manufacturing in the United States. When the embargo, nonintercourse, and war cut off the accustomed supply of foreign goods and at the same time destroyed the shipping of the country, capital was diverted perforce into manufacturing to prevent actual want of necessaries. By the end of the war very considerable sums, probably amounting to a hundred million dollars, had found investment in manufactures of various kinds, mostly textiles, which employed more than half of this total. This transfer of capital from commerce to the textile industries, John Randolph called "exchanging the trident for the distaff." These new enterprises were located chiefly in New England and the middle states. Rhode Island was the home of most of the cotton mills. But some factories were to be found in the towns of the Ohio Valley, where the difficulty of transportation across the mountains had much the same effect as the embargo and war had in the Atlantic states.

The English were uneasy over this effect of the war. Having succeeded in retaining their American market after the Revolution, they were now in danger of losing it unless means could be found to destroy the infant industries in the states. As Lord Brougham said in Parliament, "it was worth while to incur a loss upon the first exportation, in order, by a glut, to stifle in the cradle those rising manufactures in the United States which the war had forced into existence, contrary to the natural course of things." For this purpose British goods began to be "dumped" upon the American market and sold at auction for whatever they would bring.

The privations of the war period had shown others besides Madison the importance of preserving the manufactures of America until they could stand alone in spite of foreign competition. Even Jefferson overcame his antipathy to them and wrote: "There exists both profligacy and power enough to exclude us from the field of interchange with other nations; . . . to be independent for the comforts of life we must fabricate for ourselves. We must now place the manufacturer by the side of the agriculturist. . . . He . . . who is now against domestic manufacture, must be for reducing us either to dependence . . . or to be clothed in skins, and to live like wild beasts in dens and caverns."

The investments of the owners of the new plants were also at stake, but their interests were not the basis of the demand for protective legislation by the political leaders. For example, Calhoun professed to lay the claims of the manufacturers "entirely out of view." Economic independence, it was urged, was as essential as political; indeed, political independence was hardly a reality without economic self-sufficiency. As the War of the Revolution had been fought for the one, so now it was proposed to win the other by the protection of home industry.

The import duties, doubled at the beginning of the war for revenue purposes, and averaging about twenty-five per cent, were continued by the tariff act of 1816. On some classes of goods, especially cottons, the rates were increased. Imported cottons selling in the case of India prints for as little as six cents a yard were to be valued for the levy of the impost at not less than twenty-five cents. This feature of the law is known as the "minimum principle." [1]

Another recommendation of the President's message was a national system of roads and canals. An express authorization of such works by Congress was one of the omissions from the Constitution which had soon been regretted. When in 1806 Jefferson found a treasury surplus accumulating, he recommended the adoption of an amendment to confer this power, believing that Congress could not spend money raised by taxation for purposes other than those enumerated in the

[1] For discussion of the opposition to the tariff see page 458.

Constitution. A little later Gallatin prepared an elaborate report on canals and roads, and Congress appropriated money for a coast survey. No steps were taken looking towards the adoption of the suggested amendment, and with the passage of the embargo the surplus disappeared and along with it the possibility, for the time being, of a federal system.

Nevertheless the seeds of a national system of roads were planted during Jefferson's presidency. When Ohio was admitted in 1803, an agreement was made with the new state by which, in return for the exemption of federal public lands within the state from taxation, Congress pledged a percentage of the proceeds of the sales of the lands for use in building a road connecting the state with the eastern seaboard. This agreement was the origin of the Old National Road, or "Cumberland Road," as it is sometimes called, from the fact that its original eastern terminus was the town of Cumberland, in western Maryland. Its construction was begun in 1811, but at the end of the war only about twenty miles had been completed.

Madison's recommendation of internal improvements repeated that of Jefferson in 1806, including the proposal of an amendment to the Constitution. The prosecution of the war had been hampered by the lack of military roads, and the increasing population of the West laid new stress upon the importance of means of communication and transportation as bonds of union. Congress took no action, and the President renewed his recommendation in the message of 1816, particularly inviting attention "to the expediency of exercising . . . existing powers, and, where necessary, of resorting to the prescribed mode of enlarging them, in order to effectuate a comprehensive system of roads and canals."

Thus prompted a second time, Congress took up a bill reported by Calhoun which proposed to use for roads and canals the bonus paid by the bank for its charter, together with the dividends on the bank stock owned by the government. The discussion of this measure soon brought out the fact that the Republicans of the Old and New Schools had drifted far apart.

CLEAVAGE OF THE REPUBLICANS

Although the Old School Republicans had been swept into the current of the New Nationalism, they had a deep-seated respect for the letter of the Constitution and the importance of the amending process. The doctrine of implied powers which Madison was willing to accept in the erection of the bank he rejected in the case of internal improvements. When the "Bonus Bill" passed Congress and came to him for signature, he vetoed it, apparently in the hope of recalling his party to original principles.

Opinion within the Young Republican group was outrunning that of the old leaders. Taking up the ideal of economic self-sufficiency which Madison's message suggested in its recommendation of protection for manufactures, they outlined a complete national system of political economy. Clay and Calhoun were the chief exponents of this phase of the New Nationalism.

"Whenever we have the misfortune to be involved in a war with a nation dominant on the ocean," said Calhoun, in discussing the tariff bill, "the moneyed resources of the country to a great extent must fail. . . . Commerce and agriculture, till lately almost the only, still constitute the principal, sources of our wealth. . . . They both depend on foreign markets. . . . When our manufactures are grown to a certain perfection, as they soon will be under the fostering care of Government . . . the farmer will find a ready market for his surplus produce; and, what is almost of equal consequence, a certain and cheap supply of all his wants. . . . The arm of Government will be nerved; and taxes in the hour

of danger . . . may be greatly increased. . . . To give perfection to this state of things, it is necessary to add, as soon as
possible, a system of internal improvements, and at least
such an extension of our navy as will prevent the cutting off
of our coasting trade."

Discussing the Bonus Bill Calhoun made light of constitutional difficulties. Was not Congress authorized to lay taxes
to "provide for the common defense and general welfare?"
He held that this clause authorized appropriations for roads
and canals which the general welfare demanded, for the very
greatness of the country and the rapidity of its growth tended
to weaken the bonds which held together its widely separated
parts. "We are under the most imperious obligation to
counteract every tendency to disunion. . . . Whatever im-
pedes the intercourse of the extremes with this, the center
of the Republic, weakens the Union."

This scheme of things had much in common with the
thought of the English mercantilists. Both were based on a
belief in the desirability of governmental regulations to
develop national resources and industry for the sake of
strength and safety in war time. The system was implied in
Madison's recommendations, especially those relating to
protection and internal improvements; but he did not develop the implications, and on the question of the interpretation of the Constitution the President and the Young Republicans were far apart. The latter adopted implied powers
as a principle of general validity, and as sharp a difference
developed between the two groups of Republicans in their
views of constitutional construction as had once separated
Republicans and Federalists. When Monroe came to the
presidency, he, like Madison, displayed a tenderness for the
letter of the Constitution which exasperated the younger
men. In his first message (1817), while expressing his belief

in the desirability of internal improvements, he announced his conviction that a constitutional amendment was necessary to authorize Congress to establish them.

Monroe's message showed that the plans of the young Republican group as to internal improvements were blocked by the certainty of a veto of any bill which Congress might pass. They on their part would not consent to an effort to amend the Constitution. Said they, "if an amendment be recommended, and should not be obtained, we should have surrendered a power which we are bound to maintain if we think we possess it." The views of the Old School Clay called a "water-gruel regimen," an interpretation which would construe the Constitution to a dead letter and make it a bar to the country's progress. Was the Constitution by its grant of power to establish post offices and post roads and to regulate commerce between the states (in all of which he found power implied to build roads and canals) made for the Atlantic margin of the country only? "We are not legislating for this moment only, or for the present generation, or for the present populated limits of the United States; but our acts must embrace a wider scope,—reaching northwestward to the Pacific, and southwardly to the river Del Norte. Imagine this extent of territory covered with sixty, seventy, or an hundred millions of people. The powers which exist in this government now will exist then; and those which will exist then exist now." Clay seemed to have discarded altogether the necessity of the amending process.

There were many Republicans who, like Presidents Madison and Monroe, approved of national policies in themselves but could not follow Clay and Calhoun on account of constitutional scruples. There were others who, in spite of the prevailing nationalism, were still controlled by considerations of sectional interest. This division is apparent in the votes both on the Bonus Bill and the Tariff of 1816. New England Federalists and Old School Republicans voted against the Bonus Bill, which promised more benefits for other sections than for their own; and although Lowndes was chairman of the Ways and Means Committee which reported the tariff bill, and Calhoun its most eloquent supporter, many southern members could not be moved by the nationalistic arguments. Aside from the general advantage of national self-sufficiency, the benefits of protection, they perceived, would be very unevenly distributed.

John Randolph presented the sectional point of view on the tariff in his characteristic way. Said he: "It eventuates in this: whether you, as a planter, will consent to be taxed, in order to hire another man to go to work in a shoemaker's shop, or to set up a spinning jenny. . . . No, I will buy where I can get manufactures cheapest, I will not agree to lay a duty on the cultivators of the soil to encourage exotic manufactures; because, after all, we should only get much worse things at a higher price." In the vote part of the South followed Lowndes and part Randolph; it cast twenty-three votes for protection and thirty-four against it. Twenty negative votes came from the maritime districts of the North, whose carrying trade would be injured by the lessening of America's dependence upon Europe.

THE SUPREME COURT AND NATIONALISM

The decade following 1815 is memorable on account of a series of great decisions by the Supreme Court which were quite in the spirit of the New Nationalism. For the first few years after the adoption of the Constitution the judiciary was regarded as the weakest of the three branches of the Federal Government. In its first great decision the Court held that a state might be sued by the citizen of another state (Chisholm vs. Georgia, 1793) . While this decision was a sound interpretation of the words of the Constitution as they stood,[1] it was unpopular and led to the adoption of the Eleventh Amendment, which denied the jurisdiction of the federal courts in such cases.

The amendment was damaging to the prestige of the Court. Chief Justice Jay soon afterwards resigned to become a candidate for governor of New York. When a few years later President Adams offered to reappoint him, he declined. "I left the bench," he replied, "perfectly convinced that under a system so defective, it would not obtain the energy, weight, and dignity which was essential to its affording due support to the national government; nor acquire the public confidence and respect which, as the last resort of the justice of the nation, it should possess." [2]

The greatness which Jay could not foresee was achieved under John Marshall (appointed January 31, 1801), to whom Adams turned upon receiving Jay's declination. The appointee, while known as an able lawyer, had up to this time given little evidence of peculiar fitness for the Supreme Bench. Adams lived to regard his "gift of John Marshall to the people of the United States as the proudest act of his life." Indeed, as Hamilton ranks as the greatest master of finance in our history, so Marshall stands preëminent among our jurists.

Marshall, although a Virginian, was one of the small group of southern men who remained steadfast in the principles of Federalism in spite of the cross currents which carried both political parties so far from their original courses. Jefferson thoroughly distrusted him, and we have already seen how the Republicans attacked the court system of which he was head.

---

[1] "The judicial Power shall extend to all Cases . . . between a state and Citizens of another State."—Const., Art. III, Sec. 2.

[2] Jay especially disliked the circuit-court duty required of members of the Supreme Bench. He was actually confirmed by the Senate and his commission made out before his declination was received.

In the hope of counterbalancing the weight of his opinions, the Republican Presidents Jefferson and Madison appointed men of their own political faith to the bench as vacancies occurred. But these fell under the spell of Marshall's powerful mind, and the ablest of them, Joseph Story, of Massachusetts, became a worthy second to his great chief as a nationalistic expounder of the supreme law.[1]

The first of Marshall's great decisions was the opinion in the Marbury case, holding an act of Congress to be unconstitutional. In Fletcher *vs.* Peck (1810) the Court held void an act of the Georgia legislature; the decision applied that provision of the Constitution which forbids a state to pass any act impairing the obligation of contracts. In Martin *vs.* Hunter's Lessee (1816) the Court upheld the provision of the Judiciary Act of 1789 concerning appeals from the state courts in cases involving federal law. The highest court in the State of Virginia had rendered a decision in the case and denied the right of appeal, but the Supreme Court asserted its paramount authority in the face of this denial. The prohibition of state legislation impairing the obligation of contracts was again involved in the case of Dartmouth College *vs.* Woodward (1819). The State of New Hampshire had modified by act of the legislature, and against the will of the trustees of the college, the charter granted to the college in colonial days. Such a charter the Court held to be a contract which could be modified only by mutual consent of the parties. The winning of this case, as counsel for the college, his alma mater, was a step in Daniel Webster's rise to fame.

In the same year the Court gave its sanction to the doctrine of implied powers in a suit involving the United States Bank.

[1] Cæsar A. Rodney, the Attorney-General, complained in 1808: "You can scarcely elevate a man to a seat in a Court of Justice before he catches the leprosy of the Bench." Jefferson advised Madison against appointing Story, regarding him as no Republican.

Friends of local banks in several southern and western states brought about the enactment of laws taxing the branches of the United States Bank, really for the purpose of forcing them out of business. The cashier of the Baltimore branch refused to pay the tax on its notes as required by the Maryland law, and appealed from the decision of the highest state tribunal.

This case of McCulloch *vs.* Maryland involved two questions: (1) the constitutional right of Congress to incorporate the bank; and (2) the right of a state to tax an agency of the Federal Government, used in the performance of its functions. The first issue was the old one discussed by Jefferson and Hamilton while members of Washington's cabinet. Now in words really quoted from Hamilton's opinion Marshall sustained the constitutionality of the charter act and at the same time the doctrine of implied powers: "Let the end be legitimate, let it be within the scope of the Constitution, and all means which are appropriate, which are plainly adapted to that end, which are not prohibited, but consist with the letter and spirit of the constitution, are constitutional."

As to the second point, the power to tax was held to be equivalent to the power to destroy. "If the States may tax one instrument employed by the government in the execution of its powers, they may tax any and every other instrument. They may tax the mail; they may tax the mint; . . . they may tax judicial process; they may tax all the means employed by the government, to an excess which would defeat all the ends of government." The only tax which states could lay upon the branches of the bank, he concluded, was the regular property tax on their buildings and land.

By these and other decisions Marshall became one of the great builders of the American constitutional system. Unlike the jurists of later times, he was not bound by the interpretations of predecessors, for there were few of consequence. His constructive mind and his long tenure, from 1801 to 1835, enabled him to create a body of constitutional law on which all of his successors have built. The decisions discussed went far towards clarifying the limits of the powers of the states and Federal Government respectively. Some of them set restrictions on the authority of the states while others asserted the prerogatives of the national government. The Old School Republicans were alarmed by the decisions, without being able to put forward a champion who was a match for Marshall. "All wrong," groaned John Randolph, "but no man in the United States can tell why or wherein." Judge Spencer Roane and John Taylor, both of Virginia, did in fact elaborate very ably the theory first advanced by Jefferson in 1798, denying the right of the Supreme Court to pose as final judge of the constitutionality of acts of Congress and of the rights of the states. The gist of their claim was that the Constitution provided no final arbiter in such disputes. Each state was therefore the judge of its reserved powers. To these men Marshall's decisions seemed to be undermining the rights of the states and bringing about a "consolidated" republic.

Friends of popular government, moreover, saw in such decisions as that in the Dartmouth College case a sympathetic disposition of the Court towards vested interests which threatened to handicap the state governments in regulating corporations of their own creation. Thus the problem of controlling corporate enterprise—"big business"—appeared above the horizon in these years.

Some of Marshall's decisions have since been modified. While they struck out the first bold outlines of our constitutional law, the finer shading was added by later hands. Especially under Taney, his successor, the court took a more liberal turn.

BEGINNINGS OF A NATIONAL LITERATURE

Another evidence that national consciousness was stirring in this period is found in the appearance of the first signs of a truly American literature. The first generation after independence was an era of political writing. The controversy with England, the establishment of the Constitution, the contests of parties, furnished themes which filled men's minds, and left little energy for productive effort in the field of polite literature.

Then came, with the opening of the nineteenth century, writers of fiction and verse who were, for the most part, dull and uninspired imitators of English models. In the next decade, however, a new American school appeared in which the names of Washington Irving, James Fenimore Cooper, and William Cullen Bryant stand foremost.

Irving's *History of New York, by Diedrich Knickerbocker* (1809) drew its inspiration from local sources, and displayed a quality of humor which stamped its author as a genius; and while he later allowed himself to be diverted from native to foreign themes, some of the best of his work, such as the story of *Rip Van Winkle* (1819), found its setting in the Hudson Valley or Catskill Mountains. *The Sketch Book* (1820) revealed America as a land of legend and romance, equal in interest to the Old World. He was the first American writer of fiction to command respect abroad. The abundant literary output of his riper years, instinct with grace and charm, caused Thackeray to call him "the first ambassador whom the New World of letters sent to the Old."

After an attempt at a novel of the conventional English type, Cooper published *The Spy* (1821). It was a tale of the Revolution, and won immediate popularity. Next came *The Pioneers*. James K. Paulding had already published, in 1818, a poem, *The Backwoodsman,* which won the praise of critics because the writer forsook the giants, castles, and distressed maidens of European romances and portrayed the simple life of the American frontier. *The Pioneers* gave a vivid prose picture of the same life. Cooper's own experience provided the background for the book, as his father, an early settler of central New York, had brought him as an infant into what was then the wilderness. Although the stories of this pioneer among our novelists include tales of the sea, their significance in the history of our literature lies in the fact that they were products of American influences, little affected by English traditions. In the series entitled *Leatherstocking Tales,* published from 1823 to 1841, Cooper made the pioneer, Natty Bumpo, and the silent-footed Indian chief Uncas, permanent figures in world literature.[1]

With Bryant our poetry began. A few men before him had written a poem or two each; he was our first poet who wrote both much and well. *Thanatopsis,* written when the author was but a lad of seventeen, appeared in 1819.

The beginning of good work in literature is properly associated with the founding of *The North American Review,* in 1815. Innumerable magazines had sprung up in the years preceding, only to wither away after a few issues for lack of root and nourishment. The essays on natural and moral philosophy, and the "agreeable and entertaining moral tales" with which they were filled, were substitutes for real literature which bored even the long-suffering reader of those days. In the hands of Jared Sparks as editor, the *Review* set a new standard of excellence, drawing both contributions and subscriptions from the young intellectuals of New England in sufficient numbers to give it a place as a permanent factor in the developing culture of the nation.

---

[1] *The Pioneers* (1823), *The Last of the Mohicans* (1826), *The Prairie* (1827), *The Pathfinder* (1840), *The Deerslayer* (1841).

SELECT BIBLIOGRAPHY

After-War Readjustment. Adams, *History,* covers the attempts at reorganization during the last months of Madison's term. See McMaster on the currency situation. Babcock has chapters on the Second Bank, the Tariff, Internal Improvements, and the Supreme Court. See also Dewey, *Financial History,* Bogart, *Economic History,* and Coman, *Industrial History.*

Taussig, *Tariff History of the United States,* is a standard work by a leading economist. The political aspects of the tariff are brought out more fully by Stanwood, *American Tariff Controversies in the Nineteenth Century.*

Von Holst, *John C. Calhoun,* has a brief account of Calhoun's congressional career.

Cleavage of the Republicans. This topic has been little developed by writers. In this connection Gilman, *James Monroe,* and Adams, *John Randolph,* may be studied along with the lives of Clay and Calhoun. See also Hockett, *Western Influences,* Chap. IV.

The Supreme Court and Nationalism. Corwin, *John Marshall and the Constitution,* is a handy summary of the topic. Beveridge, *Life of John Marshall,* is a monumental work both in bulk and value. *Cf.* Fuess, *Daniel Webster.* See also Hockett, *Constitutional History,* I, Chap. XVIII.

Beginnings of a National Literature. Wendell, *Literary History of America.*

Chapter XX

EXPANSION

THE legislation of 1816–1817 was enacted while the country was still in the shadow of the war, and all that Congress did was colored by the supposed necessity of preparing for other wars which might come. As it turned out, nearly a century was to pass before the United States again found itself embroiled in hostilities with a European nation. The year 1815 marked the beginning of a new era, in which for the first time the government found itself free from international entanglements. Peace permitted both government and people to "turn their backs on Europe" and devote their energies as never before to the settlement and development of their own vast, rich territory. Out of domestic activities were to arise most of the public questions of the "middle period" (1815–1860).

THE WESTWARD MOVEMENT

The westward movement of population had been somewhat retarded by the war, but with the Peace of Ghent it rose to unprecedented volume. The entire Atlantic seaboard was affected by conditions which stimulated migration to the newer regions. The thin soils of the New England hillsides were incapable of producing grain in competition with the cheap and fertile lands already opened farther west. The decline of shipping added its quota of men upon whom altered economic conditions forced a readjustment in manner of life. The opportunity to earn wages in the factories which were increasing in number under the stimulus of protective legislation did not attract these sturdy seamen and sons of the soil.

466

They preferred a hazard of new fortunes elsewhere, leaving the indoor toil of the mills to women and children.

Equally conducive to migration were conditions in the southern states. The inhabitants of the back settlements of the Carolinas and Virginia were handicapped by the lack of roads and canals giving access to the markets of the coast, and they still suffered under the discriminations which since colonial days had maintained the political dominance of the tide-water planters. Many of them, moreover, belonged to religious sects, like the Quakers, which abhorred slavery. In the eighteenth century these interior settlements had been a region of small farms and free labor, but the cultivation of cotton by slave labor was spreading into the South Carolina Piedmont, while tobacco planting was encroaching upon the area of small farms in Virginia and North Carolina.

The original region of cotton growing was the coast of Georgia and South Carolina. In this limited belt flourished the sea-island, or long-staple variety. Short-staple cotton throve in almost any southern soil, but was not a profitable crop before the invention of Whitney's cotton gin (1793), which reduced the cost of removing the seed to a negligible figure. Then, under the stimulus of the increasing demand of the European factories, its cultivation rapidly increased and it soon became a more important crop than any of the older staples, rice, indigo, or even tobacco.

As if to meet the demand of the restless population, the early years of peace saw the opening of new lands in the West. Even before the Treaty of Ghent was signed, the Creeks paid the price of their defeat at the hands of Jackson's men, by the cession of a large portion of their lands in Alabama, a district stretching northward from Mobile Bay almost to the Tennessee River.

In the Northwest the soldiers who followed Harrison had cast hungry glances upon the fertile fields of the Maumee

Valley, reserved to the natives by the Treaty of Greenville; and the tribesmen, no longer having the moral support of the British in Canada, were soon persuaded to part with nearly all of their possessions in Ohio. Other treaties, some of them after wars, opened large tracts in Indiana, Illinois, Michigan, Wisconsin, Iowa, Georgia, Alabama, Mississippi, and Florida. As a corollary of this policy of opening up the Indian country, there was developed the plan of removing the dispossessed tribes to tracts west of the Mississippi, where, as was fondly imagined, they might forever remain untroubled by the white man's cupidity. The execution of the removal policy was accomplished in the thirties.

An additional incentive to migration was given in 1820 by new land laws. From the viewpoint of the federal treasury the law of 1800 had not worked well. Many purchasers under the credit system, expecting to meet deferred payments through the profits of resale or cultivation, defaulted in their obligations. Since whole communities were sometimes delinquent, eviction proved impracticable. The land code was therefore revised. The credit system was abolished, but to offset the hardship of cash payments the minimum price of lands was reduced from $2 to $1.25 per acre, and the size of the tract which might be bought to eighty acres. The auction system was retained, but it was now easier than ever before for the poor man to obtain possession of land.

For a decade or more after 1815 the chief force in pushing the frontier onward was the Piedmont stock. From the interior counties of the South Atlantic states, and from Kentucky and Tennessee to which this stock had contributed Boone and the other transalleghany pioneers of the eighteenth century, thousands of settlers poured into both Northwest and Southwest. From the same Kentucky neighborhood the families of Abraham Lincoln and of Jefferson Davis removed, the one to Indiana, the other to Mississippi.

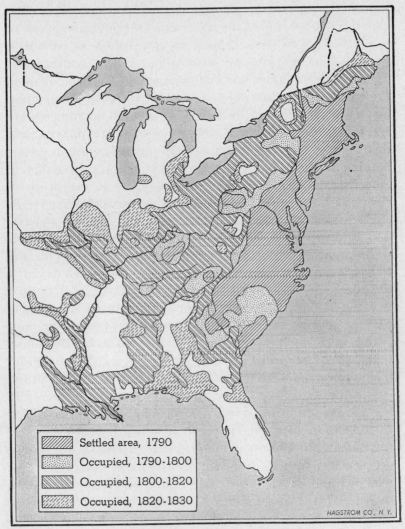

SPREAD OF POPULATION, 1790–1830

Quakers, Baptists, and other antislavery sects from Virginia and the Carolinas chose new homes in the Northwest because slavery was not allowed. The steamboat appeared on the western waters (1812) and gave command of up-stream navigation on the important rivers. The bottom lands of southern Indiana and Illinois filled up with small farms.

After 1820 any man who possessed a hundred dollars could exchange it for eighty acres of government land and become the owner of a farm in fee simple. Want of this small sum was hardly a deterrent, however, to thousands of poor men, and squatting became extremely common; the public domain was so vast that the practice had the sanction of public opinion in the West, and even the government was lax in enforcing the law against trespassers. The advantage which the auction system of disposing of lands gave to speculators, the squatters overcame by banding together in land-claims associations. Such organizations generally succeeded, by collusion or intimidation where necessary, in preventing any except actual occupants from bidding for occupied lands at the sales.

Many of the people who came to the Northwest in these years were extremely poor. Some of them brought their entire worldly possessions in wheelbarrows or packs upon their backs, and spent their first winter in "half-faced camps." These were rude shelters of poles, backed by a huge fallen log, with the southern face open to the weather. Such a camp was the home of the Lincolns for a year after their removal to Indiana in 1816, when Abraham was a boy of seven. It was replaced by a one-room log cabin which had no floor, and no covering, even of deerskin, for the holes which served as windows and door. The table and chairs were mere slabs with legs fitted into holes. Abraham's bed was "a heap of dry leaves in the corner of the loft, to which he mounted by means of pegs driven into the wall."

Prior to 1830 most of New England's emigrants went to central and western New York or to the shores of Lake Erie in Ohio. After the opening of the Erie Canal they began to reach the remoter Northwest. The project of the canal to join the Lakes and Hudson River had long been discussed by New Yorkers, who cherished the hope—until Madison vetoed the Bonus Bill—that it would be adopted as part of a comprehensive national system. Disappointed by the veto the work was begun as a state enterprise. It was ready for use in 1825 and became a great route for westward-bound emi-

THE ERIE CANAL

grants. Steamboats, in use on the Lakes after 1819, connected with the canal at Buffalo and brought the pioneers to southern Wisconsin and northern Illinois. Approaching from the northeast, they entered the prairies and became the first successful cultivators of lands which from their lack of trees had been regarded as infertile.[1]

The "Piedmontese" carried the small farm of the pioneer type into Alabama and Mississippi as well as into the Northwest. But here was an opportunity for the planter, and the small farmer was not able to hold his ground. Capitalism in the form of the seeker after good cotton lands bid up the price at the auctions to $20 or $30 per acre, and occasionally much more. Choice lands already in the hands of small farmers were secured by the offer of prices which the owners could

---

[1] A beginning had been made in southern Illinois in cultivating the prairie lands adjoining the wooded bottoms of the streams.

not afford to refuse, when other good lands farther on were to be had for so much less. Thus the planter pushed the farmer onward to a new frontier, or crowded him, if thriftless, back into the hills to join company with "poor whites." Excluded from the Northwest by antislavery legislation, the plantation spread over the Gulf states, and by the middle thirties the alluvial soils of this new South had become "black belts" in a double sense, since the slaves outnumbered the whites.

An important consequence was that, by the middle forties, the South Central states became like those of the South Atlantic division in economic life and interest, while the Mississippi Valley, which had been at first a homogeneous section (see page 529) was divided.

On the south, from the time of the purchase of Louisiana, settlers had been pressing upon the Florida boundary and chafing under the Spanish control of the coast, which barred them from their natural outlets by way of the small rivers flowing into the Gulf. The American advance-guard passed the boundary of the United States during the twenties and settled in Texas under Mexican jurisdiction. Within our limits the extreme western frontier of agricultural settlement in this decade was on the Missouri River in the "Boone's Lick country," opposite the mouth of the Osage River.

Americans had begun to settle in Missouri immediately after the purchase of Louisiana. Even before this came the aged Daniel Boone, seeking the "elbow room" no longer to be found in Kentucky or western Virginia. When Missouri Territory was organized in 1812, however, he already had twenty thousand "neighbors" along the river below his settlement, and on the west bank of the Mississippi. Missouri Territory gained population rapidly during the rush after 1815. Lying beyond the Old Northwest, it was open to the planter with his slaves. No ordinance such as barred him from Illinois operated here. Consequently, from Virginia, North Carolina, Kentucky, Tennessee, slaveholders went thither in numbers.

The tremendous shift of population in the early decades of the nineteenth century led to the division of old territories and the drawing of new boundaries with bewildering rapidity. Then as new states were admitted the political map was stabilized east of the Mississippi. Within a half-dozen years as many states were created. The appearance of Indiana (1816), Mississippi (1817), Illinois (1818), Alabama (1819), Maine (1820), and Missouri (1821), however, because statehood was granted when the population of each numbered only a few thousands, really marks only an early stage of the movement which was to convert the frontier settlements into populous commonwealths. These new states (except, of course, Maine) were the fruit chiefly of the Piedmontese migration, and were already members of the Union before the main movement of New Englanders and planters set in.

THE FAR WEST

Save for the migration into Texas beyond the bounds of the United States, the westward march of the agricultural frontier did not pass Missouri until after 1840. The admission of the new states named was followed by a process of filling in and compacting of population east of the Missouri River. While this was in progress the Far West became a field of great activity in the fur trade. The Americans infused new life into the trade which the Spanish and French had carried on in rather desultory manner from St. Louis, and soon made that town the outlet for the whole Rocky Mountain area.

William Clark was one of the organizers of the Missouri Fur Company (1809), the chief promoter of which, however, was the Spaniard, Manuel Lisa. A dozen years later (1821) the Rocky Mountain Fur Company was founded by General William H. Ashley. About the same time John Jacob Astor, a rich New York merchant, extended the operations of his American Fur Company to the transmississippi country. During the best days of the trade furs worth many hundreds of thousands of dollars were annually collected by the employés of these companies and brought to market through St. Louis. The industry was short-lived, and by 1840 the beaver trade was declining. For several decades more there was an immense traffic in buffalo hides, but by the middle of the century the West of the fur trader was giving way before the advance of the farmer and miner.

The significance of the fur trade in the history of the Far West is not found in the value of the skins which were collected. As in the first days of French exploration in the Mississippi Valley—indeed, as in the first steps of the English and Dutch westward from the Atlantic coast—the trader was the pathfinder for the settler. The French engagés and Scotch-Irish "free trappers" of the companies in the West explored the great rivers and their tributaries and found all of the passes of the Rockies and Sierras. General Ashley penetrated to the Great Basin in 1824, and within the next few years his associate, Jedediah S. Smith, several times traversed the mountains and deserts to the shores of the Pacific. Through the knowledge they gained of the geography of the western regions the traders made possible the overland migrations of the forties and the later occupation of the interior.

While the fur industry was at its height another type of commerce was opened with the Spanish settlements of the Southwest. Pike's involuntary visit in 1807 revealed the possibility of profitable relations between Santa Fé and the Missouri River settlements, but the strict Spanish law thwarted all efforts to open trade until the revolt of Mexico against Spain inaugurated a more liberal régime. In 1821 came the first successful expedition, and thereafter the "commerce of the prairies" gradually attained considerable magnitude. The outbound wagons carried cotton and woolen cloth and garments, hardware, and other manufactures, and brought back hides, mules, and silver coin or bullion.

Beyond the Rockies, which formed the boundary of the Louisiana Purchase, the United States was one of four powers which contested the possession of the basin of the Columbia River, known as the "Oregon country." Spain claimed it by right of priority of exploration of the Pacific coast; Russia by virtue of the activities of her traders who operated southward from Alaska as far as Bodega Bay, just above San Francisco. English traders had also been active in the last two decades of the eighteenth century, not only on the coast north and south of Vancouver Sound, but inland. The enterprise of the Canadian fur companies covered western Canada from the Arctic Ocean to the Pacific.

To the valley of the Columbia itself the claims of the United States seemed to its government paramount. The mouth of the river was first entered by Captain Gray, the first exploration of a considerable part of its course was made by Lewis and Clark, and its trade was first opened by Americans. In 1810 John Jacob Astor organized the Pacific Fur Company for operations on the northwest coast. The post of Astoria was established for this purpose near the mouth of the Columbia. But the War of 1812 was at hand, and the men at Astoria sold out to the British Northwest Company, which was also now ready to exploit the Oregon country, rather than run the risk of capture by a hostile warship.

After the Peace of Ghent the fate of Oregon was involved in the interpretation of the clause of the treaty which required the mutual restoration of occupied territory. Astoria could not be reclaimed under this provision, because it had been sold, not captured. However, the respective rights of England and the United States to the region as a whole were left as before the war, and in 1818 a settlement was postponed by a treaty in which it was agreed that for ten years the citizens of both countries should enjoy equal rights of trade and occupation.

The "joint occupation" agreement, renewed in 1828, worked in the long run to the advantage of the United States. The trade of the Northwest Company (absorbed in 1821 by the Hudson's Bay Company) declined with the passing years. On the other hand the thirties saw the beginning of a migration of permanent settlers from the United States which by the forties gave the Americans the major interest in the country. Thus the way was prepared for a final adjustment with England in 1846.

By the treaty of 1818 the boundary between the United States and Canada from the Lake of the Woods to the Rocky Mountains was fixed along the forty-ninth parallel. West of the mountains the line remained undetermined under the joint occupation agreement, but both England and the United States were alarmed when in 1821 a Russian ukase forbade all foreigners to trade on the Pacific coast north of the fifty-first parallel. In 1824 and 1825, however, by separate treaties with England and the United States, Russia agreed to claim no territory south of 54° 40′. In 1819 Spain had yielded to the United States her interest in everything above latitude 42°. Thus after 1824 the joint occupiers of Oregon were the remaining rivals for the region between 42° and 54° 40′, with the rights of the United States strengthened by the acquisition of Spain's claims.

THE ACQUISITION OF FLORIDA

The same treaty which dealt with the Spanish claim to Oregon transferred Florida to the United States. The situa-

tion along the Spanish border was not much improved by
the Peace of Ghent.   Amelia Island, at the mouth of the St.
Mary's, was a nest of smugglers and freebooters; runaway
slaves escaped to the Seminoles; British adventurers told the
Creeks that the lands ceded by them in 1814 were restored

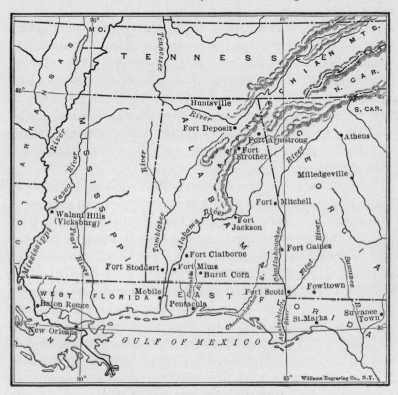

THE GULF REGION, 1812–1818

by the treaty of peace;[1] raids against the settlements in
Georgia and Alabama brought on border warfare.

[1] The interpretation of the treaty accepted by both governments was that
the United States was to make peace at once with the tribes still at war, and
that these should not be deprived of lands as punishment for their share in
the war.   It had no bearing upon the terms of earlier treaties with the Indians.

Spain's impotence threatened a chronic state of confusion and uncertainty. Late in 1817 the United States government decided to take matters into its own hands. Amelia Island was occupied by troops, and Jackson, as major-general of the southern department, was dispatched to the Florida border with the Georgia and Tennessee militia. His instructions from the Secretary of War permitted him to "adopt the necessary measures to terminate" the conflict, and authorized him to pursue the Indians across the borderline into Florida.

Jackson, moved by his old desire to conquer Florida, sent a letter to President Monroe, saying: "Let it be signified to me through any channel (say Mr. J. Rhea) [1] that the possession of the Floridas would be desirable to the United States and in sixty days it will be accomplished." He afterwards asserted that he received the President's approval of his plan. Monroe on his part denied that he made any reply, being ill at the time. Supposing that he had the President's sanction, Jackson crossed the line, seized the Spanish posts, deprived the governor of his office, and even court-martialed and executed two British subjects whom he believed to be guilty of stirring up the Indians.

This vigorous conduct made Jackson more than ever a hero, especially with the people of the West. But it stirred the wrath of England and Spain and created a delicate situation for the administration to deal with. For several days the cabinet deliberated on the course to be pursued. They agreed that Jackson had exceeded the discretion allowed him. Calhoun, Secretary of War, held that he should be punished for insubordination. In the Secretary of State, however, he found a defender. Even the extreme measure of seizing the posts, Adams held, was the logical consequence of such a punitive expedition as Spain's neglect of duty had

---

[1] One of the congressmen from Tennessee. Monroe's dilatoriness in neglecting to reply to Jackson's letter was in harmony with the negligent conduct which allowed Mathews to violate the proprieties in East Florida in 1811.

necessitated. She had drawn the consequences upon herself.

Upon Adams fell the task of satisfying the complaints of the foreign governments. To England he represented that the traders whom Jackson had put to death had by their bad conduct forfeited their right to the protection of their government. This view the British at length accepted. Spain was not so easily appeased. Her minister angrily declared that negotiations on all other matters would await the disavowal and punishment of Jackson and the restoration of the posts. To his surprise, Adams, instead of adopting a conciliatory tone, in reply declared that the President would not punish Jackson, although he had acted without authority, because the Spanish commandant had made himself "a partner and accomplice of the hostile Indians." The posts would be restored whenever a sufficient garrison was sent to control the Indians.

This was the crux of the whole matter. In a dispatch to the minister of the United States at Madrid, the Secretary of State reviewed the conduct of Spanish officials in Florida, detailed the long series of abuses which they had condoned, and ended with an ultimatum: "The United States can as little compound with impotence as perfidy, and Spain must immediately make her election, either to place a force in Florida, adequate at once to the protection of her territory and to the fulfillment of her engagements or cede to the United States a province of which she retains nothing but the nominal possession, but which is in fact a derelict, open to the occupancy of every enemy, civilized or savage, of the United States, and serving no other earthly purpose than as a post of annoyance to them."

Of the two alternatives the maintenance of order was quite beyond the resources of the Spanish government. Of necessity cession was chosen, and negotiations were begun with this in view. In February, 1819, a treaty was signed which made final disposition of all phases of the vexatious question of the two Floridas. As compensation for the cession, the United States agreed to cancel all claims of itself or citizens against Spain for damages or injuries up to the date of the treaty, assuming the payment of private claims to an amount not to exceed five million dollars.

Besides the Florida question, the treaty of 1819 settled the the boundary between the Louisiana Purchase and the territory of Spain in the Southwest. Under the French treaty of 1803 the United States had a good claim to Texas, but having insisted upon its title to West Florida it now seemed best to concede the Spanish right to the region west of the Sabine River. Up that river the line agreed upon ran to the thirty-second parallel; thence north to the Red River, which it followed to the hundredth meridian; thence north to the Arkansas River and along its right bank to its source; thence due north to the forty-second parallel, and along that line to the Pacific.[1]

Although signed in 1819, the Spanish treaty was not ratified by the Cortes until October, 1820, and not until July, 1821, was Florida formally transferred to the new owner. It was thereupon organized as a territory with Andrew Jackson as governor.

THE MONROE DOCTRINE

By the treaty of 1819 the United States tightened its hold upon the shores of the Pacific and reached out to the waters of the Gulf of Mexico. It is rather as a phase of its expanding interests in the western hemisphere than as a matter of Euro-

---

[1] This boundary provision, in connection with the French treaty of 1803, has sometimes been construed to mean that the Oregon country was a part of the Louisiana Purchase. This is an error. The Rocky Mountains were the western limit of Louisiana, and the treaty of 1819 gave us Spain's claim to a region above 42° which had never been a part of either French or Spanish Louisiana.

pean relations that the government now formulated that
unique statement of policy known as the "Monroe Doctrine."
There were three elements in this policy, all of which,
separately, were already well-recognized American principles.
Washington had contributed the germ of the principle of
isolation in his Farewell Address; Jefferson had emphasized
the same idea when he advised against "entangling alliances";
Madison, even in his war message of 1812, had carefully disavowed all entanglement "in the contests or views of other
Powers." [1]

Jefferson had brought the second element, the doctrine
of the paramount interest of the United States in the fate
of neighboring territory, to the fore, when he protested
against the transfer of Louisiana by Spain to any other power
than the United States; in 1808 he foreshadowed the extension of this solicitude to more remote regions by writing to
Gallatin that the United States desired Cuba, and Spanish
America generally, to remain in "its present condition of
dependence upon Spain"; in 1811 Madison applied the doctrine of paramount interest specifically to East Florida. Moreover, it underlay the demand which Adams made for the
proper government or the cession of Florida, and nerved
him in the negotiations with Russia relating to the northwest
coast.

The third element arose in large part from the sympathy
which the people of the United States felt for the inhabitants
of the Spanish-American colonies in their struggle for independence. It was the principle of self-determination.

Ever since the English colonies had gained their freedom
the hope of a like liberty had stirred the breasts of the peoples
of Latin America. For more than twenty-five years following
the American Revolution, Francisco de Miranda, a Vene-

[1] *Cf.* the habitual reference to the enemies of Germany in the World War
as our "associates," not "allies."

zuelan patriot, sought with remarkable persistence to arouse the interest of one European court after another in the freeing of the Spanish colonies. Captured at last, he died in a Spanish prison in 1816, but not before the fires of revolution which he had kindled had burst into flame.

Rising against the Napoleonic domination about 1810, the Spanish-Americans resumed their allegiance upon the restoration of the Bourbon dynasty by the Congress of Vienna, only to rise again when reforms were refused. King Ferdinand attempted to coerce his rebellious subjects into submission, but under the leadership of José de San Martin and Simon Bolivar, of Argentina and Venezuela, the South American states won by 1822 an independence which the proud Dons refused to recognize. The Spanish Empire, like that of ancient Rome, declined and fell. Revolution spread to Central America and Mexico, leaving only Cuba and Porto Rico in the West Indies as sad reminders of the departed glory of Castile.

To the people of the United States it seemed that their Latin neighbors were treading in their footsteps, and enthusiasm ran high for their cause. In Congress Clay led a demand for the immediate recognition of the revolutionary republics. Again and again the chamber resounded with his eloquent appeals on behalf of "eighteen millions of people struggling to burst their chains," but the administration could not be hurried into premature action. President Monroe showed his sympathy with the revolutionists by sending agents to investigate conditions, but he would not recommend recognition until he had satisfied himself that they were able to maintain their independent status. Besides, the Florida question was pending, and there was danger that precipitate acknowledgment of Spain's colonies as independent states would interfere with the success of the negotiations. In March, 1822, the President at last announced his readiness to send ministers to the new states as soon as appropriations were made for their maintenance. Thus he proclaimed that the time for recognition had come.

In the freedom of the Latin-American countries Clay saw, the possibility of a New-World association of republics, united by ties of kindred institutions and of commerce. Such an association built upon liberty would stand in sharp contrast with the despotisms of the Old World. "We look too much abroad," he said. "Let us break these commercial and political fetters; let us no longer watch the nod of any European politician; let us become real and true Americans, and place ourselves at the head of the American system."

This enticing prospect of a group of free states was threatened by the policy of the European powers. Under the lead of the Czar, the rulers of Russia, Prussia, and Austria formed an association, upon the fall of Napoleon, sometimes called the "Holy Alliance," for mutual aid in the spirit of Christian brethren. After the restoration of the Bourbon dynasty in France that country was also admitted.

The real purpose of these powers, under this fair name, was to guard the "legitimate" rulers of Europe against revolution. To invert a famous modern watchword, the intention was "to make the world safe for autocracy." Adopting the practice of intervening in countries where popular movements threatened the thrones of monarchs, they hoped to prevent the spread of revolution into their own dominions. This policy was the very antithesis of the American principle of self-determination. In carrying it out, at one Congress of the allies Austria was commissioned to put down with arms democratic movements in the Italian states of Naples and Piedmont, while at another France was allowed to send troops into Spain on a like errand. Finally, at the Congress of Verona in 1822 the French representative sought to have the Spanish-American situation discussed.

Action was postponed, and it is doubtful whether intervention would ever have been seriously advocated. But rumors that another congress might be summoned to consider the colonial problem set in motion efforts to prevent the possibility of intervention. England had acted with the other powers in the after-war period, because of her interest in the steps taken for composing the affairs of Europe, but she consistently discountenanced intervention as a violation of the rights of the invaded states.[1] The suggestion of interference with the *status quo* in America was objectionable to her both on this ground and for economic reasons. In proportion as Spanish domination in the western hemisphere declined British trade increased; and the independence of the colonies was much more favorable to her commerce than the colonial status could possibly be.

It seemed quite probable also that any power which incurred the burden of intervention on behalf of Spanish authority would be compensated by the grant of territory in the New World. England feared that France, if commissioned to intervene, would seek Cuba as her reward. She was almost as fearful of the growing interest of the United States in the island. In the summer of 1823, therefore, Canning, the Foreign Secretary, proposed a joint declaration by England and the United States against any project of intervention or territorial acquisition in Spanish America by any European power. To add weight to the declaration Canning proposed that both parties should disavow all designs on their own part of acquiring any portion of the possessions of Spain.

This proposition, several times urged by Canning, the American minister in London referred to the President. He consulted Jefferson and Madison, and the three great Vir-

---

[1] Strictly speaking, a distinction is to be made between the Holy Alliance and the Quadruple Alliance. Of the latter, formed for the purpose of general readjustment of Europe, England was a member.

ginians concurred in the judgment that the moment had
come to depart from the traditional policy of isolation and
form an entente with Great Britain. Said Jefferson, "Our
endeavor should surely be, to make our hemisphere that of
freedom. One nation, most of all, could disturb us in this
pursuit; she now offers to lead, aid, and accompany us in it."
At this juncture it was Adams, the Secretary of State, who held
fast to isolation, and insisted that the United States should
give no pledges concerning its own future policy towards
Spanish America. But he favored an "earnest remonstrance
against the interference of European powers by force with
South America." With the doctrine of isolation he thus
joined those of paramount interest and self-determination
(or non-intervention). The advice of the masterful Secretary
triumphed over that of the ex-presidents, and shaped the
famous message which Monroe sent to Congress in December,
1823.

With this background it is possible to interpret the message. Russia had not yet consented to limit her claims on the
Pacific coast (see page 476). Referring to the negotiations
then in progress with her, the message declared that "the
American continents, by the free and independent condition
which they have assumed and maintain, are henceforth not
to be considered as subjects for future colonization by any
European powers." This declaration against further colonization, a phase of the doctrine of paramount interest, has since
been construed to forbid the acquisition of territory in America by any foreign power even by purchase with the free
consent of the seller.

The intervention of the Holy Alliance in the Spanish
peninsula gave the opportunity for the message to reiterate
the principle of isolation: "In the wars of the European
powers, in matters relating to themselves, we have never
taken any part, nor does it comport with our policy so to do.

It is only when our rights are invaded, or seriously menaced, that we resent injuries, or make preparations for our defence."

Then comes a passage in which the doctrines of paramount interest and non-intervention are closely interwoven. "With the movements in this hemisphere, we are, of necessity, more immediately connected, and by causes which must be obvious to all enlightened and impartial observers. The political system of the allied powers is essentially different, in this respect, from that of America. This difference proceeds from that which exists in their respective governments. And to the defence of our own, which has been achieved by the loss of so much blood and treasure, and matured by the wisdom of their most enlightened citizens, and under which we have enjoyed unexampled felicity, this whole nation is devoted. We owe it, therefore, to candor, and to the amicable relations existing between the United States and those powers, to declare, that we should consider any attempt on their part to extend their system to any portion of this hemisphere, as dangerous to our peace and safety. With the existing colonies or dependencies of any European power, we have not interfered, and shall not interfere. But with the governments who have declared their independence, and maintained it, and whose independence we have, on great consideration, and on just principles, acknowledged, we could not view any interposition for the purpose of oppressing them, or controlling, in any other manner, their destiny, by any European power, in any other light than as the manifestation of an unfriendly disposition towards the United States."

The Monroe Doctrine is not a doctrine of indifference to Europe. On the contrary, the message of 1823 expressly affirmed that "of events in that quarter of the globe, with which we have so much intercourse, and from which we derive our origin, we have always been anxious and interested spectators." The policy of the Holy Allies in Spain and Italy was an especial cause of anxiety to the United States, which nevertheless adhered to its own policy of isolation, "adopted at an early stage of the wars which have so long agitated" Europe. The autocratic system of the Old World, maintained through forcible prevention of the exercise of the right of self-determination by weak peoples, was, however, not to be allowed to extend to the western hemisphere. Left to themselves the new republics would maintain their independence and establish popular forms of government. Through the preservation of the right of self-determination the New World, at least, should be made safe for democracy.

Canning afterwards claimed credit for Monroe's stand, and boasted, "I called the New World into existence to redress the balance of the Old." But Canning claimed too much. Our analysis of the antecedents of the message shows how deep-rooted its elements were. Through the pen of Monroe the international situation in 1822–1823 combined and welded them into the form in which they were given to the world.

The immediate effect of Monroe's message on the European powers seems to have been slight. The danger of intervention, if there ever had been any, had already passed. England's manifest opposition would have been a factor of great if not decisive importance in preventing any undertaking of the sort. These facts, of course, do not lessen the importance of the Monroe Doctrine in later times.

THE PANAMA CONGRESS

Two years later Adams as President had further opportunity to define the policy of the United States with reference to Latin America, in a way which indicated that at the time it was not eager for the rôle of protector of weaker states. Spain had not recognized the independence of the revolted repub-

lics.   Under the lead of Bolivar these planned a congress to
meet at Panama with the purpose, as was supposed, of organizing a sort of League of American Nations.   Such a league
could offer united resistance to Spain's attempts at reconquest,
or to efforts of other powers at intervention or colonization.
Moreover it would make possible the conquest of the remaining Spanish possessions, Cuba and Porto Rico, the freeing of
the slaves, and the independence of the islands or their annexation to Mexico or Colombia.

Clay, now Secretary of State, was disposed to accept the invitation to participate in the congress.   He saw in it the possibility of promoting his visionary plan of an American system
under the leadership of the United States.   President Adams
was less enthusiastic.   He did not welcome the idea of a strong
union of the other states of the western hemisphere, which
might become a formidable counterweight to the influence of
his own country, and the possibility of annexing Cuba to any
of the Latin states was only less repugnant to him than the
idea of its transfer to a European power.   He tried to dissuade
Colombia and Mexico from attacking Cuba and Porto Rico,
and through the European powers he and his Secretary of
State endeavored to induce Spain to avert the danger by recognizing the independence of her lost colonies.

Nevertheless he was willing to send delegates to Panama,
under instructions which would safeguard our neutrality and
independence of action.   He saw no objection to an agreement that each American nation should "guard by its own
means against the establishment of any future European
colony within its borders."

The President's enemies in Congress professed to see the
danger of a surrender of sovereignty or at least of an entangling alliance in participation at Panama, and southerners
took alarm at the possibility of a discussion of slavery (which
they regarded as a purely domestic concern) in an interna-

tional gathering. The Senate at last approved the mission, but one delegate died while on the way to the isthmus and the congress adjourned before the other arrived. Disagreements among the Latin states themselves prevented further sessions.

SELECT BIBLIOGRAPHY

The Westward Movement. Babcock's story of the migration of population is continued by Turner, *Rise of the New West.* McMaster supplies many episodes and illustrative incidents, while Turner gives a masterful interpretation of the significance of the movement. The essays in his *Frontier in American History* are even more brilliant as interpretations. Paxson, *History of the American Frontier,* is especially good for these years. Pertinent here is Schafer, *The Social History of American Agriculture.* As an illustration of the effects of the westward movement of the plantation, see Abernethy, *From Frontier to Plantation.*

The importance of mountain, forest, stream, and other physiographic features as forces in American development is discussed by Semple, *American History and Its Geographic Conditions,* and Brigham, *Geographic Influences in American History.* See also Schlesinger, *New Viewpoints,* Chap. II. The importance of the Ohio River as a way to the West is revealed in Ambler, *History of Transportation in the Ohio Valley.*

The Far West. See references for Chap. XVI. Very useful are Coman, *Economic Beginnings of the Far West,* Paxson, *The Last American Frontier,* and *History of the Frontier.* See also Goodwin, *Trans-Mississippi West, 1803–1853.* More recent are two books by W. J. Ghent, *The Early Far West . . . 1540–1850,* and *The Road to Oregon.* The classic history of the fur trade in the United States is the work by Chittenden, *The American Fur Trade of the Far West;* the history of the Hudson's Bay Company is the theme of MacKay, *The Honourable Company;* the life of its manager in the Oregon country, Dr. McLoughlin, is told in Montgomery, *The White-Headed Eagle,* and Johnson, *John McLoughlin;* Astor's activities are recounted in Porter, *John Jacob Astor.* Skinner, in *Beaver, Kings and Cabins,* essays a history of the fur trade of four centuries in one small volume. See also Laut, *Pioneers of the Pacific Coast.*

The Acquisition of Florida. The standard monograph is Fuller, *The Purchase of Florida.* For the larger aspects of Spanish relations, see Chadwick, *Relations of the United States and Spain,* I.

The Monroe Doctrine. A good account of the revolutions in the Spanish-American states is Paxson, *Independence of the South American Republics.* See also Rydjord, *Foreign Interest in the Independence of New Spain.*

There is a considerable literature on the Monroe Doctrine, most of it dealing with interpretation and later applications. Reddaway, *The Monroe Doctrine,* is the best monograph on its origins. Turner's discussion in *Rise of the New West,* is excellent. Perkins, *The Monroe Doctrine,* convincingly appraises the effect of the President's message upon the European powers. A different angle is taken by Tatum, *The United States and Europe, 1815–1823;* he holds that Monroe's message was directed chiefly against England. Perkins presents the story of the later evolution of the doctrine in *The Monroe Doctrine, 1826–1867.* See also Griffin, *The United States and the Disruption of the Spanish Empire.*

Chapter XXI

SLAVERY AND THE MISSOURI COMPROMISE

SECTIONAL RIVALRY IN THE WEST

BY MIGRATING to the West the democratic frontiersmen of the back country of the old states escaped from the domination of the aristocratic class. According to the conception of the eighteenth century, only such white men might vote as owned real estate, or possessed some other substantial property interest in the orderly progress of society (see page 232). A larger amount of property was required for holding office than merely for voting. In some states, in addition, certain religious requirements for officeholding were imposed. The result was that in the early years of independence the electorate constituted much less than half of the adult white male population.

But as new states were settled west of the mountains, by men who had formed the population of the interior of the coast states, their philosophy of government was put into actual practice. As a man of those times asserted, "our community is an association of persons—of human beings—not a partnership founded on property." By 1821 ten new states had been added to the original thirteen, eight from the western country and two from the northern frontier. In all these communities the approximation to economic and social equality was conducive to the belief that political equality was a natural right of all white men. Accordingly all the new states entered the Union with white manhood suffrage, absolute or virtual, and officeholding was put on the same basis as voting.[1] By their constitutions, moreover, judges as well as governors and legislators were made elective.

The democracy of the West and its devotion to the party of Jefferson in the early years of the nineteenth century had aroused the apprehension of the Federalists, as has been shown. They regarded even the New England emigrants to the West as the refuse of society.[2] Nevertheless the New England settlers carried with them many of the ideals and institutions of the states from which they came. The same was true of the southerners, and in a sense the whole process of colonizing the West was an expansion of rival sections. The southerners transplanted the county as the unit of local government, while the men of the Northeast were equally tenacious of the town. As a result Illinois, for example, adopted the county system for that portion of the state where the Piedmont stock predominated, while the New Englanders succeeded in introducing many features of the township system into the region which they occupied later. The educational ideals and methods of the two classes presented another occasion for dispute.

The rival stocks showed persistent sympathy with the sections from which they sprang. Even as late as the Civil War the southern element in the Northwest retained a partiality for the Confederacy, as the Copperhead movement shows. The affinity of the people of the upper Mississippi Valley with the South was enhanced by geographical influences, since the

[1] It is to be noted that New Hampshire, a state possessing many frontier characteristics, had provided in its constitution of 1792 for white manhood suffrage. "Virtual" manhood suffrage refers to the fact that in some states the right was conditioned upon some such requirement as enrollment in the militia, a provision with which everyone could easily comply.

[2] Timothy Flint, one of the contemporary authorities on conditions in the West, wrote about 1826: "The people in the Atlantic states have not yet recovered from the horror inspired by the term 'backwoodsman.' This prejudice is particularly strong in New England, and is more or less felt from Maine to Georgia."

river and its branches formed the natural system of communication, while the mountains were a barrier to intercourse with the East. To some extent artificial factors tended to modify the original bias of the people. The construction of the Erie Canal turned the course of the Mississippi, as it were, and made New York rather than New Orleans the chief *entrepôt* of the interior. Thereafter the East gained relatively in influence over the West. The Ordinance of 1787 had a profound influence upon this rivalry, for by interposing a legal barrier to the expansion of slavery into the Old Northwest it discouraged proslavery men from becoming residents in any great numbers, and thus gave a decisive advantage to the free states in the contest for institutional control.

Because slavery was excluded from this northwest region where the streams of migration met, their rivalry was not too intense to permit adjustments and compromises. If slavery had been tolerated, this would not have been the case. Experience proved that slavery and free labor could not prosper together in the same community. The inevitable effect of the one had been to degrade or expel the other. Many of the southerners in the lower counties of the states north of the Ohio were driven from their former homes by the irreconcilable character of the two systems of labor.

HISTORY OF SLAVERY IN AMERICA

As has been observed in previous chapters, chattel slavery disappeared from western Europe long before the discovery of America. However, when the expansion of Europe brought Spaniards, Frenchmen, and Englishmen into contact with primitive, non-Christian races, the institution was revived in their colonial possessions. There was some Indian servitude in the possessions of all of the powers which colonized America. It was especially common in the Spanish dominions until prohibited by the government, which inconsistently encouraged the importation of Negroes to serve in the stead of the natives.

The rise of the plantation in the English colonies was accompanied by the use of servile labor—red, white, and finally black. But by the time Negro slavery had become the established labor system of the plantation American opinion began to turn against it. Repeatedly during the eighteenth century provincial legislatures tried to restrict the importation of blacks, but the trade was a source of profit to British merchants, and the colonial acts were set aside. When the Revolution brought freedom of action, the Association of 1774 included Negroes among the forbidden imports, and later regulations of the Continental Congress continued the non-importation until the end of the war. Then control over the whole matter passed to the states.

Jefferson's first draft of the Declaration of Independence included in its charges against the British crown that of vetoing the colonial acts relating to the slave trade, but this clause was dropped out of deference to South Carolina and Georgia, where alone at that time were to be found apologists for human bondage. Under the influence of the revolutionary philosophy of the rights of man the belief was quite general that slavery was iniquitous. Patrick Henry affirmed that "every thinking honest man rejects it in speculation," and Jefferson exclaimed, "I tremble for my country when I reflect that God is just; that his justice cannot sleep forever."

There were slaves in every state when independence was declared. Above Mason and Dixon's line they were employed chiefly as coachmen, butlers, cooks, and body-servants in well-to-do families, and their numbers were relatively few. In the years following the Revolution, consequently, the northern states found slavery a simple matter to deal with. In one case, that of Vermont, the state constitution abolished it outright.

In Massachusetts emancipation resulted from judicial interpretation of the constitution of 1780, which declared that all
men are by nature free. This clause, the court ruled, was in-
compatible with the existence of chattel slavery within the
commonwealth. Most of the northern states adopted some
plan of gradual emancipation. Pennsylvania was the first to
take such action (1780), and its law is typical. It left unchanged the status of persons already held in bondage but
gave their children freedom when they attained adult years.

Southern states also discussed plans of emancipation. The
depression of the tobacco, rice, and indigo industries after the
Revolution made the support of the laborers burdensome to
the masters, and fostered the growth of humanitarian sentiments. But the large number of blacks in the southern
states made emancipation a much more difficult undertaking
than in the North. In some regions they outnumbered the
white inhabitants, and it was feared that freeing an ignorant
and undisciplined race would result in an idle, vicious, un-
controllable population. Slavery had at least the merit of
keeping the Negro under management.

Emancipation in the South, therefore, waited upon some
practicable plan of dealing with the free blacks. In 1816 the
American Colonization Society was formed for the purpose of
transporting freedmen to Africa. For a time its program
awakened some enthusiasm, especially in the South, where its
chief support was found. The little republic of Liberia was
the fruit of its activities, but its means proved to be quite insufficient for an undertaking of such magnitude, and its efforts
in sum made no appreciable impression upon the black mass
of American slavery.[1] Then as cotton culture spread and
southern prosperity increased conditions demanded a greater
labor supply and sentiment changed.

[1] In the best days of the Society, the number of Negroes transported did not
equal one twenty-fifth of the natural increase of the race by birth.

From the close of the Revolution slavery was regarded as a question for the states. The fathers of the Constitution have been criticized for not incorporating in the supreme law a provision for gradual emancipation. Such criticism rests on an entire misconception of the task of the Convention. It was believed that the states separately would provide for emancipation; any such antislavery provision would have insured the rejection of the Constitution; above all, the intent of the Convention—to intrust to the Federal Government only matters of general concern—excluded from its sphere the relation of master and slave as naturally as it did that of employer and employé.

Yet the Constitution touched slavery at many points—in restricting the control of Congress over commerce, in fixing the rule of apportionment of taxes and representatives, in defining the obligations which states owed to one another as members of the federation, such as the rendition of fugitives from justice and service, and otherwise. The first Congress was confronted with petitions from antislavery societies, praying it to use its powers to further the cause of freedom. The petitions led to the appointment of a committee of inquiry into the scope of the powers of Congress. The report set forth that that body could not interfere in any way with slavery in the states; that it could not prohibit the importation of slaves prior to 1808 but might lay a duty of ten dollars per head upon such importation and regulate the conditions of ocean transportation in the interests of humanity; and that the slaveholders were entitled to the enactment of a law for the rendition of fugitive slaves escaping into other states.

This report led to some legislation for the mitigation of the horrors of the "middle passage," by way of securing for the miserable blacks reasonable air space and of preventing needless suffering—much like provisions of our own times regulating shipments of live stock in railway cars. Another result was the Fugitive Slave Law of 1793. Any white person who claimed a Negro as his runaway property had merely, by oath, to satisfy a federal or state magistrate of the validity of his claim. The law made the recovery of fugitives easy, but it did not safeguard the rights of free persons of color, whom unprincipled white men were willing to enslave by perjuring themselves.

As the year 1808 approached, Jefferson congratulated Congress that the time was near when it might constitutionally make an end of the African slave trade. Accordingly an act was passed to take effect January 1, 1808. It laid heavy penalties in fines and imprisonment upon slave importers, but found no better disposition for the blacks illegally brought into the country than to turn them over to the state concerned to be sold. An act of 1819, however, intended to promote the work of the American Colonization Society, provided for the return of such Negroes to their African homes. Despite the law, the smuggling in of cargoes of "black ivory" continued more or less actively. In 1820 the trade was made piracy, punishable by death, but it is not recorded that any execution occurred for transgression of the law before 1861.

THE MISSOURI COMPROMISE

The discussions in Congress accompanying the passage of these early bills, while sharp, did not produce any alarming clash of sectional opinion. Northern and southern men agreed that slavery was an evil. Perhaps Jefferson voiced a general sentiment when he likened it to a wolf held by the ears, equally dangerous to hold or to let go.

Down almost to 1820 the rivalry of the North and South for the institutional control of the West did not involve slavery. In general the expansion of sections tended to follow lines of longitude, and the Ordinance of 1787 divided the territory of the Union into two spheres, the northern one open only to free labor. The new states had entered the Union in pairs, as it happened, each new slave state balancing a free state. This equality of the sections was deceptive, however, for it did not hold true in Congress. While in the Senate there was an actual balance, in the House of Representatives the preponderance had long since passed to the North. Beginning in 1790 with an equilibrium in both houses, the North, through more rapid growth, had, by 1820, 105 representatives as compared with 81 from the slave states.

The disparity would have been greater still but for the advantage which the South derived from the three-fifths ratio, under which sixty per cent of its slaves were counted in apportioning representation. By virtue of this clause the southern states enjoyed twenty more votes in the House and in the electoral college than their white population would have given them. The numerical superiority of the North, moreover, had hitherto been partially offset by the division of its strength between two political parties, while the South and West had been united. The opposition of the Federalists to the admission of new states and their grumbling over the three-fifths provision had been only the ineffectual declamation of a minority.

The situation was full of danger for the slave states, in case an issue should arise to unite the people of the free North against them. So long as the South could preserve its equality in the Senate, however, no legislation affecting its interests could be enacted without a concurrent majority of the two houses. The preservation of equality in the Senate was therefore a vital consideration.

This was the general situation when Missouri applied for statehood in 1818. Although beyond the river, in the territory purchased from France in 1803, Louisiana had already been admitted (1812) with slavery, largely because of its southern position and the fact that its inhabitants held slaves at the time of the purchase. In contrast, Missouri lay almost wholly above the latitude of the mouth of the Ohio, in the zone of the free states of the Northwest, as did the major portion of the Purchase, and the decision on its admission was likely to determine the fate of slavery in the rest of the territory acquired from France.

Northern leaders therefore judged that the time had come to make a stand against the spread of an institution attended by so many evils; and when a committee of the House reported a bill for the admission of the new state, James Tallmadge, a member from New York, proposed (February 13, 1819) a restrictive amendment. One clause forbade the further introduction of slavery into the state, and a second provided that "all children of slaves, born within the said state, after the admission . . . thereof . . . shall be free, but may be held to service until the age of twenty-five years."

The Tallmadge amendment aroused the South. Here was a measure which promised both to unite the North and to deprive the slave section of its equality in the Senate. If the amendment prevailed, bounds would be set to the expansion of slavery, and as new states were carved from the territory of Louisiana, the South would be more and more hopelessly outweighed in the political scale. On the other hand the slave states might gain a permanent preponderance through unrestricted expansion.

The vote on the amendment followed sectional lines. On the first clause the House stood 87 to 76. All of the yeas were cast by northern members, but eleven northerners—contemptuously called "doughfaces" by John Randolph—voted with the South. The Senate rejected the amendment and the session ended in a deadlock.

The debate on the Missouri bill startled the aged Jefferson "like a fire bell in the night." It was no moral issue that awoke his fears, but the sectional alignment, which threatened the severance of the Union. "In the gloomiest hour of the Revolutionary War," he declared, "I never had any apprehensions equal to those which I feel from this source."

The whole country was greatly stirred. During the summer recess of Congress a whirlwind of anti-Missouri feeling swept the North. Everywhere mass meetings were held and resolutions passed against the perpetuation of slavery by permitting its spread to new states. Legislatures resolved, pamphlets poured from the press, and newspapers teemed with articles indicative of the public excitement. Doughfaces were burned in effigy, and great mass meetings at Boston, New York, Philadelphia, Trenton, and Baltimore appointed committees of correspondence to distribute literature and organize the people against the admission of a new slave state.

In Congress the contest was renewed in the session of 1819–1820. Tallmadge having retired, John W. Taylor of the same state led the anti-Missouri forces in the House. Maine, hitherto a part of Massachusetts, was with the latter's consent seeking separate statehood. The Senate therefore joined bills for the admission of Maine and Missouri, hoping to compel northern congressmen, especially those from the Maine district, to forego the Tallmadge-Taylor program of restriction.

The situation which developed was critical in the extreme. The dissolution of the Union was openly discussed and to many seemed imminent. But the very danger was an incentive to compromise. At the end of six weeks of acrimonious debate, Senator J. B. Thomas, of Illinois, offered an amendment to the Maine-Missouri bill proposing that Missouri be admitted without restriction, but that in all the remainder of the territory ceded by France, north of 36° and 30′ north latitude, "slavery and involuntary servitude, otherwise than in punishment of crime whereof the party shall have been duly convicted, shall be and is hereby forever prohibited."

In the Senate the vote of the slave states on Thomas' motion stood 14 to 8, that of the free states 20 to 2. The House at first rejected it; but some of the northern Republicans were becoming suspicious that the slavery issue cloaked a design of certain of the leaders of the nearly defunct Federalist party to unite the North in a new party under their leadership. Although at first zealous supporters of the Tallmadge restriction, this suspicion led a few of them to change sides. The change broke the anti-Missouri phalanx, and the Thomas amendment (generally spoken of as the "Missouri Compromise") was then accepted, 134 to 42. On this final ballot the North was almost unanimous in the affirmative, casting only five negative votes. The South was divided, 38 to 37. Virginia cast 18 of her 22 votes in the negative.

Throughout the debate northern speakers contended that the clause in the Constitution reading "New states may be admitted by Congress into the Union," authorized that body to prescribe the terms of admission. The most notable speech upholding this opinion was made by Senator Rufus King, of New York. He had been one of the members of the Federal Convention who had sought to empower Congress to restrict the privileges of the new states. The reason for the exercise of the power now he found in the injustice of extending the three-fifths ratio of representation of new states created out of territory not originally a part of the United States. King's prominence in the Federalist party was one of the main reasons for the Republican suspicions of a new party movement.

Senator William Pinkney, of Maryland, replied to King, basing his argument upon the concept that the Union is composed of equal states. The words of the Constitution, he held, might warrant Congress in rejecting the application of a territory for statehood, but if statehood were granted, the new state must possess all of the powers of the original ones. Consequently Missouri must be as free as any of the older states to determine her domestic institutions.

The balance of power in the nation was the chief political issue in the contest, and this question of the right of a new state to control its domestic institutions was the chief legal one. The extreme states' rights men denied the power of Congress to prohibit slavery even in the territories, since they were the common property of the states both slave and free. This accounts for the considerable southern vote against the compromise.

During the summer of 1820 a convention met at St. Louis and framed a constitution for Missouri. One provision made it the duty of the legislature to pass laws to prevent the immigration of free Negroes. This clause brought on a new debate in Congress. Did the provision for the exclusion of free Negroes abridge the privileges and immunities of citizens (Constitution, Article IV, Section 2)? The outcome of much debate was a signal demonstration of the ability of statesmen to evade difficulties. Although no agreement was reached on the points in dispute, a second compromise was adopted, largely through Clay's efforts, which directed the President to announce by proclamation that Missouri was a state, upon receipt of a promise from the legislature that it would never pass a law abridging the privileges and immunities of citizens of the United States. Meaningless as this pledge was, the legislature complied with the requirement, and on August 10, 1821, the admission of the state was proclaimed.

SELECT BIBLIOGRAPHY

History of Slavery in America. Phillips, *American Negro Slavery*, is the most elaborate work on the subject. There is a brief sketch in the first volume of Rhodes, *History of the United States from the Compromise of 1850*. Hart, *Slavery and Abolition*, contains a brief sketch. Of value is Du Bois, *The Suppression of the African Slave-Trade*. See also Locke, *Anti-Slavery in America, 1619–1808*, and Adams, *Neglected Period of Anti-Slav-*

ery in America, 1808–1831. For the colonization plan, see Fox, "The American Colonization Society, 1817–1840."

The Missouri Compromise. All of the general histories give this topic considerable space. One of the best accounts is that by Gordy, *Political History,* II. Turner's brief chapter in *Rise of the New West* is marked by keen interpretation. On the constitutional aspects see Hockett, *Constitutional History,* II, 148–168.

Chapter XXII

SECTIONALISM AND POLITICAL PARTIES, 1816–1828

THE CONFLICT OF SECTIONAL INTERESTS

THE West was not merely a bone of contention between the older sections; its rapid growth soon made it a third section comparable in population and importance with the groups of states on the Atlantic. By the census of 1790 the population of the country was somewhat less than four millions, and of these only one person in fifteen dwelt west of the mountains. By 1830, however, six out of every fifteen of the inhabitants were west of the Alleghanies, and the population of the new section alone exceeded five millions. Measured by increase in population the West had grown in importance six times as fast as the rest of the country.

The great shift westward caused a radical readjustment of the nation's life. As circumstances connected with the war had impaired the shipping interest and stimulated the growth of manufactures, so now the farming, manufacturing, and planting interests had to adjust themselves to the changing geographical basis.

The West was predominantly agricultural. Cheap land was the lure which drew to it the great majority of its inhabitants. The first-comers had found themselves cut off from the rest of the world by stretches of unpeopled forest and mountain. Their isolation was even greater than that of the back-country folk of the coast states, and the privations and perils of frontier life were intensified. Theirs was the task of building society from its very foundations. Thrown upon their own resources, their first productive efforts were devoted to securing the rudest necessities of existence.

But with astonishing rapidity the clearing about the pioneer's cabin widened, and the huts which clustered here and there upon the river banks grew into towns. The very isolation of the West acted like a duty on imports; the difficulty of intercourse with the remote East was a stimulus and protection to the manufactures which it was compelled to set up for itself. By the beginning of the War of 1812 a few factories were appearing at Pittsburgh, Steubenville, Cincinnati, and Louisville. These led the people to dream of a self-sufficing western world, maintained by exchange between town and country, the farmer supplying the wants of the townsman in the way of food and receiving in return the products of the craftsman's art.

But the local market was not sufficient to absorb the surplus yield of the fields. The growth of manufactures did not keep pace with that of agriculture, and it became the chief problem of the farmer to find an adequate market. The quest for a market broke down the provincialism of the West and brought it into closer relations with other sections and countries. From the beginnings of settlement in the Ohio Valley some of the grain and meat of Kentucky and Tennessee found an outlet down the Mississippi, in spite of Spanish policy, to the West Indies and Europe. Western grain was also converted into whisky for easy carriage to the eastern seaboard. Cattle and hogs, too, were driven in increasing numbers across the mountains as time passed. The expansion of the plantation area in the South enlarged the market for the western farmer.

The difficulties of transportation were a great impediment to all intercourse, and the western states were for a long time too poor to shoulder the burden of improving the streams or building roads. They looked to the Federal Government as

506   GROWTH OF THE AMERICAN PEOPLE

the only agency by which the country could be provided with the roads and canals which were essential to their progress and to the general welfare.

Unfortunately the period of rapid expansion of western agriculture coincided with years of increasing production in Europe. The end of the wars allowed soldiers by thousands to resume their normal occupation as tillers of the soil. The supply of farm produce in the world market increased much more rapidly than the demand for it, and prices fell. European governments took pains to protect their own agriculture. For example, England revived her Corn Laws, which had been relaxed during the war period. These forbade the importation of foreign grain except when the price of the domestic crop reached an abnormal height. Under these conditions American agriculture suffered severely from overproduction and low prices during the years around 1820.

When the western farmers learned the causes of the hard times, they began to believe that a protective tariff would help them, on the theory that if a larger proportion of the people were encouraged to engage in manufacturing and a smaller part in agriculture, the farmer would find a profitable home market in supplying the needs of the manufacturing population. "Agriculture has been pursued to its acme," runs the comment of a western editor. "The number employed in it is disproportionate to that of the mechanical branch—and the true interest of the whole community will be promoted by producing an equilibrium between them."

The growth of the West was a serious matter for the eastern states. While its population rose by leaps and bounds, that of the old states, except those which, like New York and Pennsylvania, had broad unsettled spaces within their limits, came almost to a standstill. New England, which had formerly felt concern about the West for political reasons, now grew anxious on economic grounds. In 1817 Governor Wolcott, of

Connecticut, recommended that the legislature investigate the causes of the "Ohio fever," as by far the most important subject that could engage its attention. Southern legislatures also made investigations, seeking means of counteracting the attractions of the newer regions. Some of them proposed to improve the facilities for marketing the produce of their own inland counties by constructing roads and other means of transportation.

Partly because it would be one way of inducing their people to remain at home, several of the old states amended their constitutions or adopted new ones extending the suffrage to the wage-earners who had hitherto been denied the ballot. Another reason was that a new generation had grown up since the achievement of independence, for whom the old aristocratic tradition had lost much of its meaning. Just as these later Americans discarded the colonial breeches and wigs for the more practical long trousers and short-cropped hair, so they abandoned many political ideas that were sacred to the Fathers of the Republic.

Maryland and South Carolina led in the democratizing movement, enfranchising all adult white male citizens by constitutional changes in 1810. Connecticut took a similar step in the constitution of 1818, which replaced her old colonial charter. It removed all restrictions except the requirement of tax payment or military service. Next Massachusetts discarded all qualifications except a nominal tax (1821). New York followed the liberal example of Maryland and South Carolina (1826). Rhode Island framed a constitution to supercede her charter, but it was rejected by the voters (1824). Virginia extended the franchise somewhat in 1830, but did not adopt full white manhood suffrage until twenty years later.

While these changes were being made many prominent men stubbornly defended the older order. Daniel Webster and Justice Joseph Story united with the venerable John Adams in resisting the reform in Massachusetts. In New York the leading jurist of the state, Chancellor James Kent, insisted that manhood suffrage would put it "into the power of the poor and the profligate to control the affluent," and that "every department of the government" would be "at the disposal of those who are ignorant of the importance and nature of the right they are authorized to assume." In Virginia the opponents of manhood suffrage were led by such distinguished personages as Madison, Monroe, Marshall, and Randolph.

The depression of the commerce and agriculture of the states of the northern seaboard made them more and more dependent for their prosperity upon the new manufacturing industries. These looked hopefully to the West and South for their markets, and desired the extension of the protective system to give them the advantage over foreign competitors in the home market. The hard times following 1819 especially were years when the manufacturers were clamorous for additional protection. The demands of the manufacturer and farmer were kindred in the matter of the tariff, and brought the northeastern states into economic alliance with the Northwest. The Southwest, on the contrary, tended towards the plantation system too strongly to be attracted into this combination.

The interests of the eastern factory owners and the western farmers were not entirely in harmony. The westward movement made labor scarce and wages high, and the abundance of land open to settlement was looked upon as a retarding factor in the growth of manufactures. Men whose capital was invested in factories were therefore tempted to seek legislation to restrict sales of public lands, a desire with which the frontier population was not at all in sympathy.

The desire of the West for improved means of transportation was seconded by the seaboard cities of the middle states. New York, Philadelphia, and Baltimore foresaw a profitable commerce in handling the export business of the interior, and the policy of federal internal improvements received hearty support in the neighborhood of these cities. The Erie Canal enriched New York, which soon outstripped the other coast towns in population, and Pennsylvania was led, in emulation, to construct a competing route across the Alleghanies, consisting partly of canals and partly of roads. Baltimore agitated the completion of the Cumberland Road and projected a Chesapeake and Ohio Canal. But New England was indifferent. No transportation route was likely to bring freight to her ports from beyond the Hudson.

Even Norfolk and southeastern Virginia were interested for a time in a James River Canal project, but most of the Old South had nothing to gain from internal improvements except of a purely local character. The high Appalachians effectually fenced off the coast of the Carolinas from the great central valley of the continent until the era of the railroads dawned. Charleston then discovered her interest in a rail connection with the cities of the Ohio Valley. During the twenties, however, the states of the southern seaboard were the seat of opposition to federal internal improvements, which would mean the expenditure of public funds on works from which they would derive little or no benefit.

The old planting states felt the full force of the competition of the fresh, cheap lands opened up as the area of cotton cultivation expanded across the Gulf plains. The lowering of the cost of producing cotton on the fertile alluvial lands newly opened made the crop unprofitable on the thin soil of many a Carolina plantation, and the owners had no such alternative as the people of the maritime states of the North. The cotton planters devoted their energies more and more to the production of their one crop. All that they produced went to market elsewhere, and all that they consumed came from without in the course of direct or indirect exchange.

Many planters neglected even to raise hay for their animals or grain for their families and slaves, deeming it better economy to supply all of the needs of the plantation from the proceeds of the sale of their staple crop. Their political economy was consequently that of "free trade." Manufactures came most cheaply from England, where most of the cotton was sold. Any interference with this intercourse, such as a duty for the encouragement of domestic manufactures, increased the price of what the planter purchased, whether he bought imported or domestic goods. The steady demand for cotton abroad, moreover, left him little motive for creating a home market, such as the farmer needed.

The interests of North, South, and West, or to put it in economic instead of geographical terms, the interests of the manufacturing, planting, and farming sections, were inharmonious. For this reason the nationalism which was so pronounced just after the War of 1812 did not long survive. The votes against the tariff bill in 1816 foreshadowed a renewed conflict of sections growing out of economic divergences. Within a few years the planting region, especially, showed a marked reaction to localism, and revived the strict interpretation of the Constitution to offset the nationalizing tendencies of the Federal Government.

The history of the United States from 1817 to 1828 is largely a record of the rivalry of the three sections in their attempts to deal with the great domestic questions of the day, such as the tariff and internal improvements. The political weight and aggressiveness of the West in these contests is particularly noteworthy. States carved from what had been wilderness when Washington was inaugurated sent 57 members to the House of Representatives under Jackson. During that interval of forty years the representation of New England increased only from 29 to 38; that of the South Atlantic states from 45 to 60. Only the middle states showed an advance at all comparable with that of the West, with an increase from 29 to 75. We must trace the sectional conflict in the chief questions of the period.

Although the Young Republicans controlled the House of Representatives during Monroe's presidency, they lacked a sufficient majority to pass bills for internal improvements over his veto. But they studied the question. In 1818 at the request of the House Calhoun, then Secretary of War, submitted a report which outlined a system of internal improvements with national defense as the object. No attempt at legislation followed, but Congress and the executive clashed a few years later on a bill for the Cumberland Road.

The road had been completed as far as Wheeling, on the Ohio River. After a period of suspended activity due to financial embarrassment following the panic of 1819, the survey was made for the extension of the road, and in 1822 a bill passed Congress for the collection of tolls to be used in the upkeep of the highway. Since violators of the regulations would have to be dealt with, the President saw in the bill an infringement on the jurisdiction of the states and vetoed it. In Congress it had received the vote of all but two members from western states, and of nearly every member from districts along the route.

In 1824 a General Survey Bill was enacted, authorizing the President to employ the engineering corps of the army in making surveys of routes for any roads and canals which he deemed of national importance. This measure received the vote of all members who favored any of the numerous local projects, and Monroe signed it. Most of the opposition came from New England and the Old South, while the West was a unit in its support.

Republicans of the Old School, the southern seaboard

group, saw in the Survey Bill another evidence of the trend towards nationalism. Randolph denounced it as an abuse of power, and threatened opposition by every means short of actual insurrection. Jefferson was ready in 1825 to have the Virginia legislature declare federal legislation regarding internal improvements null and void, following the example of Virginia and Kentucky in 1798. But it was the tariff which, next to the Missouri question, caused the chief sectional conflict of the period.

The Tariff of 1816 had produced sufficient revenue for a year or two, and had made possible the repeal of internal taxes. The panic of 1819, however, called forth a demand for a new tariff with higher rates, both because treasury receipts were falling off and because the factories felt the pinch of the hard times. Friends of protection organized to procure the desired legislation, and a new bill passed the House in 1820. In the Senate it was defeated by a single vote.

Although the chairman of the committee which reported this bill tried hard to meet the criticism of those who contended that protection favored particular interests at the expense of the nation as a whole and the South in particular, it is evident from the vote that the spirit of sectionalism had already replaced the nationalism of 1816. The alignment of the agricultural West and the manufacturing areas of the East in support of the measure was almost perfect; while the union of the maritime interest with the cotton, tobacco, and cane growers in opposition was no less so.

The battle was now joined in earnest, and year after year the protectionists returned to the attack, under the prod of continued hard times. In 1824 they succeeded in carrying through a new act, with increased duties. The debate on this bill is noteworthy because of speeches by Webster, Clay, and Robert Y. Hayne. The first, whose constituency was still

maritime in interest, argued cogently against legislative interference with the natural course of trade. Clay on his part
elaborated the home-market theory, and advocated protection
as a means of creating a genuine "American system."

"We have shaped our industry, our navigation, and our
commerce, in reference to an extraordinary war in Europe,
and to foreign markets which no longer exist," said he. "The
consequence of the termination of the war of Europe has been
the resumption of European commerce, European navigation,
and the extension of European agriculture and European industry in all its branches. Europe, therefore, has no longer
occasion, to anything like the same extent as that she had during her wars, for American commerce, American navigation,
the produce of American industry."

Explaining that the surplus produce of the United States
was increasing much more rapidly than the consuming power
of Europe, even if the foreign states received American food
products, he argued that "a genuine American policy" would
create a home market for the products of our agriculture "in
all its varieties, of planting, farming, and grazing." The establishment of manufactures would create a home market for
the planter and farmer, and a source of supply for their necessaries. "But this home market . . . can only be created and
cherished by the protection of our own legislation against the
inevitable prostration of our industry which must ensue
from the action of foreign policy and legislation."

Clay professed to speak for all sections. "The inquiry
should be in reference to the great interests of every section of
the Union. . . . If they come into absolute collision . . . a
reconciliation, if possible, should be attempted, by mutual
concession, so as to avoid a sacrifice of the prosperity of either. . . ." But Clay's logic was the logic of the farm and
factory, not the plantation. His scheme of sectional reci-

procity was rejected by the planter. Senator Hayne, of South Carolina, spoke for the last, protesting against a system which for the South meant only burdens.

In this debate the southern speakers began to invoke the Constitution against the tariff, urging that import duties were permissible only as a means of regulating commerce or raising revenue and not for the purpose of protection. In general they spoke with moderation, but Randolph, with his usual eccentricity, threw off all restraint. "A fig for the Constitution!" he cried. "When the scorpion's sting is probing to the quick, shall we stop to chop logic?" With a sarcastic fling at the West, he exclaimed: "Men in hunting-shirts, with deer-skin leggings and moccasins on their feet, want protection for manufactures!"

The Tariff of 1824 proved unsatisfactory to the woolen manufacturers, who found that the duty on English woolens was evaded by deliberate undervaluation of the goods, to deceive customs officials. To prevent this, a new bill was introduced in Congress in 1827, known as the "Woolens Bill," which proposed to apply the minimum principle to woolen as well as cotton goods. Passing the House, it was defeated in the Senate by the casting vote of the Vice-President, Calhoun.

This rebuff led the friends of protection to call a convention at Harrisburg, in July, 1827, for the purpose of agreeing upon the features of a new bill to be presented at the next session of Congress. The Tariff of 1828, however, did not follow the Harrisburg plan. Its provisions were shaped for political ends, as will be seen later, and as an economic measure it was such a monstrosity that it was dubbed the "Tariff of Abominations."

In the antitariff agitation South Carolina eclipsed Virginia. The heroic age of the Old Dominion ended with the generation of Washington, Jefferson, Madison, and Monroe, and hegemony in the South passed to the cotton belt. Tobacco yielded the scepter to cotton as king of the staples, and the premiership was seized by the ministers of the new monarch. Dr. Cooper, of sedition trial fame, now president of South Carolina College, declared that the time had come to calculate the value of the Union. Agitation spread throughout the state and the temper of the discussions became alarming to Union men.

The development of the issues of the years 1815 to 1828 played havoc with the reputation for consistency of many a public man. Jefferson changed ground twice, once when he indorsed the tariff, and again when he reverted to states' rights. Webster supported the Tariff of 1828 and explained his new stand by saying that the interests of his constituents had changed since 1824. No statesman of the time showed a greater reversal than Calhoun. His last public utterances before entering Monroe's cabinet were strongly nationalistic. In 1816 and 1817 his advocacy of protection and internal improvements was quite on a par with Clay's speech on the Tariff of 1824. As Secretary of War his report on internal improvements fixed his place in the public mind as a foremost champion of such measures. Then after a long interval during which he was silent his vote against the Woolens Bill revealed him as the enemy of protection and the champion of sectional interests.

This somersault was due primarily to disappointment at the way in which protectionism had grown. Calhoun's original idea had been that protection for a few years would establish manufactures so firmly that they would be able to hold their own against foreign competition without further aid. But having tasted government bounty the manufacturing interest seemed to him to have become insatiable, and, aided by the votes of the representatives of agriculture, to have determined to lay the planters under permanent tribute. His chief concern, therefore, became the defense of the rights of the minority section.

Loving the Union and feeling alarm at the temper of his own state, he set himself, about the time of the passage of the Tariff of 1828, to formulate a plan by which a single state might constitutionally prevent an abuse of power by the Federal Government. The outcome was the South Carolina Exposition of 1828. It was presented to the state legislature, late in the year, in the form of a committee report.

Like Jefferson, Calhoun built the doctrine which the Exposition advanced upon the compact theory of the Constitution. Indeed, he claimed to be reasserting the doctrines of 1798. But he was much more explicit than the authors of the Virginia and Kentucky Resolutions. Rejecting completely the generally-held theory of divided sovereignty, he maintained that sovereignty rests solely in the state as a political community. The several sovereignties had united for certain purposes by entering into the constitutional compact, but the government set up under the Constitution was merely the agent of the states, in executing the powers intrusted to it for the common welfare. It was the right of each state to judge whether acts of the agent encroached upon its reserved powers. This right, Calhoun held, appertained not to the legislature of the state, but to a delegate convention, especially chosen for the purpose. Such conventions had been the organs employed by the states in ratifying the Constitution, and were the most proper channels through which the sovereign might express its will.

If such a convention adjudged an act of Congress to be unwarranted by the Constitution, that act became null and void within the nullifying state. Such nullification, however, was not the final determinant of the validity of the act, for under the constitutional compact there existed a higher power, namely, the judgment of three fourths of the sovereignties. Nullification by a single state, in short, merely suspended the congressional act until the power which could amend the Constitution passed upon the particular issue. If the judgment of the state convention were upheld by this final authority, Congress was thenceforth inhibited from employing the power in question. If, on the contrary, the amending power upheld the act of Congress, the nullifying state was bound to acquiesce—unless, indeed, it preferred to withdraw from the Union, a right which Calhoun believed to be inherent in sovereignty.

Calhoun substantially restated Jefferson's views of thirty years before, making clear that a *single state* might nullify (a point which Jefferson had left uncertain), and adding the doctrines that nullification was properly to be accomplished by a *convention,* and that the final arbiter was the *amending power*.

The Exposition gave much space to the statement of southern grievances, and the nullification theory was appended to serve as a warning to the northern majority, to show that each state held in its hand a weapon with which to defend itself against oppression. Calhoun and his friends did not think the time had come to use the weapon. When the committee's report came before the legislature, the election of Jackson, himself a cotton planter, was already assured, and in this fact Calhoun's friends saw the prospect of a change of policy with regard to the tariff. Therefore, without even adopting the Exposition, they contented themselves with publishing it.

THE RESHAPING OF PARTY LINES

The dozen years following the War of 1812 witnessed the dissolution of the old Federalist and Republican parties and the emergence of the National Republican and Democratic parties. The original divisions had grown out of social and economic problems which found their geographical basis in the strip of territory between the Atlantic and the Alleghanies. Their disintegration and the rise of the new political groupings were the natural consequences of the growth of the West, and the divergence of sections over the new problems.

The Federalist organization was the first to dissolve. The acceptance by the Republicans of so much of its nationalism —Josiah Quincy said that they "out-Federalized Federalism" —left it nothing to stand for which had distinctive value. It was undermined by the growth of the West and discredited by its aristocratic temper and opposition to the war. The campaign of 1816 was its death struggle. "If we cannot make any impression upon the presidential election, this time, I see no hope for the future," wrote one of the leaders to Rufus King. King himself thought the party should not continue a hopeless contest, and conceded that "it has probably become the real interest and policy of the country, that the Democracy should pursue its own natural course." The only possible way for the Federalists to be of use, he thought, was as a makeweight in support of the "least wicked section of the Republicans."

In somewhat this way the Federalists were factors in local and congressional politics for another decade or more—the "Indian summer of Federalism"—but they kept up no general organization. Even in 1816 there was no formal nomination of a party candidate. Their thirty-four electors cast their ballots for King. Monroe, the Republican candidate, received 183 votes.

Monroe had been indorsed by the Republican caucus, thanks to the support of Madison, triumphing over William H. Crawford. Although not a man of the caliber of Washington, Jefferson, or Madison, he had learned much by experience. The impulsiveness of his youth had given way to a

poise which passed with admirers for wisdom, and caused him
to be likened to Washington himself. He proved capable of
giving the country a safe and sane, if not brilliant, administration, thanks to a judicious selection of official advisers. To
John Quincy Adams he intrusted the State Department, to
Crawford the Treasury, which had been in his charge for a
time under Madison, and to Calhoun the portfolio of war.
Crawford was ranked as an able man by contemporaries,
but appears to the historian to have played the rôle of politician rather than statesman. Clay, somewhat disappointed at
not receiving the State Department, refused any other cabinet
office, and continuing in Congress was soon at odds with the
administration, especially on the questions of Latin-American
relations and internal improvements.

The party antagonisms of other years faded into complete
oblivion with Monroe's election. During a tour which he
made soon after his inauguration, he was received even in the
old strongholds of Federalism with enthusiasm and assurances
of the fraternal affection with which New Englanders regarded their countrymen. The *Boston Centinel,* which had
appeared in mourning upon Jefferson's elevation to the presidency and had hailed the Hartford Convention as the beginning of a new federal edifice, now commented on the President's visit under the headline "The Era of Good Feelings,"
a phrase by which Monroe's eight years of office have come to
be designated. The new temper of New England was one
manifestation of the widespread sentiment of nationalism.
At the end of four years no opposition appeared to Monroe's
reëlection; even John Adams served as a Republican elector
in Massachusetts; and the President would have shared with
Washington the honor of a unanimous vote but for the dislike
of one elector.[1]

[1] William Plumer, of New Hampshire, who cast his vote for John Quincy
Adams.

This appearance of calm in 1820 was an illusion. The Republican party was undergoing dissolution as certainly as the Federalist but more slowly. The forces of disintegration were not of the obvious kind, although during Monroe's second term a number of factions sprang up favoring the pretensions of the several candidates for the succession. It was the conflict of sectional interests which worked quietly and almost unseen to divide into antagonistic groups men who continued to call themselves by the same party name. The personal rivalries of Monroe's second term must be interpreted with due regard to these more fundamental rivalries of sections.

The Republican party of 1816 really comprised two incipient parties. The Young Republicans, with their strength in the West, formed the national wing and inherited the Federalist conception of the powers and functions of the general government. Although it was more democratic in spirit than Federalism, to it gravitated, for economic reasons, the capitalists of New England and the middle states. Many of them had been Federalists.

The Old School Republicans, zealous for a conservative construction of the Constitution, formed the nucleus of the other party, which reacted towards localism as the sectional conflict developed. This faction of the planters found its strength in the seaboard South, and in the Southwest as the plantation area spread in that direction.

The party was still outwardly intact in the campaign of 1824, but these internal differences foreshadowed an early break-up. Being without a rival, a problem arose as to how candidates were to be named. Obviously a nomination by a congressional caucus in the usual way would be equivalent to election if the nomination were regarded as binding on all members of the party. Dissatisfied with the caucus, the sections began to nominate their favorites by resolutions of the state legislatures. South Carolina led in 1821, naming William Lowndes. Tennessee followed the next year with Jackson, while Kentucky indorsed Clay and Massachusetts put forward Adams. In 1824 Crawford received the nomination of a small congressional caucus which the friends of the other candidates refused to attend.

Other states later indorsed one or other of these men. Calhoun waited in vain for a nomination, but finding himself favored for the vice-presidency by the friends of several of the other candidates, he decided to accept the certainty of the second place rather than made a doubtful fight for the first.

In deciding which of the candidates to support, the voters were not deceived by the fact that all called themselves Republicans. They were not, as has often been said, influenced merely by the personalities of the men. Each section endeavored to determine which one best represented its interests. "It will be recollected that the promotion of domestic manufactures is the ground we assume as the criterion of our choice," wrote one western editor whose comment is typical. The candidates made the voters' task difficult, however, for in their efforts to please everyone they obscured their views more or less by ambiguous language. "Is Mr. Adams really a friend to the limited interpretation of the constitution—does he stick to the doctrines of Virginia—is he opposed to the Bank of the U. S.—to a general system of internal improvement? We cannot make out from his address." So wrote the editor of the *Richmond Enquirer*.

The candidacy of Jackson was more than that of any of his rivals a matter of personality. Lacking the experience in civil affairs which the others possessed, and scorned by the upper class as an ignorant, hot-headed frontiersman, he was nevertheless the most popular candidate of all. His military successes had endeared him to the people of the West and his

candidacy expressed the popular confidence in the political
capacity of the common man. It bespoke the growing spirit
of democracy, with its antipathy to machine politics (as embodied in the caucus method of nomination, for instance)
and to the control of the Federal Government by an "aristocracy" of trained officeholders. The West took it for
granted that he held western views on economic questions.
The South took it for granted that he held southern views
because he was a cotton planter.

The division of the electoral vote among so many candidates prevented any one of them from receiving a majority.
Jackson led with 99 votes, Adams came next with 84, and
Crawford third with 41. Clay had sacrificed all hope of support in the planting states by his outspoken nationalism, and
Jackson divided with him the vote of the middle and western
states where the alliance of manufacturing and agriculture
was strongest. He received but 37 electoral votes, and his
name was excluded from the balloting in the House of
Representatives, upon which the choice devolved under the
provisions of the Constitution.

Clay was now generally believed to be in position to play
the part of "king-maker," for the congressmen of the states
which had supported him (Kentucky, Ohio, and Missouri)
were likely to vote as he did. In fact the situation was not so
simple. Crawford had suffered a stroke of paralysis during
the campaign, and his physical disability made it likely that
his friends would abandon his cause after giving him a compli-
mentary ballot. The contest would then narrow down to
Jackson and Adams, and the action of the four Crawford
states (Virginia, Georgia, North Carolina, and Delaware)
would be as important as that of the Clay states in determining the result.

As between Jackson and Adams, Clay's mind had long been
made up. The former he regarded as a mere "military chief-

tain," unfitted for the presidency. With Adams he had had
sharp personal differences, but they were in agreement on
current questions. For his own satisfaction he sought an in-
terview with Adams, which confirmed his determination to
give him his vote, but he maintained a discreet silence until
some of the western delegations announced that they would
support Adams.

In the House election in February, 1825, contrary to general expectation, enough doubtful states supported Adams on
the first ballot to give him the thirteen votes needed for election. The realignment of political groups followed with
great rapidity. Adams appointed Clay as his Secretary of
State, a personal alliance which was the true index of a tendency of their followers to fuse into an administration party;
for Adams was the second choice of the Clay states, so far as
can be judged from the available evidence. The administration program as set out in the first message to Congress was
all that the manufacturing-agricultural alliance could wish.
The Adams party, which came to be known as the National
Republicans, was a political coalition of these economic
groups. In its sectional aspect it represented an alliance between the Northeast and the northern portion of the West.

Jackson's friends of course formed the nucleus of an opposition party, which the nationalism avowed in Adams's
inaugural address and first message led most members of the
Crawford and Calhoun factions to join. This incipient party
of Jacksonian democracy was composed of incongruous elements, for it united the planters, whose views were local,
with many westerners whose economic views agreed with
those of Adams and Clay. The adherence of Van Buren of
New York, leader of the Crawford group, brought to the new
party the aid of a political manager who had already demonstrated a very unusual skill in such matters.

A great many persons were ill-disposed towards the administration because of the means used, as they believed, to defeat Jackson. Some of the latter's clever political friends, foreseeing the appointment of Clay if Adams became President, had discounted that event in advance. George Kremer, a dull-witted member from Pennsylvania, used as the tool of these schemers, alleged a few days before the election in the House, that Adams had offered Clay the post of Secretary of State in return for his support, and that Jackson might have had it if he had been willing to pay the same price. "None of Jackson's friends would descend to such mean barter and sale," ran the statement.

Clay demanded an investigation by the House, which Kremer evaded. But when Adams actually did appoint Clay, uncritical people believed, as the plotters had intended, that the charge of bribery was proved. Jackson was one of these. He had taken his defeat with equanimity up to this point, but convinced that he had been defrauded, he denounced Clay as the "Judas of the West," and withdrew his decision not to stand as a candidate in the next election.

The "bargain and corruption" charge gave Jackson's managers a capital campaign issue for 1828. Reasoning on the basis of the plurality vote in the electoral college in 1824, and incomplete statistics of the popular vote, they argued that Jackson was the people's choice, and that their will had been defeated by the alleged agreement between "corrupt" politicians. With this plea they made a powerful appeal to the growing sentiment in favor of popular government, and identified the cause of Jackson with that of democracy itself. "Vindicate the people's right to govern by electing Jackson," was well nigh the whole of their platform. By this cry they won the mass of the plain people, both of the new states and of the old ones where so many of them had recently been enfranchised.

At the same time they kept economic issues in the background. To win the election it was necessary to unite the South and West and this could not be done on economic grounds. Many of the planters believed the bargain charge. But with their aristocratic traditions they had little enthusiasm for the issue of popular government. It was Adams's nationalism which made him unacceptable. As their only alternative, they were ready to try Jackson even without knowing his views on public questions.

Few issues of the four years of Adams's term were dealt with on their merits. His administration was one long campaign for the election of 1828. Not since the 1790's had party malice gone to such extremes. When the antimasonic frenzy broke out, Adams was falsely alleged to hold high rank in the Masonic order. Baseless scandals were spread of immoral conduct while he was minister of the United States in Russia. His attitude and purpose relative to the Panama Congress were grossly misrepresented in the congressional debate by partisans who thought less of the important interests at stake than of their desire to discredit the President.

The masterpiece of manipulation came in the framing of the Tariff of 1828. The House committee composed of opponents of the administration reported a bill designed to please the western producers of raw materials—wool, hemp, flax, and iron—but to leave New England manufacturers without the protection they wished. Southern members, of course, would vote against the bill, as would (it was supposed) those from New England. It would be defeated, and the West would appear to be sacrificed by the President's own section. Thus the seeds of discord would be sown between the protectionists of the two sections. Randolph declared that "the bill referred to manufactures of no sort or kind, but the manufacture of a President of the United States." The plan miscarried, for enough of the New Englanders accepted the bill to secure its passage.

Against Jackson, in whose behalf all of this electioneering was carried on, Adams was a candidate for reëlection. Son of the second President, he had spent his life in almost continuous service of the public. At the age of fourteen he had accompanied the envoy to Russia as private secretary. Next he was a member of the secretariat of the commission which negotiated peace with England in 1782, and was still young enough after that task was done, to become a Harvard student.

During his father's presidency he was sent successively to Holland, Portugal, and Prussia as minister. Under Jefferson he represented Massachusetts in the United States Senate. On the embargo issue he broke with the Federalists and lost his seat. Thereafter he considered himself a Republican. Minister to Russia during the War of 1812, he came thence to Ghent to serve on the peace commission. Eight years more of intimate contact with public affairs as Secretary of State gave him an equipment for the chief magistracy equaled by that of few statesmen before or since.

In intellectual caliber few contemporaries approached him, and his code of private and public morality had lost little of the strictness of his Puritan ancestors. He felt keenly responsible for the administration of his high office in such a way as to promote the lasting welfare of the nation. He planned a national university, desired to promote scientific explorations, and especially wished to manage the public domain as a national trust and with expert efficiency. He would have made grants for the promotion of road- and canal-making in such wise that the ungranted land would be enhanced in value by the improvement at the same time that the country's resources were developed and brought within reach of the people. His plans were comprehensive and statesmanlike, but far beyond the grasp of the masses upon whose will hung the fortunes of public men in this dawning day of the new democracy. Besides, they involved stretches of power to which strict constructionists could never consent.

Adams firmly believed that office should seek the man, but his coldly intellectual temperament was not calculated to win friends, and his rejection of the arts of the politician deprived him of the effectual means of winning votes. He would not use his control over appointments to create a party machine. He would not remove from office men who had worked for Jackson and Crawford in 1824–1825. He would not remove the Postmaster-General when it became an open secret that he was laboring in Jackson's behalf in the campaign of 1828. He would not even deny the calumnies of his enemies. Small wonder that a friend, after vainly endeavoring to persuade him to dismiss a disloyal officeholder, warned him that he would find himself "dismissed" in the election.

And so it proved. The West and the South were solidly for Jackson, who received, besides, the votes of Pennsylvania and 20 out of 36 in New York. The New England states were loyal to their native son; but Adams received no votes south of Maryland and Delaware. The figures stood 178 to 83. Calhoun was reëlected Vice-President.

Thus did the last of the old-line statesmen depart from the capitol, making way for a crowd of politicians whose advent signalized the triumph of the people.

SELECT BIBLIOGRAPHY

The Conflict of Sectional Interests. The fifth volume of Channing, *United States,* opens with a survey of social and economic conditions in the period 1815–1845, which formed the basis of sectional rivalries. The climax of the tariff controversy is the theme of Houston, *Nullification in the United States.* See also histories of the tariff. Hunt, *John C. Calhoun,* follows the strife of sections from the biographical point of view. See also Lodge, *Daniel Webster.* The earlier phases of the economic rivalry which gradually disintegrated the Republican party are discussed by Hockett, *Western Influences,* 112–126.

On the extension of the suffrage, the best work is Porter, *A History of Suffrage in the United States.* See also Merriam, *A History of American Political Theories,* Chap. V.

The Reshaping of Party Lines. Hockett, *Western Influences,* Chap. V. McMaster gives a wealth of detail on such episodes as the House election of 1825. The lives of the statesmen of the period give the personal aspects of politics. Standard biographies are Morse, *John Quincy Adams,* Sumner, *Andrew Jackson,* and Bassett, *Andrew Jackson.* See also the newer biographies: Clark, *John Quincy Adams,* and James, *Andrew Jackson.*

Chapter XXIII

JACKSONIAN DEMOCRACY

DEMOCRACY TRIUMPHANT

THE stark, crude, self-reliant backwoodsmen who had built the new commonwealths west of the Alleghanies had written into their constitutions the democratic ideas of the frontier. By 1828 the backwash of their philosophy had undermined the "liberalism" of the fathers and brought about the enfranchisement of the masses in most of the old states. During the War of 1812 the West had held the balance of power in the Union, and in the following years the political center of gravity, like the center of population, definitely left the seaboard. The election of Jackson meant that the youthful democracy of the West, aided by the newly-enfranchised voters of the East, had placed the man of its choice in the first magistrate's chair. Jackson was the very personification of the spirit of the frontier, and by this token commanded the vote of the pioneer farmers of the new Mississippi Valley states. The new voters of the old states turned to him instinctively as a "man of the people," in preference to the trained statesmen of the old school. Astute politicians, moreover, who were already at work organizing the democratic movement, perceived that the path of success for them lay in following his banner. Still another factor in his triumph was his relative acceptability to the southern planters, who preferred any alternative to another term for John Quincy Adams.

The West of 1828 possessed a unity of outlook and interest and a political solidarity that were to be conspicuously absent twenty years later. Throughout the Mississippi Valley, along the line of settlement, the frontiersmen struggled with the same tasks of subduing the wilderness and creating social conditions fit for the rearing of a family. The valley was still a section by itself, with interests and needs quite as well defined as those of the "North" and "South" of the seaboard.

The same discontent with the restraints of old communities, the same love of freedom which had led European peasants to the thirteen colonies, had later attracted to the Mississippi Valley men and women of initiative, energy, and ambition. Outstanding traits of the people of the West were their individualism, their belief in the capacity of the common man, their hatred of special privileges for individuals or classes, and their nationalism. Their nationalism was in part the result of their diverse origins. Coming from many states and even from lands across the seas, they could find common ground only in their allegiance to the government of all the states—that government which had permitted them to acquire their lands upon easy terms and had granted them full rights of self-government through admission into the Union. An even more potent cause of nationalism was their feeling of dependence upon that government for works of internal improvement too costly for states to undertake, and for legislation which would promote a home market for their agricultural surplus.

Thus their nationalism tempered their individualism. They desired nothing so much as to be let alone and to act for themselves, so long as their objects did not exceed their powers. When the latter was the case, they showed capacity for practical coöperation, in industry as well as government, and were inclined to make of government an agency for attaining ends beyond private reach. However, by 1829 a distrust of federal activity in such matters as internal improvements and banking had begun to show itself, since such

activity often smacked of special privilege; but as yet they had been little concerned over details of political organization or fine distinctions in constitutional interpretation.

The broadening of the suffrage throughout the Union enfranchised thousands of men who had previously been sheer outsiders in the management of the government. Many of them were uneducated, untrained in political thinking, and apt to follow a magnetic leader irrespective of the policies he advocated. White manhood suffrage introduced a new and incalculable factor into the conduct of public affairs.

Boisterous scenes accompanied Jackson's inauguration. Ten thousand visitors from all parts of the country thronged Washington to witness the event. The President-elect, tall and thin, and with a military bearing, walked to the capitol with a small company of friends, his erect figure and uncovered white head in plain sight of the cheering hosts. The oath of office was administered by the venerable Chief Justice, John Marshall, whose misgivings on this occasion must have exceeded those with which he regarded Jefferson's inauguration nearly a generation earlier. After the ceremonies the impatient multitude broke into the White House, where an official reception was being held, stood in muddy boots on the damask-covered chairs, and mobbed the waiters carrying refreshments. The government was theirs at last!

Jackson had by this time outgrown the uncouthness of his earlier years, and acquired an impressive dignity of manner. His sincerity and integrity were undoubted, and his private morals without blemish. He was in no sense responsible for the unruly behavior of his admirers at the inauguration, but in making his appointments to office, he acted frankly upon the principle that the government belonged to the people. Though a man of strong personal convictions, he perceived the wisdom of selecting the heads of the executive departments from the principal factions which had supported him. Three of those chosen were political friends of Calhoun.[1] John H. Eaton of Tennessee, Secretary of War, and William T. Barry of Kentucky, the new Postmaster-General, were personal friends of the President. The Crawford element was recognized by the appointment of Van Buren as Secretary of State.

In the course of a long public career Martin Van Buren had, by sheer force of ability and skill, risen from humble beginnings to the political leadership of the important state of New York. Tactful and urbane in his personal relationships and adroit in manipulation, he was regarded by many of his contemporaries as a mere crafty politician. That he was more than that, however, his later career was to prove.

With the exception of the Secretary of State, the members of the cabinet were not strong men. Jackson did not care to lean heavily upon them for advice. Hence he gathered about him a number of intimates who enjoyed his complete confidence and who were derisively dubbed the "Kitchen Cabinet" by the National Republicans. The dominant personality in this group was Amos Kendall, an astute politician and former editor of Kentucky, and with him were associated Isaac Hill, editor of the *New Hampshire Patriot,* William B. Lewis of Tennessee, who for many years had been Jackson's political mentor, and Duff Green, editor of the *United States Telegraph.* All these men had been active in state politics, and nearly all belonged to what Webster called "the typographical crowd." Indeed, Jackson was the first President to realize the importance of being on cordial terms with the newspaper men of the country. The fact that he bestowed many offices upon newspaper editors throughout the land was no doubt a powerful assistance to him in interpreting public

[1] S. D. Ingham of Pennsylvania, Secretary of the Treasury; John Branch of North Carolina, Secretary of the Navy; and John M. Berrien of Georgia, Attorney-General.

opinion and in securing wide publicity and popular support for his policies. With the exception of Duff Green, the men named were favorable to Van Buren's political aspirations. Van Buren and Eaton of the official circle may be regarded also as members of the Kitchen Cabinet.

Jackson's accession to the presidency was marked by the adoption of a new principle in the selection of federal office-holders. Under the earlier Presidents, public officials had ordinarily continued their tenure during good behavior. To be sure, the spirit of partisanship had never been wholly absent in making appointments. Thus, when Jefferson in 1801 found the government positions monopolized by the Federalists, he filled all vacancies with members of his own party. But as the Federalist party declined, Republican Presidents had little temptation to make numerous changes, and men grew old in the service; Richard Rush once spoke of the War Department as the "octogenarian department."

In most of the northern and western states, however, the practice grew up of basing appointments and removals upon party service. In New York and Pennsylvania this system attained its greatest development, and party organization in those states anticipated the modern "political machine." The revival of factional divisions under John Quincy Adams, presented conditions favorable to the extension of the system to the Federal Government; but the high-minded Adams sternly set his face against it.

The triumph of the democratic forces under Jackson, however, opened the way for the nationalization of the "spoils system." The idea of an official aristocracy was repugnant to the common man, and most people were ready to indorse the doctrine that "to the victor belong the spoils." Furthermore, many people felt that "rotation in office" would give the newly-enfranchised masses a chance to receive training in the actual conduct of public affairs. Jackson announced the

new creed in his first annual message to Congress. Averring
that public office had come to be regarded as "a species of
property," he insisted that long continuance in office was
likely to breed indifference to the public welfare. This
danger, he believed, outweighed any advantages that might be
derived from the experience or training of the officeholder,
especially since any man of intelligence could quickly qualify
himself to perform the duties of any government position.

It was evident that the President contemplated numerous
removals from office as a measure of reform. His message
created more alarm among the official class, and in the
country at large, than his actual performance warranted.
While he removed more officeholders than any previous
President, the changes were not nearly as extensive as the
outcries of the opposition represented. The best available
evidence shows that, in the first year and a half of his administration, removals were made for all purposes of approximately
one eleventh of the entire federal civil list. Although most
of these changes were made for partisan reasons, some of
them were caused by misconduct in office and others by resignation or death. Jackson's appointments were made exclusively from the ranks of the Democratic party; and among
the men who received positions were fifty-six editors of influential newspapers. By the close of his eight years in office,
it is estimated that about one fifth of all federal officeholders
had been replaced.[1]

Jackson adopted the new practice in the spirit of reform
and without any appreciation of its dangers and abuses. It
received the unwavering support of all Presidents and parties
until the administration of President Grant, forty years later.

[1] The spoils system was accompanied by the vicious practice of levying as-
sessments on the salaries of officeholders for party purposes. Previous to elections, they were asked to contribute a percentage of their salaries for party expenses in the campaign. At first voluntary, the custom hardened in the course
of a few decades into a form of taxation, unjust and burdensome to the helpless victims.

THE QUESTION OF INTERNAL IMPROVEMENTS

When Jackson entered office, his views upon many national questions were unknown even to his close friends, and were perhaps not clearly formulated in his own mind. But in the course of his first administration a series of important problems arose for settlement, and his action with regard to them was so clear-cut and decisive that no one could remain in doubt as to his sentiments when he came up for reëlection in 1832. Since his party was made up of heterogeneous elements, it was inevitable that his spirited course should result in alienating from him a portion of his original supporters.

The first of these great questions was the old problem of the proper policy of the Federal Government in regard to roads, canals, and other public works. The National Road, now penetrating eastern Ohio, was as yet the only practicable wagon route over the mountains. Monroe, in his message of 1822 vetoing the Cumberland Road Bill, had laid down the rule that federal aid to projects of internal improvement should be confined to such works as were of general, rather than merely local, importance, and at that time Jackson, then in private life, had written to him commending his stand. Van Buren, also, had sympathized with Monroe's constitutional scruples, and had introduced a resolution in the Senate in 1825 for a constitutional amendment such as the President desired, but that body had taken no action.

After the earlier veto, by Madison, of the Bonus Bill, the states, thrown back upon their own resources, had begun to act for themselves, either directly or through subsidies to private companies. New York's Erie Canal was only the greatest of the state projects. Under John Quincy Adams the Federal Government had given assistance to some of these state projects, either by subscribing for stock or by grants of public land. The administration party would gladly have gone further, and instituted an elaborate federal system, but found the opposition too strong.

When Jackson became President, his own followers were divided on the issue. Vice-President Calhoun, though he had sloughed off most of his earlier broad-construction convictions, probably still favored federal activity in this field. Van Buren, on the other hand, disapproved of the policy. Jackson himself, while a member of the Senate (1823–1825), had not always voted consistently with the view he had expressed to Monroe. After his election Van Buren took an early occasion to discuss the matter with him, and ascertained that the Monroe letter represented his real convictions.

Jackson was soon given an opportunity to make a public announcement of his position. On May 20, 1830, Congress passed a bill authorizing the government to buy stock in a company which was planning to build a road from Maysville to Lexington, two towns in Kentucky. The bill seemed to represent a popular demand, and the proposed improvement lay in a section of Kentucky that was friendly to the President. Van Buren stated afterwards that not one in twenty believed that Jackson would dare to reject it. Against the advice of many of his western friends, he prepared a ringing veto message which Van Buren helped to compose. In this message, dated May 27, choosing to ignore the facts that the promoters of the Maysville Road contemplated extending it beyond the state line on the south, and that it would connect on the north with an Ohio route which led to the National Road, thus forming Kentucky's main overland way to the East, he asserted that the Maysville Road, as a work of merely local utility, was not entitled to federal aid under any reasonable construction of the Constitution. He furthermore called attention to the selfish "scramble for appropriations," which was an inevitable feature of the policy of federal help, and declared that the paramount object of the government should be retrenchment and economy in order to pay off the national debt. He concluded by repeating the familiar injunction that, if the people really desired federal aid, the Constitution should be amended to that end.

Jackson's opposition proved a strong deterrent to further expenditures by Congress during his presidency for roads within the boundaries of the states. The chief, though not only, exceptions were the continued aid given to the Cumberland Road and an appropriation for a highway in Alabama in 1833. In Jackson's mind, subsidies for roads in the territories and for the improvement of navigable rivers and harbors possessed greater constitutional justification, and expenditures for such purposes during his presidency actually exceeded the total appropriations under John Quincy Adams for internal improvements.

Jackson's stand against public improvements at federal cost did not cause the great popular outcry that Clay and the National Republicans had so confidently expected. The President's instinct proved a better guide to an understanding of the common man than the judgment of the experienced politicians. Within his own group of followers the Maysville veto had the effect of drawing the President closer to his Secretary of State. The southerners generally applauded Jackson's veto, and were encouraged to believe that he could be relied upon to back up strict-construction principles.

THE GEORGIA-INDIAN CONTROVERSY

The popular belief that Jackson was a strict constructionist was strengthened by his action in the Georgia-Indian controversy. In 1825 the Creeks and Cherokees still held nearly ten million acres in Georgia, and, together with the Choctaws and Chickasaws, owned a total of more than nine million acres in the near-by states of Alabama, Tennessee, and Mississippi. These tribes exercised complete rights of self-government within their domains, and were not subject to the laws of the states wherein they dwelt. Their privileged position and their possession of some of the best cotton lands excited the utmost impatience of the white planters.

In 1802, when Georgia ceded its western lands to the Union, the Federal Government had agreed to extinguish the Indian title to lands within the state "as soon as the same can be peaceably obtained upon reasonable terms." The considerable cessions obtained by the United States in the spirit of this agreement did not satisfy the land-hungry Georgians, who took the lead in a movement against the Indians in which the people of the neighboring states had almost as great an interest.

Early in John Quincy Adams' administration Georgia began a bitter controversy over the matter with the Federal Government. The treaty of Indian Springs, negotiated under President Monroe in 1825, which ceded a large portion of the Creek lands in Georgia and Alabama, was disregarded by President Adams as having been obtained by fraud. In Georgia this was looked upon as a bit of misdirected Puritan conscientiousness, and before a satisfactory adjustment was reached, threats of warlike action were exchanged between the state and federal governments. However, in 1827, the Creeks consented to a treaty ceding the last of their lands in Georgia to the United States.

The Cherokees, the most highly civilized of all the southern tribes, with whom farming had become an important industry, realized that their turn would come next. Although their rights were protected by a series of treaties with the United States, they sought to render security more secure by adopting a constitution in 1827, which asserted their position as one of the sovereign and independent nations of the earth. This bold defiance led the Georgia legislature to pass a law in December, 1828, providing that after June 1, 1830, all

Indians should become subject to the laws of the state. Mississippi and Alabama followed a little later with similar legislation.

President Jackson, who, through his own life as a frontiersman and Indian fighter, knew the red man, believed that the Indian would be debased rather than uplifted by constant association with the more advanced race. Moreover his sympathy was with Georgia. In his first annual message to Congress on December 8, 1829, he denied that the Indians had any constitutional right to an independent government within the limits of a state,[1] and asserted that they must either agree to migrate beyond the Mississippi, with the help of the United States, or submit to the laws of the state and give up all their lands not under cultivation. In accordance with Jackson's recommendation Congress passed an act on March 10, 1830 which authorized him to remove to lands west of the Mississippi, all Indians who surrendered their holdings. The sum of $500,000 was appropriated for the expense of this action.

The resolution of the Cherokees remained unshaken by these developments. When the Georgia authorities took the necessary steps to extend their jurisdiction over the Indian land, they acted upon the advice of white friends and turned to the Supreme Court for protection.[2] In the case of Worcester *vs.* Georgia, Chief Justice Marshall roundly declared that the Cherokees possessed the status of "a nation" under protection of the Federal Government and that the action taken by Georgia against the Indians was unconstitutional and void. When Jackson learned of this judgment, he is reported to have said, "John Marshall has made his decision;

[1] The Constitution (Art. IV, Sec. 3) says that "no new State shall be formed . . . within the Jurisdiction of any other State . . . without the consent of the Legislatures of the States concerned as well as of the Congress."

[2] There were three cases in all: Cherokee Nation *vs.* Georgia (1831), Worcester *vs.* Georgia (1832), and Graves *vs.* Georgia (1834).

now let him enforce it!" Jackson was not willing to concede on this or any other occasion that the executive, as a coördinate department of the government, did not have as good a right as the judiciary to decide questions of constitutionality.

Since the Supreme Court was helpless to act effectively without executive support, the Indians had to bow to the inevitable. The Cherokees eventually made a treaty with the United States in 1835, surrendering their lands for five million dollars plus a tract beyond the Mississippi and the expenses of transportation. The Choctaws and Chickasaws accepted the liberal terms offered by the United States in 1830 and 1832, and began their removal westward. In the case of the Sac and Fox Indians in Illinois, and the Seminoles in Florida, the United States had to resort to forcible measures of ejection. The former incident, known as the "Black Hawk War," occurred in 1832. In the case of the Seminoles, fugitive slaves in large numbers had joined them, and their unwillingness to migrate was due in part to the fear that those fugitives might be apprehended. The struggle dragged on from 1834 to 1842 before the United States succeeded in forcing a part of the tribe to remove.

The idea of removing the eastern tribes, both northern and southern, had occurred to Jefferson at the time of the Louisiana Purchase. Some preliminary steps had been taken under Presidents Monroe and Adams, such as the making of treaties with the western tribes, to make room for the newcomers. The final measures were adopted under the leadership of Jackson. An extensive territory in the fertile valley of the Arkansas was set up as a home of the dispossessed southern tribes, while several from the Northwest were removed to the valley of the Kansas River. By a law of 1834 and certain supplementary acts, Congress guaranteed to the removed Indians, who in the past had constantly been subject to the encroachments of the whites, the permanent possession of their new lands, as well as full rights of tribal government. No white man could go into the Indian country without a license, and no spirituous liquors were to be sold there. The office of the Commissioner of Indian Affairs was created, with special oversight of the Indians, and provision was made for supplying the tribes with domestic animals, agricultural implements, and teachers. By 1840 the whole region west of Iowa, Missouri, and Arkansas, as far as the Rocky Mountains, was established as permanent Indian country. Yet within fifteen years the white man was clamoring for the opening of the region and for the organization of territorial governments.

THE GREAT DEBATE ON THE NATURE OF THE UNION

The internal-improvements question and the Georgia-Indian dispute were hardly more than opening skirmishes in the great struggle over the nature of the Union and the respective rights of the states and the Federal Government under the Constitution. On December 29, 1829, Senator Samuel A. Foot of Connecticut offered a resolution in Congress, suggesting the desirability of stopping the survey of the public domain, and of restricting the sale of public lands, for a certain period, to those already on the market. The proposal touched a point at which the interests of Northeast and West were in conflict, and was at once assailed by Thomas H. Benton of Missouri. In an elaborate speech he declared that the material prosperity and political security of the West depended upon the rapid settlement of the country. He charged that Foot's resolution was provoked by the jealousy of the seaboard North, and by the self-interest of the manufacturers who wished to check the migration of their underpaid employés to the frontier.

On the matter of the protective tariff, as we have seen, the eastern manufacturers and western farmers had come to-

gether, and the alliance had furnished much of the support of
the National Republican party of Adams and Clay. On the
issue of government by the people, in the campaign of 1828,
this alliance had been partially severed, and much of the
West had joined with the South in support of Jackson. Now
the breach between Northeast and West on the land question
raised in the southerners who had long been smarting under
the protective-tariff policy of the northeastern industrialists,
the hope of detaching the West permanently from the alliance, and of welding the interests of the transappalachian
states and the seaboard South, by showing that the two sections were equally sufferers at the hands of the same exploiter.

With the introduction of this new element into the situation, the question of the public lands receded into the background. Thenceforward the divergent needs and interests
of sections were debated. John C. Calhoun was the logical
spokesman for the South Atlantic section, but as Vice-President he could not assume the rôle. His place was therefore
taken by Senator Robert Y. Hayne, an able and persuasive
orator from Calhoun's state. Hayne's severe indictment of
New England brought into the arena Senator Daniel Webster
of Massachusetts, the ablest constitutional lawyer in the
country and the greatest public speaker that the nation had
yet produced. From January 19 to 27, 1830, these two
giants engaged in a forensic contest that crowded the galleries
of the Senate with excited auditors.

Senator Hayne condemned the steady trend toward national consolidation, and particularly the employment of this
enlarged national power for selfish sectional advantage. Restriction of land sales, he said, would not only curb the growth
of the agricultural states, but would contribute to the up-
building of manufacturing and thus perpetuate the unconstitutional protective system. Obviously the states must look
to themselves for protection against encroachments by the

federal authority. The means for so doing had already been pointed out by the Virginia and Kentucky Resolutions of 1798–1799 and the South Carolina Exposition of 1828. He then reiterated the doctrine which Calhoun had expounded.

Webster, while protesting that New England had always been friendly to the West, directed his chief attack against Hayne's constitutional arguments. He denied that the Union was a compact formed by states, and asserted that the national Constitution had been made by the people of the entire country just as the people within each state had instituted their state constitutions. The Federal Government could not be regarded, therefore, as occupying a subordinate relationship to the states, since "the general government and the state governments derive their authority from the same source." Furthermore, the people had provided in the federal Constitution for a judiciary vested with the authority to settle all questions of constitutional law.[1]

In his view, the doctrine of nullification was not only unconstitutional but impracticable, for under its operation the tariff would be void in South Carolina, but in Pennsylvania and Kentucky, where protection was in favor, it would be in force. There would thus be "four and twenty interpreters of constitutional law, each with a power to decide for itself, and none with authority to bind anybody else," and the Constitution would be reduced to a "collection of topics for everlasting controversy." The states were not without redress, he pointed out, if the acts of the general government seemed oppressive to them, for they might lawfully amend the Constitution at their pleasure or choose new officers for the government at the elections. They might even appeal to the right of revolution, the inherent right of every people. But

[1] Webster referred to the provisions that the Constitution and the federal laws made pursuant thereto shall be the supreme law of the land, and that the jurisdiction of the federal courts shall extend to every case arising under the supreme law. See the Constitution, Art. VI, Par. 2, and Art. III, Sec. 2, Par. 1.

the South Carolina doctrine of defying the Union while remaining within it meant inevitably armed defiance of the Federal Government, or treason.

The Webster-Hayne debate was the formal opening of the historic controversy concerning the nature of the Constitution, which thirty years later was to plunge the nation into civil war. The debate of 1830, of course, did not decide the vital issues at stake, but the adherents of each side claimed a victory for their champion. That both of the great debaters loved their country and were stating the only principles upon which they believed the Union could survive, we may well believe. That both spoke with full knowledge of the selfish sectional advantages to be derived from their constitutional contentions is also true.

Hayne pleaded for the states, Webster for the nation. Hayne's arguments breathed the spirit of the past, and may have been nearer to the views most current when the Constitution was adopted. Whatever may have been the true legal character of the Constitution in 1787, it would almost certainly have failed of acceptance if the ratifying conventions had believed the Federal Government was made as independent of state control as Webster claimed, or that the Supreme Court would be the final interpreter of the Constitution in cases involving even the reserved powers of the states.

Webster, on the other hand, held that the Federal Convention had devised a truly national system—a position with which modern students are inclined to agree. Though ingenious arguments could be, and were, urged against his view, the tide of American development had set strongly in its favor. The American people·had been undergoing a process of nationalization since 1787. The heritage of a common history, the habit of working together for common purposes, the patriotic pride born of wars against a common enemy, the strong nationalism of the new western states, and Marshall's great constitutional decisions had combined to bring into being a Union that was quite unlike the one that many of the people of 1787 had thought they were creating.

THE SPLIT IN THE DEMOCRATIC PARTY

The appearance of this portentous issue boded ill for continued harmony within the Democratic party. Other influences, however, were already at work to drive a wedge between the Jackson-Van Buren following, on the one hand, and the Calhoun faction, on the other. The friends of Calhoun looked upon the South Carolinian as the logical successor of Jackson to the presidency in 1836, but this plan did not accord with the desires of the men in the Kitchen Cabinet, who were grooming Van Buren for the position. Events now occurred in rapid succession, which firmly established Van Buren in Jackson's regard while leading to his complete alienation from Calhoun.

The first of these incidents·was known as the "Eaton Affair." Shortly before his appointment as Secretary of War, John H. Eaton had married a lively young widow who, under her maiden name of Peggy O'Neil, had been the life of her father's tavern in Washington and whose free manners had set tongues wagging. The leaders of Washington society determined to ostracize Mrs. Eaton, and at cabinet functions and official receptions they studiously ignored her. The whole affair might have been merely a tempest in a teapot except for the fact that Jackson, who believed the wife of his intimate friend to be unjustly accused, resolved to make himself her champion. On every occasion he showed her marked courtesy; he even lectured his cabinet members on the attitude that their wives should take toward her. Very conspicuous in the campaign against Mrs. Eaton were Mrs. Calhoun and the wives of the Calhoun members of the cabinet, and

Jackson soon began to think of the Calhouns as abetters in an intrigue to discredit his administration. Van Buren, who as a widower was free from family restraints, won new favor with his chief because of his chivalrous attentions to Mrs. Eaton.

The breach between Jackson and Calhoun was widened by an event that occurred at the anniversary celebration of Jefferson's birthday on the evening of April 13, 1830. The southern Democrats planned to make the affair a nullification demonstration; and as Jackson had not yet committed himself on the issues raised in the Webster-Hayne debate, they hoped to surprise him into an utterance favorable to the southern position. Jackson and Van Buren took counsel in advance, and agreed that the occasion would give the President an effective opportunity to disclose his real convictions. Therefore, when Jackson was called upon for a toast, he declared in ringing tones: "Our federal Union: it must be preserved!" Calhoun sought in vain to retrieve the situation by offering as his sentiment: "The Union: next to our liberty most dear! May we all remember that it can only be preserved by respecting the rights of the states. . . ."

The final break between the two men was precipitated by an incident relating to the discussion, in 1818, by Monroe's cabinet, of Jackson's course in invading Spanish Florida. Since Jackson believed that, in this affair, he had merely carried out the wishes of the government, he had felt angered and humiliated by the criticism of his conduct. For many years he thought that he had escaped official censure only through the stout friendship of Calhoun, then Secretary of War. The time being now propitious, the Kitchen Cabinet managed to get before him, sometime in May, 1830, the fact that Calhoun, instead of being his defender, had been his most aggressive critic. To a man of Jackson's temperament, only one course was possible. After giving Calhoun a chance to explain, he sent him a letter, terminating their relations and venting his bitter disillusionment in Cæsar's reputed words to his false friend, *"Et tu Brute!"*

The President next proceeded to reorganize his administration frankly upon a Jackson-Van Buren basis. Always alive to the importance of an active newspaper support, he abandoned the *United States Telegraph* as the administrative organ because of its pro-Calhoun leanings, and induced Francis P. Blair, a Kentucky friend of Amos Kendall, to come to Washington in December, 1830, to found a new organ. Blair proved to be a prince of partisan editors, and throughout the administrations of Jackson and Van Buren, his newspaper, the *Washington Globe,* thundered forth Jacksonian policies, giving the cue to the Democratic press the country over.

Jackson's next step was to purge his cabinet of the Calhoun element. Van Buren and Eaton readily saw the wisdom of the move, and prepared the way by tendering their resignations early in April, 1831. In view of all the circumstances the three Calhoun members could but follow their example. The President then chose a cabinet composed of men who enjoyed his confidence, headed by the distinguished jurist, Edward Livingston of Louisiana, as Secretary of State, and Louis McLane of Delaware, as Secretary of the Treasury.[1] Thereafter the Kitchen Cabinet, as such, played a less important rôle, though Kendall and Blair came closer to the President than ever before, and Kendall was eventually (1835) taken into his official family as Postmaster-General. An English visitor in America at this time called Kendall a

[1] The other members were: Lewis Cass of Michigan, Secretary of War; Levi Woodbury of New Hampshire, Secretary of the Navy; Roger B. Taney of Maryland, Attorney-General; and W. T. Barry of Kentucky, Postmaster-General. Barry was the only holdover from the previous cabinet.

"twilight personage" who was supposed by Jackson's critics to be "the moving spring of the whole administration; the thinker, planner, and doer."

Jackson sought to promote Van Buren's interests by sending him as minister to Great Britain; but his nomination was defeated by the casting vote of Vice-President Calhoun. When the result was announced, Benton shrewdly remarked to a Senator who had voted against the nomination, "You have broken a minister and elected a vice-president." This occurrence undoubtedly stiffened the President's determination to secure a public vindication of Van Buren.

SELECT BIBLIOGRAPHY

Democracy Triumphant. The general events of Jackson's presidency receive detailed treatment in the comprehensive works already cited: Channing, V; McMaster, V–VI; and Schouler, III–IV. To these should now be added von Holst, *The Constitutional and Political History of the United States,* III, and Wilson, *A History of the American People,* IV. Reliable single-volume surveys are MacDonald, *Jacksonian Democracy,* and Ogg, *The Reign of Andrew Jackson.* Dodd's discussion of the period in his *Expansion and Conflict,* is valuable for an insight into the interplay of social forces and political conduct. The recent study, Bowers, *The Party Battles of the Jackson Period,* places chief emphasis upon the picturesque aspects of the epoch.

The influence of the frontier upon the rise of democracy is dealt with in Turner, *The Frontier in American History,* and Paxson, *History of the American Frontier. Cf.* Hockett, *Constitutional History,* II, 74–91.

The biographies of the statesmen of the period usually include a full discussion of pertinent political events. Of particular value are Bassett, *The Life of Andrew Jackson,* Hunt, *John C. Calhoun,* Jervey, *Robert Y. Hayne and his Times,* Lodge, *Daniel Webster,* Meigs, *Life of Thomas Hart Benton,* and *The Life of John Caldwell Calhoun,* Schurz, *Henry Clay,* and Shepard, *Martin Van Buren.* See also Smith, *The Francis Preston Blair Family in Politics,* and biographies listed in Bibliography for Chap. XXII.

The origin of the spoils system is best set forth in Fish, *The*

Civil Service and the Patronage. See also Ostrogorski, *Democracy and the Organization of Political Parties.*

The Question of Internal Improvements. The political phases of this problem are analyzed in Wellington, *The Political and Sectional Influence of the Public Lands, 1828–1842.* Hulbert, *The Paths of Inland Commerce,* gives a good account of the development of roads, canals, and early railways, summarized from the same author's *Historic Highways of America.* Paxson, *History of the American Frontier, 1763–1893,* is also of importance.

The Georgia-Indian Controversy. Phillips, "Georgia and State Rights." On the Indian wars and removals see Abel, "The History of Events Resulting in Indian Consolidation West of the Mississippi," Cole, *I Am A Man: The Indian Black Hawk,* and Foreman, *Indian Removals.* The latter continues the story of the Indians in their new homes in *The Five Civilized Tribes.* Bass, *Cherokee Messenger,* is the story of Rev. Samuel A. Worcester, the plaintiff in Worcester *v.* Georgia.

The Great Debate on the Nature of the Union. The biographies of Webster and Hayne cited above are useful. Burgess, *The Middle Period,* gives an incisive analysis of the constitutional problems of the years from 1817 to 1858. Merriam, *A History of American Political Theories,* Chap. VII, is the best objective study of the growth of political theory concerning the nature of the Union.

KING ANDREW THE FIRST.

Chapter XXIV

JACKSON'S FIGHT FOR NATIONALITY AND POPULAR RIGHTS

SOUTH CAROLINA NULLIFICATION

THE discord within the Democratic party helped to prepare the way for South Carolina's dramatic defiance of the Federal Government in 1832–1833. The hope of the South Carolinians that Jackson would use his power as President for a removal of the tariff injustices against which they had protested in the Exposition of 1828 had proved vain, for his messages to Congress had, from the outset, shown that, while he favored a modification of the Tariff of 1828, he did not share the southern view of the unconstitutionality of protection. Indeed, his position was that of a moderate protectionist.

When Congress enacted a new tariff law in July, 1832, he signed it without hesitation. The new rates, which were to go into effect on March 3, 1833, were in many respects an improvement over the "Tariff of Abominations" of 1828, but they were frankly based upon the protective principle. The average level of duties was reduced from forty-one to about thirty-three per cent. In the House of Representatives, the bill received overwhelming support from the middle states and the states west of the Appalachians. New England was evenly divided. South Carolina and Georgia voted strongly in the negative, but Virginia and North Carolina voted as strongly in the affirmative, not from sympathy with protection, but because they preferred the new measure to the one which it replaced.

The people of South Carolina had been closely following

550

the course of events. During the summer of 1830 the nullifiers, calling themselves the "State Rights party," had agitated
for a convention to consider the propriety of nullification,
but their efforts had been defeated by the Union party under
the leadership of Joel R. Poinsett. In the subsequent months,
to aid the State Rights party, Calhoun issued a series of
addresses and papers in which he restated and clarified the
nullification theory for the people at large.

The new tariff of 1832 brought matters to a crisis. Immediately after its passage, the South Carolina members of
Congress issued an address to their fellow-citizens, asserting
that "all hope of relief from Congress is irrevocably gone."
The election campaign for the state legislature which followed, on the express issue of nullification, was won by the
State Rights party, and as soon as the new legislature met it
summoned a convention. This body assembled on November 19, 1832, and five days later adopted by an overwhelming
vote an "Ordinance of Nullification." This measure declared
the tariff laws of 1828 and 1832 unconstitutional and void
within the state from and after February 1, 1833; it required
all state officials (except members of the legislature) to take
an oath to obey the Ordinance, prohibited appeals to the
United States courts in cases arising under it, and instructed
the legislature to pass the necessary acts to make these provisions operative. It closed with a threat of secession from the
Union in case Congress should pass any law for the employment of force against the state.

On November 27, three days after the adjournment of the
convention, the legislature met and passed the acts called for
by the Ordinance, including provisions for defense in case
of armed intervention by the Federal Government. Shortly
afterwards, Calhoun resigned the vice-presidency, and was
chosen to Hayne's seat in the Senate, in order that he might
act as the champion of the state in the national arena.

Jackson had been kept fully informed of these proceedings. His own instinct was to deal vigorously and decisively with the recalcitrants, but since he believed that behind the nullification program lay a genuine grievance, he was not disinclined to listen to Van Buren and other counselors, who advised that South Carolina be afforded some relief from her economic distress. The policy of the administration became thus a mixture of principle and expediency.

In November, 1832, Jackson strengthened the garrison at Fort Moultrie in Charleston Harbor. Seven revenue cutters and a ship-of-war were sent to Charleston with orders to be ready for instant action. Arms and munitions were placed at convenient and safe places, some of them across the North Carolina border, and Jackson intimated his intention of personally leading the forces against the South Carolina rebels if the crisis came. On December 10, he issued a resounding proclamation against the nullifiers.

This pronouncement, distinctly nationalistic in tone, was the joint production of the two westerners, Jackson and Livingston. South Carolina, the President declared, stood on "the brink of insurrection and treason," and he appealed to the people of the state to reassert their allegiance to that Union for which their ancestors had fought and bled. Like Webster, he affirmed that instead of being "a compact between sovereign States," the United States was "a Government in which the people of all the States, collectively, are represented." As for his own course of action, the laws of the United States must be executed, and armed resistance is treason! "I have no discretionary power on the subject; my duty is emphatically pronounced in the Constitution." Acting in the spirit of this proclamation, he asked Congress on January 16, 1833, for additional legislation to enable him to enforce the tariff law.

Jackson's bold stand for national supremacy came as a

surprise to many who had observed his earlier course in championing a strict construction of the Constitution. But it is only fair to note that he was fully as consistent in his constitutional convictions as Webster or Calhoun. He held with the former that the Union was indestructible, and with the latter that the powers of the Federal Government should be construed narrowly; but he failed to find in a literal reading of the Constitution any justification for Calhoun's nullifying doctrine. He occupied, as Calhoun admitted, a position "between the parties." His treatment of South Carolina contrasted sharply with his attitude toward Georgia during the Indian controversy, due to his conviction that the executive department was as competent as the Supreme Court to decide questions of constitutionality. In the Georgia affair he regarded the pronouncements of the federal judiciary as unconstitutional, whereas in the nullification controversy he held that a protective tariff was warranted by the Constitution.

In accordance with Jackson's desire, a "force bill" was promptly introduced in the Senate. It empowered the President to change the location of customs houses, extended the jurisdiction of the United States Circuit Courts to all cases arising under the revenue laws, and authorized the President to employ the armed forces of the United States to enforce federal laws and the processes of the federal judiciary.[1] Denounced as the "Bloody Bill," the proposed law met with the bitterest opposition of John Tyler of Virginia, Calhoun, and other southern leaders, but found an equally ardent advocate in Daniel Webster.

Meantime, Jackson's friends in Congress were pressing a plan for scaling down the tariff duties. Their efforts, embodied in the Verplanck Bill, made little progress, however,

---

[1] The provisions authorizing the employment of force were limited in duration to the end of the next session of Congress.

and it soon became clear that, in the critical juncture, there was only one man who could pilot a compromise measure through Congress. This was Senator Henry Clay, the great advocate of protection and father of the "American System." On February 12, 1833, he introduced his compromise tariff bill; even Calhoun lent his assistance, and the act was ready for Jackson's signature on March 1. It provided for an enlargement of the free list, and for a biennial reduction of all other duties until they should reach a general level of twenty per cent in 1842. On the same day the "Force Bill" was adopted by Congress.

The nullification leaders had been anxiously watching the progress of events at the capital. They had felt certain of receiving support from other southern states, but to their surprise these without exception denounced the course of South Carolina as unwise and unconstitutional. The Ordinance of Nullification was to go into effect on February 1, 1833; but on January 21 a public meeting of State Rights leaders in Charleston voted, on their own responsibility, to suspend the Ordinance until the action of Congress should be learned. On March 11, after the adjournment of Congress, the South Carolina convention reassembled and formally rescinded the Ordinance of Nullification. But as a last gesture of defiance, the convention adopted an ordinance nullifying the "Force Bill."

Each side derived encouragement from the outcome of the dispute, and it is not easy to decide where the victory rested. The Jackson administration had stood firmly for the supremacy of the Union, but, on the other hand, South Carolina had secured a large measure of the practical relief she had demanded. There can be no doubt that the controversy deepened and strengthened the conviction that the interests of the slave states and free states were diametrically opposed.

The nullification episode had a profound effect on the later development of the states' rights theory. The southern leaders saw that nullification was certain to be ineffective in practice, for in a test of force the general government would always be able to execute federal law in a nullifying state. Accordingly, talk of nullification gradually dropped into the background, and Calhoun and his followers during the next thirty years placed chief stress upon the right of an aggrieved state to secede from the Union. The episode also had the effect of estranging many southern Democrats from Jackson's leadership. Unwilling to support the President, they had either to form an antiadministration *bloc* within the party or to cast their political fortunes with the party of Clay and Webster. Those who chose the latter course played an important part in the formation of the Whig party in 1834.

THE UNITED STATES BANK CONTROVERSY

The democracy which had triumphantly elected Jackson was at base an agricultural democracy. It temporarily displaced the political control of a society which had originally rested on commerce. The latter shifted its interest, as commerce declined in the years following the War of 1812, to manufacturing and banking enterprises, which tended more and more to take the corporate form.

The conservative and democratic groups were mutually suspicious: the former feared that manhood suffrage would lead to government by incompetent demagogues using unscrupulous methods to control the ignorant voters, while the masses were equally fearful of the influence on government of a plutocracy seeking selfish ends. Because they viewed askance contractors desiring public money for constructing works of internal improvement, they hailed Jackson's Maysville Road veto with delight. The outstanding representative of corporate capitalism in the Jacksonian era, however, and the most odious, was the Second United States Bank.

The masses were indeed distrustful of banks in general, because they were everywhere incorporated by special acts of the legislatures, frequently as rewards for party service or for similar reasons. Banks founded under such circumstances were apt to lack the control needed to insure their financial soundness. Add to this the dire need of the western settlers for money to buy implements, build roads, and improve their properties, and one can understand why banks were inclined to loan freely, make excessive issues of paper notes, and employ other "wild-cat" methods. Suspensions and failures were frequent, entailing great suffering upon the whole community, especially upon the farmers, wage-earners, and other poor people into whose pockets the worthless bank notes found their way.

In particular, the great bank at Philadelphia with its various branches was the object of this popular antagonism, notwithstanding the strict regulations in its charter. It aroused much hostility during the panic of 1819 by foreclosing mortgages on large quantities of real estate, especially in the West, which were later sold at an advance. Naturally, it became a target of the state banks. Among other things, these institutions strenuously objected to the attempts of the federal bank to keep their paper issues within conservative limits by promptly returning their notes to them for redemption. Several states passed laws intended to hamper or destroy the branches of the United States Bank within their boundaries, but as we have seen, the federal Supreme Court upheld the constitutionality of the bank and its immunity from state interference.[1]

Meantime the bank had been handling the funds of the government, assisting in the collection of taxes and the ne-

[1] A decision similar to that in the case of McCulloch *vs.* Maryland was rendered in 1824 in one arising under an Ohio law (Osborn *et al. vs.* The Bank of the United States).

gotiation of public loans, and performing other valuable fiscal services. Under direction of its capable president, Nicholas Biddle, it became a prosperous and powerful institution. It intrenched itself firmly in the affections of the older sections of the country, particularly among the business classes and men of capital. But the violent democratic surge which swept Jackson into office served to give new life to all the old objections to the bank, and supplied a fresh argument against it. Democracy, being based upon the principle of equality, is always opposed to all forms of privilege, and to none more than a financial monopoly. The name of the United States Bank befitted a government institution; but, it was, in reality, a private corporation, although the government was a minority stockholder and appointed one fifth of the Board of Directors. As the one overshadowing monopoly in the country, against it was directed all the passionate hatred that a half-century later fell upon trusts and railways.

This popular fear was not altogether without foundation. At the outset, the stock of the bank had been distributed among more than thirty-one thousand holders; but by 1831 the number of stockholders had dwindled to a little more than four thousand, and the majority control had gravitated into the hands of Biddle and two members of the Board of Directors. More than four hundred of these stockholders lived in Europe, and of the remainder, the vast majority lived in the financial centers of the seaboard. Whether or not the bank had ever abused its functions, it was in a position to do so by reason of the exclusive privileges it enjoyed under its charter and its vast economic power. In the eyes of the new democracy the existence of this great moneyed monopoly, with its closely centralized control, constituted a menace to free government.

Jackson entered office with the frontiersman's prejudice against banking corporations; and his antipathy was sharp-

GROWTH OF THE AMERICAN PEOPLE

ened by the suspicion, probably unfounded, that the bank
had worked against his party in several states during the campaign of 1828. Without loss of time he announced in his
first annual message that it was none too soon for Congress
to consider whether the bank charter should be renewed at
its expiration in 1836. For himself he questioned both its
constitutionality and the desirability of its continued existence. In his next two annual messages he returned to the
subject.

His attitude was not wholly negative, for he proposed to
substitute for the existing institution a bank of limited
powers that would be a branch of the United States government, and that would, among other duties, handle the public
funds. His ideas were somewhat vague, but his proposal,
as we shall see, was eventually worked into definite form by
the Van Buren administration as the Independent Treasury
System. In these official pronouncements Jackson expressed
himself as yet with a degree of caution, for the leaders of his
party, including Secretary McLane of the Treasury Department, were far from united in support of his views. Indeed,
two committees of Congress, controlled by the Democrats,
reported in 1830 in favor of both the constitutionality and
expediency of the bank.

The approach of the presidential election of 1832 brought
matters to a crisis. Clay and Webster urged Biddle to apply
for a recharter without further delay, for they believed that
Jackson would be unwilling to hazard his chances of reëlection by a veto. If he were so foolhardy, they were convinced
that his action would spell certain victory for the National
Republicans in the campaign. Biddle readily fell in with
the plan. Being a man with an eye for the main chance, he
had long been prepared for the occasion. Through heavy
loans to prominent newspaper editors, hitherto unfriendly

to the bank, he had secured their powerful help in creating a favorable public opinion.[1] He had placed many congress-men under personal obligations to the bank through the extension of loans, accommodating in this manner thirty-four members in 1829, fifty-two in 1830, and fifty-nine in 1831.[2] Furthermore, the bank had a political tower of strength in Daniel Webster, who was one of its directors and salaried attorneys.

The application for recharter was made early in 1832, and on July 3, Congress passed the bill. On July 10 came the President's flaming message of veto. If Jackson showed in this message little knowledge of the principles of banking and finance, he at least made it unmistakably clear to the "farmers, mechanics, and laborers" that he was unalterably opposed to legislation that would "make the rich richer and the potent more powerful." Reasserting his earlier belief that the bank was unconstitutional, he emphasized the great danger to free government from "such a concentration of power in the hands of a few men irresponsible to the people"; and he further pointed out that the profits of the bank, derived from loans to western farmers, went into the pockets of capitalists in the East and Great Britain.

The veto created a profound sensation. The *Washington Globe* heralded it as a "second Declaration of Independence," freeing the country from the grasp of a moneyed monopoly and frustrating the plot of "the aristocracy of England to raise a revenue in America." But to Biddle and his associates,

[1] Thus, the *New York Courier and Enquirer,* originally an opponent of the bank, changed its attitude after it had borrowed $53,000 from Biddle. Other newspaper editors who were heavy borrowers were Duff Green of the *United States Telegraph* and Gales and Seaton of the *National Intelligencer.*

[2] The total amount of loans to congressmen was $192,161 in 1830, $322,199 in 1831, $478,069 in 1832. Biddle declared in 1833 that in half an hour he could remove all the scruples in the District of Columbia against the bank by giving positions "to worthy friends who have no character and no money."

the message was "a manifesto of anarchy." Whether Congress or the President had correctly gauged the will of the people remained to be decided in the impending presidential election.

THE PRESIDENTIAL CAMPAIGN OF 1832

The campaign of 1832 was opened by the Anti-Masons. This party was new to the national political scene. It had originated under strange circumstances. In 1826, William Morgan of Batavia, New York, a former member of the Masonic order, had published a pamphlet purporting to reveal its secrets. Soon afterwards he was abducted by certain overzealous members, who carried him as far as Niagara Falls; what befell him thereafter has never been revealed. The belief spread like wild fire through the rural districts of New York, Pennsylvania, and New England that he had been murdered, and all the latent democratic prejudice against exclusive secret societies was galvanized into active hostility. Churches took up the matter, deprived Masonic clergymen of their pastorates, and expelled Masonic laymen from membership. Other secret organizations were involved only in less degree; the honorary scholarship society, Phi Beta Kappa, founded in 1776, felt obliged to abandon its secret character at this time.

The movement quickly found its way into local and state politics, and Anti-Masonic parties were formed in several states. So popular did the new issue seem that certain astute young political leaders believed they might use it as a rallying point for the forces opposed to Jackson. Under the direction of such men as William H. Seward and Thurlow Weed of New York and Thaddeus Stevens of Pennsylvania, the party was organized on a national basis. At a national convention held on September 26, 1831, candidates were nominated and a platform adopted. William Wirt, former Attorney-General, was named for the presidency notwithstanding his statement to the convention that he had joined the Masons early in life and would not favor any "blind and unjust proscription" of the order.

This effort to fuse the anti-Jackson elements proved a failure, largely because of the personal popularity of Henry Clay, whom the National Republicans proceeded to nominate by unanimous vote in a convention at Baltimore on December 12, 1831. John Sergeant of Pennsylvania was named for the vice-presidency. The platform condemned Jackson's attitude on the great questions of the day. Jackson's renomination by the Democrats was, of course, a foregone conclusion, but in order to give a semblance of wide popular sanction to the vice-presidential choice, a national convention was held in Baltimore on May 21, 1832. Van Buren was triumphantly named for the second place, and Jackson's reëlection was recommended to the country.

In the campaign that followed, the Anti-Masons did not play an important part; the real contest occurred between Jackson and Clay. The issue that occupied the foreground was the bank question. The Democrats accused the bank of attempting to influence the voters by calling in loans and contracting the currency. But beneath the consideration of specific questions lay a fundamental division of opinion between the merchant, manufacturing, and financial classes, on the one hand and the laboring and agrarian elements on the other—between those who feared the new democratic upheaval and those who desired to give Jackson their *carte blanche* approval. The outcome was an enthusiastic indorsement of "Jacksonism." The President received 219 electoral votes, Clay 49, Wirt 7. To Jackson fell most of the electoral votes of the West, the middle states, and the South Atlantic states. The Calhoun party in South Carolina, unwilling either to vote for Jackson or to join the opposition, cast the eleven votes of the state for John Floyd of Virginia.

This campaign is notable for the appearance of several new practices which have survived to the present time. In nominating candidates party conventions, representative of the rank and file of the voters, replaced for the first time the old congressional caucus, which had broken down in 1824, and the haphazard system of nominations by state legislatures and popular conventions, which had prevailed in 1828.[1]

The adoption of platforms was likewise an innovation, essentially democratic in its purpose of giving the voters advance notice of the policies and plans to be pursued by the party if successful in the election. Nor is it to be overlooked that this election marked the first widespread use of campaign cartoons. By means of this shrewd and sometimes grotesque symbolism, political parties found it possible to instruct countless voters whose interest could have been excited in no other way.

THE TRANSFER OF DEPOSITS

Jackson interpreted his reëlection as a mandate from the people to crush the bank beyond hope of recovery. He moved as quickly as circumstances permitted, for he feared that delay would give Biddle an opportunity to cause a commercial depression through a sudden contraction of loans. A depression due to contraction apparently necessitated by the approaching expiration of the charter might deceive the people into believing that, after all, the bank should be rechartered. Jackson's weapon lay at hand in that provision of the bank charter which authorized the removal of the public funds at the discretion of the Secretary of the Treasury. Find-

[1] The Democratic convention chose to make its nominations contingent upon a two-thirds majority vote, a custom followed until recently.

ing that Secretary McLane was unwilling to take this step, he appointed William J. Duane of Pennsylvania to the office, and when the latter refused to issue the order, he replaced him with a bitter anti-bank Democrat, Roger B. Taney of Maryland.

Late in September, 1833, Taney ordered that no more government funds should be deposited in the United States Bank, and that the ten million dollars already in its custody should be gradually withdrawn in the ordinary course of meeting the expenses of the government. As a substitute depository a careful selection was made of the stronger state banks, and stringent restrictions were imposed upon them in order to preclude the possibility of financial irregularities. In general, the favored banks were required to perform the services hitherto rendered by the nearest branch of the United States Bank. The administration hoped, by these measures, to insure a gradual contraction of loans on the part of the great bank, and to provide relief to borrowers through the gradual expansion of the facilities of the sound state banks. Twenty-nine deposit banks were designated by January 1, 1835, and the number rose to eighty-nine by November 1, 1836.

In spite of Jackson's precautions, the winter, spring, and summer of 1833–1834 witnessed a severe business depression, a condition which Jackson's friends attributed to the malice of "Nicholas I." The National Republicans and the Calhounites condemned the transfer of the funds to the "pet banks." When Taney in accordance with the law reported his action to Congress, the Senate pronounced his reasons insufficient and refused to confirm him as Secretary of the Treasury. Moreover, the upper chamber denounced Jackson's part in the business; but the House approved of the transaction, and as a result of Benton's dogged loyalty, the resolutions censuring Jackson were eventually expunged from the Senate journals (1837).

FOREIGN AFFAIRS UNDER JACKSON

Jackson's conduct of foreign affairs lacked much of the ceremonial and formalism of earlier administrations, but it was marked by vigor and crowned with success. One difficult problem was presented by the unsatisfactory trade relations with the British West Indies. Ever since the close of the Revolutionary War the United States had coveted the direct trade with them, which had contributed so largely to the prosperity of the thirteen colonies. Repeated attempts had been vainly made, from Washington's time down, to obtain the privilege.

Soon after Jackson entered office, Congress at his request authorized him to open the ports of the United States to British vessels as soon as England accorded us similar privileges in her American possessions. If this move failed, Jackson planned to recommend a non-intercourse law between the United States and Canada. Great Britain, however, willingly met the terms offered. Jackson's success was no doubt facilitated by growing doubts in British official circles of the wisdom of the old monopolistic commercial system.

The settlement of long-standing claims of American citizens against France proved more difficult. These claims had arisen from the injuries sustained by American commerce under the Berlin and Milan decrees and other arbitrary orders of France during the Napoleonic wars, and ever since 1815 had been the subject of negotiation between the two countries. The accession of Louis Philippe to the throne by the July revolution of 1830 invited a reopening of the question, and in 1831 a treaty was concluded, whereby France agreed to pay the United States $5,000,000 in six annual installments in full satisfaction of the claims.

The treaty proved to be unpopular in France, however, and the French Chamber of Deputies persistently refused to vote the necessary funds. Finally, in exasperation, Jackson in

December, 1834, urged Congress to authorize reprisals on French property in the United States. Although Clay persuaded Congress to withhold the desired legislation, France was greatly irritated by the President's action. The French minister at Washington was recalled, and the American minister at Paris was given his passports.

In April, 1835, France, with a characteristic Gallic touch, authorized payment of the spoliation claims provided that a suitable apology were offered for the President's words. Jackson responded by recommending the employment of commercial coercion against France, but in the course of his message to Congress, he expressly disclaimed any intention "to menace or insult the Government of France." On the basis of this avowal good relations were restored and the payment made.

A foreign problem of a quite different kind was presented by the Texan war for independence in 1836. Beginning in the early twenties, American settlers had flocked over the border into Texas, allured by the generous land policy of Mexico. The immigrants accepted Mexican jurisdiction, of course, and were required to profess the Catholic faith. Soon they formed a majority of the sparse population of the region. It was not long before the profound differences in race, political methods, and ways of thinking and living resulted in friction. The Mexican government presently became uneasy and began to adopt regulations which irritated her new subjects. By a series of measures, she sought to provide for the gradual extinction of slavery. In this she was in part following the example of other Spanish-American republics, but some of the acts were aimed directly at Texas. Next, Texas was united with the adjoining state of Coahuila, making a new state in which the Mexican population outnumbered and therefore governed the Americans. Trade restrictions followed, designed to end all direct commercial relations between Texas and the United States; and in 1830 the policy of granting lands to immigrants was suspended. Finally, additional military posts were established and troops were dispatched to enforce these obnoxious regulations.

The discontent of the Texans had already involved some armed clashes when a revolution in Mexico precipitated a general insurrection. The revolutionary leader, Santa Anna, abolished (1836) the federal system of government which Mexico had copied from the United States in a constitution adopted ten years before, and substituted a centralized form which made an autocrat of himself. The new constitution, by which the states were reduced to mere administrative subdivisions, he succeeded in forcing upon all of them except Texas. The people of that state took up arms in defense of the federal constitution, and when Santa Anna undertook to reduce the uprising, insurgency turned into a fight for independence.

The Mexican leader invaded Texas threatening death to all rebels. Success marked his early campaign. On March 6, 1836, he stormed the Alamo at San Antonio, where every one of the nearly two hundred defenders perished. This bloody episode angered the insurgents beyond measure, and with the cry "Remember the Alamo," the leaders aroused the people to a desperate struggle for freedom. In the same month a convention had declared independence and adopted a constitution. It is significant that the declaration of independence was signed by three Mexicans and fifty-three Americans, and that forty-eight of the latter hailed from the slave states. Under Sam Houston, who had begun his public career as a congressman from Tennessee, the Texan army led Santa Anna into a trap at San Jacinto, and on April 21, 1836, made good the declaration of the convention. Santa Anna himself was taken prisoner, along with more than seven hundred of his men, but obtained his release by agreeing to recognize the independence of Texas with the boundary claimed at the Rio Grande River. Although Mexico later denied that she was bound by Santa Anna's promises, and he himself repudiated them as given under duress, the country was unable to send another army to reconquer the lost province.

The official attitude of the United States towards the war had been one of neutrality, but ardent popular sympathy with Texas prevented a strict enforcement. Volunteers were openly recruited and ships-of-war fitted out within American jurisdiction. Without their help it is doubtful if Texas could have defeated her opponent.

In July, 1836, the new republic made overtures to the United States for annexation, and in September its people approved of annexation by an almost unanimous vote. In view of efforts to purchase Texas, which the United States had made under both Adams and Jackson, annexation might have been expected to meet with hearty approval in Congress. But sentiment in the United States had changed. To the antislavery men in the North, the whole history of the settlement and revolt in Texas bore the appearance of a plot to increase the slave area of the United States. Furthermore, under the existing circumstances, annexation threatened a war with Mexico. Former President John Quincy Adams, rounding out a distinguished career in the House of Representatives, declared against the acquisition of additional slave territory. Daniel Webster counseled delay until it was known whether Texas had a *de facto* government. Calhoun, on the contrary, advocated immediate recognition of independence and admission into the Union.

Torn by conflicting counsels, Congress contented itself with authorizing the President to appoint a diplomatic agent whenever he believed that Texas independence should be recognized. This step Jackson took on March 3, 1837, the day before he left office. In this whole affair the President had acted with unusual circumspection. His enemies ascribed it to his desire to preserve party harmony and facilitate the election of Van Buren in 1836.

SELECT BIBLIOGRAPHY

South Carolina Nullification. The best detailed accounts are Houston, *A Critical Study of Nullification in South Carolina,* and the more recent one by Boucher, entitled *The Nullification Controversy in South Carolina.* See also Hockett, *Constitutional History,* II, Chap. II and III. For a different approach to the subject, see Stanwood, *American Tariff Controversies in the Nineteenth Century,* I. The general relationship of state's rights doctrines to regional self-interest is discussed in Schlesinger, *New Viewpoints,* Chap. X.

The United States Bank Controversy. The most thorough treatment, Catterall, *The Second Bank of the United States,* emphasizes the fiscal elements of the controversy. The account in Sumner, *Andrew Jackson,* is suggestive and informing, but prejudiced. White, *Money and Banking,* sheds much light on the general banking methods of the times.

The Presidential Campaign of 1832. Gammon, Jr., *The Presidential Campaign of 1832,* discusses the election in detail, including the rise of the convention system. The relation of the Anti-Masonic party to the complex political situation is authoritatively set forth in McCarthy, "The Anti-Masonic Party." See also Stanwood, *History of the Presidency,* I.

Foreign Affairs under Jackson. This subject in its general bearings is lucidly discussed in Bassett, *The Life of Andrew Jackson,* II. See also the various diplomatic histories cited in the bibliographies for preceding chapters. An authoritative work on the commercial negotiations with England is Benns, *The American Struggle for the West India Carrying Trade, 1815–1830.*

Of the many works on Texas, among the most useful for an understanding of American interest in the Texan Revolution are Smith, *The Annexation of Texas,* and Rives, *The United States and Mexico, 1821–1848.* See also Stephenson, *Texas and the Mexican War,* James, *The Raven,* and *Andrew Jackson,* the admirable biography by Barker, *Stephen F. Austin,* and Callahan, *American Foreign Policy in Mexican Relations.* Castañeda, *The*

Mexican Side of the Texan Revolution, gives a different view-point. Callcott, *Santa Anna,* is a popular and fair account of that man's career.

Joel R. Poinsett played a prominent part in the nullification episode and in the efforts to purchase Texas. There are lives by Rippy and Putnam.

Chapter XXV

THE RISE OF THE WHIGS

FACTIONS OPPOSED TO JACKSON

THE political factions opposed to Jackson had no hope of success so long as they remained divided. Hence another attempt was made early in his second administration to bring together all the dissatisfied elements. The chief of these groups were the National Republicans and the Anti-Masons; they found ready allies in those Democrats, particularly in the South, who had been antagonized by the President.

Like the factions which had rallied around Jackson in 1828 because of opposition to John Quincy Adams without any other bond to unite them, the malcontents now drew together to oppose Jackson. Agreeing in implacable antagonism to his imperious ways, they nicknamed him "King Andrew I," and began to call themselves "Whigs" (about 1833 or 1834). Like the parliamentary party in England which had opposed the king's claims, the American Whigs stood for the supremacy of the legislative branch and against "executive usurpation." But as to their constructive principles and program they prudently kept silence, for their views were too diverse to permit a formulation which would command the support of all elements in the party. For this reason they refrained for several campaigns from the attempt to draw up a platform.

In Clay and Webster the Whigs possessed two of the most able and brilliant statesmen of the time. John Tyler of Virginia was the chief spokesman of the southern wing, and Calhoun counted himself a Whig so long as Jackson remained in office, although never quite at ease in the party. In point of organization and discipline the Whigs were inferior to the Democrats. They relied chiefly on the magnetic personalities of their leaders to hold their membership. The major group in the party, numerically and intellectually, was the National Republican strain, which included both Clay and Webster; but even its distinguished leadership could not promise electoral success without the support of its southern allies. In general, the people of substance and position were to be found within Whig ranks, for they were the classes whose interests were promoted by banks, the protective tariff, and internal improvements, or imperiled by the radical doctrines of Jacksonian Democracy.

THE LAND QUESTION

In Jackson's second administration the public land question became a prominent issue, involving many conflicting interests and calling forth many proposed solutions. Land sales were increasing by leaps and bounds. The newer states wished to accelerate settlement in order to promote the development of their material resources, while eastern capitalists felt that their labor supply was being drawn off. Any measure tending to cheapen the lands was therefore certain to incur the disapprobation of the representatives of the business classes of the North Atlantic seaboard. Their attitude was revealed by Foot's resolution of 1829. On their side the westerners found allies in the southern planters, who favored any plan that would restrain the growing power of the northern manufacturers, and in the working class of the cities, who saw in cheap lands a chance to escape from wage labor.

The question assumed acute form in Congress in 1832. It being the year of a presidential campaign, Clay's political enemies sought to force him, as a presidential aspirant, to commit himself on the issue on which Northeast and West were so sharply divided. With this intent a proposal to reduce the price of lands was referred in the Senate to the Committee on Manufactures, of which he was chairman. In reporting, Clay shrewdly suggested a measure which he believed would win him the political support of both sections. He declared that the existing price, $1.25 per acre, was not too high, as the heavy sales proved, and that to lower it would depress values of real estate in the older western states as well as in the East. Since Congress was pledged to dispose of the lands for the common benefit, his bill provided for the distribution of the land revenues among all the states (in proportion to their representation in the electoral college) for a period of five years, each state's share to be expended substantially as it might choose. The plan appealed to the eastern manufacturers because it left the price of public land unchanged, and to the West because it promised a substantial revenue to the state treasuries.

This bill passed the Senate in July but died in the House. In his first message after his reëlection (December, 1832) Jackson put himself squarely on record against Clay's scheme. Since 1824 Senator Benton of Missouri had been introducing bills embodying the graduation and donation principle,[1] and the President adopted his policy, urging that "as soon as practicable" the public lands should cease to be a source of revenue and be sold at nominal cost to settlers. Tracts remaining unsold should "in convenient time" be ceded to the states within whose borders they lay.

[1] The main features of Benton's plan were: a reduction of the price of lands not sold when offered at $1.25, to $1.00 after the lapse of a year; a similar reduction of twenty-five cents at the end of the second and third years; the donation to actual settlers of lands which remained unsold after being offered at fifty cents an acre; and the cession to the states in which they lay, of all lands which were still unsold and untaken a year after they had been offered at twenty-five cents an acre. The details varied considerably in the several bills. The plan partially met a western demand that the lands should be ceded to the states within which they lay.

The various elements of the Whig party, including the southern contingent, rallied to the support of Clay. The Calhounites had earlier favored a reduction in the price of lands, but had experienced a change of heart, partly because they began to perceive that cheap lands meant that the West would be occupied by free settlers. On March 1, 1833, Clay's new bill passed both houses, only to receive a pocket veto.

Soon afterwards a new factor was introduced into the situation by the extinction of the national debt. In spite of the falling rates under the Compromise Tariff, the revenue from duties and lands was large, and the excess over expenditures was applied to the debt until in January, 1835, the last of it was paid. A surplus of government funds then began to pile up in the "pet banks," and Congress was faced with the problem of disposing of the excess income. It was not feasible to tamper with the duties on imports, which had been fixed by the compromise; nor was it any more practicable to reduce the price of government lands. For the third time, therefore, Clay offered a distribution bill, and although it passed the Senate by a party vote it failed in the Democratic House.

Calhoun now assumed the leadership and advocated a plan of disposing of all surplus funds irrespective of origin. As adopted in June, 1836, his plan provided that all money in the treasury on January 1, 1837, in excess of five million dollars, should be deposited with the states (in proportion to their electoral vote) in four equal quarterly payments. Although Jackson's constitutional scruples were quieted by the fiction that the money was a loan rather than an outright gift, he signed the bill with palpable reluctance. The impelling reason for his approval was probably his desire to do nothing to injure Van Buren's chances in the approaching presidential election. The distribution of the surplus, amounting to $37,469,000 on January 1, 1837, was never completed, for the execution of the law was interrupted by the Panic of 1837.

The plans of the Democratic organization for the election of 1836 had long been laid. Jackson's dominant will had consolidated his miscellaneous following of 1828 into a compact organization though at the cost of defections from the ranks. Jackson's mind was fixed upon Van Buren as his successor, and at the national convention held at Baltimore on May 20, 1835, he had his way. The western membership was recognized by the choice of Colonel Richard M. Johnson of Kentucky, a well-known frontier fighter, for the vice-presidency. By authorization of the convention, a committee later issued a statement of Democratic principles pledging the candidates to a continuation of Jackson's policies.

The Whigs were too heterogeneous to unite upon a single man or upon a common platform; therefore all thought of a national convention was abandoned. Instead the plan was adopted of nominating several men for President, each of whom might be expected to win the electoral votes of the states in his own geographic section. In this way it was hoped that Van Buren would be prevented from receiving a majority in the electoral college, and, as in 1824, the election be thrown into the House of Representatives. Webster was put forward by the Massachusetts legislature; Senator Hugh L. White, a former Democrat of Tennessee, by the legislatures of Tennessee and Alabama; and William Henry Harrison, the military hero of the Northwest, was nominated by a state convention in Pennsylvania.

The central figure throughout the canvass was not Van Buren but Jackson, and the old political battles were fought out anew before the people. The working class rallied to the Democratic ticket, attracted by Jackson's overthrow of the "Money Monster" and his action in establishing a ten-hour day in the Philadelphia navy yard in 1836. The outcome of the election was a surprise to the Whigs. Van Buren received 170 electoral votes, forty-six more than the total vote polled by all his opponents. Johnson, however, had only 147 votes against a combined opposition vote of the same number. For the first and only time in our history, the choice of a Vice-President devolved upon the Senate, which proceeded to elect Johnson by a vote of 33 to 16. As in 1832, South Carolina chose to bestow her eleven electoral votes on candidates of her own selection.

VAN BUREN AND THE MONEY QUESTION

Martin Van Buren has not received his just dues at the hands of posterity, partly because his merits were obscured by the picturesque personality of his predecessor, and partly because his administration coincided with a period of economic depression. By his contemporaries he was known as the "Little Magician," and his enemies asserted that his political genius consisted chiefly of the ability to straddle public issues. Yet his record as chief executive, though lacking in creative statesmanship, was that of a man of strong convictions and stubborn purpose. The fact that he preferred to persuade rather than antagonize an opponent argued no absence of moral courage.

The Panic of 1837, which crashed upon the country shortly after Van Buren entered office, was due, at bottom, to the orgy of speculation and overexpansion through which the nation had been passing. Astonished at the evidences of feverish enterprise in all parts of the country in this period, a European visitor remarked that whereas his own countrymen boasted of their past the Americans bragged of their future. The phenomenal development of the western country has already been alluded to. The increased purchase of public lands after 1830, however, was less the result of actual settlement than of the operations of speculators who borrowed wildly to invest in lands for the purpose of reselling at a profit. In the planting states much the same sort of thing was going on. A rise in the price of cotton in 1835 caused thousands of south-western planters to buy slaves and lands on credit, in the expectation of paying for them out of their profits. The fever of speculation also infected the older sections of the country, and sent real estate values soaring in the cities.

In a similar fashion, public improvements were everywhere being carried out on an extensive scale. Between 1830 and 1834 the number of steamboats rose from 130 to 230. Canals were projected and begun in many parts of the country, especially in the Old Northwest. State governments were involved in these enterprises as well as private persons and companies. The newly invented steam railway came in for special attention. Since 1826 "rail" roads or tramways, operated by horse power or stationary engines, had been in use for local commercial purposes in certain parts of the country, but in 1829 the importation of a steam locomotive from England revealed the vast possibilities of the railroad for general public use. Peter Cooper and other American inventors improved upon the English model, and state legislatures granted charters and appropriations to assist in developing the new mode of transportation. The railway mileage increased from 23 miles in 1830 to almost 1500 at the close of Jackson's administration.

In general, the construction of public works far outran the needs of the country, and tied up millions of borrowed capital in enterprises that would for many years be unproductive. Moreover, the carnival of speculation was based largely on bank credits and paper money of doubtful value. The number of state banks had increased from 329 in 1829 to 788 in 1837, and under the loose laws of the time, the specie reserve of many of the banks was entirely inadequate to support the paper money they put out. The destruction of the United States Bank removed a conservative influence, and the deposit banks loaned out public funds to borrowers with a liberal

BALTIMORE AND OHIO PASSENGER CAR, 1830

hand, as, indeed, the government encouraged them to do, to offset the contraction of the currency due to the calling in of loans by the United States Bank as it prepared to wind up business under its expiring charter. Unfortunately this policy was inconsistent with other measures which the government presently saw fit to adopt.

The artificial prosperity would have collapsed sooner or later, but the crisis was hastened by the measures alluded to. Since 1834 President Jackson had become increasingly alarmed at the amount of doubtful paper money which the government was receiving for lands and taxes. Benton had sought to get Congress to declare that "hard money" only would be accepted in payment for lands, but beyond winning for himself the sobriquet of "Old Bullion," he had been able to accomplish nothing. In April, 1835, Jackson, on his own authority, began to issue orders forbidding public officers to accept bank notes of the smaller denominations, hoping thereby to increase the circulation of specie and check the unbridled speculation. This device proving insufficient, he issued, on July 11, 1836, the famous Specie Circular, which directed all government agencies to receive only gold and silver in payment for public lands. Since "hard money" was scarce, especially in the West, an acute check was given at once to land speculation, discredit was cast upon all paper notes, and private creditors began to demand coin for payments due them.

The effects of the Specie Circular were sharpened by the withdrawal of federal funds from the "pet banks" for apportionment among the states under the Distribution Act. This forced the banks, in order to accumulate the money needed for the installment payable January 1, 1837, to call in many of their loans, and money began to grow tight. They succeeded in meeting the calls for the payment of two of the quarterly installments and half of the third, but then the payments ceased.[1] The situation was aggravated by poor crops in the West in 1835 and 1837, and by the failure of certain great business houses in Great Britain, which had invested heavily in American securities and now threw them upon the market.

Now came the failure of cotton merchants in the South, followed by that of northern factories and warehouses. On May 10, 1837, the banks of New York City suspended, and in all, 618 banks failed during this fatal year. Bankruptcies multiplied in every direction. The discredited bank notes depreciated in value, and prices shrank to a hard-money level. Twenty thousand wage-earners were thrown out of work, wages were cut, and the cities were crowded with the unemployed. For the organized labor movement, which had attained considerable proportions (see page 597) this was a death blow; it was not revived for many years. The depression continued during the remainder of Van Buren's administration; indeed, business did not return to normal conditions until 1842.

President Van Buren summoned a special session of Congress on September 4, 1837, to deal with the situation. His recommendations revealed his accord with the financial ideas of Jackson and Benton and his adherence to doctrines which were becoming popular with the urban wage-earners.[2] At his suggestion Congress authorized the borrowing of ten million dollars to tide over the immediate stringency. To safe-

[1] Eventually the Federal Government recovered all but $50,000 from the deposit banks.

[2] Since 1835 a struggle had been raging in New York within the Democratic party over fiscal policies. By this message Van Buren placed himself on the side of the Loco-Focos (so-called) and the workingmen. Aided by the President's favor, the Loco-Focos gained control of the New York Democracy; and in 1838 a law was passed, providing for ample specie reserves for state-bank notes, and permitting any group of qualified men to establish a bank under a general law. During the next decade Massachusetts, Maryland, South Carolina, and other eastern states followed New York by instituting safe and conservative banking systems. The new system spread to the Old Northwest, beginning with Illinois in 1851. These laws furnished a model for the national bank legislation of 1863–1864.

guard the public funds in future, he recommended the plan known as the "Independent Treasury" or "Subtreasury." Under this system the government would hold its own moneys. An Independent Treasury, the President believed, would not only keep the public funds safely but would prevent their use for the encouragement of private speculation. Finally he urged that the principle of the Specie Circular should be extended to all taxes and payments due to the government.

The Whigs, led by Clay and Webster, hotly opposed this scheme. They accused the President of being indifferent to the suffering of the people. They insisted that, if the United States Bank had been rechartered, the panic would never have occurred. With an eloquence born of renewed hope, they directed their efforts towards the establishment of a third United States Bank. Calhoun, however, now abandoned his erstwhile allies, and gave his support to the Independent Treasury and the Van Buren administration.

The Independent Treasury bill passed the Senate in 1837 and again in 1838, failing both times in the House of Representatives. Van Buren persisted nevertheless, and in 1840 his plan was accepted by both houses. The act as passed provided for vaults and safes in certain specified cities as depositories for government funds, and the requirement was added that after June 30, 1843, all payments to or by the United States should be made in gold or silver. The Whigs, though overborne, were not convinced, and six years more of political controversy were necessary before the plan became firmly engrafted into the federal fiscal system.

THE OVERTHROW OF THE DEMOCRATS

In dealing with the public issues of the day, Van Buren faithfully kept the pledge, made in his inaugural address, to tread in the path of his "illustrious predecessor." Indeed, some historians have gone so far as to speak of his administration as "a third term of Andrew Jackson." In the matter of internal improvements Jackson's policy was continued for another four-year period. Van Buren showed his interest in labor welfare by issuing an order in 1840 for the establishment of the ten-hour day on all government works.

As respects the public lands, Van Buren, like his predecessor, recommended a reduction of the price, with the eventual transfer of unsold lands to the states in which they lay. He also advocated granting the right of preëmption to settlers (or "squatters," as they were called) who occupied public lands in advance of sale. As earlier, Benton championed the rights of the western pioneers; but he had to meet the vigilant opposition of Clay, who continued to agitate for the distribution of the land revenue among the states. Three times the Senate passed Benton's graduation bill and three times it met defeat in the House. Likewise all efforts to enact a general preëmption law failed for the time being.

Van Buren's public acts awakened no enthusiasm among the masses. He lacked the ability to impart the dramatic quality to his measures which marked the "Old Hero's" every move. It may well be doubted, however, whether even Jackson's popularity, had he still been President, could have survived the widespread feeling that the administration was responsible for the industrial depression. The tactics of the Whigs in the campaign of 1840 were cleverly designed to take advantage of these facts.

The Whig convention, the first in the history of the party, met at Harrisburg on December 4, 1839. Henry Clay confidently expected the nomination, but the practical politicians feared that his well-known record would alienate some of the groups whose support was necessary for victory. When the voting began he was in the lead, but after repeated balloting the prize went to William Henry Harrison of Ohio. General

Harrison met the requirements of the situation perfectly. During the quarter of a century which had elapsed since the War of 1812, in spite of some service in Congress, he had done nothing to excite active antipathy, and his fame as the hero of Tippecanoe and the Thames was national. To insure the support of the southern Whigs, John Tyler was nominated as his running-mate. Because of the divergent views of the factions composing the party, the convention adjourned without adopting a platform. Democratic appreciation of the predicament of the Whigs was shown by the scornful suggestion of the *Hartford Times* that the nominee be called "the federal-whig-abolition-amalgamation-conservative-anti-masonic-striped pig-foreign missionary candidate."

The Democrats at their Baltimore convention on May 4, 1840, unanimously renominated Van Buren but were unable to unite upon a candidate for the vice-presidency. The platform indorsed the Independent Treasury, and declared against the exercise of "doubtful constitutional powers" by the Federal Government. Specific condemnation was visited upon the proposed United States Bank, the protective principle, and federal appropriations for internal improvements. A third party, organized by antislavery enthusiasts, took part in the campaign, but its proceedings were unimportant save as a harbinger of the future.

The Democrats were on the defensive throughout the campaign. They were sorely pressed to justify the policies of Jackson and Van Buren, which the Whigs charged had brought on the hard times. The Whigs either avoided a discussion of their own program or adapted their public utterances to the section in which they spoke. The Democrats attempted to ridicule these tactics and the Whig candidate: one of their prominent newspapers tried to belittle Harrison as a man who would be content to remain on his backwoods farm in a log cabin if he might have a pension and a barrel of

hard cider. No remark could have been more imprudent at
a time when the mass of the western people lived in log cabins.
Harrison regarded himself as, like Jackson, a true representative of the democratic West; and the Whig appeal to the
masses to vote for him as a man of the people was more effective than any platform would have been.

"The battle is now between the log cabins and the palaces,
between hard cider and champagne," declared Henry Clay in
campaign speeches. Daniel Webster apologized publicly because he had not been born in a log cabin, but eagerly claimed
that honor for his elder brother and sisters. "If ever I am
ashamed of it," he thundered, "may my name and the name of
my posterity be blotted forever from the memory of mankind!" Horace Greeley, a young New York journalist whose
newspaper career had been interrupted by the Panic of 1837,
established a campaign sheet called *The Log Cabin,* which
quickly attained a weekly circulation of eighty thousand
copies.

The log cabin became the election symbol of the Whigs,
and the campaign was turned by them into a joyous romp.
Giant mass meetings and barbecues were held everywhere,
torchlight processions paraded the streets of towns, "Tippecanoe and Tyler too" became the popular slogan. Women
were almost as active as men. The enthusiasm easily lent itself to song, and such ditties as "Old Tippecanoe" and "Little
Van is a used-up man" were on everyone's lips. In contrast
with the "Honest Farmer of North Bend," Van Buren was
pictured as a man who used gold spoons and dressed himself
before costly French mirrors. "The campaign was an apoth-
eosis of tomfoolery," declared Andrew D. White in after
years.

The outcome was a sweeping victory for the Whigs, Van
Buren receiving only 60 votes out of the 294 in the electoral
college. The Whigs had made politics so entertaining that

the popular vote was nearly twice as great as in the previous election. In reality, the victors had little cause for jubilation. Harrison had received only about six per cent more of the popular vote than Van Buren, and the Whigs faced the responsibility of office, divided among themselves as to a program of public policy.

THE QUARREL BETWEEN TYLER AND THE WHIGS

Clay declined Harrison's offer of the post of Secretary of State, preferring his regnant position in the Senate, and the cabinet post went to Webster. Four of Clay's intimate friends, however, were appointed to cabinet positions.[1] But of Harrison's capacities for the presidency the country was never to learn, for he died within one month of his inauguration. Sixty-eight years of age when he took the oath of office, his strength was taxed beyond endurance by the demands of the hungry Whig office-seekers.

The Whigs now paid the penalty for their non-committal opportunism in the campaign. It had served to hold together enough discordant groups to win the election, but the best promise of party harmony in carrying on the government vanished with Harrison's death. That event brought to the presidency John Tyler, a strict-constructionist, antiprotectionist, antibank Democrat, who had left his party because of Jackson's dictatorial course. His views were at variance with those of Clay and Webster. Apprehending disagreement with the new President, Clay determined to seize the command and impose his views upon him. On June 7, 1841, he offered in the Senate a series of resolutions which outlined a program of legislation. These resolutions, the National Republican faction of the Whigs, which doubtless composed a majority of

[1] Thomas Ewing of Ohio, Secretary of the Treasury; G. E. Badger of North Carolina, Secretary of the Navy; John Bell of Tennessee, Secretary of War; and J. J. Crittenden of Kentucky, Attorney-General.

the party, regarded as a belated announcement of the platform which the national convention had feared to adopt in advance of the election. Clay's main proposals were: the repeal of the Independent Treasury Act, the distribution of the proceeds of public land sales, revision of the tariff, and the incorporation of a bank. In his mind they were inseparable parts of a system; the fourth proposal, especially, he considered as the logical complement of the first. Since the representatives of the party as a whole had not indorsed these policies, and since Tyler had not been pledged to them as a candidate, he can be criticized for acting on his own judgment concerning them only if one holds that a President is bound by the opinion of a majority of his party in Congress.

The Independent Treasury Act was quickly repealed with the President's assent on August 13, 1841. Clay's pet measure for distributing the land revenues encountered greater difficulty. To many persons it seemed unwise to give away a portion of the national income when the government was borrowing money for its current expenses. Furthermore, the pioneer West, now as earlier, preferred to have the price of lands reduced; and Tyler was known to oppose distribution for fear that the resulting loss of revenue would be used as an excuse for raising the tariff.

To win enough votes for passage, the distribution bill, as adopted on September 4, 1841, contained important concessions to the opposition. The right of preëmption, so dear to the hearts of westerners, was established by an act intended to be permanent and of general application.[1] It was further enacted that the proceeds of sales of public lands should be distributed among the states provided that the tariff rates

---

[1] A squatter was granted the right to purchase the quarter-section on which he lived at the minimum rate of $1.25 per acre, when the lands were offered for sale by the government, before any other would-be purchaser was allowed to bid.

were not raised above the twenty-per-cent level fixed by the Compromise of 1833. Clay agreed to the proviso because he believed that, if once the principle of distribution was accepted by Congress, he might later induce that body to repeal the restricting clause.

Clay underestimated Tyler's deep-seated convictions. In 1842 Congress twice passed measures for raising the tariff while retaining the distribution feature, but both bills were vetoed. Forced to decide between a high tariff and distribution, the Whigs chose the former. On August 30, 1842, they enacted a law which rendered inoperative the distribution clause in the act of 1841, by restoring the tariff duties to the general level of those of 1832. The new law was generally satisfactory to the protectionists, and could be justified in the eyes of others because of deficiencies in the existing revenues.

These concessions and compromises had sadly marred the program advanced by Clay. An open break was now precipitated between Tyler and the Clay Whigs by the struggle to create a new centralized bank. No measure was more important in the eyes of Clay's followers, but it was scarcely to be expected that they could win the approval of a man of Tyler's constitutional views. When he vetoed a bill in August, 1841, for creating a "Fiscal Bank," they tried to erect a "Fiscal Corporation." This new measure was framed with an insincere show of effort to meet his supposed objections, and proved no more acceptable, but his second veto brought down upon his head a tempest of wrath and charges of party treachery. In a formal manifesto the Whig members of Congress disavowed all further political connection with him. The members of the cabinet resigned, except Webster, who lingered on until May 8, 1843, chiefly because he wished to complete certain delicate negotiations with Great Britain (see page 588).

The President, repudiated by the party which had elected

him, reorganized his cabinet by the appointment of five former Democrats, who had left their party for the same reasons
as himself. The stormy contests of this administration killed
the bank project beyond possibility of resurrection, and
robbed the distribution question of its vitality as a Whig
issue. In the absence of the Independent Treasury, state
banks were once more resorted to as depositories of the public
funds.

THE UNITED STATES AND CANADA, 1837–1842

In international affairs the anomalous position of the
Texan Republic, refused annexation by the United States
and denied recognition by Mexico, continued to excite attention in the United States, but the most critical relations in
these years were with our neighbor to the north, Canada.
One set of difficulties was a by-product of the Canadian rebellion of 1837. In 1791 the greater part of Canada had been
divided into two provinces, each with its own government:
Lower Canada, controlled by descendants of the original
French settlers along the St. Lawrence, and Upper Canada,
north of the Great Lakes, populated largely by Loyalists who
had fled from the United States during the Revolutionary
War. In the former province racial antipathy and religious
jealousy were productive of much ill feeling; in the latter the
pioneer farmers became increasingly resentful of the selfish
sway of the large landed interest and the Anglican clergy.

In 1837 the smouldering discontent flared up in an armed
attempt for independence. The uprising had slight popular
support and was easily crushed by Great Britain, but while it
lasted, it aroused much sympathy in the United States. Furthermore, it proved to be a turning point in the evolution of
British colonial policy, for, on the basis of an investigation
made by Lord Durham, Upper and Lower Canada were

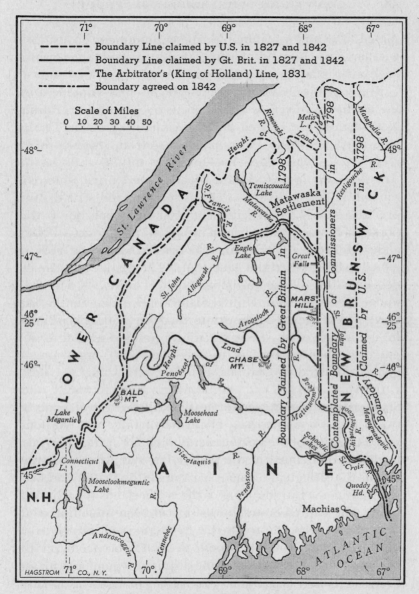

THE MAINE BOUNDARY CONTROVERSY

joined in 1840, for common purposes, under one government with large autonomous powers. Modern Canada thus owes its beginning to an unsuccessful revolt.

The Van Buren administration did its best to prevent the use of American soil as a base of insurrectionary operations. Nevertheless, the United States became involved in December, 1837, when the *Caroline,* an American steamer in the rebel service, was seized by Canadian militia while on the American side of the Niagara River. One United States citizen was killed, and the vessel was set afire and sent drifting over the Falls. The excitement aroused among our border population was presently intensified by the arrest of Alexander McLeod, a Canadian, who boasted in a New York saloon of having killed the American. The British government demanded his release on the plea that, if guilty, he had acted under orders, but the United States replied that the Federal Government lacked authority to interfere with the proceedings of a state court. The situation promised to lead to serious consequences, but fortunately the New York court acquitted McLeod in October, 1841.[1]

In April, 1842, Lord Ashburton arrived in the United States as special minister to clear up all matters at issue between the two countries. The chief of these was the long-vexed question of the northeastern boundary, which had been inadequately defined in the treaty of 1783. After earlier attempts to reach an agreement had failed, the matter had been referred in 1827 to the King of the Netherlands for adjudication. The United States, however, had been unwilling to accept the settlement proposed. In 1838–1839, armed collisions, dignified as "the Aroostook War," occurred on the Maine border in a portion of the disputed region, and for the

---

[1] Webster, in order to prevent the same difficulty from rising in the future, secured an act of Congress providing that a subject of a foreign power on trial in a state court might be brought into a United States court on a writ of *habeas corpus.*

time being, the northern frontier bristled with warlike preparations.

The adjustment of the boundary question proved to be a complicated matter since Maine and Massachusetts insisted on being represented in the negotiations along with the Federal Government.[1] But all difficulties were eventually surmounted. The treaty, signed on August 9, 1842, established a compromise line somewhat less favorable to the United States than the one proposed by the King of the Netherlands. To offset this disadvantage, the people of Maine received special trading privileges in the adjoining province of New Brunswick, and the United States agreed to make special payments to Maine and Massachusetts. Thus, for the first time, the northeastern boundary was defined in intelligible terms, and no disputes of importance have since arisen concerning it. Two other provisions of the treaty arranged for joint action of the two countries in suppressing the slave trade and for the extradition of criminals.

SELECT BIBLIOGRAPHY

The Rise of the Whigs. A helpful discussion of the subject in its general bearings appears in Fiske, *Essays Historical and Literary*, I. The tangled relations of the southern Whigs with the national organization are straightened out in Cole, *The Whig Party in the South*. The operations of the party in two northern states receive special study in Fox, *The Decline of Aristocracy in the Politics of New York,* and Mueller, *The Whig Party in Pennsylvania*.

The story of the western Democrat who won the vice-presidency in 1836 is told by Meyer, in *Life and Times of Colonel R. M. Johnson*.

The Land Question. For a connected account of the development of public-land policy, see Sato, *History of the Land Ques-*

---

[1] When Maine separated from Massachusetts, the latter retained part ownership of Maine's public lands, a considerable portion of which lay in the disputed region.

tion in the United States. The intricate politics of the land question is given penetrating analysis in Wellington, *The Political and Sectional Influence of the Public Lands, 1828–1842.* The history of the land question is carried forward in Stephenson, *Political History of the Public Lands, from 1840 to 1862.* Paxson, *History of the American Frontier,* should also be consulted.

Van Buren and the Money Question. Van Buren's presidential policies are sympathetically expounded in Shepard, *Martin Van Buren.* Political rather than economic in its interest is Alexander, *The American Talleyrand* (Van Buren). Johnson and Van Metre, *Principles of Railroad Transportation,* and Jones, *Principles of Railway Transportation,* contain useful information on early railway development.

For an understanding of fiscal problems, Dewey, *Financial History of the United States,* and *State Banking before the Civil War;* Scott, *The Repudiation of State Debts;* Bourne, *The History of the Surplus Revenue of 1837;* and Kinley, *The Independent Treasury of the United States and its Relations to the Banks of the Country,* are of special value.

The Overthrow of the Democrats. The picturesque features of the campaign of 1840 have made it a favorite subject for the standard historians and the biographers of the period. As in the case of all other campaigns to 1916, a convenient summary appears in Stanwood, *A History of the Presidency.* A special work written from the Whig point of view, with source extracts, is Norton, *The Great Revolution of 1840.*

The Quarrel between Tyler and the Whigs. Fiske discusses the Whig schism in his *Essays Historical and Literary,* I. Tyler, *The Letters and Times of the Tylers,* gives a strong presentation of the Tyler case. Recent reëxaminations of the controversy are given by Chitwood, in *John Tyler,* Lambert, in *Presidential Politics,* and Poage, in *Henry Clay and the Whig Party.*

The United States and Canada, 1837–1842. The evolution of Canadian self-government forms the theme of Tilby, *British North America, 1763–1867,* and Morison, *British Supremacy and Canadian Self-Government, 1839–1854.* Tiffany, *Relations of the United States to the Canadian Rebellion of 1837–1838,* is the most satisfactory treatment of this subject. For a detailed study of the boundary dispute, Sprague, *The Northeastern Boundary*

Controversy and the Aroostook War, and Burrage, *Maine in the Northeastern Boundary Controversy,* should be consulted. Callahan, *American Foreign Policy in Canadian Relations,* is a scholarly work on the whole subject of the relations of these Anglo-American neighbors.

Chapter XXVI

THE RISE OF THE COMMON MAN

THE democratic revolution which brought Jackson to the presidency was part of a movement which affected the entire western world. In France a revolution led by Lafayette drove out Charles X in 1830 and set up a middle-class monarchy resting upon a popular although highly restricted suffrage. In the same year Belgium, which had been forced upon the king of Holland by the diplomats of Vienna, raised the flag of independence, and established a monarchy based upon the most liberal constitution on the European continent. In Germany, Italy, and Poland, revolutionary ardor flared up and achieved slight gains for democracy.

The changes that took place in Great Britain were perhaps the most significant of all. Additional civil and political rights were conferred upon the Roman Catholics in 1829. Three years later, Parliament enacted the Reform Law—one of the landmarks of English constitutional history. The scheme of representation in Parliament was made more equitable, and the landowners and merchants were required to share the franchise with householders in the towns. The electorate was nearly doubled by these changes, and the first great step was thus taken toward confiding the control of the government to all the people. Within two decades came other reforms, including the liberalization of the government of Canada, the abandonment of most of the old mercantilist practices, and protective legislation for women and children in industry.

THE AWAKENING OF LABOR

While the forces which democratized American political life were generated in large part by the conditions accompanying the westward spread of the population, the broader reform movement was thoroughly in harmony with the current of European development. The champions of British reform, especially, corresponded with American leaders and both gave and received inspiration and encouragement. Reformers of the thirties and forties believed in the perfectibility of mankind, and sought to emancipate the intellectual and spiritual as well as the material life of the masses. The masses, too, gave evidence of a new faith in the worth of the common man and strove not merely to preserve existing privileges but to extend them.

One important manifestation of the new attitude was the beginning of labor organization in the urban centers of New England and the middle states. Industrial conditions were changing. In the earlier days skilled work had been carried on under simple conditions. A youth learned a trade during an apprenticeship of several years, and was then prepared to take his part in the bustling life of the town as an independent workman or "journeyman." Owning the simple tools of his trade, he sometimes associated himself with other journeymen under the direction of a "master workman," and worked with them on terms of personal intimacy and substantial economic equality. If the trade was of an indoor nature, the work was usually performed in the house of one of the workmen.

Such craftsmen were content to supply the needs of their own small communities. But the westward spread of population and the extension of highways and canals to every part of the country vastly widened the potential market. The new conditions called for the capitalist, who could purchase and hold large quantities of raw materials and extend attractive terms of credit to customers.   Few workmen or groups of workmen possessed the necessary capital, and as a result enterprising men who had never themselves been workmen took the lead in the expansion of industry.   Seeking profits, they bought from the workmen who produced most cheaply; and since women and children worked at lower wages than men, they were drawn into the trades in unprecedented numbers.

In consequence, the skilled workers found themselves dependent for employment upon the favor of the "merchant-capitalist," and the new conditions of competition demanded longer hours of labor while wages fell.   The work day ordinarily extended from "dark to dark," which meant an average of about twelve hours, six days a week, the year round. Such conditions prevailed throughout the towns of the northern seaboard, and to a lesser degree in a few western towns like Cincinnati, Louisville, and Pittsburgh.

In those parts of New England and the middle states where the factory system had taken root in the textile industries, the lot of the wage-earners was even harder.   Before 1814, the simple processes of spinning and weaving had been largely carried on in the home by the housewife and her children, to supply local needs.   Then the introduction of the power loom inaugurated the "industrial revolution," and the factory system replaced the simpler domestic industry.   Men who had large capital owned costly machines housed in great structures where they were driven by water or steam power. The workers became wage-earners, dependent upon the factory owner and subject to his dictation as to wages, hours, and other conditions of work.

The factories, with a few exceptions, were gloomy buildings without proper ventilation, light, or sanitation.   The wages were low; the work day long. In 1831 about sixty per cent of all workers in cotton mills of the Atlantic seaboard from Virginia northward were women. Seven per cent were children under twelve years of age. The plight of the little workers was not overstated in an address issued by the workingmen of Massachusetts in 1834: "To look at the pale and dirty, and spiritless beings, as they pour out of the factory to their hurried meals at the sound of a bell; and . . . to see the lazy motion of their jaded limbs, and the motionless expression of their woebegone countenances, must give a pang to the feeling heart which can never be forgotten."

Since the mills depended for their motive power upon near-by waterfalls or easily available deposits of "stone coal" (anthracite) , the introduction of the factory system stimulated the growth of cities at strategic points. Thus, the city of Lowell, Massachusetts, which in 1820 had only 250 people, possessed in 1840 a population of over 20,000, collected there largely to work in the mills. In such cities the wage-earners dwelt in congested quarters amidst surroundings which were unwholesome physically and morally.

Other conditions not directly connected with the problem of making a living imposed hardships on the common people. Many laws were survivals from earlier times when the idea of discrimination between social classes was universally accepted. Thus, educational advantages were virtually denied to the masses of the people, either through lack of provision for free, public schools, or because the long working hours of child wage-earners made attendance impossible. In 1833 probably one million children from six to fifteen years of age were not in any school; eighty thousand of these were in the state of New York.

The militia laws were another source of discontent. The well-to-do could escape service through payment of a fine, while the man less fortunately situated must serve or go to prison. Furthermore, state laws continued to provide imprisonment as the penalty for indebtedness, and debtors' prisons swallowed thousands of worthy but unfortunate men. Legal fees were so high that poor people were discouraged from seeking protection for their rights in the courts.

The banking system also aroused bitter criticism from the working class. Chartered by the states, these banks were permitted to conduct business without adequate safeguards for the depositors or the public, so that laborers were often forced to accept their wages in bank notes of doubtful or fluctuating value.

The campaign of the wage-earners to secure greater rights for their class began in the latter part of the twenties. Before that time chronic discontent had occasionally flared up in strikes. Attempts had been made also to form local trade unions, but these had soon withered. Individuals sometimes escaped from the hard conditions in the East by moving to the frontier; but most of the wage-earners were prevented from taking this step by large families, poverty, or lack of ambition. They were accordingly forced to work out their salvation at home.

In the year of Jackson's election to the presidency, a "Working Men's" party was organized in Philadelphia. The next year one appeared in New York, and within a short time Working Men's parties of varying strength were to be found in all the seaboard states north of Maryland. These local parties nominated candidates for local and state offices and for Congress, conducted campaigns, and founded more than fifty newspapers to acquaint the public with the grievances of the wage-earning class. They lacked incentive to combine into a national organization, for they were primarily interested in reforms that could be secured through action of the states. They sought legislation that would make life less burdensome for the poor people and create broader opportunities for the common man. The main items in their program were summarized by the *Mechanics' Free Press* of Philadelphia on April 16, 1831: "Universal education, abolition of chartered monopolies, equal taxation, revision or abolition of the militia system, a less expensive law system, all officers to be elected directly by the people, a lien law for laborers, no legislation on religion." The abolition of imprisonment for debt might properly have been included in this list.

Most of the Working Men's parties soon disappeared, but the "Workies" succeeded in arousing the public to the need of changes in the existing laws. Their voting strength was very largely taken over by the Democratic party, which under Jackson's vigorous leadership combated all class distinctions, and most of the reforms which they sought were carried into effect by action either of the states or the Federal Government.

The dissolution of the Working Men's parties was followed by a more intensive organization along economic lines. Trade unions or "trade societies" sprang up in many cities. At first these were unconnected, but in 1833 New York succeeded in linking all the societies of the city into a stable central body called a "General Trades' Union." Other large cities did likewise, and in 1834 the General Trades' Unions of the various cities joined together in a central federation or "National Trades' Union," not unlike the American Federation of Labor of our own day.

About the same time, some of the stronger crafts, like the handloom weavers and the printers, began to organize on a national basis as separate trades. By 1836 the union membership in the cities of the northern seaboard had climbed to something like three hundred thousand. Through the use of the strike and other methods of pressure, they succeeded in securing more humane conditions of employment. By winning a decisive strike in Philadelphia in 1835, involving seventeen different trades and occupations, the organized labor forces succeeded in establishing, in the leading mechanical branches, their most cherished reform, a ten-hour workday. In 1840 President Van Buren ordered the adoption of the ten-hour day on all government works, giving further impetus to the reform. The question of the statutory limitation by the states of the factory workday was much discussed, without result until 1847, when New Hampshire enacted the first ten-hour law for factory labor. In the next five years similar measures were adopted in Pennsylvania, Maine, Rhode Island, Ohio, and California.

THE STRUGGLE FOR FREE PUBLIC SCHOOLS

The activity of the working class and their zeal for humanitarian reform were indispensable factors in the forward movements of the time. The struggle of labor for democracy in education merits special consideration. Its success far exceeded that attained by similar efforts abroad, although few questions have aroused more bitter controversy in America. Nor have any been of more significance for the welfare of the people.

In the opening years of the nineteenth century, the idea prevailed that only a minority of the population needed to be educated, and this function was still regarded as a duty of the Church or as a matter of private enterprise rather than as an obligation of government. Although the principle of free public education had been recognized since colonial times, especially in New England, even there the practice fell sadly short of the theory. Wherever there were free schools they were regarded as charitable institutions for pauper children. The instruction offered was extremely rudimentary. A person who had mastered the "three R's" ranked as an educated man, while the lack of this knowledge was by no means a matter of reproach.

The spread of manhood suffrage and the growing importance of the common man led to a new conception of education. Clear-sighted statesmen perceived the danger of universal suffrage based on universal ignorance. Said one: "We think it more important that the many should be well informed than that the few should be learned." De Witt Clinton in New York, Thaddeus Stevens in Pennsylvania, and Abraham Lincoln in Illinois were among those to raise their voices for an educated electorate as a safeguard of democratic government. Educational leaders like Horace Mann in Massachusetts and Henry Barnard in Connecticut and Rhode Island gave a wise direction and practical application to the new trend. The efforts of these reformers were supported by the vigorous and incessant agitation carried on by organized labor in the cities of the northern seaboard. The labor leaders demanded free, tax-supported schools open to the children of all classes without taint of charity. "Our government is republican; our education should be equally so," declared the Workingmen's Committee of Philadelphia in 1830 after five months spent in investigating educational conditions in Pennsylvania.

The great battle for free public education was fought out in the second quarter of the nineteenth century. The friends of the new system were at first regarded as visionaries or dangerous fanatics, while they in turn considered their opponents as conscienceless conservatives and foes of progress. A Rhode Island farmer threatened to shoot Barnard if he ever caught him on his land advocating "such heresy as the partial confiscation of one man's property to educate another man's child." In state after state the agitation was conducted. Hard legislative fights were waged, and bitter contests took place with religious and private-school interests which held that their vested rights were being disturbed. The increase of taxable property during the years of struggle favored the cause by making possible a support by government which had not previously been practicable.

The first steps in the direction of reform were tentative and experimental; various substitutes for government owner-ship and operation were tried. For example, denominational and pauper schools were subsidized out of public funds, pri-vate schools were exempted from taxation, grants of land were made for their endowment. But gradually these makeshifts gave way in one state after another to free tax-supported education, provided by legislative enactment. Throughout the North and the Northwest, by 1850, the battle may be said to have been won. America led the world in this respect; and even today few countries can compare with the United States in facilities for free education.

The demand for tax-supported schools embraced secondary as well as elementary instruction, and led to a great enrich-ment of the curriculum. Emphasis was placed on the study of civics, and states passed laws prescribing the subject of his-tory. The South, with its plantation economy, caste system, and Negro slavery, lagged in its response to these new influ-ences. Some progress was made, but the real awakening did not occur in that section until after the Civil War.

Higher education also received a tremendous impulse in this period. The great pioneers in this field were the reli-gious denominations, though they were often aided by land grants and subsidies from the states. Between 1820 and 1850, eighty-seven private colleges were founded in all parts of the country, and in the next decade the number was swollen by ninety-one more. It is clear that the public school system had to be firmly established before the people could envisage higher education as a proper function of the government. Nevertheless, beginning with the University of Virginia in 1819, fifteen state universities were founded by 1850, mostly in the West and the newer parts of the South. They were as yet inadequately supported, and the great epoch of state-university expansion did not come until after the Civil War.

HUMANITARIAN CRUSADES

The new spirit of the times was evinced also by a new sense of public responsibility for the weak and unfortunate members of society and for the betterment of morals. Up to this epoch the use of intoxicants was well nigh universal. Liquor was even served at funerals, and was sold openly from booths at the chief colleges on public days. In 1826 began the first organized movement against strong drink. Starting in Boston with the formation of societies pledged to total abstinence, it spread so rapidly that within five years more than one thousand of these bands were formed in all parts of the country. After 1840 the agitation fell under the direction of the "Washington Societies," which soon recruited a membership of half a million.

The policy of self-imposed abstinence, however, proved disappointing in its results, and under the leadership of Neal Dow of Maine, the reformers began to demand the passage of state prohibitory legislation. As a consequence Maine in 1846 passed the first prohibition law in American history. By the end of 1856, thirteen states in the North and West had abolished the sale of alcoholic stimulants. But in most of these states the laws were later repealed or modified,[1] and prohibition did not again become a vital issue for a generation.

This period saw substantial progress toward prison reform, the care of the insane, and abolition of imprisonment for debt. It was the era also of the movement for the abolition of slavery, which subject will be discussed at length in the next

---

[1] New Hampshire and Vermont remained "dry" until 1904; and Maine, save from 1856 to 1858, retained prohibition until the Eighteenth Amendment was adopted (1919).

chapter. It may here be noted, however, that in 1835 Oberlin
College threw open its doors to Negro students. It thus became one of the earliest coracial colleges, and was soon reputed to be a center of abolitionist propaganda. The idealism underlying these humanitarian efforts was mirrored in
numerous experiments in social organization. These enterprises received their main inspiration from the writings and
teachings of the leaders of the rising Socialist movement in
Europe, while cheap land and sparse settlement permitted a
degree of experimentation which was impossible in the
crowded Old World. In 1825 Robert Owen, a Scotch manufacturer, established at New Harmony, Indiana, a community
where labor and property were to be in common.

Such communities multiplied under the influence of Albert
Brisbane's book, *The Social Destiny of Man* (1840), and
Horace Greeley's editorials in the *New York Tribune*. Both
men were disciples of the French Socialist, Charles Fourier.
More than forty projects were attempted between 1840 and
1850, all based upon an illimitable faith in humanity, and,
like the Owenite communities, all unsuccessful in their effort
to transform society overnight. Of these, the best known was
Brook Farm, near Boston, which counted among its members
and friends Emerson, Thoreau, Hawthorne, and Margaret
Fuller. It continued from 1841 to 1846; subsequently Hawthorne gently satirized it in *The Blithedale Romance*.

Another effect of the idealism of the time was the launching
of the first organized non-sectarian movement for the prevention of war. In 1815 peace societies had been formed in New
York, Ohio, and Massachusetts, the first of the kind in the
world. The movement spread to other states, and in 1828
the American Peace Society was founded in New York by
William Ladd, through a merger of nearly fifty local organizations. Its program called for a congress of nations, meeting periodically, the codification of international law, and the

establishment of a permanent world court with power to make decisions, though not to enforce them, in disputes arising between nations.

Meantime the peace movement had taken root abroad, particularly in England, and in 1843 a congress held in London was attended by thirty-seven American delegates. An international congress, held at Brussels in 1848, endorsed the American peace plan, and for some time congresses were held almost yearly. The hopes of the peace advocates rose high, but the movement was badly disrupted by the Crimean War (1854–1856) and the American Civil War. The organized peace movement did not become important again until the first decade of the twentieth century.

THE BEGINNING OF THE WOMAN'S RIGHTS MOVEMENT

The democratic idealism which freed white men from so many of their ancient fetters awakened women to the realization that they were denied many of the rights enjoyed by men. Their status was still fixed by the principles of the old English common law and social custom. The unmarried woman, in most respects, enjoyed the same legal rights as a man; but custom required her to marry early, and with marriage she virtually lost her separate identity in the eyes of the law. She forfeited title to all her personal property, even if it had been acquired before matrimony, and she was deprived of all control over her real property for the duration of the marriage. A husband had the right to control his wife's conduct and punish her as he did his children, and to appropriate to his own uses any wages that she earned outside the home.

The father was the sole guardian of the children during his lifetime, and could dispose of them by will at his death. Conversely, the husband was held responsible for many of the crimes and torts committed by his wife, and was entitled to

collect damages for injuries inflicted upon her. Feminine
education was considered unnecessary, except in the well-
to-do classes, and even there it was confined to needlework,
dancing, and the cultivation of manners and morals. Susan
B. Anthony's teachers refused to instruct her in long division,

THE ORATOR OF THE DAY DENOUNCING THE LORDS OF CREATION
Harper's Weekly, 1859

and were at a loss to understand why a girl should want to
learn it. Of course, women were not permitted to vote.

The call to women to awake began with the visit of Frances
Wright, a Scotchwoman of advanced views, to this country
in 1827. Her appearance before audiences to deliver lectures
on slavery, theology, and woman's rights shocked the public,
unaccustomed to seeing a woman in such a rôle; but her example soon aroused to action such great figures in the American feminist movement as Sarah and Angelina Grimké from
South Carolina, Lucretia Mott, a Quaker of Philadelphia,
and Mrs. Elizabeth Cady Stanton of New York. Keenly alive

to the humanitarian trend of the times, these women devoted their energies not only to feminism but also to antislavery, labor welfare, and temperance reform. They had to brave the contempt of most of their own sex as well as that of the men, and they stood in constant peril of physical violence at the hands of mobs because of their bold and "unwomanly" conduct.

On July 19, 1848, at Seneca Falls, New York, the first woman's rights convention in the world launched a militant crusade. The delegates drew up a declaration patterned after the Declaration of Independence. They asserted "that all men and women are created equal," and demanded equality with the male sex before the law, in educational and economic opportunities, and in voting. Though greeted by the ridicule and condemnation of press and pulpit, woman's rights conventions came to be almost yearly occurrences until the outbreak of the Civil War.

The feminist leaders were not altogether without friends among the men. Prominent at their meetings were the great antislavery agitators, William Lloyd Garrison and Wendell Phillips. Ralph Waldo Emerson, John Greenleaf Whittier, and Horace Greeley wrote and lectured in their behalf. Young Abraham Lincoln, beginning a legislative career in Illinois, announced his approval of the principal of sharing the government with those who bore its burdens, "by no means excluding the women."

Although the period was one of agitation rather than of achievement, there was some improvement in the position of women. In 1839 Mississippi granted to married women the control of their own property, and similar laws were enacted in the next decade by Texas, Indiana, Pennsylvania, New York, California, and Wisconsin. In 1821 Emma Willard had opened a seminary for girls at Troy, New York, and in 1837 the first women's seminary of college rank, Mt.

Holyoke, was opened by Mary Lyon in Massachusetts. These marked the beginnings of higher education for women. By 1860 the number of such institutions increased to sixty-one.

Coeducation was an even more venturesome undertaking; Oberlin College in 1833, Urbana University in 1850, and Antioch College in 1853, all in Ohio, led the way. Not till the University of Iowa acted in 1858 were women admitted to any state university. These were promising beginnings, but women were still far from the goal of sex equality. A long and discouraging struggle loomed ahead before success was to crown their efforts.

THE IMPROVING STANDARD OF LIFE

The welfare of the masses and their comfort of living were greatly improved by a number of important inventions between 1825 and 1850. Kerosene lamps were devised, the friction match superseded the use of flint, improved cookstoves were put on the market. The shortage of wage labor in the farming districts proved an incentive to the invention of labor-saving implements. After 1825 the threshing machine began to supplant the flail and roller, and shortly thereafter the Fairbanks platform scale, the mower, and the reaper were invented.

In 1825 the first successful attempt was made to generate steam with anthracite coal, and in 1837 the first furnace for smelting iron with anthracite was built. The English "Great Western," a wooden-hulled side-wheeler with coal to heat its boilers, inaugurated regular steam navigation across the Atlantic in 1838, although the bulk of ocean freight continued to be carried in American sailing vessels.

Outside of the plantation states, the material conditions of American life were singularly even, and generous in promise. "Go-ahead-ativeness" characterized the typical American, causing Dickens to remark, "whenever an Englishman would

cry 'All right!' an American cries 'Go ahead!' which is somewhat expressive of the national character of the two countries." A livelihood might be gained by almost every industrious person, and few great private fortunes existed. Most
business and industry still operated on a small scale. The
money for great works of internal improvement and development came chiefly from foreign investors, especially British
capitalists.

The difficulty of maintaining a united nationality in the
face of rapid geographical expansion was somewhat eased by
the mechanical ingenuity of the people. Railway mileage
steadily progressed from the first steam railroad of 1829. By
1850 one could travel over the iron highways from Maine to
North Carolina, from the Atlantic seaboard to Buffalo on
Lake Erie, and from the western end of Lake Erie to Chicago
or Cincinnati. The electric telegraph, invented in 1835 by
S. F. B. Morse, was first practically applied in 1844, and from
the outset possessed vast social and political significance. In
1847 the rotary printing press, devised by Richard M. Hoe,
revolutionized newspaper publishing, and made possible the
important position the press now has in American life.

RELIGIOUS READJUSTMENTS

The stern Calvinistic theology, already tempered by the
Great Awakening of the eighteenth century, now felt again
the softening influence of a new spirit. Under the leadership
of W. E. Channing, Unitarianism was organized about 1825
by dissenting members of the Congregational Church, on a
creed opposing the somber doctrines of total depravity and
predestination and affirming the infinite possibilities of man's
development. The new system exerted an influence altogether out of proportion to the number of its adherents, and
attained its loftiest expression in the philosophic movement
known as "Transcendentalism," of which Emerson was the

foremost exponent. The spread of Unitarianism throughout New England was checked only when men like Horace Bushnell sought to reconcile the Calvinistic theology of the old Congregational system with the gentler humanitarianism of the new era.

Other sects experienced similar changes. The Quakers were rent in twain by the teaching of Elias Hicks. The Campbells, father and son, led a departure from the old Presbyterian order. Universalism began a rapid expansion, and in the West there occurred a swift growth of the Methodists, Baptists, Presbyterians, and other denominations which were able to satisfy the spiritual cravings of a people impatient of theological hair-splitting. Itinerant preachers penetrated into the wilderness, bringing messages of hope and faith to the isolated inhabitants. Bishop Francis Asbury of the Methodist Church (died in 1816), forerunner of the group of leaders of the 1830's and 1840's, traveled nearly three hundred thousand miles in the course of his labors, preached more than sixteen thousand sermons, and ordained some four thousand ministers. In the more settled western communities, the religious enthusiasm of the frontiersmen found fervid expression in revivals and camp-meetings.

Of the many new sects that arose in this period, the most extraordinary, in the light of its subsequent history, was the Church of Jesus Christ of Latter-day Saints, commonly known as the Mormons. It was organized at Fayette, New York, in 1830, by Joseph Smith, who asserted that he had found, inscribed on golden plates, the story of a Hebrew prophet who had led his followers from Jerusalem in the year 600 B.C., to the western shores of America. In time, greatly increased in numbers, this company spread northeastward as far as the present state of New York, but became extinct about 400 A.D. A prophet, Moroni by name, a last survivor, wrote the record of the wanderings, and as a resurrected being, gave it to Smith. The sect, though Christian in its tenets, professed too many odd beliefs to be acceptable in established American communities, accustomed as they were to innovations in religion. Driven from state to state, its members were finally (1847) led by Brigham Young to the "promised land" in the valley of Great Salt Lake, Utah. There they built up a thriving commonwealth.

THE FIRST FLOWERING OF AMERICAN LITERATURE

It was not strange that the spirit of national self-confidence and democratic aspiration should find utterance in a great outpouring of literature. The decade of the thirties brought a full harvest of American letters. As might be expected, the chief center of literary activity was the old settled portion of the country; Massachusetts was particularly prominent. Henry Wadsworth Longfellow, John Greenleaf Whittier, Oliver Wendell Holmes, and James Russell Lowell commenced at this epoch their creative work, glorifying the commonplace things of life in poems of simple and genuine feeling. Emerson began to preach the doctrine of individualism and the nobility of man in imperishable prose and verse. Nathaniel Hawthorne and Edgar Allan Poe exemplified the versatility of American genius by giving literary expression to the somber and supernatural in man's experience, the former finding his inspiration in the annals of New England Puritanism, and the latter in the self-absorption of a morbid mind. Irving had already discovered the possibilities of the short story as a form of literary art; at the hands of Hawthorne and Poe America reached preëminence in literature of this type.

The trend of the times awakened a new interest in the history of the Republic, and marked the beginnings of his-

torical scholarship. In the thirties Jared Sparks took up the
task of editing historical documents, publishing, notably, collections of the writings of Washington and Franklin and the
diplomatic correspondence of the Revolution (and carefully
eliminating or softening such phrases or allusions in the writings of the Fathers as seemed to him unsuited to their dignity). He planned to write a history of the Revolution, but
it was never completed. In 1834, however, George Bancroft
published the first volume of a history of the United States
from the earliest discoveries to the adoption of the Constitution—the first comprehensive American history based upon
a laborious examination of source materials. Unfortunately,
it was colored by the author's enthusiastic championship of
democratic institutions. Before the close of the decade Irving
and William H. Prescott had amply shown, in their works on
Spain and Spanish America, the ability of American scholars
to write history with literary distinction.

In 1837 Emerson delivered a Phi Beta Kappa address at
Harvard on "The American Scholar," which has been called
"America's intellectual Declaration of Independence." In
view of the achievements just sketched, this eloquent appeal
for individuality, sincerity, and realism in the intellectual
life of America was an expression of the new literary ideals
of the whole group of contemporary writers.

Although the authors mentioned derived their enduring
fame from their writings, most of them took an active interest
in the humanitarian and political struggles of the age. Whittier was preëminently the poet laureate of the antislavery
crusade, throwing himself into the contest with a militant
fervor belied by his calm Quaker exterior. Longfellow published his *Poems on Slavery* in 1842. Lowell acted for a time
as editor of the *Pennsylvania Freeman,* and later mercilessly
lampooned the proslavery politicians in the *Biglow Papers*

(1848). Henry D. Thoreau, our first great nature writer, went to jail during the Mexican War rather than pay a tax which would help the government in what he regarded as a war of conquest.

Cooper showed his interest in the agitation for political democracy by writing a series of propagandist novels, now forgotten, in behalf of the cause in the early forties. Bancroft was an ardent anti-bank man; drawn into the maelstrom of Democratic politics, he was rewarded by Polk with a cabinet position, and subsequently given various diplomatic appointments. In the case of William Cullen Bryant, a brilliant poetic career was seriously hampered by his distinguished editorship of the *New York Evening Post* from 1826 to 1878.

As protagonists of the democratic movement, Bryant, Bancroft, and other literary men explained and interpreted Jacksonian Democracy to the educated classes of the East, and helped to make democracy respectable in their eyes. Even the unworldly Hawthorne held various political offices in the customs service, and when, in 1852, he wrote a campaign biography of his college friend, Franklin Pierce, he was repaid by the lucrative post of consul at Liverpool.

SELECT BIBLIOGRAPHY

Democracy and Social Reform. Excellent chapters on the social, intellectual, and humanitarian aspects of the democratic upheaval may be found in Channing, *A History of the United States*, V, and McMaster, *A History of the People of the United States*, V. The entire volume by Fish, *Rise of the Common Man*, is devoted to these topics. They are discussed in smaller compass in Schlesinger, *New Viewpoints*, Chap. IX, and in Faulkner, *American Economic History*, Chap. XV. Branch, *The Sentimental Years*—a book which deserves a wide reading—interprets the activities of the middle class.

The Awakening of Labor. This subject is thoroughly discussed by Sumner and Mittelman in Commons, *History of Labour* *in the United States,* I. Good summary accounts appear in Beard, *A Short History of the American Labor Movement,* and Perlman, *A History of Trade Unionism in the United States.* See also Ware, *The Industrial Worker, 1840–1860.*

The Struggle for Free Public Schools. The educational awakening is set forth with reference to its social and political background in Cubberley, *Public Education in the United States.* Other works of value in this connection are Dexter, *A History of Education in the United States,* Brown, *The Making of Our Middle Schools,* and Slosson, *The American Spirit in Education.* The great fathers of the public school system are treated in Hinsdale, *Horace Mann and the Common School Revival in the United States,* and Monroe, *The Educational Labors of Henry Barnard.* See also Finney, *Brief History of the American Public School.* On the development of colleges and universities, the most important treatise is Thwing, *A History of Higher Education in America.*

Humanitarian Crusades. Much information concerning the temperance movement appears in Woolley and Johnson, *Temperance Progress of the Century,* Fehlandt, *A Century of Drink Reform in the United States,* and Clark, *History of the Temperance Reform in Massachusetts, 1813–1883.* Prison reform is historically considered in Wines, *Punishment and Reformation,* and McKelvey, *American Prisons.* Barnes, *A History of the Penal, Reformatory and Correctional Institutions of the State of New Jersey,* is a study of more than local importance. On the treatment of the insane, consult Hurd and others, *The Institutional Care of the Insane,* and Tiffany, *Life of Dorothea Lynde Dix.*

Detailed descriptions of the Utopian communities appear in Noyes, *History of American Socialisms,* Nordhoff, *The Communistic Societies of the United States,* and Hinds, *American Communities and Coöperative Colonies.* Noyes tells the story of his own boyhood in the Oneida Community in *My Father's House.* A succinct account may be found in Hillquit, *History of Socialism in the United States,* part 1. The early peace movement is best dealt with in Curti, *The American Peace Crusade,* and *Peace or War.* Galpin, *Pioneering for Peace,* is also a contribution. The subject is given a sketchy chapter in Moritzen, *The Peace Movement of America.*

The Beginning of the Woman's Rights Movement. The legal aspects receive attention in Hecker, *A Short History of Women's Rights*. Squire, *The Woman Movement in America,* and Bruce, *Woman in the Making of America,* though popular accounts, throw light on the early phases of the feminist movement. Graham, *Ladies in Revolt,* gives intimate pictures of the activities of the women engaged in the movement. See also Beard, *America through Women's Eyes,* and Spruill, *Women's Life and Work in the Southern Colonies.* The following biographies should be consulted: Marshall, *Dorothy Dix,* Anthony, *Margaret Fuller,* Birney, *The Grimké Sisters,* and Hallowell, *James and Lucretia Mott.* Hare, *The Greatest American Woman: Lucretia Mott,* adds little to Hallowell and is uncritical. See also Gamaliel Bradford's readable *Portraits of American Women.* Taylor, *Before Vassar Opened,* is a valuable work on the early history of higher education for women. A sketch of coeducation at Oberlin is given in Hosford, *Father Shipherd's Magna Charta.*

The Improving Standard of Life. For the inventions of the period, Byrn, *The Progress of Invention in the Nineteenth Century,* is very satisfactory. Iles, *Leading American Inventors,* and Thompson, *The Age of Invention,* tell the story of several important inventors and their work. Bogart, *Economic History,* gives an excellent compact account of economic conditions. The lighter phases of life are treated, in a somewhat flippant manner, in Minnigerode, *The Fabulous Forties.*

Religious Readjustments. Information regarding religious life and doctrinal controversy may be gleaned from Dorchester, *Christianity in the United States,* Bacon, *A History of American Christianity,* and Rowe, *The History of Religion in the United States.* The *American Church History Series* contains denominational histories and also an historical account of the Roman Catholic Church in the United States.

The First Flowering of American Literature. The literary awakening is a favorite theme of the historians of American letters, and is most fully treated in *The Cambridge History of American Literature.* A convenient summary is given by Pattee in *The First Century of American Literature.* A charming phase is charmingly recorded by Brooks, in *The Flowering of New Eng-*

land. Long, *American Literature,* is valuable for showing the relationship of political and social conditions to literature.

Interesting light is thrown on conditions in the United States by the observations of foreign visitors. See Tuckerman, *America and Her Commentators,* and Nevins, *American Social History as Recorded by British Travellers.*

Chapter XXVII

SLAVERY AND SECTIONALISM

THE GROWTH OF THE SLAVERY SYSTEM

FROM the time that Tyler found himself a President without a party to the crushing of the South on the battlefield in 1865, slavery was the overshadowing question in American politics. Many of the developments of these years were due solely to the normal and expanding energies of the American people, but such matters inevitably became entangled in the skein of sectional politics, and were usually dealt with from the standpoint of proslavery or antislavery advantage.

The formation of the black belts in the Southwest (see page 472) destroyed the unity of the transappalachian country; differences in climate, soil, economic interest, and social characteristics gradually divided the Mississippi Valley into opposing parts. Instead of the small frontier farm, the great plantation became the unit of economic and social life in the Southwest. The center of cotton cultivation shifted from the South Atlantic states. In 1824 the annual cotton production of the seaboard states was almost double that of the interior South, but by 1841 this ratio was reversed. From this time on, it is safe to regard the South, from the Atlantic to the Mississippi River and even beyond (save for the inarticulate poor white element) as a compact political unit agreeing on all fundamental policies affecting cotton culture and slavery, though still superficially divided in allegiance between the two great national parties. The northern states did not undergo a similar welding process, the frontier farming regions of the Northwest and the manufacturing and financial dis-

615

tricts of the older states differing in interests at several points.

Cotton culture was singularly adapted to the employment of slaves. The work was simple, requiring only primitive implements. It gave employment for nine months in the year, and permitted the use of women and children as well as "prime field hands." White overseers were able to superintend large gangs of laborers working at the same time. Under such circumstances the planters came to regard their material prosperity as inseparably connected with the system of forced labor. Unable to conceive of a free black population living harmoniously with the white race, the southerners of that day could not foresee that Negroes could be employed as wage-earners, and indeed that the cost to the planter under such circumstances would be considerably less.

With slavery grown profitable and forming the very foundation of the South's economic life, its political leaders, professional classes, and clergy ceased to deplore it as a thing of evil, and became ardent champions of the "peculiar institution." It was said to have the sanction both of the Bible and the Constitution. It was held to shower benefits upon the Negro, and was proclaimed as the only secure basis for white civilization. Its advocates were men of gentle breeding and fine character; their sincerity and good intentions are not to be judged by the conception of human rights that prevails in our own day. Indeed, southern publicists insisted that the relations of capital and labor were more humane under slavery than under the wage system of the North, where the factory hands earned a bare subsistence, toiled amidst unsanitary conditions, and suffered in old age from unemployment and poverty.

The question of the well-being of the Negroes under the system of enforced servitude cannot rightly be disposed of with a few generalizations. Nevertheless, it seems safe to say that the material conditions of slave life were considerably easier in the three decades prior to 1830 than in the three decades thereafter, and that at all times the house servants were better treated than the field hands. The old patriarchal system of plantation government, with easy-going methods of management and personal oversight of the slaves by a beloved master, was still characteristic of southern life in the earlier period.

After 1830, however, a change became apparent, not so much in the border slave states, where the Negroes were still regarded as a convenience rather than as an economic necessity, as in the states farther south where the "Cotton Kingdom" was strongly intrenched. With the introduction of large-scale methods of cotton production in the Lower South, the master ceased to supervise his slaves himself, employing instead professional overseers whose success was measured by their ability to exact a maximum amount of work. Under such a régime the system tended to become commercialized and to lose its patriarchal character.

Moreover, after a slave uprising in Virginia in 1831 (the Nat Turner rebellion) in which sixty whites were murdered, fear of similar insurrections led southern lawmakers to pass drastic restrictive legislation.[1] The determination of the planters to protect their labor system from the rising tide of antislavery propaganda in the North tended to increase the severity of these "Slave Codes."

Many planters nevertheless treated their slaves with great indulgence, and every provident master was mindful of the necessity of keeping them in efficient working condition. But instances of heartless cruelty are on record, and the system inevitably involved the frequent breaking of family ties. The most trenchant criticism of slavery, however, was not the ac-

[1] Some typical provisions forbade Negroes to carry guns, to be absent from the plantation without written permission, to be taught to read and write, or to assemble without the presence of a white man. The Slave Codes were most severe in the states having the largest number of blacks.

tual brutality of masters; the repression inherent in any system of human bondage was in itself a brutality. The slave was merely a piece of property, an "animated tool"; no effort was made to develop his higher capacities, his self-reliance, or his intellect.

Southern society was distinguished by a high degree of stratification. Of the five or six million white people in 1841, the number in slaveholding families formed about one third. In South Carolina, Alabama, Mississippi, and Louisiana, exclusive of the largest cities, the number reached one half of the total population. But only about two per cent of the slaveholding families owned great plantations and fifty or more slaves. This small fraction formed a highly privileged class, but its primacy was maintained by force of intellect, political acumen, and the social prestige which resulted. The generous life of the great planters was distinguished by a chivalry and hospitality the charm of which is still preserved in the traditions of the old South.

Next in the scale came the well-to-do farmers who owned only a few slaves, and the professional classes—the lawyers, physicians, clergymen, and teachers—who were dependent upon the aristocracy for their incomes and were in close alliance with them. Most of the farmers, however, were unprogressive and indigent, and made up a somewhat lower stratum in society. They lived in poor houses, their food was unwholesome, and in general their lives lacked comfort and refinement.

The most degraded members of the dominant race were the "poor whites," a poverty-stricken, slaveless, illiterate, outcast element which lived in remote valleys of the mountains or sought half-heartedly to wrest a livelihood from the lands which the planters had abandoned or refused to occupy. In a society differently composed, such folk might have found opportunities for employment and eventually for rising in the social and economic scale; but in a social organization which deemed manual toil a badge of inferiority, their lot was well nigh hopeless. Only once in a generation could a man of indomitable spirit, like Andrew Johnson of eastern Tennessee, break the fetters of poverty and ignorance that bound this class and reach high political station. Generally speaking, the "poor whites" were a happy-go-lucky set of people, and in political matters they were usually willing to follow the lead of their economic and social superiors.

With the passage of years, cotton culture and its labor system came to represent a vast investment of capital. From a crop of negligible importance, its production had grown in 1800 to about thirty-five million pounds; it rose to one hundred and sixty million pounds in 1820, and in the following twenty years leaped to more than eight hundred and thirty-four million. The monetary value of the crop in 1850 was $105,600,000, and at that date seven eighths of the world's supply was grown in the South. The slaves increased correspondingly in number and value. About the time of the invention of the cotton gin the price of a good field hand was $300, in 1828 it had become $800, and in 1853, $1200. In 1850 the value of slave property in the entire South amounted to more than one and one-quarter billion dollars.

Thus was built up the structure of cotton capitalism, as significant in its influence upon national destinies in the years before the Civil War as industrial capitalism has been in the period since. Inevitably the major purpose of southerners in national politics came to be the protection and enlargement of the vested interests represented by the cotton-slavery system. As will presently be seen, one of their main objects was to extend the cotton-growing area beyond its existing confines, for, because of the wasteful system of cropping land until it was exhausted, cotton culture was ever on the move, and unlimited quantities of fresh and fertile lands were required. Furthermore, the South needed new territory out of which additional slave states might be created to offset new free states. Antislavery northerners became quickly aware of this growing influence in national affairs; they called it the "Slave Power" or the "Slavocracy," and pictured it as a never-sleeping, malevolent conspiracy for proslavery aggrandizement.

THE RISE OF ANTISLAVERY AGITATION

Antislavery agitation in the North did not become militant until the fourth decade of the century. Prior to this time there existed abolitionist newspapers and societies, which conducted a quiet, persistent campaign of education on the subject, trusting thereby to bring a gradual end to slavery. Much of this work was carried on by people who lived in the slave states or neighboring ones, and who hoped to persuade the slaveowners to adopt voluntary emancipation. The chief organization of the kind was the American Colonization Society, but the impracticability of its program quickly became apparent. Indeed, antislavery men soon began to charge that the slaveholders favored the plan as a means of getting rid of ambitious and troublesome individual bondsmen.

The new phase of abolitionism, which began about 1830, owed much to the dynamic democratic idealism of the times and to the awakened interest in social justice for all classes. It was, in a sense, the American counterpart of a world-wide movement which had achieved the abolition of human bondage in Mexico and the other Spanish-American republics in the preceding decade, and which inspired Parliament in 1833 to provide for gradual emancipation in the British West Indies. The new antislavery movement in America was combative and uncompromising, defying all the constitutional and legal guarantees protecting the slavery system.

It took no account of the difficulties and dangers involved in wholesale liberation, and valued emancipation above the preservation of the Union.

These extremists found a leader in William Lloyd Garrison, a young man of Massachusetts nativity, who possessed the fanatical heroism of a martyr with the crusading ability of a successful demagogue. He was ably seconded by Wendell Phillips, who was ostracized by his Boston friends when he lent his eloquent tongue to the unpopular cause. In 1831, Garrison founded his newspaper, the *Liberator,* and this at once became a rostrum from which he poured vitriolic editorials upon the slaveowners and all their practices. In 1832, he established the New England Anti-Slavery Society, and within a year this grew into a national body called the "American Anti-Slavery Society," pledged to a program of immediate, uncompensated emancipation.

Garrison's sensational methods awakened many northerners to the evil character of an institution which they had long since come to regard as established and unchangeable.[1] Not all of them, however, were willing to subscribe to his law-defying tactics, for they held that reform should be accomplished by legal and peaceful means. The chief spokesman of this more moderate element was William Ellery Channing, a Unitarian minister of Boston.

Still another antislavery element consisted of quiet churchgoing citizens, who, under cover of night, helped to spirit escaping slaves away to safe refuges in the North or over the border into Canada. Known as the "Underground Railroad," an elaborate network of secret routes for the fugitives was firmly established in the thirties in all parts of the North. A formal organization of the Underground Railroad work-

[1] Recent studies indicate that Garrison's influence may have been overrated in the past, at the expense of the fame of quieter reformers like Theodore Weld.

ers, with Robert Purvis as president, was effected in Philadelphia in 1838. Their most successful operations were in the Old Northwest. In Ohio alone, it is estimated that not less than 40,000 fugitive slaves were assisted to freedom during the years from 1830 to 1860. By 1840 there were about two thousand local antislavery societies with a membership of perhaps 200,000. Women took an active part by circulating antislavery petitions, holding prayer-meetings and conventions, and raising money.

In 1840 certain antislavery leaders, acting against the wishes of Garrison, gave a new turn to the movement by organizing the Liberty party and nominating J. G. Birney of New York and Thomas Earle of Pennsylvania as candidates for the approaching election. The platform proposed a more practical program than that of the Garrisonians. It called on Congress to abolish slavery in all the territories and in the District of Columbia, and branded the Fugitive Slave Act of 1793 as unconstitutional. The Liberty ticket polled only 7000 votes in 1840, but in the next few years men like Salmon P. Chase of Ohio and Charles Sumner of Massachusetts, joined the party, adding to the idealism of the founders a knowledge of the arts of political manipulation. Others, like Abraham Lincoln and Horace Greeley, who sympathized with its purposes, refused to join because they believed that its objects could be more speedily accomplished through the agency of the old parties.

The northern public as a whole held aloof from active participation in the antislavery movement. They were busy with their own concerns. Besides, they thought of slavery as a problem of the southern people, to be solved through state action, and as a moral question rather than a political issue. The unbridled zeal of the antislavery fanatics seemed to them to threaten the integrity of the Union, and the latter was dearer to their hearts, even in 1860, than the cause of freedom for the Negro. In the early stages of the militant movement, agitators in northern cities were harshly dealt with. At Alton, Illinois, in November, 1837, Elijah P. Lovejoy, an abolitionist editor, was murdered by a pro-slavery mob. Even Abraham Lincoln, then a Whig member of the Illinois legislature, felt called upon to declare in a formal protest in 1837, that while he believed slavery to be "founded on both injustice and bad policy, . . . the promulgation of abolition doctrines tends rather to increase than abate its evils."

The Federal Government sought to avoid the slavery question, but could not long do so. In 1835 a mob in Charleston, South Carolina, seized a sack of abolitionist literature which they found in the post office and burned it. The Charleston postmaster reported the affair to the Postmaster-General, who ruled that postmasters might withhold such papers from delivery. The right to use the mails was restored however, by a law of 1836.

The proslavery forces were also determined to check the flood of antislavery petitions which poured into the House of Representatives. These memorials generally asked for the abolition of slavery in the District of Columbia. In 1836 the House passed a "gag resolution" to prevent consideration of such petitions. At each subsequent session, the readoption of the "gag resolution" was fought by Joshua R. Giddings of Ohio and ex-President Adams, until, in 1844, they had the satisfaction of seeing the rule abandoned by a vote of 108 to 80.

These efforts of the proslavery element to suppress discussion defeated their purpose. The apparent denial of the constitutional guarantees of freedom of the press and the right of petition stirred many northerners, who had remained indifferent to the plight of the Negro, to resent the assaults of the "Slave Power" on the rights of white men.

As the foremost moral issue of the age, the antislavery question inevitably challenged the attention of the great religious bodies. In 1844 the Methodist Church split upon the issue of whether a bishop could hold slaves, and the southern members organized the "Methodist Episcopal Church South." In the same year the Baptists divided over the question whether slaveowners might be sent out as missionaries, and a Southern Baptist Church resulted. An increase in the membership of the sectionalized branches seemed to attest the conviction of churchgoers in each section that they were right, respectively, in their views as to the relation of Christianity to slavery. In 1853 the New-School Presbyterians divided over the same question, but the other great national churches ignored it, condoned the practice of slaveholding, and remained united until the Civil War.

SELECT BIBLIOGRAPHY

The Growth of the Slavery System. Among the best discussions of slavery and its significance in American history are Hart, *Slavery and Abolition,* Dodd, *The Cotton Kingdom,* and Jenkins, *Pro-Slavery Thought in the Old South.* The general histories of the South should be consulted, among them Cotterill, *The Old South,* and Hesseltine, *History of the South.* The colored man's point of view is set forth in Brawley, *A Social History of the American Negro.*

On the political aspects of the controversy, Boucher, *"In Re That Aggressive Slavocracy,"* represents a reaction from the overdrawn statements of the older historians of antislavery leanings. The economic phases of the cotton-slavery system are authoritatively examined in Phillips, *American Negro Slavery,* and *Life and Labor in the Old South.* Hammond, *The Cotton Industry,* is the standard work on that subject. For the tobacco industry see Robert, *The Tobacco Kingdom.* For southern economic and social conditions, there is much of value in the coöperative work edited by Chandler and others, *The South in the Building of the Nation,* V and VII. See also Ingle, *Southern Sidelights: a Picture of Social and Economic Life in the South a*

Generation before the War, and Brown, *Lower South in American History.* A shrewd analysis of the sources of strength of the "Slave Power" may be found in Holcombe, *The Political Parties of To-day,* Chap. V.

The Rise of Antislavery Agitation. Hart, *Slavery and Abolition,* is excellent on the general bearings of the antislavery movement, as is also Macy, *The Antislavery Crusade.* Barnes, *The Antislavery Impulse,* represents the new emphasis on Weld's influence. On Nat Turner's uprising and other slave insurrections, see Carroll, *Slave Insurrections.* Siebert, *The Underground Railroad from Slavery to Freedom,* is the most detailed treatment of this subject, and contains valuable maps. For a discussion of the religious ramifications of the controversy, consult Norwood, *The Schism in the Methodist Episcopal Church, 1844.*

Additional information on the antislavery movement may be gleaned from the biographies of the leaders, notably Garrison, *William Lloyd Garrison,* Sears, *Wendell Phillips, Orator and Agitator,* Kennedy, *John G. Whittier, the Poet of Freedom,* Channing, *The Life of William Ellery Channing, D.D.,* Morse, *John Quincy Adams,* and Commager, *Theodore Parker.* For a notable proslavery leader see Coulter, *William G. Brownlow.*

Chapter XXVIII

SLAVERY AND EXPANSION, 1843-1848

THE ANNEXATION OF TEXAS

BOTH Whigs and Democrats sought to keep the slavery question out of party politics, for the issue crossed party lines and threatened to disrupt the old organizations. Their efforts were defeated, however, by the revival, under Tyler, of the movement for the acquisition of Texas. Texas had again offered herself to the United States in 1837, shortly after the American recognition of her independence; but her overtures had been rebuffed, and in 1838 she formally withdrew her offer. Unlike Van Buren, President Tyler strongly favored annexation, and when Webster retired from the State Department in May, 1843, he felt free to prosecute his designs.

The case for annexation was greatly strengthened by the interest which Great Britain had been showing in Texas, and by the consequent fear that Texas might become a British protectorate organized on a basis of free trade and free labor. This apprehension was not entirely unfounded, but for political purposes it was perhaps exaggerated by the administration. On the other hand, the desire to acquire Texas was warmly assailed by the antislavery men as a scheme of the cotton capitalists to gain more slave territory. Furthermore, Mexico notified the United States that annexation would be regarded as an act of war.

Tyler appointed Abel P. Upshur of Virginia, an ardent annexationist, as Webster's successor. Negotiations with Texas were pushed though Upshur's sudden death in February, 1844, left the completion of the arrangements to the deft hands of Calhoun, his successor in office. As signed on April 12, 1844, the treaty provided for the annexation of Texas as a "territory." The Senate debated the treaty behind closed doors, and on June 8 finally rejected it by a vote of 35 to 16. There were various reasons for this action. Some Senators who favored annexation were unwilling to take the step at the cost of war with Mexico; others wished the matter to go over until the voters had expressed their will in the approaching presidential election.

The major parties had already held their national conventions when the vote on the treaty was taken in the Senate. For some months, Henry Clay and Martin Van Buren had been regarded as the logical candidates of their respective parties. Both deplored the intrusion of the Texas question into the campaign, and acting probably by prior agreement, each announced in April that he was opposed to immediate annexation. In the case of Van Buren this was, of course, merely a reaffirmation of the policy he had pursued when President.

So great was the popular demand for Clay's candidacy that when the Whigs met on May 1 they nominated him unanimously. In the interest of political expediency the platform omitted all reference to the Texas question. Theodore Frelinghuysen of New Jersey was named for Vice-President. The Democratic convention meeting on May 27 proved to be a theater of intrigue. Although a majority of the delegates were pledged to Van Buren, his Texas pronouncement had made him unacceptable to the southern contingent. Calhoun's supporters wished to secure the prize for their chief, but while not strong enough to do this, they were able to keep Van Buren from getting the necessary two-thirds vote. The outcome was the nomination of a "dark horse," James K. Polk, ex-governor of Tennessee, a strong annexationist, who had not been deemed a presidential aspirant prior to the convention. The second place on the ticket went to George M. Dallas of Pennsylvania.

The platform was the acme of political adroitness. Instead of avoiding the pivotal issue, the party boldly announced its support of "the re-occupation of Oregon and the re-annexation of Texas." By using the words "*re*-occupation" and "*re*-annexation," the Democrats sought to clear these demands of the stigma of aggression, and by coupling Oregon with Texas, hoped to establish the non-sectional character of the demand for expansion.

Tyler allowed himself to be nominated by a convention of officeholders on a platform of "Tyler and Texas," but withdrew when he saw that his candidacy would only draw votes away from Polk. The Liberty party again offered a ticket, headed by James G. Birney, and the platform declared unequivocally against the extension of slavery.

In the campaign that followed, the Democrats made their appeal to the country upon the basis of national expansion rather than slavery extension. Clay, on the other hand, began to fear the loss of southern votes because of his preconvention declaration against immediate annexation; and in letters, designed for southern reading, he explained and equivocated until no one knew definitely where he stood. Polk was victorious by a popular plurality of less than 40,000 and an electoral vote of 170 to 105. Although it polled no electoral votes, the Liberty party won 62,000 popular votes. The popular strength of Polk and Clay was so closely divided that the balance of power lay with the Liberty party in New York, Ohio, and Indiana. Had the members of that party in New York chosen to vote for Clay, he would have won the thirty-six electoral votes of that state and a majority of the electoral votes of the country.

Van Buren's repudiation by the Democratic national convention, followed by Polk's election, marked a turning point in the history of the Democratic party. Henceforth every Democratic candidate for President down to the Civil War was either a southerner or a "doughface," that is, a pro-southern northerner. The radical democracy of the Jackson-Van Buren régime succumbed to the resolute southern leaders intent on advancing cotton culture and its peculiar labor system. The death of Jackson in 1845 removed a potent counter-influence, and his great lieutenants, Van Buren and Benton, soon found themselves at cross purposes with the new leadership of the party.

Tyler, who still had four months in office after the election, hastened to capture for himself the honor of acquiring Texas. Declaring to Congress in December, 1844, that the American people had spoken in the election, he recommended that, since a two-thirds Senate majority for a treaty was out of the question, Congress should annex Texas by a joint resolution, which required only a majority vote in each house. Notwithstanding a flood of petitions and memorials from the free states against annexation, Congress followed the President's advice on February 28, 1845. Their action authorized the admission of Texas as a state of the Union. It further provided that the Texan constitution should be submitted to Congress for approval, that all boundary disputes in which Texas was involved should be adjusted by the United States, and that the public debt of the new state should not become a charge on the Federal Government.

Although the acquisition of Texas was to result in intensified sectional antagonism in American politics, the action of the United States was fully justified in international law. Texas had maintained a separate existence for nine years without any serious attempt on the part of Mexico to reconquer her. Moreover, her independence had been recognized by the leading European powers as well as by the United States. On July 4, 1845, a Texan convention summoned for that purpose accepted annexation with only one dissenting vote, a decision later confirmed by a popular referendum. At the next session of Congress, annexation was completed by the passage of a formal resolution admitting the state (December 29). The national territory was thereby enlarged by an area more than three times the size of present-day Italy.

THE PARTITION OF THE OREGON COUNTRY

James K. Polk, the new President, was not the nonentity that history often pictures him. Lacking in personal magnetism and dramatic qualities, he was a serious, methodical man of inflexible purpose and great executive capacity. His term was crowded with important events, and judged by his record, he was the greatest expansionist who ever occupied his high office. His cabinet appointments, headed by James Buchanan of Pennsylvania in the State Department and Robert J. Walker of Mississippi as Secretary of the Treasury, evidenced the dominance of southern influence in his administration.[1] Unwilling to trust Blair who had been editor of the official Democratic organ in Washington since Jackson's first administration, Polk forced him to sell his paper, the *Washington Globe,* by taking away the government printing. In its place was established the *Washington Union* with a trusted friend, Thomas Ritchie, in charge.

Since the campaign pledge respecting Texas had been virtually carried out by the time Polk took the oath of office, he was free to give his attention to the settlement of the Oregon question. That vast domain, held by Great Britain and the United States since 1818 under the joint-occupation agreement, was remote both from Great Britain and the settled parts of the United States, and for a number of years neither

[1] The other members of his cabinet were: William L. Marcy of New York, Secretary of War; George Bancroft of Massachusetts, Secretary of the Navy; John Y. Mason of Virginia, Attorney-General; Cave Johnson of Tennessee, Postmaster-General.

country had made any serious effort to colonize it. British interests were largely confined to the Columbia River Basin where the Hudson's Bay Company carried on fur-trading. American energies were mainly engaged in handling the commerce between Oregon and China.

Missionary enterprise paved the way for the coming of permanent American settlers. In 1834 the first band of farmers went overland under the lead of Methodist missionaries, and two years later another company, led by Presbyterian or Congregational missionaries, made the journey. Other parties followed, although up to the end of 1841 the total number of settlers probably did not exceed four hundred. Their situation necessitated some provision for government, and upon their own initiative they adopted (1843) a temporary plan to remain in effect until Congress should act. The American settlements were located almost exclusively south of the Columbia.

Beginning as early as 1826, the two governments had exchanged views with respect to a division of the Oregon country. The United States insisted on a westward extension of the forty-ninth parallel, which already formed the international boundary east of the Rockies. But since this arrangement would deprive the British of trading and fishing advantages in the Columbia River and of the control of the ocean outlet of the waters east of Vancouver Island, the latter demanded the Columbia River as the dividing line.

By 1843 it was apparent that a final adjustment of the rival claims could not be much longer delayed. In that year at least one thousand American settlers crossed the plains and mountains to the fertile valleys of the northwestern coast. Petitions for American occupation of the entire domain began to reach Congress. This popular interest, the Democrats shrewdly capitalized by inserting the plank in their platform of 1844 calling for the "re-occupation of Oregon," and "Fifty-

Four Forty or Fight" proved to be a telling campaign slogan with the western voters.

The campaign demand for the entire Oregon country was not, however, taken very seriously by the Democratic President. At any rate, he felt that he must first renew the earlier offer to divide the country at the forty-ninth parallel. When Great Britain again declined, he took his stand on the demand in the platform, and in his message of December 2, 1845, asserted the claim to the whole of Oregon, appealed to the Monroe Doctrine, and asked Congress to authorize the termination of the joint occupancy. Congress acquiescing, the President in May, 1846, served upon Great Britain the one year's notice required by the treaty.

Fortunately, liberals were in control of the British government who did not regard the issue as sufficiently important to justify meeting defiance with defiance, especially in view of the declining importance of the fur trade in the disputed region. Negotiations were reopened, and on June 15, 1846, a treaty was signed for the partition of the Oregon country at the forty-ninth parallel on the mainland, and along a line running through the middle of the channel between Vancouver Island and the mainland to the Pacific Ocean.[1] The Hudson's Bay Company was granted freedom of navigation of the Columbia. Polk's game of bluff had proved successful, and the United States received an expanse of territory equal in size to the combined areas of France, Portugal, and Greece.

THE WAR WITH MEXICO

The United States escaped war with Great Britain only to plunge into hostilities with Mexico. Ill feeling had long existed between the two countries, and the annexation of Texas aggravated it. Since the winning of independence a

[1] The water boundary later gave rise to disputes over the ownership of certain islands, and the matter was finally adjusted by arbitration under the Treaty of Washington (1871).

THE OREGON COMPROMISE AND THE MEXICAN CESSIONS, 1846–1848

633

succession of revolutionary governments had ruled Mexico, resulting in political instability at home and irresponsibility in foreign relations. The American Department of State labored from 1825 to 1835 before it obtained confirmation of the boundary, defined in the Spanish Treaty of 1819. Even more annoying delays attended the establishment of commercial relations, and after a satisfactory treaty was finally arranged in 1831, the Mexican authorities obstructed or forbade the execution of many of its provisions.

Citizens of the United States engaged in lawful pursuits in Mexico often were imprisoned and treated with the greatest inhumanity. In 1835 twenty-two Americans suspected of being abetters of a revolution were summarily executed without trial. The property losses of American citizens soon came to represent a large sum. In February, 1837, Jackson notified Congress that the failure of Mexico to pay American claims "would justify, in the eyes of all nations, immediate war." [1] At length, in 1839, Mexico agreed to arbitrate the claims; but she failed to comply with the award until a new treaty was made in 1843. Then after paying one or two instalments she defaulted on the remainder.

On the other hand Mexico had her grievances against the United States. She regarded the establishment of the Texan Republic as largely the work of Americans. When her troops attempted some forays across the Rio Grande in 1842, American adventurers shouldered their muskets and again rushed to the defense of Texas, and an American squadron off California, believing that war was at hand, temporarily occupied the town of Monterey. The annexation of Texas in 1845 convinced the Mexicans that the United States was engaged in a systematic dismemberment of their country.

Texas in revolt laid claim to a greater area than had been

[1] Other nations were similarly involved with Mexico. In 1838 France lost patience and collected her claims at the cannon's mouth.

included in the Mexican province of that name. As annexed by the United States, the boundary on the south and west followed the Rio Grande River from mouth to source and thence ran due north to the forty-second parallel, whereas Mexican Texas had not extended beyond the Nueces River.[1] Most of the intermediate area was sparsely populated, but within it were the Mexican settlements at the mouth of the Rio Grande and the ancient Spanish city of Santa Fé in New Mexico.

Recent students have maintained that the prospect of war with the United States in 1845 was welcomed by Mexico. Her generals, experienced in numerous revolutions, had an inflated idea of their own prowess, and counted heavily on the advantage of fighting on their own soil. Misled by the patient diplomacy of the United States during twenty years, they believed that the American people would never support a war.

Polk was obsessed with the desire to acquire Mexico's northwest provinces. However, he intended to accomplish his purpose by pacific methods, if possible. The coveted region was remote from the Mexican capital, thinly peopled, and only loosely attached to the Mexican political system; and the national treasury, chronically empty, was in need of replenishment. Hoping that financial need would induce Mexico to entertain his proposals, Polk, in November, 1845, sent John Slidell of Louisiana as minister to induce that country to concede the Rio Grande boundary in return for the cancellation of our claims against her; and to offer $5,000,-000 for New Mexico, as the country westward to California was called. As for California, he was told that "money would be no object when compared with the value of its acquisi-

[1] "The boundary was probably asserted partly in the hope of making it good, and partly with the idea of having a liberal basis for compromise in the final settlement with Mexico."—Justin Smith, *The Annexation of Texas*, p. 19.

THE WAR WITH MEXICO ON ALL FRONTS

1846	NORTHEASTERN MEXICO	NORTHWESTERN MEXICO	CENTRAL MEXICO
May 8	Taylor's victory at Palo Alto		
May 9	Taylor's victory at Resaca de la Palma		
May 13	U. S. declares war		
June 14		Uprising of American settlers at Sonoma, California	
June 26		Kearny leaves Leavenworth for Santa Fé	
July 7		Commodore Sloat takes Monterey, California	
July 9		Naval seizure of San Francisco	
July 14	Taylor occupies Camargo		
Aug. 13		Commodore Stockton takes Los Angeles	
Aug. 18		Kearny takes Santa Fé	
Sept. 20–24	Taylor captures Monterey, Mexico		
Sept. 25		Kearny leaves Santa Fé for California	
Nov. 15	Commodore Conner takes Tampico		
Nov. 16	Taylor occupies Saltillo		
Nov. 18			Scott is appointed to command Vera Cruz expedition
Dec. 6		Kearny's victory at San Pascual, California	
Dec. 29	Taylor occupies Victoria		

THE WAR WITH MEXICO ON ALL FRONTS—*Continued*

1847	NORTHEASTERN MEXICO	NORTHWESTERN MEXICO	CENTRAL MEXICO
Jan. 3			Scott orders troops from Taylor
Jan. 28	Santa Anna begins march against Taylor		
Feb. 19			Scott reaches Tampico
Feb. 22–23	Taylor's victory at Buena Vista		
March 1	Doniphan occupies Chihuahua		
March 9–29			Scott's operations against Vera Cruz
April 8			Advance on Mexico City begins
April 17–18			Scott's victory at Cerro Gordo
April 19			Scott occupies Jalapa
May 15			Scott occupies Puebla
Aug. 19			Scott's victory at Contreras
Aug. 20			Scott's victory at Churubusco
Aug. 24– Sept. 7			Armistice
Sept. 8			Scott's victory at Molino del Rey
Sept. 13			Scott's victory at Chapultepec
Sept. 14			Scott enters Mexico City

tion." But the Mexican government, having severed diplomatic relations after the annexation of Texas, refused to receive Slidell, who returned to the United States in March, 1846, with his mission unaccomplished.

In Polk's mind the situation now justified war. Already, on January 13, 1846, troops under General Zachary Taylor had been ordered to the banks of the Rio Grande. On Saturday, May 9, 1846, the President notified his cabinet of his intention to recommend war to Congress within the next few days. That night news came that on April 24 Mexican forces had crossed the Rio Grande, and fought a skirmish with some American troops.

This event enabled Polk to put the cause of war before the country in a most appealing light. On Monday, May 11, he sent a message to Congress in which he adverted only briefly to the long-standing grievances of American citizens, the violation of treaty rights, and the wrongful interferences with American trade. All former grievances were pushed into the background when he declared that Mexico had "shed American blood upon the American soil. . . . War exists, and, notwithstanding all our efforts to avoid it, exists by the act of Mexico herself." Congress responded with an authorization of men and money. On Wednesday Polk told his cabinet that "In making peace with our adversary, we shall acquire California, New Mexico, and other further territory, as an indemnity for this war, if we can."

The military operations lasted for about a year and a half. The Mexican forces outnumbered the invaders, and, for the most part, offered a stiff resistance; but they were overcome by the superior morale and stamina of the American soldiers, most of whom were volunteers. The fighting occurred in three distinct geographic areas. In order to assure the territorial objectives of the war, an American squadron in the Pacific seized the ports of California, and an overland expedition under Colonel S. W. Kearny, setting out from Fort Leavenworth on the Missouri, obtained control of New Mexico through the occupation of Sante Fé on August 18. Simultaneously with these operations, General Taylor began an invasion of northern Mexico from his point of vantage on the Rio Grande, gained victories at Palo Alto and Resaca de la Palma on May 8 and 9, took Monterey on May 24, and defeated a Mexican relief expedition under General Santa Anna at Buena Vista on February 22 and 23, 1847.

Polk, who was responsible for the plan of campaign, had hoped that these blows might bring the enemy to terms, but now saw that it was necessary to strike at the heart of the country. In March, 1847, an army under General Winfield Scott was transported to Vera Cruz, and a direct overland march begun on the capital city. Every step of the way was contested. The scaling of the mountain wall beyond Vera Cruz involved a severe struggle at Cerro Gordo on April 17 and 18; and finally, when the central plateau of Mexico was reached, there was hard fighting at Contreras, Churubusco, and Chapultepec in August and September. On September 14, 1847, Mexico City was taken, and the country lay at the mercy of the invaders.

Not desiring to prolong the war unnecessarily, Polk had sent Nicholas P. Trist of Virginia with Scott's army, under instructions to negotiate a peace the moment the Mexicans were willing to make the required territorial concessions. But the sweeping victory of the American forces caused an outburst of imperialistic sentiment in the United States, which found expression in a demand for the annexation of the whole of Mexico. Even Polk's cabinet was divided over what should be done, and Secretary of State Buchanan, with a hopeful eye on his chances in the approaching presidential election, declared in a public letter, "Destiny beckons us to hold and civilize Mexico." Polk, however, was not to be moved from his original purpose, and when Trist obtained a treaty on the original terms, at Guadalupe Hidalgo, on February 2, 1848, he accepted it and the Senate followed his action.

By the provisions of the treaty Mexico acknowledged the Rio Grande boundary of Texas, and ceded to the United States the territories then known as "New Mexico" and "Upper California." The international boundary thus established was the same as that of today, except for the strip added by the Gadsden Purchase (1853) south of the Gila

River. In return, the United States agreed to pay fifteen million dollars and to assume the payment of all American claims against Mexico.[1]

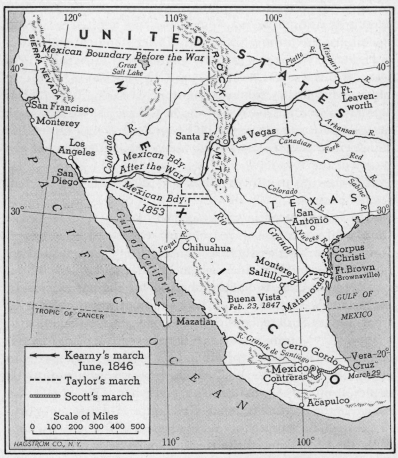

MILITARY OPERATIONS OF THE MEXICAN WAR

Thus, at a cost of twelve thousand lives and nearly one hundred million dollars, the United States gained a domain nearly two and one half times as great as France, and deprived

[1] These claims were later adjudged to amount to $3,208,315.

the Republic of Mexico of two fifths of her territory. In this connection, it may be noted that although, only twenty-five years before, the Latin-American republics had been assured by the United States of protection against European territorial expansion, they now learned that the United States did not regard the Monroe Doctrine as a self-denying ordinance.

Polk's craving for territory was not yet appeased. In a message to Congress in April, 1848, he hinted at the desirability of annexing the strife-afflicted Mexican province of Yucatan, in order to forestall similar action by Great Britain or Spain. A month and a half later he tried to buy Cuba from Spain, alleging that as her power there declined European powers were watching the island with covetous eyes. Polk's offer was met by the reply that Spain would rather see Cuba "sunk in the ocean."

Polk's plans of expansion coincided with a widespread belief that it was the manifest destiny of the United States to absorb all of North America. Northerners cherished a hope that the time would come when Canada might be brought under the flag, while "Manifest Destiny" became the slogan of the Democratic party from this time to the outbreak of the Civil War. Unfortunately, it was corrupted by the party leaders into a purely sectional purpose of acquiring semitropical lands suitable for slavery. Not all southerners possessed this aggressive temper, for there were many who deplored measures which were certain to aggravate the sectional conflict. Nevertheless the question of the extension of slavery was inextricably bound up with that of territorial expansion, and the immediate result of the great enlargement of the national area under Polk was sectional discord.

POLITICS AND PUBLIC OPINION UNDER POLK

Although foreign affairs occupied the dominant place in Polk's administration, he did not fail to give due attention to those well-established articles of Democratic faith, the Independent Treasury and a tariff for revenue only. In his first annual message he called for the restoration of the Independent Treasury, discarded by the Whigs in 1841. Congress accordingly passed an act on August 6, 1846, which, in the main, was the same law that Van Buren had labored so long to secure. The system, thus again set in motion, proved its worth, and remained continuously in existence until abandoned under the provisions of the Federal Reserve Act of 1913.

In pursuance of recommendations made by Secretary of the Treasury Walker, Congress enacted a new tariff law on July 30, 1846, which had as its ideal the raising of revenue rather than the protection of industry. While the bill was before Congress, reduction of duties was opposed by members from New England and the middle states, but favored by the farmers and planters of the West and South. The Walker Tariff enlarged the free list, and made the average rate on dutiable imports 26.5 per cent. Financially the new act proved a marked success. The average annual yield was forty-six million dollars as compared with twenty-six million dollars under the Whig tariff of 1842.

After the conflict with Mexico began, much of the time of Congress was taken up with discussions of war-time legislation. In the first flush of enthusiasm the war was extremely popular with the country; but the Whigs in Congress, while voting the necessary military appropriations, quickly adopted the policy of criticizing the causes and purposes of the struggle. The most resolute opposition came from antislavery sources, for men of this stripe regarded the conflict as an arrogant proslavery war of conquest. In this spirit, for example, the Massachusetts legislature resolved in April, 1847, that the war, "unconstitutionally commenced by the order of the President," was being waged "for the dismemberment of Mexico" with "the triple object of extending slavery, of strengthening the Slave Power, and of obtaining the control of the Free States."

Irrespective of party, the antislavery forces in Congress resolved to exclude slavery from any territory that might be acquired from Mexico. On August 8, 1846, Polk asked Congress to vote him two million dollars in order that he might be ready at any time to treat with Mexico for territorial cessions. David Wilmot, a Pennsylvania Democrat of the antislavery wing of the party, moved in the House of Representatives an amendment to the appropriation bill, providing that in all acquired territory slavery should be forever prohibited. The issue was now joined. In August, 1846, and again in February, 1847, the "Wilmot Proviso" was adopted by the House after a severe struggle, but notwithstanding the support of Webster and other northern Whigs in the Senate, the measure failed of passage there on both occasions.

At length the House was persuaded to vote the appropriations without restriction in March, 1847. By this time, however, the Wilmot Proviso had served its purpose of arousing the country to the importance of the question of slavery in the Mexican cessions. Northern legislatures indorsed the exclusion of slavery; southern legislatures just as roundly condemned the proposal. In general, the Democrats in Congress met the issue with a united front, but the Whigs were badly shaken by the contest. On every significant vote the southern Whigs voted solidly with the Democrats against the Wilmot Proviso, and the northern Whigs took the antislavery side.

The principle underlying the Wilmot Proviso was also evoked in the discussions in Congress over the territorial organization of Oregon. In messages of 1846 and 1847, Polk urged Congress to establish a regular territorial government in Oregon in place of the provisional government set up by the settlers. Although everyone recognized that Oregon was certain to be free soil, the southern members did not wish to yield the point without obtaining some corresponding sectional advantage. Bills passed by the House to organize Oregon as a free territory failed in the Senate in 1846 and 1847; but a third bill, of 1848, was approved by the Senate with an adroitly conceived amendment to the effect that the Missouri Compromise line should be extended to the Pacific. The Senate hoped in this way to commit Congress in advance to the policy of permitting slavery in the Mexican acquisitions south of 36° 30′. The House was adamant, the need for action great, and on August 13, 1848, an act was adopted authorizing a free-soil government in Oregon with no mention of the Missouri Compromise provision.

As the presidential election of 1848 drew near, the leaders of the great parties found themselves confronted with the same dilemma that had dismayed them in 1844: forces beyond their control had thrust forward the question of slavery extension as the paramount issue of the campaign. Since this question cut across party lines, the old-party managers determined, if possible, to evade it. The Democrats, holding their national convention at Baltimore on May 22, adopted a platform which defended the Mexican War as "just and necessary" but said nothing about slavery in the new accessions. For President the party nominated Lewis Cass of Michigan, a zealous expansionist and anti-Wilmot man who had recently proposed "squatter sovereignty" (see page 651) as a solution for the question of slavery in federal territories. With his name was coupled that of General W. O. Butler of Kentucky, a Mexican War veteran.

The Whigs, meeting at Philadelphia on June 7, resorted again to the plan of staking their chances on a military hero. Notwithstanding the lukewarm support of the Whigs, the Mexican War had yielded greater popular credit to them than to the party in power. The guilt of starting the war belonged to the latter, but the glory of victory belonged to the former, for both Taylor and Scott were nominally of the Whig persuasion. Although Clay was as usual an aspirant for the honor, the presidential nomination went with great enthusiasm to Zachary Taylor of Louisiana. Besides his war fame, the fact that Taylor was the owner of three hundred slaves would, it was thought, make an especial appeal to southern voters.

The true character of the nomination was amply evidenced by the General's bald announcement prior to the convention that he would run, even if the Whigs failed to nominate him, and that he would be their candidate only if "allowed to maintain a position of independence to all political parties." Millard Fillmore of New York, a suave man of moderate ability, was nominated for second place. The Ohio delegation made a determined but fruitless effort to put the convention on record in favor of the Wilmot Proviso, and the convention adjourned without framing a platform.

The opportunity for a third party based on an antislavery program was the best that had yet presented itself. Deeply stirred by the debates in Congress on the Mexican War and the Wilmot Proviso, the antislavery members of the old parties had become discontented with their traditional affiliations. In the pivotal state of New York, the Democratic party split wide open, one wing under Van Buren's leadership espousing Wilmot's plan of dealing with the Mexican cessions, and the other, led by William L. Marcy of Polk's cabinet, taking the opposite position. Van Buren's followers were called the "Barnburners," because, like the old Dutch farmer, it was said they were willing to burn the barn in order to get rid of the rats; whereas the administration Democrats, for some obscure reason, were known as the "Hunkers." Angered by the treatment they received at the hands of the Democratic national convention, and its refusal to take a stand on slavery, the Barnburners repudiated the nomination of Cass, and presently shared in the organization of a new party.

Another element of the new party appeared in the organizations of eastern wage-earners, who were just beginning to recover from the shattering effects of the Panic of 1837. These bodies undertook an aggressive agitation for free homesteads for actual settlers.[1] Their purpose was to extend a helping hand to the struggling white workingmen in the East, but their cause was eagerly championed by the antislavery men who favored any measure calculated to keep the territories free.

In order to present a united front, these several groups came together in a national convention at Buffalo on August 9 and formed the Free Soil party. Senator John P. Hale of New Hampshire and ex-President Van Buren had already been nominated respectively by the old Liberty party and the Barnburners. They now agreed to defer to the will of the convention, which named Van Buren as its candidate. Charles Francis Adams, son of John Quincy Adams, was named for the vice-presidency. An eloquent platform, written mainly by Salmon P. Chase, was adopted. It denounced the "Slave Power," declared that Congress must convert all federal territories into free soil, and indorsed the policy of free homesteads for landless settlers.

The campaign of 1848 was marked by no such enthusiasm as that of 1840 or 1844. The old-party managers effectually hushed up any discussion of dangerous issues. Though many citizens were dissatisfied with this temporizing policy, most of them either voted a "regular ticket," or stayed away from the polls, in preference to voting the third-party ticket. Under

---

[1] Petitions for this purpose poured into Congress from 1846 to 1852. In the latter year Senator Walker of Wisconsin presented a petition with so many signatures that it was fifty-two feet in length.

pressure, Taylor issued a public letter in which he described himself as a Whig, "decided but not ultra." He was victor over Cass by an electoral majority of thirty-six votes—just the vote of New York. The Free Soilers evinced remarkable strength. Although Van Buren received no electoral votes, he polled nearly 300,000 popular votes, and the new party held the balance of power between the two old parties in eleven northern states, including all those of the Old Northwest. If Van Buren had not split the Democratic vote in New York, Cass would have carried the state and won the Presidency.

SELECT BIBLIOGRAPHY

Slavery and Expansion. Garrison, *Westward Extension,* and Stephenson, *Texas and the Mexican War,* are excellent general surveys of the expansion movement which closed with the Peace of Guadalupe Hidalgo. See also Coman, *Economic Beginnings of the Far West,* Goodwin, *Transmississippi West,* and Bolton, *Spanish Borderlands.*

The Annexation of Texas. A detailed treatment is Smith, *The Annexation of Texas.* The chapters on Texas in Rives, *The United States and Mexico, 1821–1848,* are valuable. Adams studies a special phase of the subject in his *British Interests and Activities in Texas, 1838–1846.* There is back-stage history in Hill, *The Texas Navy.*

The Partition of Oregon. See references for Chaps. XVI and XX. McCormac, *James K. Polk,* sheds much light on all the problems of Polk's presidency, domestic and foreign. Excellent accounts of the Oregon episode may be found in Schafer, *A History of the Pacific Northwest,* and Paxson, *History of the American Frontier, 1763–1793.* See also Skinner, *Adventurers of Oregon,* and Ghent, *The Road to Oregon.* Very helpful is the discussion in Reeves, *American Diplomacy under Tyler and Polk.* Drury gives an excellent account of one of the pioneer missionaries of the Pacific Northwest in *Marcus Whitman, M.D.*

The War with Mexico. This subject is carefully treated in McMaster, and in the second volume of Rives, *The United States and Mexico.* See also Rippy, *United States and Mexico.* Though an exhaustive treatment, Smith, *The War with Mexico,*

is somewhat marred by the author's controversial tone.   See also
Priestley, *The Mexican Nation*.   The exuberant expansionism
of the West is brought out in Weinberg, *Manifest Destiny*, and
Fuller, *Movement for the Acquisition of All Mexico*.   The chief
general in the war is dealt with in Elliott, *Winfield Scott*.

Politics and Public Opinion under Polk.   In addition to the
general histories and biographies, such works should be consulted
for fiscal and tariff measures as Kinley, *The Independent Treasury*, Stanwood, *American Tariff Controversies*, and Taussig, *The
Tariff History of the United States*.

On elections and platforms, Stanwood, *A History of the Presidency*, I, is good, as usual.   Of special interest is Smith, *The Liberty and Free-Soil Parties in the Northwest*.   Wilmot's life has
been written by Going.   Information on George Henry Evans
and his land-reform movement may be gleaned from Commons
and others, *History of Labour in the United States*, I.

Chapter XXIX

A NATIONAL CRISIS, 1849–1852

THE UNION IN DANGER

ZACHARY TAYLOR, the new President, was a man of high character, sturdy honesty, and strong personality, with extensive experience in war but none in statecraft. He consulted leading southern Whigs before naming his official advisers, and finally selected a cabinet composed of three northerners and four men from the slave states.[1] Since the presidential election had settled nothing, Taylor was free to act as he would on matters of public policy. To the disappointment of his southern supporters, he honestly sought to weigh public questions without regard to partisan or sectional bias. Indeed, he formed a warm personal liking for William H. Seward, the antislavery Whig Senator from New York, and in August, 1849, he declared in a public speech, "The people of the North need have no apprehension of the further extension of slavery."

With the exception of Lincoln, never was a newly-elected President confronted with such grave problems. Most of them had been created and left unsettled by the Polk administration, and all were intimately connected with the slavery system. The question of major importance concerned the policy which Congress should adopt toward slavery in the new Southwest, and on this issue the members of Con-

---

[1] John M. Clayton of Delaware, Secretary of State; William M. Meredith of Pennsylvania, Secretary of the Treasury; George W. Crawford of Georgia, Secretary of War; William B. Preston of Virginia, Secretary of the Navy; Reverdy Johnson of Maryland, Attorney-General; Jacob Collamer of Vermont, Postmaster-General; Thomas Ewing of Ohio, Secretary of the Interior (a newly created department).

gress were sadly divided. Indeed, during the heated Oregon debates four distinct and mutually antagonistic views had been enunciated.

One group proposed to divide the territories once more between slavery and freedom, as had been done in 1820 by the Missouri Compromise. This was preëminently a practical man's solution. Moreover, it was sanctioned by precedent, for the Joint Resolution of 1845 had extended the original line of 36° 30′ through Texas in case additional states should be created out of the area. Polk was one of those who believed that the compromise line should be carried through the Mexican cessions to the coast.

A second group insisted upon the total exclusion of slavery from the territories. The Wilmot Proviso embraced this plan, which also had historic precedent in the Ordinance of 1787. But it was essentially an extremist position. Its supporters not only maintained that Congress should forbid slavery in the territories as a matter of humanity but also contended, in the words of the Liberty platform of 1844, that "the fundamental truth of the Declaration of Independence, that all men are endowed by the Creator with [the inalienable rights of] life, liberty, and the pursuit of happiness, was made the fundamental law of our national government by that amendment of the Constitution which declares that no person shall be deprived of life, liberty, or property without due process of law." As respects the new accessions, the advocates of congressional prohibition enjoyed a strategic advantage. Slavery had been illegal in them while they formed a part of Mexico, and it was argued that under international law this condition of freedom persisted until changed by an express act of Congress.

According to a third group, the fate of slavery should be left to the decision of the respective territorial legislatures. Since this method involved settlement by local action before

the territory became a state, it was termed, somewhat derisively, "squatter sovereignty." Yet the proposal appealed to
the democratic instincts of a people accustomed to making
vital decisions by a majority vote of those most closely concerned; at the same time it promised to relieve the federal
legislature of all responsibility in the matter. When Cass
announced his espousal of this solution, it found warm
support among the self-reliant farmers of the Northwest.
Within a few years Stephen A. Douglas of Illinois, who happily renamed the doctrine "popular sovereignty," was to become its foremost champion.

The fourth group denied absolutely that slavery could
legally be prohibited in the federal territories under any con-
tingencies or circumstances. Among the chief upholders of
this view were Calhoun and his disciple, Jefferson Davis of
Mississippi, and the doctrine became indelibly associated with
their names. These men maintained that, since the states
were joint owners of the territories, the people of each state
were entitled to equal rights in all of them, including that of
removing to them with their property, whether it consisted of
slaves or chattels of other kinds. In other words, the right
of property in slaves subsisted in the federal territories irrespective of congressional or local enactments to the contrary. In the 1840's this doctrine was held only by southern
extremists in the Democratic party, for most of the leaders
favored squatter sovereignty as a compromise acceptable
to both the northern and the southern wings.

Before Polk left office, he sent a special message to Congress urging the immediate formation of territorial governments in California and New Mexico,[1] but his recommendation brought no action. The House of Representatives

[1] The New Mexico of that time included most of the present state of that
name, all of Arizona except the part later included in the Gadsden Purchase
(1853), all of Utah and Nevada, and parts of Colorado and Wyoming.

would not accept the President's suggestion of extending the Missouri Compromise line to the Pacific, nor could the two branches agree on any other disposition of the question.

An unforeseen event now supplied a new and urgent reason for the speedy organization of the Southwest. In January, 1848, gold was discovered in the Lower Sacramento Valley in California. Settlers already on the coast rushed to the "diggings," and in the excitement, soldiers and sailors deserted from the service of the United States. The news spread like a contagion, precipitating a headlong rush of gold-seekers from all parts of the world, in which many desperate and lawless men joined. In the single year 1849, more than eighty thousand immigrants arrived in the new El Dorado. The few officials who represented the authority of the United States were unable to cope with the conditions. There were no land laws, no legal tribunals to decide disputed mining titles. In San Francisco and elsewhere organized bands of ruffians terrorized the community. It was imperative, the President declared, "to substitute the rule of law and order . . . for the bowie-knife and revolvers." The need in the remainder of the ceded territory, known as New Mexico, was less urgent, but it was plainly desirable that its political organization be effected without unnecessary delay.

Without waiting for Congress to assemble, Taylor with soldierly directness advised the people of California and New Mexico to frame state constitutions and seek immediate admission to the Union. His purpose was to spare Congress the necessity of deciding the status of slavery in the territories, since all parties recognized the right of the people to make their own decision when ready for statehood. California needed no urging, and in October, 1849, a constitution prohibiting slavery was framed and ratified. In May, 1850, New Mexico also was ready with a free-soil constitution. When Congress met in December, 1849, Taylor recommended statehood for both districts as soon as their constitutions should be submitted to that body.

But the situation was not susceptible of so simple a solution. The fiercest sectional antagonism had been kindled by the discussions of the last few years in Congress, and the original problem of territorial adjustment had become complicated by certain collateral questions. One of these concerned the boundary between Texas and New Mexico. Although the Federal Government had claimed the Rio Grande boundary from mouth to source for Texas in its dealings with Mexico in 1845, it had, during the war, recognized New Mexico as including Santa Fé and its tributary area. The Texans bitterly resented this attempt to deprive them of territory, while the antislavery members of Congress, since Texas was slave soil, sought to confine it within the narrowest possible limits. Texas harbored an additional grievance because the United States refused to assume her war debt at the time of annexation, when she surrendered her chief source of revenue, the customs duties, to the Federal Government.

Another question involved slavery in the District of Columbia. To the southerners slaveholding seemed right and proper in this area, since the land had originally belonged to Maryland, and the capital city was inclosed on all sides by slave territory. But to their opponents it seemed an ugly blot on the national escutcheon, since the District was under the direct control of Congress; and for many years antislavery petitions had besought Congress to end slaveholding there.

A final source of contention arose from the growing difficulty encountered by slaveowners in the recovery of runaway slaves. In the case of Prigg vs. Pennsylvania, the Supreme Court had held in 1842 that the master of a slave had a right to regain him under the Act of 1793 without obstruction from any conflicting state laws, but it had also decided that the federal statute did not require state authorities to assist in the rendition of fugitives. Some northern legislatures thereupon withdrew the use of state magistrates, prosecutors, and jails in fugitive-slave cases. Such acts, along with the heightened efficiency of the Underground Railroad, led southerners to demand a new and stronger fugitive-slave law, to make effective the provision of the Constitution concerning fugitives.

The excitement over these questions was by no means confined to the halls of Congress. Throughout the South, resolutions denouncing the demands and acts of the antislavery element where adopted by mass meetings and state legislatures, and threats of disunion were heard with increasing frequency. A state convention in Mississippi called a southern "popular convention" to meet at Nashville, Tennessee, in June, 1850, to consider what action should be taken in the crisis. Northern sentiment was equally tense. The legislatures of all the free states except Iowa passed resolutions favoring congressional prohibition of slavery in the territories, and a number of them demanded the abolition of slavery in the District of Columbia. The responsibility of harmonizing these jangling interests fell upon a Congress whose passions were deeply stirred by the reiterated appeals to sectional prejudice.

THE COMPROMISE OF 1850

Perhaps no session of the United States Senate has contained more distinguished men than the one which met in December, 1849. In it were Webster, Clay, Calhoun, and Benton, giants of an era fast departing, and Jefferson Davis and Stephen A. Douglas, who within a decade were to head the factions of a hopelessly divided Democracy. There, too, were Chase and Seward, destined to become the chiefs of a party not yet formed. The Free Soilers, led by Joshua R. Giddings, held the balance of power in the House, and a contest of three weeks was necessary before Howell Cobb, a Georgia Democrat of moderate views, was chosen Speaker.

The hopes of the nation rested on the aged Henry Clay, who had just been reëlected to the Senate after an absence of seven years. Viewing the troubled scene with eyes illumined with the calm wisdom of his years, he arose on January 29, 1850, and offered a series of compromise resolutions. His main proposals may be summarized as follows: California should be admitted with her free-soil constitution; territorial governments should be established in the remainder of the Mexican cession, and "as slavery does not exist by law and is not likely to be introduced" there, Congress should take no action either for the introduction or the exclusion of slavery; Texas should yield in her boundary dispute with New Mexico, in return for which the United States would assume the Texan debt contracted prior to annexation; Congress should enact a more effective fugitive-slave law; and the slave trade, but not slavery, should be abolished in the District of Columbia.

A memorable debate followed, lasting through many weeks. In a speech of February 5 and 6, Clay, beginning with faltering voice but gaining strength as he warmed to his theme, pointed to the ominous spectacle of the state legislatures, "twenty-odd furnaces in full blast generating heat and passion and intemperance," and called upon the two sections to make mutual concessions for the sake of the Union. He denied vigorously the right or possibility of peaceful secession. Analyzing the compromise resolutions in detail, he maintained that the proposals formed a middle ground honorable to both groups. When he concluded, a great throng of men and women, many of whom had come long distances to hear him, rushed forward to shake his hand and embrace him.

On March 4, Calhoun with the shadow of death already upon him appeared, too ill to read his own address but still full of that grim energy which had made him the foremost champion of cotton capitalism in his generation. He charged that the present crisis had been brought about by northern aggression, which had succeeded in banishing slavery from nearly three fourths of the territory added to the original states. In the recent schisms in the Methodist and Baptist churches, he saw the first snapping of the cords of union. As for the proposed compromise, he branded it as a betrayal of his section. The southerners could be satisfied with nothing less than a stoppage of antislavery propaganda, a faithful execution of the Fugitive Slave Act, the enjoyment of equal rights with northerners in the territories, and an amendment to the Constitution restoring the former equality of the sections. In making this last proposal, he had in mind a provision for the election of dual presidents, one from the slaveholding and one from the free states, each with a veto on the acts of Congress.

On March 7, Webster, the third of the great triumvirate, entered the lists. Clay had consulted him before offering his resolutions to the Senate, and Webster now marshaled his vast oratorical powers on behalf of conciliation. He met Calhoun's charge of northern aggrandizement by pointing out that "the general lead in the politics of the country, for three-fourths of the period . . . since the adoption of the Constitution, has been a Southern lead." In words reminiscent of his reply to Hayne, he denied that peaceful secession was possible. But he addressed himself particularly to the task of making the compromise acceptable to the free states. He deplored the violence of abolition agitation, admitted that the northern people had failed in their duty in the matter of returning fugitive slaves, and declared that "an ordinance of nature" had settled, "beyond all terms of human enactment, that slavery cannot exist in California or New Mexico."

The "Seventh-of-March Speech" came as a thunderclap to
the antislavery men of New England, who had hoped that
Webster would assume the leadership of the opponents of
slavery extension. He was denounced by public meetings
on every hand, and Whittier expressed the thought of thousands when he wrote in his poem, "Ichabod": [1]

> All else is gone; from those great eyes
>   The soul has fled:
> When faith is lost, when honor dies,
>   The man is dead!

But such people strangely misapprehended the real significance of Webster's career. Though he had shown his personal convictions by disapproving of the Mexican War and
supporting the Wilmot Proviso, devotion to an indivisible
American nationality had become the religion of his life.
To him, politics was a matter of patient adjustment of interests, and when the Union was in jeopardy, he subordi-
nated all lesser issues to the greater one. Indeed, his speech
struck a responsive chord in the hearts of people of moderate
views throughout the land.

The debate over the compromise now became general.
Douglas, the Illinois Democrat, gave it his support, while the
Mississippi Democrat, Jefferson Davis, joined Calhoun in
opposition. Benton denounced the compromise as pro-
southern. The antislavery extremists found spokesmen in
two Senators serving their first terms—Seward, the New
York Whig, and Chase of Ohio, who owed his election to a
combination of Free Soilers and Democrats. Denying that
the Constitution recognized human bondage, these men demanded that the territories remain free soil, and Seward
created a sensation with his defiant assertion that for antislavery men "there is a higher law than the Constitution."

[1] See I Samuel, 4:21.

These words, in the succeeding decade, were to become a rallying cry of the opponents of slavery.

On April 18, the Senate referred the compromise resolutions to a committee of thirteen with Clay as chairman. On May 8 the committee made its report in the form of three bills, which embodied the essence of the original proposals. The first of these—at once dubbed the "Omnibus Bill"— dealt with all the questions affecting the newly acquired Southwest. California should be admitted with its free-soil constitution; the remainder of the region should be divided at the thirty-seventh parallel into the two territories of New Mexico and Utah, and organized without mention of slavery; and the claims of Texas to a portion of New Mexico should be satisfied by a payment of ten million dollars. The second bill provided for a stringent fugitive-slave act, and the third, for the prohibition of the slave traffic in the District of Columbia.

These definite proposals seemed for the time to have little effect on the Senate. The tempests of sectional passion continued to rage unabated, and although there were majorities for the separate measures of the "Omnibus Bill," it proved impossible to secure a majority vote for all of them taken together. Fortunately, other conditions and events now began to make their influence felt. The convention of nine slave-holding states, which met at Nashville on June 3, was dominated by moderates, and called merely for the westward extension of the line 36° 30′. On July 9 the President died unexpectedly, and was succeeded by Fillmore, who, unlike Taylor, favored the compromise, and whose approval plainly appeared in his appointment of Webster as Secretary of State. Under these circumstances the various proposals were embodied in separate measures, and, one after another, passed Congress, in most cases by decisive majorities. Between the ninth and twentieth of September all the bills became laws with the President's signature.

It may well be asked which side gained the major advantage from the sectional bargain of 1850, and the answer is not easy to give. The outlawing of the slave traffic in the District of Columbia might be balanced against the drastic Fugitive Slave Act. The boundary concession of Texas was offset by the federal gift of ten million dollars. But the crux of the settlement was the provision made for the newly acquired Southwest, since by the admission of California as a free state the nation-old balance of free and slave states in the Senate was destroyed. Here the North won a clear advantage.

In the case of New Mexico and Utah, however, the essence of the compromise lay in a postponement of the issue. Governments were authorized, with the proviso that the territories should eventually be admitted as states "with or without slavery, as their constitution may prescribe at the time of their admission." But Congress did not specify whether slavery might or might not exist in these regions prior to statehood, providing only that all cases involving title to slave property should be referred to the Supreme Court. To that tribunal, then, was left the question of the legality of slavery in the new territories. In this disposition of the matter, the various factions found crumbs of comfort, for each was convinced that its own peculiar interpretation of the Constitution would be sustained by the judiciary.

From the standpoint of posterity, the fact of supreme importance was that a peace had once more been patched up between the sections and the fateful crisis postponed. Had the South seceded in 1850, it may well be doubted whether the northern people were as yet sufficiently united in opinion to wage a war to preserve the Union.

THE APPEAL TO THE COUNTRY

Whether the public would acquiesce in the decision of Congress remained to be seen. Material conditions were conducive to a cessation of sectional bickering, for the country was entering on an era of great prosperity, and the commercial and financial interests wished to be rid of a controversy which was "bad for business." The political leaders left no stone unturned to make the compromise settlement permanent. In January, 1851, a pledge was signed by forty-four congressmen of both parties, declaring their opposition to any candidate for public office who did not accept it as a final disposition of the slavery question. Thirty-four of the signers were from the slave states. In the North, under the leadership of Webster, Douglas, and Cass, huge "union meetings" were held in numerous places to voice approval of the compromise measures and pledge a rigid enforcement of the Fugitive Slave Act.

This act proved to be the chief stumbling block in the way of acceptance of the compromise by the North. Based on the decision in the Prigg case, that the obligation to enforce the constitutional provision for the rendition of fugitives rested solely upon the Federal Government, the act created federal commissioners to apprehend fugitives, and required all citizens to assist them if called upon. Moreover, Negroes seized as runaway slaves were denied the customary safeguards of personal liberty, such as trial by jury. These drastic provisions gave great offense to the antislavery element, and many of them refused to recognize the act as binding upon them.

Even more southerners hesitated. In 1850–1852, special state conventions met in Georgia, Mississippi, Alabama, and South Carolina to consider the advisability of secession. The admission of California was an especially bitter pill for the

9(

nnipeg

S

L. of the Woods

T A

Y

St.Paul. WI

E D   Mississippi

IOWA

es Moines

S

MISSO

Arkansas

ARK
Little Rock

R.

Sabine R.

LO

U L F

95°   f

pted from An

southerners. The stormiest contests occurred in South Carolina, Georgia, and Mississippi, but gradually the sober second thought of the people asserted itself everywhere in favor of conciliation. The temper of the section was best expressed in the resolutions of the Georgia convention in 1850, widely known as the "Georgia Platform." These resolutions yielded grudging adherence to the compromise measures, but served notice on the North that a lax enforcement of the Fugitive Slave Act or any further congressional restrictions on slavery would be resisted, "even to the disruption of the Union."

The presidential election of 1852 revealed that the irreconcilables were comparatively few, and that the voters in general acquiesced in the legislation of 1850. The Democrats entered the campaign with a united front, for the Van Buren faction, which had bolted in 1848, was now back in the fold. At their Baltimore convention of June 1, they adopted a platform which affirmed the compromise measures, including the Fugitive Slave Act, to be a final settlement of the slavery question. Cass, Buchanan, and Douglas were the chief contenders for the nomination.

With scant respect for the gray hairs of the veteran statesmen, Douglas' candidacy was represented by his supporters as a contest between "Young America" and "Old Fogyism." So evenly was the convention divided that none of the three could be chosen, and after forty-nine ballots the nomination went, almost by default, to Franklin Pierce, a small-town New Hampshire lawyer. Pierce was a handsome and prepossessing man of average attainments, who had supported Polk's imperialistic policy, had served in the legislature of his state and in Congress, and had taken some part in the Mexican War. William R. King of Alabama was named for Vice-President.

The Whigs came together two weeks later in the same city. Through superior strategy, the southern delegates managed to foist a platform on the convention, which committed the party of Webster and Clay to the doctrine of states' rights. Like their opponents, the Whigs declared for the maintenance of the compromise measures. The northern faction, however, succeeded, after fifty-three ballots, in nominating its candidate, Winfield Scott of Virginia, over the heads of Fillmore and Webster, either of whom would have represented in a special sense the inviolability of the compromise. William A. Graham of North Carolina was chosen for the second place.

The remnants of the Free Soil party, calling themselves "Free Democrats," nominated John P. Hale of New Hampshire, on a platform which repudiated the compromise and demanded free labor and free homesteads in the federal territories.

From the first, Democratic victory was assured. The southern Whigs were openly suspicious of Scott's antislavery support in the North, and northern Whig opinion was best expressed in the popular saying, "We accept the candidate but spit upon the platform." Scott exerted himself to curry favor with the new German and Irish voters, but his fulsome compliments only exposed him to the ridicule of the Democrats. Equally futile were the efforts of his party managers to create enthusiasm for him as the hero of two wars. Pierce received 254 votes to 42 for his opponent, the largest majority in the electoral college since Monroe's almost unanimous election in 1820. The support of the Free Democrats showed a loss of nearly one half of the Free Soil strength of 1848. The people had declared unqualifiedly for the finality of the compromise, and apparently a new era of good feeling was at hand. The events of the next few years were to prove, however, that the intersectional agreement was only a truce instead of a permanent peace.

SELECT BIBLIOGRAPHY

A National Crisis, 1849–1852. The best account of the Compromise of 1850 and its background is perhaps that found in Rhodes, *History of the United States,* I. A better understanding of the slavery adjustments in Utah and New Mexico may, however, be gained from von Holst, *The Constitutional and Political History of the United States,* III, or Schurz, *Henry Clay,* II. Volume VI of Channing's *History* treats the period 1848–1865 in the light of the latest researches.

White's readable volume, *The Forty-Niners,* is a dependable treatment of the California gold-rush. Coy, *The Great Trek,* carries the story into the fifties. Hulbert, *Forty-Niners,* puts the story in the form of a series of letters written by a man on the way to the gold fields.

On party politics the standard histories and biographies are helpful. A special study is Nichols, *The Democratic Machine, 1850–1854.* White, *The Secession Movement in the United States, 1847–1852,* contains much of value on that subject. For the contest in the crucial state of Georgia, see Shryock, *Georgia and the Union in 1850.*

Chapter XXX

THE UNDOING OF THE SECTIONAL TRUCE

MID-CENTURY AMERICA

THE general prosperity of the fifties brought contentment to all classes and seemed to promise the permanence of the new era of good feeling. President Pierce, in his inaugural address, referred to the "unparalleled progression" of the country in population and wealth. Thanks to Polk's masterful handling of foreign affairs, the national territory now stretched continent-wide over forest, plain and mountain, and within its far-flung limits dwelt a hardy, industrious people numbering in 1850 twenty-three millions. The Union comprised thirty-one states. The land of promise seemed to have become the land of achievement. In the East every branch of industry flourished; in the Midwest and the South agriculture returned unusual profits; the railways were fast knitting the settled areas more closely together, and the mines of California were pouring a golden stream into the channels of trade.

To the compilers of the census of 1860, the advance in the output of the mills and mines of New England and the Middle Atlantic states during the decade 1850–1860 was one of "startling magnitude." The capital invested in manufacturing (including fisheries and mines) had doubled, totalling more than a billion dollars. First in importance was the making of flour and meal; then came boots and shoes, cotton textiles, and lumber products, with clothing, machinery, leather and woolen goods forging rapidly forward. In 1849 patents granted for new inventions passed the thousand mark for the first time; in 1860 the number was nearly six times as great.

Among the new mechanisms employed in industry was the sewing machine, characterized by the census officials in 1860 as "altogether a revolutionary instrument." Elias Howe of Massachusetts had invented it in 1846, and other ingenious persons had added improvements which greatly widened its usefulness. The contrivance simplified one of the age-old tasks of the housewife; and, introduced into the factory and driven by steam or water power, it ushered in the era of cheap ready-made clothing.

Shipping reached the high noon of its prosperity in these years. Sailing vessels flying the American flag plied the seven seas, outstripping the British as carriers of the wares of all nations. American genius had produced a superior kind of craft, the clipper ship, long of beam, graceful and speedy. Designed in 1845, the shipyards at Boston, New York, and other northern ports were soon busy constructing the new type of vessel to meet the demand due to the migration to California, the growing China trade, and the commerce with the British East Indies, thrown open to the world in 1849.

Meanwhile, beginning in 1845, Congress sought to promote steam navigation on the ocean by liberal subsidies. New lines were established, including one connecting the Atlantic ports with the Isthmus of Panama and another joining the isthmus with California and Oregon.[1] For a time the American Collins line competed with the British Cunard company in the transatlantic trade, but a series of disasters culminating in the Panic of 1857 forced Collins into bankruptcy.

The improvements in navigation and the developments on the Pacific coast brought the Asiatic countries, in effect,

[1] Besides, a railway for transporting passengers and goods across the isthmus, undertaken with American capital, was completed in 1855.

nearer to our own and awakened American interest in the Far East. In 1844 the United States had concluded its first treaty with China, opening certain Chinese ports to trade and obtaining for American merchants extraterritorial privileges (that is, the right to be tried by American tribunals in China, according to American law).

In 1850, in order to make certain that a waterway to the Pacific across Central America would be kept open at all times by international guarantee, the United States made the Clayton-Bulwer treaty with Great Britain.[1] The next year the Government, suspicious of French intentions, affirmed its opposition to the seizure of Hawaii by any European power. So vital did the Hawaiian group seem to the growth of American interests in the Pacific that in 1854 the Government planned to annex the islands. The project miscarried because of the death of the well-disposed insular monarch. This same year Commodore Perry persuaded Japan, by a display of force, to depart from its ancient seclusion and open two ports to American trade—an event which marked the advent of the modern era in the island kingdom. Regardless of party, "Young America" visioned possibilities of trade and even of territorial gains in the great Pacific basin. But for the renewal of the slavery controversy and the exhausting war that followed, the United States might have embarked upon a career of colonial empire a half-century before it did.

While manufacturing and shipping flourished in the East, prosperity smiled with equal favor upon the South. There, despite the attention given to rice culture along the coast, sugar growing in Louisiana and tobacco raising in the border states, not to mention scattered local manufacturing, the chief fount of wealth was the cotton crop. The develop-

[1] The treaty was designed also to check encroachments by the British on territory near their base at Belize, in British Honduras.

ment of the rich black lands of the Gulf plains doubled production during the decade, but the world's demand for cotton grew still faster and the price rose steadily. From all parts of Dixie wagon, steamer and railroad brought the bulky bales to the points whence they were dispatched to remote markets. Cotton furnished more than half of the nation's exports, most of it going to England. At the same time it shed benefits upon northern mill owners, merchants and bankers and, by centering southern energies upon its cultivation, created a demand for the farm produce of the Midwest. In the South itself the wealth invested in cotton culture and its peculiar labor system represented a power which ramified into all phases of political, economic and social life. Little wonder that the people south of Mason and Dixon's line attached an almost fantastic importance to their great staple. "What would happen if no cotton was planted for three years?" asked Senator J. H. Hammond of South Carolina in a speech in 1858. "I will not stop to depict what every one can imagine, but this is certain, England would topple headlong, and carry the whole civilized world with her save the South. No, you dare not make war on cotton. No power on the earth dares to make war on it. Cotton is King."

The Midwest with its boundless prairies and swiftly growing population shared fully in the good times. Thanks to the Irish famine of the late forties and the Crimean War of the fifties, Britain as well as the older parts of America demanded its wheat and other cereals, while the rapid introduction of labor-saving implements made possible an unexampled increase of production.[1] Of the new devices the most important was the McCormick reaper. Patented originally in 1834 by Cyrus H. McCormick, a Virginia black-

[1] The act of Parliament repealing the "corn" laws in 1846 had thrown open the door to foreign cereals, but its full effect on the normal grain trade with America was not felt until the sixties.

smith, the first model had been continually improved until it became possible for one person with a team of horses to cut as much grain as seven men swinging cradles in the customary fashion. When McCormick in 1848 removed to Chicago, then a town of hardly seventeen thousand but near the center of the prairie grain belt, a new era opened in the mechanization of agriculture. He manufactured 500 machines for the harvest of 1848, but by 1860 over 100,000 reapers of his and other makes were in use, caring for a grain crop which swelled from 100,000,000 bushels in 1850 to 171,000,000 in 1860.

An important stimulus to western prosperity was the great improvement in transportation facilities. Until the mid-century, the chief outlets for western produce were by way of the Great Lakes and the Erie Canal or down the Mississippi and through the Gulf. The latter was still the more important, and the economic connections of the Midwest were with the South rather than the East. Between 1850 and 1857, however, the Appalachian barrier was pierced by five railway trunk lines, and these, by their connections in the interior, reached the Ohio River at eight points and the Mississippi at ten.

The railroads diverted to the eastward much of the traffic which had previously gone down the river. Railroad building became a mania, cities and towns vying with one another in subsidizing new roads. The national government assisted by granting lands to states for transfer to projected lines. In 1850 Stephen A. Douglas helped to secure a princely grant for the Illinois Central Railroad to link Chicago with Mobile on the Gulf. Soon he was dreaming of the advantages to his home city of like communications with California. By 1860 Illinois had more track completed than any other state in the Union. The iron bonds uniting East and West not only gave rise to mutually profitable trade, but, by emphasizing the economic interdependence of the two regions, tended to create a harmony of political outlook as well. This fact, as much perhaps as abolitionist agitation, accounts for northern unity when southern guns boomed out against Fort Sumter in 1861.

In the expansion of the railway net the South, with her capital tied up in land and slaves, had much less part. Despite their strict-construction objections to internal improvements at national cost, a number of southern states secured federal land grants to aid railroad construction. But not until late in the decade did a continuous line through the mountains, running from Memphis to Norfolk, connect the lower Mississippi with the southern seaboard. A series of commercial conventions met in the fifties to arouse enthusiasm for railway building, particularly for a road linking the South with California. The speakers also urged the promotion of manufactures and the establishment of direct steamship lines to Europe. But such efforts to keep pace with the North and free the South from "vassalage" to that section met with little success.

In keeping with the march of events in other fields, journalism took a new trend during the middle years of the century. The old type of official party organ, located in Washington and subsidized by government printing, disappeared. Journals of this kind made dull reading for all but bigoted partisans, and their high subscription price further narrowed the circle of their influence. The assumption by the government itself of the task of executing the public printing foreshadowed the end. But the end was inevitable in any case, for the masses educated in the free public schools demanded a different type of newspaper, and New York City, thanks to the improved news facilities afforded by the telegraph and the railroad, was fast replacing Washington as the principal news center of the nation.

The new journalism flowered most luxuriantly in New York and the East. Selling at a price within the reach of all, the papers sought to make a broad popular appeal with headlines, sprightly news "stories" and trenchant editorials.[1] The period produced the greatest editorial writers in our history. Unlike those of today they usually owned the journals they directed—men such as Horace Greeley of the *New York Tribune*, Henry J. Raymond of the *New York Times*, James Gordon Bennett of the *New York Herald*, Samuel Bowles of the *Springfield* (Massachusetts) *Republican* and Joseph Medill of the *Chicago Tribune*. William Cullen Bryant, who at the helm of the *New York Evening Post* had steered a course of vigorous independent journalism since 1826, continued to make a special appeal to the educated classes in the East. In national circulation and influence no other newspaper equaled the *Tribune*, edited by the brilliant but eccentric Greeley.

FOREIGN INFLUENCES

A new factor, and one of a significance which could not be correctly estimated at the time, was introduced into American life in the forties and fifties through the swelling of the tide of immigration. The liberal revolutions of the years around 1830 had been followed in Europe by a period of reaction, which was succeeded in turn by a new series of revolutions. A popular upheaval in France in 1848 was the spark which fired a powder train reaching from the English Channel to the Russian border. Within a few months half of the monarchs of Europe were deposed or forced to grant constitutions to their subjects. The kings of Prussia, Holland, Denmark and Sardinia made important concessions to popular

---

[1] The change had begun as early as 1833 when the *New York Sun* was founded as a "penny paper" catering particularly to working-class readers. Of the newspapers here named, the *Times* (1851) was the only one established after 1850. Medill formed his connection with the *Chicago Tribune* in 1855.

demands, and the Swiss communities set up a federal government modeled after that of the United States. In Great Britain the "Chartists" demanded a government based upon universal manhood suffrage. The remnants of feudal privilege were swept away in many lands, and within two decades nationality and democracy made substantial gains in nearly every great state in Europe.

The people of the United States watched sympathetically these stirrings across the Atlantic. In many of the larger cities public meetings and parades celebrated the tidings of each liberal victory. The national Democratic convention of 1848 sent "fraternal congratulations" to the new French republic, and rejoiced that the spirit of popular rule was "prostrating thrones and erecting republics on the ruins of despotism in the Old World." Whenever the popular cause suffered reverses, its leaders were prone to take temporary refuge in the New World, engaging in such occupations as promised to afford a livelihood. New York City in 1850 presented the strange spectacle of such leaders acting as porters and dancing masters. An ex-member of the German parliament worked as a barber, and the Italian revolutionist Garibaldi made tallow candles in a back street on Staten Island. Yet the American people, notwithstanding their interest in the aspirations of Europeans, considered the Atlantic a bar to active participation in Europe's affairs. President Fillmore, at the behest of Congress, sent a warship to Turkey to convey the exiled Hungarian patriot, Louis Kossuth, to the United States. Arriving in December, 1851, he received great ovations in the eastern cities, was dined by the President, and formally greeted by each House of Congress. Yet, despite his enthusiastic reception, he had to be content with the moral support and financial contributions of private individuals.

As in 1830, the revolutionary outbreaks sent thousands of

refugees to the United States as a permanent abode. The mid-century immigration was due mainly, however, to bad economic conditions. "America letters," written by successful migrants to their countrymen at home, extolled the advantages of life in the New World, while steamship and railway representatives and agents of western states added their efforts to swell the flow of immigration. From 23,000 in 1830 the number of annual arrivals rose to 84,000 in 1840 and to 297,000 in 1849, reaching high tide five years later with 428,000. Approximately three million came in the decade from 1845 to 1855—three times as many as in the whole preceding period of national independence. Between 1850 and 1860 the total number of foreign born leaped eighty-four per cent, a rate of increase far surpassing that of the native stock. "There has been nothing like it," wrote a sympathetic observer in the *Democratic Review* in 1850, "since the encampment of the Roman empire, or the tents of the Crusaders." Many of the newcomers were desperately poor; the great majority of them were peasants from southwestern Germany, discouraged by crop failures and oppressive laws, or from Ireland, forced to flee because of the potato famine of the late forties.

By 1860, nearly a million Teutons had arrived in the United States. Among them were such prominent "Forty-eighters" as Carl Schurz, Franz Sigel, and other men of education and talent. Most of the Germans settled in the newer parts of the country north of the Ohio or beyond the Mississippi. St. Louis, Milwaukee, Chicago, Cincinnati, and Cleveland attracted them in numbers. In about half of the cities of Ohio the Germans and "Pennsylvania Dutch" (descendants of German immigrants of colonial days) nearly or quite held the balance of political power. Wherever they went they carried with them their zeal for schools and education, their love of music and the liberal social customs of

THE GERMANIA MUSICAL SOCIETY

the Fatherland. In large degree, they planted the first seeds of aesthetic appreciation in the raw West. Staunch believers in legislation for free homesteads, they were ever ready to do what they could to support that cause. The Irish, on the other hand, hived in the cities of the East, or became workers on turnpikes, canals, and railroads. Indeed, the hard manual labor upon the great public improvements of the era was performed mainly by their brawn. They lived, for the most part, in wretched poverty in city tenements; and wherever they settled they added to the traditional anti-British feeling of Americans their own bitterness towards England—a fact quickly observed and capitalized by vote-seeking politicians.

The increase in the number of newcomers begot a strong nativist sentiment on the part of Americans of older stock. In the seaboard industrial districts the workingmen were dismayed by the competition of Irish laborers with a lower standard of living. Moreover, most of the Irish were Catholics, and Catholic churches, convents, and parochial schools multiplied to the alarm of the Protestants of New England and the Middle Atlantic states. The ease with which unscrupulous native politicians corrupted newly naturalized voters gave further cause for fear, seeming to threaten the integrity of American institutions. In the West, the social customs of the Germans, especially their beer drinking and lax observance of the Sabbath, offended the Puritan austerity of the older inhabitants.

As early as the thirties the hostility towards the Irish had broken out in mob violence. In 1834 a convent in Charleston, Massachusetts, was burned. A few years later the Irish quarter in Boston was sacked. Similar outrages occurred in other cities, and on one or two occasions Native American parties in New York and Philadelphia undertook to prevent the election of naturalized citizens to municipal office. In 1845 a national organization of Native Americans was effected, with a membership, it was claimed, of more than a hundred thousand. In 1850 the movement assumed the form of a secret society under the name (known at the time only to its members) of the Supreme Order of the Star-Spangled Banner. For a few years the society showed little vitality, but presently, under unexpected circumstances, it became the backbone of the spectacular Know Nothing movement.

THE REVIVAL OF SECTIONAL DISCORD

The promise of intersectional harmony with which the decade of the fifties began was not to be fulfilled. Even the material prosperity in which all regions shared did not harmonize the interests of the sections, and as the years passed it became more and more painfully evident that the economic systems of North and South were irreconcilable. The backwardness of the latter section in railway building has been noted. Most immigrants avoided the slave states, where they were not likely to find employment, and the planters saw with alarm that the newcomers were swelling the population of the free states, with a consequent increase in their congressional representation, and threatening to populate the territories with settlers hostile to slavery. Thus the deeper significance of the peaceful invasion of aliens appears in the influence upon the growing sectional antagonism. The newcomers' conception of American nationality was patterned upon that of the North, since nine tenths of them dwelt in the free states and territories. The Irish excepted, they gravitated to the party that opposed slavery, favored free farms, and espoused an indivisible Union, for slavery was unknown in western Europe, most of them were farmers, and many had fought in wars for national unification. Temporarily some of them joined the Democratic ranks because of the appeal of the party name; but as the issue sharpened, the Germans in particular, but the Scandinavians and Hollanders also, flocked into the antislavery party. The Irish, for the most part, remained incurable Democrats.

The varied industry of the North yielded profits which sought reinvestment, while many southern plantations were conducted on a credit basis, with capital drawn from the free states. Southerners resented this dependence on northern capital, resented the fact that so large a part of the profits of their labors accrued to the capitalists, resented, in short, their economic vassalage. "In one way or another," protested a southern writer in 1857, "we are more or less subservient to the North every day of our lives. In infancy we are swaddled in Northern muslin; in childhood we are humored with Northern gewgaws; in youth we are instructed out of Northern books; at the age of maturity we sow our 'wild oats' on Northern soil; . . . in the decline of life we remedy our eye-sight with Northern spectacles . . .; in old age we are drugged with Northern physic; and, finally, when we die, our inanimate bodies, shrouded in Northern cambric, are stretched upon the bier, borne to the grave in a Northern carriage, entombed with a Northern spade, and memorialized with a Northern slab!"

In the North, the antislavery irreconcilables had never abandoned their opposition to the Fugitive Slave Act of 1850. Its energetic utilization by slave owners prevented these extremists from forgetting their hatred. In some instances fugitives who had been living on free soil for many years and had married there were seized and carried off into bondage again. Northern communities, which thus saw some of the harshest features of the slavery system enacted before their very eyes, were easily incited to riotous opposition. One case that attracted nation-wide attention occurred in Boston in February, 1851, when a runaway named Shadrach was forcibly taken from the United States marshal and spirited away into Canada. Some months later, in October,

the seizure of Jerry McHenry, for several years a resident of
Syracuse, New York, led to another lawless rescue, under
Gerrit Smith's leadership, followed by the Negro's flight
across the border.

Slave rescues gave the South another cause for discontent.
The new Fugitive Slave Act was its reason for accepting the
compromise of 1850, and its nullification was not to be endured. The mood of mutual forbearance which marked the
leaders of both sections in 1850 was endangered by such affairs. Moreover, a new generation was coming forward in
political life, a generation which was less inclined to compromise than the elder statesmen.

THE RISE OF A NEW GENERATION

By the close of 1852 the master figures of the older generation had passed from the scene. Calhoun died in the Compromise year; Clay and Webster followed before Pierce's
election. Van Buren definitely dropped out of politics after
his unsuccessful run as Free Soil candidate in 1848, and
Benton retired from the Senate in 1851 after thirty years'
service. With the possible exception of Calhoun, the distinguishing trait of these men had been their devotion to the
Union. Their public life had been shaped by the great surge
of nationalism which followed the second war with Great
Britain. The new leaders, on the contrary, had been reared
in an era of sectional controversy. Younger in years and experience, they lacked the poise and caution of the seasoned
statesmen. They faced the problems of the age with all the
jaunty assurance which fresh generations are apt to bring to
a consideration of grave public issues. On the central question of the time they held intense convictions, and felt lightly
the obligation of maintaining a patchwork peace that had
been dictated by leaders of a departed era.

Both sections, with their radically different points of view, were represented in the new leadership. From the free states came William H. Seward of New York, Salmon P. Chase of Ohio, Charles Sumner of Massachusetts and Thaddeus Stevens of Pennsylvania, all of whom entered Congress in the years 1849–1851 as uncompromising foes of slavery extension and of the "Slave Power." While ever professing to cherish the Union, they were ready to risk its harmony and peace for the sake of advancing the cause to which they were committed. Southern interests were no less stoutly championed by Jefferson Davis of Mississippi, on whom fell the mantle of Calhoun, and by W. L. Yancey of Alabama, and Alexander H. Stephens, Robert Toombs and Howell Cobb of Georgia. These men frankly calculated the value of the Union in terms of sectional advantage, proclaiming on every occasion the right of secession as a means of southern redress. The compromise ideals of the preceding era found spokesmen in John J. Crittenden of Kentucky, Clay's successor in the Senate, and in Senator John Bell of Tennessee, men of lesser stature, however, than the sectional chieftains.

Stephen A. Douglas, the Illinois Senator, is harder to classify, but he was one of the dominant political figures of the decade. Short in stature but with powerful shoulders, idolized by his western followers as the "Little Giant," he embodied the two ideals dear to the frontier: ardent attachment to nationality and an unfaltering faith in local self-rule as a solvent of human ills. He was also interested in the rapid economic development of the West and particularly in the growth of Chicago where he had heavy real-estate investments. As the foremost Democrat in the free states, his position gave him an unusual opportunity to act as conciliator and arbiter between northern radicals and southern "fire-eaters." A believer in the destiny of Middle America and an exemplar of its aspirations, he retained his hold on his section unshaken until Abraham Lincoln emerged from private life in 1858.

The new antislavery leaders found an effective ally in Horace Greeley, editor of the *New York Tribune,* and the foremost among the new school of journalists. He was by temperament a reformer, and none of the agitations of the time, from spiritualism to scientific farming and Irish freedom, failed to challenge his interest. But his soul-consuming passion was hatred of slavery, and to this cause he gave increasing devotion during the fifties. The *Tribune's* circulation grew five-fold from 1850 to 1860; but its sectional character is evidenced by the fact that virtually all of its subscribers lived in the free states. The weekly edition was preëminently the journal of the rural districts which regarded it as a sort of political Bible. The antislavery forces could hardly have found a more potent vehicle of agitation and education.

No less effective in molding northern opinion, though in a different way, was the appearance of that great propagandist novel, *Uncle Tom's Cabin,* written by Harriet Beecher Stowe of Cincinnati. Others had long inveighed against slavery in the abstract, but Mrs. Stowe portrayed concretely and with moral intensity the cruelty and injustice that the system could inflict even upon a faithful liegeman like the lovable Uncle Tom. She depicted not the average condition of slaves but, rather, the melodramatic contrast between the best and worst possibilities of their existence. Appearing originally as a serial in an antislavery newspaper at the capital, the story was published in book form in March, 1852. It began its record-breaking career with a sale of three hundred thousand copies in the first year. The stage possibilities of the story appealed first to theatrical managers, then to political managers. Presently thousands of men and boys who would not have read the book were thrilled and swayed by the dramatized version. Mrs. Stowe's interpretation of slavery deeply influenced the thinking of northern youths who came of voting age in the years from 1852 to 1860. In the South it was anathema.

From this survey it is evident that when Franklin Pierce came to the presidency forces were already at work which portended a renewal of sectional strife. The new chief magistrate lacked both the experience and the ability to meet the dangers which his administration faced, and the course pursued hastened rather than delayed the new crisis.

When taking the oath of office on March 4, 1853, he expressed the fervent hope that "no sectional or ambitious or fanatical excitement may again threaten the durability of our institutions or obscure the light of our prosperity." Yet a definite proslavery influence was reflected in his choice of a cabinet. Under southern pressure he withdrew his offer of the post of Secretary of State, first made to a New Yorker with antislavery leanings, and appointed instead another New Yorker, William L. Marcy, who more nearly met the southern requirements. Jefferson Davis, noted as an implacable opponent of the Compromise, received the important office of Secretary of War.[1]

Moreover, in his inaugural address Pierce, while expressing interest in developing "new channels of trade," placed chief emphasis on his intention not to have his course as President deterred "by any timid forebodings of evil" from territorial expansion. The reference, as everyone knew, was to the scheme of annexing Cuba, which Polk and his Secretary of State, James Buchanan, had fostered but which their

---

[1] The other members of the cabinet were James Guthrie of Kentucky, Secretary of the Treasury; James C. Dobbin of North Carolina, Secretary of the Navy; Robert McClelland of Michigan, Secretary of the Interior; James Campbell of Pennsylvania, Postmaster-General; Caleb Cushing of Massachusetts, Attorney-General.

Whig successors had failed to press. This proposal to enlarge the slave area greatly pleased southern extremists who during the Whig lease of power had helped fit out filibustering expeditions in a fruitless endeavor to free the island from Spain. With Marcy's assistance Pierce prepared to translate his words into action. In August, 1854, Buchanan, Pierre Soulé and John Y. Mason, the American Ministers to Great Britain, Spain and France, were instructed to confer as to the best means of acquiring Cuba. In Belgium in October, they drew up a remarkable document, known as the Ostend Manifesto, which asserted that, if Spain refused to sell the island and our national interests required, we would be justified "by every law, human and divine," in wresting it from her by force. The President was not prepared to go to such lengths, but the proposal produced wild excitement in the free states when its contents leaked out.

The administration also coveted territory across the Mexican border, including Lower California, but succeeded only in purchasing a tract south of the Gila River.[1] By this acquisition a boundary difficulty was settled with Mexico and, at the same time, land acquired which Secretary of War Davis deemed desirable for a southern railway route to the Pacific.

Pierce's imperialistic program would have precipitated a new sectional controversy if he had adopted the recommendation of the Ostend Manifesto. He avoided that pitfall only to witness the renewal of conflict between North and South by events which at first seemed innocent enough. The region between the Rockies and the western boundary of Missouri, Iowa and Minnesota had never been given territorial organization, remaining, for the most part, a vast reserve for wild Indians and roving buffaloes. As population thick-

---

[1] The treaty was negotiated by James Gadsden, in 1853, and involved the payment of $10,000,000.

ened in the upper Mississippi Valley, more and more people turned their eyes towards this virgin land. By 1850 the need for opening the country to settlers was fast becoming urgent. Furthermore, national security made desirable a continuous zone of settlement from the heart of the continent to the distant communities on the Pacific Coast, and the extinction of the Indian title would facilitate plans for a transcontinental railway.

On January 4, 1854, Douglas as chairman of the Senate committee on territories offered a bill for organizing the whole domain as the "Territory of Nebraska." Although the region was free soil under the Missouri Compromise of 1820, he proposed that the status of slavery in the territory should be determined by the principles underlying the Compromise of 1850. These recognized, he said, the right of the territorial legislature to admit or exclude slavery (popular sovereignty), and left final determination of all questions involving the legality of slave ownership to the Supreme Court. Greeted by a storm of criticism and protest, Douglas was obliged to change the bill in certain particulars. In its final form it provided not for one territory but for two, Kansas and Nebraska, with the fortieth parallel dividing them. The Missouri Compromise was explicitly repealed, and the people of the territories were authorized to regulate their domestic institutions as they chose, "subject only to the Constitution of the United States." All questions involving title to slaves might be appealed to the Supreme Court.

From the standpoint of practical politics Douglas undoubtedly won favor for his cause by claiming that the regulations in the Compromise of 1850 as to slavery in New Mexico and Utah had been intended as a rule of universal application; but historians find no warrant for this assump-

tion.   He was on unsafe ground even when he alleged that
these regulations embodied the principle of popular sovereignty.   Indeed, not all who supported the Kansas-Nebraska
act believed that it established popular sovereignty in the

KANSAS AND NEBRASKA, 1854

proposed territories.   Senator A. G. Brown of Mississippi
said: "If I thought that in voting for the bill as it now stands
I was conceding the right of the people in a territory to exclude slavery, I would withhold my vote. . . .   It leaves the
question where I am willing it should be left—to the ultimate
decision of the courts." [1]   The provision for two territories
instead of one aided passage, for it was believed that Kansas,

---

[1] Douglas himself later said of the Kansas-Nebraska act: "We did not pre-
tend to decide the question whether the Territorial Legislature had the
power or not to prohibit slavery, but we did agree to give them all the power
we had; and, if they exercised it in such manner as to violate the constitutional
rights of any portion of the people, their remedy is to be found in an appeal
to the Supreme Court, and not to Congress."

lying next to Missouri, would become slave soil while Nebraska would fall to the antislavery Northerners.

The passage of the bill through Congress precipitated a desperate struggle. Though Congress possessed the legal power to undo what it had once done, the proposal for repeal deeply outraged the moral sense of the North. The opposition in the Senate was directed by Chase and Sumner, but the Little Giant, ceaselessly active, proved more than a match for them. In the House the shrewd assaults of ex-Senator Benton were counteracted by the parliamentary adroitness of the proslavery Whig, Alexander H. Stephens. President Pierce, abetted by Jefferson Davis, used his control of patronage in favor of the bill. Its success was assured by the support of an almost solid South, seconded by Democrats from the Midwest. The bill, signed by the President on May 30, 1854, was avowedly a Democratic measure, but throughout the stormy contest sectional rather than party advantage had been the prime consideration.

So far-reaching were the effects of the Kansas-Nebraska act that the motives which led to its introduction are a matter of continuing interest. At the time, Douglas was accused by his antislavery foes of making a conscienceless bid for southern support for the presidency, but it is hardly probable that a man of his political acumen would have risked northern defections to gain additional favor in the South. Douglas himself found ample justification for his course in the democratic character of his plan and in the belief that popular sovereignty would permanently "withdraw the question of slavery from the halls of Congress and the political arena." In any case, as he pointed out, climate would make impossible the deep rooting of slavery in the new territories. It is only fair to say that nothing in his career, either before or after 1854, warrants us in doubting his unselfish devotion to the principle of local self-determination.

Other factors, however, were involved. The agitation for a transcontinental railroad had created rivalry between the Northwest and the Southwest, each seeking new means of nourishing its own sectional prosperity. Though an engineering survey of the War Department reported the superior feasibility of a southern route, enterprising men in the Northwest were not willing to yield the point, and believed that rapid settlement of the Nebraska country would be a potent argument for a centrally located line. Douglas, eager for the commercial preëminence of Chicago, was a natural leader in any such movement. Thus the economic interest of the Northwest, as well as its democratic idealism, favored the bill. The South was willing temporarily to weaken its chances of a southern railroad because of the opportunity for slavery extension afforded by popular sovereignty.[1] As it turned out, sectional rivalry prevented federal aid to any transcontinental project until after secession caused the withdrawal of southern representatives from Congress and left the North in control.

SELECT BIBLIOGRAPHY

The Ordeal of Nationality. For the period following the Compromise of 1850 Rhodes' *History of the United States* becomes the standard treatise. McMaster, Schouler, and Channing continue to be useful general histories.

Mid-century America. Cole, *The Irrepressible Conflict,* treats the subject as a whole. Some scholars believe that the war was not inevitable. See Craven, *The Repressible Conflict,* and Milton, *The Eve of Conflict.* Industrial and technological changes

[1] Additional support for the bill resulted from a factional fight in Missouri within Democratic ranks. Senator D. R. Atchison, seeking reëlection and finding a bold course necessary to rally his slaveholding constituents, publicly promised that when he returned to Congress in December, 1853, he would work to have the rich prairie lands west of the state opened to settlers without the Missouri Compromise restriction. Besides, like the Illinois Senator, he desired to connect his state with California by rail. Had not Douglas fathered the Kansas-Nebraska bill, it seems certain that Atchison would have.

may be followed in Clark, *History of Manufactures in the United States,* and Byrn, *The Progress of Invention in the Nineteenth Century.* Burlingame, *March of the Iron Men,* is a history of invention, which attempts to show the effect in unifying the nation. Johnson and others, *History of the Domestic and Foreign Commerce of the United States,* the most extensive general account, should be supplemented by Spears, *The Story of the American Merchant Marine;* and works dealing with the era of the sailing vessel, of which there are several, including Albion, *Square-Riggers on Schedule;* Clark, *The Clipper Ship Era, 1843– 1869;* Cutler, *Greyhounds of the Sea;* and Lubbock, *Romance of the Clipper Ship.* Morison, *The Maritime History of Massachusetts, 1783–1860,* joins scholarship with unusual literary charm. On railway development the standard works are Sanborn, *Congressional Grants of Land in Aid of Railways;* Haney, *A Congressional History of Railways in the United States, 1850–1887;* MacGill and others, *History of Transportation in the United States before 1860;* and Riegel, *The Story of the Western Railroads.* Bidwell and Falconer, *History of Agriculture in the Northern United States, 1620–1860,* and Gray, *History of Agriculture in the Southern United States to 1860,* contain much information in regard to the fifties. Hutchinson, *Cyrus Hall McCormick, Seed-Time, 1809–1856,* describes the rôle played by the chief inventor and maker of farm implements. Phillips, *Life and Labor in the Old South,* includes material on economic and social conditions in the fifties, while Ingle, *Southern Sidelights,* supplements Phillips at various points. Bancroft, *Slave-Trading in the Old South,* is the best treatment on its subject. Russel, *Economic Aspects of Southern Sectionalism, 1840–1861,* and Wender, *Southern Commercial Conventions,* show, with full documentation, the importance of economic inferiority as a factor in the movement for southern independence. Diplomatic phases of the era are treated in Dennett, *Americans in Eastern Asia;* Treat, *Diplomatic Relations between the United States and Japan, 1853–1865;* and Williams, *Anglo-American Isthmian Diplomacy, 1815–1915.*

Foreign Influences. The interest of the American people in the mid-century European revolutions appears in Curtis, *The French Assembly of 1848 and American Constitutional Doctrines;*

Gazley, *American Opinion of German Unification;* and Marraro, *American Opinion on the Unification of Italy, 1846–1861.* General accounts of immigration include Fairchild, *Immigration;* Garis, *Immigration Restriction;* Stephenson, *A History of American Immigration;* and Wittke, *We Who Built America.* For particular racial elements Adams, *Ireland and Irish Emigration to the New World,* Faust, *The German Element in the United States,* and Blegen, *Norwegian Migration to America, 1825–1860,* should be consulted. The nativist movement is discussed in Billington, *Protestant Crusade.*

The Rise of a New Generation. For biographies of Northern leaders, see Bancroft, *The Life of William H. Seward;* Hart, *Salmon Portland Chase;* Haynes, *Charles Sumner;* Woodburn, *The Life of Thaddeus Stevens;* Johnson, *Stephen A. Douglas;* Milton, *The Eve of Conflict* (deals with Douglas) ; and Linn, *Horace Greeley.* Lives of outstanding southern figures include Dodd, *Jefferson Davis;* Winston, *High Stakes and Hair Trigger* (Davis) ; Cutting, *Jefferson Davis* (by an ardent admirer) ; Pendleton, *Alexander H. Stephens;* Phillips, *The Life of Robert Toombs;* Craven, *Edmund Ruffin, Southerner;* White, *Robert Barnwell Rhett;* Merritt, *James Henry Hammond;* and Flippin, *Herschel V. Johnson of Georgia.* Bleyer, *Main Currents in the History of American Journalism,* portrays the new era in the newspaper world.

The Revival of Sectional Discord. Political development and party conflict during the decade are traced in Smith, *Parties and Slavery;* Cole, *The Irrepressible Conflict,* deals with the divisive economic and social forces. Nichols, *Franklin Pierce,* appraises Pierce's presidency with relentless honesty. Two phases of foreign policy are treated in Garber, *The Gadsden Treaty,* and Ettinger, *The Mission to Spain of Pierre Soulé, 1853–1855.* Difficulties of enforcing the Fugitive Slave Act may be followed in Siebert, *The Underground Railroad from Slavery to Freedom.* The question of the motives behind the Kansas-Nebraska act has provoked considerable discussion among historians. Rhodes lays it all to Douglas's personal ambition for the presidency. According to Ray, *The Repeal of the Missouri Compromise,* the act should be understood as the execution of a campaign pledge made by Senator Atchison of Missouri in his contest for reëlection. Hodder in his "Genesis of the Kansas-Nebraska Act," and elsewhere, represents the act as one phase of the rivalry between northern and southern commercial interests to secure the terminus of the proposed Pacific railway.

Gilbertson, *Harriet Beecher Stowe,* is a study of Mrs. Stowe's emotional reactions rather than of the influence of her writings.

Chapter XXXI

THE DRIFT TOWARD DISUNION, 1854–1860

THE PARTY REVOLUTION

NO law ever passed by Congress produced such momentous consequences as the Kansas-Nebraska act. While the bill was yet before Congress, Chase predicted, "It will light up a fire in the country which may, perhaps, consume those who kindle it." The reasons are not far to seek. The measure not only revived all the old rancors over slavery extension, which Pierce had promised were at an end, but did so at the cost of annulling a long-standing sectional pact which, in the North at least, had assumed an almost sacred character. Hardly less important was the fact that the self-interest of the northern farmers, both native and foreign-born, was directly threatened by the law. Accustomed to think of the new territories as a Promised Land to which their class would fall heir, they now faced possible competition with slave labor there. Nor were they made less apprehensive by the fact that, while the Kansas-Nebraska measure was under consideration, a bill which would have encouraged northern settlement through free homesteads had been blocked by the proslavery Senate after passing the House. Greeley declared that Douglas and Pierce had made more abolitionists in three months than William Lloyd Garrison and Wendell Phillips could make in half a century.

To the Whig party the act dealt a death blow. Already weakened by sectional differences, the two factions of the party now found themselves occupying opposing camps.

Most of the southern members in Congress had voted for the measure while every northern one had opposed it. The next few years witnessed the dispersion of the Whigs into the ranks of other parties. The Democrats also suffered, though in less degree. If their numbers were diminished in the North by the desertion of "Anti-Nebraska" Democrats, the loss was in considerable degree offset by accessions from the southern Whigs. A. H. Stephens and Robert Toombs who now turned Democrat were hosts in themselves. Under the circumstances the party became more firmly allied than ever with the interests of cotton capitalism.

The most significant outcome of the Kansas-Nebraska contest, however, was the rise of two new organizations. One was the Republican party. While the act was yet pending in Congress, antislavery leaders there had issued an appeal to the people, branding it as "a gross violation of a sacred pledge" and "an atrocious plot to exclude from a vast unoccupied region immigrants from the Old World and free laborers from our own States." Three political factions were ripe for union on a program opposed to slavery extension: most of the northern Whigs, the old Free Soilers (who had called themselves Free Democrats in the campaign in 1852) and the Anti-Nebraska Democrats. Another source of strength lay in the immigrant farmers of the Midwest, whose probable political course was charted by the anti-Nebraska editorials in eighty out of eighty-eight German newspapers. Horace Greeley took a leading part in urging independent political action, but the party actually sprang into being from a spontaneous uprising of the people. On February 28, 1854, a local gathering at Ripon, Wisconsin, heralded the new party; other localities fell into line; and on July 6 a giant mass meeting in an oak grove near Jackson, Michigan, organized the party on a state-wide basis. By the fall of 1854 the new organization was active in all the western states and in some eastern ones, though the name Republican was not yet everywhere employed.

In the East progress was slower because of the powerful competition offered by the newly formed American party. The nucleus of this party was the Supreme Order of the Star-Spangled Banner. It was organized as a secret society with grips, passwords and ritualistic ceremonies, and since members declined to satisfy outside curiosity in regard to the organization, they were popularly called "Know Nothings." As a matter of fact, each member swore a solemn oath to support only American-born Protestants for office. The secrecy and charm of novelty won many persons to the party, especially in the East where aliens were least welcome and most in evidence. At the same time, important accessions came from people all over the North, who hoped by magnifying the new issue to drive the slavery question out of politics. Many southern Whigs joined because they were loath to make common cause with their traditional enemies, the Democrats; indeed, to oppose immigration seemed a means of curbing the growth of antislavery power.

The fall elections of 1854 revealed the remarkable advance of the two new parties. With no public campaign the Know Nothings cast over a fourth of the total vote in New York and more than two fifths in Pennsylvania. In Massachusetts they elected every state officer and nearly the entire legislature. Elsewhere they won lesser successes. The Republicans swept Maine, Vermont and all the midwestern states but Illinois. The Democrats lost control of the House of Representatives and of nine states. Nearly everywhere the Whigs revealed great weakness, their success in New York being due to Seward's reluctance to leave the party until after his reëlection as Senator.

Elated by their fine showing, the Know Nothings laid plans to capture the presidency two years later. In order to con-

solidate the support which had come from voters averse to
sectional strife, they added to their ritual a "Union oath,"
pledging all members to resist the election to office of disunionists as well as immigrants. But with the political
waters in turmoil it was impossible for any party to steer a
middle course. The northern and southern sections fell into
contentions over slavery, and by 1856 the Know Nothings
found themselves officially committed to popular sovereignty.
Since this doctrine belonged in a political sense to the Democrats, the fate of the party was sealed. Its activities in local
politics, however, were not without effect, for Know Nothing influence was responsible for the enactment of literacy
tests for voting in Connecticut in 1855 and in Massachusetts
two years later—the first laws of the kind in our history.[1]
The object was to reduce the number of naturalized voters.

Meantime the Republican-controlled states proceeded to
take whatever legal steps they could to impede or defeat the
operation of the Fugitive Slave Act. Such statutes usually
prohibited the use of local jails to confine fugitives and punished severely the seizure of a free Negro with intent to enslave him. The personal-liberty laws, as they were called,
were hailed by the South as proof positive of the aggressive
and lawless character of the party. In the free states, however, the Republicans steadily gained in popular favor. Seward, a giant of strength, took over leadership in the East
in 1855; the fiery partisan discussions in Congress helped to
educate the northern masses; and a brutal assault on Senator
Sumner in May, 1856, aided the Republican cause in a different way. A few days after Sumner had made a violent
speech against southern machinations in Kansas, he was attacked and caned into insensibility by Preston Brooks, a
member of the House and nephew of a southern Senator

[1] These states stood alone until 1889 when Wyoming, followed presently
by other commonwealths, imposed literacy requirements.

whom Sumner had assailed with particular venom. The deed enraged the North which saw in it additional evidence of the ruthlessness of the "Slave Power." An attempt to expel Brooks from his seat failed, every southern member but one voting to sustain him.

The Republicans faced the campaign of 1856 in a resolute mood, meeting at Philadelphia on June 17, the anniversary of Bunker Hill. The presidential nomination went to John C. Frémont of California, a popular figure by reason of his explorations in the Far West and at the same time a man unhampered by antipathies such as embarrassed Seward and Chase because of their political records. For second place W. L. Dayton of New Jersey was chosen over Abraham Lincoln, the midwestern candidate. The platform denied that the Constitution permitted the legalization of slavery in the territories, flayed the Pierce administration for the efforts it was making to impose slavery on Kansas (see p. 683), and stigmatized the Ostend Manifesto as "the highwayman's plea that 'might makes right.'"

The convention of the Know Nothings was marked by angry debates, ending in the withdrawal of most of the antislavery delegates. Their platform denounced the election of immigrants and Catholics to office, demanded twenty-one years' residence for naturalization, and advocated an indestructible Union with popular sovereignty in the territories. Millard Fillmore, whose signature had given legal effect to the Compromise of 1850, was nominated for President with A. J. Donelson of Tennessee as his running mate. Later in the year these nominations were indorsed by a national convention composed of remnants of the old Whig party.

The Democrats, fearing to nominate either Pierce or Douglas as too deeply tainted by their sponsorship of the Kansas-

Nebraska bill, chose instead James Buchanan of Pennsylvania, who had been minister to Great Britain during most of the controversy. With him was associated John C. Breckinridge of Kentucky. The platform defended popular sovereignty and the Kansas-Nebraska act as consistent with the Compromise of 1850, while condemning the "political crusade" of the Know Nothings as contrary to the American "spirit of toleration and enlightened freedom."

The campaign was a thrilling one. In the North the Republicans conducted a canvass rivaling that of 1840 in enthusiasm and having behind it what the earlier campaign lacked—a dynamic moral drive. With the slogan of "Bleeding Kansas" they sought to arouse the latent fear of every northerner against the proslavery "Buchaneers." They made an especial appeal to the wage-earners, circulating literature which represented slaveholders as declaring, for example, that "Slavery is the natural and normal condition of the *laboring man,* whether WHITE or *black.*" Alarmed by the success of such tactics, the conservative elements of the country assailed the Republicans as a radical sectional party. Both Buchanan and Fillmore maintained that Frémont's election would cause a break-up of the Union. It was repeatedly declared in Philadelphia that, if Buchanan should be defeated, the South would decline to pay the $60,000,000 which it owed the merchants and manufacturers of that city. Southern pamphleteers recklessly charged that the antislavery men were "committed to Socialism and Communism—to no private property, no church, no laws, no government—to free love, free lands, free women and free churches."

Conservatism triumphed. Buchanan polled 174 electoral votes, including every slave state except Maryland whose eight votes alone Fillmore succeeded in winning. Frémont received 114 votes from eleven northern states. Though the

Democratic party was returned to office, the surprising vote polled by the Republicans marked them as a political force to be reckoned with.

THE DRIVE FOR SLAVERY EXTENSION

The new President had held public offices of one sort or another for forty years without attaining real distinction in any of them. A northerner by birth and upbringing, he had always been favorable to the political objects of cotton capitalism. Reaching the goal of his ambitions at the age of sixty-six, he surrounded himself with advisers who shared his point of view. Lewis Cass of Michigan was given the chief place in the cabinet. Four other members were from slave states and two from free states.[1]

The most difficult task confronting the new administration was that of healing the renewed breach between the sections. This was a course for which Buchanan was ill fitted. The admission of California as a part of the Compromise of 1850 had destroyed the "sacred balance" of free and slave states in the Senate, and the rapid increase of northern population produced two more free-soil states during Buchanan's term—Minnesota in 1858 and Oregon in 1859. In the President's mind the permanence of the Union depended upon a restoration of the old equality. Moreover, like his two Democratic predecessors, he espoused a policy of territorial expansion. Since the westward movement had built up the domain of the free states, why should not Manifest Destiny now direct the course of slavery's empire southward?

In three annual messages Buchanan urged upon Congress the acquisition of Cuba "by fair purchase." Central America, he predicted in his message of 1858, would fall to the United

[1] Howell Cobb of Georgia, Secretary of the Treasury; J. B. Floyd of Virginia, Secretary of War; Isaac Toucey of Connecticut, Secretary of the Navy; Jacob Thompson of Mississippi, Secretary of the Interior; A. V. Brown of Tennessee, Postmaster-General; Jeremiah S. Black of Pennsylvania, Attorney-General.

States "at no distant day" by the natural course of events. Upon the same occasion he proposed a protectorate over northern Mexico. Repeating his recommendation the next year, he asked authority to invade Mexico to restore order, but Congress refused to heed his call to foreign adventure.

Buchanan's proposal was ill-timed; the country was already embroiled over the question of extending slavery within its existing boundaries. The experiment with popular sovereignty on the Great Plains had reached a critical stage before he entered office.

If the new territory had contained a settled population when Pierce signed the Kansas-Nebraska Act, the slavery question might perhaps have been peaceably decided. Since the region was virtually unoccupied, however, the act precipitated a mad scramble on the part of each section for political control. Organizations were formed in the North, among which the New England Emigrant Aid Company was outstanding, to urge colonization and assist settlers with reduced transportation fares and necessary equipment. While the southern planters, less mobile because of their slave property, could not meet this competition by speedy migration, sympathizers along the Missouri border were ready to cross into Kansas and stuff the ballot boxes. The intense rivalry resulted in the establishment of two groups of settlements. The northerners flocked into the Kansas River Valley, naming their principal town Lawrence in honor of the chief patron of the New England Emigrant Aid Company. The proslavery strongholds, on the other hand, were Atchison and Leavenworth on the Missouri River and Lecompton on the Kansas.

The free-soil settlers outnumbered their antagonists when the first territorial legislature was chosen on March 30, 1855, but the pro-southern forces carried the day with the illegal help of the "Border Ruffians." The legislature thus elected

adopted laws establishing slavery, while the free settlers set
up a government of their own and, in October, held a constitutional convention at Topeka which drew up a state constitution banning slavery.[1] President Pierce might at this
juncture have solved the difficulties by declaring both governments irregular and holding a fresh election under the
protection of federal bayonets. Instead, he sided with the
proslavery legislature and pledged the full power of his office
"to support public order." Emboldened by such high sanction, the pro-southern leaders took vigorous steps to crush
the Topeka government. The free-soil "governor" and his
chief associates were indicted for treason and on May 21,
1856, a proslavery force, acting as a posse, invaded Lawrence
and sacked it.

A few days later the country heard the name of John
Brown. Born in Connecticut, he had grown to manhood
amidst frontier conditions in northern Ohio. His character
is probably to be interpreted in the light of the fact that his
mother and grandmother, a sister and five cousins, suffered
from insanity. Imbibing an intense hatred of slavery in
childhood, he became convinced that he was divinely appointed to accomplish its doom. In August, 1855, he set out
in a one-horse wagon filled with guns and ammunition, to
join five sons in Osawatomie, Kansas. Incensed by the attack
on Lawrence, he resolved, in the spirit of Old Testament
justice, to slay five proslavery men to atone for an equal number of deaths of free-soilers. On the night of May 24 he and
his band fell upon a settlement on Pottawatomie Creek and
ruthlessly executed his purpose. For several months parties
of men from each side roamed the country, plundering and
killing. In all, two hundred lives were lost and two million
dollars' worth of property destroyed. Only by a vigorous

[1] A bill to admit Kansas under the Topeka constitution passed the House
of Representatives on July 3, 1856, but received scant consideration in the
Senate.

employment of United States troops was the guerrilla warfare finally brought to an end in November, 1856.

Though the proslavery party at first occupied the seats of power in the territory, it was certain that the second election would go against them. In anticipation of the event they summoned a constitutional convention which met at Lecompton in September, 1857, and drew up a proslavery constitution. To make assurance doubly sure, the convention refused to give the people a clear choice between accepting or rejecting the instrument. The voters were, in effect, permitted merely to affirm whether they favored the Lecompton constitution with or without the further introduction of slaves. Outraged by this fresh perversion of popular sovereignty, the free-soil partisans, who had already declined to participate in the election of delegates, once more stayed away from the polls. The constitution was ratified with the extreme slavery clause by a vote of 6226 to 569. When the free-soilers captured the new legislature in October, they resubmitted the constitution to the people on the express issue of acceptance or rejection. It was defeated by 10,226 to 162, the southerners this time refusing to vote.

However irregular these proceedings, it was clear that a large majority opposed the proslavery constitution. Yet President Buchanan urged Congress to grant statehood to Kansas under the Lecompton instrument. One Democratic chieftain, however, none other than the great proponent of popular sovereignty himself, warned Congress that he would not consent to have the doctrine used as "trickery and jugglery to defeat the fair expression of the will of the people." In bold defiance of the administration Douglas set about to defeat the President's recommendation. Feeling ran high in Congress, Buchanan personally threatened the Little Giant with political oblivion, and the administration press charged him with having turned "Black Republican." In spite of

Douglas's efforts the Senate followed the President, but the proposal was lost in the House (April 1, 1858).

A month later the Kansas deadlock was broken by a compromise measure, the so-called English bill. This act authorized a third submission of the Lecompton constitution to popular vote, with the provision that, in case of acceptance, Kansas should receive a grant of government lands within the state, but that, in case of rejection, statehood should be postponed until the population reached the number (93,560) necessary for a representative in Congress. The bill in effect offered a bribe to Kansans to induce them to accept the instrument, and Douglas voted against it. Nevertheless it gave the voters a chance to reject the work of the antislavery element. This they proceeded to do in August, 1858, by a majority of 11,300 to 1788.

Kansas remained a territory until the withdrawal of southern congressmen made possible its admission as a free state (January, 1861). The protracted conflict over Kansas stirred the nation deeply and added immeasurably to sectional ill will. The contest was conducted by fanatics on both sides; but the law-abiding citizens in each section unfortunately mistook the extremists as representative of the people of the other.

THE SUPREME COURT AND SLAVERY EXTENSION

In his inaugural address Buchanan voiced the hope that all contention over the status of slavery in the territories would be stilled by a forthcoming judgment of the Supreme Court. Two days later (March 6, 1857), the famous decision in the case of Dred Scott v. Sandford was announced. Dred Scott was a Missouri slave who some twenty years before had been taken by his master, an army surgeon, to reside at various posts in the free state of Illinois and, later, to a fort in the northern part of the Louisiana Purchase where slavery was

DRED SCOTT

forb
Mi
on
ab
ri

idden by the Missouri Compromise. After his return to ssouri a suit was begun on the ground that his residence free soil had liberated him.[1] Meantime he was sold to an sentee master residing in another state. After a long pe-.od of litigation the case finally reached the federal Supreme Court. The Negro's right to sue there rested upon the constitutional provision granting the federal judiciary jurisdiction in cases arising between citizens of different states. The Supreme Court, therefore, had to decide whether Dred was a citizen before it could consider whether he was a freeman. If it decided against his claim to citizenship, the practice of the court dictated that it should not pass upon the more important question of his freedom.

The majority of the court held that he was not a citizen, asserting that Negroes had not been citizens of any state at the time of the formation of the Constitution, and that the Constitution, in their judgment, was intended to apply only to the white race. Here, according to precedent, the decision should have ended, but Chief Justice Roger B. Taney and his associates felt that an opinion on the merits of the case from the preëminent judicial tribunal would remove a dangerous question from the political arena. The court, therefore, went on to declare that the Missouri Compromise had all along been void, for Congress lacked the constitutional right to enact a law which arbitrarily deprived persons of their property, slave or otherwise, in the territories of the United States.[2] Accordingly, Dred Scott was not entitled to freedom and, by the same token, masters had a constitutional right to hold slaves anywhere in the territories. The court attached no importance to Dred Scott's sojourn in Illinois,

[1] The fact that the Missouri Compromise was repealed in 1854 had, of course, no bearing upon Dred Scott's rights under that law while it was still in force.

[2] "Nor shall any person . . . be deprived of life, liberty, or property, without due process of law." Constitution, Amendment V.

arguing that, since his residence was only temporary, his
tus as slave or freeman depended upon the laws of Misso
not Illinois.

The decision created fierce excitement throughout
North, increased by the fact that the court itself had not be
in agreement, two members from the free states dissenting
Mr. Justice B. R. Curtis, challenging the assumption that Negroes had never been citizens in any of the states, insisted that
Dred Scott was a citizen within the meaning of the Constitution.   He justified the Missouri Compromise by the constitutional power of Congress to "make all needful rules and
regulations" for the federal territories, rejecting Taney's view
that this grant of authority was limited to the original area of
the United States.   He further contended that the judgment
of the court in regard to the Missouri Compromise was an
obiter dictum, that is, a pronouncement on matters not properly before the judges, and that, as such, it had no legal binding effect.

· For the southern Democrats the decision was a great victory, since it gave judicial sanction to the extreme theory
concerning slavery in the territories.   If the decision was binding, the Republican position was without constitutional sanction.   The Republicans had a way of escape, however, in
Curtis's opinion that the pronouncement against the Missouri Compromise was an *obiter dictum* which might be disregarded.   Torrents of abuse were therefore poured upon
the court for its "error."   Not even in Jefferson's time had
the judiciary come in for such bitter condemnation.   Greeley
declared in the *Tribune* that Taney's decision was "entitled
to just so much moral weight as would be the judgment of a
majority of those congregated in any Washington bar-room."
Republican spokesmen attributed the decision to partisanship, making the most of the fact that seven of the nine judges
were Democrats and five of them from the slave states.   Thou-

sands of copies of the dissenting opinions were printed and circulated as campaign documents. Even northern Democrats accepted the decision with mental reservations, for Douglas and his followers could not fail to see that the doctrine set forth ran counter to, if it did not outlaw, the theory of popular sovereignty.

THE WIDENING OF THE SECTIONAL BREACH

The Republicans, confident that the appeal of their party was reaching the people in the North, looked forward eagerly to a new trial of strength in the fall elections of 1858. To northern wrath over "Bleeding Kansas" was now added resentment over the Dred Scott decision; and both meant converts to the party. In 1857 occurred another event the blame for which the unthinking placed on the shoulders of the party in power: a financial storm burst upon the country that did not entirely clear away during Buchanan's term. The Panic of 1857 was the price exacted for the excessive commercial and industrial development which had marked the preceding years. Flush times had produced the usual orgy of speculation and imprudent investment. In anticipation of the future growth of the country, railroads, manufacturers and promoters of all kinds had burdened themselves with indebtedness beyond their actual power to repay. The crash came in the summer and autumn. Fourteen railway corporations failed; banks and insurance companies suspended; factories closed their doors. As untold numbers of wage-earners faced the winter of 1857–1858 without work, "hunger meetings," often tinged with revolutionary bitterness, took place in eastern centers. The western farmers, too, were involved in the disaster. Crops were scarcely moved in some localities and grain exports diminished by half. Even the South, despite the relative absence of speculation there, did not wholly escape. According to Senator Hammond of South Carolina,

the northern failure to advance money as usual to market its
crops inflicted a loss of $35,000,000.   Many southerners dis-
covered in this default a fresh reason why their section should
live its economic life apart from the North.

As the country recovered from the shock of the panic, the
autumn elections were at hand.   In every northern state but
Illinois and Indiana the Democrats lost ground.   Even the
President's own state of Pennsylvania turned from him because of umbrage at the tariff of 1857 (see page 751 n.) and
the inroads of the panic on the iron industry.

Throughout the North the Republicans waged an active
campaign.   The senatorial contest in Illinois possessed features of unusual interest.   The Republicans there had nominated Abraham Lincoln, a lawyer of local repute with some
slight experience in the state legislature and Congress.   Opposed to him was the veteran Douglas whose recent break with
Buchanan over the Lecompton constitution had prompted
Greeley and other easterners to advise their Illinois brethren
not to put up a candidate against him. . They saw in the Little Giant a possible accession of strength to their own party.

As the new Senator was to be chosen by a legislature not yet
elected, the rival candidates went before the voters of Illinois
in a series of seven joint debates to acquaint them with the
issues.   Upon the lean and ungainly Lincoln rested the burden of the attack.   Not only was he challenging Douglas's
right to continue in the Senate, but he was also spokesman
for the new party.   Striking the first blow in his speech accepting the nomination, he undertook to convince the people of
the aggressive proslavery purposes of the Democrats.   Before
it was too late, he asserted, the free-soil North must take a
bold stand against the "Slave Power," for the Dred Scott decision was merely an entering wedge for a later pronouncement that would legalize slavery throughout the land.   " 'A
house divided against itself cannot stand.'   I believe this gov-

ernment cannot endure permanently half slave and half free.
. . . It will become all one thing or all the other." Lincoln,
of course, was expressing not a purpose but the perception of
a great truth; but Douglas made an adroit countercharge
that the Republicans were plotting to destroy slavery within
the southern states.

Lincoln next undertook to show that Douglas, despite his
stand against the Lecompton constitution, was unworthy of
Republican support. Douglas's opposition, he pointed out,
had been actuated not by antislavery motives but by his attachment to popular sovereignty. With fine rhetorical effect
he quoted Douglas's own words in Congress: "If Kansas
wants a slave-state Constitution, she has a right to it; if she
wants a free-state Constitution, she has a right to it. . . . I
care not whether it [slavery] is voted down or voted up."
Finally, Lincoln took occasion to bring to sharp public notice
the contradiction between the Dred Scott pronouncement,
which legalized slavery in all federal territories, and Douglas's
doctrine of 1854, which left the matter to the territorial legislature. By asking Douglas to reconcile the two positions Lincoln placed him in a dilemma.[1] If he reaffirmed the right of
popular sovereignty, he would retain the loyalty of the Illinois farmers, imbued with frontier ideals of democracy, but
such a declaration would deprive the Dred Scott decision of
its force and alienate southern backing for the presidency in
1860. On the other hand, a confession that popular sovereignty had been outlawed by the action of the Supreme Court
would insure his defeat in the election at hand.

Douglas's reply is known as the Freeport Doctrine or, as
the southern Democrats called it, the Freeport Heresy. He
drew a distinction between theory and practice in the application of the Dred Scott decision. In theory, slavery might

[1] Lincoln's question was: "Can the people of a United States territory, in
any lawful way, against the wish of any citizen of the United States, exclude
slavery from its limits prior to the formation of a state constitution?"

exist throughout the federal domain; in practice, no master would go where his right of slaveholding was not fully protected by territorial law. Therefore, he concluded, the failure of a legislature to enact such a body of law, or "slave code," would have the practical effect of excluding slavery.[1] Whatever other motives may have influenced him, Douglas's stand at Freeport revealed his fidelity to cherished convictions long held. Taking the side of his neighbors and friends, he won reëlection to the Senate, but his utterance caused dismay in the ranks of the southern members of his party.

The year 1859 found sectional strife once more assuming ominous form. Since his gory exploit three years before in Kansas, John Brown's ill-balanced mind had continued to brood over the evils of slavery. Now, aided and abetted by a few antislavery extremists in the Northeast, he planned a more desperate stroke against it. Gathering a band of twenty-one followers, five of them Negroes, he seized the federal arsenal at Harpers Ferry, Virginia, on Sunday night, October 16. His scheme was to summon the slaves of the South to his standard and, from the mountain fastnesses near by, dictate the terms of their liberation. When dawn came, men armed with a medley of weapons poured into the village and, with the help of some militia companies, began a counter-attack. That night Colonel Robert E. Lee arrived with a company of United States marines, and early the next morning Brown and his surviving men were overpowered and made prisoners.

A thrill of horror ran through the nation. For many southerners Brown's fanatical attempt confirmed their worst fears as to the hidden purposes of the "Black Republicans." In

[1] This was his soundest contention, but, as a matter of fact, he also claimed that, since the Dred Scott decision merely forbade *Congress* to exclude slavery from the territories, the *territorial legislature* still retained that power, at least until the Supreme Court should declare to the contrary. In other words, a free-soil legislature might prevent the existence of slavery by "unfriendly legislation."

retaliation, governors of several states recommended opening southern ports to foreign trade and levying high excise
taxes on northern-made goods.   Antislavery zealots, on the
other hand, hailed Brown as a noble martyr to a great cause.
Most northerners, however, repudiated the exploit, for they
rightly saw in it an assault not against the South but upon all
organized society and democratic methods of securing progress.   Brown was promptly tried for conspiracy, treason and
murder.   Seventeen affidavits by neighbors and friends attest-
ing their belief that he was insane were not considered, and
on December 2, 1859, he was publicly hanged.   The dignity
of his bearing in these last weeks impressed all who saw him.
To the end he believed he was an instrument in the hands of
God.

THE CRUCIAL ELECTION OF 1860

In the new Congress which met a few days after John
Brown's execution, the northern and southern members faced
each other like enemies belonging to hostile nations rather
than like brethren of a common country.   Charges and
countercharges punctuated the discussions.   Threats of secession were made with increasing vehemence by southern
"fire-eaters," and Senator Seward was openly accused of having instigated Brown's criminal adventure.   "The members
on both sides are mostly armed with deadly weapons," Senator J. W. Grimes of Iowa wrote to his wife, "and it is said that
the friends of each are armed in the galleries."   On several
occasions violent clashes between members were only narrowly averted.   While the administration party still controlled the Senate, in the House a Democratic majority of
twenty-five had changed to a Republican plurality of twenty-
one.   The Republicans lacked an absolute majority, however, and it required nearly two months before they could
elect one of their number as speaker.

The bitterness of the struggle over the speakership was sharpened by angry allusions of southern members to an abolitionist tract, Hinton R. Helper's *The Impending Crisis of the South,* which sixty-four Republican Congressmen had formally indorsed in print. The animus of this latest assault on slavery was different from that of *Uncle Tom's Cabin.* The author, himself a nonslaveholding North Carolinian, asked the pregnant question: for whose good does slavery exist? Fortified by a mass of facts gleaned from the census reports, he answered that its direct benefits accrued to but a fraction of the white population, the "lords of the lash." This minority alone possessed the wealth, luxury and culture of which the Southland boasted, leaving the bulk of the people in "galling poverty and ignorance," deprived of equal economic, social and political opportunities. The slavery system had cursed Dixie with "comparative imbecility and obscurity," while the North without this incumbrance had attained "almost unexampled power and eminence." Helper's book was a forthright and convincing argument on behalf of the southern white proletariat against cotton capitalism and all its works. Though virtually without circulation in the slave states, the Republicans printed a hundred thousand copies for northern reading in the approaching presidential campaign, winning many converts to their cause among voters who had been left untouched by the real or fancied wrongs of the Negro.

The basic antagonism between slavery and the free-labor system was further impressed upon the northern farming and wage-earning classes by Buchanan's veto of a homestead bill in June, 1860. For more than a decade efforts had been made to secure a law giving actual settlers free farms of 160 acres from the public domain. In the House Andrew Johnson, a "poor-white" member from Tennessee, had pressed the matter, workingmen's associations in the North had championed it, and it will be recalled that in 1854 a bill for the purpose had passed the lower branch, only to suffer defeat in the upper. Again in February, 1859, a similar proposal, adopted by the House, failed in the proslavery Senate. The southern members, viewing the measure through the distorting lenses of sectional hostility, saw truly that such a law, if enacted, would quickly fill the federal territories with antislavery northerners who would lightly brush aside court decisions opposed to their interests or convictions.

When the matter came before Congress once more, in the spring of 1860, the Democrats had to tread warily for fear of offending possible northern support in the coming national election. The demand for free land was particularly popular in the Midwest, and everywhere it enlisted the enthusiasm of the Germans and other recently naturalized citizens. The Senate, however, could not quite bring itself to accept a new House bill for free homesteads. It finally compromised upon a measure authorizing the sale of tracts of 160 acres at the low price of twenty-five cents an acre, one fifth of the existing rate. But Buchanan, bolder than his party associates in Congress, vetoed the bill, alleging that it would tend to depopulate the older states, sap the frontiersmen's "noble spirit of independence," and even propagate "pernicious social theories which have proved so disastrous in other countries."

Meantime, while fighting the common enemy, the members of the President's party had sought vainly to patch up their internal differences. Douglas's independent course, begun at the time of the Lecompton fight and continued in the debates with Lincoln, had made him a frail reed for the planting interests to lean on. Without delay the proslavery leaders notified him of the price he must pay for their backing in the impending Democratic convention: he must agree to support the passage of a congressional slave code applicable to all the federal territories. This was their reply to his assertion at Freeport that slavery could be barred from a territory by the failure of the local legislature to enact protective laws. Resolutions framed by Jefferson Davis and declaring the obligation of Congress to provide a territorial slave code were presented in the Senate in February, 1860, and eventually adopted by the Democratic majority. But Douglas disregarded the ultimatum.

When the party convention met on April 23 at Charleston, South Carolina, the matter was pressed to a decision. Two platforms were submitted to the delegates, one embodying in substance Davis's demand and the other phrased in the spirit of Douglas's Freeport utterance. The northern faction carried the day, though at the cost of the withdrawal of eight southern delegations. In the voting for the presidential nomination Douglas led on all fifty-seven ballots, but could not command the necessary two thirds of the convention's original membership. His nomination, however, was accomplished several weeks later at an adjourned session in Baltimore under a rule requiring a two-thirds majority only of those present. As a sop to the South, Herschel V. Johnson of Georgia was associated with him as running mate. Meantime, the southern Democrats, deciding to place their own ticket in the field, held a convention at Richmond and unanimously adopted the proslavery platform rejected at Charleston. They chose as their candidates John C. Breckinridge of Kentucky and Joseph Lane of Oregon. Apart from the central question, the rival platforms agreed in demanding the acquisition of Cuba on "honorable" terms and the building of a Pacific railway.

While the Democrats were quarreling among themselves the Republicans proceeded exultantly to their own nominations. The chief aspirants for head of the ticket were Seward and Lincoln. The former, an easterner long prominent in national affairs, seemed to have a prior claim to the honor. Though generally moderate in his views, he had recently won northern applause by his resounding declaration that the quarrel between North and South was "an irrepressible conflict between opposing and enduring forces." Lincoln's greatest asset was his relative obscurity. Unlike the New Yorker, he was not handicapped by old political enmities; he bore no burden of past antagonisms likely to prove harmful in doubtful states. Besides, as a self-made man, the son of "poor-white" parents, "Honest Abe, the Rail-Splitter," promised as a candidate to appeal strongly to the plain people of the North.

When the convention assembled in Chicago on May 16, Lincoln's friends left nothing undone to bring success. The Indiana and Pennsylvania delegations were won over by promises of cabinet positions, agreements to which Lincoln himself was not a party though he later carried them out. Seward's supporters were no less active, but on the third ballot the westerner captured the prize. The second place went to Hannibal Hamlin of Maine. The platform was marked by moderation, being framed especially to attract northern voters who had not yet identified themselves with the party. Reaffirming opposition to slavery in the federal domain, it demanded statehood for Kansas and denounced "the new dogma that the Constitution, of its own force, carries slavery into any or all the territories." With an eye to the Midwest the party promised free homesteads and, with a squint at the Pennsylvania iron districts, advocated a tariff to encourage "the industrial interests." No mention was made of the Fugitive Slave Law, and John Brown's raid was branded as "among the gravest of crimes." Like their opponents, the

Republicans indorsed a transcontinental railway. As for threats of disunion, they declared that "the union of the States must and shall be preserved."

Still another convention was held on May 9, composed mostly of old men who were one in spirit with the venerable statesmen who had saved the nation in 1850. Adopting the name of the Constitutional Union party, they drew up a brief platform recognizing "no political principle other than the Constitution of the country, the union of the States, and the enforcement of the laws." They hoped to settle the sectional question by ignoring it. As candidates they named John Bell of Tennessee and Edward Everett of Massachusetts.

Though the ensuing campaign was less exciting than that of 1856, James Russell Lowell in the newly established *Atlantic Monthly* rightly called it "a turning-point in our history." The shrewdness of the Republican tactics became quickly evident. Everywhere profiting by northern resentment against the "Slave Power," the party found the tariff a particularly potent issue in Pennsylvania and New Jersey, while the slogan, "Free Homes for the Homeless," proved equally effective among the western farmers. Special efforts were made, with the help of Carl Schurz and other immigrant leaders, to mobilize the German and Scandinavian vote. Seward, campaigning vigorously for his erstwhile rival, took occasion in St. Louis and other appropriate places to praise the "onward striving, freedom-loving German inhabitants." [1]

The large moneyed interests of the East, on the other hand, feared that the Republican victory would precipitate secession and a general derangement of business. William B. Astor and other financial magnates are said to have raised

---

[1] It is noteworthy that shortly before the Republican convention a group of representative Germans, meeting in Chicago, had called upon the party to favor a homestead law, oppose the extension of slavery and resist measures unfriendly to naturalized citizens. Lincoln himself, while angling for the nomination, had found it expedient to become owner of a German paper in Springfield for a period lasting until after his election as President.

two million dollars to defeat the ticket in New York state. In most of the South the Republicans made no efforts, for their platform "could not cross the Ohio River." Indeed, many voters in Dixie believed that Lincoln's running mate was a mulatto. As election time drew near, Douglas, alarmed by the increasing violence of southern threats of secession in

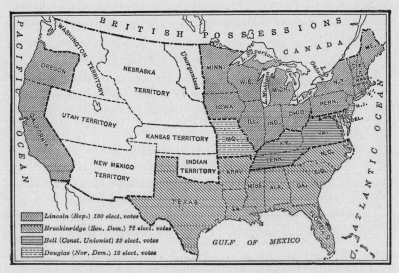

Lincoln (Rep.) 180 elect. votes
Breckinridge (Sou. Dem.) 72 elect. votes
Bell (Const. Unionist) 39 elect. votes
Douglas (Nor. Dem.) 12 elect. votes

THE ELECTORAL VOTE IN 1860

the event of a Republican triumph, made a speaking tour through five slave states. Everywhere he pledged his support to an undivided country. At Norfolk, Virginia, he declared flatly that the next President, "whoever he may be, should treat all attempts to break up the Union by resistance to its laws, as Old Hickory treated the nullifiers of 1832."

In the electoral count Lincoln received 180 votes, all from free states, Breckinridge 72, all from slave states, while Bell and Douglas divided the border states between them, receiving 39 and 12 votes respectively. These figures do not correctly reflect the relative popular following of each candidate, for Lincoln polled only about forty per cent of the popular vote. Douglas won more than twenty-nine per cent, Breckinridge eighteen and Bell nearly thirteen. Lincoln's three opponents commanded a total vote of almost a million more than he received. Yet if all the ballots cast for them had been given to any one of the three, the Republican candidate would still have won a majority in the electoral college. However, the party failed to carry either branch of Congress.

SELECT BIBLIOGRAPHY

The Party Revolution. The disintegration of the old Whig organization is treated in Cole, *The Whig Party in the South,* and Mueller, *The Whig Party in Pennsylvania.* Scisco, *Political Nativism in New York State,* is the best of the state studies of the Know Nothing movement. The other new party is the special theme of Crandall, *The Early History of the Republican Party, 1854–1856,* while further light is thrown on it by Nevins, *Frémont,* and Bartlett, *John C. Frémont and the Republican Party.*

The Drive for Slavery Extension. Curtis, *Life of James Buchanan,* is useful for this period. Efforts to secure Cuba receive detailed discussion in Callahan, *Cuba and International Relations.* Of the many accounts of the Kansas struggle perhaps the most objective is Spring, *Kansas; the Prelude to the War for the Union.*

The Supreme Court and Slavery Extension. Discussions of the Dred Scott decision may be found in Warren, *The Supreme Court in United States History,* Beveridge, *Abraham Lincoln,* and Swisher, *Roger B. Taney.* Cf. Hockett, *Con. Hist.,* II, 232–250.

The Widening of the Sectional Breach. The Panic of 1857 is given special study in Dunbar, *Economic Essays.* The Lincoln-Douglas debates are fully treated in Beveridge's *Lincoln,* II. This work is a detailed biography carrying its subject through the year 1858. The next two years of Lincoln's life are covered in Baringer, *Lincoln's Rise to Power.* Of the numerous lives of Brown, Villard, *John Brown, 1800–1859,* is the best balanced.

The Crucial Election of 1860. The efforts for a homestead law are painstakingly traced in Stephenson, *The Political History of the Public Lands from 1840 to 1862.* The major aspects of the presidential contest of 1860 can be followed in Fite, *The Presidential Campaign of 1860,* which has an anti-Douglas bias, and the early chapters of Dumond, *The Secession Movement, 1860–1861.*

Chapter XXXII

THE GREAT DECISION, 1860–1861

THE MOVEMENT FOR SOUTHERN INDEPENDENCE

MANY southerners were warmly devoted to the Union, but the election of an antislavery President by northern votes was an ominous event. Separation had been repeatedly threatened, especially after the Compromise of 1850, if southern interests could be protected in no other way, and the success of the Republicans raised again the question whether the time for secession had not come. But a decision involving dismemberment of a nation which southern statesmen had done so much to build was not lightly to be made. In an address before the Georgia legislature on November 14, Alexander H. Stephens declared that no such action should be taken unless the new chief executive should violate the Constitution. He pointed out that the President could "do nothing unless backed by power in Congress," and in that body the Republicans lacked a majority. There were other leaders who counseled delay for the purpose of insuring that the slave states would act as a unit if they acted at all. Still others favored secession, not as an irrevocable step, but as a temporary expedient, believing with the Georgian, T. R. R. Cobb, that "We can make better terms out of the Union than in it."

On the other hand extremists argued that it was better to secede before the abolition party completely dominated the Federal Government. Fear of what *might* happen under a "Black Republican" administration begot the conviction that calamity was inevitable. Lincoln's kindly and essentially conservative nature was unknown to most southerners, but

714

THE REPUBLICAN PARTY GOING TO THE RIGHT HOUSE.

CARTOON FROM THE CAMPAIGN OF 1860

they were well apprised that he had said the Union must become all slave or all free. Thus the psychology of the situation played into the hands of this group. For twenty-five years press, church, and school had propagated distrust, fear, hatred between southerners and northerners. Though they spoke the same language they no longer understood each other.

The secessionists were strongest in the seaboard and Gulf states from South Carolina to Texas. Here, where the slave population was densest and King Cotton reigned supreme, sensitiveness to antislavery criticism was keenest. Under the urging of such men as Toombs in Georgia, Yancey in Alabama and R. B. Rhett in South Carolina, the movement for disunion forged ahead. Jefferson Davis at first advised cautious action, but soon cast in his lot with these "fire eaters."

There was a difference of opinion as to whether the right to secede was reserved by each state under the Constitution, or whether it was simply the inalienable right of revolution. Nevertheless, in severing the bonds of union the seceding states took care to observe the form of legal action. In conformity with the teachings of Calhoun, special state conventions were summoned to adopt ordinances of secession, thus reversing the process by which the Constitution had originally been accepted. Appropriately enough, South Carolina took the lead. Upon receiving word of Lincoln's election, the legislature, which had remained in session for the express purpose, issued a call for a state convention. On December 20, 1860, that body formally repealed the act of 1788 ratifying the Constitution, and "dissolved" the "union now subsisting between South Carolina and other States, under the name of the 'United States of America.'" By February 1, 1861, similar action had been taken successively by Mississippi, Florida, Alabama, Georgia, Louisiana and Texas.

The ordinances of secession were usually accompanied by

a formal statement justifying the action. In general, four reasons were assigned. The growing preponderance of the North in Congress was pointed to as the prolific source of policies and legislation designed to promote northern economic welfare at the expense of the South. Much was made, also, of the waxing strength and increasing aggression of the antislavery forces, as exemplified by the personal liberty laws, defiance of the Supreme Court and John Brown's raid. Such acts were held to violate the "constitutional compact" and thereby to release the southern states from their obligations. Next, slavery was justified as a positive good. In the words of the Mississippi convention, slave labor "supplies the product which constitutes by far the largest and most important portions of the commerce of the earth . . . and by an imperious law of nature none but the black race can bear exposure to the tropical sun. These products have become necessities of the world, and a blow at slavery is a blow at commerce and civilization." But the most fundamental justification of all, in the minds of southerners, may be summed up in the modern expression: the right of self-determination. The South demanded the right to live its own life in its own way under such social institutions as it found satisfactory. In this sense, the official statements of causes may be regarded as declarations of independence. As Mississippi said, "We must either submit to degradation and to loss of property worth four billions of money or we must secede from the Union framed by our fathers, to secure this as well as every other species of property. For far less cause than this our fathers separated from the Crown of England."

That the seceding states, although they acted separately, were drawn together by a strong sense of southern nationality became quickly apparent. Delegates from the several states met at Montgomery, Alabama, on February 4, 1861, and organized a new federal government under the name of the

Confederate States of America. Davis was chosen President, though much against his wishes, for he aspired to command one of the armies of the new nation. As a concession to the moderates, the vice-presidency was bestowed upon Stephens, who had done more than any other southerner to postpone and defeat secession. The Confederate Constitution was closely modeled upon that of the United States, but there were certain significant differences. One body of provisions aimed to establish beyond question the southern position on the various sectional questions that had arisen in the past. Congress was forbidden to subsidize internal improvements (except as an aid to navigation), or to lay protective tariffs, or to grant bounties. Negro bondage was to be safeguarded in all territories, and property in slaves was never to be impaired. Nothing specific, however, was said about the right of secession, though three distinct proposals to affirm the right had been presented in the convention. A second group of clauses provided for certain reforms in governmental procedure, suggested by experience under the old Constitution. For example, the President was limited to a single six-year term, he could veto individual items in appropriation bills, and an executive budget system was provided for.

Only seven states were represented at Montgomery, but the architects of the new republic expected the early adhesion of the eight slave states which, as yet, continued loyal to the old Union. Indeed, in their high enthusiasm, they anticipated an extension beyond these natural limits. Stephens, who with secession an accomplished fact had promptly become an ardent supporter of the Confederacy, predicted in a notable speech at Savannah, that it was "not beyond the range of possibility, and even probability, that all the great states of the north-west will gravitate this way." The sequel was to show that the Confederate leaders were too optimistic, even as to those states which had domestic institutions like those of the Lower South.

THE NORTH AND SECESSION

The northern people watched these developments in the Lower South with bewilderment and indecision. Few had anticipated such an eventuality, for southern threats of secession had been looked upon as mere bombast and bluster. Nor was the North a unit on the slavery question—a fact amply evident from Douglas's success in polling well over a million votes in the free states. In any contingency, many people preferred a permanent disruption of the Union to the terrible alternative of a fratricidal war. Antislavery radicals, for their part, declared publicly that the departure of the slave states was good riddance. "If the cotton States shall decide that they can do better out of the Union than in it," asserted the *New York Tribune,* "we insist on letting them go in peace." A national convention of workingmen at Philadelphia in February, 1861, agreed that "our Government never can be sustained by bloodshed but must live in the affections of the people; we are, therefore, utterly opposed to any measures that will evoke civil war." On the other hand, there were those who could declare, like Senator E. D. Baker of Oregon, "We of the North are a majority of the Union, and we will govern our Union in our own way."

The responsibility for formulating a policy to cope with the crisis devolved upon the outgoing President and his Congress, but their course was inevitably influenced by the uncertain state of public opinion. Buchanan was at this time nearly seventy years of age. He was by nature timid, and accustomed to view public questions through southern spectacles. His dominant desire was to avoid any action which might precipitate civil conflict; he felt also an obligation to maintain the *status quo* until the new administration took

over the reins of government.   In his message of December
4, 1860, he outlined his policy.   He denied absolutely the
constitutionality of secession, but at the same time declared
that the Constitution nowhere gave the Federal Government
authority to compel a state to remain in the Union.[1]   Placing
the chief blame for the difficulties upon the North, he proposed an amendment to the Constitution, which would concede the extreme southern contentions in regard to the Dred
Scott decision, the Fugitive Slave act, and the unconstitutionality of the personal-liberty laws.

Unfortunately for the President's peace of mind the situation called for more than well-intentioned words.   What
should be done about the seacoast forts and other federal
property within the borders of the Confederacy?   Buchanan
was torn alternately between the advice of proslavery disunionists and nothern nationalists.   The most critical situation existed at Charleston, South Carolina, where Major
Robert Anderson and a small body of men occupied Fort
Sumter on an island in the harbor.   Old General Winfield
Scott urged swift and decisive action, seeking to stiffen the
President's resolution by recounting the military measures
he had taken years before at Jackson's behest to meet the
nullification crisis in South Carolina.   Buchanan's indecision
caused Cass's resignation as Secretary of State in December.
Finally Buchanan dispatched an armed steamer, the *Star of
the West*, to Fort Sumter with military supplies and reënforcements of two hundred men.   Upon her arrival at day-
break on January 9, 1861, the Confederate batteries on the
shore opened fire.   Since Major Anderson, ignorant of the

---

[1] In one portion of his message, he alluded to the obligation of the President to enforce the laws throughout the land, but failed to find in this duty
power to suppress an unlawful movement against federal authority.   In this
he was unlike Jackson in 1832, and Lincoln, who followed Jackson's example
when he entered office.   Yet, if Buchanan had begun a second term in March,
1861, it is not impossible that his course might have been much like Lincoln's.

government's plans, was unprepared to lend prompt support, she hurried back to New York. The firing upon the *Star of the West* was really an act of war, but Buchanan did not make an issue of it. Meantime, the secessionists took peaceable possession of two unoccupied forts in Charleston Harbor and of the customhouse and arsenal. Elsewhere in the Confed-

THE BEGINNING AND THE END OF JAMES BUCHANAN'S ADMINISTRATION
Lithograph of 1861

eracy the federal forts and arsenals, left unprotected, were also quietly taken over, save only Fort Pickens at Pensacola, which remained in Union hands throughout the war.

Buchanan's inaction may be accounted for in part by the belief of statesmen in both sections that civil war might yet be averted, as in 1850, through compromise measures. The most conspicuous champion of this solution was Crittenden of Kentucky, Clay's successor in the Senate. He proposed a constitutional amendment reëstablishing the Missouri Compromise line in the territories and guaranteeing slavery south of the line. But the Republican Congressmen would have none of it, believing with their President-elect that such an arrangement would merely redouble proslavery exertions for territorial expansion southward. "The tug has to come, and better now than later," advised Lincoln. While countless other proposals were aired in Congress, the only measure actually adopted fell pathetically short of the needs of the occasion—the submission to the states on March 2, 1861, of an amendment pledging Congress never to interfere with slavery within a state.

Meanwhile, efforts for conciliation had been undertaken outside of Congress. In December, 1860, seven Republican governors, meeting in New York, agreed to recommend to their legislatures the repeal of the personal liberty laws. Rhode Island complied in January, Massachusetts and Vermont soon following with drastic changes in their statutes. Had any real hope inhered in this plan, other northern states would probably have taken like action. A final attempt at adjustment was made at a "Peace Convention," presided over by ex-President John Tyler of Virginia and attended by delegates from twenty-one states. Assembling in Washington on February 4, 1861, at the call of Virginia, the gathering drafted a series of proposed amendments. The principal one provided that no new territory should be acquired without the consent of a majority of the Senators from both the free and the slave states. Apart from Crittenden and Douglas, however, the proposals found little favor when they were offered in the Senate.

As James Russell Lowell wrote in the *Atlantic Monthly*, the "panacea of palaver" had failed. Nevertheless, the months of discussion served the purpose of convincing the northern people that, peaceable means of settlement having come to naught, no alternative remained but war. Responsibility for the next move fell upon the man whose election had precipitated the crisis. It was the act of an inscrutable providence that Abraham Lincoln should have been called to the helm of state to undertake a task which, as he told his neighbors in Springfield upon departing for the capital, was "greater than that which rested upon Washington." Born in 1809 in the border state of Kentucky, there coursed through his veins the blood of a vigorous stock inherited on the one side from New England and on the other from Virginia. Migrating with his parents to Indiana and then to Illinois, he inbibed from his youthful pioneer surroundings a passionate belief in American nationality and an ardent faith in the common man. His broad humanity arrayed him instinctively on the antislavery side. Yet he had little patience with the precipitate methods of the abolitionists, who, he believed, hurt rather than helped their cause, and even less with those zealots who valued the freedom of the Negro above the preservation of the nation.

To the great majority of his countrymen Lincoln was but an uncouth backwoodsman when he entered the presidency. Indeed, his true greatness did not dawn on most men until after his death. Of the common clay himself, his mind was attuned to the unspoken hopes of the masses. "The Lord must love the plain people," he once said in his whimsical way, "that's why he made so many of them." But unlike the first great American commoner, Jackson, he regarded himself as an instrument, rather than the dictator, of events. Conscious of his political inexperience, he counseled with all sorts and conditions of men. Yet, once having formed his political principles, he never yielded them. He displayed endless tact and patience in the management of his cabinet with its contentious personalities, and for the good of the cause submitted to discourteous treatment from overbearing men like E. M. Stanton and G. B. McClellan. He had a deep understanding even of those who were seeking to destroy his beloved Union, adjudging them misguided rather than depraved. "Destruction for the idea, infinite clemency for the

person—such was his attitude." Lincoln would have been
the first to protest against the attempts of posterity to idealize
him. Human in every pore, homely to the verge of ugliness,
awkward in manner, he sometimes shocked dignified statesmen by receiving them in slippered feet. His humorous
stories, not always in the best taste, won him a reputation for
flippancy on grave occasions. His greatest mistakes were
made as an administrator, for he was often unfortunate in his
judgment of men. But these qualities made him resemble
the average man and endeared him to the plain people.

Lincoln arrived in Washington ten days before the close
of Buchanan's term, escaping a plot to assassinate him as he
passed through Baltimore. The day of the inauguration
dawned, disagreeable and stormy. Most of the participants
were agitated and apprehensive. General Scott kept an
anxious eye upon the crowd, which was commanded by
cannon. Chief Justice Taney, author of the Dred Scott
decision, administered the oath of office in words made
scarcely intelligible by emotion. Then came Lincoln's inaugural address, delivered with deep feeling and a trace of
nervousness, and containing his long-awaited announcement
of policy. The address was phrased cautiously, with the
object of preventing the secession movement from spreading
to the eight slave states which were still loyal. Yet he announced the principle upon which the Federal Government
was soon to wage war against the South.

Dwelling first upon the nature of the Union, he affirmed
that it was "older than the Constitution," for it grew out of
the fundamental sense of nationality which had animated the
colonies in their struggle against Britain. The so-called ordinances of secession were "legally void," from which it followed that violent efforts to uphold them were "insurrectionary or revolutionary." In his mind the situation reduced
itself to the relations between the national authority and

citizens in insurrection. This view, he held, was in accord with the central principle of the Constitution, that the Federal Government operates directly upon individuals. Although he dwelt on his constitutional duty to execute the laws in all parts of an indivisible country, he closed with an eloquent and touching plea for a restoration of the ancient bonds of affection.

Lincoln chose a cabinet that at once commanded confidence in the North. All elements which had contributed to Republican success were represented, including his chief rivals for the nomination. Seward was appointed to the State Department, Chase, head of the Treasury, Simon Cameron of Pennsylvania, Secretary of War, and Gideon Welles of Connecticut, Secretary of the Navy. Two border slave states were recognized by the choice of the Missourian, Edward Bates, as Attorney-General and of Montgomery Blair of Maryland as Postmaster-General.[1] Almost at once events forced the President to enter upon the course he had forecast in his inaugural address. Word came from Major Anderson that he would have to surrender Fort Sumter unless he were reënforced and provisions sent. All the members of the cabinet, except Chase and Blair, advised evacuation, while General Scott gave his weighty opinion that to relieve the fort now would require a force of twenty thousand—which did not exist.

Lincoln, almost without support, pitted his judgment against that of his more experienced counselors. It seemed to him that the abandonment of Sumter without resistance would not only impair northern morale, but would in a sense constitute a recognition of the Confederacy. He therefore served notice on the government of South Carolina that he intended to reprovision the fort without adding to the garri-

[1] Caleb B. Smith of Indiana was appointed Secretary of the Interior. Cameron was succeeded by Edwin M. Stanton of Pennsylvania as Secretary of War in January, 1862. There were also other changes.

son or supply of munitions. By this means he avoided any warlike move, knowing that, if the southerners decided to fire the first shot, they would incur the discredit of becoming the aggressors.

Upon receipt of the President's notice the Confederates summoned Anderson, the commander of Fort Sumter, to surrender, and when he refused, opened fire with their batteries. By the next day (April 13) his position had become untenable, and just as the relief ships appeared he surrendered with the honors of war.

THE APPEAL TO ARMS

The bombardment of Fort Sumter had a galvanic effect upon the men of both sections. The period of irresolution was ended. The nation—"a house divided"—faced the certainty of a brothers' war. On April 15 President Lincoln issued a call for 75,000 volunteers for three months, followed early in May by a request for 42,000 more for a term of three years. Other proclamations added about 23,000 men to the regular army and 18,000 to the navy, and declared the coast of the Confederacy under blockade. As the drums beat in every town and village, the young men rushed to arms. Greeley and other editors, casting aside their earlier timidity, rallied strongly to the cause of preserving an undivided nation. Douglas, who as it turned out had but a few months more to live, declared in a great speech in Chicago, "There can be no neutrals in this war; only patriots—or traitors." "For my own part," wrote Lincoln, "I consider the central idea pervading this struggle is the necessity of proving that popular government is not an absurdity. We must settle this question now, whether, in a free government, the minority have the right to break up the government whenever they choose."

Meanwhile, with equal fervor, the people of the seven

726   GROWTH OF THE AMERICAN PEOPLE

seceded states responded to President Davis's appeal for 100,-
000 men. Regiments sallied gayly forth from the southern
towns and hamlets, as if on holiday parade, little dreaming
how terrible the impending struggle was to be.

Even the religious world felt the shattering blow. The
Methodists and Baptists had split along geographic lines
nearly twenty years before. As the fifties advanced, six
southern synods comprising 15,000 communicants withdrew
(1857) from the New School Presbyterian Church; and sectional antagonisms plagued other sects as well. A contributor
to the *Southern Presbyterian*, writing shortly after the fall
of Sumter, believed, "This revolution has been accomplished
mainly by the churches." While B. M. Palmer, the southern
Presbyterian divine, proclaimed that "In this great struggle,
we defend the cause of God and religion," the Philadelphia
synod of the same denomination prayed for the suppression
of "the most groundless, cruel, and wicked rebellion in the
history of any people." The outbreak of war precipitated the
division of the Old School Presbyterians and the Protestant
Episcopalians into sectional bodies. Of the principal nation-
wide religious groups, only the Roman Catholics, held together by a central authority outside the national borders,
escaped organic rupture.

Both sections anxiously awaited the action of the eight
slave states which had thus far continued loyal. Bordering
the Confederacy on the north were Arkansas, Tennessee,
North Carolina and Virginia. These states were less identified with cotton production than the Lower South, having
fewer slaves as well as a larger proportion of slaveless whites.
The majority of the inhabitants believed in the right of
secession, yet until now had denied that sufficient provoca-
tion existed. But their doubts were dispelled by the attempt
to relieve Sumter, followed by Lincoln's call for troops. To
them this action seemed to be an attempt to coerce states.

Virginia took the fateful step on April 17, Arkansas on May 6, North Carolina two weeks later and Tennessee on June 24.

No state left the Union with greater reluctance than the Old Dominion. Her statesmen had been among the foremost in winning independence and framing the Constitution, and

THE PROGRESS OF SECESSION

she had furnished five Presidents. On April 5 her state convention had rejected secession, but had been swept into reversing its action by the whirlwind of disunionism raised by Lincoln's proclamations. With Virginia went Colonel Robert E. Lee, a man of noble character and superb military ability, who declined the command of the Union army out of loyalty to his state. The importance of Virginia's action to the South is indicated by the prompt removal of the Confederate capital from Montgomery to Richmond.

The mountaineers of northwestern Virginia, however, refused to abide by the decision of the state. These folk, prevailingly Scotch Irish and Pennsylvania German in stock, owned few slaves, and had long been pitted against their tidewater brethren in state politics. Shielded from southern interference by federal troops, they determined to erect a state of their own. As a preliminary move, a convention at Wheeling in June, 1861, set up a loyal government of Virginia, composed chiefly of men from the upland counties and those districts under federal military control adjoining Washington. Later a convention representing only the people of forty-six northwestern counties was held (in November), which, with the consent of the rump "state government," made application for admission into the Union as the state of West Virginia. Congress acted tardily, statehood being finally granted in June, 1863, with a constitution providing for gradual emancipation. Since West Virginia runs up like a wedge between Ohio and Pennsylvania, the loyalty of the inhabitants had the important military result of securing to the federal authorities the command of essential rail and telegraph facilities between the East and the Ohio Valley.

Between the enlarged Confederacy and the free-soil North lay the four remaining slave commonwealths—the border states of Maryland, Delaware, Kentucky and Missouri. Cotton capitalism was negligible in these states, and slaves, being relatively scarce, were regarded as only one among many forms of property. Torn in their affections between South and North, and bound to both by substantial economic ties, these states knew not which way to turn. Vigorous action by the federal authorities saved Maryland to the Union. Hemming in the District of Columbia on three sides, it would have been a fatal military blunder to permit the state to pass under hostile control. When Maryland disunionists severed telegraphic communications between Washington and the North and sought to prevent the passage of Union troops, Lincoln suspended the writ of *habeas corpus,* ordered the arrest of suspects, and stationed troops at strategic points throughout the state. As the result of these vigorous measures all danger of secession had vanished by the middle of May, 1861. With Maryland went Delaware, as a matter of course; in any case, slaves formed an insignificant fraction of the latter's population.

Farther to the west, Lincoln's native state of Kentucky lay athwart the military highway between North and South. Rent by internal dissension, she attempted to solve her difficulties by declaring her neutrality (May, 1861). Lincoln's policy here was in marked contrast with his treatment of Maryland. Feeling confident of Kentucky's eventual decision, he respected her negative attitude, while quietly laboring to promote the spread of nationalist sentiment. His faith was rewarded, for when Confederate troops violated her neutrality by occupying Columbus (in September) the newly chosen legislature declared for the Union.

In Missouri, on the other hand, the state government was openly disunionist. But the special convention, called to consider secession, proved unexpectedly nationalist in sentiment. Each body claimed to voice the true will of the people, and each summoned military force to its support. Led by Francis P. Blair, Jr., and Captain Nathaniel Lyon, and supported by militia companies of St. Louis Germans, the forces of nationalism triumphed. The state convention in July, 1861, deposed the pro-southern governor and established a loyal government. Thus the crisis was safely passed, although conflict between the antagonistic elements continued throughout the war. In all the border states save Delaware, thousands of citizens, unwilling to accept the decision of the majority, flocked into the Confederate armies.

THE EMBATTLED HOST

The people of each section entered the war with high hopes for an early victory. In material resources, however, the North enjoyed a decided advantage. Twenty-three states with a population of twenty-two million, including about half a million slaves, were arrayed against eleven states containing nine million people, of whom three and a half million were slaves. Though the southern white population was more homogeneous, the diversified make-up of the northern people proved a source of strength rather than weakness, for, in proportion to their numbers, more English, German and Irish immigrants served in the Union armies than native-born northerners.[1] The industrial superiority of the North was even greater than its preponderance in man power. The South had remained a rural region, while the free states had developed abundant facilities for the manufacture of arms and ammunition, clothing and other supplies.

Indeed, three of the most powerful allies of the North were mechanical agencies—the reaper, the sewing machine, and the railroad. The Secretary of War declared in 1861: "The reaper is to the North what slavery is to the South. By taking the places of regiments of young men in the Western harvest fields, it releases them to do battle for the Union at the front, and at the same time keeps up the supply of bread for the nation and the nation's armies." Hardly less important was the sewing machine. Besides providing factory-made garments in unlimited quantities, its adaptation to leather made possible the large-scale production of well-made, low-priced shoes. Though factory workers joined the army in large num-

---

[1] Franz Sigel, Carl Schurz and other Germans prominent in the Revolution of 1848 gave the benefit of their military experience to the untrained federal armies and rose high in the service. Count Zeppelin, who later perfected the dirigible airship in Germany, served as a cavalry officer and engineer from 1863, making his first ascent in a military balloon in this country.

THE GREAT DECISION, 1860–1861

THE GREAT DECISION, 1860–1861   731

bers, the output of clothing, undergarments and shoes, so necessary for the comfort of both soldiers and civilians, actually increased during the war.

The spread of rail mileage in the North after 1850 had an even more direct relationship to federal military success. Assisted by the telegraph, the railroad promoted the rapid movement of troops and supplies. Among the early war-time laws was one of January, 1862, giving the President authority to commandeer the rail and telegraph lines, if necessary for military purposes. A director of railroads was appointed, charged with responsibility for more than two thousand miles of track, chiefly in the border states, which were taken over and operated by the government during the conflict.[1]

The principal advantage of the South was geographic. Its people fought almost wholly on their own soil, and in spite of inadequate railway facilities could protect the military front of its compact territory with a minimum of exertion and expense. The Union forces, on the other hand, operated on unfamiliar ground, and constantly drew farther away from their base of supplies. It should be added that the aristocratic social system of the South was conducive to the development of natural leaders and the cultivation of the martial spirit. Many of the Confederate generals had fought in the Mexican War and resigned federal commissions in 1861 to join the South.

It was a common boast in Dixie that any Confederate could lick three Yankees. Thoughtful men, however, agreed with

[1] Curiously enough, another invention was neglected, which would have greatly increased the offensive power of the army adopting it. This was the breech-loading rifle. In 1857 a board appointed by the Secretary of War had reported unanimously in favor of a single-shot breechloader. Since the old muzzle-loader required sixty seconds to load and fire as against four seconds for the new gun, the superiority of the latter would seem obvious. After the battle of Gettysburg 18,000 muzzle-loaders were picked up with two or more unexploded charges in them. Yet the purchase of the newer type did not become a regular policy until 1864. Perhaps 100,000 breechloaders were in use when the war closed.

President Davis that "Only fools doubt the courage of the Yankees or their willingness to fight when they see fit." In fact, the chief hope of the Confederacy lay in a speedy victory, or in foreign intervention. Its leaders believed in the probability of intervention because the South virtually monopolized the world's cotton supply, and this product was indispensable for the operation of British textile mills. Time fought on the side of the North, for, given sufficient time, raw armies could be whipped into shape, material resources utilized and effective military leadership developed. From a military point of view, neither section was prepared at the beginning for a great war. Few officers on either side had ever commanded so much as a regiment. Many of the opposing generals were West Point men, oftentimes classmates; but the regimental and company officers in the volunteer armies were commissioned by the governors. Though this system was quickly altered in the South, politicians continued to secure high military posts in the North, where 2537 generals of all grades made their appearance during the war. Moreover, the insistent clamor and officious meddling of Greeley and of busybodies in Congress hampered northern military plans, sometimes even serving as a source of information to the enemy. In the Confederacy, too, there was lacking that unity of support so necessary for an infant nation struggling for existence. The old conception of states' rights constantly battled with the new ideal of southern nationalism.

Both sides faced the task of creating efficient fighting units out of the ranks of a people who, however warlike, were essentially unmilitary in their habits. In the first flush of enthusiasm the call for troops was met in both sections by an excess of volunteers. The raw recruits, many of them mere youths, were hastily taught the manual of arms in training camps and rushed to the front. Enthusiasm began to wane when the war showed signs of lasting much longer than was at first expected, and individuals saw a chance to reap unusual profits in civilian jobs. The private's pay of $13 a month (later raised to $16) proved to be insufficient to counteract such influences. Hence in order to raise sufficient troops, both governments found it necessary to supplement the system of voluntary enlistments, first by offering bounties, and finally by resorting to the draft.

The bounty system was first employed in July, 1861, when the Federal Government offered a bonus of $100 to each volunteer. This sum was increased during 1863 to $302 for raw recruits and $402 for veterans. States, counties and cities granted additional amounts. In 1864 a volunteer in New York county could obtain $300 from the county and $75 from the state, besides the still larger federal bounty. At the same time an Illinois district paid an average bounty of $1056. The system was bad, for it encouraged the crime of "bounty-jumping." Unprincipled men would enlist, claim the bounty, desert and reënlist elsewhere under a different name, repeating the process indefinitely. In all, the federal government paid out $300,000,000 in bounties, while the state and local governments expended an additional $286,000,000.

Conscription was first employed on August 4, 1862, when President Lincoln ordered a draft of 300,000 militia through the medium of the states. The results were unsatisfactory, and on March 3, 1863, Congress enacted the statute upon which all later drafts were based. This law operated directly upon the people of the nation. It applied only to those districts which failed to furnish their quota of volunteers—a fact which helps to explain the generous bounties offered by local authorities. All unmarried men between the ages of twenty and forty-five and all married men between twenty and thirty-five were made subject to compulsory enlistment at the President's call, the names in each draft to be selected by lot. Certain classes were exempt: high public officials, men who were the sole support of dependent families, the physically unfit and criminals. A drafted man might avoid service by providing a substitute or by paying $300.

The conscription act provoked much discontent in the North, for it ran counter to the traditional military policy of the nation. Moreover, the laboring classes and poor people generally objected to the provision which made it easy for the well-to-do to purchase exemption. When the first draft under the new law was undertaken, the provost marshal general admitted that "Every imaginable artifice was adopted to deceive and defeat the enrolling officers. Open violence was sometimes met with. . . . In certain mining regions organized bodies of men openly opposed the enrollment, rendering it necessary that the U. S. authorities should send troops to overcome their opposition." The most notorious resistance took place in New York in July, 1863. When it appeared that most of those drafted in that city were workingmen, rioting ensued. For four days the citizens were at the mercy of a mob which pillaged, burned and, in particular, vented their hatred against Negroes, who were blamed as the cause of the war and the draft. No less than a thousand persons were killed or wounded. In most parts of the North, however, the draft went quietly into effect. While it did not directly furnish many new soldiers, it did serve to speed up volunteering.

In the South, also, bounties were offered to accelerate enlistments. Conscription was resorted to earlier than in the North. By acts of April and September, 1862, President Davis was empowered to impress into service all able-bodied male whites between the ages of eighteen and forty-five. The exempted classes included state and Confederate officials, preachers and teachers, persons employed in rail transportation and important war industries, newspaper proprietors and overseers on the larger plantations. Toward the end of the war an act of March, 1865, even provided for the enforced military service of Negro slaves. The exercise of conscription by the Confederate government violated the strong states' rights tradition, and produced spirited opposition by Rhett and Stephens as well as some of the states. Governor J. E. Brown of Georgia, pronouncing the law unconstitutional, refused to permit its enforcement within his jurisdiction, though he was zealous enough in raising troops by state action. The North Carolina legislature, after formally protesting against conscription, passed an act, in contravention of the Confederate law, exempting additional classes from military service.

Faulty statistics make it impossible to know just how many men actually served under the opposing flags. Yet it is probably within the range of truth to assume that approximately 800,000 individuals fought on the southern side, and from two to three times as many on the northern. It should not be overlooked that over 50,000 whites and more than 100,000 Negroes were recruited for the North from the seceded states.

SELECT BIBLIOGRAPHY

The Movement for Southern Independence. Stephenson, *The Day of the Confederacy*, gives a good general account. Carpenter, *The South as a Conscious Minority, 1789–1861*, traces the evolution of southern political thought to the goal of secession. Dumond, *The Secession Movement, 1860–1861*, is a detailed, analytical study. Cf. Phillips, *The Course of the South to Secession*. Dumond is also author of *Antislavery Origins of the Civil War*, in which he holds that the conflict was the result of a moral crusade. Biographies of southern leaders are listed at the end of Chap. XXX.

The North and Secession. A special study is Scrugham, *The Peaceable Americans, 1860–1861.* In *James Buchanan and His Cabinet on the Eve of Secession* Auchampaugh offers an antidote to the received opinion of Buchanan as timorous and time-serving. Among the best of the many biographies of the war President are Charnwood, *Abraham Lincoln;* Stephenson, *Lincoln;* and Barton, *The Life of Abraham Lincoln.*

The Appeal to Arms. Smith, *The Borderland in the Civil War,* is a special study of the rôle of Kentucky, Missouri, northwestern Virginia and the southern halves of Ohio, Indiana and Illinois in the secession movement and the war. Further consideration is given certain of these states in McGregor, *The Disruption of Virginia;* Coulter, *The Civil War and Readjustment in Kentucky;* and McElroy, *The Struggle for Missouri.* The impact of the secession movement on organized Christianity is discussed in Vander Velde, *The Presbyterian Churches and the Federal Union, 1861–1869;* Heathcote, *The Lutheran Church and the Civil War;* and Sweet, *The Methodist Episcopal Church and the Civil War.* Ambler is the biographer of the leader of West Virginia's separation from the Old Dominion; his volume is entitled *Francis H. Pierpont.*

The Embattled Hosts. In *The Organization and Administration of the Union Army* Shannon deals authoritatively with the problems of raising, equipping and maintaining the armed forces, with particular reference to the common soldier. Lonn, *Desertion during the Civil War,* is the standard treatment of that embarrassing subject. Northern military ligislation is summarized in Huidekoper, *The Military Unpreparedness of the United States.* The military problems of the Confederacy behind the lines are dealt with in Moore, *Conscription and Conflict in the Confederacy;* economic problems in Schwab, *The Confederate States of America;* and political problems in Owsley, *State Rights in the Confederacy.*

CHARLESTON
MERCURY
EXTRA:
THE
UNION
IS
DISSOLVED!

Facsimile of a Charleston newspaper extra,
December, 1860

Chapter *XXXIII*

THE WAR OF AMERICAN NATIONALITY

NAVAL OPERATIONS IN THE CIVIL WAR

THE Confederate armies, for the most part, fought on the defensive in the Civil War. To the North fell the task of invading and conquering a country three times the size of France. Success required not only a clear military preponderance on land, but also the closing of southern ports against munitions and supplies from abroad. Yet when Lincoln proclaimed the blockade in April, 1861, to guard a seacoast 3,500 miles in length, the federal navy consisted of but ninety-odd vessels, most of them small and antiquated and some of them absent on distant cruises. Nevertheless, by pressing all sorts of vessels into service, the blockade was made reasonably effective by summer. Blockade running, with all its dangers, was a lucrative business; occasional boats, like the steamer *Kate* which made forty-four successful trips, disclosed the possibilities of the traffic. Charleston and Wilmington were the principal ports for this irregular trade, but it never assumed formidable proportions. As prewar supplies became depleted, the southern people began to suffer acute discomfort. Coffee, tea, soap, paper, clothing and matches were extremely hard to get at any price. Even more serious was the scarcity of common medicines, like quinine and morphia, indispensable for the treatment of sick and wounded soldiers. Lack of salt also created difficulties, for salt meat formed a large part of the army ration.

For one brief moment it seemed that the Confederates might succeed in breaking the blockade which threatened to strangle them. On March 8, 1862, there suddenly appeared off Hampton Roads, Virginia, a vessel which the Confederates had made over and covered with plates of iron.[1] Against this monster the wooden ships of the blockading fleet were helpless; two were rammed and sunk on this one day, and a third was driven aground. But by a striking coincidence another ironclad appeared on the very next morning, before the *Merrimac* could resume its work of destruction. The federal authorities had also been experimenting with a new type of vessel, and, thanks to the ingenuity of John Ericsson, a Swedish immigrant, had contrived a low-decked ironclad with a revolving turret carrying heavy guns. The *Monitor*—some one called it "a Yankee cheesebox on a raft"—took up the gage of battle, and while it did not win a decisive victory, it damaged the *Merrimac* sufficiently to keep it from doing further mischief.

This first battle between ironclads was epoch-making, for it proved what the naval constructors of leading maritime powers abroad already knew—that the day of the wooden warship was past. A fleet of "monitors" was presently built by the United States, and performed valuable service during the remainder of the war.

The work of the navy was not confined to maintaining the blockade, for vessels of war coöperated with the land forces in opening up the Mississippi and other rivers. In Lincoln's expressive language, "Uncle Sam's web-feet" were present not only on "the broad bay, and the rapid river, but also up the narrow, muddy bayou, and wherever the ground was a little damp." The navy was also responsible for the eventual destruction of the Confederate raiders engaged in harassing northern commerce on the high seas.

---

[1] This vessel was the former United States frigate *Merrimac*. The Confederates had renamed it the *Virginia,* but it is more commonly known by its original appellation.

LOCOMOTIVE "HERO"
WRECKED BY CONFEDERATES WHEN ATLANTA WAS EVACUATED

U. S. SIGNAL SERVICE BALLOON CORPS, CIVIL WAR

CONFEDERATE IRONCLAD RAM "STONEWALL," 1865

MILITARY ACTIVITIES IN THE WEST

The federal operations on land were determined in part by the objectives of the fighting and in part by the physical contour of the country. From the early days of the war, one of the major purposes was the capture of the Confederate capital. Other important military objectives were the control of mountain passes and navigable streams and the seizure of railway junctions, by which means the economic life of Dixie and the transportation of troops and munitions might be paralyzed. The Appalachian system, one hundred and fifty miles wide, divides the South into two unequal parts: each area became promptly a theater of war. During the first three years and more, simultaneous campaigns were waged on opposite sides of the mountain barrier, usually with little or no relation to each other. West of the Mississippi River lay a third area of conflict, involving military movements of distinctly minor consequence.

The subjugation of the South proved to be a slow and difficult process. After it was blockaded by sea, the Confederacy was gradually cut off from its western territory and deprived of its main internal lines of communication. The southern capital, against which the North began to move within the first three months of the war, did not fall until nearly four years later, after the victorious Union army in the West, sweeping all before it, had rounded the southern end of the mountains and advanced northward along the coast, to join forces with the troops assailing Richmond.

The North enjoyed an initial advantage in the West. The Confederates succeeded in gaining control of a good part of Missouri in 1861, but the struggle went definitely against them at Pea Ridge, in northwestern Arkansas, on March 5–8 of 1862. General S. R. Curtis, the victor in this fight, rapidly enlarged the area of his authority until by the close of the year

1861	In the West	In the East
April 12–14		Attack on Fort Sumter.
June 3		Engagement at Philippi, W. Va.
June 10		Engagement at Big Bethel W. Va.
July 5	Engagement at Carthage, Mo.	
July 8		Engagement at Laurel Hill, W. Va.
July 21		First battle of Bull Run, Va.
Aug. 10	Engagement at Wilson's Creek, Mo.	
Aug. 28–29		Capture of Fort Hatteras, N. C.
Sept. 2	Capture of Fort Scott, Mo.	
Sept. 12–15		Fighting at Cheat Mt., W. Va.
Oct. 21		Engagement at Ball's Bluff, Va.
Nov. 7	Battle of Belmont, Mo.	Capture of Port Royal, S. C.
1862		
Jan. 19–20	Battle of Mill Springs, Mo.	
Feb. 6	Capture of Fort Henry, Tenn.	
Feb. 16	Capture of Fort Donelson, Tenn.	
March 5–8	Battle of Pea Ridge, Ark.	
April 6–7	Battle of Shiloh, Tenn.	
April 7	Capture of Island No. 10.	
April 28	Capture of New Orleans, La.	
May 4		Capture of Yorktown, Va.
May 5		Battle of Williamsburg, Va.
May 25		Battle of Winchester, Va.
May 30	Capture of Corinth, Miss.	
May 31– June 1		Battle of Seven Pines, Va.
June 5	Capture of Fort Pillow, Tenn.	
June 6	Occupation of Memphis, Tenn.	
June 25– July 1		Seven Days' Battles, Va.
Aug. 9		Battle of Cedar Mt., Va.
Aug. 30		Second battle of Bull Run, Va.
Sept. 14–16	Battle of Munfordsville, Ky.	
Sept. 14		Battle of South Mt., Md.
Sept. 17		Battle of Antietam, Md.
Sept. 19	Battle of Iuka, Miss.	
Oct. 3–4	Battle of Corinth, Miss.	
Oct. 8	Battle of Perryville, Ky.	
Dec. 13		Battle of Fredericksburg, Va.
Dec. 29	Sherman's repulse at Vicksburg, Miss.	

1863	In the West	In the East
Dec. 31– Jan. 2	Battle of Murfreesboro, Tenn.	
May 2–5		Battle of Chancellorsville, Va.
May 16	Fighting at Champion Hill, Miss.	
June 13–15		Fighting at Winchester, Va.
July 1–3		Battle of Gettysburg, Pa.
July 4	Capture of Vicksburg, Miss.	
July 9	Capture of Port Hudson, La.	
Sept. 7		Capture of Fort Wagner, S. C.
Sept. 9	Occupation of Chattanooga.	
Sept. 19–20	Battle of Chickamauga, Ga.	
Nov. 23–25	Battle of Chattanooga, Tenn.	
Dec. 6	Occupation of Knoxville, Tenn.	

1864		
Feb. 14	Occupation of Meridian, Miss.	
April 8	Battle of Sabine Cross Roads, La.	
May 5–6		First battle in Wilderness, Va.
May 8–12		Battle of Spottsylvania C. H., Va.
May 13–16	Fighting at Resaca, Ga.	
May 18	Fighting at Rome, Ga.	
June 1–3		Battle of Cold Harbor, Va.
June 19		Siege of Petersburg, Va., begins.
June 27	Battle of Kenesaw Mt., Ga.	
July 22	First battle before Atlanta, Ga.	
Aug. 5	Capture of Mobile Bay, Ala.	
Sept. 2	Capture of Atlanta, Ga.	
Sept. 19		Battle of Opequon, Va.
Sept. 21		Battle of Fisher's Hill, Va.
Sept. 26–27	Fighting at Ironton, Mo.	
Oct. 19		Battle of Cedar Creek, Va.
Nov. 30	Battle of Franklin, Tenn.	
Dec. 15–16	Battle of Nashville, Tenn.	
Dec. 20	Capture of Savannah, Ga.	

1865		
Jan. 15		Capture of Fort Fisher, N. C.
Feb. 17		Capture of Columbia, S. C.
Feb. 18		Capture of Charleston, S. C.
Feb. 22		Capture of Wilmington, N. C.
March 19		Fighting at Goldsboro, N. C.
April 1		Battle of Five Forks, Va.
April 2		Occupation of Petersburg, Va.
April 3		Occupation of Richmond, Va.
April 9		Lee's surrender at Appomattox, Va.
April 26		Johnston's surrender at Hillsboro, N. C.
May 26	Kirby Smith's surrender at Baton Rouge, La.	

the northern half of Arkansas was in Union hands. The center of Confederate power west of the Mississippi was at Shreveport in the Red River Valley in northwestern Louisiana. Various unsuccessful attempts were made by the Union forces to dislodge the foe from this region in 1863 and 1864, but General Kirby Smith retained possession until the end of the war. The fighting west of the Mississippi had little effect upon the campaigns farther East, most of it being desultory and guerilla in character.

East of the river, the decision of Missouri, Kentucky, and West Virginia to remain with the Union placed the original battle front on a line somewhat north of the center of those states. The Confederates were thus deprived of the Ohio River, which would have formed an excellent boundary for defense and offense. When the campaign of 1862 began, the federal forces set about to open up the Mississippi, and thereby accomplish the double purpose of isolating the Confederate states west of the river and of providing the upper Mississippi Valley with its accustomed channel of commerce.

The key to the situation was the control of the Tennessee and Cumberland rivers, two tributaries of the Ohio, which penetrated southward toward the heart of the enemy country. The first major movement, therefore, was an expedition up these streams by a combined gunboat fleet and army under command of General U. S. Grant. In the early weeks of February, 1862, Forts Henry and Donelson, situated on these rivers near the Kentucky-Tennessee border, surrendered with more than 14,000 prisoners. The expedition pushed on, capturing Nashville, the Tennessee capital, on the Cumberland, while continuing the southward advance along the Tennessee. Grant's objective now was the village of Corinth in northern Mississippi, one of the principal railway centers of the South, lying at the junction of lines from Memphis, Vicksburg, Mobile and Chattanooga. After desperate fighting on

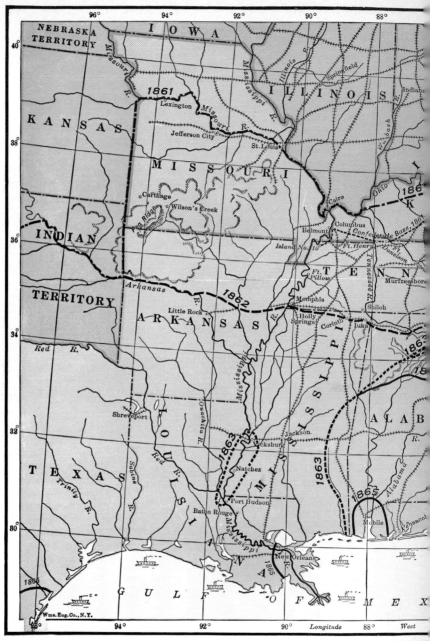

THE THEATER C

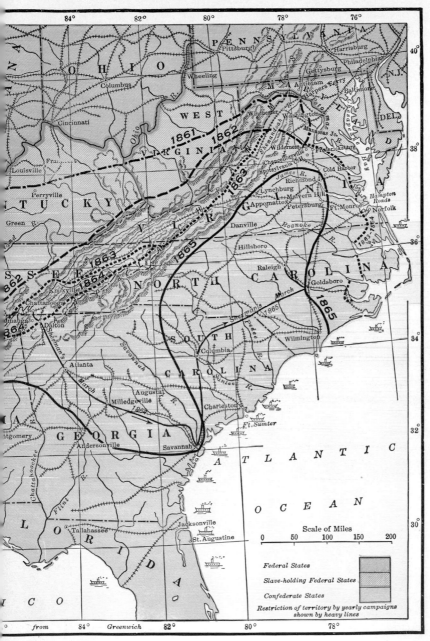

April 6–7 at Pittsburg Landing and at Shiloh, where the federals departed from the river, the advance was resumed under General H. W. Halleck. On May 30 Corinth was occupied.

Meantime, progress had been made towards breaking the Confederate hold on the Mississippi itself. Union forces operating from the North under General John Pope captured Island No. 10 (April 7), an important river fort near the Kentucky-Tennessee border, while the occupation of Corinth obliged the Confederates to abandon Fort Pillow and Memphis. A northward thrust from the Gulf by a naval force under D. G. Farragut secured also the fall of New Orleans on April 28 after ten days' fighting. In September and October the Confederates made a bold attempt to compel the withdrawal of the Union forces by a raid into the North. Braxton Bragg and Kirby Smith, moving rapidly into Kentucky, actually approached within a few miles of Cincinnati. But the Kentuckians failed to rally to the Confederate cause; and, fearing disaster, the invaders retreated, fighting notable battles at Perryville, Kentucky, and at Murfreesboro in Tennessee. The year 1862 closed with the North in possession of the western half of Tennessee, and in control of the Mississippi River save for a two-hundred-mile stretch guarded at one end by the Confederate stronghold of Vicksburg and at the other by Port Hudson.

The first business of the campaign of 1863, on the part of the North, was to complete the task begun in the preceding year—that of opening the Mississippi for navigation. The undertaking was one of the most difficult operations of the war, for Vicksburg was a natural fortress, perched on a high bluff commanding the Mississippi, and almost unapproachable from the north or northeast because of swamps. In April Grant began his active movement against Vicksburg, assisted by a gunboat flotilla. Many weeks passed with no results but blocked attacks, heavy losses in battle and deaths from malaria and smallpox. Finally, on July 4, the Confederates, themselves stricken with disease and on the verge of starvation, gave up the fight. Thirty thousand men surrendered. Five days later, when Port Hudson was taken, the "Father of Waters," in Lincoln's phrase, again flowed "unvexed to the sea."

The Union forces were now ready to press the conquest of the remainder of Tennessee. Their special objective was Chattanooga in the extreme southeastern portion, which commanded the shortest rail route between Richmond and Atlanta. A skillful campaign, conducted by General W. S. Rosecrans, brought the desired culmination on September 9; but General Bragg's army, strengthened by reënforcements from Lee, turned on the federals at Chickamauga Creek on September 19–20, driving them back into Chattanooga and laying siege to the place. Grant, now taking command in person, waged a hot battle from November 23 to 25, dislodging the Confederates and forcing their retreat into Georgia.

The campaign of 1863 marked a turning point in the war. Not only did it complete the conquest of Tennessee, but it rent the enemy country in twain, crippled the southern transportation system, and placed the Union army in a strategic position to rive the Confederacy in a new direction. Hardly less significant was the fact that it revealed Grant as the greatest military genius on the northern side, and led Lincoln to appoint him to the supreme command of the nation's armies. With his removal of the eastern theater of war, William Tecumseh Sherman, who had proved to be one of his ablest generals, took charge at Chattanooga as the campaign of 1864 got under way. To him fell the task of breaking through the mountains of northwestern Georgia and capturing Atlanta, the principal railroad center and manufacturing city left to the Confederacy. Although his army out-numbered the foe almost two to one, it took him from May to July to arrive before Atlanta, and more weeks of hard fighting there before he gained possession on September 2. The Confederate general, J. B. Hood, who saved his army only by evacuating the city, set about to imperil Sherman's line of communications and base of supplies at Nashville, and thus compel his withdrawal. But Hood suffered irreparable defeat at the battle of Nashville on December 15–16 at the hands of General George H. Thomas.

Meantime Sherman, undeterred by Hood's operations in his rear, resolved upon a southeasterly march across Georgia to the ocean. This would enable him to establish a safe base which could be supplied by sea from the North, and, at the same time, to strike a disastrous blow at the granary which fed Lee's army. He believed that if the war in all its frightfulness and ruin were brought home to the people of the Lower South their morale would break and the Confederate armies melt away. Beginning the advance on November 12, 1864, his army of sixty thousand, marching in four columns and foraging off the country, destroyed 265 miles of railway, and left in its wake a belt sixty miles wide in which nothing of military value remained. According to Sherman's own estimate, the damage amounted to a hundred million dollars, four fifths of it "simple waste and destruction." He met with no opposition worthy of the name and, on December 20, took possession of Savannah. Thus the campaign of 1864 ended with the Confederacy cut into three parts, and Sherman in a position to sweep northward along the coast toward the Union forces massed in Virginia.

THE CAMPAIGNS IN THE EAST

Meanwhile the eastern theater of war presented a different story. From the very first both sides had realized the importance of decisive action in Virginia. The rival capitals stood only a hundred miles apart, one on the Potomac, the other on the James—rivers running approximately parallel to each other. To reach Richmond the Union armies must traverse a rough and wooded country, crossing streams which lay athwart their path like moats defending the Confederate position. The Confederates, on the contrary, had a natural passageway into the North, through the Shenandoah Valley. The Shenandoah River, reaching the Potomac from the South between protecting mountain ridges, enabled the southern commanders constantly to harry the rear of the federal armies and to threaten Washington.

Lincoln's promptitude in preventing the secession of Maryland in the spring of 1861 had the strategic value of saving to the United States the control of the Potomac River. Spurred by the popular cry of "On to Richmond," General Irvin McDowell attacked the enemy at Manassas Junction on the little stream of Bull Run, twenty-five miles west of Washington, on July 21, 1861. Both armies were raw and undisciplined, but the superior leadership of the Confederate general, Joseph E. Johnston, threw the Union forces into confusion, causing a disgraceful rout. Lincoln now placed General George B. McClellan in command. Though he showed marvelous energy and success in whipping his armed mob into an efficient fighting unit, the remainder of the year passed without offensive operations.

The campaign of 1862 opened with McClellan's decision to launch a drive against Richmond from an unexpected quarter—the shore of Chesapeake Bay—thereby avoiding the difficult overland march. His plan was to ship his army to Fortress Monroe, then advance up the peninsula between the York and James rivers and capture Richmond. The Peninsular campaign was marked by timidity and overcaution. It required a month for McClellan to take Yorktown, his first objective. Proceeding slowly in the teeth of stubborn resistance, he battled his way across the Chickahominy and, by early

June, came within sight of Richmond. Though his force out-numbered Lee's army of defense by thirty thousand, he allowed the latter to assume the offensive. In the Seven Days' Battles (June 25–July 1), the Union troops were driven steadily backward, both sides suffering terrible losses.

Realizing the moment for victory had passed, Lincoln recalled the army, replacing McClellan with Pope who was enjoying temporary fame for his capture of Island No. 10 on the Mississippi. Boastful and overconfident, Pope began the overland march against Richmond, only to meet needless disaster at the second battle of Bull Run on August 30, 1862. Lee, seizing the opportunity, undertook a counterinvasion of the free states, crossing into Maryland by way of the Shenandoah Valley. With such a bold stroke he might hope to incite a pro-southern uprising in Maryland, capture the federal capital, and force the war to an abrupt close. But as Lee advanced northward, McClellan, again in command, paralleled his movements with a force vastly superior in numbers. On September 17 the two armies met at Antietam Creek, near Sharpsburg, Maryland. Desperate fighting ensued with heavy casualties. Lee was forced to give way, but, thanks to McClellan's inactivity, he effected an orderly retreat into Virginia. Late in October, when the federals once more undertook the overland march on Richmond, McClellan was replaced by General A. E. Burnside. Oddly enough, the latter had protested against his own appointment on the plea of incapacity, and the sequel justified his candor, for he was defeated with heavy slaughter at the battle of Fredericksburg on December 13. The Eastern campaign of 1862 thus ended in a draw, though with the advantage distinctly on the side of the South.

The campaign of 1863 began badly for the North. Under "Fighting Joe" Hooker, the Union forces once more attempted the overland advance on Richmond. At Chancellorsville a bloody battle from May 2 to 5, resulted in a severe repulse for the federals. The Confederate victory was gained at a high price, however, for it cost the life of General Thomas J. ("Stonewall") Jackson, who, next to Lee, was the ablest southern commander. The engagement opened the way for a new invasion of the North, and Lee, again using the Shenandoah Valley, crossed the Potomac late in June. Meantime the Union army, with General George G. Meade in command, occupied the heights at Gettysburg, which commanded several important highways, and awaited attack. Here, in southern Pennsylvania, occurred three days of terrific fighting on July 1–3, involving casualties of nearly forty thousand men, shared almost equally by the two sides. In the end Meade won the advantage.

The Confederacy had reached high tide and its fortunes began to ebb. Yet Lee retired from Gettysburg in such good order that the Union general dared not risk another battle. The remaining months passed with small skirmishes but no general engagement, and the close of the year 1863 saw the northern army as far from Richmond as when the war began.

The federals had all along possessed an advantage over the enemy in man power and equipment, but had suffered from inferior leadership. With unexampled patience Lincoln had tried a succession of generals, but without satisfactory result. The campaign of 1864 opened with the choice of yet another commander, Ulysses S. Grant. A former West Pointer, he had entered the war in 1861 as a colonel of Illinois volunteers and, through his military successes in the West, had won rapid promotion. On March 9, 1864, he was appointed to the newly revived position of lieutenant general with supreme command, under the President, of all the Union armies. Grant differed from his predecessors mainly in his pertinacity and in his resolution to crush the South by his superiority in men and resources. Furthermore, his plans embraced concerted movements by the armies East and West.   For himself he reserved the eastern command.

On the night of May 3, 1864, Grant began the oft-attempted march on the Confederate capital by crossing the Rapidan, encamping the next day in the Wilderness, a densely wooded, marshy tract ten miles across.   Here Lee measured his strength with his new opponent in an inconclusive two days' battle (May 5–6).   Grant now moved southeastward toward Spottsylvania Court House and, for the next month, was almost constantly engaged in desperate combat while stubbornly battering his way toward Richmond.   Lee, the abler strategist, fell back slowly, protecting his forces at each step by well-chosen intrenched positions, strengthened by the new device of wire entanglements.

Two costly engagements—at Spottsylvania on May 8–12, and at Cold Harbor on June 1–3, the latter near the scene of McClellan's misadventure—caused Grant to shift his base to the James River, south of Richmond, and lay siege to Petersburg, an important railroad junction connecting Richmond with the South.   By this time he had lost 55,000 men, about half of his original force, but fresh troops kept his ranks full. Still, repeated attacks failed to pierce the Confederate defense. Lee sought to draw him off in July by sending General Jubal A. Early down the Shenandoah Valley in a raid against Washington, but Grant retaliated by dispatching General Philip H. Sheridan with a force which defeated Early by weight of numbers at Opequon Creek and elsewhere.   Sheridan ravaged the valley so thoroughly that it could never be used again for a Confederate invasion.   The year closed with Grant still before Petersburg, twenty-two miles from Richmond.

Grant's advance in 1864, slow though it was, foreshadowed the end.   From all sides Yankee troops were closing in on Richmond.   On February 1, 1865, Sherman began his march northward from Georgia.   Opposed constantly by a desperate enemy, hindered by innumerable streams swollen by spring freshets, and almost without supplies, the march was marked by pillaging, destruction of railways and machinery, and general lawlessness. On February 17, the Confederates abandoned Columbia, the South Carolina capital, and in the disorder attending federal occupation it was partly destroyed by fire. Charleston fell into the hands of the federal fleet without a battle when her railroad connections with the interior were cut. On March 19 Sherman's advance ran into the Confederate forces under General J. E. Johnston at Goldsboro in central North Carolina, and was temporarily checked.

Meantime, the Confederate positions in Petersburg and Richmond had become untenable, and on April 2 Lee abandoned them, intending to effect a junction with Johnston or, if that failed, to secure himself in the mountain fastnesses. But northern cavalry got ahead of him, tearing up railways he had hoped to use, and blocking possible mountain passes. On April 9 he found himself at Appomattox Court House, some seventy miles west of Petersburg, hemmed in by the enemy and with no course open but surrender. A conference ensued between the two generals—Lee, erect in a new full-dress uniform of Confederate gray with a jeweled sword; Grant in the shabby blue of a private, wearing the straps of lieutenant general but no sword. The terms of surrender were magnanimous. The officers were permitted to retain their sidearms, and both officers and men rode off on their own horses. As Grant remarked, the animals were needed for the spring plowing. On his return from the conference, Grant quieted the noisy demonstrations of his soldiers by reminding them, "The rebels are our countrymen again."

When the news of Lee's surrender reached Johnston, he asked Sherman for terms. The two men met at Hillsboro, and on April 26 Johnston yielded on the same conditions as Lee. The two events occurred within ninety miles of each

THE SURRENDER AT APPOMATTOX

other.   A month later Kirby Smith at Baton Rouge surrendered his force of 18,000 men.   The war for southern independence had become the "Lost Cause."

FILLING THE WAR PURSE

The financing of the war placed an enormous burden upon
a people unused to heavy taxation.   In the four years the
government's expenditures overtopped those of the whole
previous period of national independence.   Yet, when Lincoln entered office, customs receipts were almost at a standstill,[1] the treasury was nearly empty and public credit on the
ebb.   In December, 1861, the banks of the North suspended
specie payments, an action soon followed by the government.
People promptly began to hoard gold and silver coins, and
the country went on a paper-money basis.   In a frantic effort
to meet the mounting war costs and restore confidence, Secretary of the Treasury Chase and Congress resorted to every
known device for obtaining revenue.   There were three principal sources to draw upon: taxation, legal-tender issues and
loans.   In all these respects the crying need for funds caused
the government to depart widely from time-honored policies.

Beginning in 1862, hardly a session of Congress passed without some increase in the tariff until by 1864 the average rate
had been advanced to forty-seven per cent, an unprecedented
figure at that time.   A total of $305,360,000 was raised from
tariff duties during the war.   An important purpose of tariff
legislation, however, was to protect northern industrialists
from foreign competition in order to enable them to pay high
domestic taxes.   The first comprehensive internal tax law,
that of July, 1862, left hardly anything untouched, from tobacco, liquors, and billiard tables to advertisements, occupations, manufactures, railroads, and inheritances.   Two years

---

[1] In 1857 Congress had scaled down the already low duties of 1846 by about
five per cent, and had enlarged the free list.

later the rates were increased.   Internal taxation had been unknown for more than a generation.

On the whole, war taxation broke sharply with the past.
An income tax had never been tried; but in 1861 such a tax
levied three per cent on incomes above $800.   By 1865 the
rates had risen to five per cent on incomes between $600 and
$5000, and to ten per cent on larger ones.   The total yield
from internal taxes of all kinds during the war was $356,-
846,000.

A second financial expedient—one the effects of which were
to plague the country for years to come—was the issue of
legal-tender notes or "greenbacks."   Time was required before returns could be obtained from the new tariff and tax
legislation, while the need of cash was immediate.   Therefore,
by the simple process of working the printing press, the
United States acquired funds for soldiers' wages and war supplies.   These notes were like the continental currency of revolutionary days, being merely the government's promises to
pay and lacking the support of a gold reserve.   Creditors were
required to take the greenbacks at face value, and their ultimate redemption in gold depended on the good faith and future financial ability of the nation.   In February, 1862, Congress authorized $150,000,000 worth of these notes, to be
receivable for all debts due to or from the Federal Government, except import duties and interest on bonds.   Further
inflation was provided for in 1862 and 1863 until, at the close
of the war, greenbacks to the amount of $431,000,000 were in
circulation.   In addition, the government issued $50,000,000
in fractional currency in denominations as low as three cents.
These shinplasters, as they were called, were needed to replace
the smaller metal coins that, as the war went on, disappeared
from use.   From a fiscal point of view, all such issues
amounted to a forced loan from the people, for the notes
quickly declined in value, both because of their superabun-

dance and because of the people's wavering faith in the government in times of military misfortune. As is always the case, there resulted a rapid rise in the cost of living. In July, 1864, a hundred greenback dollars were worth thirty-nine dollars in gold; in April, 1865, with victory assured, the gold value of that sum in greenbacks had advanced to sixty-seven dollars.

Although large sums were obtained by the means described, the government's main reliance was on borrowing money through the sale of bonds and treasury notes. In order to compete with commercial investments, high rates of interest had to be offered. The two issues of "five-twenties" (bonds redeemable at the government's option from five to twenty years after date), authorized in 1862 and 1864, bore interest at six per cent; the "ten-forties," issued in 1864, paid five per cent. Short-term loans were effected through treasury notes, offered in smaller denominations, and sometimes carrying interest as high as 7.3 per cent (the "seven-thirties"). In all, the government obtained a revenue of $2,621,917,000 by such means—nearly three times as much as from all other sources combined.

Although other causes were more fundamental, the need for speeding up the sale of bonds hastened the adoption of the national banking act. On January 1, 1862, there were fifteen hundred banks that issued notes. Chartered by the several states, the restrictions under which they operated varied widely. There was no uniformity in the quality or amount of the securities required as the basis of their circulating notes. In some states, they possessed different privileges and operated under different restrictions, their bank notes being based on a wide variety of securities, unlike in quality or amount. In some states, boards of bank commissioners made frequent and thorough examinations, while elsewhere no such boards existed or existed in name only. All told, about seven thousand different kinds of notes were in circulation apart from successful counterfeits. While the situation was not as bad as in Jackson's day, depositors in many states were uncertain as to the security of their funds, and bank notes in constant use might, or might not, be worth their face value. Some system of federal regulation and control was clearly called for. The national banking act of 1863 (amended in 1864) did away with these irregularities, supplied a safe and uniform bank currency, and at the same time provided a new market for government bonds. Incidentally, it enlisted a strong and active financial interest for the preservation of the Union.

Banks chartered under the system were required to buy federal bonds to the extent of a third of their capital stock, and to deposit them with the Secretary of the Treasury. On the basis of this security they might issue bank notes up to ninety per cent of the market value of the bonds they owned. They must also keep on hand a cash fund for the redemption of notes on demand and as a safeguard for their depositors. Depositors were further protected by the provision for periodical examination by federal inspectors. Though a large number of state banks, because of the many restrictions, at first held aloof from the national system, Congress brought most of them into line by providing in March, 1865, for a ten per cent tax on their bank notes, thus reserving the note-issuing function for national banks alone. The legislation of 1863–1865 remains the foundation of our national banking system to this day.[1]

Federal expenditures for the army and navy from 1861 to 1865 amounted to more than three billion dollars. This fig-

[1] The system was changed in detail by subsequent acts, notably the one of 1908, which permitted a national bank to deposit certain other securities besides United States bonds as a basis for its note circulation. It was also affected, in certain respects, by the establishment of the federal reserve system in 1913.

ure does not include the interest on the war debt. Furthermore, several years elapsed after the peace before the appropriations for military and naval purposes returned to a normal level, and in the last year of the conflict pensions began to swell the government's outlay. In 1879 an estimate of the expenditures growing out of the war down to that date showed a total of $6,190,000,000. But even this amount does not take into account the extraordinary expenses for war purposes borne by the state and local governments.

The financial difficulties of the Confederacy were incomparably greater. While the North had the revenue machinery of the United States government to work through, the South had to build from the ground up. At the outset, however, the Confederacy had over a million dollars in its treasury, nearly all of it confiscated from federal mints and customhouses within its borders. Like the United States, the Richmond government expected to obtain a substantial revenue from customs duties. The blockade, however, quickly put an end to this expectation. The Confederate Congress then asked each state to levy a property tax for the general treasury —the old requisition system of the Articles of Confederation —but the results proved disappointing. Finally, in April, 1863, the Congress adopted an internal revenue measure, comparable to the federal act of 1862, and including even a ten per cent tax on farm produce, payable in kind. The levy on farm products caused bitter resentment among the agricultural classes, particularly in North Carolina.

Borrowing was also resorted to, through long-term bonds and short-term treasury notes, but this method proved less successful than in the North where money for investment was plentiful. Since the first bond issue, in 1861, absorbed most of the available specie, the issue of 1862 was made payable in produce. As a result, the government came into possession of vast stores of cotton, tobacco and other commodities that

had no sale. In 1863, however, some success was met in selling a bond issue of $15,000,000 abroad. As in the North,
the tempting expedient of irredeemable paper money was
adopted. In its extremity, the Confederacy printed nearly a
billion dollars of this currency, with the inevitable sequel of
rapid depreciation and inflated prices. The total volume of
such money was swollen by unrecorded issues of state governments, banks and private business firms. The enormous war
debt of the South was outlawed by the failure of the rebellion,
and the Fourteenth Amendment of the federal Constitution,
adopted in 1868, forbade either the United States or any state
to pay any part of it.

SELECT BIBLIOGRAPHY

Naval and Military Operations. Well-balanced, brief accounts
may be found in Rhodes, *History of the Civil War* (condensed
and revised from his more elaborate work) ; Hosmer, *The Appeal
to Arms,* and his *Outcome of the Civil War;* Wood, *Captains of
the Civil War;* Paxson, *The Civil War;* Eggleston, *The History
of the Confederate War;* Dodge, *A Bird's Eye View of Our Civil
War;* Wood and Edmonds, *A History of the Civil War in the
United States;* and Fish, *The American Civil War.* Randall, *The
Civil War and Reconstruction,* the latest contribution on the subject, is a thorough, calm, dispassionate survey. It is valuable also
for its elaborate bibliographies. Among the best war biographies
are Henderson, *Stonewall Jackson and the American Civil War;*
Maurice, *Robert E. Lee, the Soldier;* Winston, *Robert E. Lee;*
Coolidge, *Ulysses S. Grant;* Burne, *Lee, Grant and Sherman;*
Eckenrode, *James Longstreet;* and Myers, *General George Brin-
ton McClellan.* The most elaborate, if not definitive, study of
Lee is Freeman, *Robert E. Lee.* Preston, in *Lee—West Point and
Lexington,* gives an excellent account of his career as an educator.
Meneely, *The War Department: 1861,* is a special study. The
war on the water in its various aspects is the concern of Baxter,
The Introduction of the Ironclad Warship; Mahan, *Admiral Far-
ragut;* Porter, *The Naval History of the Civil War;* Scharf, *History of the Confederate States Navy,* and Hill, *Sea Dogs of the*

Sixties (biographical sketches). Bradlee, *Blockade Running during the Civil War and the Effect of Land and Water Transportation on the Confederacy,* is the best treatment of its subject. In *The Irrepressible Conflict* Cole gives an intimate picture of the conditions of fighting.

Filling the War Purse. A concise analysis of federal finances and the new national banking system appears in Dewey, *Financial History of the United States.* A biographical approach is afforded by Hart, *Salmon Portland Chase;* Oberholtzer, *Jay Cooke, Financier of the Civil War;* and Burton, *John Sherman.* For southern finances, Schwab, *The Confederate States of America,* is important.

Chapter XXXIV

SOCIAL AND POLITICAL CONDITIONS IN WAR TIME

LIFE BEHIND THE LINES

SECESSION came as a severe blow to northern industry. As the banks suspended specie payments, mercantile failures multiplied until over 12,000 firms were driven to the wall. Not only was business subjected to the usual shocks incident to the outbreak of a great war, but merchants and bankers were confronted with the loss of $300,000,000 owing them from the South—private debts which the Confederate and state authorities promptly outlawed. After 1861, however, a boom set in, which lasted through the remainder of the conflict. The enormous purchases and high prices paid by the government for uniforms, munitions and other supplies kept factories running; the movement of troops and supplies augmented the freight traffic of the railroads; currency inflation and the tariff acted as powerful stimulants to industry.

The cost of living shot upward also, while the wage-earner's pay lagged far behind. A widespread revival of trade unions resulted and an increasing resort to strikes, by means of which labor succeeded in maintaining its relative position. Meanwhile, the farmer made rich profits, thanks to the needs of the army and to bad crops abroad. Wheat production had never been so great as during the war. The general well-being was mirrored in the growth of savings-bank deposits in the five-year period from $149,278,000 to $242,619,000; the number of depositors rose from 694,000 to 981,000. In only one respect did northern enterprise suffer a serious setback.

758

The increased hazards to shipping from the depredations of the *Alabama* and other Confederate raiders enabled the British to take over much of the trade hitherto carried in American vessels. All together, there was a decline of a million tons during the war years. From this injury the merchant marine never recovered, for, when peace returned, capitalists preferred the certain profits to be gained from factories and railways to the doubtful attempt to restore it.

In the train of prosperity came the usual brood of war-time evils: corruption, profiteering and fast living. The government was cheated without conscience in its purchases of military supplies. A committee of the War Department in 1862 exposed frauds of $17,000,000 in contracts amounting to $50,000,000. The Michigan legislature formally charged that "traitors in the disguise of patriots have plundered our treasury," and James Russell Lowell, agreeing, asserted, "Men have striven to make the blood of our martyrs the seed of wealth." The term, "shoddy aristocracy," came to stigmatize those who reaped fortunes out of government contracts, particularly from supplying the soldiers with inferior clothing. In the mad strife for gain northerners even engaged in illicit traffic in cotton with the enemy, often with the corrupt connivance of army officers in the field. Not only food and money but also powder and bullets reached the Confederates by this means. Before the trade was effectively regulated in 1864, the South had sold more cotton to the North than it managed to send through the blockade to England. As profiteers multiplied and wealth piled up, luxury flaunted itself in American cities as never before. "The indulgence in every variety of pleasure, luxury, and extravagance is simply shocking," reported the correspondent of the *London Times* in 1863. "Washington is mad with gayety, reeling in the whirl of dissipation," declared the *Springfield Republican* a year later.

Against this unedifying picture, however, must be set another and more inspiring one. No war in history had called
forth such heroism and self-sacrifice on the part of noncom-
batants associated with the troops or civilians behind the
lines. The army casualties mounted so rapidly that the medical department was obliged to make use of volunteer nurses.
Clara Barton, future founder of the American Red Cross, who
resigned a government clerkship to take up nursing and the
work of organizing hospital supplies, was merely more famous
than the countless others whose labors were no less devoted.

Just in time to relieve the suffering of soldiers whose
wounds required surgical attention, came the epochal discovery of anaesthetics.[1] Chloroform was most widely used
for this purpose during the war. Unfortunately, the use of
antiseptics was still unknown, and, in order to prevent wound
infections, surgeons resorted freely to amputations. Of the
thirty thousand that were performed in the Union army, the
great majority were successful. For many years following the
war, armless and legless veterans were a pathetic reminder of
the great conflict. Sanitary science also lingered in the dark
ages, with the result that, despite the heavy losses incurred in
fighting, deaths from dysentery, camp fevers, pneumonia and
other diseases proved almost twice as great.

In no armed conflict in history before the World War was
civilian relief work organized on so vast a scale. Every local
community in the North had its Ladies' Aid Society for making bandages, shirts and other necessaries and comforts; and
these groups coöperated with a national body, the United
States Sanitary Commission, which the government created in

---

[1] In 1844 Horace Wells, a dentist in Hartford, Connecticut, demonstrated
that nitrous oxide gas might be used to deaden the pain of operations. Two
years later a Boston dentist, W. T. Morton, acting upon the advice of C. T.
Jackson, a chemist, employed ether as an anaesthetic. A Georgia physician,
C. W. Long, had made the same discovery in 1842, but failed to publish his
results. The third common anaesthetic, chloroform, was first used for this
purpose in 1847 by Sir James Y. Simpson of Edinburgh.

June, 1861, to help in looking after disabled soldiers and their dependent families. The Sanitary Commission developed an elaborate organization, employing at times five hundred agents. Storehouses were maintained in Boston, New York, Cincinnati, Chicago and other centers, to which local branches sent their supplies with the assistance of free transportation by the railroads and express companies. Through its labors, conditions of camp life were greatly improved, and assistance was given in caring for the wounded on the field of battle and in hospitals. In the few days following Gettysburg, clothing and food valued at $75,000 were distributed among the men, including such delicacies as poultry, butter, eggs, milk and ice. To provide funds for the Commission's activities, "sanitary fairs" were held in all the leading cities, a total of $7,000,000 being raised chiefly in this way. The services rendered by the countless women connected with the work inspired Lincoln's oft-quoted eulogy: "If all that has been said by orators and poets since the creation of the world in praise of women were applied to the women of America, it would not do them justice for their conduct during this war."

Nor were the soldiers' spiritual needs neglected. To serve these, the United States Christian Commission was formed in November, 1861, upon the initiative of the Young Men's Christian Association. Besides providing the camps with free reading rooms containing magazines, newspapers and religious literature, it set up for injured soldiers a system of diet kitchens extending to every corps of the army.

In the South the burdens borne by the noncombatant population were even heavier than in the free states, for a larger proportion of the white men were at the front. Relief work was not organized; but the proud southern women brought into use old spinning wheels and looms in order to make clothing for the soldiers; they denied themselves meat and drink that it might be sent to the army, and, like their northern sisters, they nursed the wounded and worked in munition plants. Living in an invaded country, they experienced the horrors of war all about them—homes destroyed, fields ravaged, hostile soldiers on every side. Nothing was more remarkable perhaps than the peaceable labor of the several million slaves, whose presence in the South had caused the "irrepressible conflict" and whose freedom became a major purpose of the invading hosts.

THE RESTRAINT OF CIVIL LIBERTY

Among the most perplexing problems that confronted the government was the question of the limits to which criticism might be allowed to go. The democratic system is better adapted to peace than to war, for the efficient conduct of war requires the exercise of extraordinary powers by the government, and the suspension of the usual safeguards of rights and liberties. During the Civil War President Lincoln performed acts which in peace time would have been unconstitutional, and which could be justified only by his authority as commander-in-chief of the army and navy. Not only was the administration determined to permit nothing to cripple its efforts to maintain public safety, but, under guise of his war powers, Lincoln even attempted the great humanitarian feat of freeing the slaves. President Davis, although more cautious, was, like Lincoln, denounced by a minority as an intolerable despot.

Lincoln's suspension of the writ of *habeas corpus* called forth particular condemnation. Early decisions of the Supreme Court had implied that this cherished safeguard of liberty could be suspended only by Congress. But without consulting that body, Lincoln temporarily forbade the use of the writ in Maryland in 1861, at a time when the arbitrary arrest of suspects seemed necessary to crush the incipient secession movement. In a proclamation of September 24, 1862, he went even further, denying the privilege of the writ in the case of all persons, wherever found, who sought to discourage enlistments or were guilty of any other "disloyal practice," and setting up military courts for their trial. Thousands of men in all parts of the North were arrested upon suspicion and imprisoned without a hearing, or sentenced by military tribunals without jury. To quiet criticism, Congress passed a law on March 3, 1863, providing that suspects should not be detained longer than twenty days unless indicted by a grand jury. The President ignored this statute and arrests continued to be made by executive or military order. On the other hand, Lincoln sought to mitigate the rigors of this policy by paroling many political prisoners.

That the government acted with excess zeal, and often unlawfully, was the opinion of the Supreme Court in the case of *ex parte* Milligan. The defendant, an Indiana Democrat, had been sentenced to death by a military tribunal in 1864, on a charge of conspiracy to liberate southern soldiers held as prisoners. In 1866 the Supreme Court annulled the judgment, holding that the President could not establish military courts, and that a civilian could not be tried by such a tribunal in places where the regular civil courts were open and "in the proper and unobstructed exercise of their jurisdiction."

Meanwhile, in the South, President Davis had declared martial law (in February, 1862) and suspended the writ of *habeas corpus* in disaffected districts and at important military points. Though, unlike Lincoln, he acted with express sanction of his Congress, strong opposition developed against this interference in the accustomed sphere of state action. The North Carolina courts contested its legality, freely issuing the writ to persons imprisoned by Confederate authority. A Georgia statute in 1864 declared that refusal to grant *habeas corpus* would subject the judge to a penalty of $2500. In this campaign of protest Vice-President Stephens took an active part; and "military despotism" was roundly denounced by public meetings and legislatures. The Confederate Congress gradually restricted the President's authority in this respect, finally withdrawing it entirely on August 1, 1864.

THE ABOLITION OF SLAVERY

The freeing of the Negro was by no means a necessary consequence of the collision of arms. The avowed object of the victorious party in the election of 1860 was only to confine slavery to the states where it already existed. Even after the war began, Congress announced in July, 1861, that the government was actuated by no "purpose of overthrowing or interfering with the rights or established institutions" of the South, but sought merely "to preserve the Union with all the dignity, equality, and rights of the several States unimpaired; and that as soon as these objects are accomplished the war ought to cease." In the same session, acts were passed to organize the territories of Colorado, Dakota and Nevada with no restriction against slavery. When the popular outcry for emancipation rose high in 1862, Lincoln took further occasion to define his position in a letter of August 22, elicited by a sharply critical editorial in Greeley's *Tribune*. "My paramount object in this struggle," he declared, "is to save the Union, and is not either to save or destroy slavery. If I could save the Union without freeing any slave, I would do it; and if I could save it by freeing all the slaves, I would do it; and if I could save it by freeing some and leaving others alone, I would also do that."

Lincoln's personal convictions as to the evil of human bondage had not altered since his debate with Douglas in 1858; but as President of the whole American nation, he shrank from righting one wrong at the cost of another, and no principle of the federal system went deeper than the right of each state to control its own domestic institutions. Furthermore, he realized the folly of committing the northern people to a policy which many of them were not yet prepared to accept. Not only had he divided the vote of the North with Douglas, but those who supported him had voted against the extension, not the existence, of slavery. Many who sprang to the defense of the Union would have refrained had they believed they were fighting a "nigger war." Nor did he ever lose sight of the fact that the four border slave states had sided with the North. Abolition would not only be an act of injustice to the loyal whites in those states, but might drive them into the arms of the enemy. Had Lincoln been permitted, undisturbed by men or events, to work out his own solution, he would have instituted everywhere a program of gradual emancipation, with compensation to the masters and removal of the freedmen to Liberia or Latin America.

Under the prod of circumstances, however, steps were taken, almost from the beginning of the war, looking to the further restriction or eventual doom of slavery. On April 16, 1862, Congress provided for the compensated liberation of the three thousand slaves in the District of Columbia. Two months later (June 19) the Republicans enacted into law the principle which had brought their party into being eight years before—the exclusion of slavery from the federal territories. Lincoln desired, further, to bring about emancipation in the border states, for he realized that their permanent loyalty could not otherwise be assured. At his suggestion, Congress in April, 1862, offered to aid these states financially in a program of gradual abolition, and Lincoln held earnest conferences with the border-state Congressmen to the same end. The latter, however, remained unmoved, asserting their constitutional right to hold slaves, and declaring that any scheme of compensation, even with federal help, would inflict ruinous taxation on their people.

The problem of dealing with the question in the seceded

states proved far more difficult. To antislavery extremists the war presented a providential opportunity to deal a death-blow to slavery in the South, for, in their minds, the disloyal conduct of the planting class absolved the government from all obligations to respect southern property rights. They entirely misunderstood Lincoln's legal scruples and political caution, fiercely assailing him as a traitor to the holy cause of freedom. Such Republicans called themselves Radicals, and their quarrel with the President over emancipation led them to criticize him on other scores as well. In the cabinet they had an outspoken champion in Chase; in the House, in Thaddeus Stevens. Outside of Washington their great spokesmen were Greeley of the *Tribune* and John C. Frémont, the latter an ambitious politician as well as a mediocre soldier.

The matter was not merely one for abstract disputation. The invasion of the South brought the troops into direct contact with the slaves, raising questions which called for immediate decision. In the early weeks of the war an overwhelming number of Negroes flocked into the camp of General Benjamin F. Butler in Virginia. Should these be returned to their masters under the fugitive slave act? Butler propounded the ingenious doctrine that the fugitives were contraband of war, being a form of property used by the foe for war purposes, and hence subject to confiscation. His position was promptly approved by the War Department, and, when Congress passed a confiscation act on August 6, 1861, it provided for the seizure of slaves as well as other property when used to promote the southern insurrection.

No sooner was this question decided then General Frémont, then in command in Missouri, raised the issue in a different form. By a proclamation of August 30, 1861, he decreed the forfeiture of all property, including slaves, belonging to disloyal citizens there. This overstepped the provisions of the confiscation act, for the cause he assigned for liberation was the hostile service of the master, not of the slave. Lincoln, believing the action premature, overruled it. When General David Hunter, commanding the recovered territory around Beaufort, imitated Frémont's example in May, 1862, by declaring free the slaves of South Carolina, Georgia and Florida, Lincoln again intervened and revoked the order. On July 17, however, Congress passed a second confiscation act, which applied, in modified form, the principle for which Frémont and Hunter had stood. After inflicting drastic penalties on all persons convicted of treason, the law declared that, when the slaves of rebel masters fell into federal hands, they should "be forever free of their servitude." Two months later Lincoln said, "I cannot learn that that law has caused a single slave to come over to us."

In revoking General Hunter's order, Lincoln had declared, "Whether it be competent for me, as Commander-in-Chief of the Army and Navy, to declare the slaves of any State or States, free, and whether at any time, or in any case, it shall have become a necessity indispensable to the maintenance of the Government . . . , are questions which, under my responsibility, I reserve to myself." This pivotal question was never absent from his mind. He was constantly weighing the political considerations involved, at home and abroad, and particularly whether an act of liberation would prove effective in weakening the enemy. At a cabinet meeting on July 22, 1862, he at last announced his readiness to take the fateful step. But Seward counseled delay until a success should be won on the battlefield, lest, in view of recent military reverses, a proclamation of emancipation be regarded as a "last shriek on the retreat." The wisdom of this advice was at once recognized. The Confederate repulse at Antietam provided a fit occasion, and on September 22 the President issued the preliminary

proclamation. Justifying his action as a "necessary war measure," he declared all slaves free in those parts of the Confederacy that should be still in rebellion on January 1, 1863.
When New Year's Day came, he issued the final proclamation, designating the states and districts affected, and inviting
ex-slaves to join the armed forces of the nation. The procla-

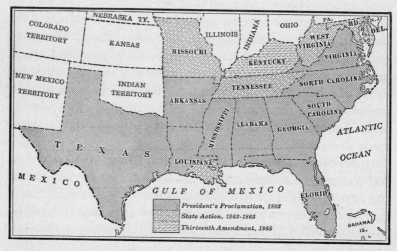

THE PROGRESS OF EMANCIPATION, 1863–1865

mation, of course, did not apply to the four border states, nor
did it involve the status of slavery in Tennessee or those parts
of Virginia and Louisiana already occupied. Elsewhere Negroes became free by the executive edict, though actual liberation had to await the victorious advance of the Union forces.
The propriety of emancipation as an exercise of war powers
can be gauged only by the results which flowed from it.
While it is doubtful whether more slaves than before sought
refuge within federal lines, over 100,000 southern Negroes enlisted as soldiers, performing services as fighters and in guarding and repairing railways, which, in Lincoln's judgment,

hastened the final victory. Of even greater import was the effect of the proclamation on public opinion abroad, for, as we shall see, it ended the danger of foreign intervention.

Lincoln's action led by swift stages to the eradication of slavery everywhere. Several of the states unaffected by the proclamation fell into line. The Missouri convention, after providing in June, 1863, for a gradual process, changed its plan to immediate freedom in January, 1865. During 1864 abolition was decreed by Maryland and by conventions of unionists in Virginia, Arkansas and Louisiana, with Tennessee following shortly after. Meanwhile, a strong sentiment had been developing to make abolition both universal and irrevocable by a provision in the federal Constitution. In April, 1864, the Senate approved the Thirteenth Amendment, forbidding slavery or involuntary servitude save as a punishment for crime. Though the House was unable at first to marshal the necessary two-thirds majority for its passage, the nation spoke unmistakably in the presidential election of 1864, causing the House in January, 1865, to reverse its earlier vote. The amendment became a part of the organic law on December 18, 1865. Its direct practical effect was to free the slaves in Kentucky and Delaware, and to substitute immediate for gradual emancipation in West Virginia.

POLITICAL DIVISIONS IN THE NORTH

Largely because of strife over the emancipation question, the Republican party throughout the war was plagued by internal dissension. The Radical wing also criticized Lincoln's management of the war, while the Conservatives stoutly defended the President and agreed with him in placing national preservation before Negro freedom. In elections the two factions maintained a united front and, since the Republicans early in the war adopted the practice of nominating candidates under the name of the Union party, they also succeeded in commanding the support of one section of the Democrats. These War Democrats, as they were called, retained their belief in the historic economic doctrines of their party, but believed that, in the existing crisis, the question of the Union overshadowed all other issues.

Most Democrats, however, continued in the regular party organization, doggedly contesting the political control of the administration forces. The great majority of them supported the war, but charged Lincoln with incompetence and condemned his assumption of autocratic power. Their slogan became, "The Constitution as it is and the Union as it was," and in Horatio Seymour of New York they possessed their ablest leader. A militant minority, headed by C. L. Vallandigham, an Ohio Congressman, opposed the war and demanded immediate peace without terms. The stronghold of the Peace Democrats was the old Northwest, particularly those parts whose inhabitants, like Vallandigham himself, were descended from settlers of southern origin. In order to carry on their propaganda more effectively, many of their number joined a secret, oath-bound order variously known as the Knights of the Golden Circle, the American Knights and the Sons of Liberty. Execrated by the public at large, this pacifist element quickly won the name of Copperheads, an epithet soon applied indiscriminately to all Democrats.

The first test of strength between the contending forces came in the fall elections of 1862. The voters, suffering a reaction from the buoyant patriotism of 1861, were dismayed by the almost unbroken succession of military defeats as well as by the disclosures of graft in government contracts. The increasing number of arbitrary arrests gave additional cause for dissatisfaction, while many were disconcerted by Democratic jibes that the Emancipation Proclamation had changed the struggle to an "abolition war." [1]   As a result, the Republicans lost ground in many parts of the country. Besides electing Seymour governor of New York, the Democrats carried New Jersey, Pennsylvania and the northwestern states from Ohio to Wisconsin. The administration, however, managed to save its majority in Congress.

The next year proved to be an even more critical one. In Indiana the Peace Democrats in the legislature blocked every measure for the support of the war, and the lower house of the Illinois legislature declared for an immediate armistice and a peace convention. The President told Sumner he feared "the fire in the rear" more than he did the enemy's military prowess. In the fall of 1863 the efforts of the defeatists reached a dramatic climax. The Democrats in Ohio chose as their candidate for governor Vallandigham, who at the time was under sentence of exile because of his denunciations of "King Lincoln." Conducting his campaign from a safe refuge in Canada, it seemed for a while that he might be successful.[2] Though he received 187,000 votes, he lost the election by a majority of 101,000. The federal victories at Vicksburg and Gettysburg proved a decisive argument against him.

Vallandigham's defeat marked the turning of the tide, though Lincoln still had much opposition to encounter both within and without his party. A mass convention of Radical Republicans at Cleveland on May 31, 1864, even tried to prevent his renomination by putting forward Frémont as their

---

[1] A favorite bit of Democratic verse ran as follows:
> Honest old Abe, when the war first began,
> Denied abolition was part of his plan;
> Honest old Abe has since made a decree,
> The war must go on till the slaves are all free.
> As both can't be honest, will some one tell how,
> If honest Abe then, he is honest Abe now?

[2] Edward Everett Hale's famous story, "The Man without a Country," was written for the purpose of affecting public sentiment at the time of this campaign.

candidate on a platform demanding sterner prosecution of
the war and a constitutional amendment against slavery. But
the maneuver failed. When the Union party convened a
week later at Baltimore, they named the President on the
first ballot, thus deciding, in Lincoln's homely phrase, that
it was "best not to swap horses while crossing the river."
With him was associated a War Democrat, Andrew Johnson,
then military governor of Tennessee. The platform praised
Lincoln's conduct of the war and promised universal freedom
by constitutional amendment. The ticket, however, evoked
little popular enthusiasm. Due to the military misfortunes
of July and August, the prospects for success were for awhile
decidedly gloomy. Advised by Greeley and others of his
almost certain defeat, Lincoln recorded his own impressions
on August 23. "This morning as for some days past," he
wrote in a private memorandum, "it seems exceedingly probable that this Administration will not be reëlected."

The party's chances were somewhat improved by the blundering of the Democrats. The convention, held at Chicago
on August 29, declared the war a failure; the platform, written under Vallandigham's influence, called for an immediate
armistice and a peace convention to restore the federal Union.
But the candidate, General McClellan, victor of Antietam,
virtually repudiated this pronouncement in his letter of acceptance. The effect of such divided counsels upon the country was indicated by the *New York Tribune's* version of the
platform: "Resolved that the war is a very good war, and
most unrighteous war, and while it should be stopped at once,
it must be carried on with vigor." Yet the success of the
Union ticket was not assured until Sherman, Sheridan and
Farragut won their great victories in September. The news
of their successes, as Seward said, "knocked the bottom out
of the Chicago nominations." Frémont withdrew from the
contest, and Lincoln was chosen by an electoral majority of

212 to 21. His popular vote was only fifty-five per cent of the total.

EUROPE AND THE AMERICAN WAR

Most of the nations of the Old World sympathized with the South, and it was the purpose of the Confederacy to convert this sympathy into a recognition of independence, coupled, if possible, with armed intervention. The government at Washington, on the other hand, strove to defeat this effort and to keep the South from procuring supplies of any kind, especially war vessels, abroad. The efforts of both sides centered upon Great Britain since it was known that Napoleon III of France would not act alone.

British opinion on the American conflict was far from unanimous. The ruling class was friendly to the Confederacy, for the nobility and landed gentry looked upon the southern planters as fellow aristocrats, and rejoiced that the great American experiment in popular government seemed on the verge of collapse. Citing Congress's own declaration at the opening of the war, they denied that the North was fighting to abolish slavery, and held with the *London Times* that "The contest is really for empire on the side of the North and for independence on that of the South." On the other hand, the manufacturing and commercial classes were divided. They heartily disliked the northern protective tariff system and greatly feared a cotton famine, but a prewar surplus of cotton tided them over for more than a year, and the shipping interests reaped golden profits from their inroads on the northern merchant marine.

From the outset the United States had influential friends in Parliament, who, though in the minority, were strong enough to prevent the government from taking extreme measures. Reform leaders like John Bright, Richard Cobden and William E. Forster identified the contest with their own struggle for greater democracy, and declared insistently that the cause of the South was the cause of slavery and the "Slave Power." In this position they were joined by the wage-earners despite the fact that the latter became the chief sufferers from the cotton stringency. It is possible, too, that pro-northern sentiment was strengthened by English crop failures in 1860–1862, which caused northern grain for a time to be in greater demand than southern cotton.[1] Tennyson and Darwin were warm supporters of the Union, offsetting Dickens and Carlyle, who sided with the Confederacy.

Relations between the two countries were sorely strained in the early years of the war. On May 13, 1861, the British government issued a proclamation of neutrality, an action quickly followed by other countries. Such a proclamation did not amount to recognition of southern independence, but it granted Confederate ships of war and commerce the same privileges in British ports all over the world as those accorded northern vessels. It also contravened Lincoln's contention that the struggle was in the nature of a rebellion rather than a war between nations—a position not easy to reconcile with his own act in establishing the blockade. The British proclamation bore the appearance of action taken precipitately, since it was issued on the very day the American Minister, Charles Francis Adams, arrived in England.

Six months later occurred the *Trent* affair, which brought the two nations dangerously near war. Captain Charles Wilkes commanding an American warship stopped the British steamer *Trent* on the high seas on November 8, and forcibly removed the Confederate commissioners, James M. Mason and John Slidell, who had taken passage from Havana for Southampton, both neutral ports. The news, greeted with extravagant joy in the North, set England ablaze with

---

[1] In a speech in Parliament in 1863 Forster declared that, if Britain had an economic motive for intervention because of the cotton shortage, "it was allowable to ask, 'What would be the cost of the war in corn [grain]?'"

resentment. Peremptorily demanding liberation of the prisoners, the British government hurried eight thousand troops to Canada and engaged in naval preparations. Since the seizure had been unauthorized and, indeed, ran counter to all previous American policy as to freedom of the seas, Lincoln allowed sufficient time to pass for public sentiment to cool and then, on December 26, ordered the men surrendered with a suitable explanation.

No sooner was this incident closed than a new difficulty arose from Great Britain's lax interpretation of her neutral duties toward the clandestine construction of Confederate cruisers. In March, 1862, the authorities allowed the newly built *Florida* to slip out of Liverpool, and in July the *Alabama* departed in a similar manner. In both instances Adams protested vigorously, presenting evidence in advance to prove Confederate ownership of the raiders. That the officials were swayed by friendship for the South cannot be gainsaid. Indeed, in September, Lord Palmerston, the Prime Minister, deciding that the time had arrived to recognize Confederate independence, arranged for a cabinet meeting with a view to proposing joint action to France and other powers. But before the meeting was held, the situation changed. For one thing, Adams let it be known that the United States would sever diplomatic relations. A more important influence was the Union victory at Antietam on September 17, followed by the emancipation proclamation. With her own strong antislavery traditions, Great Britain could not adopt a policy which would serve to perpetuate human bondage in America. From this time to the close of the war, the government stringently enforced its neutrality obligations. In 1863 the authorities seized three vessels destined for the Confederacy, two of them ironclad rams of great destructive power. Meantime, the *Florida* and the *Alabama,* engaged in their mission of harassing northern commerce, inflicted damage to the extent of more than fifteen million dollars before they were captured.

Napoleon III was even more friendly to the South than were the British leaders. He encouraged Confederate emissaries to build commerce destroyers in French shipyards, though only one, the *Stonewall,* was actually completed and delivered. Though the cotton shortage caused unemployment in certain sections of his country, Napoleon's chief motive was to cripple the military strength of the United States, so as to create conditions favorable to the realization of the long-cherished dream of reëstablishing a French empire in the New World. About six months after the war began, he induced Great Britain and Spain to join him in an armed expedition against Mexico to collect the unpaid claims of their subjects. In April, 1862, after the allied forces had occupied a number of customhouses, Great Britain and Spain came to terms with Mexico and withdrew. The French, left to their own devices, proceeded to overthrow the existing Mexican government and place Maximilian, an Austrian archduke, on a throne supported by French bayonets. All this, of course, was in direct violation of the Monroe Doctrine, but America, engaged in a struggle for national existence, could do nothing but protest and bide her time. With the return of peace she became mistress of the situation. Napoleon was warned once more, and the French troops finally withdrew in the spring of 1867. Without foreign support Maximilian's bubble monarchy collapsed.

Like France, Spain sought to profit by America's preoccupation with internal embroilments. In 1861 she annexed the Dominican Republic, a part of the island of Santo Domingo. Three years later, having declared war on Peru, she seized the Chincha Islands, valuable for guano. The United States protested sharply, announcing again the principles of the Monroe Doctrine. Early in 1865 Spain quietly relinquished both claims. On the other hand, Russia, Prussia and the Scandinavian countries were favorable to the North, Russia conspicuously so. Czar Alexander II, who had emancipated the serfs in 1861, was strongly influenced by antislavery sympathies, and even more so by the fact that the European powers friendly to the South were unfriendly to his own country. At a critical time in the war (September, 1863), one Russian fleet visited New York and another San Francisco, where their presence gave much moral support to the cause of the Union both at home and abroad.

THE SIGNIFICANCE OF THE CIVIL WAR

The decision that the United States should remain one nation marks an epoch in the history of the American people. The great constitutional issue upon which the war was avowedly fought was resolved, once for all, in favor of the supremacy of the Union. Though this conclusion was reached under purely American conditions, it coincided with a world-wide movement for the consolidation of nationality. In 1861 the Austrians were driven out of Italy and the several states of the peninsula were united under a king of their own choosing. In 1867 the dual monarchy of Austria-Hungary was founded with rights of self-government for both peoples. Three years later the third French Republic came into being, and the next year brought the achievement of German unification. America was the first to recognize the new French government; and President Grant told Congress that he saw in the united German Empire "an attempt to reproduce some of the best features of our own Constitution." Meanwhile, to the north of the United States, the provinces from Ontario east (Newfoundland excepted) combined in 1867 to form the Dominion of Canada, with full local autonomy and provision for enlarging the Dominion by the admission of the western territories. Northern triumph in the Civil War accorded with a deep-flowing historical trend.

The war resulted also in the destruction of slavery and of the power of cotton capitalism—the real, though unconfessed, cause of the struggle. Yet posterity may properly ask whether the gains repaid the terrific expenditure of blood and treasure. Slavery could hardly have lasted very much longer in any case: it was a costly system for the master, and it flew in the face of the conscience of the nineteenth century. The United States was the last of the great western nations to do away with human bondage; even Russia preceded her by a few years.

The success of the North was accompanied, moreover, by problems such as the nation had never before faced. The seceded states had to be restored to their proper position in the Union, and the love of a common nationality once more brought into being. An unprecedented debt awaited payment, and some means had to be found to cure the ills arising from greenback inflation. The presence of several million ex-soldiers among the voters portended a political influence that would not only keep alive war-time bitterness, but would burden the country for more than a generation with a staggering debt for pensions.

Even the abolition of slavery solved one problem only to create another, that of the Negro, which was to vex the nation for many years. Finally, while the undoing of the "Slave Power" removed from the political stage an aggressive force seeking purely sectional objects, its going hastened the emergence of a new and more powerful economic class, domiciled in the North and intent on molding the entire nation to its will. The collapse of plantation capitalism made way for the rise of industrial capitalism.

Yet no forebodings ruffled people's minds when the war ended at Appomattox. All was rejoicing in the North. Even in Dixie the sense of disappointment and blighted hopes was mingled with a feeling of relief. The disbanding of the troops and their dispersion into peace-time employments occurred without shock or incident. Nearly a million northern soldiers were mustered out in 1865. Most of them took their final payment with them as a "nest egg" and, with free farms awaiting in the West and abundant jobs in the new manufacturing industries, they were quietly absorbed into the ranks of civil life. The Confederates wandered home, on foot and horseback, penniless. Bereft of their slaves, their plantations laid waste or unworked, peace meant to them the building of a new South.

SELECT BIBLIOGRAPHY

Life behind the Lines. Fite, *Social and Industrial Conditions during the Civil War,* is the best guide for the free states; Wesley, *The Collapse of the Confederacy,* for the South. Stephenson, *The Day of the Confederacy,* also gives a good picture of southern life and politics. A detailed discussion of the discovery of anæsthetics is appended to Packard, *The History of Medicine in the United States . . . to the Year 1800.* The most complete account of the principal relief organization is Stillé, *History of the United States Sanitary Commission;* and the services of women are more particularly treated in Brockett and Vaughan, *Woman's Work in the Civil War,* and Underwood, *The Women of the Confederacy.* Wiley, *Southern Negroes, 1861–1865,* is concerned with the degree of loyalty shown by slaves to their masters.

The Restraint of Civil Liberty. Randall, *Constitutional Problems under Lincoln,* supersedes all earlier treatments of the subject. Fahrney, in *Horace Greeley and the Tribune in the Civil War,* portrays the great journalist at his worst. On the morale of the Confederacy, see Owsley, *State Rights in the Confederacy,* and Tatum, *Disloyalty in the Confederacy.*

Political Divisions during the War. The Peace Democrats receive careful study in Benton, *The Movement for Peace without Victory during the Civil War,* which should be supplemented by Kirkland, *The Peacemakers of 1864.* Other aspects of the political scene are treated at length in the standard histories by Channing, McMaster, Rhodes and Schouler.

Europe and the Civil War. The most useful accounts are Adams, *Great Britain and the American Civil War;* Jordan and Pratt, *Europe and the American Civil War;* West, *Contemporary French Opinion on the American Civil War;* and Thomas, *Russo-American Relations, 1815–1867.* Additional material may be gleaned from Perkins, *The Monroe Doctrine, 1826–1867;* Bancroft, *W. H. Seward;* Adams, *Charles Francis Adams;* and Harris, *The Trent Affair.* For the Confederate side, consult Owsley, *King Cotton Diplomacy;* Callahan, *The Diplomatic History of the Southern Confederacy;* Bonham, *The British Consuls in the Confederacy;* and Thompson, *Confederate Purchasing Operations Abroad.* Martin, *Maximilian in Mexico,* is the standard treatment of that subject; Harding, *The Phantom Crown,* has the same theme.

In *Flight into Oblivion,* Hanna tells of the dispersion of the Confederate cabinet after the fall of Richmond.

On Seymour, see Mitchell, *Horatio Seymour of New York.*

Significance of the Civil War. Agar, *Land of the Free,* and Carman, *Social and Economic History of the United States,* are among the works whose authors see in the Civil War the triumph of industrialism over the simple agrarian ideals of Jefferson.

APPENDIX

LIST OF BOOKS

For convenience of reference all of the books and articles mentioned in the Select Bibliographies at the close of each chapter are here listed in one alphabet according to the names of the authors.

Abbott, Wilbur Cortez, *Expansion of Europe; a History of the Foundations of the Modern World.* 2 v. New York, 1918.

Abel, Annie Heloise, "The History of Events Resulting in Indian Consolidation West of the Mississippi" (American Historical Association *Report* for 1906, I, 233–450).

Abernethy, Thomas Perkins, *From Frontier to Plantation in Tennessee: A Study in Frontier Democracy.* Chapel Hill, N. C., 1932.

——, *Western Lands and the American Revolution.* New York, 1937.

Adams, Alice D., *The Neglected Period of Anti-Slavery in America, 1808–1831.* Boston, 1908.

Adams, Charles Francis, Jr., *Charles Francis Adams (American Statesmen).*

Adams, Ephraim D., *British Interests and Activities in Texas, 1838–1846.* Baltimore, 1910.

——, *Great Britain and the American Civil War.* 2 v. New York, 1925.

Adams, Henry, *History of the United States of America during the Administrations of Jefferson and Madison.* 9 v. New York, 1890–1891.

——, *John Randolph (American Statesmen).*

Adams, James Truslow, *The Adams Family.* Boston, 1930.

——, *America's Tragedy.* New York, 1934.

——, *The Founding of New England.* Boston [c. 1921].

——, *The Living Jefferson.* New York, 1936.

Original Narratives of Early American History. See Jameson, John Franklin, editor.

Osgood, Herbert Levi, *The American Colonies in the Eighteenth Century.* 4 v. New York, 1924–1925.

——, *The American Colonies in the Seventeenth Century.* 3 v. New York, 1904–1907.

Oskison, John M., *Tecumseh and His Times: The Story of a Great Indian.* New York, 1938.

Ostrogorski, M., *Democracy and the Organization of Political Parties.* 2 v. New York, 1902.

Owsley, Frank L., *King Cotton Diplomacy.* Chicago, 1931.

——, *State Rights in the Confederacy.* Chicago, 1925.

Packard, F. R., *The History of Medicine in the United States . . . to the Year 1800.* Philadelphia, 1901.

Paine, Ralph Delahaye, *The Fight for a Free Sea* (*Chronicles of America,* XVII).

Palfrey, John Gorham, *A Compendious History of New England.* 4 v. Boston, 1884.

Palmer, John M., *General von Steuben.* New Haven, 1937.

Parkman, Francis, *Works.* Centenary edition. 13 v. Boston, 1922.

Parrington, Vernon L., *Main Currents in American Thought.* 3 v. New York, 1927–1930. Reprint in one volume, 1939.

Pattee, Fred Lewis, *The First Century of American Literature.* New York, 1935.

Paullin, Charles O., *Atlas of the Historical Geography of the United States* (Carnegie Institution *Publications,* No. 401, J. K. Wright, ed.). Washington, 1932.

——, *The Navy of the American Revolution.* Cleveland, 1906.

Paxson, Frederic L., *The Civil War* (*The Home University Library*). New York, 1911.

——, *History of the American Frontier, 1763–1893.* Boston, 1924. Reprint, 1925.

——, *The Independence of the South American Republics.* Philadelphia, 1903.

——, *Provincial Society* (*History of American Life*, III).

——, *Revolutionary New England, 1691–1776.* Boston, 1923.

Adams, Randolph Greenleaf, *History of the Foreign Policy of the United States.* New York, 1924.

Adams, W. F., *Ireland and Irish Emigration to the New World* (*Yale Historical Publications. Miscellany*, XXIII). New Haven, 1932.

Agar, Herbert, *Land of the Free.* Boston, 1935.

Albion, Robert Greenhalgh, *Square-Riggers on Schedule: The New York Sailing Packets to England, France, and the Cotton Ports.* Princeton, 1938.

Alexander, Holmes, *Aaron Burr: The Proud Pretender.* New York, 1937.

——, *The American Talleyrand: The Career and Contemporaries of Martin Van Buren.* New York, 1935.

Allen, Gardner W., *A Naval History of the American Revolution.* 2 v. New York, 1913.

Alvord, Clarence Walworth, *The Illinois Country, 1673–1818* (*Centenary History of Illinois*, I). Springfield, 1920.

——, *The Mississippi Valley in British Politics.* 2 v. Cleveland, 1917.

——, and Bidgood, Lee, *First Exploration of the Trans-Alleghany Region by the Virginians, 1659–1674.* Cleveland, 1912.

Ambler, Charles H., *Francis H. Pierpont: Union War Governor of Virginia and Father of West Virginia.* Chapel Hill, N. C., 1937.

——, *George Washington and the West.* Chapel Hill, N. C., 1936.

——, *A History of Transportation in the Ohio Valley, with Special Reference to Its Waterways, Trade, and Commerce from the Earliest Period to the Present Time.* Glendale, Calif., 1932.

American Church History Series. 13 v. New York, 1893–1897.

American Crisis Biographies. See Oberholtzer, E. P., editor.

American History Told by Contemporaries. See Hart, A. B., editor.

American Nation, The. See Hart, A. B., editor.

American Statesmen. See Morse, J. T., Jr., editor.

Anderson, Frank Malloy, "Contemporary Opinion of the Virginia and Kentucky Resolutions," *American Historical Review,* V, 45–63, 225–252.

Anderson, Troyer S., *The Command of the Howe Brothers during the Revolution.* New York, 1936.

Andrews, Charles McLean, *Colonial Background of the American Revolution.* New Haven, 1924.

——, "Colonial Commerce," *American Historical Review,* XX, 43–63.

——, *Colonial Folkways (Chronicles of America,* IX).

——, *Colonial Period of American History.* New Haven, 1934–.

——, *Colonial Self-Government, 1652–1689 (American Nation,* V).

——, *Fathers of New England (Chronicles of America,* VI).

——, ed., *Narratives of the Insurrections, 1675–1690 (Original Narratives,* XVI).

——, *Our Earliest Colonial Settlements; Their Diversities of Origin and Later Characteristics.* New York, 1933.

Andrews, Matthew P., *The Founding of Maryland.* Baltimore, 1933.

——, *History of Maryland, Province and State.* New York, 1929.

——, *Virginia: The Old Dominion.* New York, 1937.

Anthony, Katharine, *Margaret Fuller.* New York, 1920.

Ashe, Samuel A'Court, *History of North Carolina.* 2 v. Greensboro, 1908–1925.

Auchampaugh, Philip G., *James Buchanan and His Cabinet on the Eve of Secession.* Lancaster, Pa., 1926.

Avery, Elroy, *History of the United States.* 7 v. Cleveland, 1904–1910.

Babcock, Kendric Charles, *Rise of American Nationality, 1811–1819 (American Nation,* XIII).

Bacon, Leonard W., *A History of American Christianity (American Church History Series,* XIII). New York, 1897.

Baker, John Norman Leonard, *A History of Geographical Discovery and Exploration.* Boston, 1932.

Baldwin, Leland D., *Whiskey Rebels; the Story of a Frontier Uprising.* Pittsburgh, 1939.

Bancroft, Frederic, *The Life of William H. Seward.* 2 v. New York, 1900.

——, *Slave-Trading in the Old South.* Baltimore, 1931.

Bancroft, George, *History of the United States.* Author's last revision. 6 v. New York, 1883–1885.

Baringer, William, *Lincoln's Rise to Power.* Boston, 1937.

Barker, Eugene C., *The Life of Stephen F. Austin, the Founder of Texas, 1793–1836.* Dallas, 1925.

Barnes, Gilbert H., *The Antislavery Impulse, 1830–1844.* New York, 1933.

Barnes, Harry Elmer, *A History of the Penal Reformatory and Correctional Institutions of the State of New Jersey.* Trenton, 1918.

Barnes, Viola F., *The Dominion of New England.* New Haven, 1923.

Barrett, Jay A., *Evolution of the Ordinance of 1787* . . . (University of Nebraska, Department of History and Economics). New York, 1891.

Bartlett, Ruhl J., *John C. Frémont and the Republican Party* (Ohio State University *Contributions in History and Political Science,* No. 13). Columbus, 1930.

Barton, W. E., *The Life of Abraham Lincoln.* 2 v. Indianapolis, 1925.

Bass, Althea, *Cherokee Messenger.* Norman, Okla., 1936.

Bassett, John Spencer, *The Federalist System, 1789–1801 (American Nation,* XI).

——, *Life of Andrew Jackson.* 2 v. New edition. New York, 1916.

Baxter, J. P., 3d., *The Introduction of the Ironclad Warship.* Cambridge, Mass., 1933.

Beard, Charles Austin, *An Economic Interpretation of the Constitution.* Revised edition. New York, 1935.

——, *Economic Origins of Jeffersonian Democracy*. New York, 1915.

Beard, Charles A. and Mary R., *The Rise of American Civilization*. New edition, revised and enlarged. 2 v. in one. New York, 1933.

Beard, Mary R., *America through Women's Eyes*. New York, 1933.

——, *A Short History of the American Labor Movement*. New York, 1920.

Beazley, Charles Raymond, *Dawn of Modern Geography, a History of Exploration and Geographical Science*. 3 v. Revised edition. London, 1905–1906.

——, *Prince Henry the Navigator*. Abridged as *Discoveries of Prince Henry the Navigator and Their Results*. London, 1877.

Becker, Carl Lotus, *The Declaration of Independence; a Study in the History of Political Ideas*. New York [c. 1922].

——, *The Eve of the Revolution* (*Chronicles of America*, XI).

Beer, George Louis, *British Colonial Policy, 1754–1765*. New York, 1907.

——, *Commercial Policy of England towards the Colonies* (Columbia University *Studies in History, Economics, and Public Law*, III, No. 2). New York, 1893.

——, *The Old Colonial System, 1660–1754*. New York, 1912.

——, *The Origins of the British Colonial System, 1578–1660*. New York, 1908.

Bell, Herbert C., "The West India Trade before the American Revolution," *American Historical Review*, XXII, 272–287.

Bell, Margaret, *Women of the Wilderness*. New York, 1938.

Bemis, Samuel Flagg, ed., *The American Secretaries of State and Their Diplomacy*. 10 v. New York, 1927–1929.

——, *The Diplomacy of the American Revolution*. New York, 1935.

——, *A Diplomatic History of the United States*. New York, 1936.

——, *Jay's Treaty, a Study in Commerce and Diplomacy*. New York, 1923.

——, *Pinckney's Treaty* (*Shaw Lectures on Diplomatic History*, XII). Baltimore, 1926.

Benns, F. L., *The American Struggle for the British West India Carrying Trade, 1815–1830* (*Indiana University Studies*). Bloomington, 1923.

Benson, Mary S., *Women in Eighteenth-Century America: A Study of Opinion and Social Usage*. (Columbia University Studies, No. 405.) New York, 1935.

Benton, E. J., *The Movement for Peace without Victory during the Civil War* (Western Reserve Historical Society, *Collections*, No. 99). Cleveland, 1918.

Beveridge, Albert Jeremiah, *Abraham Lincoln*. 2 v. Boston, 1928.

——, *Life of John Marshall*. 4 v. Boston, 1916–[c. 1919].

Bidwell, P. W., and Falconer, J. I., *History of Agriculture in the Northern United States, 1620–1860* (Carnegie Institution Contributions to American Economic History). Washington, 1925.

Biggar, H. P., *The Precursors of Jacques Cartier, 1497–1534*. Ottawa, 1911.

Billington, Ray A., *The Protestant Crusade, 1800–1860: A Study of the Origins of American Nativism*. New York, 1938.

Birney, Catherine H., *The Grimké Sisters*. New York, 1885.

Blauvelt, Mary Taylor, *The Development of Cabinet Government in England*. New York, 1902.

Blegen, T. C., *Norwegian Migration to America, 1825–1860*. Northfield, Minn., 1931.

Bleyer, W. G., *Main Currents in the History of American Journalism*. Boston, 1927.

Bodley, Temple, *George Rogers Clarke*. Boston, 1926.

——, *Our First Great West, in Revolutionary War, Diplomacy and Politics*. Louisville, Ky., 1938.

Bogart, Ernest Ludlow, *An Economic History of the American People*. New York, 1930.

Bolton, Herbert E., "The Mission as a Frontier Institution in the Spanish American Colonies," in *Wider Horizons of American History*. New York, 1939.

——, *Spanish Borderlands* (*Chronicles of America*, XXIII).

——, ed., *Spanish Exploration in the Southwest, 1542–1706* (*Original Narratives*, XVII).

Bond, Beverley W., Jr., *The Civilization of the Old Northwest: A Study of Political, Social, and Economic Development, 1788–1812*. New York, 1934.

Bonham, Millege L., Jr., *The British Consuls in the Confederacy* (Columbia University, *Studies*, XLIII, No. 3). New York, 1911.

Boucher, Chauncey S., *The Nullification Controversy in South Carolina*. Chicago, 1916.

——, "In Re That Aggressive Slavocracy," *American Historical Review*, VIII, 13–79.

Bourne, Edward Gaylord, *The History of the Surplus Revenue of 1837*. New York, 1885.

——, *Spain in America* (*American Nation*, III).

Bowers, Claude G., *Jefferson and Hamilton, the Struggle for Democracy in America*. Boston, 1925.

——, *Jefferson in Power: The Death Struggle of the Federalists*. Boston, 1936.

——, *Party Battles of the Jackson Period*. Boston, 1922.

Boyd, Thomas, *Mad Anthony Wayne*. New York, 1929.

Bradford, Gamaliel, *Portraits of American Women*. Boston, 1919.

Bradlee, F. B. C., *Blockade Running during the Civil War and the Effect of Land and Water Transportation on the Confederacy*. Salem, Mass., 1924.

Branch, E. Douglas, *The Sentimental Years, 1836–1860*. New York, 1934.

Brawley, Benjamin, *A Social History of the American Negro*. New York, 1921.

Brebner, J. B., *The Explorers of North America, 1492–1806*. New York, 1933.

Brigham, Albert Perry, *Geographical Influences in American History*. Boston, 1903.

Britt, Albert, *Great Indian Chiefs: A Study of Indian Leaders in the Two Hundred Year Struggle to Stop the White Advance*. New York, 1938.

Brockett, L. P., and Vaughan, Mary C., *Woman's Work in the Civil War*. Philadelphia, 1867.

Brodhead, John Romeyn, *History of the State of New York*. 2 v. New York, 1853–1871.

Brooks, Van Wyck, *The Flowering of New England*. New York, 1936.

Brown, Elmer Ellsworth, *The Making of Our Middle Schools*. New York, 1907.

Brown, Everett Somerville, *The Constitutional History of the Louisiana Purchase*. Berkeley, Cal., 1920.

Brown, William Garrott, *The Lower South in American History*. New York, 1902.

Bruce, David K. E., *Revolution to Reconstruction*. New York, 1939.

Bruce, Henry Addington, *Daniel Boone and the Wilderness Road*. New York, 1910.

——, *Woman in the Making of America*. Boston, 1912.

Bruce, Philip Alexander, *The Economic History of Virginia in the Seventeenth Century*. 2 v. New York, 1896.

——, *History of Virginia, Colonial Period, 1607–1763*. New York, 1924.

——, *The Institutional History of Virginia in the Seventeenth Century*. 2 v. New York, 1910.

——, *Social Life of Virginia in the Seventeenth Century*. Richmond, Va., 1907.

Bullock, Charles Jesse, *The Finances of the United States from 1775 to 1789, with Especial Reference to the Budget* (University of Wisconsin *Bulletin*, Economics, Political Science, and History Series, I, No. 2). Madison, 1895.

Burgess, John W., *The Middle Period* (*American History Series*, IV). New York, 1897.

Burlingame, Roger, *March of the Iron Men: A Social History of Union through Invention*. New York, 1938.

Burne, Alfred H., *Lee, Grant and Sherman: A Study in Leadership in the 1864–65 Campaign*. New York, 1939.

Burr, George L., ed., *Narratives of the Witchcraft Cases* (*Original Narratives*, XIX).

Burrage, Henry Sweetzer, ed., *Early English and French Voyages* (*Original Narratives*, II).

——, *Maine in the Northeast Boundary Controversy.* Portland, 1919.

Burton, Theodore E., *John Sherman* (*American Statesmen*).

Byrn, Edward W., *The Progress of Invention in the Nineteenth Century.* New York, 1900.

Calder, Isabel MacBeath, *The New Haven Colony.* New Haven, 1934.

Callahan, James M., *American Foreign Policy in Canadian Relations.* New York, 1937.

——, *American Foreign Policy in Mexican Relations.* New York, 1932.

——, *Cuba and International Relations* (Johns Hopkins University, *Studies in Historical and Political Science,* extra volume, XXI). Baltimore, 1899.

——, *The Diplomatic History of the Southern Confederacy* (*Shaw Lectures on Diplomatic History,* II). Baltimore, 1901.

Callcott, Wilfred Hardy, *Santa Anna: The Story of an Enigma Who Once Was Mexico.* Norman, Okla., 1936.

Cambridge History of American Literature. See Trent, W. P., editor.

Cambridge History of the British Empire. See Rose, J. Holland, editor.

Carman, Harry James, *Social and Economic History of the United States.* 2 v. Boston, 1930–1934.

Carpenter, Edmund James, *Roger Williams.* New York, 1909.

Carpenter, J. T., *The South as a Conscious Minority, 1789–1861.* New York, 1930.

Carroll, Joseph C., *Slave Insurrections in the United States, 1800–1865.* Boston, 1938.

Carter, Clarence Edwin, *Great Britain and the Illinois Country, 1763–1774.* Washington, 1910.

Castañeda, Carlos E., translator, *The Mexican Side of the Texas Revolution.* Dallas, 1928.

Catterall, Ralph C. H., *The Second Bank of the United States.* Chicago, 1903.

Chadwick, French Ensor, *Relations of the United States and Spain.* 3 v. New York, 1909–1911.

Chambers, Henry E., "West Florida and its Relation to the Historical Cartography of the United States (Johns Hopkins University *Studies,* XVI, No. 5). Baltimore, 1898.

Chandler, Julian A. C. and others, *The South in the Building of the Nation.* 13 v. Richmond, 1909–1913.

Channing, Edward, *History of the United States.* 6 v. New York, 1905–1925.

——, *The Jeffersonian System (American Nation,* XII).

Channing, William Henry, *The Life of William Ellery Channing, D.D.* Boston, 1899.

Caughey, John Walton, *History of the Pacific Coast.* Los Angeles, 1933.

——, *McGillivray of the Creeks.* Norman, Okla., 1938.

Chapman, Charles Edward, *Colonial Hispanic-America: A History.* New York, 1933.

——, *The Founding of Spanish California; the Northwestward Expansion of New Spain, 1687–1783.* New York, 1916.

——, *A History of California: Spanish Period.* New York, 1921.

——, *Republican Hispanic-America.* New York, 1937.

Charnwood, Lord, *Abraham Lincoln (Makers of the Nineteenth Century,* Basil Williams, editor). London, 1917.

Cheyney, Edward Potts, *European Background of American History (American Nation,* I).

Chinard, Gilbert, *Honest John Adams.* Boston, 1933.

——, *Thomas Jefferson, the Apostle of Americanism.* Boston, 1933.

Chittenden, Hiram M., *The American Fur Trade of the Far West.* 3 v. Revised edition. Elmira, N. Y., 1935.

Chitwood, Oliver Perry, *A History of Colonial America.* New York, 1931.

——, *John Tyler, Champion of the Old South.* New York, 1939.

Chronicles of America. See Johnson, Allen, editor.

Chronicles of Canada. See Wrong, George M., editor.

Clark, A. H., *The Clipper Ship Era, 1843–1869.* New York, 1910.

Clark, Bennet C., *John Quincy Adams, "Old Man Eloquent."* Boston, 1932.

Clark, Dan Elbert, *The West in American History.* New York, 1937.

Clark, Dora Mae, *British Opinion and the American Revolution.* New Haven, 1930.

Clark, George Faber, *History of the Temperance Reform in Massachusetts, 1813–1883.* Boston, 1888.

Clark, George L., *A History of Connecticut.* New York, 1914.

Clark, Thomas D., *The Rampaging Frontier: Manners and Humors of Pioneer Days in the South and Middle West.* Indianapolis, 1939.

Clark, Victor S., *History of Manufactures in the United States* (Carnegie Institution *Contributions to American Economic History*). 3 v. Revised edition. New York, 1929.

Cleland, Robert Glass, *Pathfinders.* Los Angeles, 1929.

Cobb, Sanford Hoadley, *The Rise of Religious Liberty in America.* New York, 1902.

Colby, Charles W., *The Fighting Governor* (*Chronicles of Canada*, VII).

——, *The Founder of New France* (*Chronicles of Canada*, III).

Cole, Arthur C., *The Irrepressible Conflict, 1850–1865* (*A History of American Life*, VII).

——, *The Whig Party in the South.* Washington, 1913.

Cole, Cyrenus, *I Am a Man—The Indian Black Hawk.* Iowa City, 1938.

Coman, Katharine, *Economic Beginnings of the Far West.* 2 v. New York, 1912.

——, *Industrial History.* Revised edition. New York, 1912.

Commager, Henry Steele, *Documents of American History.* 2 v. in one. New York, 1934.

——, *Theodore Parker.* Boston, 1936.

Commons, John R., ed., *History of Labor in the United States.* 2 v. New York, 1921.

Coolidge, L. A., *Ulysses S. Grant.* Boston, 1917.

Corwin, Edward Samuel, *French Policy and the American Alliance*. Princeton, 1916.

——, *John Marshall and the Constitution* (*Chronicles of America*, XVI).

Cotterill, R. S., *A Short History of the Americas*. New York, 1939.

——, *The Old South*. . . . Glendale, Calif., 1936.

Coulter, E. Merton, *The Civil War and Reconstruction in Kentucky*. Chapel Hill, N. C., 1926.

——, *A Short History of Georgia*. Chapel Hill, N. C., 1933.

——, *William G. Brownlow, Fighting Parson of the Southern Highlands*.

Coupland, Reginald, *The American Revolution and the British Empire*. New York, 1930.

Cox, Isaac J., *West Florida Controversy, 1798–1813* (*Shaw Lectures on Diplomatic History*, VII). Baltimore, 1918.

Coy, Owen C., *The Great Trek*. Los Angeles, 1931.

Crandall, A. W., *The Early History of the Republican Party, 1854–1856*. Boston, 1930.

Crane, Verner W., *Benjamin Franklin, Englishman and American* (*Colver Lectures*). Baltimore, 1936.

——, *The Southern Frontier, 1670–1732*. Philadelphia, 1929.

Craven, Avery, *Edmund Ruffin, Southerner*. New York, 1932.

——, *The Repressible Conflict, 1830–1861*. Baton Rouge, 1939.

Crouse, D. E., *The Ohio Gateway*. New York, 1938.

Cubberley, Ellwood P., *Public Education in the United States*. Boston, 1919.

Curti, Merle Eugene, *The American Peace Crusade*. Durham, N. C., 1929.

——, *Peace or War: The American Struggle, 1636–1936*. New York, 1936.

Curtis, E. N., *The French Assembly of 1848 and American Constitutional Doctrines* (Columbia University *Studies*, LXXIX, No. 2). New York, 1918.

Curtis, George Ticknor, *Life of James Buchanan*. 2 v. New York, 1883.

Cushing, Harry Alonzo, *History of the Transition from Provincial to Commonwealth Government in Massachusetts* (Columbia University *Studies,* VII). New York, 1896.

Cutler, Carl C., *Greyhounds of the Sea: The Story of the American Clipper Ship.* New York, 1930.

Cutting, Elisabeth, *Jefferson Davis, Political Soldier.* New York, 1930.

Dellenbaugh, Frederick S., *Breaking the Wilderness.* New York, 1905.

Dennett, Tyler, *Americans in Eastern Asia.* New York, 1922.

Dewey, Davis R., *Financial History of the United States (American Citizen Series,* A. B. Hart, editor). Revised edition. New York, 1936.

——, *State Banking before the Civil War.* Washington, 1910.

Dexter, Edwin Grant, *A History of Education in the United States.* New York, 1904.

Dexter, Elizabeth Williams, *Colonial Women of Affairs.* Second revised edition. Boston, 1931.

Dexter, Henry Martyn, and Morton, *The England and Holland of the Pilgrims.* Boston, 1905.

Dickerson, Oliver Morton, *American Colonial Government, 1696–1765, a Study of the Board of Trade in its Relation to the American Colonies.* Cleveland, 1912.

Dodd, William E., *The Cotton Kingdom* (Chronicles of America, XXVII).

——, *Expansion and Conflict (Riverside History,* III).

——, *Jefferson Davis (American Crisis Biographies).*

——, ed., *Riverside History of the United States.* 4 v. Boston, 1915.

Dodge, T. A., *A Bird's-Eye View of Our Civil War.* Revised edition. Boston, 1917.

Dorchester, Daniel, *Christianity in the United States.* New York, 1895.

Dow, George Francis, *Domestic Life in New England in the Seventeenth Century.* Topsfield, Mass., 1925.

Downes, Randolph C., *Frontier Ohio, 1788–1803.* Columbus, 1935.

Doyle, John Andrew, *English Colonies in America.* 5 v. New York, 1889–1907.

Driver, Carl S., *John Sevier, Pioneer of the Old Southwest.* Chapel Hill, N. C., 1932.

Drury, Clifford Merrill, *Marcus Whitman, M. D., Pioneer and Martyr.* Caldwell, Idaho, 1937.

Du Bois, William Edward Burghardt, *Suppression of the African Slave Trade to the United States of America (Harvard Historical Studies,* I). New York, 1896.

Duff, Charles, *The Truth about Columbus and the Discovery of America.* New York, 1936.

Duffus, Robert Luther, *The Santa Fé Trail.* New York, 1930.

Dumond, Dwight L., *Antislavery Origins of the Civil War in the United States.* Ann Arbor, 1939.

——, *The Secession Movement, 1860–1861.* New York, 1931.

Dunbar, C. F., *Economic Essays* (O. M. Sprague, editor). New York, 1904.

Dutton, Charles J., *Oliver Hazard Perry.* New York, 1935.

Dyer, Walter A., "Embattled Farmers," *New England Quarterly,* IV, 460–481.

Earle, Alice Morse, *Child Life in Colonial Days.* New York, [c. 1899].

——, *Colonial Dames and Goodwives.* Boston, 1895.

——, *Colonial Days in Old New York.* New edition. New York, 1926.

——, *Customs and Fashions in Old New England.* New York, 1896.

——, *Home Life in Colonial Days.* New York, 1898.

——, *The Sabbath in Puritan New England.* New York, 1891.

——, *Stage Coach and Tavern Days.* New York, 1901.

East, Robert A., *Business Enterprise in the American Revolutionary Era.* New York, 1938.

Eckenrode, H. J., and Bryan, Conrad, *James Longstreet, Lee's War Horse.* Chapel Hill, N. C., 1936.

——, *The Revolution in Virginia.* Boston, 1916.

Egerton, Hugh Edward, *Causes and Character of the American Revolution.* Oxford, 1923.

——, *Short History of British Colonial Policy.* Second edition. London, 1905.

Eggleston, Edward, *The Transit of Civilization from England to America in the Seventeenth Century.* New York, 1901.

Eggleston, G. C., *The History of the Confederate War.* 2 v. New York, 1910.

Elliott, Charles W., *Winfield Scott: the Soldier and the Man.* New York, 1937.

Ettinger, Amos Aschbach, *James Edward Oglethorpe: Imperial Idealist.* New York, 1936.

——, *The Mission to Spain of Pierre Soulé, 1853–1855 (Yale Historical Publications. Miscellany,* XXII). New Haven, 1932.

Fahrney, Ralph Lee, *Horace Greeley and the Tribune in the Civil War.* Cedar Rapids, Iowa, 1936.

Fairchild, Henry P., *Immigration.* . . . Revised edition. New York, 1933.

Farrand, Max, *Fathers of the Constitution (Chronicles of America,* XIII).

——, *Framing of the Constitution of the United States.* New Haven, 1913.

Faulkner, Harold U., *American Economic History.* New York, 1924.

Faust, Albert Bernhardt, *The German Element in the United States.* 2 v. Boston, 1909.

Faÿ, Bernard, *Franklin, the Apostle of Modern Times.* Boston, 1929.

Fehlandt, August F., *A Century of Drink Reform in the United States.* Cincinnati, 1904.

Finney, Ross L., *A Brief History of the American Public School.* New York, 1924.

Fish, Carl Russell, *The American Civil War: An Interpretation.* New York, 1937.

——, *American Diplomacy.* Fifth edition. New York, 1933.

——, *Civil Service and the Patronage (Harvard Historical Studies,* XI). New York, 1905.

——, *The Rise of the Common Man, 1830–1850* (*History of American Life,* VI).

Fisher, Sydney George, *The Quaker Colonies* (*Chronicles of America,* VIII).

——, *The Struggle for American Independence.* 2 v. Philadelphia, 1908.

——, *The True Benjamin Franklin.* Fifth edition. Philadelphia, 1903.

——, *The True William Penn.* Philadelphia, 1899.

Fiske, John, *Historical Works.* Riverside Pocket edition. 12 v. Boston, 1915.

Fite, E. D., *The Presidential Campaign of 1860.* New York, 1911.

——, *Social and Industrial Conditions in the North during the Civil War.* New York, 1910.

Fitzpatrick, John C., *George Washington Himself: A Common-Sense Biography Written from His Manuscripts.* Indianapolis, 1933.

Flippin, Percy S., *Herschel V. Johnson of Georgia.* Richmond, 1931.

Ford, Henry Jones, *The Scotch-Irish in America.* Princeton, 1915.

——, *Washington and his Colleagues* (*Chronicles of America,* XIV).

Ford, Paul Leicester, *The True George Washington.* Philadelphia, 1904.

Foreman, Grant, *The Five Civilized Tribes.* Norman, Okla., 1934.

——, *Indian Removal: The Emigration of the Five Civilized Tribes of Indians.* Norman, Okla., 1932.

Forman, Samuel E., *Rise of American Commerce and Industry.* New York, 1927.

Foster, John Watson, *A Century of American Diplomacy.* Boston, 1901.

Fox, Dixon Ryan, *The Decline of Aristocracy in the Politics of New York* (Columbia University *Studies,* LXXXVI). New York, 1910.

Fox, Early Lee, "The American Colonization Society, 1817–1840" (Johns Hopkins University *Studies,* XXXVII, No. 3). Baltimore, 1919.

Frederick, J. H., *The Development of American Commerce.* New York, 1932.

Freeman, Douglas S., *Robert E. Lee: A Biography.* 4 v. New York, 1935.

French, Allen, *The First Year of the American Revolution.* Boston, 1934.

Friedenwald, Herbert, *The Declaration of Independence, an Interpretation and an Analysis.* New York, 1904.

Fuess, Claude Moore, *Daniel Webster.* Boston, 1930.

Fuller, Hubert Bruce, *The Purchase of Florida.* Cleveland, 1906.

Fuller, John Douglas Pitts, *The Movement for the Acquisition of all Mexico, 1846–1848.* (Johns Hopkins University *Studies,* LII, No. 1). Baltimore, 1936.

Gabriel, R. H., ed., *The Pageant of America.* 15 v. New Haven, 1925–1929.

Galpin, W. F., *Pioneering for Peace.* Syracuse, 1933.

Gammon, Samuel Rhea, Jr., "The Presidential Campaign of 1832" (Johns Hopkins University *Studies,* XL, No. 1). Baltimore, 1922.

Garber, P. N., *The Gadsden Purchase.* Philadelphia, 1923.

Garis, R. L., *Immigration Restriction.* New York, 1927.

Garrison, George P., *Westward Extension (American Nation,* XVII).

Garrison, Wendell Phillips, and Jackson, Francis, *William Lloyd Garrison.* 4 v. New York, 1885–1889.

Gay, Sidney Howard, *James Madison (American Statesmen).*

Gayarré, Charles Étienne Arthur, *History of Louisiana.* 4 v. Third edition. New Orleans, 1885.

Gazley, J. G., *American Opinion of German Unification, 1848–1871* (Columbia University *Studies,* CXXI). New York, 1926.

Ghent, William James, *The Early Far West.* New York, 1931.

——, *The Road to Oregon.* New York, 1929.

Gilbert, E. W., *The Exploration of Western America, 1800–1850: An Historical Geography.* New York, 1933.

Gilbertson, Catherine, *Harriet Beecher Stowe.* New York, 1937.

Gilman, Daniel Coit, *James Monroe (American Statesmen).*

Going, Charles B., *David Wilmot, Free-Soiler.* New York, 1924.

Goodwin, Cardinal, *The Trans-Mississippi West, 1803–1853.* New York, 1922.

Goodwin, Edward Lewis, *The Colonial Church in Virginia.* Milwaukee, 1927.

Goodwin, John Abbott, *The Pilgrim Republic. . . .* Tercentenary edition. Boston, 1920.

Goodwin, Maud Wilder, *Dutch and English on the Hudson (Chronicles of America, VII).*

Gordy, John Pancoast, *Political History of the United States with Special Reference to the Growth of Political Parties.* 2 v. New York, 1902.

Gottschalk, Louis, *Lafayette Joins the American Army.* Chicago, 1937.

Graham, Abbie, *Ladies in Revolt.* New York, 1934.

Grant, W. L., ed., *Voyages of Champlain, 1604–1618 (Original Narratives, IV).* New York, 1907.

Gray, L. C., *History of Agriculture in the Southern United States to 1860* (Carnegie Institution *Contributions to American Economic History).* Washington, 1933.

Green, Thomas Marshall, *The Spanish Conspiracy; a Review of Early Spanish Movements in the Southwest.* Cincinnati, 1891.

Greene, Evarts Boutell, *Provincial America (American Nation, VI).*

——, *The Provincial Governor in the English Colonies of North America (Harvard Historical Studies, VII).* New York, 1898.

Griffin, Charles C., *The United States and the Disruption of the Spanish Empire, 1810–22: A Study of the Relations of the United States with Spain and with the Rebel Spanish Colonies* (Columbia University *Studies,* No. 429). New York, 1937.

Guedalla, Philip, *Fathers of the Revolution.* New York, 1926.

Haggard, Howard Wilcox, *The Doctor in History.* New Haven, 1934.

Hall, Clayton C., ed., *Narratives of Early Maryland, 1633–1684* (*Original Narratives,* XI).

Hallowell, Anna D., *James and Lucretia Mott.* Boston, 1884.

Hammond, Matthew Brown, *The Cotton Industry* (American Economic Association *Publications,* new series, No. 1). New York, 1897.

Hanna, A. J., *Flight into Oblivion.* Richmond, Va., 1938.

Hanna, Charles Augustus, *The Scotch-Irish.* New York, 1902.

Haney, L. H., *A Congressional History of Railways in the United States, 1850–1887* (University of Wisconsin *Bulletin,* No. 342). Madison, 1910.

Harding, Bertita, *The Phantom Crown.* Indianapolis, 1934.

Hare, Lloyd C. M., *The Greatest American Woman: Lucretia Mott.* New York, 1937.

Harlow, Ralph V., *Samuel Adams, Promoter of the American Revolution.* New York, 1923.

Harris, T. L., *The Trent Affair.* Indianapolis, 1896.

Hart, Albert Bushnell, ed., *American History Told by Contemporaries.* 5 v. New York, 1897–1929.

——, ed., *The American Nation; A History from Original Sources.* 28 v. New York, 1904–1918.

——, *Salmon Portland Chase* (*American Statesmen*).

——, *Slavery and Abolition* (*American Nation,* XVI).

Hatch, Louis Clinton, *A History of the Vice-Presidency of the United States.* Revised and edited by Earl L. Shoup. New York, 1934.

Haynes, G. H., *Charles Sumner* (*American Crisis Biographies*).

Hazleton, John Hampden, *The Declaration of Independence; its History.* New York, 1906.

Heathcote, C. W., *The Lutheran Church and the Civil War.* New York, 1919.

Heatwole, Cornelius J., *History of Education in Virginia.* New York, 1916.

Hecker, Eugene Arthur, *A Short History of Women's Rights.* New York, 1914.

Henderson, Archibald, *Conquest of the Old Southwest, 1740–1800.* New York, 1920.

Henderson, G. F. R., *Stonewall Jackson and the American Civil War.* New edition. 2 v. in one. New York, 1936.

Hendrick, Burton J., *The Bulwark of the Republic: A Biography of the Constitution.* Boston, 1937.

——, *The Lees of Virginia: Biography of a Family.* Boston, 1935.

Hesseltine, William Best, *A History of the South, 1607–1936.* New York, 1936.

Hibbard, Benjamin H., *History of the Public Land Policies.* New York, 1924.

Hill, Jim Dan, *Sea Dogs of the Sixties.* Minneapolis, 1935.

——, *The Texas Navy in Forgotten Battles and Shirtsleeve Diplomacy.* Chicago, 1937.

Hillquit, Morris, *History of Socialism in the United States.* New York, 1910.

Hinds, W. A., *American Communities and Cooperative Colonies.* Chicago, 1908.

Hinsdale, Burke Aaron, *Horace Mann and the Common School Revival in the United States.* New York, 1898.

——, *The Old Northwest; the Beginnings of Our Colonial System.* Revised edition. New York, [c. 1899].

History of American Life. See Schlesinger, Arthur M., editor.

Hockett, Homer C., *Constitutional History of the United States, 1776–1876.* 2 v. New York, 1939.

——, *Western Influences on Political Parties to 1825* (Ohio State University *Contributions in History and Political Science,* No. 4). Columbus, 1917.

Hodder, Frank H., "Genesis of the Kansas-Nebraska Act," Wisconsin Historical Society *Proceedings* for 1912, 69–86.

Hodge, Frederick Webb, ed., *Spanish Explorers in the Southern United States, 1528–1543* (*Original Narratives,* III).

Hodges, George, *William Penn* (*Riverside Biographical Series*). Boston, 1901.

Holcombe, Arthur Norman, *The Political Parties of To-day.* New York, 1924.

Holst, Hermann Eduard von, *The Constitutional and Political History of the United States.* 8 v. Chicago, 1876–1892.

——, *John C. Calhoun (American Statesmen).*

Horrocks, John Wesley, *A Short History of Mercantilism.* London, [1925].

Hosford, Frances J., *Father Shipherd's Magna Charta: A Century of Coeducation in Oberlin.* Boston, 1937.

Hosmer, James Kendall, *The Appeal to Arms (American Nation, XX).*

——, *Outcome of the Civil War (American Nation, XXI).*

——, *Samuel Adams (American Statesmen).*

Houston, David Franklin, *Critical Study of Nullification in the United States (Harvard Historical Studies, III).* New York, 1896.

Howard, George Elliott, *Preliminaries of the Revolution, 1763–1775 (American Nation, VIII).*

Huidekoper, F. L., *The Military Unpreparedness of the United States.* New York, 1915.

Hulbert, Archer B., *Forty-Niners: The Chronicle of the California Trail.* Boston, 1931.

——, *The Paths of Inland Commerce (Chronicles of America, XXI).*

Hull, William I., *William Penn and the Dutch Quaker Migration to Pennsylvania.* Philadelphia, 1935.

Humphrey, Edward Frank, *Nationalism and Religion in America.* Boston, 1924.

Hunt, Gaillard, *John C. Calhoun.* Philadelphia, 1908.

——, *Life of James Madison.* New York, 1902.

Hurd, Henry Mills, and others, *The Institutional Care of the Insane in the United States and Canada.* 4 v. Baltimore, 1916–1917.

Hutcheson, Harold, *Tench Coxe: A Study in American Economic Development (Johns Hopkins University Studies, extra volume, new series, No. 26).* Baltimore, 1938.

Hutchinson, William T., *Cyrus Hall McCormick, Seed-Time, 1809–1856.* New York, 1930.

Iles, George, *Leading American Inventors.* New York, 1912.

Ingle, Edward, *Southern Sidelights* (*Library of Economics and Politics,* R. T. Ely, ed.). New York, 1896.

Jacobs, Melvin C., *Winning Oregon: A Study of an Expansionist Movement.* Caldwell, Idaho, 1938.

James, James A., *The Life of George Rogers Clark.* Chicago, 1928.

James, Marquis, *Andrew Jackson: Portrait of a President.* Indianapolis, 1937.

——, *The Raven: A Biography of Sam Houston.* New York, [c. 1929].

Jameson, John Franklin, *The American Revolution Considered as a Social Movement.* Princeton, 1926.

——, ed., *Narratives of New Netherlands, 1609–1664* (*Original Narratives,* IX).

——, ed., *Original Narratives of American History.* 19 v. New York, 1906–1917.

Jenkins, William Sumner, *Pro-Slavery Thought in the Old South.* Chapel Hill, N. C., 1935.

Jernegan, Marcus Wilson, *Laboring and Dependent Classes in Colonial America.* Chicago, [c. 1931].

Jervey, Theodore R., *Robert Y. Hayne and His Times.* New York, 1909.

Johnson, Allen, and others, editors, *The Chronicles of America.* 50 v. New Haven, 1918–1921.

——, *Jefferson and His Colleagues* (*Chronicles of America,* XV).

——, *Stephen A. Douglas.* New York, 1908.

Johnson, Emory R., and Van Metre, T. W., *Principles of Railroad Transportation.* New York, 1921.

——, and others, *History of the Domestic and Foreign Commerce of the United States* (Carnegie Institution *Contributions to American Economic History*). 2 v. Washington, 1915.

Johnson, Robert C., *John McLoughlin: Patriarch of the Northwest.* Portland, Ore., 1935.

Johnson, Willis F., *America's Foreign Relations.* 2 v. New York, 1916.

Johnston, Mary, *Pioneers of the Old South (Chronicles of America,* V).

Jones, Eliot, *Principles of Railway Transportation.* New York, 1924.

Jones, Matt B., *Vermont in the Making.* Cambridge, Mass., 1939.

Jones, Rufus M., *The Quakers in the American Colonies.* London, 1911.

Jones, Tom B., *An Introduction to Hispanic-American History.* New York, 1939.

Jordan, Donaldson, and Pratt, E. J., *Europe and the American Civil War.* Boston, 1931.

Kellogg, Louise Phelps, "The American Colonial Charter" (American Historical Association *Report* for 1903, I, 187–341). Washington, 1904.

——, ed., *Early Narratives of the Northwest, 1634–1639 (Original Narratives,* XVIII).

Kennedy, William Sloane, *John G. Whittier, the Poet of Freedom.* New York, 1892.

Kinley, David, *The Independent Treasury of the United States.* Washington, 1910.

Kirkland, E. C., *A History of American Economic Life.* New York, 1932.

——, *The Peacemakers of 1864.* New York, 1927.

Kirkpatrick, F. A., *The Spanish Conquistadores (Pioneer Histories series).* New York, 1929.

Kittredge, George Lyman, *Witchcraft in Old and New England.* Cambridge, Mass., 1929.

Knight, Edgar W., *Public Education in the South.* Boston, 1922.

Labaree, Leonard Woods, *Royal Government in America (Yale Historical Publications,* VI). New Haven, 1930.

Lambert, Oscar Doane, *Presidential Politics in the United States, 1841–1844.* Durham, N. C., 1936.

Latané, John H., *A History of American Foreign Policy.* Revised edition enlarged. Garden City, N. Y., 1934.

Laut, Agnes C., *Pioneers of the Pacific Coast* (*Chronicles of Canada*, XXI).

Leacock, Stephen, *Dawn of Canadian History* (*Chronicles of Canada*, I).

——, *Mariner of St. Malo-Cartier* (*Chronicles of Canada*, II).

Lecky, William Edward Hartpole, *American Revolution, 1763–1783; being the Chapters and Passages Relating to America from the Author's History of England* . . . edited by J. A. Woodburn. New York, 1898.

Lincoln, Charles Henry, *The Revolutionary Movement in Pennsylvania, 1760–1776* (University of Pennsylvania *Publications*, Series in History, No. 1). Philadelphia, 1901.

Linn, W. A., *Horace Greeley* (*Appleton's Historic Lives Series*). New York, 1903.

Lloyd, Arthur Y., *The Slavery Controversy, 1831–1860*. Chapel Hill, N. C., 1939.

Locke, Mary S., *Anti-Slavery in America, 1619–1808*. Boston, 1901.

Lodge, Henry Cabot, *Alexander Hamilton* (*American Statesmen*).

——, *Daniel Webster* (*American Statesmen*).

——, *George Washington* (*American Statesmen*).

——, *Life and Letters of George Cabot*. Boston, 1878.

Long, W. J., *American Literature*. Boston, 1913.

Lonn, Ella, *Desertion during the Civil War*. New York, 1928.

Lowery, Woodbury, *Spanish Settlements within the Present Limits of the United States (1513–1561)*. New York, 1905.

Lubbock, Basil, *The Romance of the Clipper Ship*. New York, 1938.

Lynch, William O., *Fifty Years of Party Warfare*. Indianapolis, 1931.

Lyon, E. Wilson, *Louisiana in French Diplomacy, 1759–1804*. Norman, Okla., 1934.

McCaleb, Walter Flavius, *The Aaron Burr Conspiracy*. Expanded edition with introduction by Charles A. Beard. New York, 1936.

McCarthy, Charles, "The Anti-Masonic Party" (American Historical Association *Report* for 1902, I, 365–574.

Maclay, Edgar S., *A History of American Privateers*. London, 1899.

McCormac, Eugene I., *James K. Polk*. Berkeley, Cal., 1922.

McCrady, Edward, *The History of South Carolina under the Proprietary Government, 1670–1719*. New York, 1897.

——, *The History of South Carolina under the Royal Government, 1719–1776*. New York, 1901.

——, *The History of South Carolina in the Revolution*. 2 v. New York, 1901–1902.

MacDonald, William, *Jacksonian Democracy* (*American Nation*, XV).

——, *Select Charters and Other Documents Illustrative of American History, 1606–1775*. New York, 1899.

——, *Select Documents Illustrative of the History of the United States, 1776–1861*. New York, 1897.

——, *Select Statutes and Other Documents Illustrative of the History of the United States, 1861–1898*. New York, 1903.

McElroy, John, *The Struggle for Missouri*. Washington, 1909.

McFarland, Raymond, *A History of the New England Fisheries*. Philadelphia, 1911.

MacGill, Caroline E., and others, *History of Transportation in the United States before 1860* (Carnegie Institution Contributions to American Economic History). Washington, 1917.

McGregor, J. C., *The Disruption of Virginia*. New York, 1922.

McIlwain, Charles Howard, *The American Revolution; a Constitutional Interpretation*. New York, 1923.

MacKay, Douglas, *The Honourable Company. A History of the Hudson's Bay Company*. New York, 1938.

McKee, Samuel, *Labor in Colonial New York, 1664–1776*. New York, 1935.

McKelvey, Blake, *American Prisons: A Study in American Social History prior to 1915*. Chicago, 1936.

McLaughlin, Andrew Cunningham, *Confederation and Constitution* (*American Nation*, X).

——, *A Constitutional History of the United States* (*The Century Political Science Series*, F. A. Ogg, ed.). New York, 1935.

McMaster, John Bach, *The Acquisition of Political, Social, and Industrial Rights of Man in America.* Cleveland, 1903.

——, *A History of the People of the United States.* 8 v. New York, 1883–1913.

——, *A History of the People of the United States during Lincoln's Administration.* New York, 1927.

Macy, Jesse, *The Antislavery Crusade* (*Chronicles of America,* XXVIII).

Mahan, Alfred Thayer, *Admiral Farragut* (*Great Commanders,* J. G. Wilson, ed.). New York, 1892.

——, *Influence of Sea Power upon History, 1660–1783.* Eighteenth edition. Boston, 1904.

——, *Sea Power in Its Relation to the War of 1812.* 2 v. Boston, 1905.

Maitland, Frederic William, *Constitutional History of England.* Cambridge, 1908.

Markham, Sir Clements Robert, *Life of Christopher Columbus.* London, 1892.

Marraro, H. R., *American Opinion on the Unification of Italy, 1846–1861.* New York, 1932.

Marshall, Helen, *Dorothea Dix, Forgotten Samaritan.* Chapel Hill, N. C., 1937.

Martin, G. H., *The Evolution of the Massachusetts Public School System.* New York, 1908.

Martin, P. F., *Maximilian in Mexico.* New York, 1914.

Mathews, Lois Kimball, *The Expansion of New England . . . 1620–1864.* Boston, 1909.

Maurice, Frederick, *Robert E. Lee, the Soldier.* Boston, 1925.

Maynard, Theodore, *De Soto and the Conquistadores.* New York, 1930.

Mayo, Bernard, *Henry Clay, Spokesman of the New West.* (Three volumes projected.) Boston, 1937–.

Meigs, William Montgomery, *Life of John Caldwell Calhoun.* 2 v. New York, 1917.

——, *Life of Thomas Hart Benton.* Philadelphia, 1904.

Meneely, A. H., *The War Department: 1861* (Columbia University *Studies*, No. 300). New York, 1928.

Mereness, Newton D., *Maryland as a Proprietary Province.* New York, 1901.

——, *Travels in the American Colonies, 1690–1783.* New York, 1916.

Merriam, Charles Edward, *History of American Political Theories.* New York, 1903.

Merritt, Elizabeth, *James Henry Hammond* (Johns Hopkins University *Studies*, XLI, No. 4). Baltimore, 1923.

Meyer, Leland Winfield, *Life and Times of Colonel R. M. Johnson* (Columbia University *Studies*, No. 359). New York, 1932.

Miller, John C., *Sam Adams, Pioneer in Propaganda.* Boston, 1936.

Milton, George Fort, *The Eve of Conflict: Stephen A. Douglas and the Needless War.* Boston, 1934.

Miner, Louie M., *Our Rude Forefathers; American Political Verse, 1783–1788.* Cedar Rapids, Iowa, 1937.

Minnigerode, Meade, *The Fabulous Forties.* New York, 1924.

Mitchell, Stewart, *Horatio Seymour of New York.* Cambridge, Mass., 1938.

Mohr, Walter H., *Federal Indian Relations, 1774–1788.* Philadelphia, 1933.

Monaghan, Frank, *John Jay.* New York, 1935.

Monroe, Will Seymour, *The Educational Labors of Henry Barnard.* Syracuse, 1893.

Montgomery, Richard C., *The White-Headed Eagle, John McLoughlin, Builder of an Empire.* New York, 1934.

Moore, A. B., *Conscription and Conflict in the Confederacy.* New York, 1924.

Morey, William C., "The First State Constitutions," *Annals of the American Academy of Political and Social Science,* IV, 201–232.

——, "The Genesis of a Written Constitution," *Annals of the American Academy of Political and Social Science,* I, 529–557.

Morison, John L., *British Supremacy and Canadian Self-Government, 1839–1854.* Glasgow, 1919.

Morison, Samuel Eliot, *Builders of the Bay Colony.* Boston, 1930.

——, *Harvard College in the Seventeenth Century.* Cambridge, Mass., 1936.

——, *The Maritime History of Massachusetts, 1783–1860.* Boston, 1921.

Moritzen, Julius, *The Peace Movement of America.* New York, 1912.

Morse, John Torrey, Jr., ed., *American Statesmen.* 32 v. Boston, 1898–1900.

——, *Benjamin Franklin (American Statesmen).*

——, *John Adams (American Statesmen).*

——, *John Quincy Adams (American Statesmen).*

——, *Thomas Jefferson (American Statesmen).*

Moses, Bernard, *The Establishment of Spanish Rule in America.* New York, 1898.

Mueller, Henry Richard, *The Whig Party in Pennsylvania* (Columbia University *Studies,* CI, No. 2). New York, 1902.

Mulvey, (Sister) Mary Doris, *French Catholic Missionaries in the Present United States.* Washington, 1936.

Munro, William Bennett, *Crusaders of New France (Chronicles of America,* IV).

——, *The Makers of the Unwritten Constitution.* New York, 1930.

——, *The Seigneurs of Old Canada (Chronicles of Canada,* V).

Murdock, Kenneth B., *Increase Mather, the Foremost American Puritan.* Boston, 1925.

Muzzey, David Saville, *Thomas Jefferson.* New York, 1918.

Myers, Albert Cook, ed., *Narratives of Early Pennsylvania . . . 1630–1707 (Original Narratives,* XV).

Myers, William Starr, *General George Brinton McClellan: A Study in Personality.* New York, 1934.

Narrative and Critical History of America. See Winsor, Justin, editor.

Nettels, Curtis P., *The Roots of American Civilization: A History of American Colonial Life.* (*American History Series,* D. R. Fox, editor). New York, 1938.

Nevins, Allan, *American Social Conditions as Recorded by British Travellers.* New York, 1923.

——, *The American States during and after the Revolution, 1775–1789.* New York, 1925.

——, *Frémont: The Pathmaker of the West.* New York, 1939. (Revision of *Frémont, the West's Greatest Adventurer.* 2 v. New York, 1928.)

Nichols, R. F., *The Democratic Machine, 1850–1854* (Columbia University *Studies,* CXI, No. 1). New York, 1923.

——, *Franklin Pierce.* Philadelphia, 1931.

Nickerson, Hoffman, *The Turning Point of the Revolution, or Burgoyne in America.* Boston, 1928.

Nordhoff, Charles, *The Communistic Societies of the United States.* New York, 1875.

Norton, Anthony B., *The Great Revolution of 1840.* Cleveland, 1888.

Norwood, John Nelson, *The Schism in the Methodist Episcopal Church, 1844.* Alfred, N. Y., 1923.

Noyes, John Humphrey, *History of American Socialisms.* Philadelphia, 1870.

Noyes, Pierrepont Burt, *My Father's House: An Oneida Boyhood.* New York, [c. 1937].

Oberholtzer, Ellis P., editor, *American Crisis Biographies.* 14 v. Philadelphia, 1905–1915.

——, *Jay Cooke, Financier of the Civil War.* 2 v. Philadelphia, 1907.

——, *Robert Morris, Patriot and Financier.* New York, 1903.

Ogg, Frederic Austin, *The Old Northwest* (*Chronicles of America,* XIX).

——, *Opening of the Mississippi.* New York, 1904.

——, *The Reign of Andrew Jackson* (*Chronicles of America,* XX).

——, *The Last American Frontier*. New York, 1910. Reprint, 1938.

Pellew, William George, *John Jay (American Statesmen)*.

Pendleton, Louis, *Alexander H. Stephens (American Crisis Biographies)*.

Perkins, Dexter, *The Monroe Doctrine, 1823–1826 (Harvard Historical Studies, XXIX)*. Cambridge, Mass., 1927.

——, *The Monroe Doctrine, 1826–1867 (Shaw Lectures on Diplomatic History, XVII)*. Baltimore, 1932.

Perlman, Selig, *A History of Trade Unionism in the United States (Social Science Text-Books, R. T. Ely, ed.)*. New York, 1922.

Phillips, Paul Chrisler, *The West in the Diplomacy of the American Revolution (University of Illinois, Studies in the Social Sciences, II, Nos. 2 and 3)*. Urbana, 1913.

Phillips, Ulrich Bonnell, *American Negro Slavery*. New York, 1918.

——, *The Course of the South to Secession*, edited by E. Merle Coulter. New York, 1939.

——, "Georgia and State Rights" (American Historical Association *Report* for 1901, II, 3–224).

——, *Life and Labor in the Old South*. Boston, 1929. New edition, 1935.

——, *The Life of Robert Toombs*. New York, 1913.

Plooij, D., *The Pilgrim Fathers from a Dutch Point of View*. New York, 1932.

Poage, George R., *Henry Clay and the Whig Party*. Chapel Hill, N. C., 1936.

Pollard, Albert F., *The Evolution of Parliament*. London and New York, 1920.

Porter, D. D., *The Naval History of the Civil War*. New York, 1886.

Porter, Kenneth W., *John Jacob Astor; Business Man*. Cambridge, Mass., 1931.

Porter, Kirk Harold, *A History of Suffrage in the United States*. Chicago, 1918.

Pound, Arthur L., *The Penns of Pennsylvania and England.* New York, 1932.

Powell, Edward Payson, *Nullification and Secession in the United States; a History of the Six Attempts during the First Century of the Republic.* New York, 1897.

Pratt, Julius W., *Expansionists of 1812.* New York, 1925.

Preston, Walter Creigh, *Lee—West Point and Lexington.* Yellow Springs, Ohio, 1934.

Priestley, Herbert I., *The Coming of the White Man (History of American Life,* I).

Putnam, Herbert E., *Joel Roberts Poinsett: A Political Biography.* Washington, 1935.

Randall, James G., *The Civil War and Reconstruction.* Boston, 1937.

——, *Constitutional Problems under Lincoln.* New York, 1926.

Ray, P. O., *The Repeal of the Missouri Compromise.* Cleveland, 1909.

Reddaway, William Fiddian, *The Monroe Doctrine.* Second edition. New York, 1905.

Reeves, Jesse S., *American Diplomacy under Tyler and Polk (Shaw Lectures on Diplomatic History,* III). Baltimore, 1907.

Rhodes, James Ford, *A History of the United States from the Compromise of 1850.* 9 v. New York, 1893–1922.

——, *History of the Civil War.* New York, 1917.

Richman, Irving Berdine, *The Spanish Conquerors (Chronicles of America,* II).

——, *Rhode Island, Its Making and Its Meaning.* 2 v. New York, 1902.

Riegel, Robert E., *The Story of the Western Railroads.* New York, 1926.

Rippy, J. Fred, *Joel R. Poinsett, Versatile American.* Durham, N. C., 1935.

——, *The United States and Mexico.* Revised edition. New York, 1931.

Riverside History. See Dodd, William E., editor.

Rives, George L., *The United States and Mexico, 1821–1848.* 2 v. New York, 1913.

Robert, Joseph Clarke, *The Tobacco Kingdom: Plantation, Market, and Factory in Virginia and North Carolina, 1800–1860.* Durham, N. C., 1938.

Roberts, Ellis Henry, *New York.* 2 v. Revised edition. Boston, 1904.

Robinson, Howard, *Development of the British Empire.* Revised and enlarged edition. Boston, 1936.

Roosevelt, Theodore, *The Naval War of 1812.* New York, 1882.

——, *The Winning of the West.* Standard Library edition. 4 v. New York, 1894–1896.

Rose, J. Holland and others, editors, *The Cambridge History of the British Empire.* 8 v. New York, 1929–1936.

Roseboom, Eugene H., and Weisenberger, Francis P., *A History of Ohio.* New York, 1934.

Rowe, Henry Kalloch, *The History of Religion in the United States.* New York, 1924.

Russel, R. R., *Economic Aspects of Southern Sectionalism, 1840–1861* (University of Illinois *Studies,* XI, Nos. 1 and 2). Urbana, 1924.

Rydjord, John, *Foreign Interest in the Independence of New Spain.* Durham, N. C., 1935.

Salley, Alexander S., ed., *Narratives of Early Carolina, 1650–1708* (*Original Narratives,* XIV).

Sanborn, J. B., *Congressional Grants of Land in Aid of Railways* (University of Wisconsin *Bulletin* No. 30). Madison, 1899.

Sanders, Jennings B., *Early American History (1492–1789).* New York, 1938.

Sato, Shosuke, *History of the Land Question in the United States* (Johns Hopkins University *Studies,* IV). Baltimore, 1886.

Schachner, Nathan, *Aaron Burr: A Biography.* New York, 1937.

Schafer, Joseph, *A History of the Pacific Northwest.* New York, 1918.

——, *The Social History of American Agriculture.* New York, 1936.

Scharf, J. T., *History of the Confederate States Navy.* Albany, 1886.

Schlesinger, Arthur Meier, *The Colonial Merchants and the American Revolution, 1763–1776* (Columbia University Studies, LXVIII). New York, 1917.

——, *New Viewpoints in American History.* New York, 1922.

——, and Fox, Dixon Ryan, editors, *A History of American Life.* 12 v. New York, 1929–.

Schouler, James, *History of the United States of America under the Constitution.* 7 v. Revised edition. New York, 1895–1913.

Schultz, William J., and Caine, M. R., *Financial Development of the United States.* New York, 1937.

Schurz, Carl, *Henry Clay (American Statesmen).*

Schuyler, Robert L., *The Constitution of the United States; an Historical Survey of Its Formation.* New York, 1923.

——, *Parliament and the British Empire. . . .* New York, 1929.

Schwab, J. C., *The Confederate States of America, 1861–1865: A Financial and Industrial History.* New York, 1901.

Scisco, L. D., *Political Nativism in New York State* (Columbia University Studies, XIII, No. 2). New York, 1901.

Scott, William Amasa, *The Repudiation of State Debts.* New York, [1893].

Scrugham, Mary, *The Peaceable Americans, 1860–1861* (Columbia University Studies, XCVI, No. 3). New York, 1921.

Sears, Lorenzo, *Wendell Phillips.* New York, 1909.

Sears, Louis M., *George Washington.* New York, 1932.

——, *A History of American Foreign Relations.* Revised and enlarged edition. New York, 1935.

——, *Jefferson and the Embargo.* Durham, N. C., 1927.

Seeley, Sir John Robert, *The Expansion of England.* Boston, 1883.

——, *The Growth of British Policy.* 2 v. Cambridge, 1895.

Semple, Ellen Churchill, *American History and Its Geographic Conditions.* Revised in Collaboration with the Author by Charles Fielden Jones. Boston, 1933.

Shannon, Fred A., *The Organization and Administration of the Union Army.* 2 v. Cleveland, 1928.

Sharpless, Isaac, *A Quaker Experiment in Government.* Philadelphia, 1898.

Shepard, Edward Morse, *Martin Van Buren (American Statesmen).*

Shryock, Richard Harrison, *Georgia and the Union in 1850.* Durham, N. C. [c. 1926].

Siebert, Wilbur H., *The Underground Railway from Slavery to Freedom.* New York, 1898.

Simms, William Gilmore, *Life of Nathaniel Greene, Major-General in the Army of the Revolution.* New York, 1859. (First edition, New York, 1849.)

Skinner, Constance L., *Adventurers of Oregon (Chronicles of America,* XXII).

——, *Beaver, Kings and Cabins.* New York, 1933.

——, *Pioneers of the Old Southwest (Chronicles of America,* XVIII).

Slosson, Edward E., *The American Spirit in Education (Chronicles of America,* XXXIII).

Small, Albion Woodbury, *Beginnings of American Nationality* . . . (Johns Hopkins University *Studies,* VIII, Parts 1 and 2). Baltimore, 1890.

Smith, Abbot E., *James Madison: Builder. A New Estimate of a Memorable Career.* New York, 1937.

Smith, E. C., *The Borderland in the Civil War.* New York, 1927.

Smith, Justin H., *The Annexation of Texas.* New York, 1911.

Smith, Theodore Clarke, *The Liberty and Free-Soil Parties in the Northwest (Harvard Historical Studies,* VI). New York, 1897.

——, *Parties and Slavery (The American Nation,* XVIII).

Smith, William Ernest, *The Francis Preston Blair Family in Politics.* New York, 1933.

Spaulding, E. Wilder, *His Excellency, George Clinton, Critic of the Constitution.* New York, 1938.

Spears, J. R., *The Story of the American Merchant Marine.* Revised edition. New York, 1918.

——, *The History of Our Navy.* 4 v. New York, 1897.

Sprague, J. F., *The Northeastern Boundary Controversy and the Aroostook War.* Dover, Me., 1910.

Spring, L. W., *Kansas; the Prelude to the War for the Union.* Boston, 1907.

Spruill, Julia C., *Women's Life and Work in the Southern Colonies.* Chapel Hill, N. C., 1938.

Squire, Belle, *The Woman Movement in America.* Chicago, 1911.

Stanard, Mrs. Mary Newton, *The Story of Virginia's First Century.* Philadelphia, 1928.

Stanwood, Edward, *American Tariff Controversies in the Nineteenth Century.* 2 v. Boston, 1903–1904.

——, *A History of the Presidency.* 2 v. Boston, 1916.

Stephenson, George M., *A History of American Immigration.* Boston, 1926.

——, *The Political History of the Public Lands from 1840 to 1862.* Boston, 1917.

Stephenson, Nathaniel W., *The Day of the Confederacy (Chronicles of America,* XXX).

——, *Lincoln.* Indianapolis, 1922.

——, *Texas and the Mexican War (Chronicles of America,* XXIV).

Stillé, Charles Janeway, *History of the United States Sanitary Commission.* Philadelphia, 1866.

——, *Life and Times of John Dickinson* (Pennsylvania Historical Society *Memoirs,* XIII). Philadelphia, 1891.

Sumner, William Graham, *Andrew Jackson (American Statesmen).*

Sweet, W. W., *The Methodist Episcopal Church and the Civil War.* Cincinnati, 1912.

Swisher, Carl Brent, *Roger B. Taney.* New York, 1935.

Tatum, Edward H., Jr., *The United States and Europe, 1815–1823: A Study in the Background of the Monroe Doctrine.* Berkeley, Calif., 1936.

Tatum, Georgia Lee, *Disloyalty in the Confederacy*. Chapel Hill, N. C., 1934.

Taussig, Frank William, *Tariff History of the United States*. Eighth edition. New York, 1931.

Taylor, James Monroe, *Before Vassar Opened*. Boston, 1914.

Thayer, William Roscoe, *George Washington*. Boston, 1922.

Thomas, B. P., *Russo-American Relations, 1815–1867* (Johns Hopkins University *Studies*, XLVIII, No. 2). New York, 1930.

Thompson, Holland, *The Age of Invention* (*Chronicles of America*, XXXVII).

Thompson, Samuel Bernard, *Confederate Purchasing Operations Abroad*. Chapel Hill, N. C., 1935.

Thwaites, Reuben Gold, *A Brief History of Rocky Mountain Exploration*. New York, 1904.

——, *Daniel Boone*. New York, 1902.

——, *France in America* (*American Nation*, VII).

Thwing, Charles F., *A History of Higher Education in America*. New York, 1906.

Tiffany, Francis, *Life of Dorothea Lynde Dix*. Boston, 1890.

Tiffany, Orrin Edward, *Relations of the United States to the Canadian Rebellion of 1837–1838*. Ann Arbor, Mich., 1905.

Tilby, A. Wyatt, *British North America, 1763–1867*. London, 1911.

Tower, Charlemagne, *Marquis de La Fayette in the American Revolution*. 2 v. Philadelphia, 1895.

Treat, Payson Jackson, *Diplomatic Relations between the United States and Japan, 1853–1895*. 2 v. Stanford University, 1932.

——, *The National Land System, 1785–1820*. New York, 1910.

Trent, William Peterfield, and others, editors, *The Cambridge History of American Literature*. 4 v. New York, 1917–1921.

Trescot, William Henry, *Diplomatic History of the Administrations of Washington and Adams, 1789–1801*. Boston, 1857.

Trevelyan, Sir Otto George, *The American Revolution*. New edition. 3 v. London, 1905.

Tryon, Rolla M., *Household Manufactures in the United States, 1640–1860*. Chicago, 1917.

Tuckerman, Henry Theodore, *America and Her Commentators*. New York, 1864.

Turner, Frederick Jackson, *The Frontier in American History*. New York, 1920.

——, *Rise of the New West (American Nation, XIV)*.

——, *The Significance of Sections in American History*. New York, [c. 1932].

Tyler, Lyon Gardiner, *England in America (American Nation, IV)*.

——, *The Letters and Times of the Tylers*. 3 v. Richmond, 1884–1896.

Tyler, Moses Coit, *Literary History of the American Revolution, 1763–1783*.

——, *Patrick Henry (American Statesmen)*.

Underwood, J. L., *The Women of the Confederacy*. New York, 1906.

Updyke, Frank Arthur, *The Diplomacy of the War of 1812 (Shaw Lectures on Diplomatic History, IX)*. Baltimore, 1915.

Vander Velde, L. G., *The Presbyterian Churches and the Federal Union, 1861–1869 (Harvard Historical Studies, XXXIII)*. Cambridge, 1932.

Van Deusen, Glyndon, *The Life of Henry Clay*. Boston, 1937.

Van Doren, Carl Clinton, *Benjamin Franklin*. New York, 1938.

Van Tyne, Claude Halstead, *The American Revolution, 1776–1783 (American Nation, IX)*.

——, *Causes of the War of Independence*. Boston, 1922.

——, *Loyalists of the American Revolution*. New York, 1902.

——, "Sovereignty in the American Revolution," *American Historical Review*, XII, 529–545.

——, *The War of Independence*. Boston, 1929.

Villard, Oswald Garrison, *John Brown, 1800–1859*. Boston, 1910.

von Holst. See Holst.

Wandell, Samuel H., and Minnigerode, Meade, *Aaron Burr, a Biography Compiled from Rare and in Many Cases Unpublished Sources.* 2 v. New York, 1925.

Ward, Christopher, *New Sweden on the Delaware.* Philadelphia, 1938.

Ware, Norman, *The Industrial Worker, 1840–1860.* Boston, 1824.

Warfield, Ethelbert Dudley, *The Kentucky Resolutions of 1798.* Second edition. New York, 1894.

Warren, Charles, *The Making of the Constitution.* Boston, 1928.

——, *The Supreme Court in United States History.* 2 v. Revised edition. Boston, 1932.

Warren, Joseph Parker, "The Confederation and the Shays Rebellion," *American Historical Review,* XI, 42–67.

Weeden, William Babcock, *Economic and Social History of New England, 1620–1789.* 2 v. Boston, 1890.

Weinberg, Albert K., *Manifest Destiny: A Study of Nationalist Expansion in American History.* Baltimore, 1935.

Wellington, Raynor G., *The Political and Sectional Influence of the Public Lands, 1828–1842.* Cambridge, Mass., 1914.

Wendell, Barrett, *Cotton Mather, the Puritan Priest.* Cambridge, Mass., 1926.

——, *Literary History of America.* New York, 1900.

Wender, Herbert, *Southern Commercial Conventions* (Johns Hopkins University *Studies,* XLVIII, No. 4). Baltimore, 1930.

Wertenbaker, Thomas Jefferson, *The First Americans, 1607–1690* (*History of American Life,* II).

——, *Virginia under the Stuarts.* Princeton, 1914.

Wesley, C. H., *The Collapse of the Confederacy* (Howard University *Studies,* No. 2). Washington, 1922.

——, *Negro Labor in the United States, 1850–1925.* New York, 1927.

West, W. R., *Contemporary French Opinion on the American Civil War* (Johns Hopkins University *Studies,* XLII, No. 1). Baltimore, 1924.

Whitaker, Arthur P., *The Mississippi Question, 1795–1803: A Study in Trade, Politics, and Diplomacy.* New York, 1934.

——, *Spanish-American Frontier, 1783–1785.* Boston, 1927.

White, Horace, *Money and Banking.* Boston, 1914.

White, Laura A., *Robert Barnwell Rhett.* New York, 1931.

White, Stuart Edward, *The Forty-Niners (Chronicles of America,* XXV).

Whitlock, Brand, *Lafayette.* New York, 1929.

Whitton, Lieutenant-Colonel F. E., *The American War of Independence.* New York, 1931.

Wiley, Bell I., *Southern Negroes, 1861–1865.* New Haven, 1938.

Wilkinson, James, *Wilkinson, Soldier and Pioneer.* The author, New Orleans, 1935.

Williams, Mary W., *Anglo-American Isthmian Diplomacy, 1815–1915.* Washington, 1916.

Williamson, James Alexander, *The Voyages of the Cabots and the English Discovery of America under Henry VII and Henry VIII.* London, 1924.

Wilson, Woodrow, *George Washington.* New York, 1897.

——, *A History of the American People.* 5 v. New York, 1902.

Wiltse, Charles M., *The Jeffersonian Tradition in American Democracy.* Chapel Hill, N. C., 1935.

Wines, Frederick Howard, *Punishment and Reformation* (revised by W. D. Lane). New York, 1919.

Winsor, Justin, *Cartier to Frontenac. . . .* Second edition. Boston, 1894.

——, ed., *The Narrative and Critical History of America.* 8 v. Boston, 1884–1889.

——, *The Westward Movement, . . .* 1763–1798. Boston, 1897.

Winston, Robert, *High Stakes and Hair Trigger: The Life of Jefferson Davis.* New York, 1930.

——, *Robert E. Lee, a Biography.* New York, 1934.

Wittke, Carl, *We Who Built America: The Saga of the Immigrant.* New York, 1939.

Wood, William, *Captains of the Civil War (Chronicles of America,* XXXI).

——, *Elizabethan Sea Dogs* (*Chronicles of America,* III).

——, *War with the United States* (*Chronicles of Canada,* XIV).

Wood, W. B., and Edmonds, J. E., *A History of the Civil War in the United States.* London, 1905.

Woodburn, James Albert, *The Life of Thaddeus Stevens.* Indianapolis, 1913.

Woolley, John G., and Johnson, W. E., *Temperance Progress of the Century.* Philadelphia, 1903.

Wright, Thomas G., *Literary Culture in Early New England, 1620–1730.* New Haven, 1920.

Wrong, George McKinnon, *Canada and the American Revolution: The Disruption of the First British Empire.* New York, 1935.

——, *Conquest of New France* (*Chronicles of America,* X).

——, *The Fall of Canada.* Oxford, 1914.

——, *The Rise and Fall of New France.* 2 v. New York, 1928.

——, *Washington and His Comrades in Arms* (*Chronicles of America,* XII).

——, and Langton, H. H., editors, *The Chronicles of Canada.* 32 v. Toronto, 1915–1921.

Young, Norwood, *George Washington, Soul of the Revolution.* New York, 1932.

INDEX

1642, 76; education act of 1647, 76; on force of acts of Parliament, 90; relations with royal commission, 91; charter of, annulled, 91; new charter granted, 94; decline of theocracy in, 95; witchcraft delusion in, 99 f.; life in Boston, at end of colonial period, 112 f.; Massachusetts Government Act, 183.
Massachusetts Circular Letter, 177.
Massachusetts Government Act, 183.
Massachusetts, state of, adopts a constitution, 229; democracy of constitution, 232; suffrage restriction under constitution, 232; land cession by, 261; contest over ratification of Constitution, 299; calls Hartford Convention, 443; emancipation of slaves in, 495; enlarges franchise, 507; literacy tests in, 691; amends personal liberty laws, 721.
Mather, Cotton, superstition of, 99 f.
Mather, Increase, as author, 100.
Mayflower, voyage of, 29.
"Mayflower Compact," 30.
Maysville Road Bill, 536.
Meade, George G., Union general, 748.
Mechanics' Free Press, 597.
Medicine, practice of, in seventeenth century, 98 f.; practice of, in eighteenth century, 119; discoveries in, 760; and use of anaesthetics, 760; practice in Civil War, 760.
Medill, Joseph, as editor, 670.
Mercantilists, ambition of, against Dutch, 54; activities under Charles II, 88, 89; influence increased after Revolution of 1688, 94; alliance with landed classes, and control of Parliament, 157; colonial policy of, 158 f.; divergence of views of, from American, 165 f.
Merchants, in Revolution, agitate against Sugar Act, 170; organize boycott, 172; alarmed by radical violence, 176; boycott against Townshend Act, 176; divided in at-

titude towards radicals and British, 180.
Merchants Adventurers, 17.
Meredith, William M., Secretary of the Treasury, 649 n.
Merrimac: see Virginia.
Mexico, Spanish conquest of, 2 f.; *encomiendas* in, 3 f.; development under Spain, 37 f.; independence, 482; policy towards Americans in Texas, 565 f.; feeling over annexation of Texas, 626; relations with U. S., to 1845, 634; refuses Polk's offer, 637; war with U. S., 638 f.; treaty of Guadalupe Hidalgo, 639; and Gadsden Purchase, 680 n.; Buchanan and M., 695; invaded by French, 776.
Mexico City, in colonial days, 7; captured, 639.
Midwest, agriculture in, 667 f.; railroads in, 668.
Milan Decree, issued, 400; revoked, 414.
Milligan case, 763.
Mining, in 1850's, 664.
Minnesota, admitted to Union, 694.
Miranda, Francisco de, Venezuelan patriot, 481.
Missions, and Spanish colonization, 3 f.; and French, 14 f.
Mississippi River, question of navigation of, 210 f.; demanded by U. S. as boundary, 220; in treaty of Versailles, 223; Jay-Gardoqui negotiations about, 275; navigation of conceded, 345; search for source of, 389; British right to navigate, 441 and n.; opened in Civil War, 738.
Mississippi, state of, admitted to Union, 473; secedes, 715.
Mississippi Valley, explorations in, 9 f.; French and English rivalry in, 11, 136 f.; Spanish interests in, during Revolution, 210 f.; settled by Piedmontese, 471 f.
Missouri Compromise, proposed, 500; adopted, 501; points in debate, 501; second compromise, 502; repealed,

Howard - Preliminaries of the Amer. Revol
Van Tyne - The American War
Carl Becker - The Eve of the Revolution
Channing - Vol. 3
D.N.B - read James Otis
Patrick Henry

94. How did the Revolution of 1688 affect the gov't of New Eng. RI.

95. What book did Montesquieu
What idea did he emphasize in the book

96. Who was supreme in the Eng. Govt - Kng or Parliament?

97 How did Geo III deal with this question of supremacy.

Slidell, John, as minister to Mexico, 637; as Confederate envoy, 774.

Small-state plan: *see* New Jersey Plan.

Smith, Adam, quoted, 159 and *n.*; advises free trade with U. S., 245.

Smith, Gerrit, rescues Negro, 676.

Smith, Jedediah S., explorations of, 474.

Smith, Joseph, and Mormonism, 608.

Smith, Kirby, in Louisiana, 742; in Kentucky, 743; surrenders, 751.

Smith, Robert, Secretary of State, 406 *n.*; dismissed, 421.

Smyth, Alexander, in War of 1812, 424.

Social conditions, in Massachusetts Bay colony, 40; in colonial times, 73 *f.*; in New England in seventeenth century, 95 *f.*; on frontier, in eighteenth century, 109 *f.*; in colonial Boston, 112 *f.*; in New York, Charleston, and Philadelphia, in colonial days, 116 *f.*; in South, in eighteenth century, 123 *f.*; in Confederation period, 240 *f.*; frontier homestead, 470; in middle of nineteenth century, 606 *f.*

"Sons of Liberty," organization at beginning of Revolution, 173; group of sympathizers with South in Civil War, 770.

Soulé, Pierre, frames Ostend Manifesto, 680.

South, decline of religious observances in, 101 *f.*; towns in, in eighteenth century, 123; commerce in, in eighteenth century, 129; migration westward in, after War of 1812, 467; contrasted economically with North, 669, 674, 675; supports Kansas-Nebraska bill, 683; endeavors to control Kansas, 695 *f.*; effect of John Brown's raid on, 704 *f.*; secedes, 714 *f.*

South Carolina, beginnings of, 64; discrimination against Piedmont section, 130. State: land cession, 261; ratifies Constitution, 300; enlarges franchise, 507; rise of State Rights party, 551; Ordinance of Nullification, 1832, 551; rescinds Ordinance, 554; secedes, 715; Sherman's march through, 749.

South Carolina Exposition, 1828, 516.

Southwest, during Confederation period, 272 *f.*; Spanish policy, 275 *f.*; negotiations with Spain over, 274 *f.*

Southwest Territory, 328.

Spain, colonization in America, 2 *f.*; war with England, 1588, 16; War of Spanish Succession, 138; cedes Florida, 144 *f.*; attitude towards American Revolution, 210 *f.*; joins France in war on England, 210; trade with U. S. in Confederation period, 247; policy in West after Revolution, 273 *f.*; negotiations concerning Southwest, 274 *f.*; policy during Washington's administration, 344 *f.*; treaty with in 1795, 345; treaty of San Ildefonso, 378 *f.*; dispute with U. S. over West Florida, 390 *f.*; position of, in Floridas, 1812, 428 *f.*; claims to Oregon country, 475; cedes claims to U. S., 1819, 476; anger over invasion of Florida, 478; treaty of 1819 with U. S., 479 *f.*; revolt of colonies, 482; refuses to sell Cuba to U. S., 641; S. and Ostend Manifesto, 680; invades Mexico, 776; annexes Dominican Republic, 776; war on Peru, 776.

Spanish-American revolutions, 482.

Sparks, Jared, as editor, 464; as historian, 610.

Speaker, office created, 306; development of office by Clay, 412 and *n.*, 413.

Specie Circular, 577.

Spoils system, under Jackson, 533.

Spotswood, governor of Virginia, 108.

Spottsylvania, battle at, 749.

Springfield, Mass., settled, 53; in Shays' Rebellion, 254.

Springfield Republican, Bowles edits, 670; on Washington during Civil War, 759.

THE UNITED STATES
IN 1865

Scale of Miles

0   100   200   300   400

HAGSTROM CO., N.Y., Map Makers